# The A–Z Guide to Expert Witnessing

**STEVEN BABITSKY, ESQ.**

**JAMES J. MANGRAVITI, JR., ESQ.**

**ALEX BABITSKY, MBA**

**S•E•A•K, Inc.**
**Excellence in Education Since 1980**

**Falmouth, Massachusetts**

*The authors would like to acknowledge Ryann Muir, Dee Netzel, and Rebecca Wilson Lundin for their assistance in the creation of this book.*

# CONTENTS

# Related Products by SEAK, Inc.

For more information, call SEAK at (508) 457-1111. Inquiries may also be addressed to SEAK, Inc. at P.O. Box 729, Falmouth, MA 02541. Fax (508) 540-8304; e-mail address: mail@seak.com; Internet address: www.seak.com.

# About the Authors

**Steven Babitsky, Esq.,** is the President of SEAK, Inc. He was a personal injury trial attorney for twenty years and is the former managing partner of the firm Kistin, Babitsky, Latimer & Beitman. Mr. Babitsky is the co-author of the texts *How to Become a Dangerous Expert Witness: Advanced Techniques and Strategies; Writing and Defending Your Expert Report: The Step-by-Step Guide with Models; How to Excel During Cross-Examination: Techniques for Experts That Work; The Comprehensive Forensic Services Manual: The Essential Resources for All Experts;* and *How to Excel During Depositions: Techniques for Experts That Work.* Attorney Babitsky is the co-developer and trainer for the "How to Be an Effective Medical Witness" seminar, the seminar leader for the "Annual National Expert Witness and Litigation Seminar," and the scriptwriter for the videos, "How to Be an Effective Medical Witness" and "The Expert Medical Deposition: How to Be an Effective and Ethical Witness." Mr. Babitsky trains hundreds of experts every year. He may be contacted at sbabitsky@aol.com.

**James J. Mangraviti, Jr., Esq.,** has trained hundreds of expert witnesses across the United States and Canada. He is a former trial lawyer with experience in defense and plaintiff personal injury law and insurance law. He currently serves as Vice President and General Counsel of SEAK, Inc. Mr. Mangraviti received his BA degree in mathematics *summa cum laude* from Boston College and his JD degree *cum laude* from Boston College Law School. His publications include the texts *SEAK Law School for Physicians; Law School for the Safety and Health Professional; The Independent Medical Examination Report: A Step-by-Step Guide with Models; The Successful Physician Negotiator: How to Get What You Deserve; How to Excel During Cross-Examination: Techniques for Experts That Work; How to Excel During Depositions: Techniques for Experts That Work; The Comprehensive Forensic Services Manual: The Essential Resources for All Experts; Writing and Defending Your Expert Report: The Step-by-Step Guide with Models; Cross-Examination: The Comprehensive Guide for Experts; How to Become a Dangerous Expert Witness: Advanced Techniques and Strategies;* and *Writing and Defending Your Independent Medical Examination Report: The Comprehensive Guide.* Mr. Mangraviti may be contacted at seakincjm@aol.com.

**Alex Babitsky, MBA,** is the Directory Manager of SEAK, Inc. Mr. Babitsky received his BS degree from the University of Massachusetts and his MBA from Northeastern University. Mr. Babitsky deals with expert witnesses and the attorneys who retain them on a daily basis as the Product Manager of SEAK's annual *National Directory of Experts* and SEAK's annual *National Directory of Independent Medical Examiners* (www.seakexperts.com). These two publications have a combined distribution of over 100,000 copies per edition. Mr. Babitsky regularly consults with experts of all fields on the subject of expert witness marketing and has designed dozens of marketing pieces for expert witnesses. Mr. Babitsky is the co-author of the 2004 SEAK text *National Guide to Expert Witness Fees and Billing Procedures.* Alex Babitsky may be contacted at alex@seak.com.

# Chapter 1  Overview

## 1.1  Introduction

The need for expert witnesses has never been greater than it is today.  Litigants rely on expert witness testimony in the vast majority of all civil cases. Unfortunately, few experts receive formal training in such subjects as the expert's proper role in the legal system; how to communicate opinions effectively at deposition, at trial, and in a written report; the law and procedure dealing with expert witnesses; ethics; how to deal with attorneys; and how to better manage the business aspects of a forensic practice.  This book has been written to provide information in all of these areas.  It is the comprehensive A–Z resource for all expert witnesses.

The authors have illustrated the points made in this work by example.  They have included 540 examples in the twenty-four chapters of this book.  Each example contains a summary headnote and many contain comments from the authors.  In addition, there are lengthier examples and model documents in the twenty-six appendices.  Many of the examples are summaries of actual court decisions.  These are provided to give context to the principles discussed in this book as examples of how certain issues have been resolved by a court in the jurisdiction in question (always keeping in mind that different jurisdictions may handle similar situations differently).  **This book is in no way intended to give legal advice to the reader.  Substantive and procedural law vary from jurisdiction to jurisdiction. Experts should consider seeking professional legal advice regarding any particular legal issue that may arise from their own forensic practices.**

The chapters in this book are grouped together in the following categories: procedure (2–4), evidence (5), qualifications (6–7), forming and expressing opinions (8–10), expert testimony (11–15), expert witness practice management (16–20), and additional topics (21–24).  A brief description of each of the chapters follows.

## 1.2  Procedure

Chapters 2–4 deal with the basic civil procedure that all experts should be familiar with. Included are an in-depth discussion of the broad-based discovery process, the limits thereto, and sanctions for its abuse.  Also included is a discussion of basic trial procedure, including motions for directed verdicts and motions for judgment notwithstanding the verdict. Appendices E–J provide sample litigation documents including a complaint, an answer, answers to interrogatories, a request for production of documents, a sample schedule from a subpoena duces tecum, and a deposition transcript.  Select Federal Rules of Civil Procedure are provided in Appendix Q.

## 1.3  Evidence

Chapter 5 provides an overview of the Federal Rules of Evidence.  This includes a discussion of the key concepts of relevancy and unfair prejudice as they relate to expert testimony.  Also explained are the "700" series of evidentiary rules that deal specifically with expert testimony.  The chapter concludes with an explanation of the evidentiary rules that govern an attorney's attempt to challenge an expert's credibility by establishing bias and confronting the witness with prior inconsistent statements. Appendix P provides the Federal Rules of Evidence.

## 1.4  Qualifications

Chapter 6 explains in detail the legal requirements to qualify to testify as an expert witness. This explanation is supported by numerous case-based examples. The latter part of Chapter 6 explains how a cross-examiner may challenge an expert's qualifications even after that expert has qualified as an expert. Closely related to the issue of qualifications is that of the expert's curriculum vitae (CV). Chapter 7 provides practical suggestions for experts to make their CVs much more resistant to challenge on cross-examination. A CV quality control checklist is provided in Appendix A. Model CVs are provided in Appendix T.

## 1.5  Forming and Expressing Opinions

Chapter 8 explains in detail the legal requirements for the expression and basis of an expert's opinion. This explanation is supported by numerous examples. Also included in Chapter 8 is an explanation of the methods a cross-examiner may use to challenge an expert's opinion. Chapter 9 explains in detail and with numerous examples the methodology requirements for expert testimony delineated by the U.S. Supreme Court in the landmark *Daubert, G.E.,* and *Kumho Tire* cases. Practical suggestions on how to defeat methodology challenges are provided. Chapter 10 discusses how to express an expert opinion in a written report in such a way that will make the expert less vulnerable on cross-examination. A report quality control checklist is provided in Appendix B. Model expert witness reports are provided in Appendix U.

## 1.6  Expert Testimony

An expert's function is to "assist the trier of fact." This can best be done when the expert communicates clearly and effectively with the trier of fact (usually the jury) at deposition and trial. Chapter 11 provides practical advice on how to "connect" with a jury of lay persons. Effective communication with the trier of fact requires preparation. How to prepare to testify at deposition and trial is covered in Chapter 12. Chapters 13–15 provide practical advice on how to better communicate while testifying. Expert depositions are discussed in Chapter 13. Because most civil cases never reach trial, depositions are the method by which the majority of expert testimony in civil cases is provided. Chapter 14 explains how to best communicate during direct examination. Chapter 15 explains specific techniques on how to deal with cross-examination and what an expert is likely to be asked. Included in Chapter 15 are numerous case examples on the extent of permitted cross-examination of an expert. Areas of common inquiry at deposition and trial are provided in Appendices C and D, respectively.

## 1.7  Expert Witness Practice Management

Experts who would like to be retained in more cases need to understand what attorneys are looking for from experts and how they select experts. This is explained in Chapters 16 and 17. Chapter 18 is a detailed explanation of expert witness marketing. Included are the benefits and drawbacks of various marketing methods including: word of mouth, speaking, writing, referral agencies, advertisements, and online marketing. Also included is a detailed discussion of how to test, track, and evaluate the effectiveness of each aspect of an expert witness's marketing campaign. Chapter 19 provides practical suggestions regarding how much to charge, what to charge for, and how to ensure collection of an expert's fees. Chapter 20 explains the protections and potential liabilities facing experts. Risk management techniques for experts are provided.

Substantial resources relevant to the business aspect of being an expert are provided in the appendices. Appendix K provides a compendium of expert witness referral organizations. Appendix L contains a list of online and print directories. Appendix M provides a list of legal journals and other publications where an expert might want to advertise or submit an article for publication. A list of forensic organizations is provided in Appendix N and a list of bar associations and other legal associations is provided in Appendix O. Appendix R contains model expert fee schedules and agreements. Appendix S contains model bills. A model consulting agreement has been provided in Appendix V and model marketing letters appear in Appendix W. Appendix X contains a brief summary of a detailed fee survey of over 1,000 expert witnesses. Appendix Z contains a list of expert witness practice consultants.

## 1.8 Additional Topics

The complex areas of privilege, work product, and expert discovery limits are discussed in Chapter 21. Numerous examples are provided to illustrate what testimony or information experts and/or consultants can or cannot be compelled to provide, including documents, communications with counsel, financial and tax records, and the situation where the expert was formerly employed by another party in the case. Chapter 22 covers how to communicate effectively with retaining counsel. Chapter 23 discusses expert ethics and provides concrete suggestions on how experts can avoid ethical violations. It is also important to understand the ethical rules that bind attorneys. Sample rules of ethics for attorneys are contained in Appendix Y. Chapter 24 describes the common abuses experts face and how to combat these abuses.

## 1.9 Using This Book

The twenty-four chapters in this book have been placed in a logical order. Although all the chapters interrelate, the authors have attempted to make each chapter stand alone as much as possible. The design allows readers to quickly target the particular areas of concern they may have. To facilitate this process, a detailed table of contents and index have been provided. Where chapters closely interrelate, cross-references have been provided.

## 1.10 Conclusion

It is the authors' hope that this book will help the expert better assist fact finders. It is further their hope that the expert's forensic work will become more rewarding and less stressful. The reader's feedback is encouraged.[1]

---

[1] Feedback can be addressed to the authors at mail@seak.com.

# Chapter 2  Fundamental Elements of a Lawsuit

## 2.1  Introduction

The expert witness needs to be familiar with the procedures involved in the civil litigation process. Effective expert witnesses understand the civil litigation process. This chapter explains the fundamental elements of a civil lawsuit that all experts should understand.

A *lawsuit* has been generally defined by the United States Supreme Court as "any proceeding in a court of justice by which an individual pursues [a] remedy which the law affords."[1] *Civil procedure* is the body of rules and practices by which justice is meted out by the legal system.[2] Although the specific rules of civil procedure vary from jurisdiction to jurisdiction (for example, from state to state), they are generally based upon the Federal Rules of Civil Procedure (FRCP). The Federal Rules of Civil Procedure "govern the procedure in the United States district courts in all suits of a civil nature."[3] The Federal Rules will be the focus of the discussions in this chapter. (See Appendix Q for the full text of the most important Federal Rules of Civil Procedure.)

> **Example 2.1: Rules vary from jurisdiction to jurisdiction**
> You are involved in a products liability lawsuit that has been filed in the U.S. District Court for the District of Massachusetts, in Boston. The Federal Rules of Civil Procedure and any local rules of the District of Massachusetts will govern the lawsuit. Had the suit been filed in a Massachusetts state court, the Massachusetts Rules of Civil Procedure would have governed. Which rules apply could affect things such as what type of disclosure you as an expert will be required to make under discovery, whether you can be deposed, how long your deposition can last, which party is responsible for paying the fee for your expert deposition, and what information you review or the communications you have with retaining counsel that will be protected from discovery.[4]

## 2.2  Complaint

A lawsuit begins or is *commenced* when a document called a *complaint* is filed with the court.[5] Generally, an attorney can file the complaint personally by going to the clerk's office in the courthouse or she can mail the complaint to the clerk, file it by fax, or file it by e-mail. The time of filing can be critically important because the statute of limitations tolls at the commencement of an action. To avoid being barred by the statute of limitations, a party needs to file the lawsuit before the statute runs.

A complaint is a document that sets out, in a plain and simple way, the facts on which the plaintiff's claim for relief is based. The complaint, as with all court documents, begins with the *caption,* which states the name of the court, the docket number, and the names of the various parties to the lawsuit. Next, the complaint contains numbered

---

[1] 91 U.S. 367, 375.

[2] Steven H. Gifts, *Law Dictionary* (1984) 368.

[3] Fed. R. Civ. Pro. 1.

[4] Note also that the Rules of Evidence and Civil Procedure that apply will (along with the jury pool, judges, and convenience) affect the strategic decision a plaintiff makes when deciding where to file a lawsuit.

[5] Fed. R. Civ. Pro. 3. (Please see Appendix E for a sample complaint.)

paragraphs stating the facts that the plaintiff alleges. The complaint concludes with a prayer for relief, a demand for a jury trial (if available), and the signature of the plaintiff's attorney or the plaintiff if the plaintiff is *pro se* (a pro se plaintiff is a plaintiff who represents himself). The purpose of the complaint is to define the lawsuit and put the defendant on notice as to why he is being sued. (Appendix E contains a sample complaint from a personal injury case.)

Usually, the expert should request a copy of the complaint and other legal documents *(pleadings)* in the case from the attorney who retained him. By reviewing the complaint, the expert will be able to understand quickly who is being sued, by whom they are being sued, and what the plaintiff in the case is alleging. This information will allow the expert to have a better understanding of the case and can help him to be a more effective witness.

## 2.3 Service of Process

After the complaint is *filed* with the court, the plaintiff's attorney still needs to have it *served* on the defendant(s). The various methods of service of process vary from jurisdiction to jurisdiction. The methods include in-hand delivery by a sheriff or process server, deposit at the last and usual place of abode, and service via the U.S. Postal Service. Court rules will usually limit the amount of time the plaintiff's attorney can wait between filing the complaint and perfecting service of process. It is generally permissible, however, to serve the complaint after the statute of limitations has run. In such a case, the suit will generally not be barred as long as the case was commenced (i.e., filed) prior to the running of the statute of limitations.

## 2.4 Answers and Pre-Answer Motions

Once the defendant has been served with a complaint, he has only a certain amount of time (20 days under the Federal Rules[6]) to file an *answer* or a pre-answer *motion to dismiss*.[7] Failure to respond in the applicable time period can result in a *default judgment* being entered against the defendant. A default judgment means that the defendant is held by the court to have lost the lawsuit for failure to respond in a timely manner. To avoid a default judgment, a defendant should immediately notify his personal attorney and insurance company if he is sued.

The various bases for pre-answer motions to dismiss include: lack of jurisdiction over the subject matter, lack of jurisdiction over the person, improper venue, insufficiency of service of process, and failure to state a claim upon which relief can be granted. If any of these motions are granted, the complaint will be dismissed. (However, in some cases, the plaintiff could be allowed by the court to refile or amend the complaint and try again.) An example of circumstances where each of these motions may be a valid basis for dismissal of a suit is provided in Box 2.41.

---

[6] Fed. R. Civ. Pro. 12(a)(1)(A).
[7] Fed. R. Civ. Pro. 12(b).

**Box 2.41**

1. **Lack of jurisdiction over the subject matter:** A plaintiff files a personal injury suit in the United States Tax Court.
2. **Lack of jurisdiction over the person:** A professional lives in New York, does no business in California and solicits no clients or business in California. The professional owns no property in California and has never even been to California. A former client who retained the professional in New York moves to California and files a malpractice suit against the professional in the U.S. District Court in Los Angeles.
3. **Improper venue:** A plaintiff and defendant live and work in county X of state A. The plaintiff sues the defendant by filing suit in county Y of state A.
4. **Insufficiency of service of process:** A defendant is sued. The complaint is left by the process server on the doorstep of a neighbor of the defendant's house.
5. **Failure to state a claim upon which relief may be granted:** A physician is working in an emergency room in 2006 and saves patient X's life. Two years later, patient X murders a father of three, Mr. Y. Mr. Y's family now sues the physician under the theory that the physician caused Y's death by saving X's life in 2006.

The *answer* is the document the defendant files as a response to the complaint. In the answer, the defendant responds to each and every numbered paragraph in the complaint by a) admitting the allegation, b) denying the allegation, or c) stating that he lacks sufficient knowledge to admit or deny the allegation. The answer will also list any *affirmative defenses* that the defendant asserts. These include defenses such as statute of limitations, consent, workers' compensation exclusivity, self-defense, and comparative negligence. A defendant asserting an affirmative defense is in effect saying, "Even assuming everything you allege is true, you still cannot prevail because…the statute of limitations has run, you were negligent yourself, I was acting in self-defense, etc." (Appendix F provides a sample answer.)

The expert should ask her retaining attorney to provide her with a copy of the answer. This document is part of the pleadings. By reviewing the answer, the expert will learn which factual issues are in dispute and what affirmative defenses the defendant is asserting. For example, the expert may learn that one of the defendant's affirmative defenses is that the plaintiff herself was negligent, such that her claim should be barred.

## 2.5 Counterclaims, Cross-Claims, and Third-Party Actions

The defendant is allowed to sue the plaintiff back. If the defendant would like to assert a claim of his own against the plaintiff, he would include a *counterclaim* in the answer. For example, let's say a defendant is involved in an automobile accident at an intersection with a traffic light. The defendant claims that her light was green and the plaintiff claims that *his* light was green. Both the defendant and the plaintiff were injured in the accident. The plaintiff sues the defendant for his personal injuries. The defendant can now sue the *plaintiff* for the defendant's personal injuries by including a counterclaim in her answer.

There are two important things to remember about counterclaims. First, they can be very effective in leveraging concessions from a plaintiff. This is especially true if the plaintiff owns property and does not carry liability insurance covering the counterclaim. Second, some counterclaims are *compulsory*. A compulsory counterclaim is waived forever if not brought forward by the defendant as part of the lawsuit when he is being sued.

Compulsory counterclaims are governed under Fed. R. Civ. Pro. 13, a portion of which is reprinted below in Box 2.51.

**Box 2.51**

> **Fed. R. Civ. Pro. 13.  Counterclaim and Cross-Claim**
> (a) Compulsory Counterclaims.
> A pleading shall state as a counterclaim any claim which at the time of serving the pleading the pleader has against any opposing party, if it arises out of the transaction or occurrence that is the subject matter of the opposing party's claim and does not require for its adjudication the presence of third parties of whom the court cannot acquire jurisdiction. But the pleader need not state the claim if (1) at the time the action was commenced the claim was the subject of another pending action, or (2) the opposing party brought suit upon the claim by attachment or other process by which the court did not acquire jurisdiction to render a personal judgment on that claim, and the pleader is not stating any counterclaim under this Rule 13.

In the automobile accident example above, the defendant's personal injury claim against the plaintiff would be a compulsory counterclaim because it arose out of the transaction or occurrence that is the subject of the plaintiff's suit, namely, the automobile accident.  The rationale for the compulsory counterclaim rule is that judicial economy is achieved by avoiding the relitigation of disputed facts.

If a defendant would like to assert a claim against a co-defendant, she would do so by means of a *cross-claim*.  For example, let's suppose that three physicians who operated on a patient are sued for medical malpractice.  The three physicians, depending upon the facts and circumstances of the case, may file cross-claims against one another for contribution and/or indemnification.  In effect, the defendants are trying to blame and collect money from each other if they are found to be liable to the plaintiff.

If a defendant feels that a person who is not a subject of the lawsuit is responsible for the plaintiff's harm, she can bring this person into the lawsuit by means of a *third-party action.*  The person so brought into the case would then be called the *third-party defendant.*  Let's reconsider the three physicians sued for malpractice.  Suppose that four physicians had operated on the plaintiff, but only three were sued because the fourth physician was the plaintiff's father-in-law.  If any of the other three physicians felt that the fourth physician was in any way responsible for the harm caused to the plaintiff, that defendant could bring the fourth physician into the lawsuit as a third-party defendant.

Counsel may seek an expert's opinion to assist in a claim, counterclaim, cross-claim, or third-party action.  Many cases have all of these elements and multiple parties.  An effective expert witness needs to understand which portion or portions of a lawsuit his opinion is being used in.  He can gather this information from the pleadings and by asking retaining counsel to explain who the parties to the case are and who is suing whom for what. The expert should find out the role retaining counsel has in mind for him as soon as possible.

## 2.6  Discovery
*Discovery* is the process by which a party to a lawsuit can find out information held by another party to the lawsuit or third-party witnesses or entities.  There are various methods of discovery including: depositions, interrogatories, requests for admissions, requests for

production of documents, inspection of real evidence, and medical examinations. Once a lawsuit has been commenced, the parties to the suit are allowed to use these discovery methods to gather information. (Chapter 3 discusses the discovery process greater detail.)

## 2.7  Motions

A *motion* is an application to the court requesting an order or rule in favor of the applicant.[8] When attorneys ask the court to do something, they do so by making a motion. Motions can be either oral or written. Common motions that all experts should understand include: motions to dismiss, motions for a directed verdict, motions for judgment notwithstanding the verdict, motions for continuances, motions in limine, and motions for summary judgment. The purpose of each of these common motions is briefly described in Box 2.71.

### Box 2.71

**Motion to dismiss:** The moving party is requesting that a cause of action be dismissed because the alleged facts, even if proven, do not constitute a valid legal claim. In effect, the moving party is responding "so what?" to the claim that has been asserted against them.

**Motion for a directed verdict:** The moving party requests at trial that a cause of action be dismissed because the party with the burden of proof has failed to establish sufficient facts so that a reasonable fact finder (e.g., the jury) could find in the claimant's favor. For example, in a complex toxic tort case, the plaintiff's only expert witness is barred from testifying as to causation under the *Daubert* rule. After the plaintiff rests, the defense moves for a directed verdict on the grounds that the plaintiff has not submitted sufficient proof of causation through an expert witness.

**Motion for judgment notwithstanding the verdict:** This motion is made by the losing party *after* an adverse jury verdict. The moving party is asking that the judge reverse the verdict of the jury. These motions may be granted if the judge determines that the jury verdict had no reasonable support in fact or was contrary to law.[9] These motions are commonly referred to by the initials J.N.O.V.

**Motion for a continuance:** The moving party requests that a scheduled event, for example a hearing or trial, be postponed or *continued* to a later date.

**Motion in limine:** The moving party requests an advanced ruling that evidence that it expects the opposing side to offer be held inadmissible. For example, a party may make a motion in limine to exclude the testimony of an expert for failure to comply with the *Daubert* rule. (See Chapter 9 on the *Daubert* rule.) A motion in limine may be used to obtain a ruling in advance that one side may not ask the expert certain questions. Retaining counsel may file motions in limine to protect their experts against certain types of irrelevant or abusive questions.

**Motion for summary judgment:** The moving party requests, prior to trial, and based solely on documentary evidence (including expert deposition transcripts, reports, and affidavits), that the court grant judgment in its favor because no material facts are in dispute.[10] This is a device used to throw an unprovable case out of court without it getting to the jury. Often, a lawyer with a weak case will seek to survive summary judgment to be able to settle on favorable terms over the threat of a jury trial.

---

[8] See 347 S.W.2d 211, 216.

[9] See 170 S.W.2d 303, 306.

[10] See Fed. R. Civ. Pro. 56.

## 2.8  Trial

Cases that do not settle or are not resolved through a pre-trial procedure, such as a motion to dismiss or a motion for summary judgment, or through arbitration or mediation[11] will need to be tried.  To be effective, experts must be familiar with common trial procedures.  (These procedures are discussed in Chapter 4, "Anatomy of a Civil Trial.")

## 2.9  Remedies

The remedy that a litigant seeks in a civil lawsuit is usually money damages or court orders.  In personal injury cases *special damages,* or "specials," refer to easily determinable damages, such as medical bills and lost wages.  *General damages* refer to all other damages, for example, damages for pain and suffering.  Interest may also be applied to an award for money damages.  *Punitive damages* are damages awarded for the sole purpose of punishing the defendant.  These damages are not based on the harm suffered by the plaintiff but are based on the defendant's conduct and economic situation.  Punitive damages are generally only available if they are specifically authorized by statute and may be limited to a multiple of actual damages.

## 2.10  Interest and Costs

The prevailing party in a lawsuit seeking money damages may also be awarded interest and/or costs.  Attorney's fees are generally not recoverable unless they are specifically authorized by a statute or a pre-existing contractual relationship between the parties.[12]  Interest is awarded, depending upon the jurisdiction, from the time of the accrual of a cause of action[13] or from the time of verdict.  For example, suppose Mr. Jones gets into an auto accident and injures a plaintiff on January 1, 2006.  On January 1, 2008, the plaintiff is awarded $1,000,000 in damages plus interest and costs.  If interest is calculated at a simple 10% per year and accrues from time of the accrual of the cause of action, then $200,000 will be added to this $1,000,000 judgment.  This interest will continue to accrue until the judgment is paid. Costs could include out-of-pocket expenses, such as expert witness fees, filing fees, deposition costs, and photocopying.

## 2.11  Court Orders

Court orders are also known as *injunctions* or *equitable relief.*  Equitable relief is not always available, but in some cases it may be the most appropriate remedy.  For example, let's say a professional signs an employment contract including a two-year covenant not to compete.  One year into the contract, the professional breaks his contract and sets up a competing practice across the street from his former employer.  An appropriate remedy for the professional's former employer may be an injunction ordering the professional to refrain from running the competing practice.  If the professional violates this order, he could be held

---

[11] Arbitration and mediation are forms of what is known as alternative dispute resolution or ADR.

[12] In light of this, it is generally a good idea to have a clause in your retention agreement stating that you are entitled to all costs associated with collecting your unpaid fees, including attorney's fees.  Of course, the best practice is to get your money up front.

[13] When it accrues from the accrual of the cause of action, this is known as *prejudgment interest.*

in contempt and fined a certain amount of money for each day of violation.[14] Note that there is generally no right to a jury trial when the plaintiff seeks equitable relief. It will be a judge, and not a jury, who grants an injunction.

## 2.12 Appeals

Generally, appeals may only be taken after a final judgment in a case. For example, say an expert is testifying in a case and is asked, over her retaining attorney's objections, to submit tax returns from the last three years into evidence. The judge overrules the objection and allows the question. The expert's retaining attorney will not be allowed to appeal this ruling until after the jury has reached an adverse judgment. *Interlocutory appeals* are appeals heard before a final judgment in a case. Interlocutory appeals are only allowed under limited circumstances.

Appellate courts generally only review questions of law, not of fact. They generally do not hear testimony and do not rule on the credibility of witnesses. Therefore, a case is not retried on appeal. The appellate court will decide if an error of law has been made based on the written arguments of the parties in their *appellate briefs,* the content of the record (i.e., the pleadings, exhibits, and testimony transcripts), and oral arguments of the attorneys (if allowed). The remedies granted by an appeals court include a vacated judgment with an order *remanding* the case back to the trial court for further action, usually another trial or a reversal or modification of the trial court's verdict of the judgment that was entered. **Because cases are not retried on appeal, expert witnesses need to perform as well as possible at trial. If an expert witness makes a mistake on the stand, she will not be afforded the opportunity to testify again before the appellate court.**

Even if the appellate court determines that an error of law was made by the trial judge, this does not mean that the appellate court must reverse the trial court's judgment. Under the *harmless error rule* the appellate court will only reverse a judgment if a substantial right of a party was affected.[15] The harmless error rule is another reason why experts need to perform as well as possible at trial. Even if the case is appealed and the issue under appeal has merit, the appellate court could deny the appeal under the harmless error doctrine. Because appeals are difficult to win and are subject to the harmless error doctrine, it is important that experts minimize the mistakes they make at trial.

When a litigant is awarded money damages, this is done by means of a *judgment.* For example, let's say that a plaintiff wins a $1,000,000 action against a defendant. A judgment for $1,000,000 would be entered in the court records in favor of the plaintiff and against the defendant. A judgment is not a court order to pay the damages. For example, if

---

[14] The fines for violating a court order can be quite substantial. For example, when the New York City Transit Workers struck and violated a return to work order in December 2005, their union was fined $1,000,000 *per day* and the head of the union was sentenced to ten days in jail.

[15] Fed. R. Civ. Pro. 61. **Harmless Error:** No error in either the admission or the exclusion of evidence and no error or defect in any ruling or order or in anything done or omitted by the court or by any of the parties is ground for granting a new trial or for setting aside a verdict or for vacating, modifying, or otherwise disturbing a judgment or order, unless refusal to take such action appears to the court inconsistent with substantial justice. The court at every stage of the proceeding must disregard any error or defect in the proceeding which does not affect the substantial rights of the parties.

the defendant does not have insurance or $1,000,000 in assets, he will not be held in contempt of court for failure to pay. In many cases, a defendant against whom a judgment has been entered can discharge his obligation to pay after filing for bankruptcy.

### 2.13  Conclusion

An expert who understands the fundamental elements of a lawsuit is well positioned to be effective and successful.

# Chapter 3  The Discovery Process

## 3.1  Introduction

The Rules of Civil Procedure generally provide for very liberal, broad-based discovery. There are two policy rationales for the liberal discovery procedures that dominate today's civil lawsuit: the elimination of surprise at trial and the encouragement of settlement. The theory is that if all parties know all there is to know about the other side's case (including their experts and their experts' opinions), they will be able to evaluate rationally the merits and weaknesses of the case and settle the matter. Additionally, if the suit does go to trial, the outcome will be less dependent on gamesmanship because the possibility of unfair surprises has been minimized through the discovery process.

Expert witnesses need to understand and appreciate that the Rules of Civil Procedure permit broad-based discovery. These broad-based and liberal discovery rules allow counsel to ask far-ranging questions at deposition, to go on "fishing expeditions," and to subpoena documents and tangible things that are in one's care, custody, or control. It is presumed by the law that allowing liberal discovery will encourage settlement and eliminate surprises at trial. Because over 90% of cases settle before trial, these liberal discovery rules can be judged to be serving much of their purpose.

## 3.2  Scope

The scope of discovery is delineated in Fed. R. Civ. Pro. 26(b)(1).

**Box 3.21**

| |
|---|
| **Fed. R. Civ. Pro. 26(b)(1).**<br>(b) Discovery Scope and Limits.<br>Unless otherwise limited by order of the court in accordance with these rules, the scope of discovery is as follows:<br><br>(1) In General.<br>Parties may obtain discovery regarding any matter, not privileged, that is relevant to the claim or defense of any party, including the existence, description, nature, custody, condition, and location of any books, documents, or other tangible things and the identity and location of persons having knowledge of any discoverable matter. For good cause, the court may order discovery of any matter relevant to the subject matter involved in the action. Relevant information need not be admissible at the trial if the discovery appears reasonably calculated to lead to the discovery of admissible evidence. All discovery is subject to the limitations imposed by Rule 26(b)(2)(i), (ii), and (iii). |

The broad-based nature of Rule 26 must be kept in mind when one serves as an expert in a case. Note that under Rule 26 the information sought need not even be admissible at trial. The discovery rules permit the acquisition of a broad range of information.

### Example 3.1: Fishing expeditions generally allowed

You are a sixty-two-year-old physician who has been retained by the defense to testify regarding an IME you performed on a plaintiff who has been involved in a motor vehicle accident. You are deposed by the plaintiff's attorney. The plaintiff's attorney spends forty-five minutes asking you every place you have lived and worked since you were sixteen years old. Such "fishing expedition" questions are generally allowable because of the broad-based discovery made available under Rule 26. The attorney asking such questions could argue that the questions may reveal information about your background that could be relevant to your credibility as a witness. If you serve as an expert witness in a case, your credibility is always a legitimate issue. Your experience and qualifications are relevant to your credibility.

### Example 3.2: Expert can be asked if she was ever a party to litigation
*Cabana v. Forcier,* 200 F.R.D. 9 (D. Mass. 2001)
The expert could be compelled to answer deposition questions regarding whether she had ever been a party to any litigation and whether she had ever been the subject of a disciplinary proceeding. The questions were likely to lead to evidence relevant to the expert's skill and her credibility.

### Example 3.3: Discovery rules should be liberally interpreted to permit wide-ranging discovery
*Ragge v. MCA/Universal,* 165 F.R.D. 601 (C.D. Cal. 1995)
The purpose of discovery is to remove surprise from trial preparation so parties obtain evidence necessary to evaluate and resolve their dispute; toward this end, FRCP 26(b) is liberally interpreted to permit wide-ranging discovery of all information reasonably calculated to lead to discovery of admissible evidence, even though discoverable information need not be admissible at trial.

### Example 3.4: Expert can be deposed about involvement in other malpractice cases
*Bockweg v. Anderson,* 117 F.R.D. 563 (M.D. N.C. 1987)
Defendants in medical malpractice actions are permitted to depose plaintiffs' expert witnesses regarding their prior or present involvement in other malpractice actions, in conformity with the purpose of Rule 26, which sanctions liberal discovery of expert witnesses, including information relevant only for impeachment.

### Example 3.5: Expert's personnel file discoverable
*Michael v. Gates,* 45 Cal. Rptr. 163 (Cal. App. 1995)
Personnel files of a retired Los Angeles police officer who was testifying as an expert witness were discoverable.

### Example 3.6: Disciplinary record of expert discoverable
*Ceramic Corp. of Am. v. Inka Maritime Corp.,* 163 F.R.D. 584 (C.D. Cal. 1995)
Information regarding an expert's employment as a master, including reprimands or disciplinary proceedings, were relevant and discoverable, but family, health, and financial documents were not.

## 3.3 Privilege
Rule 26(b)(1) provides that discovery may not be made of "privileged" matters. These include the attorney-client, husband-wife, and physician-patient privileges. A testifying expert's communications with retaining counsel are generally not protected by the attorney-client privilege because the expert witness is not being represented by retaining counsel. An expert witness should check with an attorney in her jurisdiction if she is asked through discovery to disclose information that she feels may be privileged.

### Example 3.7: Question calling for privileged information
You are an expert witness in a controversial case. At deposition, the opposing attorney asks you if you have discussed the case and the testimony you intend to give with your spouse. Such a

question could call for information protected by the spousal privilege. The attorney who retained you might instruct you not to answer this question because it calls for such privileged information.

**Example 3.8: Attorney-client privilege generally not applicable because attorney does not represent the expert**
*In re Omeprazole Patent Litigation,* 2005 WL 818821 (S.D. New York 2005)
Communication between counsel and its retained expert was relevant and discoverable.

**Example 3.9: Materials submitted to expert not privileged**
*Vitalo v. Cabot Corp.,* 212 F.R.D. 478 (E.D. Pa. 2002)
Attorney's copies of materials submitted to, and considered by, experts were not subject to attorney work-product privilege.

**Example 3.10: Personnel records "confidential" but not privileged**
*Rollins ex rel Rollins v. Barlow,* 188 F.Supp.2d 660 (S.D. W.Va. 2002)
Personnel records of state troopers who would offer expert opinions were not privileged as that term is used in civil discovery. This was true even though they were "confidential," just as personnel records of any employer should be confidential to protect the privacy concerns of employees.

## 3.4 Other Limits to Discovery

Although discovery is broad-based, it is not unlimited. As has already been discussed, privileged information is not discoverable. There are further limitations to discovery as well. Consider Rule 26(b)(2).

### Box 3.41

| |
|---|
| **Fed. R. Civ. Pro. 26(b)(2). Limitations.**<br>By order, the court may alter the limits in these rules on the number of depositions and interrogatories or the length of depositions under Rule 30. By order or local rule, the court may also limit the number of requests under Rule 36. The frequency or extent of use of the discovery methods otherwise permitted under these rules and by any local rule shall be limited by the court if it determines that: (i) the discovery sought is unreasonably cumulative or duplicative, or is obtainable from some other source that is more convenient, less burdensome, or less expensive; (ii) the party seeking discovery has had ample opportunity by discovery in the action to obtain the information sought; or (iii) the burden or expense of the proposed discovery outweighs its likely benefit, taking into account the needs of the case, the amount in controversy, the parties' resources, the importance of the issues at stake in the litigation, and the importance of the proposed discovery in resolving the issues. The court may act upon its own initiative after reasonable notice or pursuant to a motion under Rule 26(c). |

**Example 3.11: Overly burdensome request in light of the amount in controversy**
You are sued by your office cleaning company. The cleaning company alleges that you haven't paid $3,000 of their bills. Your position is that the company's work was of very poor quality. The cleaning company serves your attorney with a discovery request requesting, among other things, "all invoices and canceled checks" to and from the cleaning company for the last five years and "any and all other documents relating to the running" of your office for the last five years. You may be able to use Rule 26(b)(2) to attempt to limit your disclosure of the invoices and canceled checks.

**Example 3.12: Overly burdensome discovery request**
*Ricotta v. Allstate Ins. Co.,* 211 F.R.D. 622 (S.D. Cal. 2002)
An insured under a homeowners' policy brought suit against the insurer, alleging that it acted in bad faith in denying a claim for damage to his home caused by a wood-eating fungus. On the plaintiff's motion to compel production of documents, the district court held that the insured was not entitled to disclosure of every report prepared for the insurer by the expert whose report was the basis of the denial of his claim. The court cited Rule 26(b)(2) and reasoned that the burden and expense of requiring the insurer to respond to the request far outweighed the likely benefit of investigating potential bias. According to the defendant, responding to the discovery would require the defendant to hand-sort and manually review each and every claim file in its possession dating from 1987 (approximately 50,000 files).

Attorney *work product* is generally nondiscoverable. This exception to discovery is designed to allow the adversary process to function properly. The work product exception to discovery is governed by Federal Rule 26(b)(3) and Rule 26(b)(4). An expert needs to remember that, generally speaking, if she is disclosed as an expert who will testify at trial, she will need to respond to the other parties' discovery requests for documents and other information. If, on the other hand, she is not disclosed as an expert who will testify at trial but is merely a *litigation consultant,* she will generally not be subject to discovery by the other parties in the case. Because the work-product doctrine provides little protection from discovery to experts who are to testify at trial, such experts should be very careful about creating any documents or correspondence that may damage their credibility. **If an expert expects to be called at trial, she should assume that everything she writes regarding the case, even if she labels it "confidential," will be subject to discovery and disclosure.** (Chapter 21 discusses confidentiality and work product in greater detail.)

**Box 3.42**

---

**Fed. R. Civ. Pro. 26(b)(3). Trial Preparation: Materials.**
Subject to the provisions of subdivision (b)(4) of this rule, a party may obtain discovery of documents and tangible things otherwise discoverable under subdivision (b)(1) of this rule and prepared in anticipation of litigation or for trial by or for another party or by or for that other party's representative (including the other party's attorney, consultant, surety, indemnitor, insurer, or agent) only upon a showing that the party seeking discovery has substantial need of the materials in the preparation of the party's case and that the party is unable without undue hardship to obtain the substantial equivalent of the materials by other means. In ordering discovery of such materials when the required showing has been made, the court shall protect against disclosure of the mental impressions, conclusions, opinions, or legal theories of an attorney or other representative of a party concerning the litigation.

A party may obtain without the required showing a statement concerning the action or its subject matter previously made by that party. Upon request, a person not a party may obtain without the required showing a statement concerning the action or its subject matter previously made by that person. If the request is refused, the person may move for a court order. The provisions of Rule 37(a)(4) apply to the award of expenses incurred in relation to the motion. For purposes of this paragraph, a statement previously made is (A) a written statement signed or otherwise adopted or approved by the person making it, or (B) a stenographic, mechanical, electrical, or other recording, or a transcription thereof, which is a substantially verbatim recital of an oral statement by the person making it and contemporaneously recorded.

---

## Box 3.43

**Fed. R. Civ. Pro. 26(b)(4). Trial Preparation: Experts.**

(A) A party may depose any person who has been identified as an expert whose opinions may be presented at trial. If a report from the expert is required under subdivision (a)(2)(B), the deposition shall not be conducted until after the report is provided.

(B) A party may, through interrogatories or by deposition, discover facts known or opinions held by an expert who has been retained or specially employed by another party in anticipation of litigation or preparation for trial and who is not expected to be called as a witness at trial, only as provided in Rule 35(b) or upon a showing of exceptional circumstances under which it is impracticable for the party seeking discovery to obtain facts or opinions on the same subject by other means.

(C) Unless manifest injustice would result, (i) the court shall require that the party seeking discovery pay the expert a reasonable fee for time spent in responding to discovery under this subdivision; and (ii) with respect to discovery obtained under subdivision (b)(4)(B) of this rule the court shall require the party seeking discovery to pay the other party a fair portion of the fees and expenses reasonably incurred by the latter party in obtaining facts and opinions from the expert.

### Example 3.13: Expert consultant

You are retained as a consultant (the attorney does not intend to call you as a witness at trial) by the plaintiff in a case. You review the records in question and issue a written report to the plaintiff's attorney with your thoughts on how to best attack the opposing expert's credentials and opinions. Generally, your report will not be discoverable because you are not a testifying expert.

### Example 3.14: Testifying experts usually subject to discovery of anything they considered

You are retained as an expert witness and are expected to give testimony at trial. You send a confidential written report to the attorney who retained you. Generally, there is no protection against disclosure through discovery of this "confidential" report. The work-product doctrine does not operate to prevent discovery because the attorney intends to call you as a witness at trial.

### Example 3.15: Discovery might be allowed from a nontestifying consultant

You are retained as a consultant on a case in which a victim has died. You perform an examination of the body and issue a report to the retaining attorney. The body is then cremated and the plaintiff hires a second expert to testify at trial. The defense may be able to use Rule 26(b)(4) to force discovery of your otherwise nondiscoverable report. The defense could argue that the "exceptional circumstances" mentioned in Rule 26(b)(4) apply to a case such as this one because the other side cannot obtain the information by other means.

### Example 3.16: No exceptional circumstances, nontestifying expert's work product protected

*Hollinger Intern. Inc. v. Hollinger Inc.,* 230 F.R.D. 508 (N.D. Ill. 2005)

A corporation sued former officers and related parties for breach of fiduciary duty, unjust enrichment, conversion, and civil conspiracy, alleging systematic looting of the corporation's assets via sham non-compete payments. The court held that lack of exceptional circumstances precluded discovery of the work-product-protected opinion portion of the corporation's nontestifying executive compensation expert's report. The court reasoned that:

> exceptional circumstances require that "it is impracticable for the party seeking discovery to obtain facts or opinions on the same subject by other means." Fed.R.Civ.P. 26(b)(4)(B). Exceptional circumstances may be shown when: (1) the condition observed by the expert is no longer observable; or (2) the condition is subject to replication, but the costs would be judicially prohibitive. *Ludwig v. Pilkington North America, Inc.,* 2003 WL 22242224, at *3 (N.D.Ill. Sept. 29, 2003) (citing *Braun,* 84 F.3d at 236).

Defendants have not demonstrated exceptional circumstances justifying the disclosure of the Cook Report. Cook is not the only source of opinions regarding executive compensation. Defendants have the factual information underlying the disclosed portion of Cook's analysis and may retain their own experts to conduct their own analyses. Defendants will also have the opportunity to depose Hollinger's trial experts.

### Example 3.17: No exceptional circumstances, discovery from nontestifying expert not allowed

*Spearman Industries, Inc. v. St. Paul Fire and Marine Ins. Co.,* 128 F.Supp.2d 1148 (N.D. Ill. 2001)

This was an insurance bad faith case where the insured sued its insurer. The insured asked an appraiser to come and look at some storm damage to its roof. At issue was whether the insurance company could gain access to the report of a nontestifying expert. The court held that it could not, as the exceptional circumstances test of Fed.R.Civ.P. 26(b)(4)(B) was not met. The court reasoned:

> Under Rule 26(b)(4)(B), the party seeking discovery from the non-testifying expert consulted in anticipation of litigation "carries a heavy burden in demonstrating the existence of exceptional circumstances." Ager, 622 F.2d at 503 (internal quotations omitted). Exceptional circumstances are shown if the party seeking discovery is unable to obtain equivalent information from other sources. *Eliasen v. Hamilton,* 111 F.R.D. 396, 400 (N.D.Ill.1986) (internal quotation omitted). The party seeking discovery may meet this exceptional circumstances standard in one of two ways. First, the moving party may show that the object or condition at issue is destroyed or has deteriorated after the non-testifying expert observes it but before the moving party's expert has an opportunity to observe it. See *Disidore v. Mail Contractors of Am., Inc.,* 196 F.R.D. 410, 417 (D.Kan.2000); *Hartford Fire Ins.,* 154 F.R.D. at 207. Second, the moving party may show there are no other available experts in the same field or subject area. See *Bailey v. Meister Brau, Inc.,* 57 F.R.D. 11, 14 (N.D.Ill.1972) (party seeking discovery must prove that opinions by others on the subject are unavailable).
>
> Here, defendant fails to allege either that an alteration of the roof prevented it from obtaining necessary information about the condition of the roof, or that there are no other available experts in the same field or subject area. In fact, defendant has substantial information relating to the condition of the roof and the cause of damage. Defendant had ample opportunity to conduct whatever investigations it desired, and the site was inspected by Brian Mager of Starr Roofing and Tim Dickson of Stuart Jacobson & Associates, both hired by defendant. Thus, Kurucz is not the sole source of facts and opinions regarding the cause of damage to the roof. Defendant simply argues that exceptional circumstances exist because plaintiff is shopping for an expert. Even assuming plaintiff chose not to use Kurucz because he rendered an adverse opinion, "this is not only perfectly permissible, but...the very purpose of [Rule 26(b)(4)(B)] is to protect [a plaintiff] from having [its expert's] testimony used by [its] opponent....The Rule was intended to prevent an advisor from becoming an involuntary witness." *Eliasen,* 111 F.R.D. at 401 (internal quotations omitted). Defendant has not met its heavy burden of showing that the present situation qualifies as an exceptional circumstance. Thus, defendant is prohibited from presenting Kurucz as a witness.

### Example 3.18: Exceptional circumstances found, discovery from nontestifying expert allowed

*Bank Brussels Lambert v. Chase Manhattan Bank, N.A.,* 175 F.R.D. 34 (S.D.N.Y. 1997)

This was a financial fraud case. The defendant had hired the accounting firm Arthur Andersen as a nontestifying expert in the matter. The court held that discovery could be had from Arthur Andersen because the exceptional circumstances test was met in this case. The key records observed by Andersen 2 to 3 years before the lawsuit was filed could not be shown to have been in the same condition and as complete as they were when Andersen analyzed them. The court stated:

BPS has made the requisite showing of exceptional circumstances. Andersen was able to observe and analyze AroChem's financial condition as soon as the discrepancy was discovered in December 1991. Andersen apparently had "a broad base charge to just look everywhere and find anything and turn it over twice." The bulk of Andersen's investigation lasted from December 1991 through June 1992, consuming 10,000 hours of time, and involving eight to fifteen people. During this time, numerous other parties were given unlimited access to AroChem's books and records, as well as its personal legal files. Although there is no evidence that any documents were lost during this time, it was not until October 1993, almost two years after Andersen began its investigation, that the files from AroChem's offices were placed in storage and maintained under close supervision. The same month that the documents were placed in storage, the Bank Group sued CLS, and four months later, in February 1994, the Bank Group sued BPS.

It would be impracticable for BPS to reconstruct AroChem's financial condition, which Andersen had the opportunity to observe and analyze extensively for several months immediately after the discrepancy was discovered. BPS was sued more than two years after the discrepancy was discovered and more than one year after Andersen and numerous parties had the opportunity to observe, remove, and copy AroChem's files. AroChem's files were placed in storage only after numerous parties had unlimited access to the files over the course of a year or more. It is likely that documents were rearranged and possible that documents were lost or altered over the course of the year that the numerous parties had unlimited, unmonitored access to the files. As noted earlier, at least one of plaintiffs' officers has conceded that it would be more difficult now to reconstruct AroChem's collateral position as of December 1991 than it was for Andersen to reconstruct that collateral position when it conducted its work.

Moreover, even if it were possible to reconstruct Andersen's financial condition, the costs of hiring an expert to reconstruct that situation and then to analyze it would be judicially prohibitive. Andersen itself spent over 10,000 hours over the course of six months, utilizing eight to fifteen people, in investigating AroChem's situation. Given that BPS was sued long after Andersen had already completed the bulk of its investigation, BPS did not have the same opportunity to hire an expert to investigate the situation as the parties who hired Andersen had. Thus, given the evidence in the record, I conclude that BPS has met its burden of showing exceptional circumstances under which it is impracticable for BPS to obtain facts or opinions on the same subject by other means.

## 3.5 Protective Orders

*Protective orders* are allowed to prevent possible abuses that could occur through the rules of discovery. The court has discretion to issue *protective orders* to protect a party or person from "annoyance, embarrassment, oppression or undue burden or expense."[1] The court can also issue protective orders to protect "a trade secret, or other confidential research, development, or commercial information."[2] Protective orders are issued after a motion is made by the person or party seeking the order. A person need not be a party to the lawsuit to seek a protective order. The granting of a protective order is within the court's sound discretion. When granting a protective order, the court may rule that the discovery be limited or disallowed, rule that the discovery only be made available to certain persons, or limit the method of discovery used.[3]

### Example 3.19: Income tax returns
You are a fifty-five-year-old professional who is to be called as an expert witness in a case. The opposing side subpoenas your personal income tax returns from the last five years in an effort to establish bias. To protect yourself from the release of these sensitive documents, you can file a

---

[1] Fed. R. Civ. Pro. 26(c).
[2] Fed. R. Civ. Pro. 26(c)(7).
[3] Fed. R. Civ. Pro. 26(c).

motion with the court for a protective order. In response to such a motion, the court could issue a protective order stating that you need not produce the returns or that the returns be held in confidence by the opposing side.

**Comment:** For more on producing financial records, please see Section 21.7.

### Example 3.20: Portions of income tax returns discoverable
*State ex rel. Creighton v. Jackson,* 879 S.W.2d 639 (Mo. Ct. App. 1994)
The court of appeals held that the trial court did not abuse its discretion by requiring an expert witness to produce portions of his federal income tax returns reflecting income received for service as an expert witness or consultant over a five-year period. However, the court did not determine the admissibility of the records at trial—rather, it noted that the information would be admissible at trial only if it reflected legitimately on the expert's objectivity.

### Example 3.21: Grounds for protective order
*Grinnell Corp. v. Hackett,* 70 F.R.D. 326 (D.C. R.I. 1976)
Showing that likelihood of harassment was "more probable than not" would be insufficient to warrant a protective order against discovery without concomitantly showing that the information sought was fully irrelevant and could have no possible bearing on issues.

### Example 3.22: Cannot inquire about expert's gross income at deposition
*Rogers v. U.S. Navy,* 223 F.R.D. 533 (S.D. Cal. 2004)
The defendant (the United States Navy) filed a motion for a protective order seeking to preclude the plaintiff from discovering the amount of total gross income the government's medical expert, Dr. Schwab, derived from medical-legal work. The court granted the motion and reasoned:

> There is no controlling authority regarding the issue of the discoverability of the type of private financial information sought by Plaintiff from Dr. Schwab. Persuasive authority, however, is provided by the case of *Behler v. Hanlon,* 199 F.R.D. 553 (D.Md.2001). In Behler, the Plaintiff sought extensive private financial information regarding the defendant's medical expert. As in this case, the plaintiff in Behler contended that the defense medical expert was biased for financial reasons to provide an opinion favorable to the defense. Plaintiff sought the private financial information for use at trial to impeach the medical expert's credibility by demonstrating bias. The court in Behler closely examined the scope of relevancy of such information under Rule 26(b)(1) of the Federal Rules of Civil Procedure, as well as the proper scope of the information as impeachment testimony at the time of trial.
>
> The court concluded that the information sought by plaintiff regarding the doctor's activities as a defense expert witness was certainly relevant. *Id.* at 561. The court further concluded, however, that the scope of information sought by the plaintiff was "overkill" and thus properly limited pursuant to Rule 26(b)(2) or Rule 26(c). *Id.* at 562. In the court's view, "the jury readily should be able to assess possible bias on the part of an expert witness if they are made aware of the total percentage of his or her gross income that is earned from providing expert witness services." *Id.* The court also required defendant to disclose information regarding prior cases in which the doctor had served as an expert and the names of each insurance company for which the doctor had provided expert witnesses services in personal injuries cases, similar to the information required under Rule 26(a)(2)(B).
>
> In this case, the government has agreed to have Dr. Schwab disclose a substantial amount of information regarding the nature of his forensic work. Dr. Schwab will provide estimates of the percentage of his medical practice that involves forensic work versus clinical work, the percentage of his income that is derived from forensic work, the percentage of his forensic practice that is on behalf of plaintiffs versus defendants, the number of forensic evaluations he performs per week, and his hourly billing rate for performing forensic services. Plaintiff will also learn the actual dollar amount that Dr. Schwab has been and will be paid by the government for his services in this case. This should be more

than sufficient information to allow Plaintiff to effectively cross-examine Dr. Schwab at the time of trial regarding his opinions and the financial motive or bias that may have influenced those opinions.

In opposition to the government's motion, Plaintiff's counsel argues that while the Behler decision may be appropriate in run-of-the-mill personal injury cases, this case is "unique" based upon the dramatically unfavorable 28-page opinion rendered by Dr. Schwab. Plaintiff's counsel argues that Dr. Schwab's opinion includes irrelevant information and oversteps the bounds of the expert designation, showing that Dr. Schwab will go to any extent to reach a conclusion supportive of the party that retains his services. Plaintiff's counsel, however, does not explain how he would be unfairly limited in arguing bias unless he learns the actual dollar amount of Dr. Schwab's gross income from forensic work. Plaintiff's counsel does not explain how the information that Dr. Schwab has agreed to provide will be insufficient to show bias and prejudice.

The Court concludes that Plaintiff's counsel will be more than able to challenge Dr. Schwab's impartiality at the time of trial based upon the information he has been willing to provide without the need to learn the actual dollar amount of Dr. Schwab's annual income. Because Plaintiff does not persuasively explain the need to learn Dr. Schwab's private financial information, the scope of inquiry is properly limited pursuant to Rule 26(b)(2)(iii) and Rule 26(c).

Conclusion: For the reasons set forth herein, the government's renewed motion for protective order is GRANTED. Plaintiff's counsel shall not inquire of Dr. Schwab at the time of his deposition regarding the amount of his gross annual income from forensic work.

## Example 3.23: Protective order to keep expert's identity a secret where revelation would endanger life

*Carhart v. Ashcroft,* 300 F.Supp.2d 921 (D. Neb. 2004)

This case involved a physician expert witness who performed partial-birth abortions. The court granted a protective order to include taking the witness's testimony *in camera,* unless, by agreement of the parties, a trial deposition attended by the judge would suffice, sealing the expert report, and otherwise prohibiting undue disclosure of the identity of the witness during discovery, at trial, or after trial. The court stated, "without any question, the physician's life would truly be endangered should his or her identity be disclosed to the public during depositions, trial, or otherwise. In 17 years of dealing with questions like this in both criminal and civil cases, I have never seen a more compelling showing for the need to protect the identity of a witness."

## Example 3.24: Protective order denied for expert's other reports

*Hussey v. State Farm Lloyds Ins. Co.,* 216 F.R.D. 591 (E.D. Tex. 2003)

This was an insurance bad faith case. The plaintiffs sought all reports the insurer's expert had prepared for the insurer in other matters in the last 5 years. The insurance company sought a protective order. This order was denied. The court reasoned that the proposed discovery was relevant and that allowing the discovery would not cause the insurer undue burden or expense. It stated:

> Federal Rule of Civil Procedure 26(c) authorizes this court "[u]pon motion by a party...from whom discovery is sought,...and for good cause shown" to enter a protective order prohibiting or limiting discovery. A party seeking a protective order to prevent or postpone a deposition must show good cause and the specific need for protection. See *Landry v. Air Line Pilots Ass'n,* 901 F.2d 404, 435 (5th Cir.), cert. denied, 498 U.S. 895, 111 S.Ct. 244, 112 L.Ed.2d 203 (1990). "Good cause" exists when justice requires the protection of "a party or person from any annoyance, embarrassment, oppression, or undue burden or expense." Fed.R.Civ.P. 26(c); Landry, 901 F.2d at 435. The court is required to balance the competing interests of allowing discovery and protecting the parties and deponents from undue burdens.
>
> As stated above, State Farm has not shown that allowing the discovery requested will cause it an undue burden or expense. Accordingly, the Court finds no good cause to enter a protective order under Fed.R.Civ.P. 26(c).

**Comment:** Past reports and past deposition transcripts can be a gold mine of information for opposing counsel. Opposing counsel will use these to try to point out inconsistencies between the expert's current testimony and what the expert has said or written in past cases. Many experienced experts discard reports and transcripts once a case closes so that they will not be required to produce these materials in future cases. (Experts are not required to produce documents that are not in their care, custody, or control.) Such a policy also keeps down the expert's storage expenses.

## 3.6  Sanctions

If a party, deponent, or attorney unjustifiably refuses to disclose requested information, the party seeking the information can make a *motion to compel* the party or deponent to provide the requested discovery.  If the motion to compel is granted, the party seeking the discovery may also seek sanctions against the party, deponent, and/or attorney refusing to provide the discovery.  The potential sanctions include the costs of bringing the motion to compel, including attorney's fees.  If the motion to compel is *denied,* the party and/or attorney bringing the motion to compel may be ordered by the court to pay the attorney's fees and costs of the person or party from whom discovery is sought.  Sanctions can also be granted that affect the substance of a case.  For example, if a plaintiff fails to answer interrogatories or produce requested documents in the time specified by the rules, the court could enter judgment in favor of the defendant or bar the plaintiff from introducing certain evidence.

### Example 3.25: Potential consequences of failure to answer questions at deposition
You have been retained by a plaintiff to provide expert testimony.  The defendant is represented by the largest law firm in your city.  The firm charges $350 per hour.  At deposition, you are asked by the annoying defense lawyer in his $2,000 suit how much money you earned last year and what percentage of that income was derived from expert witness work.  You are offended that he would ask such a personal question and respond, "That's none of your business."  He asks again and you still refuse to answer.  By refusing to answer this question, you are taking a risk of sanctions.  If the defense files a motion to compel you to answer and this motion is granted, you may be forced to pay the defense's attorneys' fees ($350 per hour) associated with bringing this motion to compel.

### Example 3.26: How sanction is determined
*Cooper v. Lewis,* 719 So.2d 944 (Fla. App. 1998)
In this case, the Florida court commented on how sanctions should be assessed.  It stated:

> Our inquiry is limited to what the appropriate sanction is, what the proper procedure for that sanction is, and against whom such sanction may be imposed when the expert fails to comply with a proper request. In our case, the doctor who performed the IME appeared at his deposition without the requested information relating to his past experience as one who provides IMEs. The doctor stated that because of short notice he did not have the information available.
>
> When it is disclosed or made apparent to the trial court that such a witness has falsified, misrepresented, or obfuscated the required data, the aggrieved party may move to exclude the witness from testifying, or further, move for the imposition of costs and attorneys fees in gathering the information necessary to expose the miscreant expert.
>
> Even if the doctor wrongfully withheld the requested information, there appears to be no authority for sanctioning an innocent defendant, particularly in a personal injury action. If the plaintiff, at the direction of his lawyer, goes to a doctor, knowing the doctor will find permanent injuries when there are none, then the plaintiff, his lawyer, and his doctor have conspired to work a fraud on the court and, upon proper proof, all should be subject to sanctions. But in this case, the defendant is not alleged to have

committed any wrong. He didn't choose the doctor. For that matter, in a large majority of such cases, the defendant doesn't even choose the lawyer.

The trial court erred in striking the doctor from defendant's witness list because of procedural irregularities and because the record does not support a finding of willful violation (contempt) or a violation of a court order. The court erred in assessing attorney's fees and costs against the defendant because the record does not support the imposition of sanctions against him.

## Example 3.27: Witness pays for refusal to answer question at deposition

*Rockwell International, Inc. v. Pos-A-Traction Industries, Inc.,* 712 F.2d 1324 (9th Cir. 1983)
If a motion to compel discovery of a deponent who is not a party is granted, the deponent may be required to pay the moving party's reasonable expenses unless opposition to the motion was substantially justified. Here, a nonparty witness agreed to have his deposition taken for use in two separate cases—a state action and a federal action by the same plaintiff. When the opposing attorney in the state action had completed his questions, the witness, on the advice of counsel, refused to answer questions by the opposing attorney in the federal action on the theory that no more than one attorney may propound questions on behalf of the same party at the taking of a deposition. The court found that the refusal to answer was unjustified and that the plaintiff could be awarded reasonable expenses incurred in obtaining an order compelling the witness to submit to discovery. These expenses were awarded against the witness and the witness's attorney, who had advised him not to answer.

## Example 3.28: Refusal to cooperate with taking of deposition, expert barred from case

*Waicis v. Superior Court,* 226 Cal. App. 3d 283 (Cal. App. Dist. 1 1990)
In this medical malpractice case, the plaintiff's expert on standard of care, a D.M.D., refused to cooperate in the taking of his deposition. The expert forced a rescheduling of his deposition six times, often with little notice, and insisted that it be scheduled in the evenings and at awkward times. In the middle of a Saturday deposition, after "clear representation to the trial court that [the expert] would be available all Saturday," the expert claimed he had a personal appointment and left the deposition. The appellate court stated, "The trial court did everything it could to permit Dr. Frankel's deposition but the witness simply would not cooperate, even to the extent of directly violating the court's order that he be available for all of Saturday for his deposition." Additionally, it declared, "Not only is the evidence that [the expert] was uncooperative in permitting his deposition to be taken substantial, it is overwhelming."

The court approved the trial court's exclusion of the expert's testimony and awarded costs to the defendant, stating: "It is an affront to the orderly and expeditious disposition of cases for any witness, especially an expert witness, to be so uncooperative...[the expert's] conduct smacks of game playing."

**Comment:** Experts who act in good faith should be able to arrange convenient times for their depositions. The above result is what can happen when the expert does not act in good faith.

## Example 3.29: Sanctions assessed against plaintiff for expert's failure to answer questions at deposition after being instructed not to answer by retaining counsel

*Cabana v. Forcier,* 200 F.R.D. 9 (D. Mass. 2001)
In this case, a truck driver who worked as an independent contractor brought suit against a truck leasing business and one of its clients, seeking damages for injuries allegedly caused by exposure to hazardous waste. The defendant took the deposition of Cabana's treating physician and expert witness, Dr. Sica. On the second day of that deposition, defense counsel asked Dr. Sica whether she had ever been a party to any litigation, and whether she had ever been the subject of a

disciplinary proceeding.  Counsel for Cabana objected to those questions on the grounds that Dr. Sica's involvement in prior litigation and/or disciplinary proceedings was not relevant to the instant case and, accordingly, Dr. Sica was instructed not to answer.  Defendant then moved for an order compelling Dr. Sica to answer the two questions and to recover the "reasonable expenses incurred in making the motion."  Cabana responded by moving for a protective order on the grounds that the questions were asked in bad faith or unreasonably to annoy, harass, or embarrass Dr. Sica.

The court found that Dr. Sica's involvement in any prior litigation or disciplinary proceedings was clearly relevant to the instant suit and was, therefore, discoverable.

> Questions regarding such litigation or disciplinary proceedings are likely to lead to evidence relevant both to Dr. Sica's skill as a physician and her credibility, especially regarding her diagnosis of Cabana with multiple chemical sensitivity ("MCS").  Accordingly, the motion to compel Dr. Sica to answer deposition questions regarding her involvement in any prior litigation or disciplinary proceedings will be allowed. At 17.

The court then considered whether it should order the plaintiff to pay the defendant's reasonable expenses incurred in bringing the pending motion or if it should refrain from such an order because 1) the opposition to the motion to compel was "substantially justified," or 2) other circumstances make an award of expenses unjust.  The court found that the plaintiff's opposition to the motion to compel was not "substantially justified" and that an award of expenses would not be unjust in this case.  The court stated:

> The objections made by Cabana's attorney at Dr. Sica's deposition constitute the kind of frivolous delay of discovery that Rule 37 was designed to prevent.  Cabana's attorney was not trying to preserve a privilege or enforce a limitation on evidence ordered by this Court.  Furthermore, there is simply *no* evidence that counsel for [defendant] harassed Dr. Sica. Accordingly, the objections were inappropriate under Rule 30(d)(1), and [the defendant's] motion to compel will be allowed. At 17–18.

**Comment:** Note that the court found that the expert's involvement in prior litigation and disciplinary proceedings was "clearly relevant."  The only guaranteed way to avoid being asked such questions is to not agree to serve as an expert witness.

## 3.7  Methods of Discovery

There are several forms of discovery allowed under the Federal Rules of Civil Procedure.  These include interrogatories, requests for production of documents, depositions, subpoenas duces tecum, physical examinations, production of tangible things, and entry upon land.  Each of these discovery methods is discussed below.

*Interrogatories*

Interrogatories are written questions that are served on another party in the case.  They must be answered by the party (not the expert), in writing and under oath.  Interrogatories generally are only served on parties to an action.  Therefore, a witness who is not a party in a case will usually not have to answer the interrogatories.  (Appendix G provides a sample set of interrogatories with answers.)

The number of interrogatories one party can propound to another is limited under the Rules of Civil Procedure.  For example, under the Federal Rules, a party is limited to twenty-five.[4]  There is also a fixed time period within which the interrogatories must be answered. Under the Federal Rules, this period is thirty days.[5]  These time periods may be extended by agreement between the parties or a court order.  The failure to answer interrogatories within the applicable time period can result in judgment being entered against the party who fails to respond.

In most lawsuits each party will ask, through interrogatories, certain questions about the other side's expert witnesses.  The interrogatories will commonly ask for the name and address of the expert, a summary of her qualifications, and a summary of her opinions along with the facts upon which those opinions are based. The expert's interrogatories may also call for the expert's publications, a listing of any other trials the expert has testified in during the last four years, and the compensation paid to the expert for work in the case.  Expert witnesses should be aware that they may have to provide this information to the retaining attorney so that he can advise his client on how to answer any interrogatory seeking said information.  Failure to do so could result in a judgment being entered against the party who retained the expert or other sanctions, such as the expert being barred from testifying as an expert in the case.

## Requests for production of documents
These may only be served upon a party to the lawsuit[6] and thus will generally not be served on experts. There is a time limit to respond of thirty days under the Federal Rules.[7]  Failure to respond within the applicable time can result in sanctions being assessed against the party failing to produce the documents.  The party requesting the documents only has a right to "inspect and copy" the requested documents, he does not have the right to keep the originals.[8]  (Appendix H provides a sample request for production of documents.)

## Depositions
Depositions are arguably the most powerful form of discovery allowed.  Any person can be deposed, the person need not be a party in the lawsuit.  In addition, depositions allow for all-important follow-up questions.  The ability to ask follow-up questions makes depositions a far more powerful information-gathering tool than interrogatories. (Appendix J provides a sample deposition transcript of an expert witness.)  Since most cases settle, the vast majority of expert testimony is provided by way of a deposition rather than live testimony at trial. (Chapter 13 discusses depositions in much greater detail.)

## Subpoenas duces tecum
A *subpoena duces tecum* is a legal document requiring the person on whom it is served to provide specified documents for inspection and copying.  The person responding to the subpoena is usually allowed to charge the requesting party for reasonable copying costs. Subpoenas duces tecum are the discovery method that attorneys use to gain access to documents that are in the possession of persons who are not parties to a lawsuit, such as

---

[4] Fed. R. Civ. Pro. 33(a).
[5] Fed. R. Civ. Pro. 33(b)(3).
[6] Fed. R. Civ. Pro. 34(a).
[7] Fed. R. Civ. Pro. 34(b).
[8] Fed. R. Civ. Pro. 34(a).

expert witnesses. As with any discovery, unjustifiable failure to comply with a subpoena duces tecum can result in sanctions against the noncomplying person. On the other hand, if the subpoena seeks confidential, sensitive, or statutorily protected documents, a person can seek a protective order to stop disclosure of the requested document. In addition, the disclosure may also otherwise be prohibited by law. An expert should consult with a local attorney to determine which records he must produce in response to a subpoena duces tecum and which documents are protected from disclosure. (A sample schedule specifying the documents to be produced from a subpoena duces tecum is provided in Appendix I.)

### Example 3.30: Expert must produce list of past cases testified in

*Orkin Exterminating Company, Inc. v. Knollwood Properties, Ltd.,* 710 So.2d 697 Fla. App. 1998)
Orkin retained C. Douglas Mampe, Ph.D., as an expert entomologist. Knollwood served a notice of taking deposition of Dr. Mampe, which included the request that Dr. Mampe bring with him a list of all cases for the past ten years, including court case numbers, in which he had testified or conducted an investigation or prepared the reports as an expert witness. In his deposition, Dr. Mampe was asked if he had brought such a list with him. Dr. Mampe responded: "No. That's just an impossible job. I probably have thirty a year. Go back seventeen years, that's a lot of cases; and I don't keep track of them once the case has been settled, closed, or disposed of in one form or another."

On further questioning, it was clarified that Dr. Mampe did not necessarily testify in all of the cases in which he was engaged as an expert. The expert must supply this information if requested and if the expert wishes to testify in a Florida court.

The court ordered the expert to produce a list, even if the only sources were financial and business records.

**Comment:** In federal court cases all experts must produce as part of their report a list of all cases they have testified in at trial or by deposition within the preceding four years. Failure to produce this list will result in the barring of the expert from the case. See Section 10.2.

### Example 3.31: Subpoena for reports on other matters properly quashed

*United States v. 25.02 Acres of Land,* 495 F.2d 1398 (10th Cir. 1974)
Under Rules 26, 34, and 45(b), the trial court did not err in quashing a portion of the landowners' subpoena duces tecum that sought from the government's expert appraisal witness production of all appraisal reports that he had prepared for use of other private owners of property in the vicinity of the condemned property.

## Physical examinations

The rules of discovery allow for the physical examination of a party "when the mental or physical condition (including the blood group) of a party" is in controversy.[9] These are most commonly requested by the defense in personal injury actions and are called *independent medical evaluations* or *IMEs*. IMEs are also allowed under most workers' compensation statutes.

## Production of tangible things and entry upon land

The rules allow parties to "inspect and copy, test, or sample any tangible things within the scope of Rule 26(b) and which are in the possession, custody or control of the party upon

---

[9] Fed. R. Civ. Pro. 35(a).

which the request is served."[10]  The rules further provide "entry upon designated land or other property in the possession or control of the party upon whom the request is served for the purpose of inspecting and measuring, surveying, photographing, testing, or sampling the property or any designated object or operation thereon, within the scope of Rule 26(b)."[11]  Experts commonly assist counsel in the inspection of land and other tangible things.

> **Example 3.32: Expert allowed access to site of accident or machine in question**
> You are an expert in a slip and fall or defective product case.  The rules of discovery can be used to gain you access to the site of the slip and fall or the defective product in question.

## 3.8  Conclusion

Discovery is broad-based, but it is not unlimited.  Discovery violations may result in sanctions against the expert.  Experts should have a general idea of the limits allowed under discovery and seek independent legal advice when they feel those limits are being breached.  Experts should understand how the various methods of discovery can be used by each party in a case to gather information.

---

[10] Fed. R. Civ. Pro. 34(a).
[11] Fed. R. Civ. Pro. 34(a).

# Chapter 4  Anatomy of a Civil Trial

## 4.1  Introduction

Although all civil trials involve judges, not all civil trials involve juries. A trial in which the judge acts as the finder of fact is called a *bench trial*. A trial in which the jury acts as the finder of fact is called a *jury trial*. In either, the judge will set the schedule for the trial and any time limits; run the courtroom and make all legal rulings, including the admissibility of evidence (including expert testimony); and instruct the jury on the law to apply. The fact finder in the case weighs the evidence presented by each side, evaluates the credibility of the witnesses involved (including the expert witnesses), and comes to a determination as to the facts that are in dispute.

> **Example 4.1: Role of fact finder at a negligence trial**
> In a negligence suit, the jury will decide, based upon the evidence the judge allows it to hear, whether the defendant acted unreasonably as well as all other disputed questions of fact. The jury also decides the factual question of the plaintiff's damages, including pain and suffering. Key to the jury's function is its role in judging the credibility of all the witnesses in the case, including the expert witnesses. The judge in the negligence suit runs the trial, makes all necessary rulings, and instructs the jury on the law to apply during deliberations.

When an expert gives testimony, he should keep in mind whether the trial is to be a bench trial or a jury trial. If the trial is in front of a jury, the jurors are likely to be unsophisticated in technical matters, may be less educated than the expert, and may have a short attention span. The expert will need to tailor the delivery of his testimony accordingly. In a bench trial, the audience—the finder of fact—will be a judge who will be far more sophisticated than the average juror, but may or may not have any experience in the expert's field. Whether testifying before a judge or a jury, the expert must remember that his role is to assist or educate the judge or jury in matters that are beyond their general experience or comprehension.

## 4.2  Jury Selection and Pre-Trial Motions

A civil trial begins with jury selection (if the trial is a jury trial) and any pre-trial motions. Jury selection procedures vary from jurisdiction to jurisdiction. Generally speaking, juries are not selected, they are deselected. That means that the lawyers in the case will be able to exclude from the jury pool certain persons who are perceived to be biased. The lawyers can also exclude a certain number of jurors without stating a reason for their exclusion by using *peremptory challenges*. The number of peremptory challenges per side varies from jurisdiction to jurisdiction. Jury selection will continue until there are enough jurors left in the pool to fill the jury panel.

Prior to opening statements, the attorneys may choose to make pre-trial motions. The most common of these motions that experts should be aware of is a *motion in limine*. It is very important that experts understand the purpose, effect, and availability of motions in limine. A motion in limine is a motion that can be used to ask the court to exclude reference to anticipated evidence claimed to be objectionable.[1] The motion is made out of the jury's presence. Its purpose is to prevent any unfair prejudice that may occur if the evidentiary issue was ruled on in the presence of the jury.

### Example 4.2: Why an attorney may make a motion in limine

Suppose you are a recovering alcoholic and have been retained as an expert witness in a case. Your retaining attorney doesn't want the jury to know or even suspect that you are an alcoholic. Instead of making an objection during the trial when you are asked during cross-examination, "You're an alcoholic, aren't you?," your retaining attorney may make the motion in limine prior to trial. If granted, it would prevent the opposing counsel from even asking you about being an alcoholic. Thus, the jury would never be aware, even by inference, that you are an alcoholic.

### Example 4.3: Motion in limine used to shield expert from questions regarding his mental disorders

*Fredericks v. Hall,* 275 Ga. App. 412, 620 S.E.2d 638 (Ga. App. 2005)

In this medical malpractice case, the plaintiff filed a motion in limine to prevent his expert medical witness from being asked about his problems with panic disorder, agoraphobia, and dysrhythmic disorder. The court granted the motion, but limited the scope to preventing questions concerning the expert's claim for disability due to his agoraphobia.

If there is personal information that an expert does not want to come out at trial, she needs to tell her retaining attorney about it as soon as possible. The attorney may be able to successfully file a motion in limine that orders the opposing side not to ask the expert about the information in question. If an expert does not disclose such information to her retaining attorney, it will be much more difficult for the attorney to try to protect the expert.

The opposing side may also use a motion in limine in an effort to limit or exclude an expert's testimony. For example, *Daubert* challenges are often resolved as part of a pre-trial motion in limine.[2] Such motions in limine can be outcome determinative. This means that if the opposing side is successful in eliminating or limiting the expert's testimony, all or a portion of the case can be dismissed.

Experts should also be aware that there are often in limine orders in a case that prohibit witnesses, including expert witnesses, from testifying in certain areas that the judge has ruled must not be mentioned. To avoid violating these orders (and risking a mistrial or reversal on appeal[3]), an expert should ask retaining counsel prior to taking the stand if there are any areas that he cannot get into while testifying. When testifying, experts should concentrate and avoid blurting out information concerning these prohibited subjects.

### Example 4.4: Expert blurts out information in violation of court order

In the famous Libby Zion medical malpractice case in New York City in the 1990s, key issues in the case were whether or not the plaintiff had used cocaine on the night in question and whether or not she told her doctors that she was on cocaine. In response to a motion in limine by the plaintiff, the trial judge ruled that no evidence of the plaintiff's past use of cocaine could be presented by the defense (as this would be unfairly prejudicial). A controversy arose in the case when in response

---

[1] 220 N.W.2d 919, 922.

[2] See *Bado-Santana v. Ford Motor Co.,* 364 F.Supp.2d 79 (D. Puerto Rico 2005).

[3] *See Senters v. Black & Decker (U.S.), Inc.,* 123 Fed.Appx. 354 *(C.A. 10 Okla. 2005).*

to a question not directly on point, a defense expert included information on the plaintiff's prior use of cocaine. The expert should not have mentioned this information and his client may have been sanctioned for this statement.

## 4.3 Opening Statements

After selecting a jury, a trial begins with the plaintiff making an *opening statement*. During the opening statement the attorneys are allowed to outline their theories of the case and preview the evidence they intend to present. Attorneys are not allowed to argue during the opening statement; they can only preview the evidence. A defendant may give an opening statement or may defer the opening until the conclusion of the plaintiff's case. Failure of the plaintiff to outline all of the facts necessary to prove the plaintiff's case can result in a *directed verdict* being entered against the plaintiff.[4]

> **Example 4.5: Argumentative statements not allowed during opening statements**
> A physician is sued for malpractice. During opening statements the defendant's attorney stands up and states, "Ladies and gentlemen of the jury, physicians are not God. They should not be held responsible just because a patient has not recovered." The plaintiff's attorney objects. The judge is likely to strike this statement as being argumentative. During opening statements, the lawyers are not allowed to make arguments, they can only preview what the evidence will or will not show.

> **Example 4.6: Directed verdict after opening statement**
> During a kidney transplant operation, a physician mistakenly removed his patient's one good kidney. He is sued for malpractice. At trial, the plaintiff's attorney makes her opening statement, which is, "Ladies and gentlemen of the jury, my client has been caused to suffer greatly because of the action of Dr. Jones. We will prove that Dr. Jones should not be practicing medicine and ask that you carefully listen to the evidence in this case. Thank you for taking the time out of your busy lives to serve on this panel." The defense attorney rises and moves for a directed verdict. In this case, no specific instance of negligence was alleged in the opening statement. A judge could very well grant this motion for a directed verdict and dismiss the plaintiff's case because a plaintiff's attorney needs to lay out all the elements of a valid cause of action.[5]

## 4.4 Burden of Proof

The burden of proof in most civil cases is a *preponderance of the evidence*.[6] To satisfy this burden, the fact finder must be convinced that it was more likely than not that the event in question occurred. In percentage terms, the fact finder would have to believe that there was a 50% or greater probability that the event in question took place. Some issues in civil cases must be proven to a higher standard. This standard is usually *clear and convincing evidence*. There is no percentage number that can be assigned to this higher standard. If a claim must be proven by clear and convincing evidence, this standard is usually specified in a statute or administrative regulation and is imparted to the jury via jury instructions.

It is crucial that expert witnesses understand the burden of proof in civil cases. For the opinion of an expert to be admissible, it must satisfy the preponderance-of-the-evidence,

---

[4] In practice, this harsh rule is rarely enforced by the court.

[5] In this professional negligence case, that the doctor had a physician-patient relationship with the patient, that he violated the standard of care, and, thus, he caused harm to the patient.

[6] 397 U.S. 358.

more-likely-than-not standard explained above. Commonly accepted phrases used by experts to express these concepts include stating that their opinions are based upon "a reasonable degree of scientific (or medical) certainty." It is absolutely crucial that experts state their opinions in a legally sufficient manner. Failure to do so could result in the opinion being stricken from evidence by the judge as being speculative. (See Chapter 8 on opinions.)

## 4.5  Presentation of Evidence

After opening statements, the presentation of evidence will begin with the plaintiff calling its first witness. The plaintiff's case will continue until the plaintiff has called its last witness. After the plaintiff has called its last witness, the defense will be given an opportunity to call witnesses and present its case. Generally speaking, the witnesses each side intends to call at trial need to be disclosed to the other parties in advance. This practice allows parties to depose and seek discovery from the proposed witnesses prior to trial and helps eliminate surprises at trial. Conversely, a party may be prohibited from calling a witness at trial, especially an expert witness, if the witness's identity has not been disclosed sufficiently before trial.

## 4.6  Directed Verdicts

A *directed verdict* is a verdict entered by the court in a jury trial without consideration by the jury because the facts elicited during the trial, together with the applicable law, made it clear that the directed verdict was the only one that could have been reasonably returned.[7] When the judge directs a verdict she is in essence saying that, based on the evidence submitted, the directed verdict is the only possible one a reasonable jury could have determined. Federal Rule 50(a) governs directed verdicts. They are granted most often against the plaintiff at the close of the plaintiff's case. When plaintiff's attorneys speak of "getting over the rail" or "getting to the jury" they are referring to avoiding a directed verdict by having the judge decide to let the jury decide the case. In weak cases, plaintiffs often seek to "get to the jury" to either encourage a settlement or take a chance on a favorable jury verdict. Defendants sometimes settle after a directed verdict is denied rather than chance a jury verdict.

Box 4.61

| |
|---|
| **Fed. R. Civ. Pro. Rule 50. Judgment as a Matter of Law in Jury Trials; Alternative Motion for New Trial; Conditional Rulings**<br>(a) Judgment as a Matter of Law.<br>(1) If during a trial by jury a party has been fully heard on an issue and there is no legally sufficient evidentiary basis for a reasonable jury to find for that party on that issue, the court may determine the issue against that party and may grant a motion for judgment as a matter of law against that party with respect to a claim or defense that cannot under the controlling law be maintained or defeated without a favorable finding on that issue.<br>(2) Motions for judgment as a matter of law may be made at any time before submission of the case to the jury. Such a motion shall specify the judgment sought and the law and the facts on which the moving party is entitled to the judgment. |

---

[7] 123 F.2d 438, 440.

Many plaintiff cases depend upon certain expert testimony to avoid the entry of a directed verdict against the plaintiff. For example, let's say a plaintiff sues the manufacturer of a common shampoo claiming that the shampoo caused his hair loss. Ms. Johnson is the plaintiff's only expert witness and she is prepared to testify, based upon a reasonable degree of scientific certainty, that the shampoo did in fact cause the hair loss. When Ms. Johnson is called to the stand, the defense raises a *Daubert* challenge (see Chapter 9) and the judge rules that she cannot testify. At the close of the plaintiff's case, the defense attorney makes a motion for a directed verdict. This motion would likely be granted because the court would probably conclude that no reasonable jury could find for the plaintiff without expert testimony that established that the shampoo caused the hair loss.

Experts must be aware of and understand directed verdicts. An expert should ask his retaining attorney up front what minimum testimony is needed to avoid a directed verdict and get to the jury. An expert who is not able to provide such testimony should let the retaining attorney know as soon as possible so that she can look for another expert, settle the case, or take other needed action to protect her client's interests.

**Example 4.7: Directed verdict granted after expert barred from testifying**
*Taylor v. Mazda Motor of America, Inc.,* 2005 WL 2990900 (Fla. App. 3 Dist. 2005)
In this case the plaintiff's expert and lay witness were prevented from testifying in the trial as a sanction for them not being made available for deposition. The trial court then granted the defense a directed verdict as the plaintiff was not able to prove its case without witnesses. The appeals court reversed, saying that the barring of the plaintiff's experts from testimony was "disproportionate to the offense."

**Comment:** As in the above case, an expert witness being barred from testifying often results in the other side winning the case. It is for this reason that experts are closely challenged in an attempt to bar them for lack of qualifications or insufficient methodology. Experts need to be prepared for such high-stakes challenges.

## 4.7 Closing Arguments
After the close of evidence, each party will be allowed to make a *closing argument* or *summation* to the jury. The amount of time each party can spend for summation is decided by the judge. During summation, the parties are allowed to make arguments as to how the evidence that was presented should be interpreted.

## 4.8 Jury Instruction, Deliberation, and Decision
After summation, the judge will instruct the jury on the law it should apply in its deliberations. This is called *jury instruction*. Each of the parties will usually submit suggested jury instructions for the judge to consider. Some states require that the verdict be unanimous, others require only a specified majority, for example, ten of twelve jurors. Sample jury instructions regarding the credibility of witnesses in general and expert witnesses in particular are reprinted below.

**§ 1.14(c)  Credibility of Witnesses.**
**Instruction 1-6**
Because you are the sole judges of the facts, you are also, necessarily, the sole judges of the credibility, the believability, of each of the various witnesses who have testified. You have

seen and heard them all. You can judge, as well as any group can judge, how much credence, how much reliance, and how much weight should be given to the testimony of each.

There are certain factors that jurors may, and perhaps should, take into consideration in judging the credibility of any witness in any case. They are the following:

a. First is the demeanor of the witness. This means his or her appearance and conduct on the witness stand. How did the individual strike you? Did his or her words ring true or did they not ring true? That is the factor to consider.

b. Another factor is the interest, if any, of the witness in the outcome of the trial. You are at perfect liberty to take this into consideration in judging the credibility of that witness.

c. A third factor is a witness's relationship or feeling for or against one side or the other, or the absence of any such relationship or feeling. You may consider such in judging credibility.

d. Another factor you may consider is any prior statement that a witness may have made that is in some way inconsistent with his or her testimony on the witness stand. You may also consider any motive that a witness may have to lie or to stretch the truth.

e. When considering credibility, you may also judge the probability or improbability of the witness's testimony and also the opportunity, lack of opportunity, or extent of opportunity that the witness had to hear or to see those things about which he or she gave testimony.

As the sole judges of the facts, and therefore, the sole judges of the credibility of each witness, you may accept the testimony of any witness as completely true if you wish. By the same token, you may reject the testimony of any witness in its entirety as completely untrue if you wish to do that. Or you may accept some parts of a witness's testimony as true and reject other parts of that same testimony as untrue if that is what you find the facts to be.

In other words, ladies and gentlemen, it is your function, the function of the jury, to collectively evaluate the testimony of each witness and then to apply your good sound, common sense and intelligence in determining whether to believe or to disbelieve it, either totally or in part—in short, to determine just where the truth does lie.

### § 20.15. Expert Testimony—Qualifications of Expert.
**Instruction 20-15**

[A witness/Witnesses] who [has/have] special knowledge, skill, experience, training or education in a particular subject [has/have] testified to certain opinions. Any such witness is referred to as an expert witness. In determining what weight to give any such opinion, you should consider the qualifications and credibility of the witness, the facts or materials on which each opinion is based, and the reasons for each opinion.

An opinion is only as good as the facts and reasons on which it is based. If you find that any such fact has not been proved, or has been disproved, you must consider that in determining the value of the opinion. Likewise, you must consider the strengths and weaknesses of the reasons on which it is based.

You are not bound by an opinion. Give each opinion the weight you find it deserves.

### § 20.16. Weighing the Conflicting Testimony of Experts.
**Instruction 20-16**

In resolving the conflict in the testimony of the expert witness, you should weigh the opinion of one expert against that of another. In doing this, you should consider the qualifications and credibility of each witness, the facts and materials on which each opinion is based, and the reasons for each opinion. The opinions of expert witnesses, however, should not be considered by you as conclusive, even if no conflicting or contrary opinions are introduced. In other words, they are not binding on you, even if uncontradicted.

## 4.9  Verdict or Mistrial

After it is instructed by the judge, the jury will deliberate on each and every claim that is still in issue (that is, that hasn't been disposed of by a directed verdict, settlement, or other means) until it reaches a verdict or becomes deadlocked.  The jury's verdict may be general or special.  A *general verdict* is merely a finding for the plaintiff or defendant.  A *special verdict* is a verdict that answers specific questions of fact that were posed to the jury by the court.  For example, "Was there a design defect in product x?"  Special verdicts are often requested and used where there is a chance that the jury will misunderstand and misapply the law if they are just asked to find for the plaintiff or defendant with a general verdict.  If the jury is deadlocked, the judge will eventually declare a mistrial and the case will have to be retried.

## 4.10  Post-Verdict Motions

After the jury returns its verdict(s), the parties may choose to make post-trial motions.  A common post-trial motion is a motion for judgment notwithstanding the verdict.  A motion for *judgment notwithstanding the verdict*, or *j.n.o.v.,* is essentially a motion for a directed verdict made after the jury has returned an adverse verdict.  Under the Federal Rules, a prerequisite for making a j.n.o.v. motion is that a motion for a directed verdict was made and not granted.  Under the Federal Rules, the motion must be filed no more than ten days after entry of judgment.[8]  When a party files a j.n.o.v. motion, it is essentially asking the court to throw out the jury's verdict because no reasonable jury could have come to such a verdict.

After a jury verdict, a party may also make a *motion for a new trial.*  This may be granted for "any of the reasons for which new trials have heretofore been granted in actions at law in the courts of the United States."[9]  These reasons include irregularities in the proceedings, misconduct of the jury, newly discovered evidence, and insufficiency of evidence.  A motion for a new trial must also be made within ten days of entry of judgment.[10]  Motions for new trials and j.n.o.v.s are checks on runaway juries and jury nullification.[11]  The availability of such a motion means that litigants can lose at the trial court level even if the jury loved their experts and finds in their favor.  The granting of, or failure to grant, post-trial motions is a question of law that can be argued on appeal in an effort to reverse the judge's decision.

## 4.11  Alternative Dispute Resolution

It is important to keep in mind that many disputes are no longer resolved through formal civil litigation in state or federal court.  The cost and time required to prosecute lawsuits have driven many prospective litigants to resolve their differences through *alternative dispute*

---

[8] Fed. R. Civ. Pro. 50(b).

[9] Fed. R. Civ. Pro. 59(a).

[10] Fed. R. Civ. Pro. 59(b).

[11] Massachusetts Superior Court Judge Hiller Zobel used a similar safety valve available under Massachusetts law (Massachusetts Rule of Criminal Procedure 25(b)(2)) to reduce the conviction of nanny Louise Woodward from second-degree murder (carrying a mandatory life sentence) to manslaughter.

*resolution* or *ADR*. The most common forms of ADR are mediation and arbitration. Expert witnesses are used in varying ways in all forms of ADR.

*Mediation* is a form of ADR that involves the appointment of an agreed-upon third party to facilitate settlement negotiations. This third party is called the *mediator*. Cases can be submitted to mediation before or after suit has been filed. Mediation is a useful tool to use to reach a settlement to a disagreement. An important advantage of mediation is that the parties control the outcome and all resolutions are voluntary. If the parties do not wish to settle through mediation, they can still go to court. The qualifications and credibility of the expert witnesses on each side and the content of the testimony they intend to give at trial are important factors that affect how much a case will be settled for during mediation.

*Arbitration* is a process by which the parties in a dispute submit the dispute for resolution to an agreed-upon arbitrator (or panel of arbitrators).[12] The arbitrator is then the fact finder and decision maker. Arbitration rules of procedure vary, but are usually far less formal and strict than the Rules of Civil Procedure and Evidence. Arbitration is usually faster and cheaper than formal litigation in a court of law. Arbitration can be binding or non-binding. In *binding arbitration* the parties agree that the judgment of the arbitrator is final and can be enforced through court action. *High-low* arbitration involves setting limits on the amount of the arbitrator's award and is a way to place some control over the outcome. Experts may participate in arbitration by testifying live at the arbitration hearing or by submitting written affidavits containing their sworn opinions. When testifying at an arbitration hearing, experts need to keep in mind that the decision maker is an arbitrator who is generally far more sophisticated than the average juror. Usually, the arbitrator has experience in the matter at issue, for example, construction or environmental litigation.

In some cases, private judges are being retained to resolve cases. In these cases the private judges (attorneys or retired judges) are agreed upon by the litigants and can provide an expeditious and cost-effective resolution to a disputed matter.

### 4.12  Conclusion

Experts should have a basic understanding of the procedures of a civil trial. This will allow the expert to work well with retaining counsel and communicate more effectively with the trier of fact.

---

[12] Under some forms of arbitration, the parties do not need to agree upon an arbitrator.

# Chapter 5  Evidence

## 5.1  Introduction

The rules of evidence vary from jurisdiction to jurisdiction.  Federal courts use the Federal Rules of Evidence (FRE).  State courts have their own evidentiary rules, but, generally, these are based upon the Federal Rules.  The Federal Rules will be the basis of the upcoming discussion of evidence.

Experts should have a basic understanding of the rules of evidence.  Evidentiary matters are questions of law that are decided by the presiding trial judge.  Evidentiary rulings are within the discretion of the trial judge and are only disturbed on appeal if it is found that the trial judge abused his discretion.  This means that the trial judge most often has the last word on what is and is not admissible.  The judge will be governed by whichever rules of evidence apply in that particular jurisdiction.  The purpose of the Federal Rules of Evidence is stated in Rule 102.

### Box 5.11

**Fed. R. Evid. 102.  Purpose and Construction**
These rules shall be construed to secure fairness in administration, elimination of unjustifiable expense and delay, and promotion of growth and development of the law of evidence to the end that the truth may be ascertained and proceedings justly determined.

The purpose of the Federal Rules is therefore to seek justice and the truth, but to do so fairly and in a manner that does not result in unjustifiable expense or delay.

## 5.2  The General Structure of Evidence Law

Rules 401, 402, and 403 define the general structure of the Federal Rules of Evidence.

### Box 5.21

**Fed. R. Evid. 401.  Definition of "Relevant Evidence"**
"Relevant evidence" means evidence having any tendency to make the existence of any fact that is of consequence to the determination of the action more probable or less probable than it would be without the evidence.

### Box 5.22

**Fed. R. Evid. 402.  Relevant Evidence Generally Admissible; Irrelevant Evidence Inadmissible**
All relevant evidence is admissible, except as otherwise provided by the Constitution of the United States, by Act of Congress, by these rules, or by other rules prescribed by the Supreme Court pursuant to statutory authority.  Evidence which is not relevant is not admissible.

### Box 5.23

**Fed. R. Evid. 403.  Exclusion of Relevant Evidence on Grounds of Prejudice, Confusion, or Waste of Time**
Although relevant, evidence may be excluded if its probative value is substantially outweighed by the danger of unfair prejudice, confusion of the issues, or misleading the jury, or by considerations of undue delay, waste of time, or needless presentation of cumulative evidence.

All relevant evidence is admissible, unless it is inadmissible due to another rule of evidence or law. Relevancy is very broadly defined in Rule 401. Rule 403 is the most important of the exclusionary rules. Under Rule 403, relevant evidence may be excluded by the trial judge if its probative value (tendency to prove or disprove a relevant fact) is *substantially outweighed* by the danger of unfair prejudice, confusion of the issues, misleading the jury, or by considerations of undue delay, waste of time, or needless presentation of cumulative evidence. "Unfair prejudice" means an "undue tendency to suggest decision on an improper basis, commonly, though not necessarily, an emotional one."[1] To avoid having testimony excluded under Rule 403, an expert may have to work closely with retaining counsel to have counsel flesh out every reason it is relevant and every reason it is not confusing or misleading. Consider the following examples dealing with expert evidence.

### Example 5.1: Expert's personal practices of how he does surgery and acts post-operatively properly excluded in malpractice case

*Sosna v. Binnington,* 321 F.3d 742 (C.A. 8 Mo. 2003)

The trial court was upheld in its refusal to allow cross-examination of a defendant expert witness in this medical malpractice case. The court reasoned that the practices complained of were of limited relevance and would confuse the jury because the plaintiff's theory of liability did not involve these particular practices.

> Sosna first argues that the District Court erred when it limited the scope of her cross-examination of the defendant's expert, Dr. Drebin. The District Court granted Binnington's motion in limine and ruled that Drebin could not be questioned regarding his deposition testimony that he was critical of Binnington's actions because he personally would have administered antibiotics peri-operatively (i.e., during surgery), would have decompressed the bowel, and would not have performed an incidental appendectomy. We think the District Court properly concluded that these were Drebin's personal practices or opinions and therefore were not relevant to the standard of care and that, to the extent that they were relevant, they had a tendency to confuse the jury and to unfairly prejudice the defendant. See Fed.R.Evid. 403. Sosna's theory of liability did not involve any of the practices that Drebin was critical of Binnington for performing (or for not performing). Had Sosna pursued a theory of liability premised on one of these actions, the associated evidence might have been admissible as relevant to the standard of care. However, because Sosna's case was premised on a different theory and chain of events (i.e., the failure to relieve the obstruction or remove the compromised section of the small bowel), we see no abuse of discretion in the District Court's ruling. At 745.

**Comment:** Note that the defense in this case protected its expert from the questions at issue by filing a motion in limine in advance of the expert taking the stand. For more on motions in limine, please see Section 2.7.

### Example 5.2: Expert not allowed to testify as to credibility of other witnesses

*Nimely v. City of New York,* 414 F.3d 381 (C.A. 2 N.Y. 2005)

The appeals court in this case held that the trial judge had abused his discretion in allowing the expert witness to testify that he believed other witnesses were being truthful and by allowing the expert to explain why he believed them to be truthful. The court stated:

---

[1] *Firemen's Fund Ins. Co. v. Thien,* 63 F.3d 754, 758 (8th Cir. 1995) (quoting *United States v. Dennis,* 625 F.2d 782, 796-797 (8th Cir. 1980)).

Viewed in this light, and against the backdrop of the legal principles governing the admissibility of expert testimony more broadly, we do not believe that Dawson's testimony presents a close case. His direct testimony stated that he "rejected" the possibility that Muirhead and McCarthy had lied, and explained various reasons why police officers have no incentive to give false statements in excessive force cases. On cross-examination Dawson reiterated his conclusion that the police officers were "telling the truth as they perceived it." Even assuming that Dawson, based upon his experience or expertise, was qualified to render an opinion as to the tendencies of police officers to lie or to tell the truth in investigations of the sort at issue here (an assumption of which we are highly dubious), his statements essentially instructed the jury as to an ultimate determination that was exclusively within its province, namely, the credibility of Muirhead and McCarthy. Such testimony does not "assist the trier of fact," Fed.R.Evid. 702, but rather "undertakes to tell the jury what result to reach," and "attempts to substitute the expert's judgment for the jury's." Duncan, 42 F.3d at 101. At 397.

**Comment:** It is rarely a good idea for experts to give opinions on who is telling the truth and who is not. Such decisions are for the jury alone to make and the expert is not qualified to make them.

### Example 5.3: Exclusion of expert who would present cumulative testimony allowed

*Tran v. Toyota Motor Corp.,* 420 F.3d 1310 (C.A. 11 Fla. 2005)

In this case, the appeals court upheld as a proper exercise of discretion and application of FRE 403 the testimony of a witness whose testimony the court felt would be cumulative. The court reasoned:

Tran next argues that the district court erred in excluding the testimony of Dr. Charles Clark. Tran proposed to present Dr. Clark as an expert witness to testify about Tran's neck injury from a "micro perspective." Appellants' Brief at *1315 18. Tran was able to offer the testimony of the treating physician, Dr. Michael Cheatham. In addition, Tran presented the expert testimony of Dr. Joseph Burton, whose testimony Tran characterizes as encompassing a "macro perspective" on the collision and Tran's injury. *Id.* at 17.

After Dr. Burton testified, Toyota objected to Dr. Clark's testimony as cumulative. See Fed.R.Evid. 403. The court examined Dr. Clark's deposition and expert witness report, and extensively examined Dr. Clark's qualifications. The court concluded that Dr. Clark's opinions, and the bases for these opinions, were the same as those of Dr. Burton. The court sustained Toyota's objection and excluded Dr. Clark from testifying.

"The district court has broad discretion to determine the admissibility of evidence, and we will not disturb the court's judgment absent a clear abuse of discretion." *United States v. McLean,* 138 F.3d 1398, 1403 (11th Cir.1998).

Drs. Burton and Clark relied on the same medical evidence in forming their opinions. In addition to testimony about the collision and inertial forces, Dr. Burton testified about Tran's neck injury and the impact of the seat belt. These "micro" issues are the same as those about which Dr. Clark would have testified. Moreover, the treating physician, Dr. Cheatham, testified about Tran's injury as well. In sum, Tran presented extensive testimony to the jury suggesting that the seat belt caused her injury, and it is not at all clear that Dr. Clark would have added any different information that Tran could not have presented through Drs. Burton and Cheatham. Additionally, unlike in Johnson, Dr. Clark's qualifications are not significantly greater than the other doctors'. Finally, Tran could have called Dr. Clark when given an opportunity for rebuttal, but did not call him at that time. While we note that in Johnson we held that a third expert witness was not cumulative, whereas Dr. Clark was excluded from testifying as a second expert witness, the mere number of witnesses is not conclusive when these other factors support the district court's decision.

On this record, we cannot say that the court would have abused its discretion had it allowed Dr. Clark to testify. The testimony likely would not have unduly prolonged the trial, Dr. Clark's practice and experience was somewhat different from that of the other doctors, and Tran might have presented her evidence differently had she known earlier that Dr. Clark would be excluded. Given our deferential standard of review, however, we cannot say that the district court's decision fell outside its permissible "range of choice." *United States v. Kelly,* 888 F.2d 732, 745 (11th Cir.1989). Therefore, we affirm the court's order excluding Dr. Clark's testimony as cumulative. At 1314–1315.

### Example 5.4: Testimony regarding ethnic stereotypes unduly prejudicial (prejudicial testimony)

*Jinro America, Inc. v. Secure Investments, Inc.,* 01 Cal. Daily Op. Serv. 8116 C.A.9 (Ariz. 2001)
This case arose out of a business deal ostensibly for the international trade of frozen chicken. When the parties' deal unraveled, Jinro, the plaintiff, sued the defendants to recover millions of dollars for breach of contract, fraud, and racketeering. The defendants claimed the transaction was a sham designed to circumvent South Korean currency laws. A jury agreed with the defendants. The plaintiffs appealed. Their main contention was that the trial was prejudicially infected by ethnically biased, "xenophobic" expert testimony. The defendants relied on David Herbert Pelham as an expert witness to testify about Korean law and the business practices of Korean companies— particularly their alleged propensity to engage in fraudulent activity, including the avoidance of Korean currency laws. Pelham had no formal education or training in business or as a cultural expert. He was not a lawyer. Rather, he was a private investigator. His testimony was offered to educate the jury about the modus operandi of Korean businesses. The testimony included this exchange:

> **Q:** Would you recommend to your clients that they enter into oral agreements with Koreans?
> **A:** I would never recommend anybody rely on oral agreements.
> **Q:** Why is that?
> **A:** Well, I don't think oral agreements are a very safe way to do business anyplace, but particularly in Asia and probably more particularly in Korea.
> **Q:** Why is that?
> **A:** Well, because of the culture, dealing with Korean businessmen can end up with some pretty sorry results if you haven't safeguarded yourself. At 8–9.

On cross-examination, the expert testified:

> **Q:** You aren't telling this jury that you believe that all Korean businesses operate corruptly, are you?
> **A:** All Korean businesses? I don't think I would say all Korean business. I would say that the prevalence of corruption and fraud in the Korean business community is very great and very extensive.

The court found that the expert was not qualified to testify, then stated, "Even if Pelham's testimony might have been admissible as expert testimony, it was so tinged with ethnic bias and stereotyping that it should have been excluded under Rule 403's balancing test." At 9.

The court suggested that the real purpose of the expert's testimony was to exploit the plaintiff's status as a Korean business and to beg the jury to draw an inference adverse to Jinro based entirely on its ethnic identity or national origin.

### Example 5.5: Accuracy of testimony irrelevant to unfair prejudice determination

*Traharne v. Wayne Scott Fetzer Co.,* 2001 WL 127641 (N.D. Ill. E. Div. 2001)
In this products liability case, the manufacturer of a submersible pump that allegedly led to an electrocution death proffered the testimony of an electrical engineer. The expert testified that the sump pump left the defendant's manufacturing facility without a strain relief clamp in violation of the defendant's own manufacturing specifications. The plaintiff claimed that the expert's conclusions were inaccurate and thus the opinion was unfairly prejudicial. The court noted, "evidence is unfairly prejudicial only if it will induce the jury to decide the case on an improper basis, commonly an emotional one, rather than on the evidence presented." The court stated that

the accuracy of expert conclusions is an inappropriate objection to admissibility of expert testimony. The court rejected the claim of unfair prejudice.

## Example 5.6: Neurosurgeon's testimony on secondary gain irrelevant and unfairly prejudicial

*Rodgers v. CWR Const., Inc.,* 33 S.W.3d 506 (Ark. 2000)

The plaintiff, a contractor, sustained head, neck, and other injuries, among others, when materials fell on him at a job site. A neurosurgeon conducted a surgical consultation with the plaintiff and ultimately concluded that surgery was unwarranted. He opined that the plaintiff's current disability related to pre-existing injuries rather than the May 1994 incident. Over the plaintiff's objection, the neurosurgeon proceeded to testify regarding the issue of secondary-gain motivation (i.e., a behavior that is rewarded). The expert explained that the secondary gain is the promise of a financial settlement or award that may come after an industrial accident. However, when cross-examined, the expert admitted that he was not giving testimony that it was his opinion that any secondary gain was involved in the instant case. The plaintiff objected to the introduction of any evidence regarding secondary-gain motivation on the grounds that the expert could not say that the plaintiff had secondary-gain motivation within a reasonable degree of medical certainty and that the danger of unfair prejudice outweighed any probative value. Over these objections, the trial court allowed the testimony.

The appellate court found that the testimony was irrelevant, particularly in light of the fact that the doctor was unprepared to testify that it was a relevant issue in the case. The court went on to say:

> Further, even if the evidence had some slight relevance, the testimony should have been excluded per Ark.R.Evid. 403 because its probative value was substantially outweighed by the danger of unfair prejudice, confusion of the issues, or misleading of the jury. The jury could easily have concluded that secondary-gain issues were relevant to the case. At 511.

## Example 5.7: Relevant expert evidence

*Shekell v. Sturm, Ruger & Co.,* 14 Fed. Rules Evid. Serv. 1634 (CA.9 Mont. 1983)

In an action against a gun manufacturer arising from the discharge of a gun when it was dropped with the safety engaged, the testimony of an expert concerning accidents that occurred when an uncocked gun fired unexpectedly or when the position of the hammer was unknown was sufficiently probative on the issue of whether the gun was unreasonably dangerous to be relevant for purposes of Rule 401. The court found that a description of various ways in which a gun could accidentally fire was relevant if it promoted an understanding of how a firing mechanism works, aided in establishing whether the safety mechanism was defective, or assisted the jury in comprehending how the gun could have discharged when the plaintiff dropped it.

## Example 5.8: Relevant expert testimony

*Haney v. Mizell Memorial Hospital,* 744 F.2d 1467 (11th Cir. 1984)

A medical malpractice defendant offered evidence regarding the plaintiff's intoxication and alcohol and drug use. The court found it admissible under Rule 401, concluding that it was relevant to the plaintiff's ability to communicate with medical personnel and their ability to restrain and obtain cooperation from him; relevant to the plaintiff's prayer for damages for future mental anguish, rehabilitation care, and loss of earnings; and relevant to rebut testimony offered by the plaintiff pertaining to his lifestyle and quality of life prior to the accident.

**Example 5.9: Evidence not misleading**
*Edwards v. Liz Claiborne, Inc.,* 17 Fed. Rules Evid. Serv. 1316 (E.D. Pa. 1984)
In a products liability action, the plaintiff alleged that a terrycloth blouse retailed by the defendant was defective in design and in its failure to provide sufficient warnings of unusually hazardous burning characteristics. The defendant's expert witness performed an in-court experiment designed to show that the blouse would not have formed molten polyester drippings when burned, notwithstanding that the blouse material was 25 percent polyester and 75 percent cotton while the test material was 40 percent polyester and 60 percent cotton, and notwithstanding several departures from the standard testing procedure. The court admitted the evidence based on the facts that the experiment was specifically designed to illustrate one facet of the accident, it was highly unlikely that the jury mistook the experiment as an exact duplication of the accident itself, and the fabrics were sufficiently similar to enable the jury to find the experiment helpful to its determination of the likelihood that the fabric formed molten drippings when it burned.

**Comment:** In-court demonstrations can be extremely effective. They can also be extremely risky. Recall O.J. Simpson and his glove. If an expert plans to attempt a demonstration, he needs to make sure it will work. To avoid potential disasters, many attorneys videotape expert demonstrations and then play the videotapes in court.

**Example 5.10: Relevant evidence**
*Ventura v. Titan Sports,* 65 F.3d 725 (8th Cir. 1995)
A professional wrestler—and budding politician—sued a wrestling organization for compensation based upon illegal use of videotapes of his performance. The wrestler offered testimony by a damages expert. The court found it relevant to the wrestler's quantum meruit claim because, regardless of whether the defendant's actions rose to the level of conscious tort, the expert's testimony concerning the market value of the wrestler's videotape license related to the material facts of the value of the license to the defendant and the value of the royalties to the wrestler.

**Example 5.11: Danger of unfair prejudice outweighed probative value of testimony by "credentials" expert**
*White v. U.S.,* 148 F.3d 787, 792 (7th Cir. 1998)
In this malpractice action, the plaintiff sought to introduce the testimony of a credentials expert. The expert had reviewed the defendant physician's deposition testimony and the documents she provided regarding her degrees and licenses. The expert was prepared to testify that the physician could not have obtained certain degrees. The plaintiff wanted to show that the physician was not properly licensed. The court excluded the evidence, concluding there was no direct evidence of fraud or dishonesty, thus the probative value of the evidence was slight. The issue of credentials could have developed into a lengthy trial-within-a-trial.

**Example 5.12: Defendant's failed examinations not admissible (irrelevant evidence)**
*Campbell v. Vinjamuri,* 19 F.3d 1274 (8th Cir. 1994)
The plaintiff sued the defendant anesthesiologist for malpractice. The plaintiff sought to introduce evidence that the defendant had failed board-certifying examinations in anesthesiology. The court excluded the evidence as irrelevant, concluding that a person's performance on an examination is not determinative of that person's ability to meet a required standard of care.

**Example 5.13: Results of expert's experiment on another automobile is irrelevant evidence**
*Barnes v. General Motors Corp.,* 547 F.2d 275 (5th Cir. 1977)
This was a products liability suit arising out of an automobile crash that allegedly resulted from the defective design of the car. The court found that the plaintiff's engineer expert's testimony regarding the results of an experiment he conducted on another automobile was irrelevant to the issue at hand and presented a real danger of unfair prejudice. The experiment was conducted under circumstances very different than those existing at the time of accident, thus the engineer's testimony had no probative value.

**Example 5.14: Unfairly prejudicial expert testimony (worklife expectancy)**
*Marcel v. Placid Oil,* 11 F.3d 563 (5th Cir. 1994)
An oilfield worker sued the oil company for damages arising out of a slip-and-fall on an offshore rig. The oil company's expert economist testified on the issue of the worklife expectancy of an oilfield worker in an effort to show that the worklife was shorter than average. The defendant did not offer any other evidence comparing the worklife in the oilfield with the national average or with the worklife of any other occupation. The evidence was not admitted—its potential for unfair prejudice outweighed its probative value.

**Example 5.15: Evidence potentially confusing (employment conditions)**
*Rogers v. Raymark Industries, Inc.,* 922 F.2d 1426 (9th Cir. 1991)
The widow of a shipyard welder brought an action against an asbestos manufacturer, alleging asbestos exposure caused her husband's lung cancer. The plaintiff contended that her husband's work was less like a welder's and more like an insulation worker's. The plaintiff offered testimony from an expert in marine asbestos insulation techniques. The testimony was intended to describe the conditions under which the plaintiff's husband worked in the shipyard. The court excluded the testimony. It reasoned that the expert's description of shipyard insulation techniques would have been relevant only to that portion of the deceased's work experience that put him in close proximity to insulators. Thus, the jury might have been confused into equating the expert's description of life as an insulator with life as a welder.

**Example 5.16: Polygraph evidence unfairly prejudicial**
*Conti v. Commissioner,* 39 F.3d 658 (6th Cir. 1994)
In this case, the plaintiffs voluntarily took polygraph tests to try and prove a cash hoard claim without the tax court's or IRS counsel's knowledge. The tax court held that the polygraph results were unreliable and refused to admit them. The tax court also excluded the results under Rule 403. The Sixth Circuit affirmed the tax court on the latter basis. The *Conti* court observed that the unfairly prejudicial effect of unilateral polygraph tests outweighs their probative value because the party offering them does not have an adverse interest at stake when taking the tests.

**Example 5.17: Testimony on irrelevant matter could lead to confusion (staple gun)**
*Paradigm Sales, Inc. v. Weber Marking Sys., Inc.,* 880 F. Supp. 1247, 1252-53 (N.D. Ind. 1995)
In this patent infringement action, the patent holder for a staple gun brought an infringement action against a competitor. Expert testimony by an engineer was offered by the defendant. This expert proposed to compare the physical operation of the alleged infringing gun to the operation of the staple gun manufactured by the patent holder. The court found the testimony irrelevant. "The issue for the trier of fact is whether the Weber device performs substantially the same function in substantially the same way to achieve substantially the same result as the device *disclosed in the patent,* not as the device manufactured by the defendant." The court held that expert testimony on this irrelevant matter would confuse the issues and was thus inadmissible under Rule 403.

**Example 5.18: Expert linguist's proposed testimony was a waste of time**
*Tilton v. Capital Cities/ABC, Inc.,* 938 F. Supp. 751, 753 (N.D. Okla. 1995)
The court excluded an expert linguist's proposed testimony about how certain rhetorical devices or speech patterns convey implied meanings. It found the testimony would confuse the jury and that it was "a waste of time."

**Example 5.19: Evidence of tests relative and probative: child restraint seats**
*Gilbert v. Cosco, Inc.,* 989 F.2d 399 (10th Cir. 1993)
In this products liability action regarding the design of child restraint seats, the manufacturer introduced evidence of tests it had performed. This evidence was offered to assist the manufacturer's expert in demonstrating the physical principles that formed the basis for his opinion. The court allowed the evidence, concluding that although it would be highly prejudicial to the plaintiff's case, the tests were relevant and the plaintiff had ample opportunity to attack the expert's conclusions on cross-examination.

**Comment:** Note how the court balances probative effect versus the dangers of admitting the evidence. Here the proposed testimony was admitted because the tests were relevant.

**Example 5.20: Expert evidence irrelevant to set value of survivors' loss of companionship and society**
*Brereton v. U.S.,* 973 F.Supp. 752 (E.D. Mich. 1997)
In the damages phase of this wrongful death action arising out of a fatal airplane crash, expert evidence was proposed to set the value of the survivors' loss of society and companionship. The expert, an economist, based his figures on the value that society might place on the safety and health of a statistically average individual. The court excluded the testimony, concluding it was irrelevant to the issue of the survivors' loss of companionship and society. The only way to determine this value was to assess the type of relationship the decedent had with the survivors. The expert testimony was unhelpful in making such an assessment.

**Example 5.21: Expert testimony relevant and probative (increased risk of cancer)**
*Stead v. F.E. Myers Co.,* 785 F.Supp. 56 (D. Vt. 1990)
This action was brought against the manufacturer of a submersible pump for injuries allegedly resulting from exposure to pump oil. The plaintiff offered expert testimony by an M.D. and a Ph.D. that there was an increased risk of cancer resulting from the exposure. Neither expert could testify to a reasonable degree of medical certainty that the exposure caused cancer. This did not matter, however, because the plaintiff sought recovery for the cost of extensive medical monitoring that the increased risk of cancer made necessary. The court found the testimony relevant and probative to the issue of recovery of costs for future medical monitoring.

**Example 5.22: Evidence of when expert pilot crashed airplane unfairly prejudicial**
*In re. Air Crash Disaster,* 86 F.3d 498 (6th Cir. 1996)
Here, plaintiffs sued an airline after one of its planes crashed during takeoff. A human factors expert, also a pilot, was testifying for the plaintiffs. The defense sought to cross-examine the expert on a 1953 crash of a plane he piloted that resulted in two deaths. The court found that the proposed line of questioning would result in testimony that was unfairly prejudicial and did not allow the cross-examination: "The time lapse, the different airport, the different technology, the dubious relevance to the witness's currently-claimed expertise, and the need to avoid detailed inquiry into a separate plane crash—these all spoke for exclusion."

## 5.3  Evidence Rules Dealing Specifically with Experts

Federal Rules of Evidence 702–705 deal explicitly with expert witnesses.

The role of an expert is to "assist the trier of fact" through her "scientific, technical, or other specialized knowledge." If this opinion is not based upon reliable methodology, it may not assist the trier of fact and it may be excluded under the *Daubert* line of cases. (The *Daubert* line of cases and the legal requirements thereunder are discussed in Chapter 9 on methodology.)

To testify as an expert, an individual must be qualified by "knowledge, skill, experience, training, or education." Note the conjunction "or." An expert needs to be qualified under only one of these categories, not all. If the court holds as a matter of law that an expert is not qualified to testify in a certain area, then he will not be allowed to testify in that area. Note, however, that even if the judge does find the expert qualified to testify, his qualifications are still a legitimate line of inquiry in cross-examination because they will affect the weight to be given to the expert's testimony. (Qualifications are discussed in greater detail in Chapter 6.)

The December 2000 amendments to the Federal Rules of Evidence include amendments to Fed. R. Evid. 702 and 703. Those amendments incorporate into the Rules some of the guidance on the admissibility of expert testimony stemming from *Daubert* and its progeny.

**Box 5.31**

---

**Fed. R. Evid. 702.  Testimony by Experts**
If scientific, technical, or other specialized knowledge will assist the trier of fact to understand the evidence or to determine a fact in issue, a witness qualified as an expert by knowledge, skill, experience, training, or education, may testify thereto in the form of an opinion or otherwise, <u>if (1) the testimony is sufficiently based upon reliable facts or data, (2) the testimony is the product of reliable principles and methods, and (3) the witness has applied the principles and methods reliably to the facts of the case</u>. *[New matter is underlined.]*

---

This codification of the *Daubert* reliability determination requires both a quantitative and qualitative analysis by the trial judge. It is quantitative in that the trial court must ensure that the underlying facts or data are sufficient to support the opinion. It is qualitative because the trial court must evaluate the reliability of the expert's opinion by examining the principles and methods upon which it is based and the court must assess the expert opinion's helpfulness by scrutinizing how it is applied to the facts of the case. It is important to note that the revised Rule did not codify the *Daubert* factors (although so much post-*Daubert* commentary has focused upon them). This is purposeful in that the Supreme Court never intended those specific factors to be either "exclusive nor dispositive" (see Advisory Committee Notes at 11). In fact, the Advisory Committee Notes to the revised Rule cite the "considerable ingenuity and flexibility" that courts have demonstrated in applying *Daubert* and contemplate that such flexibility would continue under the revised Rule. *Id.* at 14. The Advisory Committee Notes to the amended Rule 702 are reproduced below.

Rule 702 has been amended in response to *Daubert v. Merrell Dow Pharmaceuticals, Inc.,* 509 U.S. 579 (1993), and to the many cases applying *Daubert,* including *Kumho Tire Co. v.*

*Carmichael,* 119 S.Ct. 1167 (1999). In *Daubert* the Court charged trial judges with the responsibility of acting as gatekeepers to exclude unreliable expert testimony, and the Court in *Kumho* clarified that this gatekeeper function applies to all expert testimony, not just testimony based in science. See also *Kumho,* 119 S.Ct. at 1178 (citing the Committee Note to the proposed amendment to Rule 702, which had been released for public comment before the date of the *Kumho* decision). The amendment affirms the trial court's role as gatekeeper and provides some general standards that the trial court must use to assess the reliability and helpfulness of proffered expert testimony. Consistently with *Kumho*, the Rule as amended provides that all types of expert testimony present questions of admissibility for the trial court in deciding whether the evidence is reliable and helpful. Consequently, the admissibility of all expert testimony is governed by the principles of Rule 104(a). Under that Rule, the proponent has the burden of establishing that the pertinent admissibility requirements are met by a preponderance of the evidence. See *Bourjaily v. United States,* 483 U.S. 171 (1987).

*Daubert* set forth a non-exclusive checklist for trial courts to use in assessing the reliability of scientific expert testimony. The specific factors explicated by the *Daubert* Court are (1) whether the expert's technique or theory can be or has been tested—that is, whether the expert's theory can be challenged in some objective sense, or whether it is instead simply a subjective, conclusory approach that cannot reasonably be assessed for reliability; (2) whether the technique or theory has been subject to peer review and publication; (3) the known or potential rate of error of the technique or theory when applied; (4) the existence and maintenance of standards and controls; and (5) whether the technique or theory has been generally accepted in the scientific community. The Court in *Kumho* held that these factors might also be applicable in assessing the reliability of non-scientific expert testimony, depending upon "the particular circumstances of the particular case at issue." 119 S.Ct. at 1175.

No attempt has been made to "codify" these specific factors. *Daubert* itself emphasized that the factors were neither exclusive nor dispositive. Other cases have recognized that not all of the specific *Daubert* factors can apply to every type of expert testimony. In addition to *Kumho,* 119 S.Ct. at 1175, see *Tyus v. Urban Search Management,* 102 F.3d 256 (7th Cir. 1996) (noting that the factors mentioned by the Court in *Daubert* do not neatly apply to expert testimony from a sociologist). See also *Kannankeril v. Terminix Int'l, Inc.,* 128 F.3d 802, 809 (3d Cir. 1997) (holding that lack of peer review or publication was not dispositive where the expert's opinion was supported by "widely accepted scientific knowledge"). The standards set forth in the amendment are broad enough to require consideration of any or all of the specific *Daubert* factors where appropriate.

Courts both before and after *Daubert* have found other factors relevant in determining whether expert testimony is sufficiently reliable to be considered by the trier of fact. These factors include:

(1) Whether experts are "proposing to testify about matters growing naturally and directly out of research they have conducted independent of the litigation, or whether they have developed their opinions expressly for purposes of testifying." *Daubert v. Merrell Dow Pharmaceuticals, Inc.,* 43 F.3d 1311, 1317 (9th Cir. 1995).

(2) Whether the expert has unjustifiably extrapolated from an accepted premise to an unfounded conclusion. See *General Elec. Co. v. Joiner,* 522 U.S. 136, 146 (1997) (noting that in some cases a trial court "may conclude that there is simply too great an analytical gap between the data and the opinion proffered").

(3) Whether the expert has adequately accounted for obvious alternative explanations. See *Claar v. Burlington N.R.R.,* 29 F.3d 499 (9th Cir. 1994) (testimony

excluded where the expert failed to consider other obvious causes for the plaintiff's condition). Compare *Ambrosini v. Labarraque,* 101 F.3d 129 (D.C. Cir. 1996) (the possibility of some uneliminated causes presents a question of weight, so long as the most obvious causes have been considered and reasonably ruled out by the expert).

(4) Whether the expert "is being as careful as he would be in his regular professional work outside his paid litigation consulting." *Sheehan v. Daily Racing Form, Inc.,* 104 F.3d 940, 942 (7th Cir. 1997). See *Kumho Tire Co. v. Carmichael,* 119 S.Ct. 1167, 1176 (1999) *(Daubert* requires the trial court to assure itself that the expert "employs in the courtroom the same level of intellectual rigor that characterizes the practice of an expert in the relevant field").

(5) Whether the field of expertise claimed by the expert is known to reach reliable results for the type of opinion the expert would give. See *Kumho Tire Co. v. Carmichael,* 119 S.Ct.1167, 1175 (1999) *(Daubert's* general acceptance factor does not "help show that an expert's testimony is reliable where the discipline itself lacks reliability, as for example, do theories grounded in any so-called generally accepted principles of astrology or necromancy."), *Moore v. Ashland Chemical, Inc.,* 151 F.3d 269 (5th Cir. 1998) (en banc) (clinical doctor was properly precluded from testifying to the toxicological cause of the plaintiff's respiratory problem, where the opinion was not sufficiently grounded in scientific methodology); *Sterling v. Velsicol Chem. Corp.,* 855 F.2d 1188 (6th Cir. 1988) (rejecting testimony based on "clinical ecology" as unfounded and unreliable).

All of these factors remain relevant to the determination of the reliability of expert testimony under the Rule as amended. Other factors may also be relevant. See *Kumho,* 119 S.Ct. 1167, 1176 ("[W]e conclude that the trial judge must have considerable leeway in deciding in a particular case how to go about determining whether particular expert testimony is reliable."). Yet no single factor is necessarily dispositive of the reliability of a particular expert's testimony. See, e.g., *Heller v. Shaw Industries, Inc.,* 167 F.3d 146, 155 (3d Cir. 1999) ("not only must each stage of the expert's testimony be reliable, but each stage must be evaluated practically and flexibly without bright-line exclusionary (or inclusionary) rules."); *Daubert v. Merrell Dow Pharmaceuticals, Inc.,* 43 F.3d 1311, 1317, n.5 (9th Cir. 1995) (noting that some expert disciplines "have the courtroom as a principal theatre of operations" and as to these disciplines "the fact that the expert has developed an expertise principally for purposes of litigation will obviously not be a substantial consideration.").

A review of the caselaw after *Daubert* shows that the rejection of expert testimony is the exception rather than the rule. *Daubert* did not work a "seachange over federal evidence law," and "the trial court's role as gatekeeper is not intended to serve as a replacement for the adversary system." *United States v. 14.38 Acres of Land Situated in Leflore County, Mississippi,* 80 F.3d 1074, 1078 (5th Cir. 1996). As the Court in *Daubert* stated: "Vigorous cross-examination, presentation of contrary evidence, and careful instruction on the burden of proof are the traditional and appropriate means of attacking shaky but admissible evidence." 509 U.S. at 595. Likewise, this amendment is not intended to provide an excuse for an automatic challenge to the testimony of every expert. See *Kumho Tire Co. v Carmichael,* 119 S.Ct.1167, 1176 (1999) (noting that the trial judge has the discretion "both to avoid unnecessary 'reliability' proceedings in ordinary cases where the reliability of an expert's methods is properly taken for granted, and to require appropriate proceedings in the less usual or more complex cases where cause for questioning the expert's reliability arises.").

When a trial court, applying this amendment, rules that an expert's testimony is reliable, this does not necessarily mean that contradictory expert testimony is unreliable. The amendment is broad enough to permit testimony that is the product of competing principles or methods in the same field of expertise. See, e.g., *Heller v. Shaw Industries, Inc.,* 167 F.3d 146, 160 (3d Cir. 1999) (expert testimony cannot be excluded simply because the expert uses one test rather than another, when both tests are accepted in the field and both reach reliable results). As the court stated in *In re Paoli R.R. Yard PCB Litigation,* 35 F.3d 717, 744 (3d Cir. 1994), proponents "do not have to demonstrate to the judge by a preponderance of the evidence that the assessments of their experts are correct, they only have to demonstrate by a preponderance of evidence that their opinions are reliable....The evidentiary requirement of reliability is lower than the merits standard of correctness." See also *Daubert v. Merrell Dow Pharmaceuticals, Inc.,* 43 F.3d 1311, 1318 (9th Cir. 1995) (scientific experts might be permitted to testify if they could show that the methods they used were also employed by "a recognized minority of scientists in their field."); *Ruiz-Troche v. Pepsi Cola,* 161 F.3d 77, 85 (1st Cir. 1998) *("Daubert* neither requires nor empowers trial courts to determine which of several competing scientific theories has the best provenance.").

The Court in *Daubert* declared that the "focus, of course, must be solely on principles and methodology, not on the conclusions they generate." 509 U.S. at 595. Yet as the Court later recognized, "conclusions and methodology are not entirely distinct from one another." *General Elec. Co. v. Joiner,* 522 U.S. 136, 146 (1997). Under the amendment, as under *Daubert,* when an expert purports to apply principles and methods in accordance with professional standards, and yet reaches a conclusion that other experts in the field would not reach, the trial court may fairly suspect that the principles and methods have not been faithfully applied. See *Lust v. Merrell Dow Pharmaceuticals, Inc.,* 89 F.3d 594, 598 (9th Cir. 1996). The amendment specifically provides that the trial court must scrutinize not only the principles and methods used by the expert, but also whether those principles and methods have been properly applied to the facts of the case. As the court noted in *In re Paoli R.R. Yard PCB Litig.,* 35 F.3d 717, 745 (3d Cir. 1994), "any step that renders the analysis unreliable...renders the expert's testimony inadmissible. This is true whether the step completely changes a reliable methodology or merely misapplies that methodology."

If the expert purports to apply principles and methods to the facts of the case, it is important that this application be conducted reliably. Yet it might also be important in some cases for an expert to educate the factfinder about general principles, without ever attempting to apply these principles to the specific facts of the case. For example, experts might instruct the factfinder on the principles of thermodynamics, or bloodclotting, or on how financial markets respond to corporate reports, without ever knowing about or trying to tie their testimony into the facts of the case. The amendment does not alter the venerable practice of using expert testimony to educate the factfinder on general principles. For this kind of generalized testimony, Rule 702 simply requires that: (1) the expert be qualified; (2) the testimony address a subject matter on which the factfinder can be assisted by an expert; (3) the testimony be reliable; and (4) the testimony "fit" the facts of the case.

As stated earlier, the amendment does not distinguish between scientific and other forms of expert testimony. The trial court's gatekeeping function applies to testimony by any expert. See *Kumho Tire Co. v. Carmichael,* 119 S.Ct. 1167, 1171 (1999) ("We conclude that *Daubert*'s general holding—setting forth the trial judge's general 'gatekeeping' obligation—applies not only to testimony based on 'scientific' knowledge, but also to testimony based on 'technical' and 'other specialized' knowledge."). While the relevant factors for determining reliability will vary from expertise to expertise, the amendment rejects the premise that an expert's testimony should be treated more permissively simply because it is outside the realm of science. An opinion from an expert who is not a scientist should receive the same degree of scrutiny for reliability as an opinion from an expert who purports to be a scientist. See *Watkins v. Telsmith, Inc.,* 121 F.3d 984, 991 (5th Cir. 1997) ("[I]t seems exactly backwards that experts who purport to rely on general engineering principles and practical experience might escape screening by the district court simply by stating that their conclusions were not reached by any particular method or technique."). Some types of expert testimony will be more objectively verifiable, and subject to the expectations of falsifiability, peer review, and publication, than others. Some types of expert testimony will not rely on anything like a scientific method, and so will have to be evaluated by reference to other standard principles attendant to the particular area of expertise. The trial judge in all cases of proffered expert testimony must find that it is properly grounded, well-reasoned, and not speculative before it can be admitted. The expert's testimony must be grounded in an accepted body of learning or experience in the expert's field, and the expert must explain how the conclusion is so grounded. See, e.g., American College of Trial Lawyers, Standards and Procedures for Determining the Admissibility of Expert Testimony after *Daubert,* 157 F.R.D. 571, 579 (1994) ("[W]hether the testimony concerns economic principles, accounting standards, property valuation or other non-scientific subjects, it should be evaluated by reference to the 'knowledge and experience' of that particular field.").

The amendment requires that the testimony must be the product of reliable principles and methods that are reliably applied to the facts of the case. While the terms "principles" and "methods" may convey a certain impression when applied to scientific knowledge, they remain relevant when applied to testimony based on technical or other specialized knowledge. For example, when a law enforcement agent testifies regarding the use of code words in a drug transaction, the principle used by the agent is that participants in such transactions regularly use code words to conceal the nature of their activities. The method used by the agent is the application of extensive experience to analyze the meaning of the conversations. So long as the principles and methods are reliable and applied reliably to the facts of the case, this type of testimony should be admitted.

Nothing in this amendment is intended to suggest that experience alone—or experience in conjunction with other knowledge, skill, training or education—may not provide a sufficient foundation for expert testimony. To the contrary, the text of Rule 702 expressly contemplates that an expert may be qualified on the basis of experience. In certain fields, experience is the predominant, if not sole, basis for a great deal of reliable expert testimony. See, e.g., *United States v. Jones,* 107 F.3d 1147 (6th Cir. 1997) (no abuse of discretion in admitting the testimony of a handwriting examiner who had years of practical experience and extensive training, and who explained his methodology in detail); *Tassin v. Sears Roebuck,* 946 F.Supp. 1241, 1248 (M.D.La. 1996) (design engineer's testimony can be admissible when the expert's opinions "are based on facts, a reasonable investigation, and traditional technical/mechanical expertise, and he provides a reasonable link between the information and procedures he uses and the conclusions he reaches"). See also *Kumho Tire Co. v. Carmichael,* 119 S.Ct. 1167, 1178 (1999) (stating that "no one denies that an expert might draw a conclusion from a set of observations based on extensive and specialized experience.").

If the witness is relying solely or primarily on experience, then the witness must explain how that experience leads to the conclusion reached, why that experience is a sufficient basis for the opinion, and how that experience is reliably applied to the facts. The trial court's gatekeeping function requires more than simply "taking the expert's word for it." See *Daubert v. Merrell Dow Pharmaceuticals, Inc.,* 43 F.3d 1311, 1319 (9th Cir. 1995) ("We've been presented with only the experts' qualifications, their conclusions and their assurances of reliability. Under *Daubert,* that's not enough."). The more subjective and controversial the expert's inquiry, the more likely the testimony should be excluded as unreliable. See *O'Conner v. Commonwealth Edison Co.,* 13 F.3d 1090 (7th Cir. 1994) (expert testimony based on a completely subjective methodology held properly excluded). See also *Kumho Tire Co. v. Carmichael,* 119 S.Ct . 1167, 1176 (1999) ("[I]t will at times be useful to ask even of a witness whose expertise is based purely on experience, say, a perfume tester able to distinguish among 140 odors at a sniff, whether his preparation is of a kind that others in the field would recognize as acceptable.").

Subpart (1) of Rule 702 calls for a quantitative rather than qualitative analysis. The amendment requires that expert testimony be based on sufficient underlying "facts or data." The term "data" is intended to encompass the reliable opinions of other experts. See the original Advisory Committee Note to Rule 703. The language "facts or data" is broad enough to allow an expert to rely on hypothetical facts that are supported by the evidence. *Id.*

When facts are in dispute, experts sometimes reach different conclusions based on competing versions of the facts. The emphasis in the amendment on "sufficient facts or data" is not intended to authorize a trial court to exclude an expert's testimony on the ground that the court believes one version of the facts and not the other.

There has been some confusion over the relationship between Rules 702 and 703. The amendment makes clear that the sufficiency of the basis of an expert' s testimony is to be decided under Rule 702. Rule 702 sets forth the overarching requirement of reliability, and an analysis of the sufficiency of the expert's basis cannot be divorced from the ultimate reliability of the expert's opinion. In contrast, the "reasonable reliance" requirement of Rule 703 is a relatively narrow inquiry. When an expert relies on inadmissible information, Rule 703 requires the trial court to determine whether that information is of a type reasonably relied on by other experts in the field. If so, the expert can rely on the information in reaching an opinion. However, the question whether the expert is relying on a sufficient basis of information—whether admissible information or not—is governed by the requirements of Rule 702.

The amendment makes no attempt to set forth procedural requirements for exercising the trial court's gatekeeping function over expert testimony. See Daniel J. Capra, The *Daubert* Puzzle, 38 Ga.L.Rev. 699, 766 (1998) ("Trial courts should be allowed substantial discretion in dealing with *Daubert* questions; any attempt to codify procedures will likely give rise to unnecessary changes in practice and create difficult questions for appellate review."). Courts have shown considerable ingenuity and flexibility in considering challenges to expert testimony under *Daubert,* and it is contemplated that this will continue under the amended Rule. See, e.g., *Cortes-Irizarry v. Corporacion Insular,* 111 F.3d 184 (1st Cir. 1997) (discussing the application of Daubert in ruling on a motion for summary judgment); *In re Paoli R.R. Yard PCB Litig.,* 35 F.3d 717, 736, 739 (3d Cir. 1994) (discussing the use of in limine hearings); *Claar v. Burlington N.R.R.,* 29 F.3d 499, 502-05 (9th Cir. 1994) (discussing the trial court's technique of ordering experts to submit serial affidavits explaining the reasoning and methods underlying their conclusions).

The amendment continues the practice of the original Rule in referring to a qualified witness as an "expert." This was done to provide continuity and to minimize change. The use of the term "expert" in the Rule does not, however, mean that a jury should actually be informed that a qualified witness is testifying as an "expert." Indeed, there is much to be said for a practice that prohibits the use of the term "expert" by both the parties and the court at trial. Such a practice "ensures that trial courts do not inadvertently put their stamp of authority" on a witness's opinion, and protects against the jury's being "overwhelmed by the so-called 'experts'." Hon. Charles Richey, Proposals to Eliminate the Prejudicial Effect of the Use of the Word "Expert" Under the Federal Rules of Evidence in Criminal and Civil Jury

Trials, 154 F.R.D. 537, 559 (1994) (setting forth limiting instructions and a standing order employed to prohibit the use of the term "expert" in jury trials).

GAP Report—Proposed Amendment to Rule 702

The Committee made the following changes to the published draft of the proposed amendment to Evidence Rule 702:

1. The word "reliable" was deleted from Subpart (1) of the proposed amendment, in order to avoid an overlap with Evidence Rule 703, and to clarify that an expert opinion need not be excluded simply because it is based on hypothetical facts. The Committee Note was amended to accord with this textual change.

2. The Committee Note was amended throughout to include pertinent references to the Supreme Court's decision in *Kumho Tire Co. v. Carmichael,* which was rendered after the proposed amendment was released for public comment. Other citations were updated as well.

3. The Committee Note was revised to emphasize that the amendment is not intended to limit the right to jury trial, nor to permit a challenge to the testimony of every expert, nor to preclude the testimony of experience-based experts, nor to prohibit testimony based on competing methodologies within a field of expertise.

4. Language was added to the Committee Note to clarify that no single factor is necessarily dispositive of the reliability inquiry mandated by Evidence Rule 702.

Please consider the following case examples, which give an idea as to how the federal courts apply the reliability requirements of Rule 702. For additional case examples dealing with the methodology and admissibility of expert testimony, please see Chapter 9.

### Example 5.23: Life-care planner's opinion admissible (sufficiently reliable)

*Marcano Rivera v. Turabo Medical Center Partnership,* 415 F.3d 162 (C.A. 1 Puerto Rico 2005)
In this case, the court held that testimony offered in a medical malpractice trial by a life-care planner regarding the projected cost of a child's future care, stemming from severe neurological injuries sustained at birth, was sufficiently reliable for admissibility. Although his projections were not subject to physician review, the life-care planner had been admitted as an expert on rehabilitation and life-care planning in numerous state and federal courts and his proposed care plan was based on a review of records from the agency providing the child with skilled nursing care, a letter from her physician, and an interview with her family and caregiver.

**Comment:** Note that the expert's track record in being admitted to testify in other courts was a factor in allowing his testimony in this case. Experts should avoid cases where they are not confident that their opinions will be admitted.

### Example 5.24: Engineer's opinion not reliable, inadmissible (Lincoln Navigator shifting out of park)

*Simmons v. Ford Motor Co.,* 132 Fed.Appx. 950 (C.A. 3 N.J. 2005)
In this products liability action, the plaintiff sought damages arising from injuries she sustained when, upon exiting her Lincoln Navigator, she was struck by that vehicle when it spontaneously shifted out of park. The case was thrown out via summary judgment because the plaintiff's expert engineer's opinion was held unreliable and inadmissible. The court stated:

> After conducting a *Daubert* hearing, the District Court determined that although Anderson was qualified to testify, the proposed expert testimony failed to satisfy the reliability requirements of F.R.E. 702 and *Daubert*. In addition, the District Court determined that Simmons failed to satisfy her burden of providing a reasonable alternative design to the defect at issue pursuant to New Jersey's product liability

law. See *Lewis v. American Cyanamid Co.,* 155 N.J. 544, 715 A.2d 967, 980 (1998). Simmons subsequently requested that the District Court enter final judgment under Fed.R.Civ.P. 54(b) because the disqualification of her expert rendered her unable to sustain her burden at trial regarding the remaining breach of express warranty and failure to warn claims. We have jurisdiction pursuant to 28 U.S.C. § 1291. For the reasons that follow, we will affirm.

Because we write principally for the parties, who are familiar with the underlying facts, we need not recite them in detail here. Simmons argues that the Navigator was defective because its park gear became disengaged by releasing itself or not holding the proper position, causing the vehicle to roll backward. She contends that the vehicle was in "false park," where a driver senses by feel and observation that she has placed the gear shift lever in park but the parking pawl does not land in the appropriate place in the transmission. This condition makes the vehicle susceptible to moving out of park into neutral or reverse and permits inadvertent movement of the vehicle to occur. To prove this theory of liability and her proposed alternative double wheel design regarding the alleged defect, Simmons relied on the opinions of Anderson, which were excluded from evidence. We apply an abuse of discretion standard when reviewing a trial court's decision to admit or exclude expert testimony. *Kumho Tire Co. v. Carmichael,* 526 U.S. 137, 152, 119 S.Ct. 1167, 143 L.Ed.2d 238 (1999).

The District Court determined from both Anderson's report and his testimony at the *Daubert* hearing that the process by which he reached his conclusions was unreliable. Calhoun, 350 F.3d at 321. Specifically, the District Court determined that he failed to provide a testable hypothesis and was never able to duplicate a scenario where the weight of the vehicle in combination with false park caused the vehicle to move; the method he utilized was not subject to peer review; he failed to produce any material or data from which a potential rate of error could be gathered; he had not established that he had used any standards when conducting his tests; and there was no assertion that he utilized a generally accepted method for determining false park.

Despite Simmons' arguments to the contrary, Anderson's conclusions derive from subjective observations and methodologies, thus failing to meet the reliability requirements of F.R.E. 702 and *Daubert. Kumho Tire,* 526 U.S. at 154- 55, 119 S.Ct. 1167. Although he opined that the vehicle was in false park when Simmons exited the vehicle, he could not identify why the car disengaged from park. Anderson admitted that he could not replicate the movement that caused Simmons' injuries and that he arrived at two theories why the movement occurred simply because he could not come up with any other causes of the movement. Anderson posited that Simmons' vehicle rolled backwards either due to Simmons' inadvertent shifting of gears upon exiting the vehicle or due to the weight of the vehicle combined with Simmons' movement. The former theory lacks evidentiary support. Simmons testified that the vehicle was placed in park, turned off, and exited by her before the spontaneous movement occurred. As to the latter theory, Anderson could not duplicate the movement experienced by Simmons. Further, when he accomplished movement by hitting the gear shift out of park, the vehicle rolled too fast to permit his exit from the vehicle.

As to whether Simmons provided sufficient evidence of a reasonable alternative design, we conclude that the District Court correctly ruled that she had not met her burden in this regard. Under New Jersey law, a plaintiff claiming that a product is defectively designed bears the burden of proving that a practical and feasible alternative design would have reduced or prevented the harm. *Lewis,* 715 A.2d at 980. The District Court must initially determine whether sufficient evidence has been presented to permit a reasonable factfinder to conclude that a reasonable alternative design could have been adopted. *H.T. Rose Enter., Inc. v. Henny Penny Corp.,* 317 N.J.Super. 477, 722 A.2d 587 (1999). Here, the District Court properly exercised its discretion in determining that the testimony offered by Anderson failed to meet the threshold for admissibility. The proposed alternative was nothing more than a sketch without a mock-up or testing of the design. Nor could Anderson affirm that the proposed alternative design was in use by any vehicle manufacturer or that any manufacturer had eliminated the possibility of false park in the design of vehicles with automatic transmissions. Anderson offered only his unsubstantiated belief as to what would be a feasible alternative design. Absent data or evidence to support such a conclusion, however, we conclude that the District Court properly exercised its discretion in excluding Anderson's testimony. See *H.T. Rose,* 722 A.2d at 595-97; *Smith v. Keller Ladder Co.,* 275 N.J.Super. 280, 645 A.2d 1269, 1272 (1994).

We have considered all of the arguments of the parties and conclude that no further discussion is necessary. For the foregoing reasons, we will affirm the judgment of the District Court. At 951–953.

**Comment:** This case was *lost* (through summary judgment) when the expert's opinion was excluded. Since the disallowance of an expert can be outcome determinative in many cases, experts can expect their opinions to be aggressively challenged.

### Example 5.25: Pharmacology expert's testimony in toxic tort case not reliable, therefore inadmissible (Metabolife)
*McClain v. Metabolife Intern., Inc.,* 401 F.3d 1233 (C.A. 11 Ala. 2005)
The court stated:

> Dr. O'Donnell, Pharm. D., testified as an expert in pharmacy, pharmacology and nutrition; he is not a toxicologist or a medical doctor. He based his opinions about Metabolife's toxicity and its ability to cause heart attacks and strokes in substantial part on ephedrine's classification as a sympathomimetic drug. He testified that drugs in the sympathomimetic family, including ephedrine, cause constriction of blood vessels that leads to increased pulse rate and increased blood pressure. The long-term use of ephedrine can cause narrowing of blood vessels, called vasospasm, a transitory constriction of a blood vessel, and also vasculitis, an inflammation or irritation of blood vessels. Vasospasm and vasculitis caused by extended use of ephedrine can lead to heart attacks and strokes. That Metabolife causes vasospasm and vasculitis, which in turn causes strokes and heart attacks, is O'Donnell's ultimate opinion that the court must analyze under *Daubert*.
>
> O'Donnell also testified that adding caffeine to ephedrine in Metabolife 356 makes ephedrine more toxic, so any amount of caffeine added to ephedrine is too much. This combination of drugs poses an "imminent risk of death."
>
> O'Donnell's opinions lack the indicia of reliability necessary to survive a *Daubert* inquiry and challenge under Rule 702. He draws speculative conclusions about Metabolife's toxicity from questionable principles of pharmacology, while at the same time, neglecting the hallmark of the science of toxic torts—the dose-response relationship. He also draws unsubstantiated analogies between ephedrine and phenylpropanolamine, infers conclusions from studies and reports that the papers do not authorize, and unjustifiably relies on government public health reports and consumer complaints to establish medical causation. In short, O'Donnell does not support his opinions with sufficient data or reliable principles, as identified by the *Daubert* rubric, and fails to follow the basic methodology that experts should follow in toxic tort cases. At 1239–1240.

**Comment:** Drug cases (especially ones that try to break new ground) are part of a category of cases where expert testimony should be expected to be very closely examined under *Daubert*. Experts testifying in such cases should take particular care in making sure that their opinions are well supported.

### Example 5.26: Economist's damages opinion too speculative
*Johnson Elec. North America, Inc. v. Mabuchi Motor America Corp.,* 103 F.Supp.2d 268 (S.D.N.Y. 2000)
In this patent infringement case, an economist's expert opinion regarding the damages an electric motor manufacturer suffered from alleged infringement of an electric motor patent was excluded by the trial court. The appellate court agreed with the trial court. At issue was the expert's report, which was a detailed economic analysis of the worldwide market for micromotors. Based upon that analysis, the expert economist estimated how many of the allegedly infringing micromotors were used within the United States and computed the damages to the alleged infringee. However, the expert had no empirical data as to the number of allegedly infringing micromotors incorporated

into products that were shipped into the United States. The court noted that the computations of that number were based on highly questionable assumptions. The court stated:

> This Court agrees that speculative economic analysis must be rejected. It can be appropriate to utilize market reconstruction to prove damages, particularly in patent cases. However, if [the alleged infringee] wishes to reconstruct the micro-motor market, that reconstruction must be grounded on the most relevant and reliable data available. At 286.

**Comment:** Experts who wish their opinions to be both admitted and believed by the jury should base those opinions on hard data and numbers rather than on subjective estimates.

### Example 5.27: Hydrogeologist's methodology reliable, factual basis goes to credibility of opinion (TCE)

*U.S. v. Dico, Inc.,* 2001 WL 1094944 (C.A. 8 2001)
Here the United States sued a landowner under CERCLA to recover response costs for cleanup of groundwater contaminated by trichloroethylene (TCE) and other chlorinated volatile organic compounds (VOCs). The district court found the landowner liable for the costs incurred by the Environmental Protection Agency in cleaning up the groundwater at the site and awarded it over $4 million in cleanup costs. The landowner appealed both the liability and the award portions of the judgment entered by the district court. On appeal, the court considered the landowner's argument that the district court erred in refusing to exclude the testimony of the government's expert hydrogeologist because "his methodology was unreliable." The court considered the expert's methodology and found it reliable under the *Daubert* standard. However, the landowner also argued that the hydrogeologist's testimony was unreliable because his findings were, in at least three instances, based upon insufficient data. The court rejected the argument and stated:

> Again, because "the factual basis of an expert opinion goes to the credibility of the testimony, not the admissibility, and it is up to the opposing party to examine the factual basis for the opinion in cross-examination," the District Court properly refused Dico's invitation to exclude Robertson's testimony on this ground. *Loudermill v. Dow Chem. Co.,* 863 F.2d 566, 570 (8th Cir.1988) (holding district court did not abuse its discretion by admitting expert testimony challenged by defendant as being "insufficiently supported by facts"); *accord Arkwright Mut. Ins. Co. v. Gwinner Oil, Inc.,* 125 F.3d 1176, 1183 (8th Cir.1997) (same). *U.S. v. Dico, Inc.,* 2001 WL 1094944.

**Comment:** Even if the expert's testimony is admitted, the factual basis of his opinion remains a prime area for cross-examination. The best experts base their opinions on sufficient data.

### Example 5.28: Methodology reliable, factual basis goes to credibility of opinion (unpaid gas royalties)

*SEECO, Inc. v. Hales,* 22 S.W.3d 157 (Ark. 2000)
In this case, royalty owners seeking allegedly unpaid royalties brought a class action suit against a gas producer. The trial court entered judgment on the jury's verdict for the royalty owners and granted certification. The gas producer appealed. One of the contentions on appeal was that the opinions of two of the royalty owners' expert witnesses were conclusory and were not based on sufficient facts. The first witness testified about the implied covenant to market, an issue regarding the interpretation of the contracts at issue. A second expert witness for the royalty owners confirmed the first's opinions and calculated the damages from the gas producer's failure to enforce the contract at issue. The court rejected this argument in affirming the award:

> This court has held that the weight and value to be given expert witnesses lies within the exclusive province of the jury, and it is the jury's decision whether to believe or disbelieve any witness. *Dixon*

*Ticonderoga Co. v. Winburn Tile Mfg. Co.,* 324 Ark. 266, 920 S.W.2d 829 (1996). Clearly, the jury in this case accorded John McArthur's and Don Ray George's testimony more weight than the appellants' witnesses, and this court will not disturb that finding on appeal. The appellants argue that McArthur's testimony was merely conclusory, but we fail to see how that was the case. Once an expert witness is qualified, the weakness in the factual underpinning of the expert's opinion may be developed on cross-examination, and such weakness goes to the weight and credibility of the expert's testimony. *Jackson v. Buchman,* 338 Ark. 467, 996 S.W.2d 30 (1999). Here, McArthur's testimony was based on the particular facts of the case. While he did reach certain conclusions, these conclusions were thoroughly explained with regard to the law and the facts surrounding this case. At 168.

Rule 703, below, deals with the types of evidence expert witnesses can rely on when forming their opinions.

### Box 5.32

| |
| --- |
| **Fed. R. Evid. 703. Bases of Opinion Testimony by Experts**<br>The facts or data in the particular case upon which an expert bases an opinion or inference may be those perceived by or made known to the expert at or before the hearing. If of a type reasonably relied upon by experts in the particular field in forming opinions or inferences upon the subject, the facts or data need not be admissible in evidence in order for the opinion or inference to be admitted. Facts or data that are otherwise inadmissible shall not be disclosed to the jury by the proponent of the opinion or inference unless the court determines that their probative value in assisting the jury to evaluate the expert's opinion substantially outweighs their prejudicial impact. |

When the Federal Rules of Evidence were first enacted in 1975, one of the important changes to the common law rules of evidence was that under Rule 703 experts could base an opinion not only on facts that were in evidence, but also on facts that were not in evidence and even on facts that might not be admissible if they were offered at trial, as long as these underlying facts dealt with the kind of information on which similar experts would rely in making nonlitigation-oriented professional judgments. Thus, under the Federal Rules of Evidence, the emphasis shifted away from the admissibility of the facts upon which an expert's opinion was based to the reliability of these facts as determined by the profession in arriving at professional judgments independent of litigation.

Rule 703 gives experts a fair degree of latitude regarding the facts or data upon which their opinions are based. This latitude is not, however, unlimited. These facts or data need not be admissible in evidence themselves (for example, hearsay) as long as they are of a type that is reasonably relied upon by experts in that field. *If a court (i.e., the trial judge) holds that an expert's opinion is based upon facts or data that are not reasonably relied upon by experts in the same field, then the expert's testimony may be excluded.* Consider the following examples.[2]

---

[2] Chapter 8 on opinions contains further Rule 703 cases.

**Example 5.29: Damages expert's opinion based upon statements from his client's employees not admissible (calculation of economic loss)**
*Loeffel Steel Products, Inc. v. Delta Brands, Inc.,* 387 F.Supp.2d 794 (N.D. Ill. 2005)
In this breach of contract action the court granted the plaintiff's motion to bar the defendant's expert from testifying because the basis of the defense expert's testimony did not comply with the requirements of Rule 703. The court stated:

> Mr. Dohmeyer's damage model and calculation of economic loss suffer from the further flaw that they violate of Rule 703 of the Federal Rules of Evidence.
> Mr. Dohmeyer's calculation of economic loss is based on the assumption that the addition of extra labor and shifts would allow the Line to yield the same productivity as it would have running at faster speeds with fewer shifts. The theory and the precise number of additional workers and shifts needed came from the defendants' employees, on whom Mr. Dohmeyer uncritically relied. It is undisputed that neither Mr. Dohmeyer nor his assistants at DVC had any expertise in blanking machines and were incapable of assessing the validity of the information provided by the defendants. (Dohmeyer deposition at 26, 33-38, 89). Cf. *Bailey v. Allgas,* 148 F.Supp.2d 1222, 1240 (N.D.Ala.2000)(unquestioning reliance on opinions expressed by plaintiff's counsel not proper).
> Proceeding from this "unquestioning reliance," *Gentieu v. Tony Stone Images/Chicago, Inc.,* 214 F.Supp.2d 849, 853 (N.D.Ill.2002) (Shadur, J.), Mr. Dohmeyer calculated the amount it would cost Loeffel to pay the additional workers in order to produce as much finished steel as would have been produced had the Line operated properly. Mr. Dohmeyer's difficulty in explaining how the additional workers would cure the situation demonstrates dramatically that he brought no expertise to bear on the underlying assumptions on which his economic loss theory was based:
>
>> Sure, just by having, you know, the kinds of things, you know—you have to, I guess, re— recalibrate the machine every time you put a new roll on it where it should have been automatic, you can have a guy standing there, you know, doing that kind of thing. You know, once again, I don't know the technical parts of it, and I understood them a lot better when I did the interview and when I prepared for this deposition last time, but I haven't gone back to re-talk to them about those specifics again for today's deposition.... (Dohmeyer Dep. at 37).
>
> Yet, Rule 703's relaxation of the usual requirement of firsthand knowledge—a rule which represents a pervasive manifestation of the common law's insistence upon the most reliable sources of information—was premised on an assumption that the expert's opinion will have a reliable basis in the knowledge and experience of his discipline. *Daubert,* 509 U.S. at 592, 113 S.Ct. 2786. When pressed, Mr. Dohmeyer could not even say whether the additional labor would solve the alleged problems and raise the level of production. For that information, one would, he said, have to check with Messrs. Barron, King and DaClue. (*Id.* at 37-38, 45, 89). Referring to his damage figure, he said:
>
>> [A]ll it really assumes is with the addition of this expense. And it would probably be labor, you know...It says with this much money thrown at the problem, probably—probably, in terms of labor, you can solve the production problems that are alleged. (Dohmeyer Dep. at 44-45).
>
> It is no answer to say that since Rule 703 allows an expert to base an opinion on inadmissible evidence, Mr. Dohmeyer must be allowed to testify, even though the basis of the information on which he relied came from the defendants. First, the defendants have made no effort to carry their burden of proving by a preponderance of the evidence that the kind of information given to Mr. Dohmeyer is the kind "reasonably relied upon by experts in the particular field in forming opinions or inferences upon the subject...." The argument is thus forfeited. *United States v. Baretz,* 411 F.3d 867 (7th Cir.2005).
> Second, and more importantly, while Rule 703 was intended to liberalize the rules relating to expert testimony, it was not intended to abolish the hearsay rule and to allow a witness, under the guise of giving expert testimony, to in effect become the mouthpiece of the witnesses on whose statements or opinions the expert purports to base his opinion. Under Rule 703, an expert may rely on hearsay in

formulating his opinion—provided the requirements of Rule 702 are met—but the evidence is not admissible for the truth of the matters asserted.

Rule 703 was never intended to allow oblique evasions of the hearsay rule. In *Dura Automotive,* the Seventh Circuit acknowledged that it "is common in technical fields for an expert to base an opinion in part on what a different expert believes on the basis of expert knowledge not possessed by the first expert." 285 F.3d at 613. For example, as the Committee Notes to the 1972 Proposed Rule 703 observed, a physician, though not an expert in radiology, may rely for a diagnosis on an x-ray. *Id.* The Seventh Circuit extrapolated from there to make its point:

> We too do not believe that the leader of a clinical medical team must be qualified as an expert in every individual discipline encompassed by the team in order to testify as to the team's conclusions. But suppose the soundness of the underlying expert judgment is in issue. Suppose a thoracic surgeon gave expert evidence in a medical malpractice case that the plaintiff's decedent had died because the defendant, a radiologist, had negligently failed to diagnose the decedent's lung cancer until it was too advanced for surgery. The surgeon would be competent to testify that the cancer was too advanced for surgery, but in offering the additional and critical judgment that the radiologist should have discovered the cancer sooner he would be, at best, just parroting the opinion of an expert in radiology competent to testify that the defendant had x-rayed the decedent carelessly.

The problem, then, is that the expert is vouching for the truth of what another expert told him—he is merely that expert's spokesman. But, "[a] scientist, however well credentialed he may be, is not permitted to be the mouthpiece of a scientist in a different specialty. That would not be responsible science." *Id.* at 614. See also *Grant v. Chemrex, Inc.,* No. 93 C 0350, 1997 WL 223071, 8 (N.D.Ill. April 28, 1997) (expert's "professional knowledge and ability" were not adequate to evaluate calculations and opinions upon which he based his opinion).

That is precisely the situation here: If allowed to testify, Mr. Dohmeyer would be "hid[ing] behind" Messrs. Barron, King and DaClue and acting as their "mouthpiece." *Id.* at 615. He would, in effect, be vouching for their labor-added methodology, when he has absolutely no knowledge of whether the theory is valid and reliable. See also TK-7 Corp., 993 F.2d 722. Thus, Mr. Dohmeyer's testimony cannot be used to prove that additional labor and shifts were in fact the medicament for the Line's ills. *In re James Wilson Associates,* 965 F.2d 160, 173 (7th Cir.1992)(Posner, J.).

The example posed by Judge Posner in *James Wilson Associates* demonstrates the problem with Mr. Dohmeyer's testimony: "If, for example, the expert witness (call him A) bases his opinion in part on a fact (call it X) that the parties lawyer told him, the lawyer cannot, in closing argument, tell the jury, 'see we proved X through our expert witness, A.'" *Id.* at 173. (Parenthesis in original).

Yet, without the testimony of Messrs. Barron, King and DaClue explaining and justifying their labor-added theory, Mr. Dohmeyer's testimony will "rest[ ] on air." *Dura Automotive,* 285 F.3d at 615. If the underlying assumptions cannot be proven by admissible, competent evidence, the very nature of which would appear to require expert testimony, Mr. Dohmeyer's analysis of economic loss would have no evidentiary support and would be irrelevant. See Rule 402, Federal Rules of Evidence. Yet, the only expert disclosure in the case on the defendants' side is Mr. Dohmeyer's. Messrs. Barron, King and DaClue have not been designated as experts. Hence, it would appear that Mr. Dohmeyer's testimony, even if initially allowed, would ultimately have to be stricken.

In the instant case, denying the motion to prohibit Mr. Dohmeyer's testimony and allowing him to testify when there will be no competent evidence to prove the truth of the underlying assumptions would result in allowing testimony that would have to be stricken as irrelevant. The law never requires an idle thing to be done. At 806–810.

**Example 5.30: Depression inventory may be used as basis of opinion, but not itself admissible**
*Leiting v. Mutha,* 2002 WL 287528 (Colo. App. 2002)
In this personal injury case, the plaintiff's testifying doctor based his opinion in part on a depression inventory prepared by a nontestifying doctor. The court held that the inventory itself was not admissible and cited Rule 703.

> Plaintiff sought admission of the depression inventory on the basis that the testifying doctor, who had not prepared the inventory, used it in his treatment of plaintiff. Defendant objected on grounds that the inventory was outside the doctor's area of expertise and constituted hearsay. The trial court admitted the inventory into evidence, presumably under CRE 703, which provides, in part, that facts or data upon which an expert bases an opinion need not be admissible in evidence if of a type reasonably relied upon by experts in the particular field in forming opinions.
>
> CRE 703, standing alone, does not provide a basis for admission of this evidence. That rule allows an expert to base his or her opinion on facts or data that are not admissible in evidence. An expert may describe the statements or reports he or she relied on, but CRE 703 does not permit otherwise inadmissible facts or data contained in the reports or statements to be admitted merely because the expert relied on them. 29 C. Wright & V. Gold, Federal Practice & Procedure § 6273, at 315 (1997)(rule 703 not intended "as a vehicle for undermining other rules of evidence").
>
> Fed.R.Evid. 703, which is otherwise similar to CRE 703, was amended in December 2000 to make clear that the facts and data relied upon by the expert are not automatically admissible. The following sentence was added to the federal rule: "Facts or data that are otherwise inadmissible shall not be disclosed to the jury by the proponent of the opinion or inference unless the court determines that their probative value in assisting the jury to evaluate the expert's opinion substantially outweighs their prejudicial effect." Although CRE 703 has not been similarly amended, this clarification to the federal rule is nonetheless instructive.

**Example 5.31: Expert can rely on data not personally collected (CERCLA)**
*Gussack Realty Co. v. Xerox Corp.,* 224 F.3d 85 (C.A. 2 2000)
Here, the lessor and lessee of a property that had allegedly been contaminated by the release of solvents from a photocopier refurbishing plant operated on an adjacent property, brought suit against the plant operator. The trial court awarded damages to the plaintiffs based on their CERCLA and negligence claims. The appellate court considered, among other issues, whether the trial court erred in admitting the plaintiffs' expert's testimony. The defendant argued that the plaintiffs' experts failed to conduct their own tests and relied only on data provided by Xerox's own experts and the Department of Environmental Conservation. However, an expert may rely on data that she did not personally collect. The court explained:

> The Federal Rules of Evidence specifically provide that an expert may rely on facts or data "perceived by *or* made known to the expert at or before the hearing." Fed.R.Evid. 703 (emphasis added). The expert need not have conducted her own tests. *See B.F. Goodrich v. Betkoski,* 99 F.3d 505, 524 (2d Cir.1996) ("Dr. Brown did not personally visit the landfills or dig up any shovelfuls of waste, but he was not required to do so."). At 94–95.

**Comment:** Experts may base their opinions on data they did not personally collect.

**Example 5.32: Road design expert can base opinion on inadmissible police reports**
*Wiley v. City of New Orleans,* 809 So.2d 151 (La. App. 4 Cir 2001)
In this personal injury case, the plaintiff called as an expert witness an expert, Clary, with expertise in land surveying and the design, construction, maintenance, and safety of public roads and streets. The court held that it was proper for the trial court to allow Clary to base his opinion on police

reports which were themselves inadmissible. The court, applying the Louisiana Code of Evidence (which tracks the Federal Rules) stated:

> The defendant argued that Mr. Clary's expert testimony should not have been admissible because it was based upon inadmissible hearsay, i.e. police accident reports. However, the 1988 official comments (d) to the Louisiana Code of Evidence Article 703 states:
>
>> Under this Article the facts or data underlying the expert witness' opinion may properly be:...(3) under designated circumstances, facts or data not admissible in evidence (because, for example, their source is inadmissible hearsay), if they are of a kind reasonably relied upon by experts in the particular field in arriving at their opinions or inferences....Whether the facts or data may be "reasonably relied upon" in this fashion is a question for the court under Article 104(A). See 3 J. Weinstein & M. Berger, Weinstein's Evidence 703[03](1984).
>
> We find no error in the trial court's ruling that the evidence was inadmissible hearsay per se, but could be used as a basis for expert testimony.

**Comment:** Experts may base their opinions on inadmissible hearsay.

**Example 5.33: Electrical expert allowed to base cause of fire opinion in part on report of deceased cause-and-origin expert**
*Ferrara & Mercurio v. St. Paul Mercury Insurance Company,* 240 F.3d 1 (1st Cir 2001)
In this insurance case, the issue was whether the fire in question was caused by arson. The court stated:

> Much of the two-week trial before Judge Harrington was a battle between the experts concerning whether the fire was accidental or of incendiary origin. Defendant's expert, John Malcolm, concluded that the fire on the TWO FRIENDS had three points of origin and was deliberately set. Plaintiff's expert, Paul Sullivan, testified that an accidental electrical fire started in the lower electrical panel and exploded in a so-called flash-over igniting everything in the super-heated compartments of the vessel.
>
> Beyond the conflicting expert opinions, the battle also raged over whether John Malcolm should be allowed to testify as St. Paul's cause-and-origin expert. It is on this issue that F&D appeals. F&D contends that John Malcolm should not have been permitted to render an expert opinion as to cause and origin because his opinion was based on unreliable data, viz, data not collected by him personally.
>
> As soon as four days after the fire, St. Paul had hired Fred O'Donnell as its expert to investigate the origin and cause of the fire. Fred O'Donnell then hired John Malcolm as an electrical systems expert to assist him in that investigation. On July 8, 1993, the two men began their investigation on site in Gloucester where the boat remained moored.
>
> O'Donnell and Malcolm worked closely with each other. Malcolm testified that together, sometimes with Malcolm holding the measuring tape for O'Donnell, the two took measurements of the vessel in preparation for producing scale drawings to assist in the investigation and their report. Although Malcolm's job for which O'Donnell had retained him was to pay close attention to the boat's electrical system, the two men worked in tandem, often double-checking each other's observations and analyses by calling each other over to various burn sites on the vessel to coordinate their data collection and inquiries.
>
> During the first two trials, O'Donnell and Malcolm both testified as experts, O'Donnell as to the fire's cause and origin and Malcolm as to related but narrower questions concerning the fire and the boat's electrical system. Unfortunately, however, between the first appeal and the third trial, O'Donnell died. For the third trial, then, instead of replacing O'Donnell with an outside cause-and-origin expert, defendant decided that Malcolm would testify as St. Paul's only fire expert, providing opinions on both cause and origin and the vessel's electrical system. This decision is the source of F&D's objection regarding the admissibility of Malcolm's testimony. F&D argued to the district court, as it does to us

now, that Malcolm was not competent to testify as to cause and origin as his testimony was principally based not on his own observations but on those made by O'Donnell.

F&D's next objection, although not crafted as such, is essentially a Rule 703 objection. F&D claims that Malcolm's opinion as to cause and origin was based on unreliable data, viz, data provided by the late Fred O'Donnell and not that which was collected through Malcolm's own personal observation.

A major problem with this argument is that Malcolm himself had visited the fire scene and examined the evidence there side by side with O'Donnell. Besides looking at burn patterns and studying the electrical system, he took measurements and photographs and wrote his own report. He also interviewed the vessel's engineer. Many photographs of evidence at the scene were entered into evidence by stipulation. Hence, it is simply not the case that Malcolm's cause-and-origin opinion rested mainly upon O'Donnell's investigations.

To be sure, Malcolm's opinion coincided with O'Donnell's and he testified that he read O'Donnell's report in preparation for his expert testimony, along with the report of the local fire department. But the opinion he rendered was his own, and, as said, he had first-hand knowledge of the fire scene and the observable facts there upon which to base that opinion. Federal Rule of Evidence 703 allows Malcolm to have taken O'Donnell's report and opinion into account when forming his own expert opinion. So long as the basis of Malcolm's opinion did not extend beyond facts or data "of a type reasonably relied upon by experts in the particular field in forming opinions or inferences upon the subject, the facts or data need not be admissible in evidence." Fed.R.Evid. 703. We think a cause-and-origin expert like Malcolm could be expected to examine the report of another expert like O'Donnell as well as the fire department's report in the course of forming his own opinion derived from a variety of sources, including his own first-hand knowledge of the primary evidence at the fire scene.

In the present case, the jury understood that Malcolm's observations coincided with those of the deceased expert hired by defendant and that, until recently, Malcolm's only job was to advise and supplement O'Donnell's conclusions as to the cause and origin of the fire with his own opinion concerning the role of the vessel's electrical system in the fire. Thus, in weighing and evaluating Malcolm's opinion, the jury was able to determine whether it was in some way weakened by reliance upon O'Donnell's.

We find no error in the district court's ruling that Malcolm's opinion as to cause and origin was properly admitted. At 7–9.

**Example 5.34: Pathologist allowed to rely on autopsy photographs taken by someone else**
*State of Nebraska v. Pruett,* 638 N.W.2d 809 (Neb. 2002)
The defendant in this criminal case was convicted of manslaughter and appealed. At trial, the state had presented the expert testimony of a pathologist. Dr. Matthias Okoye, a forensic pathologist, testified that an autopsy was performed by one of his colleagues. Okoye reviewed the autopsy reports and photographs taken at the time of the autopsy. He also examined the organs and microscopic tissue sections taken at the autopsy. He opined that the cause of death was from a gunshot wound. During Okoye's testimony, autopsy photographs, exhibits 39 through 54, were entered into evidence over Pruett's hearsay objections. Pruett requested that the jury be instructed that they could not consider Okoye's testimony about facts and data not directly perceived by him. The court did not give the requested instruction. The court held that the expert's testimony was properly admitted. It stated:

> Pruett contends that the court erred in allowing Okoye to testify regarding facts provided to him by others and not perceived by him directly. He objected on the basis of hearsay to the introduction into evidence of the autopsy photographs.

# EVIDENCE

The court held that the expert testimony was properly admitted and stated:

Neb.Rev.Stat. § 27-703 (Reissue 1995) provides:

> The facts or data in the particular case upon which an expert bases an opinion or inference may be those perceived by or made known to him at or before the hearing. If of a type reasonably relied upon by experts in the particular field in forming opinions or inferences upon the subject, the facts or data need not be admissible in evidence.

> We have held that § 27-703 contemplates admission of an expert's opinion based on hearsay supplying facts or data for that opinion, rather than requiring firsthand knowledge as the only source of information for an expert's opinion.
>
> Further, an expert may rely on hearsay facts or data that are reasonably relied on by experts in that field. Thus, a doctor who did not directly treat a patient may provide expert testimony regarding the patient, and any lack of firsthand knowledge goes to the weight of the opinion.
>
> Okoye could give his opinion because he relied on data that are reasonably given by other experts in his field. Pruett's argument that Okoye could not testify regarding facts that he did not perceive directly is without merit. At 817.

## Example 5.35: Doctor's testimony regarding psychology admissible
*Walker v. Soo Line R.R. Co.,* 208 F.3d 581 (C.A. 7 2000)
The plaintiff sued the defendant railroad company, seeking damages for injuries suffered by having been struck by lightning while working in a railroad tower. At trial, the plaintiff sought to introduce expert testimony to establish that electrical injury could have been the cause of his condition. Most of that testimony was excluded.

The plaintiff was evaluated by the Electrical Trauma Research Program at the University of Chicago. Two members of that team were prepared to testify. One of these experts was a psychologist who had examined the plaintiff. He administered tests designed to assess the plaintiff's IQ, his concentration, and other functions. The trial court permitted him to testify about the results of those tests; it did not permit his testimony about his evaluation of the plaintiff's IQ before the incident or about any decline in his IQ since the incident. The evidence was excluded because the psychologist had not evaluated the plaintiff before the incident and had relied on an erroneous account of his educational history. The appellate court, however, found that the psychologist could have been allowed to testify, because "Medical professionals reasonably may be expected to rely on self-reported patient histories." At 586. Moreover, it explained, "In situations in which a medical expert has relied upon a patient's self-reported history and that history is found to be inaccurate, district courts usually should allow those inaccuracies in that history to be explored through cross-examination." *Id.*

Secondly, the district court refused to allow any testimony by the doctor who headed the clinical team at the University of Chicago that examined and evaluated the plaintiff. The doctor concluded, based to a significant extent on her discussions with members of the team, that the plaintiff had post-traumatic stress disorder and had lost function because of an electrical injury. Although there was no dispute about the doctor's expertise on the subject of electrical trauma, the trial court found that she improperly relied on findings of other members of her team. The appellate court disagreed and stated:

> At the outset, we think that it was proper for a physician working in the role that [the doctor] held on the diagnostic and evaluation team to rely on the work of her team members in forming her opinion. Medical professionals have long been expected to rely on the opinions of other medical professionals in forming their opinions. At 588.

The court continued:

Nor do we believe that the leader of a clinical medical team must be qualified as an expert in every individual discipline encompassed by the team in order to testify as to the team's conclusions. The team approach to medical diagnosis and treatment is employed to ensure that all relevant disciplines work together for the good of the patient. The leader of that team is chosen because of her ability to assess accurately the role that each member of the team ought to play and to reconcile, when necessary, competing perspectives. In short, the expertise of the team leader is the capability to evaluate, in light of the overall picture, the contributions of each member of the team. Here, the district court found [the doctor] to be an expert on the subject of electrical trauma. As part of that expertise, she naturally would be expected to have expertise on the subject of whether electrical injuries could cause post-traumatic stress disorder. [The doctor] is not a psychiatrist and well might not be able to render an opinion about diagnosing post-traumatic stress disorder on the basis of something other than electrical trauma. However, as the leader of a clinical team specializing in electrical injury, who reasonably relied on the expert opinions of specialists who also examined the plaintiff, her conclusion that the plaintiff suffered from post-traumatic stress disorder was a professional opinion that the jury had the right to consider. *Id.* at 589.

The appellate court reversed and remanded.

## Example 5.36: Hearsay evidence from store personnel not reasonably relied upon (safe not burglar deterrent)
*Redman v. John D. Brush & Co.,* 111 F.3d 1174 (4th Cir. 1997)
A metallurgic engineer's testimony that a safe was not burglar deterrent was properly excluded. The expert relied solely on hearsay information from store personnel to identify a standard of burglar protection capacity. Experts would not rely on this hearsay as an indication of industry safety standards.

## Example 5.37: In drug case, chemist can rely upon report of testing done by another chemist
*United States v. Posey,* 647 F.2d 1048 (10th Cir. 1981)
In a drug prosecution, it was permissible for one chemist to rely upon tests run by another in testifying that the tested substance was cocaine: "It is quite reasonable for a chemist to review another chemist's analysis when forming an opinion as to the veracity of the latter's test results."

## Example 5.38: Physician could not rely on conclusory statement of another doctor made to obtain disability benefits
*Gong v. Hirsch,* 913 F.2d 1269 (7th Cir. 1990)
In this medical malpractice suit, a physician expert testified that the decedent's perforated peptic ulcer was due to Prednisone. The expert based this conclusion on a letter from the deceased's physician to a doctor at the medical department of the deceased's employer stating that the deceased's perforated peptic ulcer was due to Prednisone. The court rejected the testimony, finding that such a letter was not the type of information reasonably relied upon by an expert because it was merely a conclusory statement made by a doctor who was not a treating physician at the time of the illness in question. It was, in fact, an analysis made for the presumed purpose of obtaining employment disability benefits.

## Example 5.39: Consumer surveys may be used as basis of expert testimony
*President & Trustees of Colby College v. Colby College, New Hampshire,* 508 F.2d 804 (1st Cir. 1975)
A survey of consumers may be used as the basis for expert testimony.

**Example 5.40: Inspection of scene**
*Elgi Holding, Inc. v. Insurance Co. of North America,* 511 F.2d 957 (2nd Cir. 1975)
An inspection of the accident scene may be used as the basis of expert testimony.

**Comment:** Not only may an inspection be used, an inspection should, wherever possible, be made by the expert. An expert who opines upon the cause of an accident, but fails to personally visit an accident scene may be treated extremely skeptically by a jury.

**Example 5.41: Field agents' reports**
*United States v. Genser,* 582 F.2d 292 (3rd Cir. 1978)
Reports from field agents are sources upon which an expert witness may reasonably rely for the basis of his opinions.

**Example 5.42: Government-approved documents such as tables and codes**
*Frazier v. Continental Oil Co.,* 568 F.2d 378 (5th Cir 1978)
Facts or data upon which experts may reasonably rely, such as governmentally approved tables or codes, are acceptable bases for expert opinions.

**Example 5.43: Litigants' affidavits are self-serving and not reasonably relied upon**
*In re Agent Orange Prod. Liab. Litig.,* 611 F.Supp 1223 (E.D.N.Y. 1985)
In this mass toxic tort case, physician experts based testimony on the affidavits of their clients. The court concluded, "Although Rule 703 permits experts to rely upon hearsay, the litigants' self-serving general affidavits and checklists prepared in gross for complex litigation are not material that medical experts would reasonably rely upon and so must be excluded under Rule 703." Also, the court found that the expert physician's failure to consider and discuss any studies that address the actual population and amount of exposure involved in the case at hand supported the conclusion that his opinion was legally incompetent.

**Comment:** This expert should have based his opinion on more thorough research. This would have assisted with both the admissibility of the expert's testimony and the weight the testimony was given.

**Example 5.44: Experts are allowed to rely upon the opinions of experts in other fields**
*United States v. 1014.16 Acres of Land,* 558 F.Supp 1238 (W.D. Mo. 1983)
In this land condemnation action, the court considered the admissibility of the opinions of a real estate appraiser, a hydrologist, and a forester. The court found that despite the opposition's contention that their opinions are improperly based upon opinions of other experts, it is reasonable to expect that experts will rely on opinions of experts in other fields as background material for arriving at an opinion.

**Example 5.45: Unreasonable to rely on study with lower-end confidence interval of less than one in toxic tort case**
*Kelley v. American Heyer-Shulte Corp.,* 957 F.Supp 873 (W.D. Tex. 1997)
The court held that an expert's testimony regarding causation that was based on an epidemiology study should be excluded from a products liability case under Federal Rule of Evidence 703. The study had a lower-end confidence interval of less than one for the relative risk linking breast implants to Sjogren's Syndrome. The court found that it was unreasonable as a matter of law for an expert to rely on such a study to draw any conclusions regarding a Sjogren-implant link.

**Comment:** Experts involved in high-stakes litigation must expect aggressive challenges to their opinions. As such, experts are well advised to base their opinions on the strongest studies available.

### Example 5.46: Firearms origin expert could rely upon trade publications and company catalogs

*United States v. Harpe,* 802 F.2d 115 (5th Cir. 1986)

An expert in firearm origin, identification, and design classification could rely on trade publications and company catalogs in testifying on the origin of a firearm. Such publications were of the type reasonably relied upon by experts in the firearms field.

### Example 5.47: Native American expert could rely upon Native American oral history

*Cree v. Flores,* 157 F.3d 762 (9th Cir. 1998)

A Native American elder testified as an expert regarding the meaning of a treaty to his tribe. His testimony was based on oral history passed down through generations of tribe members. Though this oral history was inadmissible hearsay, the court determined that it was of the type of data reasonably relied upon in the elder's field.

### Example 5.48: Data provided by counsel could be used (amount of damages)

*Deghand v. Wal-Mart Stores,* 980 F.Supp 1176 (D. Kan. 1997)

The plaintiff's economic expert testified regarding the amount of damages. The defendant disputed the numbers and contended that the opinion lacked a factual foundation. The court concluded that it could presume that the plaintiff's counsel provided the expert with reliable data concerning the plaintiff's rate of pay at the time of her discharge and the average number of hours she worked per week. The court noted that the defendant's dispute with the numbers went to weight, not admissibility.

**Comment:** The fact that the expert relied upon data or information provided by retaining counsel can be expected to be a subject of close questioning on cross-examination.

### Example 5.49: Investigator's reliance upon hearsay was proper (private investigation)

*First Nat'l Bank of Louisville v. Lustig,* 96 F.3d 1554 (5th Cir. 1996)

A private investigator testified as an expert in civil fraud detection and investigation. This was a complicated bank fraud coverage case that required explanations of a lender's operations, loan approval procedures, and the transactions themselves. He reviewed documents and interviewed witnesses about the loans at issue. The district court admitted his testimony that the loan committee relied heavily on allegedly fraudulent misrepresentations in approving the loans even though he had no personal knowledge of this fact. The expert explained that his testimony in this case was derived from his conclusions from the knowledge he obtained through his investigation. The court held that the bases of the expert's opinion were proper.

### Example 5.50: Informal interviews with industry figures reasonably relied upon

*Doctor's Hosp. v. Southeast Medical Alliance,* 878 F.Supp 884 (E.D. La. 1995)

In this action against a parish hospital service district for alleged violations of federal and state antitrust laws, an expert in the field of health care and economics testified on the general business practices of managed care plans. The expert, who testified for the defendant, based his opinion partly on interviews with representatives of managed care plans. The plaintiff hospital argued that these informal conversations did not meet the requirements of a formal survey. However, the hospital did not show that the expert's interviews were not information-gathering devices reasonably relied upon by experts. Moreover, the court found that the interviews upon which the expert based his opinion went more toward the weight than the admissibility of his opinion.

**Example 5.51: Malpractice expert could not rely upon chart note written by consulting physician who did not have personal knowledge of the alleged event**
*Ricciardi v. Children's Hospital Medical Center,* 811 F.2d 18 (1st Cir. 1987)
In this medical malpractice action, the trial court ruled that a physician expert could not rely upon a note written by the consulting physician in the patient's chart where the consulting physician did not have personal knowledge of the alleged event and did not know where he obtained the information recorded in the note. The court found that, although an expert is not confined to admissible evidence in forming an opinion under Rule 703, the note contained in the chart was not of the type reasonably relied upon by experts in this particular field in forming opinions or inferences upon the subject.

**Example 5.52: Expert can rely upon hearsay, but such reliance does not make the hearsay admissible (aircraft manufacture)**
*Engebretsen v. Fairchild Aircraft Corp.,* 21 F.3d 721 (6th Cir. 1994)
In this pilot's products liability action against an aircraft manufacturer for injuries sustained in an emergency landing, the reports of the defendants' experts who investigated the cause of the incident were not admissible under either Rule 702 or 703. The court noted that Rule 702 permits expert opinion testimony, not opinions contained in documents prepared out of court. It further noted that Rule 703 allows experts to rely upon materials, including inadmissible hearsay, in forming the basis of an opinion, but it does not permit the admission of materials relied upon for the truth of the matters they contain if the materials are otherwise inadmissible.

**Example 5.53: Oil production figures reasonably relied upon**
*South Cent. Petroleum, Inc. v. Long Bros. Oil Co.,* 974 F.2d 1015 (8th Cir. 1992)
In this investors' suit arising out of an alleged breach of a purchase agreement for oil wells, the court properly admitted expert testimony to determine an offset amount. The court found that the production figures relied on by the experts were a type reasonably relied upon by experts in the field.

**Box 5.33**

| |
|---|
| **Fed. R. Evid. 704. Opinion on Ultimate Issue** |
| (a) Except as provided in subdivision (b), testimony in the form of an opinion or inference otherwise admissible is not objectionable because it embraces an ultimate issue to be decided by the trier of fact. |
| (b) No expert witness testifying with respect to the mental state or condition of a defendant in a criminal case may state an opinion or inference as to whether the defendant did or did not have the mental state or condition constituting an element of the crime charged or of a defense thereto. Such ultimate issues are matters for the trier of fact alone. |

Experts are allowed under Rule 704 to testify on areas that embrace an ultimate issue to be decided by the trier of fact (for example, valuation of the property in a condemnation case).[3] Before the adoption of this rule, experts were allowed to offer factual opinions (the

---

[3] "The reasoning behind Rule 704(a) is that if an expert provides a solid foundation and explanation on an issue in which the factfinder needs assistance, the factfinder is simply left hanging if the expert

plaintiff's inattention caused the crash with the defendant's car), but not legal conclusions (the plaintiff's negligence caused the crash).[4] The rule no longer explicitly makes this distinction, but the difference remains: experts are not allowed to tell the jury how to apply the facts to the law.[5]

The one exception to this rule has to do with testimony regarding the mental state or condition of a defendant in a criminal case. This so-called "Hinckley Amendment" was enacted after the acquittal, on the grounds of insanity, of the attempted assassin of President Ronald Reagan.

**Example 5.54: Opinion on ultimate issue allowed in tax fraud case**
*U.S. v. Whistler,* 139 Fed.Appx. 1 (C.A. 9 Ariz. 2005)
The defendant in this case was a CPA who was indicted for helping to prepare fraudulent tax returns. The court held that under the Federal Rules of Evidence, an expert can testify on an ultimate issue to be decided by the trier of fact, as long as the expert does not testify about "whether the defendant did or did not have the mental state or condition constituting an element of the crime charged or of a defense thereto." See Fed.R.Evid. 704(a)-(b); *United States v. Clardy,* 612 F.2d 1139, 1153 (9th Cir.1980). Here, the appeals court held that the testimony was not improper opinion evidence because the government's expert did not express an opinion as to the defendant's state of mind. Accordingly, the district court did not abuse its discretion when it allowed this testimony.

**Example 5.55: Testimony offering a legal conclusion excluded (ADA discrimination)**
*Burkhart v. Washington Metro. Area Transit Auth.,* 112 F.3d 1207 (D.C. Cir. 1997)
In this case, a deaf bus passenger became involved in a physical fight with the bus driver. The passenger alleged that the transit authority discriminated against him under the Americans with Disabilities Act because it failed to ensure that communications with him were as effective as communications with others. The plaintiff's expert in police training and procedures testified regarding this allegation. His testimony concluded that the communications were not as effective as communications with others, which is the statutory requirement of the ADA. In effect, the testimony stated that the defendant did not comply with the ADA. The appeals court found that the testimony was an impermissible legal conclusion rather than a factual opinion.

---

cannot cap off the testimony with a conclusion about the ultimate issue to which the expert is testifying. Sometimes, a conclusion on the ultimate issue ties the expert's testimony together into a coherent whole, and as such it will be more helpful to state the conclusion along with the rest of the opinion. The Rule also recognizes that a distinction between 'ultimate' and other issues is elusive, and that common-law decisions attempting to draw such a distinction were often arbitrary and unpredictable." Stephen A. Saltzburg, et al., *Commentary to Federal Rule 704,* U.S.C.S. Fed. Rules Evid. 704 (1999) 134–135.
[4] "It would be disingenuous to suggest that the cases reflect a nationally uniform definition of the permissible parameters of expert opinions that stray near or across the line of legal opinions." Stephen D. Easton, "Yer Outta Here! A Framework for Analyzing the Potential Exclusion of Expert Testimony Under the Federal Rules of Evidence," 32 *U. Rich. L. Rev.* (1998) 1, 55.
[5] "Notwithstanding Rule 704(a), an expert cannot go beyond her proper role and intrude upon an important function of the Trial Judge, which is to instruct the jury as to the requirements of law that apply to the particular facts of the case." *Id.*

**Example 5.56: Testimony admitted where psychiatrist expert did not state legal conclusion in repressed memory case**
*Hoult v. Hoult,* 57 F.3d 1 (1st Cir. 1995)
In this case, the plaintiff sued her father for assault and intentional infliction of emotional distress stemming from alleged childhood sexual abuse. The plaintiff based her allegations upon memories recovered during therapy. The expert psychiatrist testified regarding repression of memory caused by traumatic abuse. The psychiatrist came perilously close to testifying that the particular victim/witness could be believed. However, the appellate court did not overturn the trial court's admission of the testimony. The court noted that the psychiatrist was subjected to rigorous cross-examination; that defense counsel repeatedly attempted to elicit opinion testimony from the psychiatrist that she believed the plaintiff's allegations but she steadfastly refused to give an opinion; that the psychiatrist herself testified that she had no way of knowing whether the plaintiff's allegations were true; that the jury was presented with evidence contradicting or calling into question the psychiatrist's opinions; and that the court expressly instructed the jury that they were free to reject the psychiatrist's opinions. The psychiatrist stated no impermissible legal conclusion.

**Example 5.57: Evidence admitted because it was not a legal conclusion (IRS agent on bank fraud)**
*United States v. Duncan,* 42 F.3d 97 (2nd Cir. 1994)
The defendant was accused of bank fraud and conspiring to make corrupt payments to public officials. An IRS agent gave expert testimony regarding the type of transactions in question and the general functioning of the tax system. The court found that the agent's opinion testimony did not state a legal conclusion. The agent did not couch his opinions in terms that derived their definitions from judicial interpretations, his testimony was based on his personal knowledge, and, although he stated certain factual conclusions, he never expressed an opinion regarding the defendant's guilt of the offenses charged.

**Comment:** Experts should avoid legal conclusions. Not only are these inadmissible, they are generally outside of the expert's area of expertise and will make the expert extremely vulnerable on cross-examination.

**Example 5.58: Sleep deprivation expert testimony allowed**
*Miksis v. Howard,* 106 F.3d 754 (7th Cir. 1997)
In this personal injury action arising out of a traffic accident, the plaintiff's sleep deprivation expert testified that the defendant was fatigued and that sleep deprivation was the primary cause of the accident. The court properly allowed the testimony. It noted that the expert did not attempt to reconstruct the accident and testified to the existence of fatigue, not just its role. Moreover, there was a factual dispute whether the driver was fatigued and whether that fatigue could have caused the driver to hit the plaintiff's construction bucket.

**Example 5.59: Mental state of accused, answer to hypothetical prohibited**
*United States v. Manley,* 893 F.2d 1221 (11th Cir. 1990)
In this prosecution, defense counsel wanted to ask the expert psychiatrist a hypothetical question: whether a person with the described mental disease would "be able to appreciate the nature and quality of his actions." But the court of appeals upheld the trial judge's decision to preclude an answer to that hypothetical, on the ground that it would elicit testimony prohibited by Rule 704(b).

**Example 5.60: Mental state of accused, opinion admitted (established practice of drug trade)**
*United States v. Conyers,* 118 F.3d 755 (D.C. Cir. 1997)
In this case, the court decided whether the packaging of drugs and the possession of a firearm by the defendant were sufficient to support a finding of intent to distribute. The government expert testified that the packaging of the drugs found in the defendant's possession was consistent with the distribution in the area. He also testified that the weapon recovered from the defendant's person was the revolver of choice among local drug dealers. The court noted that an expert witness may testify about an established practice among individuals involved in the drug trade, provided that the witness does not speak directly to the guilt or innocence of the accused. The court then found that, although the testimony could support an inference of intent, it did not constitute an opinion on the ultimate issue of the defendant's guilt or innocence.

**Example 5.61: Mental state of accused, testimony admitted**
*United States v. Brown,* 32 F.3d 236 (C.A.7 Ill. 1994)
The defendant was charged with bank robbery and raised an insanity defense. The prosecution's psychiatrist testified that Brown suffered from a major depressive disorder and may have suffered some depressive episodes with psychotic features. Following the description of this diagnosis, the prosecutor asked the witness whether a person suffering from the disorder described was, by that reason alone, "unable to understand the wrongfulness of his acts." The witness answered in the negative. Brown objected that this was ultimate issue testimony as to his legal sanity, barred by Rule 704(b). The trial court allowed the testimony and the appellate court affirmed that decision. The court noted that the prosecution's expert "never testified to Brown's peculiar mental state" but rather "merely described Brown's mental disorder and that such an affliction does not preclude one from appreciating the nature or quality of his acts." The court declared that because the expert testimony was not "specific to Brown's mental state" but rather concerned "the characteristics of his mental disorder," it was permitted by Rule 704(b).

**Example 5.62: Mental state of accused, evidence admitted (schizophrenia)**
*United States v. Thigpen,* 4 F.3d 1573 (11th Cir. 1993)
Here, the court found no error in allowing the prosecutor to "ask a series of questions to elicit an opinion as to whether [schizophrenia] by necessity implies that a person would be unable to appreciate the nature and quality of his acts." The court stated that these questions were permissible because "no question by the prosecutor asked the witness to opine whether [defendant] was able to appreciate his actions."

**Example 5.63: Mental state of accused, evidence excluded (ability to appreciate wrongfulness of act)**
*United States v. Kristiansen,* 901 F.2d 1463 (8th Cir. 1990)
The defendant in this case was charged with escape from a halfway house. He claimed that he lacked willful intent due to insanity. The defendant's expert psychiatrist testified that he had been under the influence of cocaine and suffered from psychosis. On cross-examination, the prosecutor asked: "Would this severe mental disease. . .affect the individual's ability to appreciate the nature and quality of the wrongfulness of his acts?" The trial court sustained an objection, and the court of appeals affirmed, reasoning that this was a hypothetical question designed to elicit testimony on the ultimate issue of intent.

**Example 5.64: Mental state of accused, evidence excluded (hostage negotiation)**
*Salas v. Carpenter,* 980 F.2d 299 (5th Cir. 1992)
Here, the Fifth Circuit explained its exclusion of proffered expert testimony as a matter inappropriate for expert opinions:

> As an expert in the field of hostage negotiation, Dr. Greenstone can properly offer evidence on effective methods and explain to a jury faults in the methods employed by a police force. On the other hand, Dr. Greenstone is not in a better position than a juror to conclude whether [defendant's] actions demonstrated such a lack of concern for [plaintiff's] safety as to constitute deliberate indifference or conscious disregard. Opening the door to ultimate issues did not "open the door to all opinions."

**Box 5.34**

---

**Fed. R. Evid. 705. Disclosure of Facts or Data Underlying Expert Opinion**
The expert may testify in terms of opinions or inference and give reasons thereof without first testifying to the underlying facts or data, unless the court requires otherwise. The expert may in any event be required to disclose the underlying facts or data on cross-examination.

---

Under Rule 705, an expert may be subject to cross-examination regarding the underlying facts or data upon which she has based her opinion. This is allowed because an expert's opinion is only as good as the facts and data upon which it is based.

**Example 5.65: Bases for opinion (conversation with another expert) proper subject of cross-examination**
*Lewis v. Rego, Co.,* 757 F.2d 66 (3rd Cir. 1985)
A products liability action was brought against the manufacturer of a propane cylinder's safety relief valve, seeking recovery in connection with the explosion of the propane cylinder. An expert in physical metallurgy was asked on cross-examination about the bases for his opinion. One of these was a conversation he had with another metallurgist. The expert was not allowed to answer the question. This exclusion by the trial court was held to be improper. The appellate court stated: "Although it is not required that the bases for an expert's opinion be disclosed before the opinion is given, the bases of the opinion may be testified to on direct examination, and if inquired into during cross-examination, must be disclosed."

**Comment:** Experts can expect close questioning on the bases of their opinions including everything they read, everything they inspected, and everyone they talked to. The stronger the basis for the opinion, the more believable the opinion will be.

**Example 5.66: Bases for opinions could be explored on cross-examination (ADA constructive discharge)**
*Polythane Systems, Inc. v. Marina Ventures Intern., Ltd.,* 993 F.2d 1201 (5th Cir. 1993)
An employee sued his employer for constructive discharge under the Americans with Disabilities Act and for worker's compensation retaliation and defamation. The plaintiff's economics expert was to testify to back pay, using figures based upon employment history provided by plaintiff's counsel. The defendant challenged the bases of the testimony in a pre-trial motion. The court cited Rules 703 and 705 and denied the pre-trial motion to exclude the expert's testimony regarding the amount of compensation owed. The court then noted that the defendant could more fully explore the figures—and their bases—during cross-examination. The court then told the plaintiff to be prepared to proffer factual bases for the expert's assumptions during trial.

## 5.4 Credibility: Bias and Prior Inconsistent Statements

In the end, most trials boil down to one issue and only one issue—credibility. Therefore, the adverse party may try to subtly, or not so subtly, impeach or reduce the credibility of an expert witness. This is completely proper. This section is designed to teach, in a very basic way, some of the evidentiary rules dealing with an attorney's assault against an expert's credibility.

*Bias*

Although there is no federal rule addressing bias directly, the United States Supreme Court has held that a witness may be impeached on the ground of bias.[6] Judges usually give attorneys wide latitude to show a witness's potential bias. If the witness being impeached denies the bias, the judge has discretion to allow extrinsic evidence to show the bias. *An expert must expect that evidence that may tend to show her bias can and will be held to be admissible because it is relevant to her credibility.* Although bias attacks go to the weight, and not the admissibility, of expert opinions, bias attacks can be very effective as bias is something the jury is likely to understand (unlike many other aspects of expert testimony). As a practical matter, the best way for experts to deal with bias attacks is to prevent them by only testifying in cases where an actual or perceived bias does not exist. Please see the following examples of evidentiary questions regarding the potential bias of experts.

**Example 5.67: Defense expert in sentencing phase of death penalty case can be cross-examined on his personal opposition to the death penalty**
*U.S. v. Purkey,* 428 F.3d 738 (C.A. 8 Mo. 2005)
In holding the cross-examination on the defense expert's personal beliefs about the death penalty proper, the court reasoned as follows:

> Even under the traditional rules of evidence, "cross-examination regarding potential bias of a witness is proper." *United States v. Amerson-Bey,* 898 F.2d 681, 682 (8th Cir.1990); see *United States v. McCoy,* 131 F.3d 760, 760-61 (8th Cir.1997) (per curiam). If Dr. Peterson strongly disfavored the death penalty, knowledge of that would be relevant to the jury's evaluation of his credibility in testifying to factors that could mitigate Mr. Purkey's sentence; "'exposure of a witness' motivation in testifying is a proper and important function of...cross-examination,'" *Van Arsdall,* 475 U.S. at 678-79, 106 S.Ct. 1431 (quoting *Davis,* 415 U.S. at 316-17, 94 S.Ct. 1105). To the extent that the FDPA alters this rule, it relaxes it, see 18 U.S.C. § 3593; Lee, 274 F.3d at 495; a fortiori the district court did not err in allowing the government to continue its line of inquiry into Dr. Peterson's beliefs about the death penalty. At 760.

**Comment:** Experts should avoid testifying in cases where their personal bias may affect, or may be perceived to affect, their objectivity.

**Example 5.68: Cross-examination about runners, referral fees is proper**
*Flores v. Miami-Dade County,* 787 So.2d 955 (Fla. App. 3 Dist. 2001)
Here, a motorist brought an action against the county for personal injuries sustained in a collision with a county bus. The trial court entered judgment for the county and the motorist appealed, contending that the cross-examination of the motorist's treating physician and trial expert regarding the expert's referral arrangements was improperly allowed as evidence of the expert's bias.

---

[6] *United States v. Abel,* 469 U.S. 45 (1984).

At trial and over objection, on cross-examination the county brought out the fact that, at relevant times, the doctor had an agreement with the plaintiff's previous counsel whereby each would refer cases to the other. Further, the doctor and the lawyer both shared a runner who would recruit patients for the doctor and clients for the lawyer. The doctor paid the runner a monthly fee plus an additional amount for each patient that he referred. He had, over a period of time, paid the runner $80,000. The trial court allowed the testimony, and the appellate court affirmed this decision:

> [T]he doctor's sharing of a runner with plaintiff's prior counsel, his extensive payments to the runner, and his reciprocal referral arrangement are facts which could reasonably be viewed as creating a bias toward testifying favorably to plaintiffs. Interest and motive of a witness are proper subjects for cross-examination. *Id.* § 608.5, at 465. The cross-examination was properly allowed. At 957.

The plaintiff also contended that it was a crime for a physician to pay for the referral of patients and there can be no cross-examination if the conduct being inquired about amounts to a crime. The appellate court disagreed, stating:

> The jury was not told that this financial arrangement might constitute a crime. The cross-examination was pertinent to demonstrate bias, and is not defeated simply because the conduct might also constitute a crime. At 957.

Finally, the plaintiff argued that it was impermissible to cross-examine the doctor about referral arrangements on any case other than the present one; it was therefore impermissible for the doctor to be asked about his course of dealing with the plaintiff's former counsel and the financial arrangement he had with the runner. The appellate court disagreed:

> [T]here must be reasonable latitude for inquiry about the extent of a trial expert's alignment with one side, or another, of litigation practice. To that end, *Elkins* and the rule allow some discovery regarding work that the trial expert has done in other cases. *See also Allstate Ins. Co. v. Boecher,* 733 So.2d 993, 997-999 (Fla.1999). The inquiry extends not just to the compensation arrangements for the current case, *see* Fla. R. Civ. P. 1.280(b)(4)(A)(iii) 1., but also allows inquiry into the expert's work in other cases. *Id.* at 958–59.

**Comment:** An expert who can be shown to be biased will have very little credibility.

### Example 5.69: Evidence of pending malpractice case against expert admissible
*Oberlin v. Akron Gen. Med. Ctr.,* 743 N.E.2d 890 (Ohio 2001)
A patient brought a medical malpractice action against a hand surgeon. The trial court entered judgment for the surgeon. The patient appealed. The court of appeals affirmed, and the patient sought a discretionary appeal. The Supreme Court held that evidence that an expert witness is a defendant in a pending malpractice action that alleges a medical error similar to the one at issue is admissible.

The plaintiff claimed that he suffered permanent damage to his left arm, hand, and ulnar nerve due to the defendant's negligence. According to expert testimony presented on the plaintiff's behalf, the length of the inflation time was excessive, resulting in reflex sympathetic dystrophy.

The defendant's expert witness, an M.D., admitted in his deposition to being a defendant in a pending medical malpractice action. In another deposition, plaintiff's counsel again cross-examined the expert regarding the claim against him. The claim had been brought in Canada by the expert's former patient and involved an injury similar to the plaintiff's.

When the second deposition videotape was played at trial, the court refused to allow the jury to view the plaintiff's cross-examination of the expert concerning the Canadian malpractice case.

The trial court found that although the testimony "may have some probative value in terms of bias, * * * the Court feels that the prejudicial nature of this testimony far outweighs any probative value." At 892.

On appeal, the plaintiff attempted to demonstrate the probative value of the disallowed testimony, arguing that the evidence would have established potential bias on the expert's part because he was facing a very similar malpractice claim himself. The Supreme Court laid out the potential biases:

> The similarity of the area operated upon and of the resulting injury is enough to indicate bias. If [the expert] were to criticize any aspect of [the defendant's] handling of the surgery, the Canadian plaintiff might seize on that testimony and use it against [the expert] in her own suit. Therefore, [the expert] might be biased in evaluating [the defendant's] performance for fear that the testimony might be used against him later. He might be predisposed to find that the doctor here acted within acceptable bounds of competence.
>
> …Second, an expert with an active malpractice case against him might be hostile to malpractice claimants in general. He might apply what he considers the unfairness of the entire process to his interpretation of whether this particular doctor acted reasonably. At 892–93.

The court explained the balancing test at issue:

> Of course, evidence of an expert witness's potential bias will prejudice the case of the party for whom he is testifying. But that is the very reason for establishing the bias of a witness—to cause a jury to think critically about the testimony being offered. The only important inquiry is whether the evidence of bias is *unfairly* prejudicial. Were [defendant's] counsel in this case to attempt to inflame jurors by describing the horrors of the Canadian plaintiff's injury, that might be considered unfairly prejudicial. The fact the expert is simply involved in a pending malpractice action is not.
>
> Thus, the trial court in this case unreasonably minimized the probative value of cross-examination of [the expert] on his pending malpractice claim, and accorded far too much weight to the allegedly unfair prejudicial nature of that testimony. The trial judge thus abused her discretion in refusing to allow Oberlin to cross-examine [the expert] on his pending malpractice action. We accordingly reverse the judgment of the appellate court, and order a new trial in this matter. At 893–94.

## Example 5.70: Evidence regarding expert's relationship with insurer admissible despite rule prohibiting insurance evidence

*Yoho v. Thompson,* 548 S.E.2d 584 (S.C. 2001)

An automobile accident victim brought this action to recover for her injuries. The plaintiff's underinsured motorist (UIM) carrier took over the defense after the liability insurer paid its policy limits. The trial court excluded evidence of the defense expert's consulting work for the carrier and entered judgment on the jury verdict. The plaintiff appealed, the court of appeals affirmed the decision, then the Supreme Court heard the case.

Prior to trial, the driver indicated she would call to the stand a physician who had reviewed the plaintiff's medical records and who would give an opinion regarding her injuries. She moved the court to allow her to explore the expert's connections to the insurer, even though the state evidence rule precluded any discussion of insurance in front of the jury. At the hearing on the motion, the plaintiff presented the expert's deposition testimony from another case that he did "a fair amount of consulting work with [the carrier]" and had given lectures to the carrier's agents and adjusters. The plaintiff also presented evidence that ten to twenty percent of the expert's practice consisted of reviewing records for insurance companies, and that his yearly salary was based on the amount of money his practice earned, which included his consulting work. Nonetheless, the trial judge refused to let the plaintiff cross-examine the witness regarding his relationship with the insurer on the basis that the probative value of the content of the cross-examination would be outweighed by the prejudicial effect of injecting the issue of insurance into the proceedings. The court did allow the plaintiff to address the expert's bias by using generic terms such as "defense," "defendants," and "defense lawyer," but she could not discuss his possible bias by using the word "insurance."

The Supreme Court concluded that the connection between the expert and the insurer was sufficient to justify admitting evidence of their relationship to demonstrate the expert's possible bias in favor of the insurer. It stated:

> [The expert] was not merely being paid an expert's fee in this matter. Instead, he maintained an employment relationship with [the insurer] and other insurance companies. [The expert] consulted for [the insurer] in other cases and gave lectures to [the insurer's] agents and adjusters. Ten to twenty percent of [the expert's] practice consisted of reviewing records for insurance companies, including [the insurer]. Further, [the expert's] yearly salary was based in part on his insurance consulting work. The trial court erred in refusing to allow [the plaintiff] to cross-examine [the expert] about his relationship with [the insurer]. At 586.

### Example 5.71: Expert's participation in liability fund not proper subject of cross-examination

*Hoffart v. Hodge*, 609 N.W.2d 397 (Neb. App. 2000)

In this medical malpractice case, the appellate court considered whether it was an error for the trial court to have refused to allow cross-examination of the defendant physician's expert concerning his participation in the same excess liability fund in which the defendant participated. The court described the fund, which was created by state statute, as an excess liability insurer in which physicians may elect to participate.

This fund required participating physicians to maintain a certain amount of base liability coverage. Then, any settlement or judgment in excess of the base coverage was paid from the fund. Participating physicians pay a surcharge on their base liability policy premiums, which is used to maintain the fund. The plaintiff argued that because a portion of any judgment awarded to him might be paid by the fund, which in turn could cause an increase in surcharges, the defendant physician's expert's participation in the fund was a proper subject for questioning to show financial bias. The appellate court considered and rejected this argument:

> In a recent medical malpractice case, the Nebraska Supreme Court held that "a plaintiff must establish that an expert has more connection to a defendant's insurer than that of the policyholder or member in order for the evidence to be admissible." See *Reimer v. Surgical Servs. of the Great Plains,* 258 Neb. 671, 676, 605 N.W.2d 777, 781 (2000) [citations omitted] "[A]bsent evidence that a witness has a direct interest in the outcome of the litigation, such as an agent, owner, or employee of the defendant's insurer, the potential for bias is too remote and is outweighed by the prejudice its admission would cause." 258 Neb. at 676, 605 N.W.2d at 781.

> ...[The plaintiff] has shown no connection other than the fact that [the defendant physician] and his expert witnesses are subject to the same premium surcharge which is used to maintain the Fund. Applying the rule adopted in *Reimer v. Surgical Servs. of the Great Plains, supra,* we find the trial court did not abuse its discretion when it did not allow cross-examination as to [the defendant's] expert witnesses' participation in the Act. At 408.

### Example 5.72: Expert's relationship with counsel proper subject of cross-examination

*Tiburzio-Kelly v. Montgomery,* 681 A.2d 757 (Pa. Super. 1996)

The Pennsylvania Court dealt with a medical malpractice claim resulting when a child was born with disabilities. At issue was the proper scope of cross-examination of the defendant's expert medical witness in the case. Specifically, the plaintiffs sought to show bias by eliciting the fact that the expert was himself currently being represented by the defendant's law firm. The trial court did not allow the cross-examination, but the appellate court held that this information was the proper subject of a cross-examination designed to show bias. Plaintiff's counsel called the defendant's expert pediatric neurologist and sought permission to elicit from him the fact that he was then being represented in another matter by a member of the firm that was representing the co-defendant practice in the case at hand. The appellate court found that:

> …it is proper to elicit from an expert the fee he is being paid to testify. Later decisions have further indicated that it is also proper to elicit whether a personal friendship exists between the expert and either the party calling him or that party's counsel….Certainly, evidence of an ongoing relationship between the witnesses and attorneys is information which the jury would want to know about and we believe is entitled to know about.

*Note:* The court held that the trial court's failure to allow cross-examination as to the expert medical witness's bias was so serious an error that it awarded the plaintiffs a new trial.

**Example 5.73: Expert's history with defendant goes to weight of evidence, not admissibility**
*Khan v. New York State Dept. of Health,* 17 A.D.3d 938, 794, N.Y.S.2d 145 (N.Y.A.D. 3 Dept. 2005)
In ruling that bias evidence goes to weight, not admissibility, the court stated:

> Petitioner first claims that he was deprived of a fair hearing because BPMC's expert witness was biased against him. The alleged cause of this bias was that petitioner bid on a medical practice a decade earlier allegedly driving up the price the expert eventually paid for that practice. The expert testified that he recalled that a doctor with the same last name had bid on the practice and he eventually realized it may be the same person as petitioner, but that he and petitioner had never met or spoken and he had no animosity toward petitioner as a result of the alleged "bidding war." Petitioner's testimony established that his final bid on the practice was $300,000 and the expert paid $450,000, making it unlikely that petitioner was the competitor who drove the cost up to the eventual sale price. The expert's alleged bias goes to the weight of his testimony, not its admissibility (see *Matter of Lauersen v. Novello,* 293 A.D.2d 833, 834, 739 N.Y.S.2d 780 [2002] ). The Committee was presented with information of the expert's alleged bias and could use it to assess his credibility (see *Matter of Cohen v. Mills,* 271 A.D.2d 826, 828, 706 N.Y.S.2d 256 [2000]; *Matter of Brigham v. De Buono,* 228 A.D.2d 870, 644 N.Y.S.2d 413 [1996], lv. denied 89 N.Y.2d 801, 653 N.Y.S.2d 278, 675 N.E.2d 1231 [1996] ), which it did by finding no evidence of bias and largely crediting his medical testimony. At 939.

**Example 5.74: Compensation in prior related cases was fair game during cross-examination**
*Coward v. Owens-Corning Fiberglass Corp.,* 729 A.2d 614 (Pa. Super. 1999)
A group of plaintiffs filed a products liability action against an asbestos manufacturer. The court considered whether an expert physician should have been subjected to cross-examination regarding the amount of money he was paid in other asbestos litigation over the previous twenty years. The court allowed the cross-examination. Cross-examining counsel specifically asked the expert whether that compensation influenced his opinions regarding the case at trial.

**Example 5.75: Expert could be questioned on his testifying 150+ times for the same insurer**
*Brantley v. Sears Roebuck & Co.,* 959 S.W.2d 927 (Mo. App. E.D. 1998)
The plaintiff, a homeowner, sued the seller of a dishwasher, alleging the machine caused a house fire. The court considered whether the fire expert could be cross-examined on the point that he had testified for the same insurer over one hundred and fifty times. The court found the cross-examination proper and allowed it to take place in order for the plaintiff to show bias.

**Comment:** Experts who testify numerous times for the same client are likely to lose their credibility.

### Example 5.76: Expert could be asked about annual income from expert witness work
*State ex rel. Lichtor v. Clark,* 845 S.W.2d 55 (Mo. App. 1992)
The plaintiff in this personal injury case objected to being examined by a physician selected by defense counsel, complaining that the doctor was biased. The particular orthopedic surgeon had a long history of employment by insurers and the defense bar. In the context of resolving that discovery dispute, the court discussed the problem of biased expert witnesses and held that "the trial judge in this case has discretion to allow testimony as to the amount of annual income derived from employment as an expert witness."

### Example 5.77: Involvement in prior medical malpractice action fair game on cross-examination
*Underhill v. Stephenson,* 756 S.W.2d 459 (Ky. 1988)
In a medical malpractice action, it was proper for the plaintiff to cross-examine the defendant's medical expert regarding the expert's prior involvement in an unrelated malpractice action. The plaintiff, the court reasoned, had a right to cross-examine the medical expert on "all matters relating to every issue." Evidence to show bias of an expert witness, the court concluded, is relevant.

### Example 5.78: Expert's relationship with counsel (where counsel represented expert in prior malpractice case) can be explored
*Clements v. Stewart,* 595 So.2d 858 (Ala. 1992)
In this medical malpractice case, the defendant's medical expert testified that the defendant had not deviated from the appropriate standard of care. The plaintiff made an offer of proof outside the presence of the jury that showed that the defendant's medical expert had been a defendant in a medical malpractice action; that the witness had been represented in that action by the same law firm that was representing the defendant in the current case; and that that action had been settled. The trial court did not allow cross-examination on the issue. The state supreme court heard the appeal of this decision and found that the plaintiff should have been able to cross-examine the expert with respect to any bias that he may have had against plaintiffs in medical malpractice actions.

**Comment:** The court noted the rule: "Not only is there allowable great latitude on cross-examination of a witness, but this latitude is enlarged as to an expert witness." Experts should be prepared for aggressive questioning on any and all potential biases.

### Example 5.79: Cross-examination on history of negligence cases against experts not allowed
*Mazzone v. Holmes,* 557 N.E.2d 186 (Ill. App. Dist. 1 1990)
In this medical malpractice action, the plaintiff contended that the trial judge erred in refusing examination of a defense medical expert regarding the number of professional negligence cases brought or then pending against him. The plaintiff argued that the evidence was relevant to his interest or bias as the defendant physician's expert witness. The court concluded that it was proper to bar questions regarding the number of malpractice cases pending against the physician on the ground of relevancy. The only support for the plaintiff's position, the court observed, was the "general proposition that parties should have the opportunity to expose the interest or bias of medical experts through cross-examination." The court concluded, however, that such

examination should be strictly limited to matters such as "the number of referrals, their frequency, and the financial benefit derived from them."

### Example 5.80: Questions on expert's nonrenewal of privileges disallowed
*Kane v. Ryan,* 596 A.2d 562 (D.C. 1991)
The defendant physician in this malpractice case attempted to question the plaintiff's medical expert as to why her privileges at the hospital at which the plaintiff was treated were not renewed. During cross-examination, the defendant's attorney inquired as to whether the expert was upset with the subject hospital over the "manner" in which it did not renew her hospital privileges, to which the expert replied the matter was not relevant to the case at issue. The court denied any inquiry into the nonrenewal of the expert's privileges. It noted that the trial judge may properly limit bias cross-examination if it concludes that the evidence is too collateral. This rule, the court commented, allows the trial judge to direct the trial in a way that assures that the jury will focus on the central issues it must decide, rather than on a mini-trial of a marginally relevant or collateral issue. In the case at hand, the court reasoned, a further exploration of the reasons the expert was not renewed privileges would have required a "parade of witnesses on an issue that could have had only a remote bearing on possible bias against" the defendant physician, a doctor who had privileges at the subject hospital, but was apparently not among those who had a role in deciding the expert's future.

**Comment:** The trial judge has broad discretion in allowing or limiting questioning. The authors can see another trial judge potentially admitting questions on the expert's nonrenewal of privileges.

## *Prior inconsistent statements*
Another important technique used to impeach an expert's credibility is through confrontation with a prior inconsistent statement of the expert. This is allowed under the Rules and is a powerful form of impeachment because it shows that the expert has been inconsistent regarding an issue. The prior statements most commonly used to impeach an expert include the expert's published or unpublished writings and the expert's prior deposition or trial testimony.[7] Impeachment can be a powerful tool because the fact finder is likely to understand that inconsistency is often a sign of dishonesty.

Because an expert's prior writings and testimony are becoming more and more easily available with the progression of technology, he should be prepared for this form of impeachment. The best way to prevent this form of attack is to always testify truthfully. If an expert has testified seemingly inconsistently in the past, the expert should be prepared to explain why this is this case (for example, new research). Finally, the best experts insist on examining the whole document they are being impeached with to assure that the cross-examining attorney is not taking their prior statement out of context.

### Example 5.81: Example of impeachment attack on an expert
**Q.** And it's your testimony that Chemical X cannot, under any circumstances, cause pathology?
**A.** That's correct.

---

[7] It is usually not advisable for experts to retain old deposition and trial transcripts on closed files. This only makes opposing counsel's search for materials to use against the expert that much easier because he can obtain the transcripts from the expert under discovery much more easily than he could otherwise.

**Q.** Do you recall testifying in the *Todd v. Davis* case in 2002?

**A.** Vaguely.

**Q.** I have here your trial testimony from the *Todd* case. You were testifying under oath at trial and were asked, "Can Chemical X cause cancer?" Answer: "Yes." Am I reading that correctly, sir?

**Comment:** The way to deal with an impeachment attack is either to testify consistently so as to avoid such challenges, or to be prepared to explain why the testimony is inconsistent (for example, newly released research).

### Example 5.82: Impeachment not allowed where probative value is low and danger of unfair prejudice is high

*Hunter v. Ura,* 163 S.W.3d 686 (Tenn. 2005)

In this medical malpractice case the court held that the trial judge disallowed an alleged prior inconsistent statement comparing experts to whores from being used against the defense expert because the probative value of the alleged statement was low and the danger of unfair prejudice was high. The court stated:

> We next address whether the Court of Appeals correctly held that the trial court erred in denying a motion for a mistrial after the plaintiff cross-examined a defense expert witness, Dr. John Eichorn, with a prior statement in which the witness had described his role as a defense expert in an unrelated case. The trial court ruled that the cross-examination was improper but that a mistrial was not warranted. The record reveals that the following exchange occurred during the cross-examination of Dr. Eichorn:
>
> > Q. Do you perceive it as your role in participating in a case for the defense, with issues like this, that it is incumbent upon you to create a theory of defense?
> > A. No.
> > Q. That would be inappropriate, wouldn't it?
> > A. And potentially not possible.
> > Q. Do you consider it your role to be an advocate for the party for whom you're testifying?
> > A. No.
> > Q. That would be inappropriate, wouldn't it?
> > A. Correct.
> > ....
> > Q. Now let me take it like this, and make it a little bit more specific. You've testified in a case before where you were the expert witness for an anesthesiologist where the blood pressure got too low and the patient's brain died, haven't you?
> > A. I don't recall specifically, but it's certainly possible.
> > Q. Well, we're going to—let me see if I can help you. Have you ever before, Dr. Eichorn, in serving in this type of role, when serving as an expert witness for an anesthesiologist, sued because a patient came out of surgery brain dead because of low blood pressure, said to the defense lawyer who hired you, "There are big problems with what your anesthesiologist did, but I will help you create a theory to defend this case, and short of hiring an outright prostitute, I'm the best you are going to find"? Have you ever said that?
>
> After the defense objected, Dr. Eichorn denied that he made the statement.
>
> In a jury-out hearing, counsel for the plaintiff proffered a letter in which a lawyer attributed the statement to Dr. Eichorn in an unrelated case and argued that the witness could be impeached with the prior inconsistent statement and with evidence of his bias in favor of the defendants. The defendants argued that there was no factual basis upon which to find that Dr. Eichorn had made the statement.
>
> The trial court concluded that the statement was not admissible to impeach Dr. Eichorn as a prior inconsistent statement under Rule 613 of the Tennessee Rules of Evidence because its probative value was substantially outweighed by its prejudicial effect. The trial court also found that the prior statement

could not be used to show Dr. Eichorn's bias in favor of the defendants under Rule 616 of the Tennessee Rules of Evidence. The trial court's offer to instruct the jury to disregard the question was declined by the defendants. The trial court denied the defendants' later motion for a mistrial.

The Court of Appeals held that there was no reasonable factual basis for the question and that the cross-examination of Dr. Eichorn with the prior statement was reversible error under Rule 613.

The trial testimony of a witness may be impeached with a prior written or oral statement made by the witness. Tenn. R. Evid 613; see Neil P. Cohen, et al., Tennessee Law of Evidence § 6.13 (4th ed. 2000) ["Cohen, et al"]. When a witness is examined about a written or oral statement, "the statement need not be shown nor its contents disclosed to the witness at that time, but on request the same shall be shown or disclosed to opposing counsel." Tenn. R. Evid. 613(a). Extrinsic evidence of a prior inconsistent statement "is not admissible unless and until the witness is afforded an opportunity to explain or deny the same and the opposite party is afforded an opportunity to interrogate the witness thereon, or the interests of justice otherwise require." Tenn. R. Evid. 613(b).

A prior statement being used to impeach a witness "must be inconsistent with the witness's trial testimony." Cohen, et al., § 6.13[3] at 6-134. Although Rule 613(b) does not define "inconsistent," a prior inconsistent statement made by a witness must have "a reasonable tendency to discredit the testimony of the witness." Cohen, et al., § 6.13[3] at 6-133 (quoting Michael H. Graham, 1 Handbook of Federal Evidence 882 (4th ed.1996)). The trial court may exclude evidence of the prior inconsistent statement if its probative value is substantially outweighed by the danger of unfair prejudice, confusion of the issues, misleading the jury, or a risk of undue delay. Tenn. R. Evid. 403.

In our view, the trial court did not abuse its discretion in ruling that the plaintiff could not use the prior statement attributed to Dr. Eichorn for impeachment as a prior inconsistent statement. Although the plaintiff made a credible argument that the prior statement was inconsistent with Dr. Eichorn's testimony that his role as an expert witness does not include creating a theory of defense or acting as an advocate, the trial court was concerned with the reliability and probative value of the alleged prior statement. Indeed, the trial court found that the statement was a "characterization" made by a lawyer in an unrelated case and was not a prior inconsistent statement made by Dr. Eichorn. In addition, the trial court concluded that the probative value of the alleged prior statement was substantially outweighed by the risk of unfair prejudice to the defense. The record does not demonstrate that the trial court abused its discretion. At 697–699.

### Example 5.83: Impeachment from answer to interrogatory allowed even when expert did not sign interrogatory answers, later deposition was consistent with trial testimony, and expert had reason for inconsistency

*York v. El-Ganzouri,* 353 Ill.App.3d 1, 288 Ill.Dec. 529 (Ill. App. 1 Dist. 2004)
The expert in this case was confronted with prior inconsistent answers to interrogatories that were signed by the party, not the expert. The court held that the expert could be impeached with these answers even though he did not write them himself and even though his trial testimony was consistent with his deposition testimony. The court stated:

At trial, Dr. Meyer testified on direct examination, on behalf of Dr. El-Ganzouri, that Dr. York's injuries resulted from a spinal infarct, meaning a deprivation of blood and oxygen to the spine, causing the death of the deprived tissues. Dr. Meyer opined that the infarction resulted from systemic hypotension (low blood pressure) during the knee replacement surgery. He denied that an injury was caused by the entry of a needle and injection of anesthesia into Dr. York's spinal cord, explaining that he would have expected to find a "blob" or "puddle" of anesthesia around the point of insertion in MRIs of Dr. York's spine, but he did not find such a mass. The effect of this testimony was to attribute Dr. York's injuries to the knee surgery and not to the anesthesia procedures.

The following exchange occurred when Dr. Meyer was subject to cross-examination:

Mr. Clifford: Okay. And then after you got those additional records, you conferred with Counsel; did you not?
Dr. Meyer: Yes.

Mr. Clifford: And you told Counsel your opinions; did you not?

Dr. Meyer: Yes.

Mr. Clifford: And those opinions, I believe, were filed with the Court on August 14, 2001; and one of them was, "It is more likely than not that James York sustained a spinal cord infarct. This infarct more likely than not was caused by either the spinal needle, catheter, agent or a combination thereof coming in contact with a vessel, which in turn caused ischemia to the patent's spinal cord." That was one of your original opinions; true?

Dr. Meyer: Yes.

Mr. Clifford: And that is not your opinion today; true?

Dr. Meyer: That's correct, and that was clarified at the deposition.

* * *

Mr. Clifford: Doctor, just so we deal with this in a perspective of time, these opinions of yours initially to the effect that the spinal—you've always had the view that he had a spinal cord infarct, right?

Dr. Meyer: Yes.

Mr. Clifford: But you originally held the view that the spinal cord infarct was caused by either the needle, the catheter, the agent, which I take to be the Marcaine, or a combination thereof coming into contact with a vessel, which in turn caused ischemia; isn't that right?

Dr. Meyer: Yes.

Mr. Clifford: And you gave—those opinions were disclosed on August 21 of 2001 signed by that lady Irwin, right?

Dr. Meyer: By Shirley Irwin, that's correct.

Mr. Clifford: And but Shirley Irwin is not a doctor, right? You know that to be a fact; don't you?

Dr. Meyer: Yes.

Mr. Clifford: And the fact is that what she wrote down and what she filed in court she got from you and confirmed by you, correct?

Dr. Meyer: She did get that from me. I don't know that it was completely confirmed prior to those being filed.

Mr. Clifford: Okay. Fair enough. And this clarification, your word, not mine, that you're talking about here, you gave your deposition in this case on September 4, 2001, some 10, 15 days later, so say two weeks later. So you're telling us that between August 21 and September 4th, two weeks, you did further study that gave you this enlightenment about hypotensive events that contributed to the spinal cord infarct, right?

Mr. Petrek: Objection, your Honor. That assumes facts not in evidence.

THE COURT: Overruled.

* * *

Mr. Clifford: Okay. So when you tell us that you've clarified, the fact is you've not withdrawn the idea—or maybe you are. Let's get this straight. Are you withdrawing the idea that the spinal cord infarct was caused either by the spinal needle, the cath, the agent or a combination thereof coming into contact with a vessel; are you withdrawing that?

Mr. Petrek: Object to the form of the question.

* * *

Mr. Clifford: Are you withdrawing that opinion?

Dr. Meyer: I just don't know what it means to withdraw it in a legal sense, so you might—

Mr. Clifford: Drop it, give it up, throw it out.

Dr. Meyer: That's not what I think happened.

Mr. Clifford: I'm talking about the opinion now.

Dr. Meyer: Yes.

Mr. Clifford: Are you still holding to that opinion, yes or no?

Dr. Meyer: No, I don't think that that's the opinion.

Mr. Clifford: Okay. But you do think that the opinion that you came up with at your deposition two weeks later is the answer to what occurred here?

Mr. Petrek: Object to the form of the question.

79

Dr. El-Ganzouri contends that such impeachment was improper because an attorney, as opposed to Dr. Meyer himself, prepared and swore to the interrogatory answer, which should therefore not be attributable to Dr. Meyer, and that Dr. Meyer was therefore not subject to any impeachment as his deposition and trial testimony were identical. Dr. York counters first that Dr. El-Ganzouri waived this challenge by his failure to make an appropriate, timely objection, and secondly because the explicit language of Rule 213 allows for such interrogatory answers to be used for impeachment. We agree with both of plaintiff's arguments.

To begin, as Dr. York suggests, the plain language of the rule supports the availability of Rule 213(g) interrogatory answers for impeachment of an expert witness. Section (h) of the rule states: "answers to interrogatories may be used in evidence to the same extent as a discovery deposition." 177 Ill.2d R. 213(h). Supreme Court Rule 212(a)(1), addressing the use of discovery depositions, explains that "[d]iscovery depositions * * * may be used * * * for the purpose of impeaching the testimony of the deponent as a witness in the same manner and to the same extent as any inconsistent statement made by a witness." 188 Ill.2d R. 212(a)(1); see also *Estate of Whittington v. Emdeko National Housewares, Inc.,* 96 Ill.App.3d 1007, 1011, 52 Ill.Dec. 345, 422 N.E.2d 26, 30 (1981) (observing the same interrelation between the two rules).

That the interrogatory answers may have been completed and signed by an attorney, as opposed to the expert, in our view, cannot justify modification of the plain meaning of the Rule allowing impeachment. Courts have long understood that the answers to 213 interrogatories surrounding experts are a collaboration between the expert and the retaining party. At 542–546.

**Comment:** Experts should be aware of what is in their clients' answers to interrogatories. They should work with counsel to ascertain that the answers regarding their testimony are accurate.

## 5.5  Conclusion

Experts should have a fundamental knowledge of the rules of evidence.  These rules allow relevant evidence unless there is a reason to exclude it, such as danger of unfair prejudice. Expert evidence needs to be reliable (as determined by the trial judge) or it can be excluded. Evidence of bias and prior inconsistent statements are generally admissible because such evidence is relevant to the expert's credibility.  The evidence the expert bases her opinion upon need not be admissible into evidence itself if it is of a type reasonably relied upon by experts in the expert's particular field.  Experts are advised to:

- use a reliable methodology when forming their opinions,
- base their opinions on reliable facts,
- avoid any actions that could be construed as indicating that they are biased, and
- always testify truthfully and consistently unless there is an honest reason why a change of heart occurred.

Experts should strive to never have their proposed testimony excluded.  When an expert's proposed testimony is excluded because the testimony is unreliable, because the expert is not qualified, or for other reasons, this may severely affect the expert's reputation and future.  Indeed, it may permanently and adversely impact the expert's viability as a witness.

# Chapter 6  Qualifications

## 6.1  Introduction

To be effective, an expert witness must understand the requirements for his qualification as an expert.  This chapter explains the requirements experts need and reviews sample case law regarding these qualifications.

**Experts should remember to only testify in cases where they are truly qualified.** If an expert witness is found by the judge to not be qualified and is barred from testifying, this fact may be brought up in future cases and it may have the practical effect of ending the expert's career as an expert.[1]  Even if the expert is qualified enough for the judge to allow her to testify, it is best to defer opining on any matter where the expert is not completely comfortable.  An expert who is not truly qualified is likely to perform poorly and suffer damaging, serious, and permanent injury to her reputation in the legal community.  Such a result does not bode well for an expert's chances of future employment as an expert.  Experts are well advised to err on the side of caution and to never testify in an area unless they are completely confident of their qualifications in the area in question.

## 6.2  Qualifications As a Matter of Law—Legal Requirements to Qualify As an Expert Witness

Federal Rule of Evidence 702 governs the qualifications of expert witnesses.

### Box 6.21

> **Fed. R. Evid. 702. Testimony by Experts**
> If scientific, technical, or other specialized knowledge will assist the trier of fact to understand the evidence or to determine a fact in issue, a witness qualified as an expert by knowledge, skill, experience, training, or education, may testify thereto in the form of an opinion or otherwise, if (1) the testimony is sufficiently based upon reliable facts or data, (2) the testimony is the product of reliable principles and methods, and (3) the witness has applied the principles and methods reliably to the facts of the case.

The role of an expert witness is to use "scientific, technical, or other specialized knowledge" to assist the trier of fact to "understand the evidence or to determine a fact in issue."  The "trier of fact" is the jury in a jury trial and the judge in a bench trial (a trial without a jury).  The rationale for Rule 702 is that the jury may not be able to understand or correctly decide a case without assistance from experts.

Experts are qualified to testify by their "knowledge, skill, experience, training, or education."  Note the conjunction "or."  Under Rule 702, the expert only needs to have "knowledge," "skill," "experience," "training," *or* "education."  She need *not* have all five.

---

[1] What attorney would want to hire an expert knowing that a judge in a previous case had found the expert unqualified as a matter of law? Even if the expert was found qualified in the present case, she would likely face a series of difficult questions during cross-examination: "Are you the same expert that was found not qualified as a matter of law by U.S. District Court Judge Smith?" or "Isn't it true that you'll agree, for a price, to testify on anything, regardless of your true qualifications?"

Expert witnesses will routinely be qualified at the beginning of direct examination by the counsel who has retained them.  The expert can expect to be asked about her:

- profession,
- education,
- training,
- employment,
- experience,
- certifications/licenses,
- specialties,
- present title,
- practical experience,
- number of examinations/investigations performed,
- lecturing or teaching,
- research work,
- awards,
- published works,
- memberships in professional associations, and
- when and where she previously qualified to testify as an expert.

Some experts may feel uncomfortable going over their credentials and professional accomplishments in open court.  The extent of the "qualifying" testimony should be reviewed with counsel during pre-trial preparation.  It is the responsibility of counsel to decide how much of the background, experience, and expertise of the expert to put before the jury.  Counsel should attempt to impress the judge and jury without putting them to sleep.

Under Rule 702, it is the judge who initially determines if an expert's proposed testimony, as a matter of law, will satisfy the Rule's requirements.  If an expert's qualifications are challenged, the judge may have him *voir dired*.  This means that the expert will provide preliminary testimony on his qualifications via direct and cross-examination. Based on the testimony he provides during the voir dire, the judge will then make her ruling on whether the expert is qualified to testify.

If the judge holds that the expert is not qualified to testify on a particular area, then the expert will not be allowed to testify on that area.  The judge's decision in this regard is an issue that may be raised on appeal, but the standard of review is usually whether the trial judge abused her discretion in holding that the expert was not qualified.  This is a difficult standard to meet.

If the judge finds that the expert is qualified, he will be allowed to state his opinion only in the areas in which he was qualified, not on any and all matters or issues.[2]  Qualified experts are allowed to testify by expressing an opinion.  This is in stark contrast to lay witnesses, who can usually only testify to firsthand personal knowledge.  The issue of an expert's qualifications will be determined on a case by case basis.

---

[2] Of course, the expert's proposed testimony could still be challenged under the *Daubert* line of cases. (See Chapter 9 on methodology.)

The facts of a particular case will dictate the expertise needed by the proffered witness. The fact that a witness may have qualified previously in a particular case does not necessarily mean he will be found qualified in subsequent cases.

## 6.3  Factors the Judge Considers When Ruling on Qualifications

When deciding whether an expert is qualified to testify in a particular case, the judge will consider many factors. These include whether the witness has been qualified to testify on the issue in the past, the witness's specialized training and education (or lack thereof), whether the witness has published in the area in question, the expert's licenses, the expert's membership in relevant professional organizations, whether a firsthand inspection or examination was performed, the extent of the witness's real-world experience, and whether the proposed testimony is to be given in front of a jury or at a bench trial.

*Previous cases*
Was the expert's testimony previously accepted in a similar case? When counsel can demonstrate that the expert has previously been qualified in similar cases, this will be considered carefully by the trial judge.

**Example 6.1: Expert had testified in numerous other cases, found qualified**
*Green Party of New York State v. New York State Bd. of Elections,* 2003 WL 21296155 (E.D.N.Y. 2003)
An author was qualified to testify in a ballot access law case. The expert published a newsletter and was the author of numerous articles on minor parties. He had testified as an expert in numerous courts on laws that affect those groups.

**Comment:** Authoring articles and newsletters on a topic helps show qualifications. Publications can also be very effective marketing techniques. Please see Chapter 18.

**Example 6.2: Expert had been accepted previously in numerous state courts, found qualified**
*Burdette v. Drushell,* 2494 Cir. (La. App. 1.Cir. 2002)
An engineer was qualified to testify in an action that a carpenter brought seeking to enforce a lien against a property owner. The expert was a professional civil and consulting engineer with many years' experience. He had previously been accepted as an expert in the fields of construction and engineering in numerous state courts.

**Example 6.3: Thirty-plus years experience testifying, found qualified**
*Dufrene v. Willingham,* 702 So.2d 1026 (La. App. 5 Cir. 1998)
A retired police officer was qualified to testify as an accident reconstructionist. The witness had been testifying in state and federal courts since 1966 and had testified as an expert in accident reconstruction since 1964.

**Example 6.4: Qualified as expert in forty states, found qualified in case at hand**
*Labit v. D. H. Holmes Co., Ltd.,* 721 So.2d 933 (La. App. 5 Cir. 1998)
A tire expert was found qualified in part because he had qualified as an expert in forty states and in over two hundred cases.

**Example 6.5: "Significant" that expert was found qualified in a previous case**
*Magnivision, Inc. v. Bonneau Co.,* 33 F.Supp.2d 1218 (C.D. Cal. 1998)
The court calls "significant" the fact that the witness had qualified to testify in a previous case.

**Example 6.6: Court cites fact that other courts had found the expert qualified to testify, finds expert qualified to testify in case at hand**
*Colboch v. Uniroyal Tire Co., Inc.,* 670 N.E.2d 1366 (Ohio App. 8 Dist. 1996)
The court was dealing with a mechanic who was injured when the tire he was mounting exploded. The court found that the metallurgical engineer was qualified to testify, stating, "The other courts have reviewed Milner's qualifications and determined that he is qualified to testify as an expert in litigation regarding defective tires."

## Education and training

Experts with appropriate training and education will be found to be qualified. However, when a judge finds that even a highly educated expert, such as a physician, lacks required additional specialized training, that expert may be found not qualified to testify. Frequently, experts who lack training in the area in question are found not qualified to testify.

**Example 6.7: Lack of training on using impairment guidelines, M.D. not qualified to testify on whole-person impairment**
*Figlioli v. R.J. Moreau Companies, Inc.,* 866 A.2d 962 (N.H. 2005)
General and vascular surgeon not qualified to give expert opinion on homeowner's neurological impairment or on her whole-person impairment. Surgeon testified that he had no neurological training or experience and that he had never before used the guidelines.

**Comment:** Had this expert been allowed to testify, his opinion, which was based upon no hands-on experience, might have carried little weight with the fact finder.

**Example 6.8: Education cited by court when finding expert qualified**
*Rogers v. Detroit Edison Co.,* 328 F.Supp.2d 687 (E.D. Mich. S. Div. 2004)
A motorist's treating psychologist was qualified to testify as an expert witness regarding his opinion that the victim suffered from post-traumatic stress disorder as a result of his car being struck by an electric cable. Although the psychologist lacked experience in treating patients with PTSD, he was licensed as a clinical psychologist in the state of Florida; he had Bachelor of Arts and Master of Sciences degrees; he held a doctorate in psychology; he had completed his post-doctorate work; and he had engaged in group and individual therapy for over 25 years.

**Example 6.9: Lack of training and experience, not qualified**
*Citizens for a Safe Grant v. Lone Oak Sportsmen's Club, Inc.,* 624 N.W.2d 796 (Minn. App. 2001)
A firearms expert was not qualified to testify as an expert on shooting-range safety and design issues. The expert had limited training and no practical experience in those areas.

**Example 6.10: Ph.D. found qualified to testify**
*Metropolitan St. Louis Equal Housing Opportunity Council v. Gordon A. Gundaker Real Estate Co., Inc.,* 130 F.Supp.2d 1074 (E.D. Mo. E. Div. 2001)
The expert was qualified to testify in a housing discrimination case. The expert had doctoral degrees in psychology and mathematical/statistical psychology and had been involved in behavioral science data analysis since 1965.

**Example 6.11: D.D.S. qualified to testify on failure to diagnose jaw**
*Dolen v. St. Mary's Hosp. of Huntington,* 506 S.E.2d 624 (W.Va. 1998)
An oral surgeon was qualified to testify to the malpractice of physicians for failure to diagnose the plaintiff's jaw. The witness received a degree in dental surgery, a master's degree in biological

sciences with a concentration in oral surgery, and had practiced in the fields of oral and maxillofacial surgery for the last 14 years.

**Example 6.12: Lack of training, not qualified**
*Everett v. Georgia-Pacific Corp.,* 949 F.Supp. 856 (S.D. Ga. 1996)
A family physician was found to be not qualified to testify about chronic obstructive pulmonary disease. The court found his lack of training in toxicology to be determinative.

**Example 6.13: Experienced physician lacking training or experience on issue in question found not qualified**
*Cali v. Danek Medical, Inc.,* 24 F.Supp.2d 941 (W.D. Wis. 1998)
An orthopedic surgeon with thirty-five years of experience was found not qualified to testify in a pedicle screw case. The court noted that the witness had no experience or training in the area on which his opinion was to be offered.

**Example 6.14: Engineer lacking training as an accident reconstructionist found not qualified**
*Wilson v. Woods,* 163 F.3d 935 (5th Cir. 1999)
A mechanical engineer was found not qualified to testify as an accident reconstructionist. The witness did not have training or experience in this field.

**Example 6.15: Lack of formal education, RN found not qualified**
*Kent v. Pioneer Valley Corp.,* 930 P.2 904 (Utah App. 1997)
A registered nurse was found not qualified to testify that an injection caused nerve damage. The court cited lack of formal education.

**Example 6.16: Lack of training, engineer found not qualified**
*Surace v. Caterpillar, Inc.,* 111 F.3rd 1039 (3rd Cir. 1997)
An electromechanical engineer lacked training in back-up alarms and habitation and was held not to be qualified.

**Example 6.17: Lack of training, accident reconstructionist found not qualified**
*Waste Mgt of Ohio v Mid-America Tire,* 681 N.E.2d 492 (Ohio App. 2 Dist. 1996)
An accident reconstructionist was found not qualified to testify on wheel explosion due to lack of training.

**Example 6.18: Biomechanical engineer lacked medical training, found not qualified**
*Combs v. Norfolk and Western Ry. Co.,* 507 S.E.2d 355 (Va. 1998)
A biomechanical engineer with a Ph.D. was found not qualified to testify regarding the cause of a ruptured disk. The witness did not have sufficient medical training.

**Example 6.19: Physician lacking physical therapy training not allowed to testify on the standard of care of a physical therapist**
*Kirker v. Nicolla,* 681 N.Y.S.2d 689 (A.D. 3 Dept. 1998)
A surgeon was not permitted to testify on the standard of care of a physical therapist. The witness had no training or experience in the field of physical therapy.

## *Publications and writings*

Judges frequently will find qualified and defer to experts who have published extensively in their fields. For an expert, publishing not only is a powerful way to show qualifications, it can be a good way of promoting oneself. (See Sections 18.7 and 18.8.) Of course, experts can also be confronted on cross-examination with any inconsistencies between their testimony and their past writings (see Section 15.4).

### Example 6.20: Co-author of books on bicycling found qualified
*Derienzo v. Trek Bicycle Corp.,* 376 F.Supp.2d 537 (S.D.N.Y. 2005)
An electrical engineer was qualified as an expert in the areas of the history of bicycling, bicycling trends and habits, and bicycling safety. He was not qualified as an expert about matters involving bicycle design or metallurgical engineering. The expert was a certified bicycling instructor, held positions with various bicycling organizations, and co-authored books on bicycling.

### Example 6.21: Published over 185 articles, found qualified
*Santoro ex rel. Santoro v. Donnelly,* 340 F.Supp.2d 464 (S.D.N.Y. 2004)
A mechanical engineer was qualified to render an expert opinion on the adequacy of warnings for a fireplace. The engineer worked as a mechanical engineer after graduating from college, had written warnings for kitchen appliances and car signals, had conducted human factors research regarding readability and color lettering for purposes of designing warnings, and had published over 185 articles on packaging and merchandising subjects.

### Example 6.22: Pathologist author of several articles found qualified
*Axelrad v. Jackson,* 2004 WL 1440605 (Tex. App. Houston 14 Dist. 2004)
A pathologist was qualified to testify on the age of a patient's perforation. The pathologist lacked specialized training about the disease process of diverticulitis. However, the pathologist was board certified, was a full professor, held an endowed chair, wrote several articles about gastrointestinal cytology, and was familiar with the pathology of the gastrointestinal tract. In addition, the surgeon who operated on the patient testified that the pathologist was knowledgeable in the area in question.

### Example 6.23: Argonomist who wrote 150 scholarly articles "eminently qualified"
*B.F. Goodrich v. Betkoski,* 99 F.3rd 505 (2nd Cir. 1996)
The court found an argonomist who had written over 150 scholarly scientific articles eminently qualified to testify.

### Example 6.24: Contributing editor to important text (highway safety expert) found qualified
*Wood v. Minnesota Mining and Mfg. Co.,* 112 F.3d 306 (8th Cir. 1997)
A highway safety expert was permitted to testify on the safety of a railroad crossing. The expert was a contributing editor of an important text regarding traffic engineering as it applies to railroad crossings.

## Expert's firsthand knowledge, inspection, or testing
In making their decisions on qualifications, judges will consider whether the expert has firsthand knowledge of a machine, site, or condition due to an inspection. It is recommended that experts always try to test or inspect the item in question.

### Example 6.25: Numerous firearms examinations, found qualified
*Symington v. Daisy Mfg. Co., Inc.,* 360 F.Supp.2d 1027 (D.N.D. NE. Div. 2005)
A former police firearms examiner had sufficient experience, training, and education to qualify as an expert in a products liability action against the manufacturer of an airgun, alleging that the airgun was defective. During the 20 years in which he worked in a police crime laboratory, he had examined thousands of firearms to determine how they functioned, he had taken armorer courses

from numerous firearm manufacturers (which included instruction in assembly, disassembly, and testing of firearms), and he had performed numerous tests on manufacturer's airguns.

### Example 6.26: Hands-on work, vocational expert found qualified
*Campana v. City of Greenfield,* 164 F.Supp.2d 1078 (E.D. Wis. 2001)
A vocational specialist was qualified to testify as an expert regarding whether city comptroller and treasurer positions required equal effort, skill, and responsibility. The expert had reviewed job descriptions and interviewed the treasurer.

### Example 6.27: Personal inspection of site in question, civil engineer found qualified
*Burgess v. Harley,* 934 S.W.2d 58 (Tenn. App. 1996)
The court was dealing with the dangerousness of an intersection. The judge relied in part on the fact that the civil engineer had firsthand knowledge due to his personal inspection and found him qualified to testify.

### Example 6.28: Delayed visit to accident scene, engineer not qualified
*Pelzer v. United Parcel Service,* 484 S.E.2d 849 (N.C. App. 1997)
An engineer was found not qualified due to a delayed visit to an accident scene.

**Comment:** Experts are well advised to visit the accident scene as soon as possible.

### Example 6.29: Failure to inspect tractor in question, civil engineer not qualified
*West v. Sonke,* 968 P.2d 228 (Idaho 1998)
A civil engineer did not inspect the actual tractor in question. The expert was held not qualified to testify.

**Comment:** Even if the judge allowed this expert to testify, the expert would have been very vulnerable during cross-examination because he never inspected the tractor in question.

## Real-world experience
Judges may find experts with real-world experience qualified to testify, despite lacking formal education or training. Real-world experience can also weigh heavily on jurors faced with conflicting expert testimony.

### Example 6.30: Lack of formal education does not bar experienced pest control person from testifying
*Merrifield v. Lockyer,* 2005 WL 1866401 (N.D. Cal. 2005)
Expert found qualified based on more than twenty years of experience in the field of structural pest control. Lack of formal education in pest control and lack of board certification did not bar qualification.

### Example 6.31: Patent attorney not qualified because of lack of specific hands-on experience
*Kairos Scientific Inc. v. Fish & Richardson, P.C.,* 2003 WL 21960687 (Cal. Super. 2003)
A patent attorney was not qualified to render an expert opinion regarding matters covered by the client's patent regarding enzyme screening. The expert had no direct hands-on experience with manipulating enzymes or enzyme research.

**Example 6.32: Over 100 previous studies and analyses, aerospace engineer found qualified**
*Quiet Technology DC-8, Inc. v. Hurel-Dubois UK Ltd.,* 326 F.3d 1333 (C.A. 11 Fla. 2003)
An aerospace engineer was found qualified as an expert in computational fluid dynamics. The expert had worked for several aerospace companies, where he performed over 40 computational fluid dynamics analyses and assisted in roughly 80 additional computational fluid dynamics studies.

**Example 6.33: Vast hands-on experience, trademarks expert found qualified to testify**
*Betterbox Communications Ltd. v. BB Technologies, Inc.,* 300 F.3d 325 (C.A. 3 Pa. 2002)
A trademarks expert was found qualified to testify on the issue of whether consumers would likely be confused by trademarks for computer-related products sold through catalog marketing. The expert had worked actively for 20 years in the fields of direct marketing and mail-order catalogs, had extensive experience in marketing and use of logos in advertising, had published a variety of articles on direct marketing, had taken courses in graphic design, had designed corporate logos, and had approximately four years' experience as the owner of a business involved in direct marketing of computer products.

**Example 6.34: Thirteen years experience as building inspector, qualified to testify**
*Pack v. Case,* 30 P.3d 436 (Utah. App. 2001)
The expert was qualified to testify on a roofing matter. He had thirteen years of experience as a building inspector.

**Example 6.35: Lack of practical experience, shooting range safety expert not qualified**
*Citizens for a Safe Grant v. Lone Oak Sportsmen's Club, Inc.,* 624 N.W.2d 796 (Minn. App. 2001)
This expert was not qualified to testify on shooting range safety and design issues. The expert had limited training and no practical experience in those areas.

**Example 6.36: Lack of degree, but actual experience in field, criminal behavior expert qualified**
*Price ex. rel. v. NYC Housing Authority,* 706 N.E.2d 1167 (N.Y. 1998)
The court found qualified an expert in criminal behavior who lacked a degree but had actual experience in the field.

**Example 6.37: No formal education beyond high school, but 40 years experience, auto mechanic qualified**
*General Motors Corp. v. Pegues,* 724 So.2d 489 (Miss. App. 1998)
An auto mechanic with forty years of experience but only a high school education was found qualified to testify on causation in a defective ball joint case.

**Comment:** Advanced education is *not* a requirement for being an expert witness.

**Example 6.38: Lack of experience, fire investigator not qualified**
*Hamilton Mut. Ins. Co. v. Ford Motor Co.,* 702 N.E.2d 491 (Ohio App. 6 Dist. 1997)
A fire and explosion investigator with twelve years of experience was found not qualified to testify regarding an allegedly faulty design or manufacturing defect of an automotive component. The witness had no experience in the design and manufacturing of automobiles.

**Comment:** For an expert's experience to be relevant, it needs to be in the area in which the expert is testifying.

**Example 6.39: Experience not extensive, but psychologist allowed to testify**
*Sharon B.W. v. George B.W.,* 507 S.E.2d 401 (W.Va. 1998)
A psychologist was found qualified to testify in an alleged sexual abuse child custody case even though his clinical practice did not encompass a great deal of sexually abused children.

**Example 6.40: Lack of academic training not a bar**
*Price ex. rel. Price v. NYC Housing Auth.,* 706 N.E.2d 1167 (N.Y. 1998)
A criminal behavior expert was qualified by experience, skill, training, knowledge, and experience. Lack of academic training in behavioral sciences did not disqualify the witness.

**Example 6.41: No experience, master plumber not qualified to testify on warnings**
*Johnson v. District of Columbia,* 728 A.2d 70 (D.C. 1999)
A master plumber was found not qualified to testify regarding the required safety warnings on commercial heaters. The witness had no experience in the design of water heaters and their controls. His testimony showed that he was unfamiliar with and somewhat misinformed regarding regulations governing the permissible temperature ranges of hot water provided from commercial heaters.

## Licenses
The court is also likely to consider whether the expert is licensed.

**Example 6.42: Lack of license, epidemiologist not qualified to opine on individual medical histories**
*Flowers v. Union Carbide Corp.,* 610 S.E.2d 109 (Ga. App. 2005)
An epidemiologist who was not a licensed medical doctor was not qualified to render an expert opinion on medical histories of individual patients.

**Example 6.43: Counselor in the midst of licensing process not qualified in child custody case**
*Lasater v. Lasater,* 2004 WL 1172614 (Ind. App. 2004)
A counselor was not qualified to offer expert testimony in a child custody proceeding because the counselor was still in the process of completing her licensing requirements and was not yet a licensed therapist.

**Example 6.44: Attorney not licensed in state in question, not qualified to testify in legal malpractice case**
*Glaser v. Pullman and Comley,* LLC, 88 Conn. App. 615 (Conn. App. 2005)
Due to unfamiliarity with Connecticut law, an attorney was not qualified to testify as an expert in a legal malpractice action arising out of his former clients' attempted purchase of a commercial building. Issues regarding Connecticut law were important to the case, but the expert stated that he did not know whether Connecticut law differed from the law of the states where he was licensed to practice law.

## Professional society membership
The court may also be moved by the expert's membership in relevant professional societies.

**Example 6.45: Member of several relevant professional societies, accident reconstructionist qualified**
*Marron v. Stromstad,* 123 P.3d 992 (Alaska 2005)
An accident reconstructionist was qualified to testify in an automobile accident case despite formal training that was limited to courses in accident reconstruction. His coursework was both extensive

and highly specialized, he was a member of several professional societies, he was certified by the state as a police instructor in accident reconstruction, and he had been working in the field for many years.

### Example 6.46: Member of home inspectors' organization, qualified
*GSB Contractors, Inc. v. Hess,* 2005 WL 877764 (Tenn. App. 2005)
A home inspector was qualified to give expert testimony in this homeowners' action against a contractor for breach of residential construction contract. The inspector had a degree in mechanical engineering, had inspected approximately 10,000 homes, and was a member of a home inspectors' association.

## Bench trial
The court may be more liberal in admitting expert testimony when the case is not before a jury. This is because the court does not have to worry about an unsophisticated jury being led astray.

### Example 6.47: Judge more liberal in qualifying expert witness because of bench trial
*Endresen v. Scheels Hardware and Sports,* 560 N.W.2d 225 (N.D. 1997)
An expert with questionable qualifications was allowed to testify. The court stated, "I think because it is a bench trial I have the luxury of being a little more liberal at least on the initial receipt of any evidence."

## *Additional Cases*
### Example 6.48: Roofing expert with 20 years' experience qualified
*Merlin v. Fuselier Construction, Inc.,* 789 So.2d 710 (La. App. 5 Cir. 2001)
The plaintiffs sued for breach of warranty after they purchased a three-year-old house that they alleged had a defective roof. After moving in and experiencing problems, the plaintiff hired an expert to inspect the roof. This expert later testified as to the condition of the roof. The court considered the roofing expert's qualifications:

> [The expert] testified that he had worked in the roofing business for twenty years, that he was the owner of a roofing company and an inspection company, that he was licensed by the State, and that he had previously testified as an expert in both Jefferson and Orleans parishes. Under these circumstances we cannot say that the trial court was clearly wrong in qualifying Mr. Ryan as an expert. At 718.

### Example 6.49: Safety expert not qualified to opine on design defect
*Berry v. Crown Equipment Corp.,* 108 F.Supp.2d 743 (E.D. Mich. 2000)
The plaintiff sued a forklift manufacturer to recover for injuries sustained while he was driving a stand-up forklift. The defendant argued that the plaintiff's safety expert was not qualified to render an expert opinion as to any alleged design defect in this case and, therefore, that his testimony should be disregarded in its entirety. The court weighed the expert's qualifications:

> [T]he Court finds both that [the safety expert] lacks the qualifications necessary to render an expert opinion regarding the alleged design defect of the Crown stand-up forklift upon which Plaintiff's claims in this case are predicated and that [the safety expert]'s particular theory of liability in this case is not supported by sound technical reasoning or methodology. By his own deposition testimony, [the safety expert] has demonstrated that he does not possess the requisite "knowledge, skill, experience, training or education" to render an opinion on defective forklift design. He has no formal engineering education or background and is neither a mechanic nor a biomechanic, nor does he claim any expertise in human factors engineering or biomechanics. He has never published any forklift-related articles and his only experience with forklifts was more than 20 years ago, while he was working for Chrysler Corporation.

Further, his only experience with forklift design involved his placement of "a curved kind of horseshoe-shaped back guard" and a "padded seat" for comfort on one of two sit-down forklifts used at the Chrysler plant he worked at forty years ago. He has no experience with respect to safety doors to enclose the operator's area and, apparently, he is not well-versed in either the industry literature in this area or testing data related to safety doors. Although [the safety expert] has some general experience in workplace safety, that experience was principally in the area of OSHA compliance. At 752–53.

The court also refused to qualify the expert on the basis of his vague claim to previous work as an expert witness:

At the hearing on this matter, Plaintiff's counsel also argued that the Court should deem [the safety expert] qualified on forklift design because he had provided testimony as an expert on a Clark forklift in 1995 "in a court in Cleveland." However, Plaintiff's counsel did not know the specific nature of that action, and did not know whether it was in a state or federal court. Further, he did not know whether [the safety expert] was subjected to a *Daubert* inquiry in that case. Therefore, the Court finds no support for qualifying [the safety expert] as an expert in this case based on his having previously provided expert testimony concerning a forklift in a court in Ohio. At 754.

### Example 6.50: CPA qualified on damages in infringement case despite lack of specific experience in mortgage industry

*Main Street Mortgage, Inc. v. Main Street Bancorp., Inc.,* 158 F.Supp.2d 510 (E.D. Pa. 2001)
A mortgage brokerage sued a competitor for service mark infringement. The defendant moved to exclude the testimony of the plaintiff's proffered damages expert, a CPA. The defendant challenged the CPA's qualifications, citing his lack of experience performing analyses in the mortgage industry. The court described the CPA's qualifications:

[The expert] is a Certified Public Accountant (CPA) with twenty-one years of experience in the profession....For ten years, he worked as an auditor or audit manager with various accounting firms. In 1989, he became a director at Ernst and Young. In 1993, he formed his own consulting company, and for the past sixteen years he has worked as a consultant in dispute resolutions. [The expert] has been qualified as an expert in several jurisdictions, including the Eastern District of Pennsylvania [where this case was heard]. While he does have extensive general accounting experience, this dispute represents the first time that he has worked on a case concerning the mortgage or home loan industry.

We find that [the expert], although not specialized in the mortgage industry, is sufficiently qualified to make the damages estimate contained in his report. [The expert] is an experienced public accountant who has conducted valuations of various businesses and previously performed analysis similar to that done here. He discussed the mortgage industry with [...] the President of Main Street Mortgage. He also examined the historical performance of mortgages in the three dominant counties in the Philadelphia area: Bucks, Chester, and Montgomery.

Were he being offered as an expert as to the inner workings of the mortgage industry, we might conclude that he lacked the proper qualifications. However, as Plaintiff's counsel articulated at Oral Argument, [the expert] is not testifying as a trademark expert or saying that the decline in Plaintiff's business is attributable to the Defendant's allegedly infringing conduct. He is being offered to quantify the decline. [The expert's] proposed testimony concerns the area of damages, and we find that his background as a CPA and experience in analyzing financial data are sufficient to qualify him to testify on lost profits. At 513.

### Example 6.51: Railroad expert qualified, based on experience

*Wellman v. Norfolk and Western Ry. Co.,* 98 F.Supp.2d 919 (S.D. Ohio 2000)
A railroad employee who allegedly sustained on-the-job knee and back injuries after he slipped on debris that had accumulated between the track rails brought an action against his employer, alleging that it was negligent in failing to maintain a safe workplace.

The expert's qualifications were at issue. The court allowed the expert to testify on certain issues, based on his experience:

> The issues about which the expert proposes to testify concern the proper and safe maintenance of a railroad yard with respect to debris dropped from loaded cars. The Plaintiff bears the burden of establishing that the railway was in some way negligent in failing to maintain a safe workplace. The calculus of risk incumbent in an analysis of negligence in this context turns on a number of factors, including, but not limited to: a) methods of preventing or detecting debris; b) the amount of debris which will make a railway unsafe for workers; c) means of inspecting cars to prevent spills; and d) practices and procedures in place to remediate spills in a timely manner. While this list is not meant to be exhaustive, it is designed to illustrate the types of issues which the Plaintiff must establish to prove that the Defendant employer maintained an unsafe rail line and that the same constituted negligence.
>
> In the Court's view [the expert] has sufficient expertise and experience in the rail industry to opine as to these issues. He is qualified to testify as to the proper maintenance of a rail line with respect to accumulation of debris, the means of detecting and remediating such spills, methods of preventing incoming cars from causing debris, and acceptable industry methods to remediate such hazards. To the extent that he has worked in the industry, particularly as a former terminal superintendent, trainmaster, and yardmaster for the Penn Central Railroad and his later experience in the regulation and over[sight] of the industry by the FRA, he is qualified to render such opinions. At 925.

## 6.4  Case Examples by Type of Expert

There is a substantial body of reported cases dealing with (as a matter of law) the qualifications of expert witnesses. The following table provides a sampling of recent decisions. Although most experts are routinely found qualified, there has been a growing trend toward the courts being more restrictive. When reviewing the cases below, the authors recommend that you focus not so much on the results themselves, but on the reasons the courts reached the results they did.

### *Recent Cases by Type of Expert*

***Abortion:*** Constitutional challenge to the Partial-Birth Abortion Ban Act of 2003. Expert OB/Gyns were ***not qualified*** to testify because they did not have any personal experience with the late-term abortion procedures at issue, despite being eminently qualified OB/Gyn practitioners. *Planned Parenthood Federation of America v. Ashcroft,* 320 F.Supp.2d 957 (N.D. Cal. 2004)

***Accident Reconstruction:*** Accident reconstruction expert was ***qualified*** to testify in an automobile accident case despite formal training limited to courses in accident reconstruction. His coursework was both extensive and highly specialized, he was a member of several professional societies, he was certified by the state as a police instructor in accident reconstruction, and he had been working in the field for many years. *Marron v. Stromstad,* 123 P.3d 992 (Alaska 2005)

***Accident Reconstruction:*** Witness was ***qualified*** to testify as an expert on traffic accident reconstruction. Although the witness had no college degree, he spent 15 years with the Louisiana State Police and attended advanced courses in accident investigation and reconstruction. The expert's job included responsibility for reviewing serious injury and fatality accidents and he offered technical assistance to troopers conducting accident investigations. The expert had also investigated more than 3,000 accidents and testified as an expert in other trials. *Leblanc v. Baxter,* 05-33 La.App. 5 Cir. 5/31/05 (La. App. 5 Cir. 2005)

***Accountant:*** The expert was ***qualified*** to testify in an accounts receivable dispute. The expert had 17 years of experience reviewing financial documents and was retained to analyze thousands of records concerning the accounts receivable in question. *Wechsler v. Hunt Health Systems, Ltd.,* 2003 WL 22358807 (S.D.N.Y. 2003)

***Aerospace Engineer:*** Expert in computational fluid dynamics was ***qualified.*** The expert had worked for several aerospace companies, where he performed over 40 computational fluid dynamics analyses and assisted in roughly 80 additional computational fluid dynamics studies. *Quiet Technology DC-8, Inc. v. Hurel-Dubois UK Ltd.,* 326 F.3d 1333 (C.A. 11 Fla. 2003)

***Antitrust:*** An expert with general business experience unrelated to antitrust economics was ***not qualified*** to offer an opinion on complicated antitrust issues such as defining relevant markets. *Berlyn, Inc. v. Gazette Newspapers, Inc.,* 214 F.Supp.2d 530 (D. Md. 2002)

***Appliance Safety:*** A safety engineer, who held a college degree in safety and fire protection engineering technology and who worked for over 25 years in the product safety arena evaluating product safety from an accident prevention standpoint, was ***qualified*** to give expert testimony in a products liability action stemming from an incident in which a 10-month-old child climbed inside the broiler compartment of a kitchen range manufactured by the defendant. This was despite the fact that the engineer had never previously analyzed the specific safety issue of how a 10-month-old infant interacted with a broiler door. *Dewick v. Maytag Corp.,* 324 F.Supp.2d 894 (N.D. Ill. E.Div. 2004)

***Appraisal:*** This expert was ***qualified*** to render an opinion concerning the value of real estate. The expert had been a resident for many years in the county in which the development was located, had been actively involved in the real estate business in the county for over 20 years, had served on the State Board of Appraisers for seven years, and had been recognized as an expert witness qualified to render opinions as to the value of real property by the courts in the county. *Boles v. National Development Co., Inc.,* 175 S.W.3d 226 (Tenn. App. 2005)

***Appraisal:*** A real estate agent ***qualified*** to testify as to the value of real property. The expert was not a licensed appraiser, but had six years experience as a real estate agent, which included determining approximate values of real property. *In re Marriage of Perkins,* 2004 WL 112598 (Tex. App. Amarillo 2004)

***Author/Publisher:*** This expert was ***qualified*** to testify in a ballot access law case. The expert published a newsletter, was the author of numerous articles on minor parties, and had testified as an expert in numerous courts on laws that affect those groups. *Green Party of New York State v. New York State Bd. of Elections,* 2003 WL 21296155 (E.D.N.Y. 2003)

***Automobile Repair:*** A mechanic technician at an automobile dealership was ***qualified*** to testify as an expert regarding a mechanical repair. The technician had been employed at the dealership for 20 years and had extensive experience with vehicles built by the manufacturer of the owner's motor vehicle. *Buck v. Auto Shop M.D., Inc.,* 2003 Ohio 6959 (Ohio. App. 11 Dist. Portage 2003)

***Automobiles:*** An expert witness who had been an editor of several automobile magazines was ***not qualified*** to testify on a post-collision fire in an automobile. The witness had neither performed a study nor published any literature on the issue of consumer expectations of anything. He had no knowledge of the issues at hand beyond his reading of industry magazines. *Tunnell v. Ford Motor Co.,* 2004 WL 1797160 (W.D. Va. 2004)

***Bicycles:*** An electrical engineer was ***qualified*** as an expert in the areas of the history of bicycling, bicycling trends and habits, and bicycling safety. He was ***not qualified*** as an expert about matters involving bicycle design or metallurgical engineering. The expert was a certified bicycling instructor, had held positions with various bicycling organizations, and co-authored books on bicycling. *Derienzo v. Trek Bicycle Corp.,* 376 F.Supp.2d 537 (S.D.N.Y. 2005)

***Blood Alcohol:*** State trooper who investigated an accident was ***not qualified*** to testify as to the significance of the driver's blood alcohol level at the time of the motor vehicle accident. The trooper based his claim of expertise on five to ten arrests of motorists with similar blood alcohol levels, 40 hours of class instruction, and a yearly refresher course. *Am. Select Ins. Co. v. Sunnycalb,* 2005 Ohio 6275 (Ohio App. 12 Dist. Warren C 2005)

***Boat:*** A naval architect marine engineer was ***not qualified*** to testify on whether a yacht's swim ladder had a defective design. The expert had no training in metallurgy or in ladder design, had no familiarity with the ladder at issue or with swim ladders in general, and had never taken part in manufacturing ladders. *Higginbotham v. KCS Intern., Inc.,* 85 Fed.Appx. 911 (C.A. 4. Md. 2004)

***Business Valuation:*** A forensic accountant was ***not qualified*** to testify as to his expert opinion with respect to the valuation of an insurance agency that sold only long-term care insurance policies. The accountant had never appraised such insurance agencies, had no background information on the long-term care insurance industry, and had done no work in that industry in the last 10 years. He did no research or analysis of the long-term care insurance market prior to providing the valuation, except for reading some articles found on the Internet. *Sun Ins. Marketing Network, Inc. v. AIG Life Ins. Co.,* 254 F.Supp.2d 1239 (M.D. Fla. 2003)

***Business Valuation:*** This expert was ***qualified*** to provide an opinion regarding the value of a pathology business. The witness did not have a college degree, but the witness provided advice to a variety of medical concerns regarding the acquisition and sale of medical practices and physician recruitment. The witness had over 14 years of practical experience in acquisition and operation of medical practices. *Root v. Root,* 2003 WY 36 (Wyo. 2003)

***Child Custody:*** A counselor was ***not qualified*** to offer expert testimony in a child custody proceeding. The counselor was still in the process of completing her licensing requirements and was not yet a licensed therapist. *Lasater v. Lasater,* 2004 WL 1172614 (Ind. App. 2004)

***College Professor:*** An Australian professor was ***not qualified*** to testify on whether a student met a university's standards for performance on the comprehensive examination or whether the student's performance on the examination was equal or superior to that of two other students. The expert had never given an examination at the doctoral level or formulated questions for such an examination. His teaching experiences were in Canada and Australia. *Jung v. George Washington University,* 875 A.2d 95 (D.C. 2005)

***Computers:*** This expert was ***qualified*** in the field of computer forensics despite lacking a background in computer programming or the ability to read or write code. The expert had worked in the field of computer forensics for five years and had completed between 1,600 and 1,700 forensic reports based on his findings, some of which had been accepted by various courts. The expert was a member of an association for high technology crime investigators and he completed three post-graduate training courses in computer forensics. *Galaxy Computer Services, Inc. v. Baker,* 2005 WL 1278956 (E.D. Va. 2005)

***Construction:*** This expert had 40 years of experience in the construction industry, had teaching experience pertaining to wall construction, and had six years of wall building experience. He was

# QUALIFICATIONS

*qualified* even though he did not have a formal degree in engineering. *Slip Track Systems, Inc. v. Metal-Lite, Inc.,* 304 F.3d 1256 (C.A. Fed. Cal. 2002)

*Construction:* The expert was *qualified* to testify on a roofing matter. He had thirteen years experience as a building inspector. *Pack v. Case,* 30 P.3d 436 (Utah. App. 2001)

*Damages:* This CPA was *qualified* to give an expert opinion regarding lost profits from a management agreement for a casino in the Caribbean. The CPA had done hundreds of lost profits evaluations, had done several evaluations of casinos, and had analyzed businesses in the Caribbean. *Bright v. Addison,* 2005 WL 1819595 (Tex. App. Dallas 2005)

*Damages/Value of Employment Contract:* An economist was *qualified* to give expert testimony regarding the present and future value of a former employee's employment contract. The economist had a doctorate in economics, taught a university course in corporate valuation, and often acted as a consultant preparing valuations for various corporations. *KMG Kanal-Muller-Gruppe Deutschland GmbH & Co. KG v. Davis,* 2005 WL 568056 (Tex. App. Houston 1 Dist. 2005)

*Disabilities:* This expert was *qualified* to testify on the emergency evacuation of individuals with disabilities. The expert was experienced and had served as the president and CEO of an Americans with Disabilities Act (ADA) consulting firm, worked with architects and building owners in the design phase of new facilities, and reviewed existing facilities to determine their accessibility and recommend ways to improve accessibility. *U.S. E.E.O.C. v. E.I. DuPont de Nemours & Co.,* 16 A.D. Cases 1487 (E.D. La. 2005)

*Discrimination:* Vocational specialist was *qualified* to testify as an expert regarding whether city comptroller and treasurer positions required equal effort, skill, and responsibility. The expert had reviewed job descriptions and interviewed the treasurer. *Campana v. City of Greenfield,* 164 F.Supp.2d 1078 (E.D. Wis. 2001)

*Discrimination:* A Department of Corrections employee's correctional management expert was *not qualified* to testify in an employee's race discrimination action. The expert's correctional management was unrelated to California and the expert merely expected that California's procedures would be similar to those in other parts of the country. *Starrett v. State,* 2002 WL 598531 (Cal. App. 5 Dist. 2002)

*Discrimination:* A statistician, who had a Ph.D. and was well experienced, was *qualified* to undertake segregation analysis in a Title VII class action even though during his deposition he could not recall two arithmetical terms related to segregation analysis and he had never before offered a segregation analysis into evidence. *McReynolds v. Sodexho Marriott Services, Inc.,* 349 F.Supp.2d 30 (D.D.C. 2004)

*Discrimination:* This expert was *not qualified* to give his opinion on statistical evidence to show disparity in promotions of African-Americans in an employment discrimination case. The expert had no educational or professional background or experience in employment statistics. In addition, the expert's methodology could not be determined to be objectively valid or based on sound principles. *King v. Enterprise Rent-A-Car Co.,* 2004 WL 3563268 (E.D. Mich. S. Div. 2004)

*Dogs:* A veterinarian was *qualified* as an expert to testify about the characteristics of the Rottweiler breed in this dog bite case. The expert had studied the characteristics and behavioral traits of various dog breeds. In addition, he was a practicing veterinarian who had cared for approximately five hundred Rottweilers since the early 1980s. *Hill v. Williams,* 547 S.E.2d 472 (N.C. App. 2001)

***Drug Abuse:*** A psychiatrist was ***qualified*** to testify regarding amphetamine use generally and specifically by the person in question. Even though the expert had not published anything in the field and only .04 percent of his practice dealt with methamphetamine abuse, he held specialty certification in psychiatry, had numerous professional society memberships and privileges in area hospitals, and saw amphetamine abusers at least once a month. *Loram Maintenance of Way, Inc. v. Ianni,* 2004 WL 1472700 (Tex. App. El Paso 2004)

***Economics:*** An economics professor was ***qualified*** to testify on whether a state's statutory scheme regulating liquor prices promoted its avowed interest in promoting temperance. The expert had vast experience in studying and advising on drug- and alcohol-related problems and had researched the effects of price on alcohol consumption. The expert's findings were based on a large amount of alcohol-specific research, experience, and the fundamental laws of economics. *TFWS, Inc. v. Schaefer,* 183 F.Supp.2d 789 (D. Md. 2002)

***Employment:*** A rehabilitation counselor was ***qualified*** to testify that an injured employee was unable to engage in gainful work activity. The expert possessed all credentials for certification in his profession. *Standard v. Union Pacific R.R. Co.,* 34 Fed.Appx. 629 (C.A. 10 Okla. 2002)

***Engineer:*** The expert was ***qualified*** to testify in an action a carpenter brought seeking to enforce a lien against a property owner. The expert was a professional civil and consulting engineer with many years' experience. He had been accepted as an expert in the fields of construction and engineering in numerous state courts. *Burdette v. Drushell,* 2494 La.App. 1 Cir. (La. App. 1 Cir. 2002)

***Engineering:*** This expert was ***qualified*** as an expert in petroleum engineering. The expert was a registered professional engineer with nearly 30 years of experience in the petroleum industry who provided lengthy and detailed testimony. *Amoco Production Co. v. Texaco, Inc.,* 838 So.2d 821 (La. App. 3 Cir. 2003)

***Fair Housing:*** The expert was ***qualified*** to testify in a housing discrimination case. The expert had doctoral degrees in psychology and mathematical/statistical psychology and had been involved in behavioral sciences data analysis since 1965. *Metropolitan St. Louis Equal Housing Opportunity Council v. Gordon A. Gundaker Real Estate Co., Inc.,* 130 F.Supp.2d 1074 (E.D. Mo. E. Div. 2001)

***Fair Housing:*** This lawyer ***qualified*** to testify on fair housing training. The lawyer was the director of a city fair housing program and had extensive experience in training real estate agents and brokers in compliance with the requirements of Federal Housing Administration. *Metropolitan St. Louis Equal Housing Opportunity Council v. Gordon A. Gundaker Real Estate Co., Inc.,* 130 F.Supp.2d 1074 (E.D. Mo. E. Div. 2001)

***Financial:*** A stock broker/financial planner was ***qualified*** by training and experience to testify in a divorce action regarding the present value of a husband's retirement benefits. *Carter v. Carter,* 2005 WL 3557408 (Ala. Civ. App. 2005)

***Firearms:*** This witness was ***not qualified*** to testify as an expert on shooting range safety and design issues. The expert had limited training and no practical experience in those areas. *Citizens for a Safe Grant v. Lone Oak Sportsmen's Club, Inc.,* 624 N.W.2d 796 (Minn. App. 2001)

# QUALIFICATIONS

**Firearms:** A former police firearms examiner had sufficient experience, training, and education to *qualify* as an expert in a products liability action against the manufacturer of an airgun, alleging that the airgun was defective. During the 20 years in which he worked in a police crime laboratory, he had examined thousands of firearms to determine how they functioned, he had taken armorer courses from numerous firearm manufacturers (which included instruction in assembly, disassembly, and testing of firearms), and he had performed numerous tests on manufacturer's airguns. *Symington v. Daisy Mfg. Co., Inc.,* 360 F.Supp.2d 1027 (D. N.D. NE. Div. 2005)

**Firearms:** A metallurgical expert was ***qualified*** to give testimony in a products liability action regarding steel used to manufacture a gun barrel that exploded. The expert held a Ph.D. in metallurgy, was a professor of material science, performed failure analyses on metals, reviewed industrial failures in metals for 35 years, and was an amateur gunsmith. *Olympic Arms, Inc. v. Green,* 176 S.W.3d 567 (Tex. App. Houston 1 Dist. 2004)

**Forklift:** A professor of biomechanical engineering was ***qualified*** to give testimony in a forklift design case even though he did not have thorough experience with injuries resulting from forklifts. Provided that he used an appropriate methodology, the expert's knowledge and experience were enough for him to testify on the mechanics of the injury in a products liability action. *Phillips v. Raymond Corp.,* 2005 WL 799128 (N.D. Ill. E. Div. 2005)

**Fraud:** This witness was ***qualified*** to testify as an expert with respect to lock-box accounts. The expert had served as an Internal Revenue Service agent for 33 years, specializing in financial fraud investigations. Although he had no previous experience with lock-box accounts per se, the expert's testimony dealt specifically with tracking funds into and out of lock-box accounts, which was well within the expert's area of expertise. *Microfinancial, Inc. v. Premier Holidays Intern., Inc.,* 385 F.3d 72 (C.A. 1 Mass. 2004)

**Head Injury:** A biomechanical engineer was ***qualified*** to testify regarding the extent of a head injury. The expert had a number of degrees in engineering, had studied how force related to injury, and had testified approximately 50 times in court for both plaintiffs and defendants. *Compher v. The Kroger Company,* 2005 Ohio 482 (Ohio App. 5 Dist. Guernsey 2005)

**Human Factors:** The expert was ***qualified*** based on specialized knowledge to testify on the step design of a tractor. Despite possessing a degree in experimental psychology rather than ergonomics/human factors, the expert had experience in human factors via work in product design and safety, including design of steps and access/egress systems. He had written on various aspects of ergonomics and human factors. *Fedor v. Freightliner, Inc.,* 2002 WL 523927 (E.D. Pa. 2002)

**Impairment Rating:** A general and vascular surgeon was ***not qualified*** to give an expert opinion on a homeowner's neurological impairment or on her whole-person impairment. The surgeon testified that he had no neurological training or experience and that he had never before used the guidelines. *Figlioli v. R.J. Moreau Companies, Inc.,* 866 A.2d 962 (N.H. 2005)

**Insurance:** This expert ***qualified*** to testify on insurance claims handling. She had a college degree, was involved in the insurance industry for 13 years, had professional insurance designations, and was familiar with the insurance claim at issue and with the policy. *Bohanon v. Farmers Ins. of Columbus, Inc.,* 2005 Ohio 5399 Ohio App. 5 Dist. (Delaware 2005)

**Insurance:** An attorney was sufficiently ***qualified*** to offer an opinion regarding the reasonableness of an insurer's handling of an insured's claim under a fire policy. The attorney did not specialize in fire loss claims, but he did have special knowledge of the insurance claims adjustment process due to his 20 years' experience defending insurance companies against claims by policy holders. The attorney had spoken on the topic of bad faith at legal seminars and prepared materials in connection with those seminars. The essence of the insured's bad faith claim was that the insurer unreasonably denied his claim by assigning an inexperienced adjustor who did little to obtain the information necessary to adjust the claim. *Talmage v. Harris,* 354 F.Supp.2d 860 (W.D. Wis. 2005)

***Ladder Design:*** This engineer was ***not qualified*** to testify in a ladder case. The witness was not a Ph.D., he did not test any loads on the ladder itself, and he was unable to pass the Georgia mechanical engineering exam after multiple attempts. *Massok v. Keller Industries, Inc.,* 147 Fed.Appx. 651 (C.A. 9 Cal. 2005)

***Land Use:*** Despite lacking an educational background similar to that of the opposing experts, an engineer was ***qualified*** to testify that the five percent fee charged by a telecommunications provider for use of rights-of-way was a barrier to entry into the local telecommunications market and that it did not reflect the municipality's related costs. The expert had vast experience in right-of-way matters. *TC Systems Inc. v. Town of Colonie, New York,* 213 F.Supp.2d 171 (N.D.N.Y. 2002)

***Landfill:*** This was a landfill developer's suit against a county and county officials. The engineer was ***qualified*** to testify about elevated methane levels, financial considerations, and the Atlanta landfill and solid waste disposal market's practices. However, the engineer was ***not qualified*** to testify as to the operation of the county's planning department. *BFI Waste System of North America v. Dekalb County, Georgia,* 303 F.Supp.2d 1335 (N.D. Ga. Atlanta. Div. 2004)

***Landscape Architect:*** In this nuisance case, the expert's experience as a municipal planner and landscape architect did ***not qualify*** him as an expert on the operation of foster homes. *Carter v. Beech Brook, 200–Ohio,* 4225 Ohio.App.11. (Dist. Geauga. C., 2003)

***Legal Malpractice:*** Due to unfamiliarity with Connecticut law, this attorney was ***not qualified*** to testify as an expert in a legal malpractice action arising out of his former clients' attempted purchase of a commercial building. Issues regarding Connecticut law were important to the case, but the expert stated that he did not know whether Connecticut law differed from the law of the states where he was licensed to practice law. *Glaser v. Pullman and Comley, LLC,* 88 Conn.App. 615 (Conn. App. 2005)

***Lending:*** A lender's employee was ***not qualified*** to offer testimony interpreting a credit life insurance contract. The expert was not an attorney and was not qualified to testify as to legal conclusions. *MIC Life Ins. Co. v. Hicks,* 825 So.2d 616 (Miss. 2002)

***Lending/Banking:*** The expert was ***not qualified*** to offer expert testimony on the banking practices of residential loan officers. The witness supervised residential loan officers as a bank's chief financial officer and had impressive credentials regarding high-end commercial banking procedures. He did not have expertise on the exact procedures of residential loan officers. *Forte v. Citicorp Mortgage, Inc.,* 90 Conn. App. 727 (Conn. App. 2005)

***Lost Profits:*** The vice president of finance for an oilfield pump manufacturer was ***qualified*** to testify as an expert on the issue of a manufacturer's lost profits. He had a BBA in accounting and more than 30 years' experience managing the financial and accounting functions of companies engaged in the manufacture and distribution of various products. *Toshiba Machine Co., America v. SPM Flow Control, Inc.,* 2005 WL 3008433 (Tex. App. Fort Worth 2005)

*Medical Malpractice:* A doctor was ***not qualified*** to testify as an expert regarding the standard of care required for surgical removal of tissue identified for a breast biopsy. The expert's experience with biopsies was based on his residency more than thirty years ago, there was evidence that medical science and surgical techniques had changed since that time, the doctor presented no evidence that he had kept up with these advances, and the doctor's expertise was in oncology. *Lopez v. Reddy,* 2005 NMCA 054 (N.M. App. 2005)

*Medical Records:* Although the witness was ***not qualified*** as an expert in handwriting, testimony as to whether the charts of two of an ophthalmologist's patients had been altered was ***allowed.*** The court reasoned that this testimony related to specialized information, reviewing a medical record when making a medical diagnosis. *Siuda v. Howard,* 2002 Ohio 2292 (Ohio. App. 1 Dist. Hamilton 2002)

*Medicine:* A medical expert ***qualified*** to testify regarding sternal dehiscence even if the expert's practice did not include surgical treatment of patients. *Eason v. Anoka-Hennepin East Metro Narcotics & Violent Crimes Task Force,* 2002 WL 1739666 (D. Minn. 2002)

*Medicine:* A biomechanical engineer was ***not qualified*** to opine on what types of physical ailments the plaintiff may have and whether the force involved in a motor vehicle collision could potentially aggravate or cause an injury in a plaintiff with a prior injury or ailment. *Salerno v. Tudor,* 2002 WL 120608 (Cal. App. 1 Dist. 2002)

*Medicine:* A physician ***qualified*** to testify that if a cigarette not containing nicotine were designed and manufactured it would be healthier than a cigarette containing nicotine. The expert was certified in internal medicine and pulmonary medicine, was a professor of medicine, authored or edited multiple Surgeon General Reports on the health consequences of smoking, and had written numerous articles concerning health consequences of smoking. *Burton v. R.J. Reynolds Tobacco Co.,* 183 F.Supp.2d 1308 (D. Kan. 2002)

*Medicine:* A treating general surgeon was ***qualified*** to express expert opinions on whether it was unusual for head-injured patients to be unable to remember events surrounding an accident and whether it could be predicted who would regain memory. The expert general surgeon was fellowship-trained in trauma, practiced for 27 years as a trauma specialist, had taught at several academic medical centers, was very familiar with brain injury literature, and had treated hundreds of patients with similar head injuries. *Falconer v. Penn Maritime, Inc.,* 380 F.Supp.2d 2 (D. Me. 2005)

*Medicine:* This epidemiologist was ***not qualified*** to render an expert opinion on medical histories of individual patients because he was not a licensed medical doctor. *Flowers v. Union Carbide Corp.,* 610 S.E.2d 109 (Ga. App. 2005)

*Medicine:* A pathologist ***qualified*** to testify on the age of a patient's perforation. The pathologist lacked specialized training about the disease process of diverticulitis. However, the pathologist was board certified, a full professor, held an endowed chair, wrote several articles about gastrointestinal cytology, and was familiar with the pathology of the gastrointestinal tract. In addition, the surgeon who operated on the patient testified that the pathologist was knowledgeable in the area in question. *Axelrad v. Jackson,* 2004 WL 1440605 (Tex. App. Houston 14 Dist. 2004)

*Medicine:* A board-certified internist ***qualified*** to testify as an expert witness concerning a urological problem. Even though the expert was neither a urologist nor a neurologist, he had some training in urology at medical school. Internal medicine covers any type of problem that may affect the adult patient and the urological symptoms in question included the types of symptoms that the expert evaluated in his practice. *Carlson v. Okerstrom, 675 N.W.2d 89 (Neb. 2004)*

*Medicine:* An emergency medicine physician was *qualified* to render an opinion on the manner in which wounds were inflicted upon a victim. *Com. v. D'Orazio, 66 Pa. D.&C. 4th 202 (Pa. Com. Pl. 2004)*

*Medicine:* Due to experience in treating brain injury, a neurologist was *qualified* to testify regarding an injured person's brain injury. *Floyd v. McGill, 575 S.E.2d 789 (N.C. App. 2003)*

*Mental Competency:* A sheriff's training on how to handle a person with a mental disability did *not qualify* him as an expert witness on the issue of whether a father was competent to execute a deed. *Rutledge v. Wallace, 2002 Ohio 5372 (Ohio App. 7 Dist. Carroll C. 2002)*

*Nursing Home Malpractice:* A nurse was *qualified* to testify on nursing home standards of care. The case concerned a deceased nursing home resident who died as a result of injuries sustained in a run-away wheelchair accident. The nurse had extensive experience in providing expert services and had taught nursing at a public university. The nurse had experience as a staff nurse and administrator at a nursing home and had served as a consultant in nursing services administration and gerontological care. *Sunbridge Healthcare Corp. v. Penny, 2005 WL 562763 (Tex. App. Texarkana 2005)*

*Patent Attorney:* The expert was *not qualified* to render an opinion regarding matters covered by a client's patent regarding enzyme screening. The expert had no direct hands-on experience with manipulating enzymes or enzyme research. *Kairos Scientific Inc. v. Fish & Richardson, P.C., 2003 WL 21960687 (Cal. Super. 2003)*

*Pest Control:* Due to more than twenty years of experience in the field of structural pest control, the expert was found *qualified.* Lack of formal education in pest control and lack of board certification did not bar qualification. *Merrifield v. Lockyer, 2005 WL 1866401 (N.D. Cal. 2005)*

*Plumbing Inspector:* This expert was *not qualified* to opine as to a city's financial health or its building and safety department. *Shepherd v. City of Salem, 2004 WL 1273307 (D. Or. 2004)*

*Police Misconduct:* In this police brutality case involving a victim whose neck was broken during arrest, a martial arts instructor *qualified* to offer an opinion regarding the types of bodily responses generally associated with pressurized neck restraints based on his experience in martial arts. *Fultz v. Whittaker, 261 F.Supp.2d 767 (W.D. Ky. 2003)*

*Police Training:* Experience and training as a police officer of 22 years *qualified* an expert to render an opinion on police training, methods, and policies as well as the clinical signs and dangers of cocaine-induced excited delirium. *Watkins v. New Castle County, 2005 WL 1491520 (D. Del. 2005)*

*Portfolio Management:* This expert was found *qualified* due to an extensive background and qualifications in analyzing bonds, publishing several articles relating to the issues at hand, and his expert testimony on similar matters in almost 50 court or legislative appearances. *Ulico Cas. Co. v. Clover Capital Management, Inc., 217 F.Supp.2d 311 (N.D.N.Y. 2002)*

*Post-Traumatic Stress Disorder:* A licensed social worker was *qualified* to diagnose post-traumatic stress disorder. She was a licensed clinical social worker who provided psychotherapy to her patients. When seeking payment from third-party insurers, the insurance companies did not require diagnosis and treatment services to be rendered by someone with a higher medical degree. *Bourque v. Stop & Shop Companies, Inc.,* 814 A.2d 320 (R.I. 2003)

***Post-Traumatic Stress Disorder:*** A motorist's treating psychologist was **qualified** to testify as an expert witness regarding his opinion that the victim suffered from post-traumatic stress disorder as a result of his car being struck by an electric cable. Although lacking experience in treating patients with PTSD, the psychologist was licensed as a clinical psychologist in Florida; had a Bachelor of Arts, a Master of Sciences, and a doctorate in psychology; had completed his post-doctorate work; and he had engaged in group and individual therapy for over 25 years. *Rogers v. Detroit Edison Co.,* 328 F.Supp.2d 687 (E.D. Mich. S. Div. 2004)

***Power Cord Design:*** The witness was **qualified** to provide expert testimony about the cause and origin of a fire in a leased residence. The witness was **not qualified** to provide expert testimony about the design of a treadmill power cord that allegedly caused the fire. The expert was neither an electrical engineer nor an electrician, had no experience in power cord design or treadmill design or manufacture, did not know what standards were applicable to power cord design at the time the treadmill was manufactured, and had a complete lack of experience and training in the areas of electrical engineering and, specifically, power cord design. *Nationwide Mut. Ins. Co. v. ICON Health and Fitness, Inc.,* 2005 Ohio 2638 (Ohio App. 10 Dist. Franklin 2005)

***Prisons:*** The expert was **qualified** to testify regarding rehabilitation of inmates. The expert had many years of training and experience in gang identification and had personal knowledge of the prison's mission to provide inmates with an environment away from gang influences. *Koutnik v. Brown,* 2005 WL 2897446 (W.D. Wis. 2005)

***Products Liability:*** A pharmacologist was **not qualified** to testify as to whether any benefits from a certain level of weight loss outweighed risks accompanying the use of a weight loss medication. Even though the expert had attended symposia on weight loss and lectured regarding obesity, he had no special qualifications regarding the effects of certain levels of weight loss on health. *In re Meridia Products Liability Litigation,* 328 F.Supp.2d 791 (N.D. Ohio 2004)

***Products Liability:*** A cardiologist was **qualified** to testify in a Vioxx products liability action despite a short and conclusory report and that his deposition testimony revealed a lack of understanding. The expert specialized in cardiology and reviewed all the relevant materials. *In re Vioxx Products Liability Litigation,* 401 F.Supp.2d 565 (E.D. La. 2005)

***Railroads*** Locomotive engineer was qualified to testify as an expert on railroad issues. He worked as a locomotive engineer for over 20 years and had testified about or been deposed on railroad issues in multiple cases. *Haager v. Chicago Rail Link, LLC,* 232 F.R.D. 289 (N.D. Ill. E. Div. 2005)

***Residential Construction:*** A home inspector was **qualified** to give expert testimony in a homeowners' action against a contractor for breach of a residential construction contract. The inspector had a degree in mechanical engineering, had inspected approximately 10,000 homes, and was a member of a home inspectors' association. *GSB Contractors, Inc. v. Hess,* 2005 WL 877764 (Tenn. App. 2005)

***Safe Sex:*** The expert was **not qualified** on whether swingers engaged in safe sexual practices. *Recreational Developments of Phoenix, Inc. v. City of Phoenix,* 220 F.Supp.2d 1054 (D. Ariz. 2002)

***Security:*** The expert was ***qualified*** to testify on the issue of appropriate security measures for the Vice President's visit to a city (the case involved a civil rights action brought by an arrested political protester). *Blair v. City of Evansville, Ind.,* 2005 WL 697212 (S.D. Ind. Evansville Div. 2005)

***Substance Abuse:*** A social worker who treated an employee for substance abuse problems was ***not qualified*** to offer an expert medical opinion regarding the employee's condition. The social worker had no training in medicine and lacked any demonstrated ability to interpret medical records meaningfully. *Gilbert v. DaimlerChrysler Corp.,* 685 N.W.2d 391 (Mich. 2004)

***Tanning Machine:*** A licensed engineer was ***not qualified*** to render an expert opinion regarding the safety of a tanning machine. Although licensed as an engineer, the expert showed no specialized knowledge, experience, training, or education with regard to tanning equipment. *Rosen v. Tanning Loft,* 791 N.Y.S.2d 641 (N.Y.A.D. 2 Dept. 2005)

***Tires:*** The witness was ***not qualified*** to testify regarding tire manufacture and design. The witness had not published or been subject to peer review in the area of tire manufacture or design. His expertise was developed for litigation. *Prince v. Michelin North America, Inc.,* 2003 WL 1058328 (W.D. Mo. W. Div. 2003)

***Trademarks:*** An expert was ***qualified*** to testify on whether consumers would likely be confused by trademarks for computer-related products sold through catalog marketing. The expert had worked actively for 20 years in direct marketing and mail-order catalogs, had extensive experience in marketing and the use of logos in advertising, had published a variety of articles on direct marketing, had taken graphic design courses, had designed corporate logos, and had approximately four years' experience as the owner of a business involved in the direct marketing of computer products. *Betterbox Communications Ltd. v. BB Technologies, Inc.,* 300 F.3d 325 (C.A. 3 Pa. 2002)

***Trip and Fall:*** A safety engineer was ***qualified*** as an expert in a premises liability action involving a parking garage patron's fall from the curb in front of the garage elevator. He had an extensive background in the field of safety engineering, was board certified as a safety professional, and had specialized knowledge in premises safety and accident cause analysis. *Burns v. Baylor Health Care System,* 2003 WL 22161590 (Tex. App. El Paso 2003)

***Trusts:*** Despite not administering a trust or advising clients on the creation and administration of trusts, the expert was ***qualified*** to testify as an expert on trust creation and administration. The expert had more than thirty-seven years of trust and probate experience, consisting of litigation of more than thirty-five trust and probate cases. The expert educated trust officers and advised clients concerning issues of trust creation and management. *Williams v. Security Nat. Bank of Sioux City, Iowa,* 358 F.Supp.2d 782 (N.D. Iowa W. Div. 2005)

***Valuation:*** A fire department's district chief was ***not qualified*** to testify on the value of property loss from a fire because he had received very little training in estimating the value of property losses from fires. *Brantley v. State Farm Ins. Co.,* 37,601 La. App. 2 Cir. 1/28/04 (La. App. 2 Cir. 2004)

***Warnings:*** An engineer was ***qualified*** to testify on whether a paint manufacturer should have included a warning on a spray paint can. The engineer was licensed for over 40 years, had provided expert testimony sixteen times about technical issues (including warnings), and had education, professional, and technical experience in designing and implementing warnings. *Coleman v. Rust-Oleum Corp.,* 2005 WL 3448065 (W.D. Ky. 2005)

**Warnings:** A mechanical engineer was *qualified* to render an expert opinion on the adequacy of warnings for a fireplace. The engineer worked as a mechanical engineer after graduating from college, had written warnings for kitchen appliances and car signals, had conducted human factors research regarding readability and color lettering for purposes of designing warnings, and had published over 185 articles on packaging and merchandising subjects. *Santoro ex rel. Santoro v. Donnelly,* 340 F.Supp.2d 464 (S.D.N.Y. 2004)

**Warnings:** An expert in agricultural equipment design was *not qualified* to testify as to the adequacy of warnings on a tractor. The expert lacked specialized training in the adequacy of warnings and had only taken a workshop in human factors. *Schaaf v. Caterpillar, Inc.,* 286 F.Supp.2d 1070 (D.N.D. SW. Div. 2003)

**Water Rescue**: A water rescue expert was *not qualified* to opine on whether a drowning victim's life could have been saved if members of a private water rescue organization had entered the water and searched for him. The expert lacked the requisite medical training to qualify him to give this opinion. *Beck v. Haik,* 377 F.3d 624 (C.A. 6 Mich. 2004)

## 6.5 Qualifications Still a Legitimate and Important Issue After the Judge Finds the Expert Qualified

If the judge finds an expert qualified, the expert will be allowed to testify as an expert witness in a case.[3] This, however, does not in any way eliminate the issue of qualifications. **The expert's qualifications will remain a legitimate issue for direct and cross-examination because they are relevant to his credibility and to the weight the jury should give his testimony.** A discussion of some of the more common areas of cross-examination inquiry regarding an expert's qualifications follows.

*Gaps in the expert's CV*

When trying to challenge an expert's credibility, counsel may focus on any gaps in the expert's CV. An expert witness should be prepared to explain any such gaps.

**Example 6.52: Explanation of gap in CV**
Q. I see here a gap on your resume from May 1996 to September 1996. What were you doing at that time?
A. I took the summer off to volunteer in an AIDS clinic in South Africa.

*Licensing*

Many records from professional licensing organizations may be easily and readily available to a cross-examining attorney apart from the discovery process. These records could include college transcripts. An expert witness should be prepared to be questioned about any such records as they may affect her credibility. Experts are well advised to obtain and maintain all required professional licenses and to avoid any activity that may result in professional complaints being filed against them with licensing agencies.

**Example 6.53: Explanation of license suspension**
Q. I see here your license was suspended in 1997.
A. Yes, I was late paying the renewal fee.

---

[3] Assuming the expert testimony is not excluded for another reason.

## Education

If an expert witness has a questionable academic background, he can expect to be questioned about this during cross-examination. He might also be questioned about his lacking advanced education, especially if this contrasts with the opposing attorney's experts. Experts who have had long and distinguished careers should not be overly concerned with these questions for two reasons. One, they may backfire with jurors who lack stellar academic credentials. Two, how or where an expert was educated 30 or 40 years ago has very little to do with how much the expert knows about the issue at hand.

> **Example 6.54: Education questions**
> **Q.** I have here your college transcript. Isn't it a fact that your GPA was only 2.2?
> **Q.** You don't have a graduate degree in this field, do you?
> **Q.** You were asked to leave Yale twice, were you not?
> **Q.** The last formal education you had was in high school?
> **Q.** You didn't graduate with any kind of honors, did you?

## Professional writings

Publications may increase a witness's credibility with a jury. If a forensic expert "wrote the book" on a particular area, this may score points with the jury. If, however, an expert witness has not published in a particular area, this may be brought out on cross-examination as a way to lessen her credibility. This is especially true if the opposing expert is well published.[4] Publications are also an effective way of promoting a forensic practice (see Chapter 18).

> **Example 6.55: Lack of publications**
> **Q.** You haven't published anything in this area, have you?

## Experience

Practical, recent, relevant, hands-on experience—or the lack thereof—may be very important to a jury as far as an expert's qualifications are concerned. An expert witness should be prepared to answer any questions about his real-world experience. This is a particular area of concern if the expert is an academic or if he is retired and now only consults and testifies. It is also of particular concern when the expert's experience does not exactly match up with what's at issue in the case.

> **Example 6.56: Experience questions**
> **Q.** Doctor, when was the last time you actually delivered a baby?
> **Q.** I realize that you have a doctorate in mechanical engineering, sir. You don't have any experience regarding brake repair, do you?
> **Q.** You've never designed one of these, have you?
> **Q.** Is it fair to say that you have been basically retired for the last 5 years?

---

[4] If an expert has published, then her writings can be used to impeach her testimony if they contradict what she says on the stand.

*Training and certification*
Any lack of training or certification can be brought out during cross-examination. Once again, this is most likely to occur if the opposing expert has more training or certification.

**Example 6.57: Training questions**
Q. You're not board certified, are you?
Q. You haven't taken any continuing education courses in this area, have you?

*Knowledge of relevant literature*
Experts will likely be questioned on the relevant literature in the field to show that they do not keep up. Experts are well advised to keep current with the literature relating to the specific topics on which they testify.

**Example 6.58: Literature questions**
Q. Do you keep current with the literature in your field?
Q. Have you read such and such article?

*Past mistakes*
An expert will likely be questioned on any past professional mistakes. Experts who do not admit ever making any mistakes are not credible.

**Example 6.59: Past mistakes**
Q. What is the biggest mistake you have made in your professional life?
Q. Have you ever admitted that you made a mistake while testifying?
Q. You were fired from that job, weren't you?

## 6.6 Avoiding Qualifications Problems
Experts want to avoid being found to be not qualified to testify in a particular case because such a finding will be used against them in future cases. Experts should act with an abundance of caution and take all steps necessary to avoid working in cases where there is a reasonable chance of their being found not qualified.

*1. Stay within one's area of expertise*
The further an expert strays from her actual area of expertise, the more likely she is to:

- be questioned about her qualifications,
- be found not qualified,
- have her testimony limited, and
- be cross-examined at length.

Experts should aggressively police themselves and avoid any cases where they have any doubt about their qualifications. Testifying in cases where you don't feel very qualified is short-sighted and will come back to haunt you.

*2. Maintain an accurate CV*
The expert should give his retaining attorney a complete and accurate CV without any mistakes, exaggerations, untruths, or material omissions. (Please see Chapter 7 on

bulletproofing a CV.) Inaccurate CVs smack of sloppiness and dishonesty. They will devastate an expert's credibility.

*3. Discuss the role of the expert in the case at hand with the retaining attorney*
The expert should discuss with counsel what the expert's role will be and what issues and areas he will be asked to state his opinions on. An expert should decline cases in which he does not feel qualified.

*4. Tell the truth*
The expert should tell the truth when retaining counsel questions him about his qualifications, experience, and training. He should be prepared to accept the fact that he may not be qualified in the case at hand.

*5. Beware of large cases*
Qualifications are most likely to be challenged in significant cases where a lot of money is at stake. Experts should be especially careful about being truly qualified before agreeing to testify in such big cases.

## 6.7 Conclusion
The judge will initially decide, as a matter of law, whether an expert is qualified to testify. She will base her decision upon the expert's knowledge, skill, experience, training, and education. Even if an expert is found qualified by the judge, the expert's qualifications remain a legitimate area of inquiry during cross-examination. Experts should help bolster their qualifications by continuing to gain hands-on experience, publishing, teaching, maintaining professional society memberships, participating in continuing education, and keeping current with the relevant literature in their field. Experts should decline working on cases if they have any reasonable doubt concerning their qualifications.

# Chapter 7  Bulletproofing an Expert CV

## 7.1  Introduction

The expert's curriculum vitae (CV) is *crucially* important.  The CV is usually the first document retaining counsel will review when she considers whether to retain an expert.  It will also be closely scrutinized by *opposing* counsel.  A poorly drafted CV can and will provide substantial ammunition to an attorney set on discrediting an expert witness.  It is, therefore, extremely important that the CV be drafted and proofed carefully and updated as soon as an event occurs that warrants an update.  This chapter provides specific advice on how to prepare, maintain, and proof a CV.

## 7.2  Currency

The CV summarizes an individual's professional accomplishments.  It is important to keep one's CV current and up to date.  Failure to do so will make an expert witness look sloppy or lazy.  In some circumstances, it can even be used to make him look dishonest.  Experts need to find the time to keep their CVs up to date.

Many experts fail to keep CVs up to date for the simple reason that they are too busy.  To better maintain the currency of his CV, the wise expert should adopt a specific protocol for updating it and then stick to that procedure.  Mistakes and omissions are far more likely to occur with CVs that are not updated immediately upon an event which would warrant updating such as giving a talk, publishing a paper, changing employment, etc.  As such, it is best practice to get in the habit of updating your CV as soon as an event occurs which warrants an update. It is recommended that this be done personally and not be delegated to support staff.  It is also good practice to include the date on which the CV was last updated at the bottom of the document so that all readers, including the expert, are aware of this.

## 7.3  Typos

Typographical errors simply must be avoided on CVs.  When retaining counsel sees a typographical error or errors on a CV, she may conclude that the expert is sloppy and she may decline to hire the expert.  When opposing counsel finds a typographical error or errors on a CV, these will be pointed out during cross-examination to make the expert appear sloppy, as if he rushes, or is just plain stupid.  An expert does not want opposing counsel to be able to argue, in effect, that his opinion shouldn't be believed because he can't even get his own CV correct.

To avoid typographical errors in CVs it is best to carefully proof your CV *and* to have it carefully proofed by another person such as your spouse or assistant.  Typographical errors on CVs are 100% avoidable.

## 7.4  Accuracy

Mistakes, misleading impressions, and intentional or unintentional inaccuracies should be avoided.  At best, these make an individual look sloppy and, at worst, they make her appear dishonest.  In either event, her credibility may suffer dearly.

It is especially important not to intentionally exaggerate, fabricate, or be dishonest in a CV. This means that the expert needs to describe items with sufficient detail, accuracy, and clarity so that the reader is not misled. Credibility is the key to one's value as an expert witness. Veracity on a CV can and will be used to prove or disprove an expert's credibility while testifying. As noted by this book's authors in a previous work:

> You can assume that counsel will have a copy of your latest as well as prior versions of your curriculum vitae (CV). It is extremely important that your CV contain no exaggerations or inaccuracies. If you did not graduate from MIT, summa cum laude, your CV should not indicate that you did. The date that you received a degree can also be used in cross-examination. If you list yourself as an author of a book or article and you were in fact only a co-author, you are opening yourself up to be damaged during cross-examination. If counsel can show that you exaggerated your CV, he can make the argument that you are exaggerating when giving your opinion. Even worse, if there is an obvious falsehood on your CV, counsel can portray you as a liar.[1]

Problem areas with accuracy and misleading entries include:

- listing the expert as an author, where in fact she was only a co-author (see Section 7.14),
- listing under "Publications" a work that has been submitted for publication, but that has not been published (see Section 7.14),
- listing events that have not yet occurred on a CV (for example, a future presentation), and
- omitting articles or presentations from a CV.[2]

## 7.5 Gaps in the CV

The first thing any lawyer will look for are any gaps contained in a CV. For example, are the years 1982 to 1983 unaccounted for? Did the expert actually graduate college in two years, or is she trying to hide the two years that she spent at a junior college? Counsel may create a timeline to determine if any periods on a CV do not match precisely with an expert's educational and work activities. Time gaps are red flags for opposing counsel. If there are gaps in an expert's CV, she can expect to face questions at deposition or trial such as those in the following example.

### Example 7.1: Questioning gap in CV
When you left the years 1982 to 1983 out of your CV, you were attempting to mislead the jury, weren't you?

It is good practice to fill in the gaps in a CV. This is true even if a person is not particularly proud of what she accomplished during that time. An expert's most valued asset is her credibility. One's credibility is more likely to be damaged by an intentional omission on a CV than by whatever it was that the expert didn't want to report. Juries may forgive the

---

[1] Steven Babitsky and James J. Mangraviti, Jr., *How to Excel During Cross-Examination: Techniques for Experts That Work* (Falmouth, MA: SEAK, Inc., 1997) 27.
[2] Opposing counsel can easily find these through an Internet search.

fact that an expert flunked out of the first college she went to thirty years ago. They will be far less likely to forgive their being intentionally deceived.[3]

## 7.6  Unearned Titles and Certifications

The listing of what are in effect "mail order" degrees is extremely problematic. Experts should avoid obtaining and listing certifications, titles, or designations that they in effect purchased and did not truly earn. Sophisticated counsel has access to lists of organizations that offer fancy sounding titles and designations in return for the payment of a fee. When, during cross-examination, it is revealed that an expert attended no courses, took no tests, and obtained the designation by being "grandfathered in," his credibility as an expert can be destroyed quickly.[4] Most sophisticated experts avoid this potential problem by leaving this kind of unearned title, designation, or certification off of their CVs.

## 7.7  Listing Multiple Areas of Expertise

Experts may sometimes list many different areas of expertise on their CVs. This is often done in an effort to obtain more cases. The problem is, listing many different specialties on a CV can often lead to a damaging line of questioning on cross-examination which implies that the expert is a jack of all trades and master of none. Even where an expert actually has expertise in many areas, it is probably best to avoid listing each of these on the CV. Even if it's true, it may be hard for a jury to believe that the expert is a true expert on so many areas as opposed to being a hired gun.

## 7.8  Self-Serving Subjective Characterizations

Experts should avoid self-serving, subjective characterizations on their CVs. For example, referring to oneself as a "nationally known expert." Such statements can often be shown on cross-examination to be, at best, puffery and self-aggrandizing. It is far better to list objective reasons that show impressive credentials (publications, awards, lectures, etc.) than to subjectively characterize your own qualifications.

## 7.9  Extraneous Information

Experts commonly make the mistake of including superfluous information in their CVs. Extraneous matter usually only serves the purpose of making opposing counsel's job of cross-examining the expert that much easier by providing information counsel would have otherwise had no knowledge of. Examples include:

- Social Security numbers,
- birth date,
- past testimony with or without a results "scorecard,"
- political affiliations,
- religious activities and affiliations,

---

[3] It is wise for experts to point out any gaps in their CVs to retaining counsel. In this way, retaining counsel can ask the expert to explain the gaps during direct examination. The negative impact of these gaps should be diminished if they are brought out on direct rather than cross-examination.

[4] For example, "You took no test. All you did was pay the $800 and you got the designation. Isn't that the case?"

- associations with controversial, lightening rod organizations such as the NRA or NARAL, and
- names of the expert's children.

## 7.10 Multiple CVs

Many experts make the mistake of having multiple CVs. These could include a short one for quick and easy faxing, one that emphasizes certain kinds of experience or expertise, and (worst of all) one that is plaintiff- and another that is defense-oriented. Experts should assume that counsel has access to *all* their CVs. Counsel can use the existence of multiple CVs to damage one's credibility.

### Example 7.2: Intentional omission on one version of CV
Isn't it true that you intentionally omitted your work on behalf of the insurance industry from this CV?

As the above example illustrates, it is better practice to have one complete, accurate CV and to keep that CV up to date.

## 7.11 Memberships, Affiliations, and Licenses

One of the challenges for the expert who has a long, detailed CV is to keep it current. It is not uncommon for experts to list twenty, forty, fifty, or more scientific or professional societies that they are or have been involved with. If an individual just lists the affiliations without dates, he leaves the impression that he is still actively involved in all of the societies or organizations. This will often come back to haunt the expert on cross-examination.

### Example 7.3: Listing a membership that is no longer current on CV
**Q.** You listed the Managed Care Society of America on your CV under scientific societies. Are you a member in good standing of that organization?
**Q.** What about the next professional society you listed?

It is better practice to list the societies and organizations along with the dates of active involvement. When there is still active involvement, the expert can list the organization and note his membership from the date he first joined until the present.

### Example 7.4: Showing dates of membership on CV
American Cancer Society 1989–Present.

Professional memberships are proper on a CV and membership in these can be used to help prove an expert's qualifications. One should not, however, place undue emphasis on a membership that only required a fee. Overly emphasizing such memberships can be used against experts during cross-examination.

## 7.12 Honorary Degrees and Memberships

To avoid misimpressions, *honorary* memberships or degrees should be listed as such.

### Example 7.5: When a degree or membership is honorary, say so
Honorary member California Research Committee in Nutrition (2002)
Ph.D., Columbia University (Honorary) (1996)

Failure to do so may make an expert appear dishonest and can be used against her during cross-examination.

### 7.13 Expert Witness Experience

Many experts make the mistake of listing the number of cases, states, and law firms they have been involved with in their expert witness work. They want readers to think that they must be good based on their volume of work. This type of inclusion in the CV may come in many forms, such as the following.

"Has served as an expert witness or consultant on cases in 42 states,"

*or*

"Consultant to the law firms of:

Kistin, Babitsky, Latimer, and Beitman
13 Falmouth Heights Road
Falmouth, Massachusetts 02540

and

Duff, Mangraviti, and Keefe
28 State Street
Boston, Massachusetts  02110,"

*or*

"Performed over 5,000 Independent Medical Evaluations,"

*or*

Testimonial Experience
1. *Smith v. Jones* (Duff, Mangraviti & Keefe) Mass. Superior Court, Plaintiff, $3.7 million jury verdict for plaintiff
2. *Frist v. Reid* (Gordon and Babitsky) New York Supreme Court, Defense, favorable defense settlement after expert deposition

These types of entries in a CV should be avoided. They are irrelevant to one's expertise and may provide counsel with ample ammunition for cross-examination. The potential areas of cross-examination inquiry that could result from such an inclusion include bias, hired-gun status, sources and amount of revenue earned, work on previous cases, personal relationship with counsel, that the expert is "keeping score," that the expert is interested in the outcome and trying to "win," and the propensity to testify only for plaintiffs or defendants. As such, these types of entries should not be included on a CV.

### 7.14 Writing and Publications

Forensic experts often get into trouble when listing their writings and publications on their CVs. Care should be taken to be completely accurate in all claims. Was the expert the "author," a "co-author," or one of fourteen contributors to an article, chapter, or book? The differences may at first seem subtle and perhaps even insignificant. Upon cross-examination, however, the expert who exaggerates about his publications can be at risk.

**Example 7.6: Result of exaggeration on CV**
**Q.** So, when you testified that you authored six books on warning labels, you actually meant to say you contributed to these books. Would that be more accurate and less misleading to the jury?

An expert's attempts to increase the number of her publications by claiming responsibility for publications she did not write is a serious mistake. Consider the following example.

**Example 7.7: Self-aggrandizing language will backfire**
Dr. Binder's research and educational activities concentrating in hematology have resulted in over 300 publications including some 60 chapters and books.

Such an item will open up an expert to questions about what she actually wrote, why she inflated the number of publications on her CV, and why she was attempting to mislead the fact finder or jury. It is better practice to not inflate the number of publications, their importance, or their significance. The expert who understates rather than overstates is in a much stronger position to withstand close questioning by counsel on cross-examination.

Another common mistake made by experts is to list a work that has only been accepted for publication as opposed to actually being published. This is an easy inaccuracy for attorneys to discover because the publication in question will not show up on electronic literature searches. Counsel will use such a mistake to show that the expert is misleading the jury. As such, it is better practice for experts to either only list a publication once it has actually been published or to specify in a separate section writings that have not yet been published but have been accepted for publication.

## 7.15 Form
There are many ways to lay out a CV. The form is mostly a matter of personal preference. (Appendix T contains some sample CVs.)

## 7.16 CVs on Web Pages
Many experts now have their own or corporate Web pages. The CVs that are listed on the Web pages are frequently inconsistent with the hard copies distributed by the expert and filed with the court. The reason for this is simple: the person in charge of the Web page does not update the expert's CV as frequently or in the same fashion as the expert does. To avoid this problem, the expert should change the hard copy and the Web site CV at the same time and in the same fashion. The goal is to avoid having inconsistent CVs—a situation that is a fertile area for cross-examination.

## 7.17 Legal Requirements to Produce a CV
An expert who fails to provide his curriculum vitae (CV) as required by applicable discovery rules[5] or court orders can jeopardize not only the admissibility of his testimony, but, in some instances, the case itself. Consider the following examples.

---

[5] See, for example, Fed. R. Civ. Pro. 26, which requires the expert report to contain the expert's qualifications.

### Example 7.8: Failure to provide CV prior to testifying
*Seivewright v. State*, 7 P.3d 24 (Wyoming 2000)
In this criminal case, the expert, Dr. Huben, failed to provide his CV before he testified. The court pointed out the importance of the CV, which is relevant to qualifications and credibility. "In the case of an expert witness, in which qualifications go to both admissibility and weight, a vitae is material information by which the opposing party's counsel can challenge the expert's qualifications and credibility."

The Wyoming Supreme Court found that the trial court committed reversible error by allowing the expert to testify without producing his CV and report. The court stated:

> In accordance with W.R.Cr.P. 26.2, if a party elects not to comply with an order to deliver a statement, the district court has three options for sanctioning that behavior. The rule requires that the trial court "*shall* order" (1) that the witness not be permitted to testify; or (2) that the testimony of the witness be stricken from the record; or (3) if the attorney for the State elects not to comply, the court *shall* declare a mistrial if required in the interest of justice. W.R.Cr.P. 26.2(e). The rule is mandatory in all respects; it does not allow the district court any discretion to refuse to act in the face of uncontradicted allegations of discovery violations in a criminal prosecution. Allowing Seivewright to object to "particular questions" at trial is not one of the sanctions mandated by the rule. Thus, it cannot be argued that the district court's ruling was within the parameters of the rule despite its failure to determine if the discovery order has been violated.
>
> When Seivewright alleged the State failed to comply with W.R.Cr.P. 26.2, the district court should have ordered the State to submit the document for *in camera* inspection or held a hearing to determine whether the report and the curriculum vitae fell within the purview of the rule or the pretrial discovery order. Failure to take any action at all violated the rule and was reversible error.

### Example 7.9: Federal Rule 26 report, qualifications not provided, testimony barred
*Elswick v. Nichols*, 144 F.Supp.2d 758 (W.D. Kentucky 2001)
This was a medical malpractice case. The plaintiff's expert nurse was not permitted to testify in part because her Rule 26 report did not include a list of her qualifications. The court stated:

> The plaintiff's counsel submitted a copy of this report to the defense counsel. However, the defendants were never provided with Craig's qualifications, a list of her publications, any information regarding previous testimony by her, or a list of items that she reviewed in this case. Finally, there is no written report expressing Craig's opinions about the causation of Plaintiff Elswick's injury [FN4]. Discovery in this case is now closed. Clearly, these omissions indicate a substantial violation of Fed.R.Civ.P. 26(a). Therefore, Craig is unable to testify in this case as an expert witness because disclosures on this matter are clearly inadequate with respect to Rule 26(a). At 765.

**Comment:** For further information on the required contents of Federal Court Rule 26 expert reports, please see Section 10.2.

### Example 7.10: Qualifications not provided in Rule 26 report, testimony barred
*Campbell v. McMillan*, 83 F.Supp.2d 761 (S.D. Mississippi 2000)
The court found the designated expert's report inadequate and precluded the expert from testifying. The court stated:

> The fourth requirement mandates the expert to provide a list of his qualifications, including a list of all publications authored by the expert within the preceding ten years. This requirement was not met…
>
> Based on an analysis of both Federal Rule of Civil Procedure 26 and applicable case law, this Court finds that the expert designation and disclosure of the expert's report were deficient. Therefore, unless the Plaintiffs can come forward with an excusable reason for the inadequacies, the use of Murray as an expert witness at trial should be barred. *See* Fed.R.Civ.P. 37(c)(1). At 765.

**Example 7.11: Report without qualifications insufficient, expert must supplement or will be barred from testifying**

*Nguyen v. IBP, Inc.,* 162 F.R.D. 675 (D. Kansas 1995)

This case also involved an insufficient Rule 26 report.  The court stated:

> The disclosures served by plaintiff clearly and indisputably do not comply with Fed.R.Civ.P. 26(a)(2)(B).  The only document signed by the expert witness was a letter addressing the expert's opinions and the basis therefor, the data considered by the expert, and exhibits to be used as a summary of or support for the opinions.   While a curriculum vitae was provided, it was not signed by the witness and did not include publications authored by the witness within the past 10 years.  Although plaintiff, by interrogatory answer, provided the compensation agreement, this agreement was not a part of the report signed by the witness.  Plaintiff's counsel supplied a list of 137 patients about whom the witness had apparently testified during the 34 month period prior to October 28, 1994, and the dates of the deposition testimony.  No identification of the "cases" in which these depositions were given is provided.  The court or administrative agency in which the depositions were taken is not provided.  Although an attorney's name is provided as to most of the patients, in many instances the first or last name of the attorney is missing.  The telephone numbers are not supplied for the attorneys for 55 patients.  The list is not signed by the witness.  It includes entries for less than three years rather than for four years as required by the rule. At 679.
>
> Plaintiff's failure to provide a report including a statement of the expert's compensation agreement, the expert's qualifications, or an identity of the publications authored by the expert during the past 10 years, in light of the lack of any such publications, is harmless since the facts were otherwise supplied and the failure may be cured by simply having the witness sign a disclosure to these facts.  As noted above, the failure to provide the listing of cases is not harmless.  The court will allow the plaintiff to provide a supplemental disclosure which corrects the deficiencies identified herein within 40 days from the date of the filing of this order, otherwise, Dr. Shechter will not be permitted to testify at the trial of the action. At 682.

## 7.18  Conclusion

Experts who are scrupulously accurate, complete, and honest in crafting their CVs and who keep their CVs current and mistake-free enhance and protect their value as expert witnesses.

# Chapter 8  Properly Forming and Expressing Expert Opinions

## 8.1  Introduction

One of the primary responsibilities of an expert is to render an opinion that will assist the trier of fact. This opinion needs to be stated in a legally sufficient manner and must be based upon reliable facts, data, and methodology. Experts can expect to be closely questioned on their opinions, how they were formed, and the facts and data upon which they are based.

## 8.2  Properly Stating an Expert Opinion

In most civil cases, the legal requirements for stating an expert opinion is related directly to the burden of proof that exists. That burden of proof is a "preponderance of the evidence," "more likely than not," or "more than 50% likely." This is a much lesser burden of proof than the "beyond a reasonable doubt" standard with criminal cases.

The expert's opinion must satisfy the "preponderance of the evidence" burden of proof. This means that the expert must opine that it is more probable than not (there is more than a 50% probability) that his opinion is correct. Thus, an expert may give testimony in terms of an opinion that something could, or would, produce a certain result. The theory for admitting opinion testimony of this nature into evidence is that an expert witness's view regarding probabilities is often helpful in the determination of questions involving matters of science or technical or skilled knowledge.

The facts or scientific principles on which experts base their opinions must be sufficient to support reasonably accurate conclusions. Expert witnesses will not be barred from expressing opinions merely because they are not willing to state their conclusions with absolute certainty. However, expert opinions, if not stated in terms of the certain, must at least be stated in terms of the probable and not merely of the possible. The test of whether an expert's testimony expresses a reasonable probability is not based upon the use of "magic words" but is determined by looking at the entire substance of the expert's testimony. Although no magic words are required, certain phrases are commonly used by experts to express the idea that their opinions are based on at least a 51% probability. These phrases include:

- "based on a reasonable degree of medical certainty,"
- "based on a reasonable degree of scientific probability,"
- "based on a reasonable degree of scientific certainty,"
- "based on a reasonable degree of medical probability," and
- "more likely than not."

When an expert does not express the concept that she is at least 51% sure of her opinion, the opinion might be excluded by the judge. Thus, it is important to state an opinion in a way that clearly communicates that it is based upon a reasonable degree of probability and not just a mere possibility or speculation. Consider the following examples.

**Example 8.1: Magic words not required, but "conceivable" opinion not admissible**
*Daughtery v. Conley,* 906 So.2d 108 (Miss. App. 2004)
In this case, the appellate court affirmed a trial court's barring of the plaintiff's expert testimony for being speculative and not reliable. The plaintiff's experts had testified (see below) without confidence regarding causation by characterizing the causal relationship as being merely "conceivable." The court reasoned as follows:

> The central argument on appeal is whether Mississippi law requires expert medical testimony to be expressed in terms of medical probability or possibility. The issue, however, is not whether a specific word must be spoken during testimony. The Supreme Court's distinction in Pittman between the use of probability and possibility was employed in reference to the expert medical witness's ability to convey to the trial court the requisite level of reliability of the expert medical opinion. Neither Pittman nor Whittington should be misread simply as an exercise in form over substance. The mere use, or non-use, of the word probability in expert medical opinion testimony is never a substitute for determining the reliability of an expert medical opinion. The semantic illustration was not offered as a script for expert medical testimony, rather it reflects the substantive requirement that the expert medical opinion testimony must be reliable...
>
> At trial, Daughtery and Conley each presented expert medical testimony from two medical doctors. Conley's witnesses testified that the causal connection between this type of collision and an appendicitis was anecdotal and impossible respectively. Daughtery offered testimony from Steven Hayne, M.D. and Enrique Gomez, M.D. in support of his argument that there is a causal connection between the rear-end automobile collision and Daughtery's appendicitis. Dr. Gomez was the surgeon who performed the appendectomy. On direct examination, Dr. Gomez was asked the following:
>
> > **Q.**.....did you form an opinion, then, to a reasonable degree of medical probability as to whether or not in this particular case the seat belt and the—the trauma from the seat belt in the motor vehicle accident then was the cause of Mr. Daughtery's appendicitis?
> > **A.**.....given the events of this case and the timing of the onset of symptoms, it is quite conceivable that the patient's appendicitis was as a result of the vehicular accident.
>
> The following exchange occurred during the cross-examination of Dr. Gomez:
>
> > **Q.** When [Daughtery's counsel] called you for the first time, you told them, I've never seen that [causal connection] or I've never heard of that and I've never read of that, true?
> > **A.** I doubted it. I did—I did doubt it.
> > **Q.** And it wasn't until they sent you literature that you read that you came to the conclusion that it is conceivable?
> > **A.** Conceivable, yes.
> > **Q.** And that's the best word, isn't it?
> > **A.** Yes, conceivable.
>
> Dr. Gomez was then questioned about his physical examination of Daughtery:
>
> > **Q.** In addition to running tests on him, you examined his abdomen because he was complaining of abdominal pain?
> > **A.** Correct.
> > **Q.**.....you didn't find any sign of injury, did you?
> > **A.** No.
> > **Q.**.....in addition to that visual examination of the outside of his body, you did a CT examination of the inside of his body?
> > **A.** Correct.
> > **Q.** The CT scan didn't find any abnormalities in the appendix, did it?
> > **A.** Correct.

Q.....to a reasonable degree of medical certainty, did the automobile accident four days before he was originally taken to the emergency room in your opinion cause or contribute to cause the appendicitis that he ultimately suffered...?

A. It would be consistent with a product from the motor vehicle crash. It would in part meet Fowler's criteria reported in the Journal of the American Medical Association of 1938 in which he lists three criteria. The criteria would include that there was no previous abdominal pain and that—in the right lower quadrant; two, that there was a force directed upon the abdominal wall, which would be consistent in this case. And the third would not meet Fowler's criteria, that is, that the onset of pain would have occurred within [eight] hours to [forty-eight] hours. However, there's other literature, case presentations and the like that would indicate that the onset could be delayed at least five days. And that's in the British surgical literature as well as the American surgical literature. So Fowler's criteria would be met in part with the exception of the third criteria.

Dr. Haynes likewise stated his medical opinion on direct examination:

Q. And based upon the records you reviewed, the slide you reviewed, the literature you reviewed, your experience and education, to a reasonable degree of medical certainty did—in your opinion did the accident...cause or contribute to cause the appendicitis...?

A. It would be consistent with that.

Q. In the absence, then—assuming no evidence comes forward of those other [causes] of acute appendicitis, is there any other medically reasonable explanation in your opinion as to the cause of his appendicitis?

A. I do not know of any other explanation. I cannot exclude all potential causes of acute appendicitis. All I'm saying is consistent with a product of a motor vehicle crash.

On cross-examination, Dr. Haynes was questioned about his expert medical opinion and the materials on which it was based:

Q. Now, in this literature that has been provided to you [by plaintiff's counsel], can you tell me which one you think is most authoritative on the subject that acute appendicitis results more likely than not from an automobile accident?

A. I think each one of these. There are different levels of certainty described in the articles, but cumulatively I think that they indicate to my reading that there is an association in absence of other [causes].

On redirect, Dr. Hayne explained what items he relied upon in forming his expert medical opinion:

A. I think the most important thing would be looking at the standard in literature, and that was established almost [seventy] years ago in the Journal of the American Medical Association. It met two of the three criteria. The third criteria I think needs to be modified.

The trial court has "'considerable leeway in deciding in a particular case how to go about determining whether particular expert testimony is reliable.'" Mississippi Transp. Comm'n, 863 So.2d at 37(¶ 13) (quoting Kumho Tire, 526 U.S. at 152, 119 S.Ct. 1167). In the case below, the trial court allowed both parties to fully present their expert testimony. Both parties had every opportunity to fully present their arguments and evidence, and every witness was subjected to cross-examination. The evidence presented clearly reflects the existence of a theory within the medical community regarding a causal connection between automobile collisions and appendicitis. Dr. Gomez testified that the causal connection is conceivable, and Dr. Haynes testified that the appendicitis is consistent with a product of a motor vehicle crash and that his reading of the medical literature indicates that there is an association between the two events in the absence of other causes. The record also clearly reflects that the facts of this case do not even satisfy all three of the "Fowler criteria" which Daughtery presents in support of this causal theory. Even in drawing all favorable inferences from the evidence in Daughtery's behalf, the final analysis is clear. The trial court appropriately determined that Daughtery failed to present evidence sufficient to demonstrate that the theory of a causal connection between rear-impact vehicle collisions and appendicitis enjoys general acceptance within the medical community. It would have been inappropriate to charge the jury with ratifying a theory that is not generally accepted in the medical community, and which the medical community itself has not yet adopted. Therefore, we affirm the trial court's order granting a directed verdict in Conley's favor. At 110–113.

**Comment:** Better pre-trial preparation and communication with retaining counsel might have avoided this case being lost. Either the expert would have been prepared to express the opinion in a different way or counsel could have looked for another expert who would.

### Example 8.2: Speculative opinion lacking expert's confidence not admissible
*Morsicato v. Sav-On Drug Stores, Inc.,* 111 P.3d 1112 (Nev. 2005)
The court in this pharmacy malpractice case held that the trial judge had improperly admitted into evidence speculative expert testimony where the expert only couched his opinion in a legally sufficient way after he was warned by the court that his opinion would be struck otherwise. The court stated:

> The Morsicatos argue Dr. Schneck's expert testimony on causation was speculation and conjecture that failed to meet the requisite standard for expert testimony and therefore should have been stricken. We agree.
>
> A district court's decision to admit expert testimony is reviewed for an abuse of discretion. The district court's decision will not be overturned absent "a clear abuse of discretion."…
>
> Sav-On argues that even though Dr. Schneck's testimony was not made to a reasonable degree of medical probability, it was nevertheless admissible under the general standard of NRS 50.275 because it did not address an ultimate finding of fact.
>
> Not all medical expert testimony must be stated with a reasonable degree of medical probability. The standard for admissibility varies depending upon the expert opinion's nature and purpose….
>
> Since 1989, this court has held that "a medical expert is expected to testify only to matters that conform to the reasonable degree of medical probability standard." Furthermore, in dictum, this court has observed that expert testimony regarding causation must also rise to this level of certainty. As the Pennsylvania Supreme Court has recognized, one rationale for requiring such specificity with expert opinions is that "if the plaintiff's medical expert cannot form an opinion with sufficient certainty so as to make a medical judgment, there is nothing on the record with which a jury can make a decision with sufficient certainty so as to make a legal judgment." See, e.g., *Id.* at 671-72, 782 P.2d at 1304 (recognizing that testimony regarding causation must conform to the reasonable degree of medical probability standard); accord *Fitzgerald v. Manning,* 679 F.2d 341, 350 (4th Cir.1982) (in order to qualify on causation, the medical expert opinion cannot be stated in general terms but must be stated in terms of a reasonable degree of medical certainty).
>
> We conclude that medical expert testimony regarding standard of care and causation must be stated to a reasonable degree of medical probability. In this case, Dr. Schneck testified concerning an ultimate issue in the case, causation. He was not certain what caused Morsicato's injuries; however, he stated that he could offer a theory that was just as plausible as the theory that lindane caused the injury. He further testified that he ranked an autoimmune response as the most likely cause of the injury and recognized that this was inconsistent with Nevada's evidentiary standard. Only after the court explained that Dr. Schneck's testimony would be stricken unless he testified in accordance with Nevada law, did he state that more likely than not an autoimmune response was the most likely cause of the injuries. Dr. Schneck never stated his medical opinion to a reasonable degree of medical probability, however.
>
> Dr. Schneck's testimony was highly speculative and failed to meet the admissibility standard. Therefore, we conclude that the district court abused its discretion in failing to strike the testimony, and we reverse the district court's judgment and remand for a new trial on the issues of causation, contributory negligence, and damages, if any. At 1115–1116.

# PROPERLY FORMING AND EXPRESSING EXPERT OPINIONS

**Example 8.3: "Possibly," "may," and "apparently" not legally sufficient**
*Topp v. Leffers,* 838 N.E.2d 1027 (Ind. App. 2005)
This was a personal injury case evolving from an automotive accident. The court held that the plaintiff's medical expert's opinions were not certain enough to support a verdict for the plaintiff where the expert's opinion was presented in terms of "possibly" and "may." The court stated:

> A plaintiff's burden may not be carried with evidence based merely upon supposition or speculation. *Id.* at 877. Evidence establishing a mere possibility of cause or which lacks reasonable certainty or probability is not sufficient evidence by itself to support a verdict. *Id.* An expert medical opinion that lacks reasonable certainty, standing alone, is not sufficient to support a judgment. Litera, 692 N.E.2d at 901. "[E]xpert medical opinion couched in terms less than that of a reasonable degree of medical certainty; such as 'possible,' 'probable,' or 'reasonably certain,' are admissible and do have probative value. However, such medical testimony standing alone, unsupported by other evidence, is not sufficient to support a verdict...." *Colaw v. Nicholson,* 450 N.E.2d 1023, 1030 (Ind.Ct.App.1983).
>
> The expert opinions of Dr. Reecer and Dr. Schreier, standing alone, are not sufficient to sustain Topp's burden on the element of causation because they lack reasonable medical certainty. In his written report, Dr. Reecer stated, "Ms. Topp had prior spine complaints which could possibly have been aggravated by the accident." Appellant's App. at 150 (emphasis added). He went on to say, "All things considered, Ms. Topp may have had an aggravation of her preexisting spine complaints." *Id.* (emphasis added). During his deposition, Dr. Reecer again confirmed that he believed Topp may have had an aggravation of her pre-existing spine complaints. *Id.* at 211. In Litera, an expert medical witness testified that a patient's fall may have worsened his condition, and that it was possible that the patient would have reached his present condition at some point without the fall. We held that this testimony was not of sufficient certainty to sustain the judgment in favor of the injured patient. Litera, 692 N.E.2d at 901-02. Like the expert medical witness in Litera, Dr. Reecer uses the terms "possibly" and "may." Such testimony is not of sufficient certainty to show that Leffers' actions caused the aggravation of Topp's pre-existing injuries.
>
> In a letter dated May 10, 2001, Dr. Schreier wrote, "This examination and history in this 54 year old woman reveals evidence for subacute chronic mechanical spinal dysfunction, apparently due to the motor vehicle accident." Appellant's App. at 153 (emphasis added). Later, Dr. Schreier wrote that Topp "appears to have occipital neuralgia from a motor vehicle accident." *Id.* at 155 (emphasis added). On March 13, 2003, Dr. Schreier wrote, "I first saw Yvonne Topp in physical medicine clinic on 5/10/01 due to complaints suffered in a motor vehicle accident injury 11/24/00." *Id.* at 156. This last statement merely recounts facts and does not draw any conclusions regarding the cause of Topp's injuries. The first two statements draw conclusions about the cause of Topp's injuries, but these conclusions are prefaced by the use of the words "apparently" and "appears." Dr. Schreier's use of the words "apparently" and "appears" indicate that he believed it was possible that the November 2000 accident caused the aggravation of Topp's pre-existing injuries, but that he was not certain of this. Thus, Dr. Schreier's opinions are not of sufficient medical certainty to show that Leffers' actions caused the aggravation of Topp's pre-existing injuries. At 1033–1034.

**Comment:** Even if these opinions were admitted, an opinion hedged with words such as "possible" and "may" is not likely to carry significant weight with the jury. Experts are well advised to express their opinions with confidence.

**Example 8.4: Expert's testimony admissible when he used the term "reasonable degree of medical certainty"**
*Marron v. Stromstad,* 123 P.3d 992 (Alaska 2005)
The court in this case admitted an expert's testimony despite the fact that the expert did not have a complete grasp of all relevant facts. The court reasoned that the expert had expressed confidence

in his opinions and had explicitly stated that his opinions were based on a "reasonable degree of medical certainty." The court stated:

> Dr. Rubenstein's opinions were not overly speculative and they met the standards of medical certainty.
>
> Marron also claims that the superior court should have granted her motion in limine to exclude Dr. Rubenstein's testimony because "his opinions are speculative and do not meet the standards of medical certainty." Marron recites several specific facts related to her medical history and treatment of which Dr. Rubenstein was apparently unaware at the time of his deposition: whether Marron had suffered pain prior to the accident with Stromstad, "when the last time prior to his examination of her she had taken any prescription pain medication," and the half-life or length of effectiveness of her prescription drugs. We reject the argument that Dr. Rubenstein's testimony should have been precluded because it was speculative.
>
> In *Maddocks v. Bennett*, we stated that a medical expert's opinion must be within a "reasonable medical certainty" or the equivalent "reasonable medical probability" to be admissible. Maddocks indicates that "reasonable probability" is determined by the expert's own confidence in the expert's testimony. Dr. Rubenstein himself stated that he believed his conclusions to be within "a reasonable degree of medical certainty" based on Marron's medical records and MRI results. At 1008.

**Comment:** Using magic legal words is very common. The one caveat is that the expert should not use any term unless he knows what it means. Otherwise, he can be subjected to a devastating cross-examination.

**Example 8.5: "Probably" sufficient to meet reasonable degree of medical certainty standard**
*Wackenhut Corp. v. Jones*, 40 S.W.3d 333 (Ark. App. 2001)
The employer and the workers' compensation carrier brought an appeal of a decision of the Workers' Compensation Commission that the claimant's left knee replacement was a reasonable and necessary consequence of a compensable injury. On appeal, the court held that the doctor's use of the word "probably" was sufficient to satisfy the requirement that a medical opinion addressing compensability be stated within a reasonable degree of medical certainty.

The doctor who performed the knee replacement surgery testified at deposition that the claimant was bowlegged, which caused the load on the inner part of her knee to be dramatically higher than it was on the outer compartment of the knee. He further testified that over the years that he treated the claimant, the condition of her knees deteriorated.

> [The doctor] unequivocally stated that appellee's compensable injury was the start of the rapid deterioration of appellee's knee, that it was "probably predestined that this was going to occur, and the job injury just happened to be what triggered this one knee." When asked whether the deterioration would have taken place as quickly without the job injury, [the doctor] replied, "That would be a purely speculative guess, because under my very eyes the opposite knee had the same process occur. So it may well have been predestined that it was going to occur, it just so happened that the job injury started the process on the left side." When asked by appellants' attorney whether it was his belief that the job injury probably exacerbated or accelerated the need for treatment of appellee's condition, [the doctor] replied, "That's correct."
>
> On redirect examination, the following dialogue occurred between [the doctor] and appellee's counsel:
>
> Appellee's Counsel: In terms of when [appellee] would have probably faced this [knee replacement] in the future had not this injury occurred, what, in your opinion—when would this have probably manifested itself to a degree that she would have had that knee replacement?
> Doctor: You know, I can't imagine. I think—. All I can really say is that it just probably occurred sooner.

> Appellee's Counsel: Any figure, in your best professional judgment, of how much sooner because of the job-related injury?
> Doctor: Probably the best guesstimate of how to come up with that number would have to be based on the—. By January of 1999, both knees had reached a 4+ degenerative level.
> Appellee's Counsel: That's the most severe?
> Doctor: That's as bad as it can be. And this, of course, is when I referred her […] to have total replacement or osteotomy. But in any event, one knee had an injury and one knee didn't have an injury prior to that, and they both ended up at the same level at the same time. So, you know, I guess I really—. The only timetable I can give you is that I think it happened quicker than it probably would have without the job injury, but probably not a wide time span different. At 335–36.

The defendants challenged the certainty of the expert's opinion, but the court affirmed the award to the plaintiff, stating:

> An expert opinion is to be judged upon the entirety of the opinion, and it is not validated or invalidated on the presence or lack of "magic words." *Tyson Foods, Inc. v. Griffin,* 61 Ark.App. 222, 966 S.W.2d 914 (1998). In the present case, [the doctor] stated that the job injury began the deterioration process in appellee's left knee, and that the need for the total left knee replacement probably occurred sooner as a result of the compensable job injury. "Probably" is defined in *The American Heritage Dictionary,* New College Edition, as "most likely," and it was not expressly prohibited by the Supreme Court's decisions in *Frances* and *Crudup, supra.* We hold that use of the word "probably" is sufficient to satisfy the requirement of Ark.Code Ann. § 11-9-102(16)(B) (Supp.1999) that medical opinions addressing compensability must be stated within a reasonable degree of medical certainty. At 336.

### Example 8.6: Damages expert's opinion within $6 million range sufficiently certain where underlying facts in dispute

*Belleville Toyota, Inc. v. Toyota Motor Sales, U.S.A., Inc.,* 738 N.E.2d 938 (Ill. App. 5 Dist. 2000)
A Toyota dealership sued the authorized importer of new Toyota vehicles into the United States and the wholesale distributor of those vehicles for breach of dealer agreements and a violation of the Motor Vehicle Franchise Act. The trial court entered judgment on jury verdicts for the plaintiff. The defendants appealed. On appeal, the defendants claimed that the plaintiff's damages expert's opinion was not certain enough to establish causation of damages. The court disagreed:

> Defendants' next attack on the causation issue is based on the fact that [the expert] testified to eight different potential awards that encompassed a range from approximately $5 million to approximately $11 million. Defendants contend that [the expert]'s presentation of eight possibilities within a range of $6 million establishes that plaintiff was unable to establish damages within a reasonable degree of certainty. Plaintiff responds that the alternative damage estimates were entirely appropriate because the correct measure of damages depended upon the outcome of factual disputes that the jury had to resolve. For example, if the jury found that there was no shortage of vehicles, it might still consider damages based on plaintiff's theory that an order system was in existence. We agree with plaintiff that since alternative theories and different periods were involved, it was appropriate for different estimates of damages based on the different factors to be supplied to the jury. [Citations omitted.] At 946.

### Example 8.7: Equivocal statement of opinion ("suggestion" of causal relationship) not sufficient

*Wintz By and Through Wintz v. Northrop Corp.,* 110 F.3d 508 (7th Cir. 1997)
Under Illinois law, to serve as the sole basis for a conclusion that an act was the proximate cause of the plaintiff's injury, an expert must be able to testify with a reasonable degree of medical certainty that a proximate cause existed. In light of the expert's statement on cross-examination that he was not stating with any degree of medical certainty that the plaintiff's problems had "at any time" been

caused by bromide, the court concluded that his equivocal statement during direct that there was a "suggestion" that the symptoms were "related" to bromide was insufficient, standing alone, to raise an issue of fact as to proximate causation of the plaintiff's short-term problems.

### Example 8.8: Absolute certainty not required
*Nelson v. Ford Motor Co.,* 150 F.3d 905 (8th Cir. 1998)
The plaintiffs asserted that the district court erred by admitting testimony that there were no scratches in the notch where the jack was to be placed and that there was a tear elsewhere on the underbody of the car, indicating that the jack had been mispositioned. They contended that Ford's expert conceded in his deposition that it was not possible to state with absolute certainty that the jack had been incorrectly placed. The court held that the expert testimony was admissible and that any uncertainty in the expert's opinion was a factor the jury could consider in weighing his testimony.

### Example 8.9: Reasonable degree of certainty required
*Kannankeril v. Terminix International, Inc.,* 128 F.3d 802 (3rd Cir. 1997)
Under New Jersey law, medical expert testimony must be made with a reasonable degree of certainty.

### Example 8.10: Speculative expert testimony not admissible
*Crawford v. Seufert,* 388 P.2d 456 (Or. 1964)
The expert witness, an M.D., admitted that his opinion rested upon speculation. The case was an action for damages arising out of an automobile collision. The plaintiff claimed that the accident caused her to suffer from severe perforations of the diverticulum. There was other evidence that the perforations were a result of a chronic degenerative ailment. The physician was to testify that the particular perforation was induced by the collision. On cross-examination, the doctor was asked about the three different types of perforated diverticula, and he admitted that there was no difference between that which he saw and the others.

> **Q.** Diverticula do perforate into the mesentery?
> **A.** Yes.
> **Q.** And you don't know why?
> **A.** No.
> **Q.** And then you necessarily had to speculate in this case, based upon the history of the accident that had been given you, that that would be a cause?
> **A.** Yes.

The court set aside the jury verdict in favor of the plaintiff. The court held that such speculative evidence, as a matter of law, could not support a finding that the accident caused the medical condition. It stated: "For medical opinion testimony to have any probative value, it must at least advise the jury that the inference drawn by the doctor is more probably correct than incorrect."

**Comment:** Note how the expert was trapped by opposing counsel's use of the phrase "had to speculate."

### Example 8.11: Firsthand knowledge of event in question not required
*Derrick v. Norton,* 983 S.W.2d 529 (Mo. App. E.D. 1998)
At issue was why a full-length mirror fell off a closet door and injured the plaintiff. The following exchange took place with the plaintiff's expert architect:

**Q.** If there hadn't been any earthquake or some foreign object causing the mirror to fall, do you have an opinion as to the cause of the fall the mirror?

**A.** Technically I don't know why the mirror fell because I was not there. I know that it was—

**Counsel:** Your honor, let me object to any further editorialization as the witness has said he does not know why in answer to a question as to whether he has an opinion.

**The court:** Sustained.

The court found that it was an abuse of discretion for the trial judge to exclude the opinion merely because of the above exchange. The court reasoned that although the expert used the words "I don't know," it was clear from the rest of his statement that he was merely noting that he had not personally observed the occurrence and was not denying that he had any opinion at all.

### Example 8.12: Expert testimony not based on "reasonable medical probability" should not be admitted

*Antoine-Tubbs v. Local 513, Air Transport Division,* 50 F.Supp.2d 601 (N.D. Tex. 1998)

At issue was whether workplace stress caused preeclampsia in the plaintiff. The plaintiff's expert osteopath was asked if she could state with reasonable medical probability what caused the preeclampsia in the plaintiff. The witness replied, "You can't say that." The court found that the witness's testimony on this issue should not be admitted because it amounted to only subjective belief and unsupported speculation.

### Example 8.13: Mathematical certainty not required where expert offers credible support for opinion

*Boudreau v. S/V Shere Khan C,* 27 F.Supp.2d 72 (D. Me. 1998)

At issue was the cause of a fire aboard a yacht. The defendant's main attacks on the basis of the plaintiff's expert were the expert's lack of mathematical certainty about certain contributing fires in the leak and fire. The court held that the expert testimony was admissible because the expert testified credibly that such mathematical certainty was not necessary for him to render a competent opinion and explained credibly how he was able to determine the cause of the fire from his two firsthand inspections of the vessel and the crew reports of the circumstances of the fire.

### Example 8.14: "Might" or "could" sufficient

*Hawn v. Fritcher,* 703 N.E.2d 109 (Ill. App. 4 Dist. 1998)

At issue was whether an auto accident caused a plaintiff's chondromalacia. The plaintiff's orthopedic surgeon testified as follows:

**Q.** So, is your opinion, as to whether it might or could have been caused by the auto accident, is your answer yes or no?

**A.** Yes, it could.

The court held the testimony admissible. It reasoned that the witness had testified to a reasonable degree of medical certainty that the accident "might or could" have caused the condition in the plaintiff's knees.

## 8.3 Facts and Data Relied Upon

The sophisticated expert understands what she is permitted to rely upon in forming an expert opinion. Federal Rule of Evidence 703 provides that the facts or data upon which the expert bases her opinion need not be admissible in evidence if of a type "reasonably relied upon by experts in the particular field in forming opinions or inferences upon the subject." For more information on what experts can and cannot rely upon, including numerous case examples, please see Section 5.3.

## 8.4  Ultimate Issue

Except in criminal cases where the issue is the mental state of a defendant, experts are permitted to give opinions that embrace "an ultimate issue to be decided by the trier of fact."[1] Experts who are qualified to testify are permitted to offer their opinions on ultimate issues, such as causation, negligence, speed, intoxication, handwriting, value, and damages. For more information, including case examples, please see Section 5.3.

## 8.5  Foundation of an Opinion

The expert's opinion is only as strong as the facts and data upon which it is based.  The rules permit an expert to testify regarding her opinion without first testifying to the underlying facts or data.[2]  This does not mean, however, that the testifying expert will not have to disclose these facts or data.  The facts and data upon which an expert bases her opinions are legitimate areas of cross-examination that she needs to be prepared to address.  In attacking these facts and data, counsel will try to prove "garbage in, garbage out."  Counsel may also try to show that the expert did not consider key information, did not have time to do an adequate analysis, and that the information considered was flawed.  (Each of these lines of cross-examination attack is discussed below in Section 8.7 on cross-examination challenges.)

## 8.6  Methodology

Experts can expect to be scrutinized closely regarding the methodology they used in determining their opinions.  In federal court, and in some state courts, the judge will act as a gatekeeper to exclude from evidence unreliable expert testimony that was not based upon sound methodology.  Recall that under Federal Rule of Evidence 702, expert testimony is only admissible if "(1) the testimony is sufficiently based upon reliable facts or data, (2) the testimony is the product of reliable principles and methods, and (3) the witness has applied the principles and methods reliably to the facts of the case." Under the *Daubert v. Merrell Dow Pharmaceuticals, Inc.*[3] line of cases, a judge in a jurisdiction following *Daubert* will evaluate carefully the expert's methodology in forming her opinion.  The judge will consider several factors, including, but not limited to:

1.  whether the theory or technique used by the expert can be, and has been, tested,
2.  whether the theory or technique has been subjected to peer review and publication,
3.  the known or potential rate of error of the method used, and
4.  the degree of the method's or conclusion's acceptance within the relevant scientific community.

---

[1] Fed. Rule Evid. 704(a).

[2] Fed. Rule Evid. 705, Disclosure of Facts or Data Underlying Expert Opinion: "The expert may testify in terms of opinion or inference and give reasons therefor without first testifying to the underlying facts or data, unless the court requires otherwise. The expert may in any event be required to disclose the underlying facts or data on cross-examination."

[3] 113 S. Ct. 2786 (1993).

Even if the judge does not exclude an expert's opinion under Rule 702 or the *Daubert* line of cases, an expert's methodology and the reliability of the facts and data upon which the opinion is based will remain legitimate areas of inquiry on cross-examination. This is because the expert's methodology is relevant to the weight the fact finder should give the expert's testimony. (Methodology is discussed in much greater detail in Chapter 9.) Experts are well advised to form opinions based upon reliable facts and data.

## 8.7  Cross-Examination Challenges to an Expert's Opinions
Experts can expect to be cross-examined extensively about their opinions. Areas of inquiry that the expert should anticipate and prepare for (and hope to avoid through working diligently and forming well-reasoned, well-supported opinions) include the following.

*Sources of information and assumed facts*
Were they reliable? Are they biased? For example, an oral history provided by the plaintiff or by counsel.

*Cherry-picking facts and data*
Did the expert only use facts and data that fit with his conclusions and opinions?

*Literature*
What literature supports the opinion? What does not?

*Testing or research not done*
Was there anything the expert would have liked to have done that she was unable to do (for example, because retaining counsel would not pay for it)?

*Basis for each opinion*
Upon what facts and data is it based? Were there facts or data missing, or were any data or facts inaccurate?

*When each opinion was formed*
Was it before crucial information was available or before important tests were performed?

*The reliability of the assumptions upon which the opinions are based*
If these assumptions can be shown to be false, an opinion may collapse.

*The alternative opinions that were considered but rejected*
Was the expert open-minded? Does he have solid reasons for rejecting other alternatives?

*Degree of flexibility*
Is the expert willing to change his opinion if he is presented with different/new facts or assumptions?

*Degree of scientific certainty*
Is the opinion a mere speculative "guess," and thus inadmissible, or is it based upon a reasonable degree of probability?

*The methodology employed in arriving at the opinion(s)*
Is the methodology sound and reliable, or is it a methodology that was created for the purpose of the current litigation?

*Which documents were used/not used in forming the opinion(s)*
These will indicate what facts and data the expert did and did not consider.

*The equipment used*
Was it appropriate? Was it used correctly? Is the equipment reliable? (For example, was it recently serviced, calibrated, or tested?)

*Tests relied upon*
Did the expert do them personally? Were they done correctly?

*Opposing experts*
Why are the experts' opinions different?

## 8.8  Ten Tips on Forming Opinions That Will Stand Up in Court and Reflect Well on the Expert
Some suggestions for forming supportable, powerful opinions follow.

- Only testify within your true area of expertise.
- Check and recheck your math, calculations, and measurements.
- Be thorough and unbiased in your research—do not cherry-pick.
- State your opinion confidently, but do not exaggerate.
- Avoid small cases where counsel puts you on a tight budget that does not allow you to do the work necessary to form a solid opinion.
- Personally visit the scene, examine the patient, inspect the machine, etc.
- Obtain and carefully review all relevant documents.
- Leave no stone unturned.
- Verify your factual assumptions as much as possible especially those based on information provided by retaining counsel.
- Do not allow retaining counsel to influence your opinion.[4]

## 8.9  Sample Opinions
Sample opinions from experts in various disciplines are provided below.

> *Sample 1:* Physician's Opinion on a Car Accident
> *Sample 2:* Architect's Opinion on a Swimming Pool
> *Sample 3:* Engineer's Opinion on a Power Press
> *Sample 4:* Criminal Justice Expert's Opinion on Sexual Harassment
> *Sample 5:* Safety Professional's Opinion on a Slip and Fall
> *Sample 6:* Psychologist's Opinion on Emotional Distress Due to Battery
> *Sample 7:* Physician's Opinion in Medical Malpractice Case
> *Sample 8:* Emergency Physician on Failure to Meet the Standard of Care: Death Resulting
> *Sample 9:* Certified Public Accountant's Opinion on Fair Market Value of Notes
> *Sample 10:* Securities Expert's Opinion on Suitability of Investment Activities

---

[4] For detailed information on forming opinions, please see Chapter 3, "Bulletproofing Your Opinion," in *How to Become a Dangerous Expert Witness* (SEAK 2005).

# PROPERLY FORMING AND EXPRESSING EXPERT OPINIONS

*Sample 11:* Plastic Surgeon's Opinion on Informed Consent
*Sample 12:* Metallurgist's Opinion on Leaking Water Heater
*Sample 13:* Certified Fraud Examiner's Opinion on Medicare Fraud
*Sample 14:* Mechanical Engineer's Opinion on Design and Safety of Screw Conveyor
*Sample 15:* Electrical Engineer's Opinion on Dwelling Fire Analysis

## Sample 1: Physician's Opinion on a Car Accident

Based upon the available information, to a reasonable degree of medical certainty, there is probable causal relationship between Mr. Orrin's symptoms and complaints of neck pain and his 8/14/98 automobile accident.

## Sample 2: Architect's Opinion on a Swimming Pool

It is my opinion, within reasonable architectural certainty that the "front" door and yard fence gate at 11950 Harvard Road were not locked or latched because they did not have self-closing and self-locking devices that would have prevented Lee Warren from passing through them. The door and gate also did not have alarms thereon that could signal their use to Lee Warren's parents. Lee Warren was unsupervised during his passage to the pool and into the pool. It was the Warrens' responsibility, at a minimum, to have self-closing and self-latching mechanisms on the yard fence gate. Moreover, It was the installation contractor's responsibility to be aware of the gate requirements and to advise the Warrens thereof, based on his extensive experience in pool installation.

The decision to backfill under and beside the fan deck, in light of the decision to excavate, created the low fan deck configuration.

It is also my opinion that the *installation* of the subject aboveground pool at 11950 Harvard Road resulted in defective conditions. These conditions altered the safety factors designed in the pool's manufacture and stated in the installation manuals. The resultant position of the fan deck and the low height above the ground - less than 24 inches - of the fan deck created an accessible passageway onto the deck and into the pool, regardless of the placement of the step ladder. These conditions were hazardous and allowed Lee Warren to reach the pool. In the event that the filter/pump housing was used as a means to climb up to the deck (which is highly unlikely), its placement by the installation contractor was faulty, since it was located near a low point of the deck, a low height which the contractor created. ABC Pools, Inc., failed to construct a pool with a deck that was inaccessible to Lee Warren.

## Sample 3: Engineer's Opinion on a Power Press

A.) The A.B. Stamp Press, serial number 104759, was sold to ACME Metal Stamp Company, Inc., with a defectively designed and manufactured latch and latch bracket. The defect caused the press, suddenly and without warning, to begin operating continuously while in the single stroke mode.

B.) The manufacturer failed to adequately notify and warn users about the extreme hazards associated with the defective latch bracket.

C.) The manufacturer failed to furnish the press with an appropriate point-of-operation interlocked barrier guard.

D.) The manufacturer failed to provide suitable warnings and instructions to ensure that guards are in place, and interlocks functioning, prior to operating the press.[5]

## Sample 4: Criminal Justice Expert's Opinion on Sexual Harassment

1. As a result of the failure of the supervisors of the Lincoln Police Department and its Chief to enforce its own directive, General Order 200-8 (Supervisor's Responsibilities), Officer Lynn Stephens was subjected to a violation of the law (sexual harassment) by Sergeant George Johnston and Lieutenant William Thomas while she was assigned as an officer in the Mounted

---

[5] See Appendix U for the complete report.

Patrol Unit under the immediate supervision of Sergeant Johnston and the unit command of Lieutenant William Thomas.

2. Chief Tim Duncan's failure to insure the Lincoln Police Department's own directive system was followed (General Order 200-3 titled <u>INVESTIGATION OF ALLEGED MISCONDUCT BY OFFICERS</u>) in the investigation into the sexual harassment of Officer Stephens (that all complaints of serious misconduct be investigated by the Internal Affairs Division as a Class 1 complaint) sent a message to the employees of the Lincoln Police Department that sexual harassment is not considered a serious act of misconduct.

3. Chief Tim Duncan's decision to suspend for ninety days and to transfer Johnston and Thomas, but not to demote Johnston and Thomas as the Department's Administrative Disciplinary Committee had recommended, re-enforced the message already sent to the employees of the Lincoln Police Department that sexual harassment allegations would not be treated as seriously by the administration of the department as their Directives require or their employees (membership of Administrative Disciplinary Committee) expected.

Chief Duncan's failure to terminate Thomas when another complaint was sustained against him after he returned to work from his ninety day suspension (as Chief Duncan had warned Thomas he would do) and the Department's performance evaluation of Thomas (very good) during the time period of his suspension again re-enforced this message.

By neglecting to reflect the disciplinary actions taken against Lieutenant Thomas on Thomas's performance evaluation that covered the time period in which he was suspended for sexually harassing Officer Stephens, Chief Duncan and the supervisors of the Lincoln Police Department failed to insure General Order 300-8 (Performance Evaluations) was followed and properly enforced.[6]

## Sample 5: Safety Professional's Opinion on a Slip and Fall

The area of Ms. Singh's accident was, indeed, too "dark" for safe pedestrian travel. It is inappropriate for a landowner to expect guests to remember the position of exterior pathways, therefore, they must be marked and lighted adequately so that pedestrians can see their way around and avoid obstacles and follow the turns in a pathway. Ms. Singh was correct when she described the accident area as "dark", and "dark" is a quantifiable term.

Safety building codes used within the industry of rental property ownership require at least 1.0 foot candle of light at exterior walkways such as the one involved in Ms. Singh's accident (see exhibits #1, #2, and #3). Adequate lighting is very important on the accident pathway because of the 90° turn that must be negotiated and because of the 9-inch-high wall which becomes a tripping hazard if unseen. The light available at the bottom of the stairway at the time of Ms. Singh's accident was less than one-tenth that required for safe travel.

The building owner must accept responsibility for the safety of his or her tenants and invited guests and perform the necessary inspections to determine whether or not lighting fixtures which are necessary for safety are properly functioning.

## Sample 6: Psychologist's Opinion on Emotional Distress Due to Battery

I can state with psychological certainty that:

(1) Mr. S. is suffering from emotional distress, including **depression (DSM IV: 296.22)** and **undifferentiated somatoform disorder (DSM IV: 300.81)**, but not from any **post-traumatic stress disorder (DSM IV: 309.89)**, and

(2) these conditions are **not caused by** or **attributable** to the alleged battery, rather

(3) Mr. S.' symptoms may be better accounted for by alternative stresses in his life experience.

---

[6] See Appendix U for the complete report.

### Sample 7: Physician's Opinion in Medical Malpractice Case

It is my opinion, based upon a reasonable degree of medical certainty that S.B., M.D., provided markedly substandard care in:

(a.) Embarking on a course of very prolonged, poorly monitored lytic therapy in a case which required treatment by surgical thrombectomy because of the sensory and motor changes present;

(b.) Having started therapy for whatever reason, failing to use an aggressive fragmentation, high concentration, directed lytic agent infusion; and for some reason starting and continuing therapy in a demonstrably non-essential, currently and previously non-collateralizing profunda femoris artery while the condition of the right foot and leg continued to deteriorate;

(c.) Failing to recognize that the previously angiographically demonstrated major collateral, the DBrLCF was obstructed and that Mr. B.'s leg and foot were not in the same condition as before by-pass surgery and now had insufficient collateralization to maintain viability;

(d.) Continuing the infusion in a non-essential artery for 11 hours after the current patient complaint began, before trying to clear the bypass graft of clot;

(e.) Failing to pursue established principles of lytic therapy, and/or failing to observe the limitations, the indications and contraindications of the technique; and

(f.) Failing to obtain adequate supervision of his performance from the surgeons in an area of treatment he claims is beyond his ability to evaluate and conduct.

It is my further opinion that because of each and all of these incidents of failing to render care to a current medically acceptable standard, Mr. B. unnecessarily suffered the loss of his right leg below the mid-thigh.

### Sample 8: Emergency Physician on Failure to Meet the Standard of Care: Death Resulting

-On 13 July 2006, critical information from Dr. Wilson's office regarding Ms. Fisher's condition and suspected infirmities was communicated to personnel in the TMC ED, but that information was not recorded or passed on to the treating ED staff physician.

-Bonnie Halvorsen, RN, the triage nurse who attended to Ms. Fisher in the TMC ED, failed to appreciate the significance of Ms. Fisher's low pulse oximetry reading, failed to record that reading, and failed to alert the treating ED staff physician to the existence of a low reading on this patient.

-Had the essential information from Dr. Wilson's office and the triage nurse been made available to Drs. Wilson and Young: 1) a chest x-ray would have been ordered, 2) a diagnosis of pneumonia would have been made, and 3) the patient would have been admitted to the hospital for aggressive treatment of her pneumonia. None of these events happened. As a consequence, Ms. Fisher's condition deteriorated and she expired.

### Sample 9: Certified Public Accountant's Opinion on Fair Market Value of Notes

*CONCLUSION OF FAIR MARKET VALUE*

Based upon the results of our analyses and procedures, it is our opinion that as of the date of value, October 26, 2001, the fair market values of the Notes were as follows:

| | |
|---|---|
| Promissory Note of December 31, 1993: | $320,000 |
| Promissory Note of January 1, 2001 (Principle Value=$346,854.76): | $39,000 |
| Promissory Note of January 1, 2001 (Principle Value=$808,333.41): | $90,000 |
| Promissory Note of October 1, 2001: | 1,729,000 |
| **Total Fair Market Value of the Notes** | **$2,178,000** |

The narrative and schedules that follow explain our methodology and set forth the information used in arriving at our conclusions. The attached *Sources of Information* list the data and information relied upon in arriving at our conclusion.

We performed our valuation in conformity with the Appraisal Foundation's Uniform Standards of Professional Appraisal Practice. This appraisal is subject to the enclosed "Appraisal Certification and Contingent and Limiting Conditions." Also enclosed is information about SP&H, including the professional qualifications of the firm's management and SP&H's products and services.

Respectfully submitted,
*Jane Sheffler-Oliphant*

## Sample 10: Securities Expert's Opinion on Suitability of Investment Activities

As I have previously stated in this document, it is my opinion, based on a reasonable degree of securities industry certainty, that ACME, Inc. mishandled the accounts. This opinion is based on all of the information brought to light in this report. The main issues in this investigation are:

16.1    The churning of the Smithe accounts,
16.2    The total disregard ACME, Inc. had for their own policies and procedures along with NASD rules related to the products sold,
16.3    The actions that resulted in the loss of the client's whole life insurance policies,
16.4    The concentration that resulted from the actions ACME, Inc. recommended that the client place 100% of their investments in annuities,
16.5    The unsuitability of the transitions that were solicited by ABC Securities, Inc., and
16.6    The breach of fiduciary duty that occurred.

## Sample 11: Plastic Surgeon's Opinion on Informed Consent

### *STANDARD OF CARE AND CONCLUSIONS*

A physician or surgeon is not required to give the best medical care in his community to his patient, but is required to provide the patient the care normally rendered by physicians with the same or similar training and experience in his community or in a similar community.

It is my opinion that the evidence does not support the proposition that he did give proper informed consent of the procedure that he carried out and that she did not understand enough about open carpal tunnel release versus endoscopic carpal tunnel release to make a decision as to what procedure she wanted. She did not know that nerve injury could occur, nor did she know that it was easier to injure the nerve in endoscopic or limited incision procedures than open procedures with incisions large enough to completely visualize the nerve. She did not understand that surgeons who have done hundreds of these procedures are less likely to injure a nerve than residents or surgeons who have done a few procedures.

I am familiar with the standard of care in medical centers similar to Central Medical and the doctors who teach and operate in these hospitals. It is my opinion that Dr. Tyndall deviated from the standard of care by not adequately informing of the procedures and the risk of the procedures to the degree necessary for her to decide upon the proper procedure for herself.

The cause of the injury to is not a mystery. The median nerve was injured. Dr. Tyndall's medical record conclusively proves to a prudent hand surgeon that he knew a nerve was injured and he wanted to reexplore the wound to fix the problem. Ms. Franklin felt that Dr. Tyndall did something wrong in surgery and did not want him to operate on her again and therefore sought additional opinions.

This type of injury does not occur in the absence of negligence or conduct below the standard of care. It is my opinion that Dr. Tyndall deviated from the standard of care by injuring the nerve.

The Bier Block that Dr. Tyndall wisely used for the anesthesia allows the surgeon to know at the operating table usually, and certainly in the recovery room, that a nerve has been cut or injured. The nerves are only lightly anesthetized in this procedure (Bier Block) and not totally anesthetized as is the soft tissue. This allows the surgeon to know of an injury by the intense reaction of pain by the patient so he can instantly open the wound to explore the nerve visually or take the patient back to surgery from the recovery room to open the wound, visualize, and repair the damage.

If the endoscopic carpal tunnel release is done under local anesthesia, there is always an immediate response by the patient to a nerve injury and this response is more profound than when under Bier Block. If an axillary block or general anesthetic is used, there is a prolonged delay in response and the patient is deprived of the ability for the surgeon to recognize this injury and promptly respond.  Advocates of endoscopic carpal tunnel release favor either a local anesthetic or a Bier Block like Dr. Tyndall had performed.

For some unknown reason, Dr. Tyndall did not perceive sudden pain in surgery when the nerve was injured.  When the tourniquet was released, all the trapped local anesthesia escaped except that bound by the soft tissue.  The patient experienced typical nerve injury pain in the recovery room, and not at all like the light pain she had after her first operation.  Dr. Tyndall failed to appreciate this as well.  He could have immediately taken her back into the operating room, opened the incision under general anesthesia or under an axillary clock, perform an endoscopic repair of any injured fascicles, or decompress the nerve of any internal bleeding.  This would have significantly reduced her postoperative problems, and ultimate disabilities or prevented them completely.

This failure to respond to obvious signs of nerve injury and to immediately reexplore the wound and correct the problem was a deviation from the standard of care.  Malpractice requires a deviation from the standard of care and this deviation must cause damage or harm to the patient.  If Dr. Tyndall had only damaged the nerve but recognized the signs of damage as the Bier Block would have allowed and opened the wound widely to microscopically repair the wound, the patient may well have never developed a Reflex Sympathetic Dystrophy and malpractice would not exist.

Dr. Tyndall postoperative care beginning on the first postoperative visit was excellent.  He ruled out tendon injury with the ultrasound and really knew there was a nerve injury.  The severe stimuli in the median nerve, probably due to intra-neurohemorrhage in a mostly intact nerve, caused a confusing spasticity of the intrinsic muscles either due to the overload of signals caused by the medial nerve or from "crossover" to the ulnar nerve.  Dr. Tyndall unfortunately could not regain the confidence to allow him to re-operate on her hand.  It is my opinion that the majority of hand surgeons would opine that most patients with education and experience would have acted in the same or similar way and does not infer any contributory negligence on her part.

## SUMMARY

1.  Dr. Tyndall deviated from the standard of care in not explaining endoscopic and open carpal tunnel release and the complications that can result to the extent that could understand and make an informed consent to surgery.
2.  Dr. Tyndall deviated from the standard of care in injuring the median nerve and not recognizing it by direct visualization with the scope or by recognizing the signs of injury a Bier Block allows in opening the wound and carrying out a microscopic exploration and repair.
3.  The deviation of the standard of care by Dr. Tyndall from what other surgeons with the same or similar training in the same or similar communities would have done has resulted with severe permanent damage to this patient's hand and well being, has resulted in Reflex Sympathetic Dystrophy which has been resistant to treatment in spite of many experts and many institutions trying to help.  It furthermore resulted in a significant disability that she must live with.

### Sample 12: Metallurgist's Opinion on Leaking Water Heater

My findings with respect to the subject water heater can be summarized as follows:

-   The water heater was not defective or unreasonably dangerous, as virtually all water heaters eventually leak.
-   The water heater provided a lifespan consistent with industry statistics.
-   The water heater compiled with all requirements of the applicable industry safety standard UL-174 for residential electric automatic storage water heaters and was certified by Underwriters Laboratories, an independent appliance testing agency.
-   The cause of this water heater to crack and leak was a defective installation, in that it was installed in a closed system without any provision for thermal expansion.
-   The installation of the subject water heater in a closed system was also in violation of the local plumbing code for Prairieville, Louisiana, as building water pressure must be limited to 80psi.
-   There was no weld defect caused by the manufacturing process as alleged by Plaintiff's expert as there is no evidence in any of the testing or investigation of this case to date that would support such a conclusion.

Again, these are my opinions as to a reasonable degree of engineering certainty. As discovery is ongoing in this matter, I reserve the right to amend or modify the opinions stated herein as new evidence becomes available.

## Sample 13: Certified Fraud Examiner's Opinion on Medicare Fraud

Medicare is America's national funded medical and hospitalization insurance program, for the elderly and disabled. The Medicare program is governed by the United States Congress. To qualify as a Part A or Part B health service Provider, a Provider must meet certain statutory criteria and enter into Health Insurance Benefit Agreements. These agreements are known as Provider Agreements with the Secretary of the Department of Health and Human Services (DHHS).

The provider involved in this case met statutory criteria and entered into Health Insurance Benefit Agreements with DHHS. By entering into the Provider Agreements the defendants agree to accept Medicare assignment of payments and to abide by the laws established in Title 42, Public Health and Welfare, which establishes Medicare rules and regulations for health care Providers and Suppliers.

Fraud includes any intentional or deliberate act to deprive another of property or money by guile, deception or other unfair means. Medicare fraud and abuse rules clearly provide that incorrect reporting of diagnoses or procedures to maximize payments and billing for services not furnished and/or supplies not provided are considered frauds committed.

Based upon my review and examination of the above-referenced documents it is reasonable to believe that the defendants committed Medicare fraud and abuse in the form of up-ceding or up-coding.

## Sample 14: Mechanical Engineer's Opinion on Design and Safety of Screw Conveyor

The screw conveyor was suitable and safe for its intended purpose. In terms of safety, the screw conveyor was not defectively designed, manufactured, marketed, or installed. The cautions and warning location on and near the screw conveyor, which contained pictographs and text, gave specific instructions and consequences of ignoring the instructions.

This injury was caused by Mr. Thomas reaching into a moving screw conveyor. In doing so, he disregarded an open and obvious hazard, his safety training, the caution and warning signs, six Omni-Crown Safety Manuals, Policies, Process, and Procedures, and his leadership responsibilities.

There were easy to implement methods of preventing any disassembled component from falling into the inlet of the screw conveyor. However, once a component fell into the screw conveyor, there were several safe alternatives for retrieving the component which could have been performed in a reasonable amount of time. Yet, Mr. Thomas chose an extremely dangerous and unnecessary action which resulted in his injury.

## Sample 15: Electrical Engineer's Opinion on Dwelling Fire Analysis

Based upon the analysis of the remaining burn patterns, it was determined that the fire originated in the wall, near the northeast corner of the dwelling's back porch. The only items capable of causing a fire, which were located in the origin area at the time of the fire, were a light switch used to control the outside porch light and the electrical Romex wiring connected to it. It is unlikely that a failure in the switch occurred that started this fire, based upon the remaining burn patterns. Had this fire originated inside the metal box that held the outlet, S would have expected the fire to vent out the front of the box into the interior of the dwelling. The fire clearly did not initially spread inside the dwelling. Furthermore, the light switch located in the origin area had been installed to that location for at least 12 years (length of time current homeowners have lived in the dwelling), and has never had any problems. However, the wiring connected to it was new and was installed by the company contracted to replace the siding on the dwelling. This company was not licensed to perform electrical work on the dwelling. They informed the homeowner that they were able replace their old lights with new ones, as well as relocate the exterior light on the back porch, which they did. During S's site visit, several items that indicated poor electrical workmanship were observed.

This fire was caused as a result of an electrical failure of either the light switch, the electrical wiring located in the origin area, or the connection between the wiring and the switch. Since not all of the electrical evidence was recovered from the scene, however, the exact electrical failure that caused this fire remains undetermined. With the exception of the old switch, all the electrical items capable of causing this fire had been installed by ABC Company, which was not licensed to perform electrical work. Areas of poor workmanship on their behalf were observed, problems with the electrical items in that area began to occur immediately after the installation, and this fire occurred only several months after their work was completed. Combining these facts with the fact that this fire occurred as a result of an electrical failure in the area where ABC Company performed electrical work makes it probable that this fire was caused as a result of the work they performed.

Sarita Illya hereby certifies the expressed opinions and conclusions have been formulated within a reasonable degree of professional certainty. They are based upon all of the information known by Sarita Illya as of the time this report was issued, as well as knowledge, skill, experience, training, and/or education.

## 8.10  Conclusion

Experts need to be prepared to express and deliver their opinions in a legally sufficient way. Speculation and guessing are not permitted. Opinions need to be based upon reliable facts and methodology or they may be excluded from evidence. Cross-examination will challenge the expert's opinions, methodology, and the facts and data upon which the opinion is based. The expert should be prepared for such challenges.

# Chapter 9  Methodology

## 9.1 Introduction

An expert's methodology can be challenged in two ways. First, it can be challenged as being unreliable "junk science" as a matter of law. This would be decided by the judge upon motion and would be based upon the *Daubert, G.E.,* and *Kumho Tire* cases discussed below and the reliability requirements now embodied in Federal Rule of Evidence 702 (see Section 6.2 for Rule 702 and its accompanying Advisory Committee Notes).[1] In making her determination, the trial judge acts as a "gatekeeper" whose job it is to exclude from evidence unreliable expert testimony that will not assist the trier of fact.[2] Some of the factors a judge may look at in making a ruling include:

- whether the theory or technique used by the expert can be, and has been, tested;
- whether the theory or technique has been subjected to peer review and publication;
- the known or potential rate of error of the method used;
- the degree of the method's or conclusion's acceptance within the relevant scientific community;
- whether the expert is proposing to testify about matters growing naturally and directly out of research he has conducted independent of the litigation or whether he developed his opinions expressly for purposes of testifying;
- whether the expert has unjustifiably extrapolated from an accepted premise to an unfounded conclusion;
- whether the expert has adequately accounted for obvious alternative explanations;
- whether the expert is being as careful as he would be in his regular professional work outside his paid litigation consulting; and
- whether the field of expertise claimed by the expert is known to reach reliable results for the type of opinion the expert would give.

Even if the expert testimony is allowed by the judge, the expert's methodology will remain a legitimate area for cross-examination. This is because the methodology used is relevant to the weight the jury gives the expert's testimony.

If the expert testimony is excluded by the trial judge, this fact may be brought up in future cases and in effect becomes part of the expert's "permanent record." In many cases, the lawyers realize that an exclusion of the expert's testimony will result in an automatic victory in the case. Hence, attorneys in many cases put significant time and resources into challenging and excluding the opposing expert's testimony. Even so, the exclusion of expert

---

[1] Not all jurisdictions follow these cases. Federal courts do, but state laws may vary.

[2] The *Daubert* rule's purpose is to exclude merely conjectural expert testimony and to admit expert testimony of scientific knowledge that will assist the trier of fact. *Poole ex rel. Wrongful Death Beneficiaries of Poole v. Avara,* 908 So.2d 716 (Miss. 2005). The rule governing admission of expert scientific testimony requires the district court to perform a gatekeeping function to ensure that any and all scientific testimony or evidence admitted is not only relevant but reliable. *Fuesting v. Zimmer, Inc.,* 421 F.3d 528 (C.A. 7 Ill. 2005).

testimony is still "the exception rather than the rule."[3] All experts are therefore well advised to employ a reliable methodology when forming their opinions. Experts should decline to work in cases where they cannot provide a solidly reliable opinion.

**Example 9.1: Gatekeeper function of trial judge**
The defense makes a motion in limine to exclude causation expert testimony in a toxic tort case because the defense feels this testimony is unreliable. The judge finds that the expert's testimony is not unreliable and allows the testimony into evidence. The reliability of the expert's methodology may still be questioned on cross-examination because it is relevant to the weight to be given to the testimony. Had the judge ruled the testimony inadmissible, this ruling could have been *outcome determinative* and have resulted in the dismissal of the plaintiff's case.

## 9.2 Overview of the U.S. Supreme Court Case Interpretations of Federal Rule of Evidence 702

The *Daubert* line of cases interprets Federal Rule of Evidence 702 and came down long before the 2000 "reliability" amendments to Federal Rule 702 were enacted.[4] *Daubert* established that a trial court judge is to act as gatekeeper under the Federal Rules of Evidence in order to ensure the scientific validity of the expert's testimony. *Daubert* set forth several factors a trial court should consider when evaluating scientific validity. (See the *Daubert* discussion below.) At the time, the case apparently applied only to novel scientific testimony—now both the amended Rule 702 and relevant case law make clear that its analysis applies to all expert testimony, scientific or otherwise.[5]

Four years after *Daubert,* in *General Electric v. Joiner,*[6] the Supreme Court limited appellate review of the trial court's decision to admit or exclude expert testimony to an abuse of discretion standard. The expert should realize that an appellate court will seldom reverse a trial judge's admissibility determination under this abuse of discretion standard. In effect, *Daubert* required a judge to scrutinize the reliability of the expert's methodology. *Joiner* then offered increased protection and insulation of the judge's decision.

In 1999, the Supreme Court decided *Kumho Tire Company Ltd. v. Carmichael.*[7] *Kumho* directed that the *Daubert* factors be applied equally to nonscientific expert testimony as well as to scientific expert testimony.[8] The court also held that trial courts are free to apply other factors in addition to those set out in *Daubert.*[9] This is also made clear in the Advisory Committee Notes to the amended Rule 702. In effect, a trial court can now fashion

---

[3] Advisory Committee Notes to Federal Rule of Evidence 702.

[4] Fed. Rule Evid. 702, Testimony by Experts: "If scientific, technical, or other specialized knowledge will assist the trier of fact to understand the evidence or to determine a fact in issue, a witness qualified as an expert by knowledge, skill, experience, training, or education may testify thereto in the form of an opinion or otherwise."

[5] In federal court and in states following this line of cases.

[6] *General Electric v. Joiner,* 522 U.S. 136, 139 L. Ed. 2d 508, 118 S. Ct. 512, 1997 U.S. LEXIS 7503 (1997), on remand, 134 F.3d 1457, 1998 U.S. App. LEXIS 1770 (11th Cir. Ga. 1998).

[7] *Kumho Tire Co. v. Carmichael,* 143 L. Ed. 2d 238, 119 S. Ct. 1167, 1999 U.S. LEXIS 2189, 67 U.S.L.W. 4179 (1999).

[8] *Kumho,* 119 S. Ct. at 1175.

[9] *Id.* at 1176.

its own flexible standard to determine validity, subject only to review under an abuse of discretion standard. This further expands a trial judge's discretion in evaluating *all* expert testimony, scientific and non-scientific alike.[10]

## 9.3 Procedures Judges Employ When Acting as Gatekeepers

An expert's reputation and viability for future work may ride on the outcome of a *Daubert* challenge to his testimony. It is therefore important to understand the process of how these challenges are made and what analysis is applied by the courts. The procedure used in determining reliability is left to the discretion of the trial judge. These could include the following.

- Making a *Daubert* ruling in conjunction with a motion for summary judgment.
- Addressing *Daubert* in ruling on a motion in limine.
- Requiring an expert to complete a detailed affidavit describing her methodology.

Some of the procedures may result in the judge holding a *"Daubert* hearing" outside of the presence of the jury. At the hearing, the expert will testify and the judge must decide, by examining the expert's methodology, whether the expert has the "specialized knowledge" that will legally permit the witness to testify. These determinations will sometimes involve detailed and exhaustive proceedings because the result of the hearing may be outcome determinative of the entire case.

## 9.4 *Daubert*

The landmark case of *Daubert v. Merrell Dow Pharmaceuticals, Inc.*[11] interpreted Federal Rule of Evidence 702. In *Daubert,* the court held that to meet the "specialized knowledge" requirement of Rule 702, the trial judge must make a threshold finding of whether the expert's methodology was sound. The *Daubert* court identified four factors bearing on that threshold finding. The judge will consider several factors, including (1) whether the theory or technique used by the expert can be, and has been, tested; (2) whether the theory or technique has been subjected to peer review and publication; (3) the known or potential rate of error of the method used; and (4) the degree of the method's or conclusion's acceptance within the relevant scientific community. Moreover, the Ninth Circuit added a fifth factor to the list upon hearing the remanded case: whether the expert's theory existed before litigation began. The expert should note that rarely will a court exclude testimony on the basis of one factor alone. As noted above, the law is now clear that the 4 or 5 *Daubert* factors are non-exclusive, that trial judges are free to employ other factors as well, and that not all the *Daubert* factors will all apply in all cases. *See e.g. Loeffel Steel Products, Inc. v. Delta Brands, Inc.,* 387 F.Supp.2d 794 (N.D. Ill. E.Div. 2005). The inquiry into both relevance and reliability of expert testimony under *Daubert* is, of necessity, always highly fact-specific. No one factor, even when applicable, is outcome determinative. For example, the Advisory Committee Notes to Rule 702 mention the following additional factors that courts have used.

---

[10] Shubha Gosh, "Tires and Testimony: Judging the Junk: High Court Expands Trial Judges' Role in Evaluating Expert Witnesses," *Fulton County Daily Report,* April 29, 1999, 1.

[11] *Daubert,* 113 S. Ct. 2786 (1993).

Courts both before and after *Daubert* have found other factors relevant in determining whether expert testimony is sufficiently reliable to be considered by the trier of fact. These factors include:

(1) Whether experts are "proposing to testify about matters growing naturally and directly out of research they have conducted independent of the litigation, or whether they have developed their opinions expressly for purposes of testifying." *Daubert v. Merrell Dow Pharmaceuticals, Inc.,* 43 F.3d 1311, 1317 (9th Cir. 1995).

(2) Whether the expert has unjustifiably extrapolated from an accepted premise to an unfounded conclusion. See *General Elec. Co. v. Joiner,* 522 U.S. 136, 146 (1997) (noting that in some cases a trial court "may conclude that there is simply too great an analytical gap between the data and the opinion proffered").

(3) Whether the expert has adequately accounted for obvious alternative explanations. See *Claar v. Burlington N.R.R.,* 29 F.3d 499 (9th Cir. 1994) (testimony excluded where the expert failed to consider other obvious causes for the plaintiff's condition). Compare *Ambrosini v. Labarraque,* 101 F.3d 129 (D.C. Cir. 1996) (the possibility of some uneliminated causes presents a question of weight, so long as the most obvious causes have been considered and reasonably ruled out by the expert).

(4) Whether the expert "is being as careful as he would be in his regular professional work outside his paid litigation consulting." *Sheehan v. Daily Racing Form, Inc.,* 104 F.3d 940, 942 (7th Cir. 1997). See *Kumho Tire Co. v. Carmichael,* 119 S.Ct. 1167, 1176 (1999) *(Daubert* requires the trial court to assure itself that the expert "employs in the courtroom the same level of intellectual rigor that characterizes the practice of an expert in the relevant field").

(5) Whether the field of expertise claimed by the expert is known to reach reliable results for the type of opinion the expert would give. See *Kumho Tire Co. v. Carmichael,* 119 S.Ct.1167, 1175 (1999) *(Daubert's* general acceptance factor does not "help show that an expert's testimony is reliable where the discipline itself lacks reliability, as for example, do theories grounded in any so-called generally accepted principles of astrology or necromancy."); *Moore v. Ashland Chemical, Inc.,* 151 F.3d 269 (5th Cir. 1998) (en banc) (clinical doctor was properly precluded from testifying to the toxicological cause of the plaintiff's respiratory problem, where the opinion was not sufficiently grounded in scientific methodology); *Sterling v. Velsicol Chem. Corp.,* 855 F.2d 1188 (6th Cir. 1988) (rejecting testimony based on "clinical ecology" as unfounded and unreliable).

## 9.5  *G.E. v. Joiner*

*G.E. v. Joiner*[12] was the first Supreme Court case to follow up directly on *Daubert.* The *G.E.* decision established that appellate courts must review a trial judge's determination of whether to admit or exclude expert testimony under an "abuse of discretion" standard. In practical terms, this means that it will be very difficult to overturn a trial court's determination.

In the case, plaintiff Robert Joiner alleged that he developed lung cancer as a result of exposure to polychlorinated biphenyls (PCBs). Joiner claimed that while his history of cigarette smoking and his family's history of lung cancer may have predisposed him to developing lung cancer, his exposure to PCBs and their derivatives (furans and dioxins)

---

[12] *General Electric v. Joiner,* 522 U.S. 136, 139 L. Ed. 2d 508, 118 S. Ct. 512, 1997 U.S. LEXIS 7503 (1997), on remand, 134 F.3d 1457, 1998 U.S. App. LEXIS 1770 (11th Cir. Ga. 1998).

promoted the development of his cancer. The district court deemed inadmissible all of the plaintiffs' expert testimony that Joiner's exposure to PCBs, furans, and dioxins caused his cancer. After throwing out the expert testimony, the court entered summary judgment in the defendant's favor. The plaintiffs appealed to the Eleventh Circuit.

The Eleventh Circuit Court of Appeals applied *Daubert* to the plaintiffs' claims. The *Joiner* appeals court first determined that the plaintiffs' experts' methodology, procedures, and information supporting their opinions were scientifically reliable. The plaintiffs' two chief experts were Dr. Daniel Teitelbaum, a clinical toxicologist, and Dr. Arnold Schecter, a preventative medicine specialist. Both doctors were well qualified. Both experts familiarized themselves with the specifics of Joiner's health history and disease, and both reviewed pertinent medical literature. Dr. Teitelbaum examined Joiner, interviewed him, reviewed his medical records, and reviewed the depositions of Joiner's family and his coworkers. Dr. Schecter interviewed Joiner, reviewed his medical records, and viewed a videotape of Joiner's working conditions related to his alleged toxic exposure. Each doctor employed scientific studies and authorities in formulating his respective opinions.

Moreover, each expert used scientifically reliable methods and procedures in gathering and assimilating all of the information forming his opinions. Each doctor asserted that the procedures he employed in arriving at his opinions were generally accepted in the medical community, a point that the defendants did not dispute. The doctors' extensive experience in their respective fields further augmented the reliability of their methodology and reasoning.

The appellate court especially criticized the trial court's review of the bases for Drs. Teitelbaum's and Schecter's opinions. For example, the district court rejected the plaintiffs' experts' two animal studies because of their limited number, because they used massive doses of PCBs, and because they were conducted on animals instead of humans. The appellate court found that none of these reasons was sufficient to render the experts' testimony unreliable—explaining that the question was simply whether the experts' use of challenged studies represents sound methodology. The appellate court proclaimed that the number of studies is irrelevant and it is improper to deem research unreliable solely because it employs animal subjects. In sum, this court reversed the trial court because:

> Instead of reviewing the bases for the experts' opinions to screen out mere speculation, the district court excluded the experts' testimony because it drew different conclusions from their research. This it should not have done. Courts should simply satisfy themselves as to the reliability of proffered expert testimony, "leaving the jury to decide the correctness of competing expert opinions."[13]

The United States Supreme Court reversed the Eleventh Circuit. It held (1) abuse of discretion is the proper standard for an appellate court to apply in reviewing a federal district court's decision to admit or exclude expert scientific testimony at trial; and (2) because it was within the discretion of the district court in the instant case to conclude that the animal studies and the four epidemiological studies upon which the experts relied were not sufficient, whether individually or in combination, to support the experts' conclusions that

---

[13] 78 F.3d 524 533 (11th Cir. 1996).

the electrician's exposure to PCBs contributed to his cancer, the district court did not abuse its discretion in excluding the experts' testimony.

## 9.6 *Kumho Tire*

The *Kumho Tire*[14] decision established decisively that the *Daubert* factors apply to the testimony of engineers and other experts who are not scientists. The decision also established that a trial court, in its discretion, may consider the *Daubert* factors in its analysis of expert testimony, but it may also consider other factors that it determines are better indicators of reliability of the specific circumstances of the case. The decision reaffirmed that a trial court's determination will be reviewed under *G.E.*'s abuse of discretion standard.

Kumho was a products liability case. A tire on the vehicle driven by one of the plaintiffs blew out, the vehicle overturned, one passenger died and the others were injured. The plaintiffs sued the tire's maker and its distributor (collectively Kumho Tire), claiming that the tire that failed was defective. Their case hinged in significant part upon the depositions of a tire failure analyst, Dennis Carlson, Jr., who intended to testify that, in his expert opinion, a defect in the tire's manufacture or design caused the blow out. That opinion was based upon a visual and tactile inspection of the tire and upon the theory that in the absence of at least two of four specific, physical symptoms indicating tire abuse, the tire failure of the sort that occurred here was caused by a defect. Kumho Tire moved to exclude the testimony on the ground that the expert's methodology failed to satisfy Federal Rule of Evidence 702. The district court granted the motion and acknowledged *Daubert*'s mandate that it should act as a reliability "gatekeeper." The court noted that the four *Daubert* factors argued against the reliability of the expert's methodology. The Eleventh Circuit Court of Appeals held that the district court had erred as a matter of law in applying *Daubert.* Believing that *Daubert* was limited to the scientific context, the court held that the *Daubert* factors did not apply to Carlson's testimony, which it characterized as skill- or experience-based. The Supreme Court reversed the Eleventh Circuit's ruling and held that the *Daubert* factors may apply to the testimony of engineers and other experts who are not scientists.[15] It explained that the evidentiary rationale underlying *Daubert*'s gatekeeping determination is not limited to scientific knowledge: "Rule 702 does not distinguish between 'scientific' knowledge and 'technical' or 'other specialized' knowledge, but makes clear that any such knowledge might become the subject of expert testimony."[16]

The Supreme Court applied these standards to the case and found the trial court's decision to exclude the expert testimony proper. The Supreme Court explained that the trial court excluded the testimony because it initially doubted the expert's methodology and then found it unreliable after examining the transcript in some detail and considering the respondents' defense of it. The doubts that triggered the court's initial inquiry were

---

[14] 119 S. Ct. 1167 (1999).

[15] *Kumho,* at 7–13.

[16] The court further explained: "Finally, it would prove difficult, if not impossible, for judges to administer evidentiary rules under which a 'gatekeeping' obligation depended upon a distinction between 'scientific' knowledge and 'technical' or 'other specialized' knowledge, since there is no clear line dividing the one from the others and no convincing need to make such distinctions." *Kumho,* at 7–9.

reasonable, as was the court's ultimate conclusion that the expert could not reliably determine the cause of the failure of the tire in question. The question was not the reliability of the methodology in general, but whether the expert could reliably determine the cause of failure of *the particular tire at issue*. That tire, the expert conceded, had traveled far enough so that some of the tread had been worn bald, it should have been taken out of service, it had been repaired (inadequately) for punctures, and it bore some of the very marks that he said indicated not a defect but abuse. Moreover, the expert's own testimony cast considerable doubt upon the reliability of both his theory about the need for at least two signs of abuse and his proposition about the significance of visual inspection in this case. The plaintiffs argued that other tire failure experts, like their own, rely on visual and tactile examinations of tires. But there was no indication in the record that other experts in the industry used the plaintiffs' expert's *particular* approach or that tire experts normally make the very fine distinctions necessary to support his conclusions. Nor are there references to articles or papers that validate his approach. "[Plaintiffs'] argument that the District Court too rigidly applied *Daubert* might have had some validity with respect to the court's initial opinion, but fails because the court, on reconsideration, recognized that the relevant reliability inquiry should be 'flexible,' and ultimately based its decision upon Carlson's failure to satisfy either *Daubert*'s factors *or any other* set of reasonable reliability criteria."[17]

## 9.7 Case Examples
**Example 9.2: Testing blood alcohol from deceased person's vitreous humor of eye had been proven reliable, testimony admissible**
*Olson v. Ford Motor Co.,* 2006 WL 214910 (D.N.D. N.W. Div. 2006)
This was a wrongful death action. The court held that expert testimony regarding blood alcohol level determined through testing the vitreous humor of the eye was admissible where witnesses had required credentials, testimony was of value to help the jury assess whether the victim was contributorily or comparatively negligent, and the test procedure had been proven reliable.

**Comment:** Reliable testing can help bolster an expert's opinion.

**Example 9.3: Drug causation testimony admissible when published research supported opinion**
*In re Vioxx Products Liability Litigation,* 2005 WL 3105326 (E.D. La. 2005)
The victim in this case suffered a fatal cardiovascular event after taking Vioxx. The court held that the expert testimony in question was admissible where there had been at least several clinical trials and observational studies which revealed that the drug could increase the risk of cardiac incidents and a significant number of peer-reviewed articles and observational studies supporting the proposed testimony appeared in credible and well-recognized medical publications.

**Comment:** Expert testimony is at its most persuasive where (as in the above case) the expert can demonstrate that he did his homework and that respected authorities support the expert's conclusions.

---

[17] *Kumho,* at 13–19.

**Example 9.4: Failure to perform multiple testing does not bar expert testimony where expert's methodology was scientifically valid and permitted conclusion reached**
*Principi v. Survivair, Inc.,* 231 F.R.D. 685 (M.D. Fla. 2005)
This was a paramedic/firefighter's products liability action against the manufacturer of a specialized backpack used for a portable breathing apparatus. Injuries to the back of the neck from the impact of a backpack frame during use were alleged. The court held that the fact that the expert witness had conducted only kinematic analysis before forming the causation opinion (without performing further tests to determine whether the specific injuries were due to the impact of frame) did not render the expert's conclusion unreliable. The court reasoned that the expert's methodology was scientifically valid. It permitted the conclusion.

**Example 9.5: Slip and fall expert's wet or icy surface testimony inadmissible where methodology not subjected to peer review or publication and no written standards**
*Rising-Moore v. Red Roof Inns, Inc.,* 2005 WL 1081151 (S.D. Ind. Indianapolis Div. 2005)
The court in this case excluded the expert's finding that the ramp leading to a motel's entrance was unsafe when icy or wet. There were no standards written to associate safety of a walking surface with results of coefficient of friction tests, the expert's methodology had not been subjected to peer review or publication, there was no evidence as to the type of soles on the shoes the plaintiff was wearing when he fell, the ramp was not tested until two years after accident, and the expert measured the effect of water, not ice.

**Comment:** It is usually helpful to cite written standards where such standards exist. It pays for an expert to take the time to do her homework. The thoroughness an expert demonstrates will bolster her opinions.

**Example 9.6: Expert ignores clinical studies showing no link between silicone breast implants and systemic disease, testimony barred**
*Norris v. Baxter Healthcare Corp.,* 397 F.3d 878 (C.A. 10 Colo. 2005)
Proposed expert testimony was insufficiently reliable where the expert ignored or discounted without explanation epidemiological studies finding no proven link between silicone implants and systemic disease. Instead, he relied on clinical case studies and differential diagnosis.

**Comment:** This case could have turned out differently had the expert provided a cogent reason why he discounted the contrary studies. The best experts can articulate valid reasons why they did not follow contrary authority.

**Example 9.7: Expert testimony inadmissible where standards not followed**
*Fireman's Fund Ins. Co. v. Canon U.S.A., Inc.,* 394 F.3d 1054 (C.A. 8 Minn. 2005)
Expert opinions regarding a fire's origin were excluded as unreliable because the experts' hypotheses were not carefully examined against empirical data obtained from fire scene analysis and testing required by experimental testing standards of the National Fire Protection Association (NFPA).

**Comment:** Experts are well advised to follow and cite accepted written standards.

# METHODOLOGY

**Example 9.8: Testimony admissible despite no previous tests and no scrutiny from other experts**
*Seeley v. Hamilton Beach/Proctor-Silex, Inc.,* 349 F.Supp.2d 381 (N.D.N.Y. 2004)
This case involved an allegedly defective toaster. The expert had "good grounds" for opining that the toaster's design was defective and that the manufacturer knew about safer alternative designs. Tests performed by the expert were specific to the situation and thus might not have been performed before or faced scrutiny from other engineering experts.

**Comment:** This case exemplifies the flexible approach courts follow when ruling on admissibility. This opinion was admitted despite lack of peer review. Evidently, the court was satisfied on other grounds that the expert's opinion was reliable and not based on "junk science."

**Example 9.9: Testimony regarding height of flood waters sufficiently reliable where expert used slightly modified version of model approved by Army Corps of Engineers**
*Acker v. Burlington Northern and Santa Fe Ry. Co.,* 347 F.Supp.2d 1025 (D. Kan. 2004)
Expert testimony regarding the height of flood waters was admissible despite a railroad's assertion that the expert's model was inaccurate with respect to actual surveyed flood depths, that the expert calibrated his hydrologic model on an irrelevant past flood, and that the expert's use of effects of the embankment and bridge on the flood were time-barred. The expert used a slightly modified version of a model approved by the Army Corps of Engineers. It would have been impossible to model the effect of the train without also considering the bridge and embankment.

**Example 9.10: Products liability testimony admissible where hypothesis tested, published, and accepted within scientific community**
*Santoro ex rel. Santoro v. Donnelly,* 340 F.Supp.2d 464 (S.D.N.Y. 2004)
Testimony that a fireplace heater presented an unreasonable risk of contact burns, even though it met the American National Standards Institute standards, was admissible. The expert had based his opinion on work he performed for the Consumer Product Safety Commission. He tested his hypothesis, the studies were published, and his ideas had gained acceptance within the scientific community.

**Example 9.11: Testimony based on unpublished report that ignored other studies and differed with other experts in the same area not admissible**
*In re Rezulin Products Liability Litigation,* 309 F.Supp.2d 531 (S.D.N.Y. 2004)
The expert's opinions in this case regarded the ratio of liver failure induced by a drug for treating diabetes. The court barred the expert's proposed testimony where the expert admitted relying on an unpublished report by a biostatistician for the Food and Drug Administration without considering two epidemiological studies that reached drastically different conclusions. The court found that the expert had adopted an extreme view apparently not shared by other experts in the same area.

**Comment:** This is an example of where the court considered the expert to be "out in left field" and practicing "junk science." The court came to this conclusion because it found that the expert:

- ignored recognized studies,
- had opinions that were not shared by his colleagues,
- relied on specious sources such as an unpublished report, and
- ignored contrary reports.

**Example 9.12: Survey technique in discrimination case not reliable, testimony barred**
*Yapp v. Union Pacific R. Co.,* 301 F.Supp.2d 1030 (E.D. Mo. E. Div. 2004)
This was a discrimination case. The court found that the methodology employed by the employer's experts in conducting a survey regarding the employer's hiring qualifications and processes was not scientific or inherently reliable so as to be admissible as scientific evidence. The survey in question consisted of 16 interviews with representatives of the employer who were not hiring decision-makers, employer's counsel selected the interviewees, screened the interview questions, and participated in each of the interviews. The experts' study was based on a non-random sample of departments and accounted for a limited number of jobs. The experts' analysis was not grounded in a reliable method for understanding hiring processes.

**Comment:** *Daubert* challenges are most often used against plaintiff's experts and are a favorite tool of defense counsel. However, the rules apply equally to all experts and, as in the above example, *Daubert* challenges can and will also be used against defense experts.

This case also illustrates something to avoid in expert witness work: letting retaining counsel cherry-pick and control the data and information upon which the expert will base his opinion.

**Example 9.13: Citing a peer-reviewed study alone is not good enough, it depends what the study shows**
*In re Lockheed Litigation Cases,* 10 Cal.Rptr.3d 34 (Cal. App. 2 Dist. 2004)
The court held that the expert's opinion that chemicals in a workplace caused an increased risk of cancer to employees was inadmissible. The court found that the study on which the opinion was based provided no reasonable basis for the opinion. The study reviewed epidemiological studies of painters who potentially were exposed to more than 130 different chemicals, including the five found in the workplace in question. However, the study did not indicate whether persons exposed to only those five chemicals contracted cancer at a rate greater than the national average, since study subjects were exposed to many other chemicals, including known carcinogens.

**Comment:** Most likely, the opposing experts, opposing counsel, and the court will closely review the studies upon which the expert's opinion is based. As such, it is critical that the studies support the opinion as strongly as possible. Perhaps the above result could have been avoided had the expert spent the time to research and locate studies which were more on point to the case in hand (if indeed such studies exist). Success as an expert often is a function of diligent preparation.

**Example 9.14: Extrapolation from high-dosage lengthy exposure tests, inadmissible**
*Bourne ex rel. Bourne v. E.I. DuPont de Nemours & Co.,* 85 Fed.Appx. 964 (C.A. 4 W.Va. 2004)
Testimony that benomyl, a fungicide, caused birth defects was not admissible. Experts extrapolated from high-dosage, single-species testing, and lengthy exposure *in vitro* testing. No epidemiological studies supported the experts' position, and the relied-upon animal studies were far removed from the child's allegations.

**Comment:** The stronger the study for the proposition being offered, the stronger the likelihood of withstanding a *Daubert* challenge.

**Example 9.15: Opposing side could not produce evidence showing that studies relied upon by expert dealt with a different situation, testimony admitted**
*Carson Harbor Village, Ltd. v. Unocal Corp.,* 2003 WL 22038700 (C.D. Cal. 2003)
This was a CERCLA environmental contamination case regarding interaction between urban storm water and wetlands. The court found the proposed expert testimony sufficiently reliable where the

defendants failed to proffer any evidence suggesting that the owners' property was distinct from the locales that were the subject of national and local studies cited by the expert.

**Comment:** It is crucial that cited studies actually stand for the proposition the expert purports them to stand for.

### Example 9.16: Peer-reviewed study not required where other factors establish the reliability of the expert's opinions

*Clausen v. M/V NEW CARISSA,* 339 F.3d 1049 (C.A. 9 Or. 2003)

This case involved an oil spill's effects on commercial oyster farmers. The court found the proposed expert testimony admissible despite a lack of supporting peer-reviewed literature specifically addressing that subject. The expert relied upon a variety of objective, verifiable evidence, surveyed the oyster beds, conducted a clinical examination of diseased and dead oysters, relied on government reports showing that the vessel in question's oil was in oyster beds and the oysters themselves, and relied on the fact that contact toxicity was a mechanism that had occurred in every animal system studied.

**Comment:** Peer-reviewed studies, although certainly a good idea when available, are in no way an absolute requirement for the admissibility of expert testimony.

### Example 9.17: Testimony not contradicted by scientific community admitted

*Stroheim & Romann, Inc. v. Allianz Ins. Co.,* 2003 WL 21980389 (S.D.N.Y. 2003)

This case involved causation testimony against a property insurer to recover for damage to a building. The court held that the proposed testimony was sufficiently reliable to be admissible where there was no evidence that the methodology deviated from acceptable scientific standards or that the opinions were contradicted by the scientific community.

**Comment:** Expert testimony that is "out there" and not generally accepted in the field is the most vulnerable to a methodology/reliability challenge. Testimony based upon commonly accepted methodology in the relevant field is routinely admitted. Experts who wish to have their testimony admitted should base their testimony on methods commonly accepted in their field.

### Example 9.18: Prepared, experienced expert allowed to testify on home's foundation movement

*United Services Automobile Ass'n v. Pigott,* 154 S.W.3d 625 (Tex. App. San Antonio 2003)

Testimony on whether the movement of the insured's home foundation was caused by a plumbing leak was admissible where the expert relied on the same testing data relied on by the opposing expert, the witness gave several reasons for ruling out other possible causes of foundation movement, the witness relied on his experience in conducting over 6,000 forensic investigations on foundations, and the expert's testimony was grounded in his application of his engineering training to data regarding elevations and soil samples.

**Comment:** Note how this expert articulated several *reasons* for ruling out other possible causes of the foundation movement in question. This is an example of the value of diligence and preparation. Diligent, well-prepared experts usually produce opinions that hold up in court.

**Example 9.19: Testimony based on computer analysis barred where program was not properly used**

*City of Wichita, Kansas v. Trustees of APCO Oil Corp. Liquidating Trust,* 306 F.Supp.2d 1040 (D. Kan. 2003)

Expert testimony on computer modeling of groundwater flows was inadmissible. The expert failed to correlate model results with field data, assumed relevant ground conditions without obtaining confirmation, and deviated from usual modeling methodology.

**Comment:** Just as citing a peer-reviewed study will not result in admissibility unless the study actually supports the expert's testimony, use of a generally accepted computer program will not support admissibility unless that program was properly employed. Experts are well advised to be properly trained in the use of applicable computer programs and to properly use such programs.

**Example 9.20: Testimony inadmissible where expert did not bother to inspect the machine in question**

*Ortiz-Semprit v. Coleman Co., Inc.,* 301 F.Supp.2d 116 (D.C. P.R. 2004)

The court held that the expert's opinion that a fire occurring during an attempt to refuel an electric generator originated because of an electrostatic discharge was unreliable and thus inadmissible. The witness was a certified fire and explosion investigator by the National Fire Protection Association, but he did not inspect the generator, the scene of accident, or interview burned victims. In addition, the witness was unable to state whether four conditions listed in the National Fire Code volume he relied upon for his opinion were fulfilled.

**Comment:** Wherever possible, experts *must* inspect the relevant evidence in the case. Even if the expert's proposed testimony is admitted, failure to perform a hands-on inspection can open up the expert to a devastating cross-examination. This case also demonstrates the importance of preparation. A well-prepared expert would have been ready to answer likely questions regarding the text relied upon to form the opinion (in this case, the National Fire Code volume).

**Example 9.21: Expert eliminates other possible causes as improbable, causation opinion admitted**

*Bitler v. A.O. Smith Corp.,* 400 F.3d 1227 (C.A. 10 Colo. 2004)

This case involved a propane water heater explosion. The court held that an accident investigator's method of reasoning to the best inference (eliminating alternative possible causes of the gas leak as improbable) to conclude that the gas leak was caused by copper sulfide contamination on the water heater's safety valve seat was a valid scientific technique to establish causation.

**Comment:** When opining on causation, experts should always consider and provide valid reasons for eliminating other potential causes.

**Example 9.22: Conjecture opinion not allowed**

*Cook v. Sunbeam Products, Inc.,* 365 F.Supp.2d 1189 (N.D. Ala. S. Div. 2005)

In this case the court held that the expert's testimony was inadmissible. The expert testified that because the manufacturer of electrical products had made other products that were defective and because a fire started in the bedroom while an electric blanket made by the manufacturer was present, the blanket started the fire because it was defective. The court reasoned that the expert's opinions related to the fire's origin and cause were not based upon any acceptable methodology applicable to fire investigation.

# METHODOLOGY

**Comment:** The expert's methodology appeared extremely weak. The expert in this case would probably have been much better served by declining to provide an opinion in this case, thus avoiding this black mark on his record. One of the most important decisions an expert makes is which cases to accept and which to decline. Experts can avoid many potential problems by declining to give opinions where they are not truly qualified.

**Example 9.23: Conclusory, unsupported opinion not admissible**
*Hoy v. DRM, Inc.,* 2005 WY 76 (Wyo. 2005)
Testimony was not admissible against an engineering firm and construction company that allegedly damaged a leach field for a mobile home park. The experts were unable to rule out other causes for the leach field's failure, they never explained exactly how their experience and knowledge supported their opinions, and they had not undertaken any research, reviewed any relevant literature, or consulted with other experts on their theories of causation.

**Comment:** Admissible, persuasive opinions are well supported. Conclusory opinions, even if admitted, are not likely to be believed. Experts should strive to provide well-supported opinions.

**Example 9.24: Expert methodology "anecdotal," barred in multiple chemical sensitivity case**
*Bradley v. Brown,* 42 F.3d 434 (7th Cir. 1994)
Two physicians, clinical ecologists, testified that the plaintiff suffered from MCS through exposure to the defendant's spraying of a pesticide. The court excluded the testimony because the experts' opinions were "hypothetical." The experts' opinions did not establish that the etiology of MCS was known or tested. The court found that the experts could not provide testimony explaining why a person contracts a chemical sensitivity: "The method leading to [the experts'] conclusions was merely anecdotal" (438). This case illustrates the proper court focus on principles and methodology, not conclusions.

**Comment:** The methodology rules were designed to bar so-called "junk science." Experts opining in controversial areas such as multiple chemical sensitivity should expect vigorous challenges to the admissibility of their opinions.

**Example 9.25: No evidence of test to support causation opinion, testimony excluded in toxic tort case**
*Schmaltz v. Norfolk & W. Ry. Co.,* 878 F.Supp. 1119 (N.D. Ill. 1995)
Physicians offered opinions that the plaintiff's respiratory condition was caused by exposure to the defendant's chemicals. The first physician's testimony was excluded because he offered no evidence of tests that supported his theory.

**Example 9.26: No evidence that expert had conducted any studies or analyses to substantiate his views, testimony excluded in carpal tunnel syndrome causation case**
*Zarecki v. National R.R. Passenger Corp.,* 914 F.Supp. 1566, 1574 (N.D. Ill. 1996)
A physician's proffered testimony on the cause of the plaintiff's carpal tunnel syndrome was excluded on the grounds that the physician offered no evidence that he had conducted any studies or analyses to substantiate his views. This case also confirms the following: "Of these four factors [listed in *Daubert*], the first—whether the proffered theory has been tested—has been deemed the most important."

**Comment:** Not only is testing useful for the admissibility of the expert's proposed testimony, the fact that the expert conducted testing is likely to make the testimony more persuasive to the jury.

**Example 9.27: Testimony barred in power saw products liability action where expert did not offer testable alternative design**
*Stanczyk v. Black & Decker, Inc.,* 836 F.Supp. 565 (N.D. Ill. 1993)
This was a products liability action against a power saw manufacturer for a design defect. A mechanical engineer expert witness (who designed saws) testified that an alternative concept would have been safer. The court found that he offered no testable design to support this concept and excluded the evidence on that ground.

**Comment:** The strongest opinions do not have holes in them. This expert would have been much better served to have presented a testable alternative design. Products liability, pharmaceutical, and fire origin cases are some of the categories of cases that tend to draw *Daubert* challenges. When testifying in such cases, experts are best served to discuss with retaining counsel the likely *Daubert* issues and make plans to avoid problems. For example, if based on previous case law, a testable alternative design is likely to be an issue, the expert should try to develop such a testable design.

**Example 9.28: Causation analysis based on "just looking at it" not sufficient to avoid a *Daubert* exclusion in radiation-induced cataract case**
*O'Conner v. Commonwealth Edison Co.,* 13 F.3d 1090 (7th Cir. 1994)
A physician's expert testimony that he could ascertain whether a particular cataract was caused by radiation just by looking at it was not admitted because no evidence was offered to prove that radiation-induced cataracts could be identified by mere observation.

**Comment:** If the expert was able to articulate *why* he could tell by "just looking at it" this testimony may have been admitted. Experts should always be able to provide cogent reasons why their opinions are valid.

**Example 9.29: No "empirical foundation" to causation opinion where no study had been performed in drug products liability case**
*Wheat v. Pfizer, Inc.,* 31 F.3d 340, 343 (5th Cir. 1994)
This was a products liability action against manufacturers of drugs that allegedly caused the plaintiff's death. Expert witness testimony was excluded and the court noted that the expert's testimony would not have passed the first factor of a *Daubert* analysis. The expert hypothesized that the combination of two drugs may have caused the plaintiff's injury, but he admitted that no study of the combination had ever been done: "[T]hus his hypothesis lacked an empirical foundation."

**Comment:** This is a good example of the type of testimony the judge is supposed to bar in his role as "gatekeeper." The methodology rules were designed to keep unreliable testimony away from the jury.

**Example 9.30: Hypothesis, although testable, was never tested, testimony excluded in breast implant case**
*Kelley v. American Heyer-Schulte Corp.,* 957 F.Supp. 873 (W.D. Tex. 1997)
This was a products liability suit alleging the manufacturer's breast implants caused the plaintiff's injury. The epidemiologist expert witness's hypothesis, though testable, had never been tested. The court excluded the testimony on this ground, as well as others.

# METHODOLOGY

**Example 9.31: Lack of tests and testing results in exclusion of expert testimony in medical device products liability case**
*Cabrera v. Cordis Corp.,* 945 F.Supp. 209 (D. Nev. 1996)
In this products liability suit against the manufacturers of a brain shunt, plaintiffs offered several experts to support the claim that the product caused the silicone toxicity present in the plaintiff. The immunologist expert witness testified to the results of a blood test he performed on the plaintiff that revealed the presence of antibodies allegedly resulting from the brain shunt. The court found several inadequacies with the test the expert employed. The internist expert witness opined that the plaintiff's medical complaints were a result of silicone toxicity. The court excluded the testimony in part because there was no way to test the validity of the opinions. Similarly, the physical chemist expert witness was to testify regarding the presence of a defect—the use of silicone—in the shunt. The court excluded the testimony because the expert had not tested, nor did he rely upon, any tests regarding the propriety of silicone as a material for brain shunts.

**Example 9.32: Antitrust theory neither tested nor capable of testing, testimony excluded**
*City of Tuscaloosa v. Harcross Chems., Inc.,* 877 F.Supp. 1504 (N.D. Ala. 1995)
City water and public utilities sued several chlorine distributors for various antitrust violations. An economist expert witness offered an opinion that the defendants engaged in collusive behavior. The court excluded the opinion because the theory upon which it was based ("conscious parallelism") had not been tested, nor was it capable of being tested.

**Example 9.33: Method of inquiry developed for litigation and not subject to peer review, testimony excluded in pharmaceutical products liability case**
*Lust v. Merrell Dow Pharm., Inc.,* 89 F.3d 594 (9th Cir. 1996)
This products liability action was brought under the theory that the plaintiff's birth defect was caused by the plaintiff's mother's ingestion of the defendant's fertility drug. The plaintiff's expert, an epidemiologist, failed to subject his method of inquiry to peer review and to develop his opinion outside the context of litigation. His opinion was excluded.

**Comment:** The most valuable experts are those who are not full-time professional experts and who have not developed their theories in the context of litigation. Ideally, experts should maintain professional practices apart from their forensic work.

**Example 9.34: Lack of peer review in toxic tort case, testimony excluded**
*Cuevas v. E.I. DuPont De Nemours & Co.,* 956 F.Supp. 1306 (S.D. Miss. 1997)
In this action against a herbicide manufacturer, the plaintiff's expert toxicologist opined that the herbicide caused the plaintiff's medical problems. The court excluded the opinion, noting that the expert "admitted that his opinion had not undergone any type of peer-review."

**Comment:** The peer review test is a way for the court to determine whether the expert's method is accepted in the relevant professional community.

**Example 9.35: Lack of peer review in pharmaceutical products liability case, testimony excluded**
*Haggerty v. Upjohn Co.,* 950 F.Supp. 1160, 1164 (S.D. Fla. 1996)
In this products liability action against the manufacturer of a sleeping medication, the plaintiff's expert, a nonphysician pharmacologist, opined that the ingestion of the medication caused the plaintiff's injury. The court found that the expert's causation opinion had never been subjected to

peer review—her methodology had never been published nor discussed in front of a scientific audience.

**Example 9.36: Testimony excluded in vehicle products liability case where no peer-reviewed studies were cited and theory not tested**
*Navarro v. Fuji Heavy Indus.,* 925 F.Supp. 1323, 1329 (N.D. Ill. 1996)
In this products liability action against the manufacturer of a vehicle, the plaintiff's engineering expert offered his opinion that the manufacturer's design was defective and this defect caused the structural failure that caused the plaintiff's injury. The court, declaring this testimony inadmissible, stated:

> [The expert] has not provided adequate scientific support for his damning conclusions. He cites no published journals, studies, reports, or treatises, nor has he set forth the methodology employed in reaching his conclusions. He does not identify testing or research techniques. There is no reference to peer review of any results reached by [the expert].

**Example 9.37: High potential rate of error when calculating radioactive half-life based on only two samples, testimony excluded**
*In re TMI Litig. Cases Consol. II,* 911 F.Supp. 775, 795 (M.D. Pa. 1996)
In this action, residents near Three Mile Island sought damages for alleged exposure to excessive amounts of radioactive gases during the reactor accident. The court excluded a chemistry professor's proffered testimony because his method of calculating radioactive half-life for soil samples, based on only two readings, had a very high potential rate of error. A meteorologist's testimony was also excluded. He proffered testimony about a plume movie and water model of dispersion of radioactive gases emitted during the reactor accident, and the court found that the methodology had a potentially high rate of error.

**Comment:** To avoid potential rate of error challenges, experts should use an appropriately large sample size.

**Example 9.38: Due to extraordinarily high rate of error, testimony excluded where expert extrapolated from animal studies without supportive human studies**
*Wade-Gereaux v. Whitehall Lab., Inc.,* 874 F.Supp. 1441, 1480 (D.V.I. 1994)
In this products liability action brought against the manufacturer of a nasal decongestant by a mother on behalf of her child (who was born with birth defects), the plaintiff's expert, a pediatric pathologist, testified that the decongestant was the cause of the birth defect. This opinion was based upon several animal studies. The court rejected the expert's opinion, stating:

> The theory of plaintiff's expert witnesses that they can directly extrapolate from experimental animal studies without supportive positive human studies to opine as to causation in humans is one that has an extraordinarily high rate of error, and this fact weighs against the admissibility of opinions based upon those methodologies.

**Comment:** Testimony based on animal studies is often challenged. Experts who intend to testify based on animal studies should consult with counsel early on to ensure that steps are taken to help mitigate the likelihood that the expert's testimony will be excluded.

# METHODOLOGY

**Example 9.39: Testimony that is "far afield from any recognized scientific principle" excluded**
*Stalnaker v. General Motors Corp.,* 934 F.Supp. 179 (D. Md. 1996)
The court's words are illustrative:

> The Court agrees with the defendant that the plaintiff's expert witnesses do not present sufficient evidence from which a jury could reasonably conclude that there was a defect in the product, and that the so-called "skip-lock" theory is indeed a theory that is "scientific," in the sense that it relies on basic principles of physics and mechanics. Yet, it is in itself obviously so far afield from any recognized scientific principle to be completely inadmissible under the current standard for admissibility of expert testimony.

**Example 9.40: Opinion lacking general acceptance excluded**
*Dennis v. Pertec Computer Corp.,* 927 F.Supp. 156 (D. N.J. 1996)
In this products liability action by keyboard operators against a keyboard manufacturer, a certified professional ergonomist opined that the defendant's keyboard design was likely to produce cumulative repetitive motion trauma. The court did not admit the testimony: "[The expert's opinion has] simply not gained general acceptance."

**Comment:** Note that this successful *Daubert* challenge involved a controversial area—whether use of a keyboard caused cumulative repetitive motion trauma. *Daubert* challenges are most likely in controversial areas.

**Example 9.41: Economist's "willingness to pay" model for calculating loss of future enjoyment of life had been peer reviewed, but had not gained general acceptance, testimony excluded**
*Kurncz v. Honda N. Am., Inc.,* 166 F.R.D. 386 (W.D. Mich. 1996)
This was a personal injury action. The plaintiff sustained injury while riding a three-wheeler. The plaintiff offered testimony by an economist, purportedly to aid the jury in valuating the plaintiff's loss of future enjoyment of life caused by the defendant's negligence. The economist proposed a "willingness to pay" model for calculating these damages. The court rejected the testimony as unreliable: "[The] method has been subject to peer review and [the expert] is well published. The peer review, however, has not led to general acceptance—the fourth *Daubert* factor."

**Comment:** Peer review may not lead to admissibility when peers do not accept the methodology.

**Example 9.42: Inadequate testing and lack of acceptance of theories by other experts in same field dooms testimony**
*American & Foreign Insurance Co. v. General Electric Co.,* 45 F.3d 135 (6th Cir. 1995)
Here, the court affirmed a district court's determination that the plaintiff's electrical engineering expert could not satisfy at least two of *Daubert*'s four prongs. The expert's theories were not accepted by other experts in the same field and his testing and his theory were not of a type reasonably relied upon by others in his field. Moreover, his testing was woefully inadequate. He did not preserve the raw data from his tests and he never calibrated the instruments used to perform those tests.

**Comment:** Note how the expert is criticized for sloppiness. Even if the expert's testimony was admitted, a sloppy expert's testimony is unlikely to persuade a jury.

**Example 9.43: None of the research performed outside of the context of lawsuit, testimony excluded**
*Estate of Mitchell v. Gencorp, Inc.,* 968 F.Supp. 592 (D. Kan. 1997)
The estate of a worker who died of chronic myelogenous leukemia brought a products liability action against the manufacturer of chemicals that had been stored in a "flammable room" at the worker's place of employment. The plaintiff's experts—two physicians, each specializing in hematology and oncology—testified that the defendant's chemicals caused the decedent's leukemia. The court found it "significant" that the plaintiff's experts developed theory opinions expressly for the purpose of testifying, stating, "none of the witnesses has done any research on his theories outside the context of this lawsuit." This fact, combined with other inadequacies in the experts' opinions, led the court to exclude the evidence.

**Comment:** *Daubert* challenges are very common in toxic tort cases.

**Example 9.44: Testimony barred where expert had never before performed human testing**
*Braun v. Lorillard Inc,* 84 F.3d 230 (7th Cir. 1996)
A smoker who had used cigarettes with an asbestos filter sued the manufacturers of the cigarette and filter under a theory of products liability, alleging that the products caused his mesothelioma. The plaintiff's expert, a professor of biochemistry, testified that lung tissue obtained from the plaintiff (who died before the conclusion of the litigation) contained asbestos fibers. The expert was also president of a consulting firm that does environmental testing for the presence of asbestos. The court found that the expert had never tested human tissues for the presence of asbestos before being hired by the plaintiff's lawyer and that the suggestion for using the particular testing method on humans had come from lawyers rather than scientists. The court excluded the testimony and characterized the situation as abuse by the plaintiff's lawyer: "That abuse is the hiring of reputable scientists, impressively credentialed, to testify for a fee to propositions that they have not arrived at through the methods that they use when they are doing their professional work rather than being paid to give an opinion helpful to one side of a lawsuit."

**Comment:** When a retaining lawyer helps direct the expert's investigation this provides a huge amount of fodder for the opposing side. The most effective experts form their opinions based upon reliable methodology and not by taking directions from retaining counsel.

## 9.8 Treatment of Testimony by Specialty
In the following cases, the court has subjected expert testimony to a *Daubert* or *Daubert*-based analysis. The list is organized by specialty type.

*Accident Investigator:* Testimony was **admissible** although the expert did not test his theory. The testimony did not present any controversial or novel explanations concerning regularly occurring natural phenomena. *Bitler v. A.O. Smith Corp.,* 400 F.3d 1227 (C.A. 10 Colo. 2004)

*Accident Reconstruction Engineer and Auto Safety Engineer:* Expert testimony that vertical attachments on a tractor-trailer's rear bumper guard would have prevented the deaths of a driver and a child passenger (whose vehicle collided with the trailer from behind and slid underneath) did not satisfy *Daubert* standards. Testimony was **not admissible** in the surviving passenger's products liability action against the trailer manufacturer. Experts did not factor-in the added strength of the rear guard with the vertical attachments and how that would enhance injury. Underlying data only addressed the mechanics of the accident as it actually happened. The court noted that both experts relied on intuition rather than valid reasoning and reliable methodology. *Rapp v. Singh,* 152 F.Supp.2d 694 (E.D. Pa. 2001)

*Accident Reconstructionist:* This case considered the force of impact based on the use of an accelerometer to measure G forces on a vehicle. **Admissible** because the methodology was an accepted industry practice. *Perret v. Neson,* 722 So.2d 1118 (La. App. 5 Cir. 1998)

*Accident Reconstructionist:* The expert addressed the number of impacts upon a vehicle. **Admissible.** Methodology tested and generally accepted. *J.B. Hunt Transport v. General Motors,* 52 F.Supp2d 1084 (E.D. Mo. 1999)

*Accident Reconstructionist:* The opinion of a former state police officer expert regarding a collision's lateral speed lacked sufficient reliability. It was **excluded** partly because the methodology used was not testable, was not subject to peer review, had no known rate of error, and was not generally accepted within the scientific community. *Davis v. Martel,* 790 So.2d 767 (La. App. 3 Cir. 2001)

*Accident Reconstructionist:* An expert opinion regarding the cause of a motor vehicle accident was **not admissible.** The expert did not perform any calculations, did not use any mathematical formulas, made no attempt to find out the information needed to determine if the vehicle hydroplaned, did not take any measurements of the accident scene, and did not have the benefit of photographs of the accident scene. *Garcia v. Louisiana Dept. of Transp. and Development,* 787 So.2d 1142 (La. App. 4 Cir. 2001)

*Accountant:* Damages opinion of expert was sufficiently reliable to be **admissible;** expert employed acceptable methodology. Doubts regarding assumptions used in calculating damages went to weight, not admissibility. *Main Street Mortgage, Inc. v. Main Street Bancorp., Inc.,* 2001 WL 1013378 (E.D. Pa. 2001)

*Agricultural Economist:* This case involved the causes of fluctuations in the cattle market. Testimony was **excluded** because the modeling method was not generally used in the field to support causation. *Blue Dane Simmental v. American Simmental Assn.,* 178 F.3d 1035 (8th Cir. 1999)

*Agricultural Engineer:* At issue was the effect of an electric cooperative's stray voltage on a dairy herd. **Admissible** testimony because the theory was exhaustively tested. *James v. Beauregard Elec. Co-op., Inc.,* 736 So.2d 353 (La. App. 3 Cir. 1999)

*Agronomist:* This CERCLA suit involved the costs incurred in the clean up of a hazardous substance. **Admissible** opinion based on valid methodology. *B.F. Goodrich v. Betkoski,* 99 F.3d 505 (2d Cir. 1996)

*Allergist:* Testimony alleged that a carpet caused respiratory illness. **Inadmissible** opinion because no scientific studies were presented. Methodology reliable, but did not "fit" conclusion. *Heller v. Shaw,* 167 F.3d 146 (3rd Cir. 1999)

*Anthropologist:* Testimony considered the meaning of certain terms as applied by a government agency. **Admissible.** *Grand Traverse Band of Ottawa & Chippewa v. U.S.,* 46 F.Supp.2d 689 (W.D. Mich. 1999)

*Biomechanical Engineer:* Testimony on mechanism of hockey player's injury was **inadmissible** in an action against the manufacturer of the hockey helmet and mask. Expert's analysis exhibited a glaring and egregious lack of testing, an overwhelming reliance on assumed values, and a novel theory. *Mohney v. U.S. Hockey, Inc.,* 300 F.Supp.2d 556 (N.D. Ohio W.Div. 2004)

***Biomechanical Engineer (Ph.D.):*** In this products liability case, the expert opinion regarding the cause of injuries was **admitted.** Methodology was reliable. The expert reconstructed the accident by reviewing the police report, photos of the scene, Miles's medical records, Miles's radiology reports (which interpreted Miles's x-rays), witness statements and depositions, and medical literature. *Miles v. General Motors Corp.,* 2001 WL 930568 (C.A. 8 2001)

***Biomechanics:*** This case involved a guest who had fallen from an apartment balcony. The court held **inadmissible** proposed testimony that it was much more likely that a gust of wind caused the guest to fall than it was that she accidentally leaned over too far backwards and lost her balance. This testimony appeared to be based more on supposition than science. The court noted that the expert admitted that the cause of the fall was not clear. *O'Neill v. Windshire-Copeland Associates,* 372 F.3d 281 (C.A. 4 Va. 2004)

***Biomedical Engineer:*** This testimony involved a theory of "inertial release" and its relation to a seatbelt system's crashworthiness. The **admissible** theory was based on extensive testing. *Guild v. General Motors Corp.,* 53 F.Supp.2d 363 (W.D.N.Y. 1999)

***Cardiologist:*** This case considered the likelihood of future medical problems. **Admissible** opinion based upon accepted scientific principles and proven data. *Knapp v. Northwestern University,* 942 F.Supp. 1191 (N.D. Ill. 1996)

***Cardiologist:*** At issue was if a nicotine overdose caused a heart attack. **Inadmissible** opinion because no scientific evidence was presented to support the theory and there was no reference to the literature. *Rosen v. CIBA-Geigy Corp.,* 78 F.3d 316 (7th Cir. 1996)

***Ceramics Expert (Ph.D.):*** This case involved the adequacy of a warning label on a grinder. The **inadmissible** opinion was not based upon any scientific theory or empirical research. *Robertson v. Norton Co.,* 148 F.2d 905 (8th Cir. 1998)

***Certified Public Accountant:*** An insider-trading defendant found certain reports unreliable and did not pay attention to them. **Inadmissible** testimony because the methodology was speculation. *SEC v. Lipson,* 46 F.Supp.2d 758 (N.D. Ill. 1999)

***Chemical Engineer:*** An opinion considered whether asbestos manufacturers engaged in conspiracy. **Admissible.** *Burgess v. Abex Corp.,* 712 N.E.2d 939 (Ill. App. 4 Dist. 1999)

***Chemist:*** The cause of a tire failure was at issue. The **inadmissible** opinion did not present evidence explaining the methodology supporting the theory nor did it indicate the theory was tested under current manufacturing standards. *Mitchell v. Uniroyal Goodrich Tire Co.,* 666 So. 2d 727 (La. App. 4 Cir. 1995)

***Chemist:*** A farmer exposed to cattle larvacide retained it in his tissue. This opinion was **excluded** on grounds of all *Daubert* factors, particularly "common sense" testing methods. *Loch v. Shell Oil Co.,* 49 F.Supp.2d 1262 (D. Kan. 1999)

***Civil Engineer:*** Preventative maintenance on an injury-causing elevator was not done properly. **Inadmissible** opinion because no evidence was presented regarding any scientific basis for the opinion. *Jiminez v. GNOC, Corp.,* 670 A.2d 24 (N.J. Super. A.D. 1996)

***Clinical Ecologist:*** The cause of MCS was in question. **Inadmissible** opinion because no reliable scientific basis for diagnosing MCS exists. *Coffey v. County of Hennepin,* 23 F.Supp.2d 1081 (D. Minn. 1998)

# METHODOLOGY

***Clinical Social Worker:*** A terminated employee's mental anguish was at issue. The **inadmissible** opinion was neither testable nor peer-reviewed. Although it was accepted by the community for nonjudicial use, the rate of error was not explored. *America West Airlines, Inc. v. Tope,* 935 S.W.2d 908 (Tex. App.-El Paso 1996)

***Construction Expert (Construction Management & Costing):*** Testimony as to the amount of termite-related damage to an apartment complex was **admissible,** notwithstanding alleged weaknesses in the "subtraction method" employed to calculate such damage. *In re Westminster Associates, Ltd.,* 265 B.R. 329 (Bkrtcy. M.D. Fla. 2001)

***Criminologist:*** Testimony regarding the culture and practices of the New York Police Department was **admissible.** It was based upon interviews, commission reports, research articles, scholarly journals, books and newspaper reports. Such data are of a type reasonably relied upon by experts in various disciplines of social science. *Katt v. City of New York,* 151 F.Supp. 2d 313 (S.D.N.Y. 2001)

***Economist:*** In a wrongful death suit, an expert's testimony regarding loss of income was **excluded** because the expert did not prove the scientific reliability underlying the "mirror image" methodology of estimating future earnings. The expert provided no peer-reviewed publication support, no citation for a book that supported the approach, and no authority to support that the approach was generally accepted. *Ollis v. Knecht,* 751 N.E.2d 825 (Ind. App. 2001)

***Economist:*** Testimony involved loss figures for loss of guidance or counsel in the context of parents' anticipated losses of financial support due to a child's death. **Inadmissible** opinion not based on scientifically valid methodology. *Cochrane v. Schneider Nat. Carriers, Inc.,* 980 F.Supp. 374 (D. Kan. 1997)

***Electrical Engineer:*** The expert was **allowed to testify** regarding an electric blanket that caught on fire. This was based on the expert's experience as an electrical engineer, his testing, and his observations of the subject blanket. *Hildebrand v. Sunbeam Products, Inc.,* 2005 WL 2739205 (D. Kan. 2005)

***Electrical Engineer:*** At issue was if an asphalt compactor was defective because it lacked an automatic shutoff device. **Inadmissible** testimony because the "concept" in the opinion was untested. *Campbell ex. rel. Campbell v. Studer,* 970 P.2d 389 (Wyo. 1998)

***Electrical Engineer:*** Opinion that a clothes dryer thermometer caused a fire. **Admissible.** Numerous works of technical literature support the mode of analysis. *Maryland Cas. Co. v. Therm-O-Disc, Inc.,* 137 F.3d 780 (4th Cir. 1998)

***Electrical Engineer:*** Opinion that electrical wiring started a fire was **admissible** based upon reasoned elimination of other possible causes. *Doyle Wilson Homebuilder, Inc. v. Pickens,* 996 S.W.2d 387 (Tex. App.-Austin 1999)

***Electrical Engineer:*** Theory that a copier malfunction caused a fire (based on inspection of the machine) was **admissible.** *Media Logic Inc. v. Xerox Corp.,* 689 N.Y.S.2d 762 (A.D. 3 Dept. 1999)

***Electricity Expert (Physics Ph.D.):*** Theory that stray voltage caused injury to a dairy herd was **inadmissible** because it had no scientific support and was untested. *Schlader v. Interstate Power Co.,* 591 N.W.2d 10 (Iowa 1999)

*Engineer:* Alternative seatbelt design feasibility and "inertial actuation" testimony was **inadmissible** because the design concept was not subjected to peer review or testing. *Rogers v. Ford Motor Co.,* 953 F.Supp. 606 (N.D. Ind. 1997)

*Engineer:* Opinion that an airbag should only deploy at 20 to 25 mph in a frontal collision was **inadmissible.** It was unpublished, untested, and unverified. *Demaree v. Toyota Motor Corp.,* 37 F.Supp2d 959 (W.D. Ky. 1999)

*Engineer:* Cause of separation of tire belts opinion was **inadmissible.** It did not incorporate any scientific authority. *Diviero v. Uniroyal Goodrich Tire Co.,* 919 F.Supp. 1353 (D. Ariz. 1996)

*Engineer:* Testimony that a small fragment of metal caused an explosion was **inadmissible** based upon untested premises. *Stibbs v. Mapco, Inc.,* 945 F.Supp. 1220 (S.D. Iowa 1996)

*Engineer:* At issue was the identity of the manufacturer of a broken scoping line cable. **Inadmissible** because chemical analysis of the wire rope was based on unreliable methodology and there was no evidence presented regarding any of the *Daubert* factors. *Hanks by Old. Nat. Trust Co. v. Korea Iron and Steel,* 993 F.Supp. 1204 (S.D. Ill. 1998)

*Engineer:* Testimony that falling merchandise in a store aisle was caused by the store's improper stacking was **inadmissible.** The opinion was based on commonsense determinations but was not scientifically reliable because it did not rely on calculations of the weight and size of the merchandise that fell, the number of items in the stack at the time of the incident, or the degree of force that would cause the stack and merchandise to move or fall. *Brown v. Wal-Mart Stores, Inc.,* 402 F.Supp.2d 303 (D. Me. 2005)

*Engineer:* Opinion that a tire changer design was defective was **inadmissible** because the expert never designed, built, or tested a changer that incorporated a different design based upon his alternative. *Peitzmeier v. Hennessy Industries, Inc.,* 97 F.3d 293 (8th Cir. 1996)

*Engineer:* This theory that a design defect caused vibrations in a coal hauler that caused injuries in drivers was **admissible** because the haulers' "geometry" supports the opinion. *Bartley v. Euclid, Inc.,* 158 F.3d 261 (5th Cir. 1998)

*Engineer/Accident Reconstructionist:* Opinion that a motorist caused an accident and injuries to a bicyclist was **admissible.** The theory was based on physics and the tests forming the opinion's basis were sound and had nonjudicial uses. *Waring v. Wommack,* 945 S.W.2d 889 (Tex. App.-Austin 1997)

*Engineer/Ergonomist:* At issue was if a keyboard required excessive keying forces. **Inadmissible** opinion was not based on an ergonomic analysis of factors affecting the plaintiff. *Reiff v. Convergent Technologies,* 957 F.Supp. 573 (D. N.J. 1997)

*Environmental Consultant:* Confined testing results to determine the source of contamination by spilled diesel fuel was **inadmissible** due to insufficient testing methodology. *Burns Philip Food v. Cavalea Continental Freight,* 135 F.3d 526 (7th Cir. 1998)

*Epidemiologist:* At issue was whether Depo-Provera caused birth defects. **Admissible** opinion used conventional methodology for expert's field. *Ambrosini v. Labarraque,* 101 F.3d 129 (D.C. Cir. 1996)

*Epidemiologist:* Testimony based on questionable study was **not admissible.** Sample size of study was so small that the margin of error was very large, the study never reached any conclusion about

PUF-coated implants specifically, and the expert ignored certain flaws in the study. *In re Silicone Gel Breast Implants Products Liability Litigation,* 318 F.Supp.2d 879 (C.D. Cal. 2004)

*Ergonomist:* Opinion regarding the biomechanics of keystroking, the plaintiff's disorders, and the keyboard design was **inadmissible.** No methodology was presented and there was no evidence of peer review of the theory. *Dennis v. Pertec Computer Corp.,* 927 F.Supp. 156 (D. N.J. 1996)

*Ergonomist:* Testimony that a computer-aided dispatch system caused repetitive motion disorder and that workstation design was unreasonably dangerous was **inadmissible.** The expert offered no evidence regarding the source relied upon for relevant industry standards and no peer review or publication of conclusion. *Bennet v. PRC Public Sector, Inc.,* 931 F.Supp. 484 (S.D. Tex. 1996)

*Ergonomist:* Opinion stating that low-repetition occupations are associated with cumulative trauma disorders was **inadmissible.** The testing underlying the theory was insufficient. *Stasior v. Nat'l Railroad Passenger Corp.,* 19 F.Supp2d 835 (N.D. Ill. 1998)

*Exercise Physiologist:* At issue was the amount of energy an average person expended while walking a round of golf. **Inadmissible** opinion disclosed no evidence of methodology. *Olinger v. U.S. Golf Association,* 52 F.Supp.2d 947 (N.D. Ind. 1999)

*Fire Expert:* Testimony stating that a fire was caused by arson was **inadmissible.** The conclusion came as a result of eliminating other factors, no testing took place, and there was an admitted lack of scientific basis for the hypothetical cause of the fire. *Michigan Millers Mut. Ins. Corp. v. Benfield,* 140 F.3d 915 (11th Cir. 1998)

*Fire Investigator:* In this products liability suit, testimony that a design defect caused 23 clothes dryer fires was **reliable,** even though the expert did not test his theory experimentally. The expert analyzed burn patterns of each dryer and ruled out potential alternative explanations. *Travelers Property & Cas. Corp. v. General Elec. Co.,* 150 F.Supp.2d 360 (D. Conn. 2001)

*Fire Investigator:* Testimony was **inadmissible** where there was no evidence that ballast could generate enough heat to ignite a fire. Although the expert claimed he adhered to fire investigation standards requiring him to determine whether the heat source was capable of generating ignition temperature, the opinion did not meet these standards. *Truck Ins. Exchange v. MagneTek, Inc.,* 360 F.3d 1206 (C.A. 10 Colo. 2004)

*Forensic Chemist:* Testimony that 99% of U.S. currency is contaminated with drug residue was **inadmissible.** There was no peer review of the test results underlying the opinion and the tests were not replicable. *U.S. v. $141,770 in U.S. Currency,* 157 F.3d 600 (8th Cir. 1998)

*Gun Expert:* At issue was whether a gun malfunction caused a hunting accident. This **inadmissible** opinion was too speculative. *Bromley v. Garey,* 979 P.2d 1165 (Idaho 1999)

*Immigration Expert:* Opinion regarding the passport-stamping practices of Mexican immigration officials, based on "professional study or personal experience," was reliable and **admissible.** *Maiz v. Virani,* 253 F.3d 641 (C.A. 11 2001) 65 (Idaho 1999)

*Immunologist:* The opinion that a brain shunt resulted in silicone toxicity, based upon a "silicone antibody test," was **inadmissible** because the test did not meet any of the *Daubert* factors. *Cabrera v. Cordis,* 945 F.Supp. 209 (D. Nev. 1996)

***Industrial Engineer:*** Alternative designs for the braking system of a trim press were at issue. **Inadmissible** opinion because the design had never been subjected to the scientific method and had never been tested. *Cummins v. Lyle Industries,* 93 F.3d 362 (7th Cir. 1996)

***Industrial Hygienist:*** Although the expert's studies had not been conducted under conditions that were substantively similar to those experienced by plaintiff, the studies were conducted properly. **Testimony admissible.** *Clephas v. Garlock, Inc.,* 2004 WL 1699794 (Ky. App. 2004)

***Industrial Hygienist:*** Opinion stated that exposure to excessive levels of Benzene caused injury. This **admissible** opinion had generous scientific support for its causation theory. *Curtis v. M&S Petroleum, Inc.,* 174 F.3d 661 (5th Cir. 1999)

***Industrial Hygienist:*** Testimony stating that exposure to trichloroethylene caused multiple myeloma was **admissible** due to sound methodology. *Arnold v. Dow Chemical Co.,* 32 F.Supp.2d 584 (E.D.N.Y. 1999)

***Industrial Hygienist:*** At issue was a worker's level of exposure to the defendant's chemicals. The **inadmissible** opinion was based on photos of the work site and unreliable methodology. *Mitchell v. Gencorp Inc.,* 165 F.3d 778 (10th Cir. 1999)

***Industrial Hygienist:*** This case involved whether Toulene caused myelogenous leukemia. The opinion was **inadmissible** because the expert knew of no studies showing that the chemical caused the disease. *Estate of Mitchell,* 968 F.Supp. 592 (D. Kan. 1997)

***Industrial Hygienist and Environmental Engineer:*** In question was whether ethylene oxide was entrained and circulated into the plaintiff physician's office. The opinion was **admissible** because articles relied on were authoritative and methods were accepted by the medical community. *LaSalle Nat. Bank v. Malik,* 705 N.E.2d 938 (Ill. App. 2 Dist. 1999)

***Internist (M.D., Ph.D.):*** This was a products liability case. An expert opinion linking a drug's pharmacological effect to heightened cardiac risk was **excluded** as unreliable given the absence of testing, no peer review and publication, and lack of acceptance in the scientific community. *Brumley v. Pfizer, Inc.,* 200 F.R.D. 596 (S.D. Tex. 2001)

***Locomotive Engineer:*** In this case involving a railroad accident, the expert opinion that the engineer should have seen a gap in rails was **not admissible.** It was not reliable because it was not founded on facts in evidence. *Guidroz-Brault v. Missouri Pacific R.R. Co.,* 254 F.3d 825 (C.A. 9 2001)

***Marine Biologist:*** In an oil spill case, an opinion regarding the cause of death of millions of oysters was **sufficiently reliable** despite absence of prior studies. The court found the expert's science was reliable enough to address the cause at issue, that it was not feasible to conduct controlled experiments on the issue, and that the expert developed his opinion using differential diagnosis methodology. *Clausen v. M/V New Carissa,* 2001 WL 1011882 (D. Or. 2001)

***Mechanical Engineer:*** Alternative design for safety device on table saw was **inadmissible** because the methodology was "virtually nonexistent." *Tassin v. Sears, Roebuck and Co.,* 946 F.Supp. 1241 (M.D. La. 1996)

***Mechanical Engineer:*** Opinion that a corn-head device was unreasonably dangerous and should have had awareness barriers was **inadmissible** because there was no testing of the device. *Juarequi v. Carter Mfg. Co.,* 173 F.3d 1076 (8th Cir. 1999)

# METHODOLOGY

*Mechanical Engineer:* An expert **could testify** about two runs of a computer program. Although somewhat suspect, the program had been properly verified, was arguably reliable, and was widely accepted as a tool for predicting severity of automobile collisions on human occupants. *Melberg v. Plains Marketing, L.P.,* 332 F.Supp.2d 1253 (D.N.D. N.W. Div. 2004)

*Mechanical Engineer:* In this products liability case, an expert opinion that the design was defective because it failed to comply with SAE standards was **admissible.** The methodology included researching engineering standards and applying those standards to knowledge gained during field research. *Alfred v. Caterpillar, Inc.,* 2001 WL 950974 C.A. 10 (Okla. 2001)

*Mechanical Engineer:* At issue was whether a tractor's pedal design was unreasonably dangerous. The **inadmissible** opinion was based on experience, but no evidence of scientific foundation was offered. *Freeman v. Case Corp.,* 118 F.2d 1011 (4th Cir. 1997)

*Mechanical Engineer:* This products liability action was brought against a manufacturer of lift trucks. The expert's opinion regarding a design defect lacked indicia of reliability and was therefore **inadmissible.** The expert employed no defined methodology and did not provide "good grounds" for his conclusions because he did not perform any substantive testing of the allegedly defective design or of his proposed alternative. *Milanowicz v. The Raymond Corp.,* 148 F.Supp.2d 525 (D. N.J. 2001)

*Mechanical Engineer (Ph.D.):* In this construction workers' suit against a crane manufacturer for injuries suffered when a load was dropped from the crane, the opinion that the crane's hoist brake mechanism was defective (based on a review of affidavits of eyewitnesses and a crane inspector, inspection of the same type of mechanism in a different case, and a review of a letter and service bulletin from the manufacturer) was **reliable.** However, the court struck a portion of the opinion as to when the manufacturer had notice of the defect. Neither the expert's expertise nor personal knowledge provided a basis for the opinion. *Carballo Rodriguez v. Clark Equipment Co.,* 147 F.Supp.2d 81 (D. Puerto Rico 2001)

*Medical Toxicologist:* This case considered whether exposure to contaminated milk caused laryngeal cancer. The expert's opinion was **inadmissible.** There was no scientific literature drawing a connection between the type of exposure in this case and cancer and no human or animal study showed a connection. *Nat'l Bank of Commerce v. Associated Milk Producers,* 22 F.Supp.2d 942 (E.D. Ark. 1998)

*Metallurgist:* Opinion that manufacturing flaws caused premature fracturing of a guidewire tip used in an angioplasty procedure was **admissible.** The opinion was based on observation of destructive testing of the guidewire tip, testing developed and performed under the direction of the defendants' expert witness, and fractographs from scanning electron microscopic examination. *Parkinson v. Guidant Corp.,* 315 F.Supp.2d 754 (W.D. Pa. 2004)

*Microbiologist:* At issue was if certain tampons caused toxic shock syndrome. **Admissible,** although not generally accepted. *Graham v. Playtex Products, Inc.,* 993 F.Supp. 127 (N.D.N.Y. 1998)

*Naval Architect:* Expert opinion that a bend in a yacht's swim ladder was the result of the owner's normal use of the ladder was **not admissible.** The expert agreed that static forces applied to the ladder from normal use would result in applied force of less than half of that needed to cause the bend. The expert did not perform any testing on the ladder, could only speculate as to when the ladder was bent, and his calculations failed to take into account the ladder's handholds. *Higginbotham v. KCS Intern., Inc.,* 85 Fed.Appx. 911(C.A. 4 Md. 2004)

*Neurologist:* "Challenge/de-challenge/re-challenge methodology" in reaching the conclusion that a herbal weight-loss supplement containing ephedrine and caffeine caused each of the user's injuries was **inadmissible** where there were insufficient controls employed by the expert. *McClain v. Metabolife Intern., Inc.,* 401 F.3d 1233 (C.A. 11 Ala. 2005)

*Neurologist:* The causal relationship between stress and multiple sclerosis was at issue. **Admissible** opinion due to an abundance of specialized literature on the relationship. *Colell v. Mentzer Investments, Inc.,* 973 P.2d 631 (Colo. App. 1998)

*Neurologist:* The opinion involved whether a device's vibration caused carpal tunnel syndrome. The **admissible** theory was subjected to numerous scientifically valid tests. *White v. Chicago Pneumatic Tool Co.,* 994 F.Supp. 1478 (S.D. Ga. 1998)

*Neurologist:* The case involved whether exposure to silicone after a breast implant caused multiple sclerosis. The opinion was **inadmissible** because the scientifically unreliable theory failed *Daubert* analysis. *Minnesota Min. & Mfg. Co. v. Atterbury,* 978 S.W.2d 183 (Tex. App.-Texarkana 1998)

*Neurologist:* In a products liability action against a drug manufacturer, an opinion that intracerebral hemorrhage (ICH) was caused by ingestion of the drug at issue to suppress postpartum lactation, based on differential diagnosis, was **inadmissible.** It lacked a basis for "ruling in" the drug at issue as a potential cause of ICH. *Glastetter v. Novartis Pharmaceuticals Corp.,* 252 F.3d 986 (C.A. 8 2001)

*Neurologist:* An opinion that neurological problems were caused by exposure to solvents was **inadmissible.** It was based on "whole person aggravation" theory. There was no evidence that the theory had a scientific basis. Articles relied upon did not support neurotoxicity conclusions. *Schudel v. General Electric Co.,* 120 F.3d 991 (9th Cir. 1997)

*Neuropsychologist and Neurotoxicologist:* In this toxic tort case, the expert was **allowed** to testify that the injury was consistent with exposure to a toxic level of the toxin at issue. *Bonner v. ISP Technologies, Inc.,* 259 F.3d 924 (C.A. 8 2001)

*Neurosurgeon:* At issue was whether the plaintiff developed carpal tunnel syndrome because he carried signal lights. The opinion was **inadmissible** because there was no investigation or research into causes of CTS, no articulation of methodology by which conclusions might be tested, and the testimony was prepared specifically for litigation. *Dukes v. Illinois Cent. R. Co.,* 934 F.Supp. 939 (N.D. Ill. 1996)

*Nuclear Reactor Physicist:* The opinion asserted that plaintiffs were exposed to gases after a hydrogen blowout. **Inadmissible.** The expert could not explain how he reached his conclusions. *In re TMI Litigation Cases Consol. II,* 911 F.Supp. 775 (M.D. Pas. 1996)

*Obstetrician:* Administering the chicken pox virus to a mother would have protected a fetus that was born with defects. **Admissible** opinion based on scientifically valid principle even though "science" has not fully tested the expert's theory. *Williams v. Hedican,* 561 N.W.2d 817 (Iowa 1997)

*Occupational Physician:* The opinion stated that exposure to ethylene oxide caused brain cancer. **Inadmissible.** The opinion was unreliable due to inconclusive animal studies and insufficient epidemiological evidence. *Allen v. Pennsylvania Engineering Corp.,* 102 F.3d 194 (5th Cir. 1996)

# METHODOLOGY

***Ophthalmologist:*** The case considered whether ingestion of Tegison (for psoriasis) caused toxicity in the plaintiff. Opinion found **inadmissible.** The novel theory had not been tested and was not accepted by the medical community. *Golod v. Hoffman-LaRoche,* 964 F.Supp. 841 (S.D.N.Y. 1997)

***Ophthalmologist:*** Opinion that therapeutic doses of Accutane caused cataracts. Found **inadmissible** because no specific determination of how much of the drug actually reached the plaintiff's lenses nor how much need be present to produce cataracts. *Grimes v. Hoffman-LaRoche, Inc.,* 907 F.Supp. 33 (D.N.H. 1995)

***Orthopedic Surgeon:*** Expert stated that a bone screw device used in a spinal fusion caused injury. The opinion was **inadmissible.** The expert did not present a scientific basis for the opinion, thus it failed *Daubert* factors. *Smith v. Sofamor, S.N.C.,* 21 F.Supp.2d 918 (W.D. Wis. 1998)

***Orthopedic Surgeon:*** The expert's opinion that the patient's failed spinal fusion resulted from a defective spinal fusion device was **unreliable.** Methodology underlying the opinion was inconsistent with diagnostic methodology he used in his medical practice. *Cooper v. Smith & Nephew, Inc.,* 259 F.3d 194 (C.A. 4 2001)

***Orthopedic Surgeon:*** Opinion that keyboarding caused carpal tunnel syndrome was **admissible** based upon medical literature, nerve conduction tests, and experience. *Crafton v. Union Pacific R. Co.,* 585 N.W.2d 115 (Neb. App. 1998)

***Pathologist:*** The expert was **not allowed to testify** that implants accelerated breast cancer spread. No human or animal studies showed that the chemical could cause such an acceleration. There were no specific data about the possible effects of the amount of the chemical to which the plaintiff was theoretically exposed. *In re Silicone Gel Breast Implants Products Liability Litigation,* 318 F.Supp.2d 879 (C.D. Cal. 2004)

***Pediatric Neurologist:*** The expert's opinion that a prematurely born infant's cerebral palsy could have been caused by excessive *in utero* carbon monoxide exposure was **admissible.** It was based on the generally accepted scientific technique of differential diagnosis methodology by identifying possible causes of the infant's cerebral palsy and ruling out most of these causes, identifying the type of event that led to or substantially contributed to cerebral palsy, and ascertaining the timeframe within which that event occurred. *Asad v. Continental Airlines, Inc.,* 314 F.Supp.2d 726 (N.D. Ohio E. Div. 2004)

***Pediatric Ophthalmologist:*** Testimony **inadmissible** where there were no studies supporting the doctor's theory that a condition could be successfully treated outside of the 72-hour period recommended by studies. The only study cited by any of the experts in which treatment did not occur within 72 hours of the threshold showed no positive outcomes. *Gross v. Burt,* 149 S.W.3d 213 (Tex. App. Fort Worth 2004)

***Pediatrician:*** Opinion that a mother's exposure to Dursban caused birth defects in her child was **inadmissible.** It was not based on the expert's own research or any animal or human studies. *Nat'l Bank of Com. v. Dow Chemical,* 965 F.Supp. 1490 (E.D. Ark. 1996)

***Pharmacologist:*** Amount of drugs driver of vehicle consumed and time of consumption. **Admissible** based on half-life methodology that has significant support in the scientific community. *Ruiz-Troche v. Pepsi Cola of Puerto Rico,* 161 F.3d 77 (1st Cir. 1998)

***Pharmacologist:*** The expert relied on certain studies in reaching his conclusion but authors of one report admitted their studies did not offer a basis to prove causation between ephedrine and caffeine. Authors of another report indicated that their report demonstrated only a temporal, not a causal, relationship between ephedrine and adverse cardiovascular events. **Testimony barred.** *McClain v. Metabolife Intern., Inc.,* 401 F.3d 1233 (C.A. 11 Ala. 2005)

***Pharmacologist:*** At issue was whether ingestion of Halcion caused psychological injury. The **inadmissible** opinion was based upon methodology that was not scientifically sound. The expert did not review epidemiological data or actual case studies underlying opinion. *Haggerty v. Upjohn Co.,* 950 F.Supp. 1160 (S.D. Fla. 1996)

***Pharmacologist and Toxicologist:*** Testimony regarding the cause of acute symptoms was based on **reliable** methodology. *Bonner v. ISP Technologies, Inc.,* 259 F.3d 924 (C.A. 8 2001)

***Pharmacology Professor:*** Opinion that taking Floxin caused AIHA and GBS was **inadmissible** on all four *Daubert* grounds. *Willert v. Ortho Pharmaceutical Corp.,* 995 F.Supp. 979 (D. Minn. 1998)

***Physician:*** Opinion stating that an exterminator's negligence caused an office worker's MCS. **Inadmissible** because the theory of causation was too speculative to satisfy *Daubert* factors. *Coffin v. Orkin Exterminating Co., Inc.,* 20 F.Supp.2d 107 (D. Me. 1998)

***Physician:*** At issue was whether occupational diseases were caused by toxic chemical exposure. The **inadmissible** opinion proffered no evidence establishing *Daubert* factors. *Aldridge v. Goodyear Tire & Rubber Co.,* 34 F.Supp.2d 1010 (D. Md. 1999)

***Physician:*** Testimony that patient tampering took place was **admissible** based upon the knowledge of toxicity derived from and supported by peer-reviewed articles. *Gess v. U.S.,* 952 F.Supp. 1529 (M.D. Ala. 1996)

***Physician:*** Testimony that a treating physician's medical opinion on causation can be based on differential diagnosis was **admissible.** *Wesberry v. Gislaved Gummi AB,* 178 F.3d 257 (4th Cir. 1999)

***Physician:*** At issue was whether the use of Oraflex (contaminated by Benzene) caused bone-marrow disorder. **Admissible** opinion. Three physician experts based their theory on differential diagnosis methodology. There is a clear connection in the scientific literature between Benzene and MDS. *Lakie v. Smithkline Beecham,* 965 F.Supp. 49 (D.D.C. 1997)

***Physician (Expert on Lead Poisoning):*** The expert opinion considered the use of "KXRF bone lead testing" to determine bone lead levels. The **inadmissible** opinion had not gained acceptance in the medical community, except for experimental purposes. *Dombrowski v. Gould Electronics, Inc.,* 31 F.Supp.2d 436 (M.D. Pa. 1998)

***Physician, PM&R:*** Testimony that a fall caused hormonal changes resulting in fibromyalgia was **inadmissible** because there was no scientifically reliable basis for the causation opinion. *Black v. Food Lion, Inc.,* 171 F.3d 308 (5th Cir. 1999)

***Physicians, Toxicologist, Psychologists:*** Testimony that MCS was caused by exposure to environmental pollutants. **Inadmissible** opinion due to inadequate scientific foundation for conclusions regarding MCS. *Frank v. State of New York,* 972 F.Supp. 130 (N.D.N.Y. 1997)

# METHODOLOGY

***Physicist:*** Testimony **not admissible** where proposed testimony was not supported by scientific testing and three publications introduced to support the theory of long-term, low-temperature ignition were inconclusive, vague, or inapplicable. *Truck Ins. Exchange v. MagneTek, Inc.,* 360 F.3d 1206 (C.A. 10 Colo. 2004)

***Polygraph Examiner:*** At issue were the results of a polygraph exam using control question technique. Testimony was **inadmissible** because the rate of error was undetermined and there was no general acceptance. *Meyers v. Arcudi,* 947 F.Supp. 581 (D. Conn. 1996)

***Polymer Chemist:*** Testimony regarding the products of the breakdown of polyurethane foam in the body was **admissible** despite the existence of contrary studies. The expert's testimony was based on his own published peer-reviewed study and other published peer-reviewed studies *In re Silicone Gel Breast Implants Products Liability Litigation,* 318 F.Supp.2d 879 (C.D. Cal. 2004)

***Professor of Materials, Science & Engineering:*** The effects of silicone breast implants on the body were in question. The **admissible** testimony was based on the expert's own research, chemical company studies, government studies, and other expert's testimony. *Vassallo v. Baxter Healthcare Corp.,* 696 N.E.2d 909 (Mass. 1998)

***Psychiatrist:*** Testimony related to repressed memory. The **admissible** theory had been tested, subjected to peer review, and accepted by clinical psychiatrists. *Shahzade v. Gregory,* 923 F.Supp 286 (D. Mass. 1996)

***Psychologist:*** At issue was whether exposure to diesel fumes caused dementia. The **inadmissible** opinion was based on testing still in the research stage. *Summers v. Missouri Pacific R.R. System,* 132 F.3d 599 (10th Cir. 1997)

***Psychologist:*** Testimony regarding the manner in which an "all white" advertising firm's campaign affects African-Americans was **admissible** based on peer-reviewed articles and sound methodology. *Tyus v. Urban Search Management,* 12 F.3d 256 (7th Cir. 1996)

***Radiation Geneticist:*** Testimony considered the extent of radiation to which trees were exposed. The **inadmissible** opinion was based upon dendrometric study, no evidence on the methodology was employed. *In re TMI Litigation Cases Consolidated II,* 910 F.Supp. 200 (M.D. Pa. 1996)

***Rheumatologist:*** The case considered whether breast implants caused Sjogren's Syndrome. The **inadmissible** expert testimony was based upon literature that did not support the theory and the expert's own studies did not meet *Daubert* factors. *Kelley v. American Heyer-Schulte Corp.,* 957 F.Supp. 873 (W.D. Tex. 1997)

***Safety:*** Opinion **admissible** that a customer's trip and fall over a clothing rack was caused by the store owner's failure to design a rack that would not protrude into the traffic area and the owner's failure to follow safety manuals and industry practices. The expert took into account reliable publications such as a National Safety Council document and employed the same level of intellectual rigor that characterized the practice of an expert in his field. *Wisdom v. TJX Companies, Inc.,* 2006 WL 149004 (D. Vt. 2006)

***Safety Engineer:*** Testimony that a gravity grain box was dangerous and unsafe was **admissible** based on commonly used design principles. *Doblar v. Unverferth Mfg. Co., Inc.,* 981 F.Supp. 1284 (D. S.D. 1997)

***Safety Engineer:*** Expert opinion that an instruction on an adhesive remover rendered it hazardous was **inadmissible** due to insufficient testing and no studies were presented. *Kirstein v. Parks Corp.,* 159 F.3d 1065 (7th Cir. 1998)

***Safety Engineer:*** Opinion regarding an injury resulting from failure of automotive lift was **excluded** because there was no showing that the theory had been tested or reviewed by other safety experts. *Hutton v. Globe Hoist Co.,* 2001 WL 1006648 (S.D.N.Y. 2001)

***Safety Engineer:*** This products liability action stemmed from an incident in which a 10-month-old child climbed inside the broiler compartment of a kitchen range. The expert engineer had not explained how he arrived at his conclusions as to some of his proposed design alternatives. Thus, his opinions regarding these alternative designs were **not admissible.** *Dewick v. Maytag Corp.,* 324 F.Supp.2d 894 (N.D. Ill. E. Div. 2004)

***Statistician:*** Aggregated pools analyses were **admissible** because the statistician previously explained the methodology underlying his analyses. *McReynolds v. Sodexho Marriott Services, Inc.,* 349 F.Supp.2d 30 (D.D.C. 2004)

***Statistician:*** Testimony **admissible** despite opposing side's claims that the studies were done in anticipation of litigation, samples were too small, and the expert failed to perform elementary tests of reliability. Such challenges addressed the factual basis of the analysis and went to weight, not admissibility. *Marvin Lumber and Cedar Co. v. PPG Industries, Inc.,* 401 F.3d 901 (C.A. 8 Minn. 2005)

***Tire Expert:*** **Testimony barred** where opinion was based only on visual and tactile testing of a tire. No evidence indicated that other experts used the same methodology. The tire expert did not refer to any article or publication that specifically supported his approach. *Goodyear Tire & Rubber Co. v. Rios,* 143 S.W.3d 107 (Tex. App. San Antonio 2004)

***Toxicologist:*** Opinion that a "toxic reaction" was caused by inhaling powdered bleach was **inadmissible.** The expert never conducted any research to test the hypothesis, never saw the injury before, and offered no scientific basis for the opinion. *Higgins v. Diversey Corp.,* 998 F.Supp. 598 (D. Md. 1997)

***Toxicologist:*** Extrapolation from animals to humans was proper where there was no reliable epidemiological evidence and governmental public health organizations had relied on animal studies to conclude that the chemical was a probable or possible carcinogen. Testimony was **admissible.** *In re Silicone Gel Breast Implants Products Liability Litigation,* 318 F.Supp.2d 879 (C.D. Cal. 2004)

***Toxicologist:*** Opinion that exposure to Chlordane caused injury was **inadmissible.** Affidavits containing the expert's testimony offered no information about the methodology used or qualifications of the expert. *Vardaman v. Baker Center, Inc.,* 711 So.2d 727 (La. App. 1 Cir. 1998)

***Toxicologist:*** Testimony that a herbicide caused an injury was **inadmissible.** The opinion was based on a theory that had never been peer reviewed. *Cuevas v. E.I. DuPont de Nemours and Co.,* 956 F.Supp. 1306 (S.D. Miss. 1997)

***Toxicologist:*** An opinion stating that latex paint exposure caused asthma was **inadmissible.** The expert's reports, affidavits, deposition testimony, and supporting literature failed to identify what methodology he employed to reach his causation conclusion other than a temporal relationship. *Cartwright v. Home Depot USA,* 936 F.Supp. 900 (M.D. Fla. 1996)

***Toxicologist:*** At issue were levels of exposure to termiticide. Opinion was **admissible** in spite of expert not considering threshold levels of exposure. The opinion was consistent with accepted methods of toxicology. *Louderback v. Orkin Exterminating Co.,* 26 F.Supp.2d 1298 (D. Kan. 1998)

***Toxicologist:*** Testimony that potassium poisoning was used to murder decedent was **admissible** although the theory was untested and novel. (This was a bench trial, which gave the court more latitude.) *Matter of Sybers,* 583 N.W.2d 890 (Iowa 1998)

***Toxicologist, Pharmacologist (M.D.):*** Methodology underlying doctor's testimony regarding increased risk of cancer for persons exposed to butadiene and soot was **reliable,** although he conceded he could not precisely measure the plaintiff's exposure. *In re New Orleans Train Car Leakage Fire Litigation,* 2001 WL 737680 (La. App. 4 Cir. 2001)

***Tree Pathologist:*** Testimony as to contributing causes of tree's fall was **admissible** despite the expert's inability to conduct any empirical testing on the subject tree because it no longer existed. The expert was able to deduce possible causes of the tree's failure based on examination of photographs of the tree, depositions by witnesses, forestry texts, and a report by another tree expert. It was possible to test the expert's conclusions objectively. *Lesser ex rel. Lesser v. Camp Wildwood,* 282 F.Supp.2d 139 (S.D.N.Y. 2003)

### 9.9  How Experts Can Avoid or Deal with *Daubert* Challenges

An expert's opinion may be challenged at a *Daubert* hearing. If the challenge is successful, the expert's entire testimony could be excluded from evidence. This could result in the dismissal of the case and permanent damage to the reputation of the expert. What can an expert do to protect herself from a successful *Daubert* challenge?

*General assessment*
Prior to accepting the engagement, an expert should ask counsel if he anticipates a *Daubert* attack on the expert's testimony. Next, the expert should evaluate for herself if a *Daubert* attack is likely. Is the case novel? Is it complex? Is a substantial amount in controversy? Was the case filed in federal court or in one of the majority of states that follow *Daubert?*

*Specific criteria*
The expert should take a long, hard look at her work and methodology results under the *Daubert* criteria. To avoid rejection of testimony, an expert should do the following.

- Only use theories or techniques that have been tested and passed.
- Use theories or techniques that are objective.
- Specify the known error rate or potential error rate for the method.
- Use methods with acceptable error rates.
- Produce peer-reviewed literature (i.e., journal studies, reports, and treatises supporting the expert's conclusions and opinions).
- Produce reliable scientific data to prove that her methods and conclusions are generally accepted in the scientific community.
- Demonstrate that her theories existed prior to the commencement of the litigation.
- Not develop novel theories to support conclusions for specific litigation.

- Demonstrate that she maintained standards and controls (for example, good laboratory practices and simultaneous blind controls).
- Demonstrate that findings can and have been replicated by others.
- Demonstrate that her methodology followed the scientific method as it is practiced by at least a recognized minority of scientists in her field.
- Offer testimony that is sufficiently tied to the facts of the case to help the jury to resolve a factual dispute.
- Avoid relying on the coincidence of temporality.
- Avoid extrapolating unjustifiably from an accepted premise to an unfounded conclusion.
- Adequately account for obvious alternative explanations.
- Demonstrate the same care and accuracy as in regular professional work.
- Use the real-world methodology of her field.
- Use an appropriate methodology to ensure that her opinion derives from and constitutes a form of specialized knowledge.

## 9.10 Conclusion

Expert opinions must be supported by reliable methodology. "Junk science" may be excluded from evidence for being unreliable. Even if it is not excluded by the trial judge, the expert's methodology may be subject to close questioning during cross-examination. Experts should base their opinions upon sound methodology. If an expert cannot base his opinion on a reliable methodology, he should decline to offer an opinion.

# Chapter 10  Bulletproofing an Expert's Report

## 10.1  Introduction

Experts may be asked to draft reports that state their opinions and the bases for these opinions.  The expert needs to assume that anything he writes will be discoverable as part of ongoing or future litigation.  (See Chapter 21 on confidentiality and work product.)  *An expert, therefore, should never draft a written report of any kind unless he has been expressly requested to do so by his retaining counsel.*  Counsel may remind the expert not to draft a written report when she retains the expert or when she sends the expert records or documentation.  Experts should never draft written reports without checking with counsel.

## 10.2  Written Reports Required in Federal Court

There are many reasons why counsel may want an expert to draft a written report.  A written report may be required by the court or forum where the litigation is pending.  For example, under Federal Rule of Civil Procedure 26(a)(2)(B),[1] unless otherwise stipulated or directed by the court, an expert must prepare and sign a written report containing:

- a complete statement of all opinions to be expressed,
- the basis and reasons for the opinions,
- the data or other information considered,
- any exhibits to be used in summary of the opinions,
- any exhibits to be used as support for the opinions,
- the qualifications of the witness,
- a list of all publications authored by the witness in the preceding ten years,
- the compensation to be paid for the study and testimony, and
- a listing of any other cases in which the witness has testified as an expert at trial or by deposition within the preceding four years.[2]

The reason for requiring expert reports is the elimination of unfair surprise to the opposing party and conservation of resources.[3]  Failure to comply with the requirements of Rule 26(a)(2)(B) can result in the expert's testimony being stricken.  The test of compliance is whether the report is sufficiently complete, detailed, and in compliance with the rules so that surprise is eliminated, unnecessary depositions are avoided, and costs are reduced.[4]

**Example 10.1: Report missing expert's qualifications, compensation, and complete statement of opinions with reasons insufficient**
*Pell v. E.I. DuPont De Nemours & Co., Inc.,* 231 F.R.D. 186 (D. Del. 2005)
In this ERISA case the court held that the expert's report did not satisfy the requirements of Federal Rule of Civil Procedure 26(a)(2)(B) because the report did not include the expert's

---

[1] See Appendix Q for the full text of Rule 26.
[2] Fed. R. Civ. Pro. 26(2)(B).
[3] *Reed v. Binder,* 165 F.R.D. 424 (D.C. N.J. 1996).
[4] *Reed v. Binder,* 165 F.R.D. 424 (D.C. N.J. 1996).

qualifications, compensation, and a complete statement of the opinions to be offered with reasons. The court reasoned:

> I agree that the Report fails to even come close to satisfying the requirements for expert reports under Federal Rule of Civil Procedure 26(a)(2)(B). Specifically, the Report does not contain Dr. Tannian's qualifications to give expert testimony, namely an identification of his employment history, or identification of publications, or a listing of other cases in which he has testified, or an indication of his compensation from Plaintiffs. (See D.I. 105, Ex. A.) Dr. Tannian states in the Report that "[e]stimates will be made of the pension Mr. Pell would have received under the Consol Pension Plan ... [,]" but does not provide any indication of those estimates or what his conclusions based on those estimates will be. Dr. Tannian chooses 6.0% and 8.0% wage growth rates for a number of years without any explanation of how or why he chose those numbers. (D.I. 105, Ex. A. at 2 ("Had he remained at Consol, and gained wage increases of only 8.0% a year through 1990, dropping back to 6.0% a year through 2001, his pay level in 2001 under these lower (than previous actual) wage growth rate assumptions would have been $17,356 a month in 2001").) Thus, the Report fails to contain a complete statement of all opinions to be expressed and the basis and reasons therefor as required by Rule 26(a)(2)(B).
>
> Moreover, Dr. Tannian's proposed testimony and Report fail to satisfy the *Daubert* standards for the admissibility of expert testimony. Without including Dr. Tannian's qualifications, there is no way for me to determine whether he is qualified to render the expert opinions he has proposed in the Report. There are also clear analytical gaps in Dr. Tannian's opinions, namely, the methodology he used to derive the 6% and 8% wage growth rate figures. It is therefore impossible to judge the reliability of Dr. Tannian's methods. Thus, Dr. Tannian's report fails to meet the requirements of both Rule 26(a)(2)(B) and *Daubert.*
>
> Under Federal Rule of Civil Procedure 37(c)(1), [a] party that without substantial justification fails to disclose information required by Rule 26(a)...is not, unless such failure is harmless, permitted to use as evidence at a trial...any witness or information not so disclosed. In additional to or in lieu of this sanction, the court, on motion and after affording an opportunity to be heard, may impose other appropriate sanctions....[including] requiring payment of reasonable expenses, including attorney's fees, caused by the failure....
>
> Fed.R.Civ.P. 37(c)(1).
>
> If Plaintiffs choose to remedy the deficiencies of Dr. Tannian's report, DuPont will have another opportunity to depose Dr. Tannian to determine whether his report satisfies the requirements of Rule 26(a)(2)(B) and whether his testimony satisfies the standards enunciated in Daubert. The reasonable expenses incurred by DuPont as a result of Plaintiff's failures under Rule 26(a)(2)(B) will be paid by Plaintiffs, including DuPont attorney time spent in preparation for, and deposition of, Dr. Tannian, and time to make a subsequent motion to strike and preclude, should Plaintiffs be unable to remedy the deficiencies noted above. See *Tarlton v. Cumberland County Correctional Facility*, 192 F.R.D. 165, 169 (D.N.J.2000) (noting the self-executing nature of Rule 37(c)(1), i.e., there is no need for a litigant to make a motion to invoke the possible sanctions of the Rule). Should Plaintiffs choose not to remedy the deficiencies of Dr. Tannian's report and proposed testimony, DuPont's Motion to Strike and Preclude will be granted for all of the reasons discussed. The Plaintiffs must make their election within three weeks of the date of this Order. At 193–194.

**Comment:** The courts are fairly strict in requiring compliance with Rule 26(a)(2)(B). Experts may be barred from testifying if their reports do not meet the requirements of the Rule.

### Example 10.2: "Conclusionary" report, testimony barred

*Salgado v. General Motors Corporation,* 150 F.3d 735 (7th Cir. 1998)
The experts' reports were filed in an untimely manner and were markedly deficient—they appeared to be "preliminary" in nature. The first expert's report was "conclusionary" and thus insufficient. The court characterized the second expert's report as "devoid of any factual basis for its conclusionary opinions." Also, the second expert claimed the report was sparse because he had not been provided discovery materials. Then, he attempted to file a supplementary report

containing the "factual bases" for his opinion. However, this supplemental report was based solely on materials already in his possession before the filing of the first report. The court barred both experts' testimony.

**Comment:** If the expert is allowed to testify at trial, an opinion without supporting reasons will be extremely vulnerable to attack on cross-examination and will be unlikely to persuade a fact finder. The most persuasive and valuable experts offer well-supported and well-reasoned opinions that are not conclusionary.

### Example 10.3: Report without list of past testimony within last four years, expert barred
*Elgas v. Colorado Belle Corp.,* 179 F.R.D. 296 (D. Nev. 1998)
In this tort action, the plaintiff failed to provide a proper Rule 26 report for her designated expert witness. The court struck the designation of the expert, because "[the expert] has not listed other cases in which he has testified as an expert at trial or by deposition within the preceding four years." An expert's report must be "detailed and complete." The court explained:

> An expert's failure to maintain records in the ordinary course of his business sufficient to allow the disclosures to be made, does not constitute "substantial justification" for the failure to provide required disclosures as to any retained expert expected to testify at the trial of the case. The requirements of the Rule 26(a) are mandatory as to any expert retained to testify. If the expert is unable or unwilling to make the disclosures he should be excluded as a possibility for retention as an expert witness in the case.

The plaintiff argued that she was unable under her current financial situation to find another expert. However, the court rejected this and stated that "[a] party may not simply retain an expert and then make whatever disclosures the expert is willing or able to make notwithstanding the known requirements of Rule 26." The court reasoned,

> [T]he disclosure of prior recorded testimony is designed to give the other party access to useful information to meet the proposed experts' opinions. The proliferation of marginal or unscrupulous experts will only be stopped when the other party has detailed information about prior testimony. The list of other cases in which the witness has testified as an expert should include the court, the names of the parties, the case number, and whether the testimony was by deposition or at trial. At 298.

Because the plaintiff did not show how the failure to disclose was substantially justified or harmless, the court struck the designation plaintiff's expert.

**Comment:** Experts who wish to testify in federal court should, on an ongoing basis, maintain a list of the cases they have testified in at deposition and trial going back four years. Experts will not be allowed to testify without including this list in their reports. Reconstructing this list from scratch when needed could be quite difficult, especially if the expert testifies often.

### Example 10.4: All "reasonably available information" regarding past testimony not enough, expert to supplement report or be stricken
*Nguyen v. IBP, Inc.,* 162 F.R.D. 675 (D. Kan. 1995)
The plaintiff's expert's report did not contain all the data required under Rule 26. The report identified patients about whom the expert had testified, but the report provided no identification of "cases" or courts in which the expert's deposition had been taken, had incomplete or missing attorney names, had missing phone numbers for attorneys, provided no witness signature, and offered entries for the last three, rather than four, years. The plaintiff maintained that all "reasonably available information" was disclosed, but the court found no substantial justification existed for the shoddy report. "An expert's failure to maintain records in the ordinary course of

business sufficient to allow the disclosures to be made does not constitute 'substantial justification' for the failure to provide required disclosures as to any expert retained…." The court allowed the plaintiff the opportunity to submit a supplemental disclosure that corrected the deficiencies, then declared that the expert's testimony would be barred if the supplemental report did not suffice.

In some arbitration proceedings experts must present their direct testimony via a written report signed under the pains and penalties of perjury. Counsel may also want a written report to assist in settlement negotiations. A well-written and soundly reasoned report will improve the settlement value of a case. A written report may also be needed in support of or in opposition against a motion for summary judgment or as a vehicle to discourage costly expert depositions. Whatever the reason, the expert's report will become a crucially important document in a contested legal proceeding. It is, therefore, very important that it is drafted carefully.

## 10.3  The Most Common Report Drafting Mistakes

When drafting a report, the expert should only address the issues that counsel has asked her to address in the report. If she is unsure of which issues to address, the expert should call counsel and ask him what he wants addressed and what issues he does not want addressed. For example, when drafting an Independent Medical Examination (IME) report, an expert will need to know which issues and opinions should be included in the written report (for example, impairment, disability, symptom magnification, etc.) and which should not be included (for example, appropriateness of care).

The expert should address all the issues that counsel has requested her to address. Failure to do so can be very damaging to counsel's case. In some circumstances, for example, where the report was to be used to oppose a motion for summary judgment or where it was to be used in lieu of direct testimony, failure to address all the requested issues could result in the case being lost outright.

An expert should keep in mind that anything she writes in a report can and will be used against her when she testifies in the case at hand or even in some future case. In effect, each and every report an expert produces becomes a part of the expert's "permanent record." A poorly written report can be used during cross-examination to damage an expert's credibility in the case at hand and in future cases. There are several things to avoid when drafting reports that can and will come back to haunt an expert during cross-examination. These include the following.

### 1. Sloppiness

The report should be proofed carefully. It's tough to pick up your own typos, so it may be a good idea for experts to have someone else proof their work. They should also use a computerized spelling and grammar checker. A good cross-examiner will point out each and every instance of sloppiness and typos in a report. Counsel can make the argument that if an expert was sloppy in drafting his report, he was probably rushed and sloppy when he formed his opinion. She will argue that an opinion based upon sloppy or rushed work is not credible. This problem is 100% avoidable if the expert takes his time and has his report proofed.

**Example 10.5: Typo in report makes the expert look sloppy (or worse)**
It is therefore my opinion, based upon a reasonable degree of reasonable certainty that….

**Comment:** Grammatical and typographical errors are 100% avoidable. They should be corrected by careful proofing by the expert, the expert's word processor, and a third person such as the expert's assistant or spouse.

## 2. Remarks that make the expert appear to be an advocate

An expert needs to avoid making any remarks, even subtle ones, that counsel can use to show that the expert is an advocate in the case for the party that retained him. The role of the expert in the case is as an expert, not an advocate. If counsel can successfully argue that the expert is an advocate, the expert will come off as a hired gun and will lose credibility with the jury. Examples of remarks to avoid include stressing key points with exclamation points, underlining, capitalization, and remarks addressing credibility.

**Example 10.6: Emphasis in report makes expert appear to be an advocate**
The defendant in this case was <u>clearly</u> GROSSLY Negligent!!!

**Comment:** If the expert appears to be arguing a case, he will lose credibility.

**Example 10.7: Expert comments on credibility of witness in report**
This report is based in part upon the deposition of the plaintiff, John Smith, who was not a credible witness.

**Comment:** The jury, not the experts, judges the credibility of witnesses.

## 3. Improperly stating an opinion

The expert's main reason for being involved in a case is to state an opinion that will assist the trier of fact in deciding the case. This opinion must be stated in a proper, legally sufficient way. The most commonly used phrase to properly state an expert opinion follows.

**Example 10.8: Proper language to use when stating an opinion**
Based upon a reasonable degree of (scientific or medical) (probability or certainty), it is my opinion that....

Experts need to avoid using hedge words such as *may, could,* or *possible* when stating opinions.

**Example 10.9: Hedge words weaken or invalidate report and opinion**
It's my opinion that it's possible that the tire that failed on May 9, 1999 had a design defect.

Failure to state an opinion properly in a report can result in major problems. First, in some cases, it can result in the expert's opinion being excluded by the court or other forum. Second, during cross-examination it will be used against the expert to damage her credibility.

## 4. Inartfully drafted sentences or phrases

Experts need to avoid using inartfully drafted sentences or phrases that could suggest incompetence or bias.

**Example 10.10: Inartfully drafted sentence is an avoidable mistake**
Per your request, I have formed the opinion that....

**Comment:** Such sentences are best avoided by *carefully* proofing your work and having someone else proof your work as well. The best experts take the time and make the effort to ensure that their reports are carefully proofed.

Counsel will use anything and everything contained in an expert's report as ammunition during cross-examination. An expert should not give her any extra ammunition by using inartful sentences or phrases. Experts should read over their reports carefully before submission.

### 5. Sharing draft reports with retaining counsel

Experts should not share draft reports with retaining counsel. Such draft reports are generally discoverable. The fact that they were shared with counsel and changes were then made to them strongly suggests that retaining counsel influenced the contents of the expert's report.

### 6. Drawing legal conclusions

Wise experts do not draw legal conclusions (for example, "The plaintiff was guilty of contributory negligence"). This is (usually) beyond the area of one's expertise and will get the expert into trouble during cross-examination.

**Example 10.11: Consequences of using a legal term such as "negligent" in a report**
Can you please explain to the jury the four elements of negligence, Mr. Harding?

Experts should state their opinions in such a way that they do not reach legal conclusions.

**Example 10.12: Stating an opinion without using legal terms**
Based upon all of the evidence I have reviewed, it is my opinion, based on a reasonable degree of certainty, that the plaintiff was not operating her vehicle safely at the time of the motor vehicle accident in question.

### 7. Gratuitous information and opinions

Experts should not offer gratuitous information. Instead, they should address only the points they have been requested to address. Any additional information or opinions merely serve as cross-examination ammunition.

**Example 10.13: Superfluous language**
I would also like to add that I am <u>very</u> happy that my involvement in this case will soon be coming to an end.

**Comment:** Extraneous language should be aggressively edited out of an expert's report. Inclusion of such language can only hurt the expert.

### 8. Failure to be clear and concise

The less clear and concise the report, the more open an expert will be to damaging cross-examination. Ambiguities fuel cross-examination.

**Example 10.14: Vague sentence**
This is clearly a case of what you see is what you get.

**Comment:** The best experts communicate clearly and do not use vague, confusing sentences.

## 9. Failure to check with counsel

An expert should put in a courtesy call to her retaining lawyer prior to drafting a report. During this call the expert can confirm that the attorney still wants a written report. It also provides a good opportunity to discuss findings prior to drafting the written report.

## 10. Being informal or "chatty"

The expert's report is a legally significant document that needs to be formally drafted. Informality or "chattiness" is to be avoided.

> **Example 10.15: Informality**
> Dear Teddy: Thank you for this referral. What a doozey of a case! I have reviewed….
>
> **Comment:** Informal language or chattiness can be used to show that the expert is friendly with retaining counsel or is not taking his role as an expert seriously.

## 11. Failure to review the report personally

The final step before signature should be the expert's personal review of the report. Experts should not provide clients or intermediaries with a pre-signed signature page or signature stamp.

## 12. Failure to follow the strict requirements of Rule 26(a)(2)(B) when drafting a report for federal court

Reports written pursuant to Federal Rule 26(a)(2)(B) that do not follow the strict requirements of the rule may result in the expert being barred from the case. Please see Section 10.2 above.

## 13. Not citing authority

Citing competent authority will help bolster the report and help an expert's opinion survive a *Daubert* challenge.

## 14. Using pronouns

Pronouns such as "he," "she," "it," and "they" are imprecise and should be avoided.

## 15. Self-serving words that set too high of a bar

An expert should avoid self-serving language that on the surface makes her report look stronger, but in reality sets a very high bar that opens the expert up to cross-examination.

> **Example 10.16: "Meticulous" examination**
> On May 27, 2006 I conducted a meticulous examination of the accident site.
>
> **Comment:** This expert has opened himself up to cross-examination that is likely show that he is exaggerating. All the cross-examiner needs to do is point out the many things the expert did not do as part of this self-described "meticulous" investigation.

## 16. Overuse or misuse of computer-generated boilerplate language

Use of the same computer-generated language in each report is problematic. Opposing counsel can easily use this language to show that all the expert's reports are the same, that his conclusions were pre-ordained, and that the expert is lazy. If computer-generated language is used, it is best to carefully proof the report to make sure that all the computer-generated language is applicable to the case at hand.

## 17. Failure to state reasons for opinions

The most persuasive reports contain opinions that are supported by objective facts, reasons, and standards. Ideally, these reasons will be presented as a numbered list. The use of a numbered list is helpful in that even if the reader does not understand or remember the expert's reasoning, he will understand that the expert did in fact have his reasons.

> **Example 10.17: Reasons for opinions provided as numbered list**
> *Opinions*
>
> Breach of Standard of Care:
> It is my opinion that there was a breach in the standard of care in that there was a failure to:
> 1. Notify the attending physician, Dr. Lee, of the abnormalities in the fetal heart rate tracing earlier.
> 2. Have an adequately trained nurse evaluating the monitor strip.
> 3. Have the certified nurse midwife present to evaluate the monitor strip after having been notified several times.
> 4. Maintain continuous fetal monitoring with a fetal scalp electrode in light of the:
>    • decrease in the fetal baseline heart rate,
>    • decrease in the variability,
>    • late decelerations,
>    • question marks (?) denoting maternal heart beat and not the fetal heart beat,
>    • heart rate tracing in the 90 beats per minute range, and
>    • knee-chest position.
>
> It is also my opinion that the failure to monitor the fetus at this time was the proximate cause of Kim Johnson's neurological outcome. There is a window of opportunity to predict fetal asphyxial exposure before fetal decompensation and newborn morbidity. This opportunity was missed by not appropriately interpreting the monitor tracing, not placing an electrode onto the fetal scalp, and not notifying the physician sooner.
>
> **Comment:** Persuasive opinions are those opinions that are backed up with reasons. Providing a numbered list of the expert's opinions is particularly effective in communicating that the expert had good reasons for forming his opinion. Opinions that are supported by objective facts, reasons, and standards are difficult to successfully attack on cross-examination.

## 18. Failure to list documents relied upon

Experts often fail to specifically list the documents relied upon in forming their opinions. This can lead to numerous questions during cross-examination on exactly what the expert did and did not rely upon when forming her opinion. It is best to specifically list which documents were relied upon. Not only is this transparent, but this also shows that the expert was thorough when reviewing the documents, forming his opinion, and drafting his report.

# BULLETPROOFING AN EXPERT'S REPORT

**Example 10.18: Detailed list of documents reviewed**
In forming the foregoing opinions, the undersigned has reviewed the following documents and other information:

1. Third, fourth and fifth Amended Complaints
2. Certified copy of AEIC policy # 02-BO-904634 issued to Notwen Corp., *et al.*
3. Discovery items listed in Attorney Lee's letter to me dated August 8, 2005
4. Deposition of Rebecca Lewis, July 28, 2005
5. Deposition of Lisa daCosta, September 16, 2003
6. Deposition of William Newton, September 16, 2003
7. Deposition of Jennifer Hormel, June 28, 2005
8. AEIC claim file, bates # 00001-1124
9. Safeco training manual, bates #AEIC0001-311 (under protective order)
10. Oregon statutes on Trade Secrets, # 646.461, 646.463, 646.465, 646.467, 646.469, 646.471, 646.473, 646.475
11. Black's Law Dictionary (3rd edition)
12. "Insurance Contract Analysis" by Eric A. Wiening dated 9/4/2005
13. "Fire, Casualty & Surety" Bulletins (FC&S) dated 1/14/05

**Comment:** A detailed list as above has several advantages.

- It makes the expert appear thorough and precise.
- It tells the reader exactly what the expert reviewed.
- It is a useful tool for the expert to use when preparing to testify because it reminds the expert of exactly which documents he reviewed.
- It is an invaluable aid while testifying.

## 10.4  Defending a Report at Deposition and at Trial

Experts need to know their reports cold. This includes dates, names, facts, figures, and citations. The expert will lose credibility with the jury if he appears to not be thoroughly familiar with his own report. To become thoroughly familiar with the report, he will need to review it carefully and study it as part of the preparation process prior to testifying. Please see Section 12.3.

If an expert testifies in a way that is, or can be made to sound, inconsistent with his written report, he will be questioned about this. This is a process known as *impeachment.* Proper preparation is the key to surviving an impeachment attack. An expert needs to be prepared to justify any changes in opinion from what was described in his report or to correct any mischaracterizations that counsel may raise.

**Example 10.19: Expert prepared to explain apparent inconsistency between report and testimony**
**Q.** Your report stated that it was your opinion that the vehicle in question was traveling at 65–70 miles per hour at the time of impact. Now you're saying the speed was 75–80. You were obviously wrong once, when was it?
**A.** My opinion expressed in the report was based on all the information that was available to me when the report was drafted. Since then, new information, including...has become available to me. My opinion today is more valid than the one expressed in the written report because it is based on previously unavailable information.

175

**Comment:** Experts should be prepared to explain why their testimony may be inconsistent with their report. Experts should also listen very carefully to counsel's questions to ensure that counsel is not misleading the jury by accusing the expert of an inconsistency that does not in fact exist; for example, by taking an excerpt from the report out of context.

If an expert is not permitted to explain during cross-examination, he will have an opportunity to explain himself adequately on redirect. The expert should prepare his retaining attorney in advance for the areas that may have to be explained on redirect.

The report in the case at hand is not the only report the expert needs to worry about. Counsel can and will use reports from prior cases to attempt to discredit an expert in front of the jury.[5] This can be especially effective if counsel can show that the expert's opinion in this case is inconsistent from his opinion in a previous case (for example, in a previous case report he stated that fibromyalgia does not exist; in this case his testimony is that fibromyalgia was the diagnosis). There are two good ways to defeat this tactic. First, experts should call cases as they see them. This will greatly reduce potential problems with this tactic. Second, experts should keep their cool. There is most likely a very good reason why an expert's opinion has evolved ("Ah yes, that was before the landmark Cahill-Lu study on the issue showed that…"). The expert should keep his head and make sure the reason for the change gets communicated to the jury. He shouldn't get rattled or else the jury may conclude that he has something to hide.

## 10.5  Formatting

A report that is organized into sections delineated by subject headings is the easiest to read and appears to have been carefully drafted. Commonly used headings include the following.

- Introduction, Overview, or Statement of Purpose
- Executive Summary
- Qualifications
- Prior Testimony
- Investigation or Examination
- Incident, History, or Facts
- Analysis or Discussion
- Supporting Data
- Test Results
- Materials Reviewed
- Exhibits
- References
- Opinion(s) or Findings
- Conclusion(s)

---

[5] Because reports from past cases may be used against the expert, experts should be very careful when drafting their reports. Each report in effect becomes part of the expert's "permanent record."

In terms of formatting and presentation, experts should also keep in mind the following points.

- Reports should have an easy-to-read font size. This should be at least a size eleven because small print is very difficult for many people to read.
- Experts should also remember to number the pages of their reports.
- A cover page can make the report look more professional.
- A table of contents is a nice touch on longer reports.
- Inserting color digital photographs into the report can really make the report stand out. A picture says a thousand words.
- It is best to use short sentences and short paragraphs. This facilitates readability.
- A properly formatted report can be an invaluable aid to expert witnesses while testifying because they can quickly find needed information.

## 10.6  Further Resources

Two sample forensic reports have been provided in Appendix U. A report quality control checklist has been provided in Appendix B. For more detailed information on report writing, please consult SEAK's *Writing and Defending Your Expert Report: The Step-by-Step Guide with Models* by Steven Babitsky, Esq., and James J. Mangraviti, Jr., Esq.

## 10.7  Conclusion

An expert should only draft a written report if she is explicitly requested to do so by retaining counsel. Reports drafted pursuant to Federal Rule 26 must strictly conform to the requirements of the Rule or the expert may be barred from testifying in the case. Everything in the report can be used as ammunition against the expert in the case at hand and in future cases. Therefore, experts need to draft and proof their reports very carefully and study them thoroughly prior to testifying.

# Chapter 11  Connecting with the Jury

## 11.1  Introduction

In jury trials, the jury ultimately decides the case. Their job is to determine the facts of the case. A crucial part of this is determining the credibility of the witnesses.[1] This includes expert witnesses. As such, it is of the highest importance that experts are able to communicate with the jury in a credible, memorable, understandable, and persuasive way. Everything else is secondary. To connect with the jury, an expert needs to understand what jurors want and employ the best ways to communicate with them.

## 11.2  What Juries Want

Attorney Jay W. Dankner, a highly experienced and successful litigator, explains that jurors want:

1. A relevant, coherent, understandable story.
2. To keep their interest at all times.
3. To be spoken to in clear, unambiguous terms.
4. Respect and sincerity.[2]

*A relevant, coherent, understandable story*

Sophisticated counsel will establish a theme or "story" for the entire trial that will appeal "to the jurors' standard of justice and fairness, be consistent with the evidence, and [bc] easy to remember."[3] For example, the story could be "man gets in accident, fakes injury to get money," "big company makes dangerous product that doesn't perform as promised," or "company X breaks promise to company Y and company Y is devastated financially." The expert's testimony is a crucial part of the theme or story. Many times, expert testimony is the glue that holds the story together. In any event, the expert needs to understand the theme or story of the case and how her testimony fits into the story. Gaining such an understanding is an important part of the preparation process.

*Keeping the jurors' interest at all times*

Boring experts are ineffective. Boredom is likely to be an expert's number one obstacle to communicating effectively with a jury. Many jurors do not want to be on the jury and they may have little or no interest in the case. Even more importantly, they may have an overwhelming desire that everyone concerned (the lawyers, the witnesses, and the judge) move the process along as quickly as possible so that they can all go home. To keep the jurors' interest, an expert witness should do the following.

---

[1] The judge will give the jury the following typical expert witness jury instruction: "You have heard evidence in this case from witnesses who testified as experts. The law allows an expert to express opinions on subjects involving their special knowledge, training, skill, experience, or research. You shall determine what weight, if any, should be given such testimony, as with any other witness."

[2] Jay W. Dankner, *Communicating with the Jury*. Handout materials for the Fifth Annual SEAK National Expert Witness and Litigation Seminar, Hyannis, Massachusetts (June 20, 21, 1996) 2.

[3] *Id.,* 2.

- Use powerful descriptive language that paints a picture.
- Use phrases that the jury will remember.
- Use language that jurors will understand.

For example, the expert witness might want to say (to describe a fractured neck): "It was like a finger getting caught in a door as it slammed shut. His spinal cord was cut and he'll be paralyzed the rest of his life." This is far more effective than saying: "I diagnosed a C3-C4 fracture with massive cord damage secondary to blunt trauma resultant from the MVA in question. Prognosis is for severe and permanent functional impairment."

Technical language can be extremely boring because it is hard for the jurors to follow and digest. The expert should not fall into the temptation of using it to prove to the jury how smart she is. It is far more effective to use descriptive terms that jurors understand, can visualize, and will remember. The best experts remember that their role in the case is to teach the jury and not to show off.

The expert witness should keep in mind that once she has "lost" the jury through boredom, it may be difficult or impossible to regain their attention. As such, it is good practice to work with retaining counsel to be permitted to communicate the major points of an opinion to the jury as soon as possible during direct examination. For example, let's assume an average juror has a 20-minute attention span.[4] Under this assumption, it is not good practice to spend 40 minutes talking about one's impressive experience, education, and publications *before* talking about the case at hand. By the time the expert gets to the case at hand, the jury may very well not be listening any longer. Additionally, studies have shown that jurors remember most the testimony at the beginning and the end of an examination. As such, the most effective experts start their testimony off strong and end strong as well. Doing this requires preparation with and the cooperation of retaining counsel.

*Avoid jargon*
It is best to avoid technical terminology or jargon that jurors may not understand. Such jargon is a major impediment to connecting with the jury. For example, the expert shouldn't say: "A comparison of the antemortem and postmortem records through the use of forensic odontology revealed endodential at tooth #1," when she can say: "I compared his dental records from before and after he died and found a root canal had been done on the upper right third molar...which is this tooth" (demonstrating).

As part of the preparation process, the expert should lay out how she is going to explain her testimony in clear and unambiguous terms. Some experts practice their testimony with a lay person such as an administrative assistant and then ask for feedback. This is a good technique to determine whether the expert will be able to communicate with the jury effectively. A little forethought or advanced work in this area will pay major dividends on the witness stand.

*Respect and sincerity*
Most jurors do not have the education and technical knowledge of sophisticated experts. Collectively, however, they have hundreds of years of experience in spotting phonies. The

---

[4] A valid assumption in the opinion of the authors.

expert witness, therefore, needs to avoid any comments or actions that can be interpreted as insincere or as showing a lack of respect for the jury.

**Example 11.1: Unknowingly insulting the jury**
Well, I realize that most of the jury doesn't have a high level of technical education, so I'd like to explain by drawing a diagram. I think that would make it easier.

**Comment:** There was probably no malice meant in a comment like this. However, reminding the jury of their lack of education is not a good way to connect with them.

**Example 11.2: Insulting the jurors' intelligence**
No, Counselor, my $600/hour fee has nothing to do with why I'm here today. I'm here to help the jury. I really think my expertise will assist them.

**Comment:** Jurors may not understand quantum mechanics or DNA testing, but they can spot an answer that is insincere. Once the jury has labeled the expert as a phony, it is likely that his testimony will not be believed. This is not the way to connect with a jury.

## 11.3 Communicating with Jurors

Expert witnesses need to be able to communicate with the jury. The most important quality that separates the ordinary expert from the great expert is communications skills. The expert's role in the litigation is to assist the trier of fact. She cannot properly fulfill this role if the jurors cannot understand her testimony. To better communicate with the jury, Sonya Hamlin, one of the nation's leading jury consultants, recommends the following eight points.

*1. During demonstrations print and do not abbreviate.*
An expert cannot connect with the jury if they can't read her writing or if they don't understand her abbreviations.

*2. Keep your language simple and recognizable.*
Jurors are not persuaded by what they cannot understand.

*3. Make sure the jury and judge can see your visuals.*
Visual aids are useless if they can't be seen. A wise expert witness verbalizes his concern to the judge that the jurors be able to see. When the jury hears that he is concerned, this will score points with them. The expert will also find out whether they can see.

*4. Practice with videotape.*
The expert should see how he looks and determine where he needs to improve.

*5. Self-edit and speak succinctly.*
Wise experts get to the point. They assume that a juror's attention span is no more than 20 minutes. This time should not be squandered.

*6. Tell the jurors what they need to know; not all that you know.*
Experts should not risk obscuring important testimony or losing the jury's attention.

*7. Understand the problems jurors have in assimilating a great deal of technical data when it is presented orally.*
Effective experts make their presentations visual.

*8. Visualize and demonstrate to reinforce your testimony.*[5]

Today's "TV generation" is visually driven. When an expert witness lets the jurors see what he is talking about, they understand better and remember more.

Additional techniques for communicating with a jury follow.

*Analogies and similes*

Analogies and similes are perhaps the most effective ways to connect with a jury.[6] The use of analogies and similes that relate to the jurors' personal experiences will, when done well, be remembered, discussed, and used during deliberations. The case of a young man who lost both arms in a farming accident comes to mind. The expert went to dinner with the plaintiff and his wife. When asked at trial to describe how the young man ate his dinner when the plate was put in front of him the expert stated, "He ate like a dog." This story was told to the author almost thirty years ago. He has not yet been able to forget it. Another memorable case involved a cardiologist who testified that an event made the heart attack inevitable and explained that it was "like lighting the fuse to a bomb. It was just a matter of time before it went off." An expert who can use analogies effectively is a formidable (and very valuable) witness. This is true not only because of her level of expertise, but rather due to her ability to communicate. Experts who make their testimony come alive are effective communicators.

*Powerful, memorable language*

Experts who use powerful, memorable language in the courtroom can drive home their testimony. There are usually many different ways expert testimony can be expressed. The most effective experts prepare diligently to use powerful, memorable language in lieu of dry, boring, forgettable language.

> **Example 11.3: Different ways to express one concept**
> *Memorable and Powerful:* He suffered a massive heart attack and died on the spot.
> *Dry and Forgettable:* There was an acute myocardial infarction resultant in expiration of the patient.
>
> *Memorable and Powerful:* The plane crashed into the harbor.
> *Dry and Forgettable:* The pilots executed an uncontrolled water landing.
>
> **Comment:** The best experts prepare diligently and use powerful and memorable language to express their opinions. These experts understand that how they say something may be just as important as what they are saying.

*Make it easy for the jury to connect with you on a personal basis*

Persuasion of jurors is based in large part upon trust. If the jurors trust the expert they will be more likely to believe the expert. Trust can be built by bonding with the jury and getting them to relate to the expert and like the expert. This is usually best done by showing the

---

[5] Sonya Hamlin, *What Makes Juries Listen Today* (Glaser Legal Works, 1998) 556–591.

[6] Hamlin states: "…use analogies based on *familiar* objects, experiences, or concepts. If you say, 'research is kind of like trying out the keys on your key ring until you can finally find the one that fits and opens the door,' jurors will have an instant image because they've done *that* a thousand times."

jurors that the expert has many things in common with the jurors. Such things could include children, grandchildren, the local area, household chores, common ailments, hobbies, sports, fallibility, etc. If the jurors feel that you are a real person they will be more readily persuaded by you.

**Example 11.4: Show your human side**
**Q.** How did you go about starting your investigation?
**A.** Well, like my three-year-old grandson Jimmy, I started out by asking many, many "why?" questions and following up on the answers wherever they led.

**Comment:** The expert here has subtly attempted to bond with the jury by showing that he's a real person like them, one with grandchildren, family pride, and who finds children cute. The jurors will be more likely to believe experts that they can relate to. He also showed impartiality by describing his willingness to not prejudge the outcome of his investigation.

*Be a teacher*
Experienced expert witnesses act like excellent teachers would. These experts show genuine enthusiasm for the subject matter and are able to simplify and convey complex information with humility and exuberance.

*Verbal techniques*
Attorney Jay Dankner suggests that experts employ the following verbal techniques when testifying:

> Vary your pace. Keep the jury interested and awake. Use good vocal energy. Inspire confidence. Find your natural pace. Consider when to slow down or speed up. Don't rush because you're nervous. Use proper phrasing to make certain the jury understands your point. Vary your pitch. Create an impression of confidence and authority. Use proper articulation to convey competence. Use crisp language with ideas that are easy to follow. Regulate your volume for maximum impact.[7]

The expert witness also needs to speak up and use his microphone correctly. The jurors can't believe a witness if they can't hear him.

*Nonverbal techniques*
An expert witness should dress appropriately. In most cases, this means formal business attire. The witness should be well groomed and not wear any ostentatious jewelry. A Rolex watch and a $2,000 suit will not help gain the sympathy of the jury. An expert witness should not chew gum. Everything a witness does can be seen by the jury and will affect how jurors evaluate the individual's testimony.

When walking in and out of the courtroom, the expert witness should not look at or acknowledge the party who has retained her. She should not stop to shake hands, etc. Doing so can make the expert look partisan and will lose her credibility with the jury. Furthermore, the expert witness should not invade the space of the jury by leaning on the railing to the jury box. Instead, she should maintain eye contact with the jurors and key in on any easily identifiable jury leaders.

---

[7] Dankner, 5.

The expert witness should try to appear calm and self-assured.  It is important to use good posture while sitting in the witness box and to be serious and professional.  Wise experts have all their documents and notes organized so that they do not have to fumble through them.

The jury scrutinizes body language.  Therefore, effective expert witnesses will not appear uncomfortable or insecure.  Signs of insecurity include frequently moving a hand to one's mouth or face, fidgeting, toying with one's clothes or hair, and finger or foot tapping.[8]  These signs present a negative image to the jury.

*Things to avoid*

There are a number of things that can impede one's ability to connect with the jury.  The expert witness should not do the following.

- Act in a condescending manner
- Act pompous
- Appear egotistical
- Be pedantic
- Argue with counsel
- Praise oneself
- Be arrogant
- Be boring
- Be cute
- Be overconfident
- Be sharp
- Be verbose
- Change demeanor on cross-examination
- Turn her back on the jury
- Confuse the jury
- Patronize
- Engage in nervous habits
- Fumble for papers or documents
- Look or act anxious or worried
- Overwhelm the jury

## 11.4  Additional Resources

For further information on connecting with a jury, please see *Winning Over the Jury* (DVD video, 2005 SEAK, Inc.) and *How to Become a Dangerous Expert Witness* (text, 2005 SEAK, Inc.).

## 11.5  Conclusion

Communication is critical.  An effective expert is one who can connect with and persuade the jury.  Everything else is secondary.  Experts should work diligently on practicing and improving their communication skills.

---

[8] Harold A. Feder, "Methods of Challenging Forensic Fraud and Unethical Behavior," *Shepard's Expert and Scientific Evidence Quarterly* (Spring 1995) 3.

# Chapter 12  Preparing to Testify at Deposition and Trial

## 12.1  Introduction

Effectiveness when testifying is far more the result of perspiration and preparation than it is of inspiration.  Experienced experts understand the critical need to prepare completely and thoroughly before testimony is given.  Thorough preparation will most likely result in good performance.  Inadequate preparation will most likely result in poor performance.  Each time an expert testifies, her reputation and credibility are on the line.  Any oversights, mistakes, or errors she makes due to a lack of preparation will become a permanent part of her "expert witness baggage."  Not only will this affect the result in the underlying case, but the expert's future as an expert witness could be damaged permanently as well.

## 12.2  Preparation with Counsel

Experts who plan to testify at deposition[1] or trial should meet with retaining counsel to prepare.  Such a meeting, however, is a legitimate area for inquiry during cross-examination.  Any questions about the meeting with counsel before testifying should be answered truthfully, simply, and directly.

> **Example 12.1: Questioned about preparation meeting with retaining counsel**
> **Q.** Isn't it a fact, Ms. Jones, that you met with Attorney Smith prior to your testimony here today?
> **A.** Yes.
> **Q.** Tell me everything you said and everything he said at this meeting.
> **A.** I certainly couldn't provide you a verbatim transcript.  We met to review the day's schedule, the relevant law, the procedures that would be used, and the questions I would likely be asked.
>
> **Comment:** Unless the expert says something inartful, such as, "Counsel told me how to testify in this case," this line of questioning should have little effect on the jury.  Keep in mind that, as with fees, the opposing experts are in the same boat.  Like you, they are getting paid for their time and are meeting to prepare with their retaining counsel.

The following areas should be reviewed during the expert's meeting with counsel prior to testifying.

*How to state an opinion in a legally sufficient way*
The expert needs to understand any and all "magic words" necessary to render a legally sufficient expert opinion in the case at hand.  There should be *no* confusion about this fundamental proposition.  Ordinarily, a "reasonable degree of scientific/medical certainty" is legally sufficient.[2]  The expert needs to understand fully the meaning of these terms of art (for example, "51% or more likelihood") in case she is cross-examined on them.  Experts should never use words that they cannot define.

---

[1] For more information on deposition preparation, please see Section 13.4.
[2] For more on properly expressing an opinion, please see Chapter 8.

**Example 12.2: Going over the magic legal words to use**
**At pre-deposition conference:** Counselor, I am prepared to render my opinion based on a reasonable degree of scientific certainty. Is that sufficient in this jurisdiction?

**Comment:** The main reason an expert is retained in a case is to provide an opinion or opinions. Experts need to be prepared to express their opinion(s) in a legally sufficient manner.

*Questions to be asked on direct examination*
Experts can and should review the questions counsel intends to ask them during their direct examination at deposition or trial. A run-through of the answers with counsel is usually a good idea and is an accepted practice. This run-through allows the expert to develop the most effective language to communicate to the fact finder. The expert should anticipate, however, that counsel is likely to ask additional questions during the testimony if they are needed to flesh out the answers.

*Questions likely to be asked on cross-examination*
Experts should review with counsel what questions he anticipates the expert will be asked on cross-examination. The expert should also ask that he be subjected to a vigorous mock cross-examination by retaining counsel. (Please refer to Chapter 15 and Appendix D for listings of some of the possible areas of cross-examination inquiry.) Experts who have been prepared by being subjected to a mock cross-examination from retaining counsel will likely perform much better during their real cross-examination.

*The file that the expert intends to take to court or deposition*
The expert should show counsel the entire file she intends to bring to the trial or deposition.[3] Any extraneous material should be removed from the file. No relevant material should be removed from the file.

**Example 12.3: Extraneous material in file**
**Counsel to expert:** Is this a listing sheet for a 5-bedroom estate in Concord? Alex, this has no place in this file.

*Information about the judge*
Experts should discuss with counsel any habits, predilections, or biases of the presiding judge. It is always a good idea to get (and stay) on the judge's good side.

**Example 12.4: Intelligence about the presiding judge**
**Counsel to expert:** Listen, Judge Jones is a real character. He likes to make jokes. If he makes one, it is usually a very good idea to laugh at it.

*Information about opposing counsel*
Experts should ask counsel about the style, demeanor, tactics, tricks, standard questions, and predilections of opposing counsel at deposition and trial.

**Example 12.5: Gaining information about opposing counsel**
**Counsel to expert:** Listen, let me give you the lowdown on Attorney Harris. He's got a standard routine and some standard zingers for experts. For example, he loves to ask….

---

[3] Of course, the expert should not bring any files unless asked to do so via subpoena or by counsel.

# PREPARING TO TESTIFY AT DEPOSITION AND TRIAL

*Theme of the case*

Experts who are apprised by counsel of the theme of the case can, within the bounds of truth and ethical behavior, assist counsel in developing the theme. Once apprised of a case theme, experts may offer specific suggestions about areas of inquiry for direct or cross-examination, exhibits, or demonstrations to help counsel develop the trial theme.

### Example 12.6: Discussion of theme of case with retaining counsel
The theme of the trial may be that although the defendant may have made an error in judgment, there was no chance that this caused any harm to the plaintiff.

*Testimony of other witnesses*

Experts should be familiar with the testimony given by other witnesses in the case. As such, the expert may want retaining counsel to provide him with the prior depositions taken in the case. This testimony of fact witnesses may affect the assumptions that were used to formulate the expert's opinion. The testimony of other expert witnesses will show the opposing side's theory of the case.

### Example 12.7: Testimony of opposing expert telling
In a medical malpractice case, the defense experts testified at deposition that causation was lacking, but they offered no opinions on breach of standard of care. Causation is likely to be the most hotly contested issue in this case when it goes to trial.

*Information about the jury*

The expert should know as much about the jury as possible. This includes their social, educational, professional, ethnic, and religious makeup. The expert's testimony needs to be tailored so that she can communicate most effectively with the jury. (See Chapter 11 on communicating effectively with juries.)

### Example 12.8: Key information on jury
**Counsel to expert:** We've got an inner city jury here in South Central Los Angeles. They are likely to be very mistrustful of the police. Keep that in mind.

### Example 12.9: Valuable information on the jury
**Counsel to expert:** You're in rural Mississippi. Bury that damn Boston accent as much as you can—that won't go over well with this jury.

*Exhibits and demonstrative evidence*

The expert and counsel need to review together carefully all aspects of how, where, when, and which exhibits and demonstrative aids will be used during the trial. Failure to prepare can lead to delay, clumsiness, and in some cases, outright disasters. The sophisticated expert knows when the exhibits will be used, how they will be handled, where they will be placed, and what questions she will be asked about them. Most importantly, she makes sure prior to trial that everything functions properly. It is sound practice to have a backup "low tech" version of demonstrative evidence ready to go if and when the expert's high tech equipment decides not to work properly.

*Last-minute developments in the case*
Counsel needs to share with the expert any last-minute developments in the case (for instance, witness unavailability, evidentiary rulings, or motions pending).

*Timing issues*
Trial delays are endemic to the legal system. The expert should review with counsel when he is needed at the courthouse. Some experts are asked to be "on call." In this situation, counsel will call or beep the expert, who promises to come quickly to the courthouse. In some cases, the expert may want to be present at the testimony of the other witnesses.

*Dress*
How does retaining counsel wish the expert to dress? This will vary depending upon where, when, and how the testimony will be given. Experts should remember to ask retaining counsel how to dress for their testimony.

*Other areas of concern*
*Any* and *all* issues that concern the expert should be discussed with counsel at the pre-testimony conference. The stress of testifying at trial can be reduced significantly by eliminating any anxiety the expert may have due to unresolved areas of concern. A relaxed, well-informed expert is in the best position to testify effectively.

## 12.3  Preparation Alone
Experts also need to prepare thoroughly on their own. Experienced experts take the following actions when preparing to testify.

*Read everything*
The well-prepared expert touches, reviews, and reads every piece of paper in his file before the trial. This includes correspondence, witness statements, reports, the complaint, interrogatories, depositions, photos, videos, and exhibits. Frequently, an assignment has gone on so long that an expert may forget about crucial information without this review.

*Memorize key facts*
This includes the names of the parties. Not being able to recall a party's name may make a witness look callous or forgetful and can lessen the expert's credibility. Key dates should also be memorized along with citations and other facts and figures. An expert who has a command of the facts will impress the jury.

*Recheck calculations, data, and test results*
The sophisticated expert leaves nothing to chance prior to testifying. A review of calculations, data, and test results is necessary. If the expert is called upon to perform or explain these calculations or data, this review will prove invaluable.

*Organize and index file*
After reviewing the contents of her trial file with counsel, the experienced expert organizes and indexes the file to ensure ease of use while testifying. When the jury sees the file, they will note that the expert is organized, which should help bolster the expert's credibility. Unnecessary fumbling and searching through a file at trial is a rookie mistake and is to be

avoided. The sophisticated expert summarizes voluminous data and has supporting data available.

*Prepare responses for the hard questions*
The experienced expert understands the need to anticipate, reflect upon, and be able to answer the difficult questions he will face on cross-examination. A wise expert takes time to think about the most difficult questions he could be asked and he determines how he would respond to them. Such preparation is essential to excellence on the witness stand.

> **Example 12.10: Preparing answers for tough questions**
> **Thinking to self:** What if he asks me about why I don't defer to the opposition? What will I say?...I think I'll need to focus on the weight of my hands-on experience as being more valuable than the opposition's impressive academic credentials.

*Re-examine the evidence*
When an examination of evidence that may have changed was part of the basis of an opinion, the forensic expert should consider re-examining the evidence immediately prior to testifying.

> **Example 12.11: Re-examining the evidence**
> You will be testifying on the prognosis for an individual you last examined 18 months ago. It may be a good idea to set up a brief meeting to examine the person prior to testifying so that your information is up to date.

*Update research*
Experts should perform a literature search to see if any new research has been published that may change their opinions. You may be asked on cross-examination if you have done this and your answer to this question should be "yes."

*Visit the courtroom*
Visiting the courtroom prior to the day of the trial is a good idea if time permits. This pre-trial visit will acquaint the expert with the physical facility and its limitations and will increase his comfort level when arriving for trial. Removing one aspect of the fear of the unknown will help reduce the anxiety level of the expert.

*Reread deposition and reports*
Most sophisticated experts know their own depositions and reports cold. It is an absolute necessity for the expert to have a complete mastery of her prior testimony and reports in the case. Cross-examiners will use any inconsistency between deposition testimony and trial testimony to impeach a witness. Failure to master one's own testimony and reports will often result in a devastating cross-examination.

*Review the important dates*
Successful expert witnesses review the crucial dates in the case. Many commit them to memory. These dates include:

- when the expert was first contacted by counsel,
- when the expert was retained,

- when the expert received the records and from whom they were received,
- when the expert formed his opinion(s) in the case,
- the date of the accident in question, and
- the date(s) key tests were performed.

Failure to be familiar with key dates will make an expert look sloppy and will affect his credibility negatively.

*Keep CV up to date*
The expert may be asked to produce her CV. She should therefore make sure that it is updated and proofed.

*Work out any demonstrations*
The wise expert makes sure her audiovisual and other demonstrations work flawlessly. If they don't, she will lose credibility and the jury will lose interest. The "higher tech" the presentation, the more one needs to be concerned over whether it will work properly when needed. Having a backup plan in the event of system failure is a good idea.

*Relax*
The expert should *not* work and study until the moment he is called to the stand. He should complete his preparation and set aside time to relax and reflect on the task ahead. Taking a walk in the park, going for a run, or doing those things that one finds relaxing are important parts of a witness's preparation. The relaxed, confident, and prepared expert will do his best at trial.

## 12.4  Lack of Preparation
Most expert testimony is given by way of deposition. Sophisticated experts make the time necessary to prepare for deposition. If they cannot do this, they should ask that the deposition be rescheduled. If the request is made sufficiently in advance, retaining counsel should be able to reschedule the deposition. Depositions are commonly rescheduled. This is one way experts can avoid testifying unprepared.

Trial testimony is much more difficult to postpone because it will be the judge who ultimately decides when the trial will start. However, attorneys can request that trials be postponed or *continued.* If a case is set for trial during a time of year when it will be difficult to prepare properly, the expert may want to ask counsel if he can get a better trial date. The expert should let counsel know up front about any scheduled vacations or unavailable dates. This allows counsel to act before a trial date is set and helps avoid counsel having to ask for a continuance. The expert can also request that counsel call the other witnesses first, to give herself additional time to prepare.

## 12.5  Conclusion
The key to effective testimony is proper preparation. Experts must properly prepare before giving testimony. This includes preparing with retaining counsel and by oneself. Experts must find and take all the time necessary to thoroughly prepare prior to testifying.

# Chapter 13  The Expert Deposition

## 13.1  Introduction
Well over 90% of civil cases settle prior to expert witnesses being called at trial. As such, experts can expect that the majority of testimony that they give will be given at deposition.[1] It is extremely important to be effective during an expert deposition. This chapter provides a brief overview of expert depositions and provides some suggestions for being more effective at deposition.[2]

## 13.2  Deposition Basics
The ability of counsel to ask follow-up questions and pursue many lines of inquiry make the deposition counsel's most potent discovery tool in a case. (For more information, please refer to Chapter 3 on the discovery process.) As Fish and Ehrhardt note:

> It is only the oral deposition which permits the spontaneity and conflict necessary for testing perceptions by follow-up questions and immediate inquiry into peripheral matters. Most importantly, it is the only opportunity to obtain admissions directly from parties, rather than from the written words of attorneys. It provides a chance to determine the credibility and demeanor of a witness and the impression he or she is likely to create upon the jury. Under most circumstances in the [case] the oral deposition should be the focal point of the discovery plan. All other discovery devices should be utilized, at least partially, for deposition preparation.[3]

Depositions differ from trials in many important ways, including the following.

- There is no jury present at a deposition.
- There is generally no judge present at a deposition to rule on objections or other disputes amongst the attorneys.
- The only objection counsel is generally allowed to make at the deposition is an objection to the form of the question.
- Even when an objection is made at deposition, the expert generally must still answer the question. The judge will rule on the objection later.
- Counsel is given wide latitude to ask questions at deposition because these questions need only be reasonably calculated to lead to the discovery of admissible evidence. Thus, so-called "fishing expeditions" are allowed at depositions even when they would not be allowed at a trial.

---

[1] Note that some states do not allow or severely limit the use of expert depositions. Experts who work in these jurisdictions will be deposed less frequently.

[2] For comprehensive coverage of expert depositions, see Steven Babitsky and James J. Mangraviti, Jr., *How to Excel During Depositions: Techniques for Experts That Work* (Falmouth, MA: SEAK, Inc., 1999). SEAK expects to publish *The Comprehensive Guide to Expert Depositions* in 2007. For more information, please visit www.seak.com.

[3] Raymond M. Fish and Melvin E. Ehrhardt, *Malpractice Depositions: Avoiding the Traps* (Montvale, NJ: Medical Economics Co., Jan. 1987) 3.

At deposition, the expert who is being deposed is called the *deponent*. The deponent's testimony is taken under oath. The deposition may be scheduled in counsel's office, in the expert's office, or another location. The two kinds of depositions that experts face are:

- preservation of evidence depositions and
- discovery depositions.

*Preservation of evidence depositions*
In *preservation of evidence depositions,* the expert will be deposed by counsel who retained him. These depositions are often videotaped. (See Section 13.9 for a discussion of videotape depositions.) Preservation of evidence depositions are taken because counsel may want to use the deposition at trial in lieu of having the witness appear live. Preservation of evidence depositions are usually taken if counsel feels the witness might be unavailable at trial and/or to avoid the cost of paying the expert to appear at trial. In this type of deposition, the expert can expect a full direct examination by retaining counsel and a close cross-examination by opposing counsel. What is happening in effect is that the witness's trial testimony is being taken outside of the courtroom. Because preservation of evidence deposition testimony resembles trial testimony, the expert witness should follow the advice in Chapter 14 (on effective direct examination testimony) and in Chapter 15 (on effective cross-examination testimony) when faced with a preservation of evidence deposition.

*Discovery depositions*
In *discovery depositions,* the expert will be deposed by opposing counsel. Most or all of the questioning will come from the opposing attorney. Unlike cross-examination, many of the questions will be open-ended, with the goal of getting the witness to talk as much as possible. The expert witness will generally not be questioned by the attorney who retained him because she already knows what the expert is going to say at trial.

The opposing attorney at a discovery deposition may have many goals. The most important ten goals of the questioning attorney are discussed below.

## 13.3  Discovery Deposition Goals
To be effective during a discovery deposition, an expert witness needs to understand the goals of the deposing attorney. Generally speaking, counsel has one or more of the following ten goals.[4]

*1. Learn the expert's opinions*
The main reason the expert is testifying is to render an opinion or opinions. Counsel will almost certainly want to learn precisely what the expert's opinion is, the basis for her opinion, how the opinion was formed (i.e., the methodology used), when she arrived at the opinion, what future tests and evaluations she is planning, and under what circumstances she is willing to change or modify her opinion, or form and offer new opinions.

---

[4] Steven Babitsky and James J. Mangraviti, Jr., *How to Excel During Depositions: Techniques for Experts That Work* (Falmouth, MA: SEAK, Inc., 1999) 17–36.

# THE EXPERT DEPOSITION

**Example 13.1: Sample opinion deposition questions**
Q. Please state any and all opinions you will be giving at trial and the bases for each of these opinions.
Q. When did you form your opinion?
Q. Would your opinion change if it was shown that the lab report of 6/23/2006 was inaccurate?
Q. Are you planning on doing any further tests?
Q. What areas will you not be opining on?

**Comment:** Counsel has a right to this information. Opinions should be well founded and experts need to answer counsel's questions truthfully and directly. However, experts should not volunteer information that was not asked for. If asked if his opinion would change if presented with new or additional facts, the expert witness should provide an open-minded, honest answer. If the expert is inflexible when presented with new facts, he runs the risk of losing credibility.

## 2. Explore the expert's qualifications
Qualifications are relevant to an expert's credibility and are a legitimate area of inquiry. Opposing counsel will want to learn as much as possible about an expert's qualifications. Specifically, the expert may be questioned about her background, education, training, and experience.

**Example 13.2: Questions probing the expert's qualifications**
Q. How many of these types of machines have you designed over the last ten years?
Q. Please detail for me your educational background from high school to the present.
Q. Why did you leave your first college after only two years?
Q. Has your license ever been suspended or revoked?
Q. Have you received any awards for your work in this field?
Q. What have you published in this field?
Q. What, if any, certifications do you hold?
Q. Please explain to me what makes you qualified to give an opinion in this case.

**Comment:** Exaggeration of qualifications is not honest and can come back to haunt an expert. An expert should not obsess over qualifications questions. What is usually far more important to a jury in terms of credibility is whether they like the witness, how well the expert communicates, and whether the expert witness is in a reasonable position to offer a valid opinion. The fine details and points of qualifications may be very important to experts and their peers, but they may be of little interest to a jury.

## 3. Lock down the expert
One of the main purposes of depositions is to get an expert's testimony *on the record*. The stenographer at the deposition will do just that—record the expert's sworn testimony onto a written transcript. This written transcript serves to "lock down" testimony because a witness can be impeached by the deposition transcript if she later contradicts her opinion at trial.

**Examples 13.3: Locking down the expert**
Q. Are there any other opinions you will be offering at trial?
Q. Tell me everything you reviewed prior to forming your opinion.
Q. Please tell me each and every opinion you will be offering at trial.

**Comment:** Everything said on the record at deposition is recorded by the stenographer. The transcript of the deposition can and will be used against a witness who changes his testimony at trial. Counsel may also attempt to take deposition testimony out of context. Therefore, expert witnesses need to consider carefully their answers at deposition and make sure their answers are truthful and phrased artfully. An experienced expert will often slightly hedge his answers to such lockdown questions to leave some room for flexibility. For example, in response to the first question above about other opinions, the sophisticated expert may reply, "Not that I can think of at this time," instead of a simple "no."

### 4. Evaluate an expert's credibility

The expert's demeanor and communication skills will also be evaluated by counsel during the deposition. The ability to communicate and persuade is a crucial piece of information that counsel needs to prepare for trial and to properly evaluate the settlement value of the case. Counsel will want to determine the likely effect of an expert's testimony if she were to testify before a jury or fact finder. To do this, counsel will often ask questions designed not so much to find out what the answer is as *how* the answer is provided.

**Example 13.4: Sizing up how the expert is likely to present himself at trial**
Q. How much are you being paid for your testimony here today?
A. Not nearly enough.
Q. Where did you go to college?
A. Ahhh…well…, that's a tough one. I…ahhh, did two years at RPI, then I went into the army. Ahhhh…and I transferred into…no, strike that, I went back to MIT, I believe that was in 1971….
Q. You're nothing more than a whore, aren't you?
A. It takes one to know one, Counselor.

**Comment:** Experts should concentrate on presenting themselves well at deposition, even though the jury is not present. One's value as an expert witness is based more on the ability to communicate and persuade than on technical and professional qualifications. Additionally, parts of the deposition might be read to the jury at trial.

### 5. Probe for possible bias

Generally, questions concerning potential bias are allowed at deposition because they are relevant to the credibility of a witness. Counsel will attempt to discover any potential biases that a witness may have, which, if revealed to the jury or fact finder, may detract from one's credibility. Common areas of inquiry on the subject of bias include expert witness fees and income, the propensity for testifying only for plaintiffs or defendants, and any personal interest or relationship the witness may have with the subject matter of the litigation or the parties and attorneys involved in it. Bias attacks can be very effective at damaging an expert's credibility because although the jurors may not understand all the technical concepts in the case, they will understand how bias can affect objectivity.

**Example 13.5: Sample bias questions**
Q. How much are you being paid for your testimony?
Q. What percentage of your income do you earn from expert witness and forensic work?
Q. When was the last time you testified for a defendant in a case?
Q. You're Attorney Keefe's brother-in-law, correct?
Q. How many cases have you been involved in over the last five years?

Q. Do you own any stock in the defendant's corporation?

Q. You believe in getting injured workers back to work as soon as possible, don't you?

**Comment:** Bias is a legitimate area of inquiry. Expert witnesses should answer these questions simply and directly. Evasive answers will only compound any bias damage and further damage an expert's credibility. Simple, direct answers force counsel to move on to new lines of questioning.

## 6. Determine the factual assumptions that are the basis of the expert's opinion

An opinion is only as good as the facts and assumptions upon which it is based. Counsel will attempt to learn and explore the assumed set of facts upon which an expert based her opinion(s). If counsel can undermine these assumptions, the reliability of any and all of the expert's opinions will be called into question.

### Examples 13.6: Sample deposition questions regarding factual assumptions

Q. On what assumptions is your opinion based?

Q. Would you change your opinion if you were to learn that your assumptions were invalid?

**Comment:** Factual assumptions must be reasonable and accurate. An expert should be prepared to give ground if he is asked if his opinion would change under different assumptions.

## 7. Gather as much information as possible

Deposition is a golden opportunity for counsel to gather information about the expert, the science upon which her opinions are based, how her opinions will be presented to the jury or fact finder, and many other areas of inquiry.

### Example 13.7: Fishing for information

Q. What are the major texts in this area?

Q. Please tell me each and every place you have been employed since high school.

Q. Do you plan on using any demonstrative evidence at trial?

**Comment:** Counsel has the right to try to gather information. That is the whole idea behind discovery. The expert must answer truthfully but should not volunteer information.

## 8. Gain valuable concessions

Counsel may attempt to use the expert's opinion to bolster his own case. This is commonly done in three different ways. First, counsel may point out where experts for the opposing sides are in agreement. Second, counsel may try to demonstrate that if the underlying factual assumptions are changed, the expert's opinion will change to support counsel's case. Finally, counsel may attempt to push an expert's opinion to the extreme in an attempt to make it look ridiculous.

### Example 13.8: Trying to gain concessions from the expert

Q. You would agree that there is significant impairment, would you not?

Q. Let's assume that the plaintiff lied to you when describing these events. Under this assumption, would you consider changing your opinion?

Q. Does your opinion hold true in all cases, without exception?

**Comment:** A wise expert avoids extreme, all-encompassing opinions. He defends his opinions with conviction, but gives ground when appropriate. An expert who fights every point may appear to be biased. The most believable experts concede points that warrant concessions.

## 9. Intimidate the expert

Counsel may use pointed questioning at the deposition to demonstrate the professional and personal price the expert will have to pay for continued involvement in the case or for any real or arguable ethical violations. This may be designed to keep the expert off balance, make him fearful of a trial appearance, discourage him from pushing the envelope, or encourage him to end his involvement in the case.

**Example 13.9: Trying to intimidate the expert**

**Q.** Are you prepared to tell the jury why your license was suspended?
**A.** Absolutely. I'm not ashamed that I had an alcohol problem. I am extremely proud of my recovery.
**Q.** Do you know that you are testifying under the pains and penalties of perjury and that every word of your testimony in this case becomes part of your permanent record that can be used against you in this case, future cases, and in any complaints brought against you heard by professional associations and licensing authorities?
**A.** Yes.

**Comment:** Dealing with an aggressive attorney is like dealing with an aggressive dog. It is best not to show fear. Persons who are easily intimidated are probably not best suited for expert witness work.

## 10. Save some ammunition for the trial

Good attorneys will *not* ask all of their hardest questions as deposition. A good attorney will hold back on some of his toughest questions to use them as a surprise at trial. As such, experts should never assume that their trial testimony will mirror their deposition testimony and that there will be no surprises.

## 13.4  Preparing for Expert Depositions

Effectiveness at deposition may depend upon whether an expert prepared diligently for deposition. As part of the preparation process, the expert is well advised to require a full and complete pre-deposition conference with the lawyer who has retained her. Because trial lawyers are typically very busy, it may be necessary to insist on this conference taking place. Prior to the conference, the wise expert does the following.

1. Reads all materials counsel has sent.
2. Completes tests, experiments, and other necessary work.
3. Fully thinks through all of the important aspects of the case, in particular possible questions from the opposition and how to respond to them.[5]

At the pre-deposition conference with counsel, the expert should cover any areas she is concerned about. At this conference, the expert may want to do the following.

---

[5] Henry L. Hecht, *Effective Depositions* (Chicago, American Bar Association: 1997) 417.

- Review the type of questions that opposing counsel is likely to ask. In complex or challenging cases, it is not unusual to have a "run-through" with a vigorous cross-examination by counsel or an associate. In a run-through, the expert will be asked the most difficult questions and be given an opportunity to reflect on the questions and answers.
- Review the questions (if any) retaining counsel will ask.
- Review the pertinent legal standard for liability and causation. Review the applicable jury instructions and become familiar with any "magic words" that must be used to make testimony legally sufficient.
- Identify any privileged information or work product contained in the expert's file.
- Review what should and should not be brought to the deposition. This includes responses to any subpoenas the expert may have received.
- Be updated on the current status of the litigation by having counsel share documents, interrogatories, and pleadings. If these are not forthcoming, the expert may request them for review prior to deposition.
- Share with counsel any prior contrary opinions the witness may have rendered in other cases.
- Review the day's schedule and the procedures that will be followed.
- Review the expert's qualifications and opinions. Discuss the bases of these opinions and how these opinions fit into the case.[6]

In addition to the pre-deposition conference with counsel, the expert should consider taking the following actions to prepare properly for deposition.

- Review her CV to make sure that it is completely accurate and up to date.
- Review and master the crucial dates in the case.
- Review and master the important facts in the case, including names and places.
- Review and master her own reports and records.
- Prepare and practice answers to the questions the expert expects to face at deposition.
- Get enough sleep the night before the deposition.
- Set aside adequate time for the deposition itself.

Depositions are commonly rescheduled. An expert who has not had sufficient time to prepare for a deposition should strongly consider asking counsel to reschedule it. Depending upon the amount of notice and the status of the litigation, he will likely be successful in doing so. In any case, it doesn't hurt to ask. The worst thing that the other side can say is no.

### 13.5 Subpoenas and Documents

The notice of deposition is frequently accompanied by a *subpoena duces tecum*. This type of subpoena requires that the expert produce certain documents that are specified in a schedule

---

[6] Steven Babitsky and James J. Mangraviti, Jr., *How to Excel During Depositions: Techniques for Experts That Work* (Falmouth, MA: SEAK, Inc., 1999) 39–40.

attached to the subpoena. (Appendix I provides a sample subpoena duces tecum schedule.) When served with this type of subpoena, the expert should do the following.

1. In the pre-deposition conference, she should have counsel review her subpoena and her file to see if some of the information requested need not be produced under the discovery rules.

2. She should not remove or try to hide potentially damaging documents.

3. She should not produce requested documents that are not properly discoverable under the rules of discovery.[7]

When confronted with or asked to comment on documents during the deposition, the expert witness should take all the time necessary to read the entire document before responding. She should not worry about taking too much time—that's the problem of the attorney who asked the question. When referring to a document, experts should use its exhibit number, followed by a brief description of the document. This will help ensure an accurate transcript.

**Example 13.10: Describing a document to make a clear record**
Exhibit 1, the September 6, 2006 FAA report.

## 13.6 Transcript
The most important result of the deposition is the transcript or videotape. This is the "record" that can be later used as part of a summary judgment motion and at trial.[8] Expert witnesses may have the right to verify the accuracy of the transcript by reading and signing the deposition transcript. This right should be affirmatively asserted by the expert when counsel is agreeing to the stipulations at the beginning of the deposition. Stating, "I will not waive the reading and signing and would like to read and sign" should preserve this right. Failure to affirmatively assert the right to read and sign may result in a waiver of that right.

The Federal Rules of Civil Procedure allow deponents to make changes in form or substance to their testimony. Changes need to be explained on an *errata sheet.*[9] The Rules place no limitations upon the type of changes that may be made. However, the original answer to a deposition question remains part of the record and can be read at trial.[10] If significant changes are made, these can result in the deposition being reopened.[11]

## 13.7 Deposition Advice for Experts
The authors recommend the following.

*Experts should tell the truth.*
This is an expert's legal and ethical duty. Experts who tell the truth and honestly believe in their testimony are difficult to shake and should appear credible to the jury.

---

[7] Determining this may require getting legal advice.

[8] This record of the expert's testimony can and will be used against the expert in future cases as well.

[9] For example, a witness who said "1977" at a deposition, but meant to say "1997." The expert would state "mistake in date" on the errata sheet.

[10] *Podell v. Citicorp Diners Club,* 112 F.3d 98 (2nd Cir. 1997).

[11] *United States ex rel. Burch v. Piqua Eng'g,* 152 F.R.D. 565 (S.D. Ohio 1993).

# THE EXPERT DEPOSITION

*Experts should act naturally.*
An expert is likely to make a better witness if he doesn't try to be someone he is not.

*It is wise for an expert to say he doesn't know if he doesn't know.*
This is a perfectly legitimate response. No one is expected to know everything about everything. An expert should not be too proud to say, "I don't know."

*It is best to avoid arrogance.*
Juries don't like arrogant witnesses. Arrogance makes for a less valuable witness.

*Wise experts avoid absolute words.*
Experts should avoid absolute words such as *always* and *never*. Counsel may employ a counterexample to make the expert who uses absolute words look silly or as though she was exaggerating.

*It is important to avoid hedge words.*
Experts should avoid *could, I suppose,* and *possibly* in reference to their opinions. If a witness uses hedge words, her opinion might not be legally sufficient.

*Experts should take breaks when needed.*
Witnesses perform best when they are not worn down. If you need a break, ask for one. Alternatively, you can ask retaining counsel to ask for a break every 60 to 90 minutes.

*It is essential to read documents before testifying about them.*
Experts will often be asked questions about documents during a deposition. A witness can't testify accurately about a document unless he takes the time to read it carefully. Experts should take all the time they need to read and review a document before answering a question on it, especially if they have never seen it before.

*Experts should not argue with counsel.*
The expert's role is to be an expert, not an advocate. An expert who argues will appear to be an advocate and will lose credibility.

*Experts should not assume, exaggerate, speculate, guess, or estimate.*
Expert testimony needs to be based on a reasonable degree of medical or scientific certainty. Guessing is not permitted.

*An expert should not joke.*
The expert should show respect for the process or the jury will not respect her. Joking is not appropriate at deposition.

*It is best for an expert to say he doesn't remember if he doesn't remember.*
This is legitimate. It is never to be used dishonestly, however. Dishonest use of the "I don't remember" response is illegal, unethical, and will make a negative impression on the jury.[12]

*Experts should avoid slang.*
Use of slang diminishes credibility. It makes the expert appear less serious and professional.

---

[12] For example: Q: "Were you ever alone with Ms. Lewinsky?" A: "I can't recall."

*Experts should respond that they don't understand a question when that is the case.*
If an expert answers a question he doesn't understand he risks providing a misleading answer. The best experts force counsel to explain or rephrase any questions they don't understand.

*It is unwise to interrupt the questions.*
Interrupting runs the risk of providing information that was not going to be asked for. Effective experts answer the precise question asked, not the question they would like to have been asked.

*Experts should listen to all questions carefully.*
Listening carefully allows an expert witness to confine her answers to what was asked. The best experts are all exceptionally good listeners.

*It is important to pause before answering.*
This gives the witness a chance to consider his response carefully. It also gives counsel a chance to object to the question if she chooses to do so. Note that brief pauses prior to answering will not be reflected on the deposition's written transcript.

*Effective experts will not lose their temper.*
An expert witness who loses her temper is likely to say something on the record that she will later regret. Experts should never lose control.

## 13.8 Fees and Billing
See Chapter 19 for a detailed discussion of fees and billing.

## 13.9 Videotape Depositions
Videotaped depositions are permitted by the Rules of Civil Procedure[13] and are being used with increasing frequency. To excel at videotaped depositions, the authors recommend experts do the following.

- Prepare with counsel and practice before a video camera to correct annoying, distracting, or unfavorable mannerisms, methods of answering questions, or nervous habits.
- Dress conservatively.
- Men should try to get a close shave.

---

[13] Fed. R. Civ. Pro. 30(b)(4) provides: "Unless otherwise agreed by the parties, a deposition shall be conducted before an officer appointed or designated under Rule 28 and shall begin with a statement on the record by the officer that includes (A) the officer's name and business address; (B) the date, time and place of the deposition; (C) the name of the deponent; (D) the administration of the oath or affirmation to the deponent; and (E) an identification of all persons present. If the deposition is recorded other than stenographically, the officer shall repeat items (A) through (C) at the beginning of each unit of recorded tape or other recording medium. The appearance or demeanor of deponents or attorneys shall not be distorted through camera or sound-recording techniques. At the end of the deposition, the officer shall state on the record that the deposition is complete and shall set forth any stipulations made by counsel concerning the custody of the transcript or recording and the exhibits, or concerning other pertinent matters."

- Look directly into the camera when testifying.
- Avoid long, pregnant pauses that may make them look evasive or uninformed.
- Hold exhibits so they can be seen by the judge and jury.
- Avoid eating, drinking, or chewing on gum, pens, or pencils.
- Turn off pagers and cell phones.
- Avoid making unnecessary noise by rustling paper or touching the microphone.
- Avoid being goaded into flashes of anger, arrogance, or combativeness.
- Use make-up and powder.
- Watch their body language.
- Try to not appear evasive, suspicious, nervous, or anxious.
- Not be distracted by counsel.

## 13.10  Handling Abuse at Deposition
Chapter 24 discusses how to best handle abusive tactics and conduct of counsel.

## 13.11  Additional Resources
For a checklist of likely areas of inquiry at a discovery deposition, please see Appendix C. For more detailed coverage of expert depositions, please consult the additional SEAK resources below.

Texts:
> *How to Excel During Depositions: Techniques for Experts that Work* (1999)

Seminars:
> *Advanced Deposition Skills Workshop*

DVD Videos:
> *The Expert Deposition: How to Be an Effective and Ethical Witness* (2005)
> *The Expert Medical Deposition: How to Be an Effective and Ethical Witness* (2005)

## 13.12  Conclusion
Most expert testimony is given by way of deposition.  Experts need to be effective when testifying in this format. To be effective, experts need to understand the basic ground rules of depositions and the goals of opposing counsel.  Experts should thoroughly prepare for their depositions and should employ the special techniques described in this chapter.  These techniques differ in many important ways from the techniques that should be employed while testifying during direct examination and cross-examination at trial.

# Chapter 14  Direct Examination

## 14.1  Introduction

Direct examination is all about persuasion, communication, keeping the jurors' interest, and making the testimony memorable. It is an expert witness's opportunity to persuade the jury (or judge at a bench trial) that her opinion should be believed. The goal during direct testimony is to persuade the jury to find one's opinion credible. To achieve this goal, the witness will need to concentrate all of her energies on communicating persuasively with the jury or fact finder. If she does not communicate effectively with them, they will not value her opinion. The expert needs to persuade the jury to agree with her opinions. Everything else is secondary. If the expert witness cannot effectively communicate her opinion, that opinion will carry little, if any, weight with the jury.

## 14.2  Preparing to Testify[1]

*What will be asked*

It is far easier to prepare for direct examination than it is to prepare for cross-examination. During direct examination, the expert witness will be asked questions by the attorney who retained him. By meeting with that attorney prior to testimony, the expert can go over exactly what he is going to be asked. Because he knows what he will be asked, he can then prepare carefully articulated responses. Common areas of inquiry on direct examination include:

- qualifications,
- fees and other difficult areas (to defuse cross-examination on these issues),
- investigation and methodology (the bases of the expert's opinions), and
- opinions.

When preparing his responses, the expert should keep in mind that he will be attempting to persuade a jury of lay people, many of whom may be scientifically unsophisticated. It is during this preparation process that he can formulate the analogies, explanations, and powerful and memorable language that he will use to help him speak in terms that the jury will understand and remember. The expert should review the language that he intends to use with his retaining attorney prior to testifying. The retaining attorney may have some good advice on how to better communicate with the jury.

Prior to trial, a wise expert meets with the attorney who is going to examine him. The expert should insist upon meeting with the actual attorney, not one of her associates. It is only by meeting with the attorney who will question him that the expert witness can get a feel for the attorney's style in asking questions. The expert witness should practice and try to develop a smooth rhythm with the examining attorney.

Experts should prepare for testimony and think in advance of their responses. They should not memorize their responses, however. The jurors may pick up on memorized

---

[1] For additional information on preparing to testify, please see Chapter 12.

responses and may judge the testimony as staged.  It is likely that such testimony will then be discounted.

The successful witness gets his facts straight before trial.  He needs to know his facts cold.  The jury may not understand every bit of expert testimony in the case but the fact that the expert was sharp, did his homework and appeared to have a command of the facts of the case will not be lost on the jury.

He also needs to know *everything* upon which he based his opinion.  He should be prepared to discuss any and all of his written reports.  If the expert witness is unprepared and forgets or is slow to remember key facts or key bases for his opinions, he will lose credibility with the jury.

*Visual aids*

Visual aids are almost always a good idea.  Research shows that jurors retain more information if it is also presented to them visually.[2]

The expert witness should always show retaining counsel any and all visual aids she intends to use during testimony.  Visual aids that are simple and easy to read are the best.  Complicated or "busy" aids may not be appreciated by the jury.

Experts now commonly use various high-tech audiovisual aids as demonstrative evidence to help them better communicate with the jury.  Such aids can be extremely effective.  During the preparation process, experts need to check and recheck their equipment.  It is unwise to get into a situation where one's testimony is heavily dependent upon high-tech audiovisual equipment that fails to work.  The wise expert witness prepares a low-tech backup exhibit just in case of the inevitable "technical difficulties."

*Dress and personal appearance*

The jurors will have an emotional reaction to how a witness dresses.  For example, they may be offended and distracted if they notice a flashy Rolex watch on an expert's wrist.  These jurors probably earn a very small fraction of what the expert witness earns.  Additionally, they are generally being forced to serve as jurors against their choice.  Experts should not wear any flashy clothes or jewelry that will either offend or distract the jurors.  An expert witness wants the jurors to consider her testimony carefully, she does not want them to think about how much her watch costs.

Witnesses should dress neatly.  A witness should make sure that his shirt is tucked in.  Men should get a good shave the morning of the trial.  Expert witnesses want to look as though they have their act together.  A witness who doesn't look personally well organized and well kept may lose credibility with the jury.

The expert should meet with retaining counsel prior to the trial to discuss how she would like the witness to dress.  This will depend in large part upon where the trial is being held and who is on the jury.  For example, cowboy boots might be the best way to dress for a trial in some parts of Texas, but they would probably distract the jury if the trial were held in New York City.

---

[2] See Dana Basney, "The Secrets to Becoming a World Class Expert," 2006 Expert Witness Summit Seminar Handbook (SEAK) at 67.

*Mannerisms*

People often employ various nervous mannerisms when they are in a stressful situation.[3] This is commonly true of experts when they are in the stressful position of testifying in front of a jury. Nervous mannerisms are distracting and weaken one's ability to persuade the jury. They need to be avoided or the jury may think that the witness is anxious because she is not telling the truth.[4]

To eliminate nervous mannerisms, one needs to first identify what they are. A witness who has given videotaped testimony in the past should review this testimony and try to pick up any nervous or distracting mannerisms. If a witness hasn't given videotaped testimony in the past, she should consider giving some mock testimony in front of home videotaping equipment. She might consider having a relative or friend watch the tape(s) with her. Once the expert has identified her distracting mannerisms, she should practice testifying while attempting to eliminate these mannerisms. By eliminating as many distracting mannerisms as possible, an expert witness will be in a much better position to communicate with and to persuade the jury.

*Documents*

A wise expert organizes his files and documents before going to court. He does not want to take the stand with a file spilling out with loose and dog-eared documents. If an expert is asked to find a document on the stand, he needs to be able to find it right away. If he looks disorganized, he will lose credibility with the jury. The expert witness should think about the jury deliberations. He wants the jury talking about his opinions, not the fact that his file was a mess and that it took him five minutes to locate a document.[5]

## 14.3  Testifying Techniques

*Communicating with the jury*[6]

As a rule of thumb, expert witnesses should think of the jury as a group of eighth graders. Like eighth graders, jurors are generally not highly educated in the expert's field of expertise and generally have a very short attention span. They can, however, be intelligent, extremely perceptive at determining when someone is being dishonest with them, and truly want to do a good job. First impressions are important. If a jury's first impression is that an expert is arrogant, his entire testimony will likely be tainted. Jurors respond best to analogies and visual aids. Therefore, an expert should try to use analogies and visual aids to better communicate with and persuade the jury.

Jurors make decisions based largely on emotion and by analyzing the testimony in light of their own life experiences. Experts need to recognize this to properly communicate with jurors. If an expert is biased, arrogant, or pompous, jurors may be offended by him and, based on emotion, discount his opinion. If, on the other hand, an expert appears likeable and unbiased, the jurors' emotions will tell them to listen carefully to what is said and to give it

---

[3] For example, tapping fingers, twirling hair, shaking a leg or knee, etc.
[4] See Lindsley Smith, "Juror Assessment of Veracity, Deception, and Credibility." At 6–7.
[5] And also wasted five minutes of the jurors' time.
[6] For additional information on communicating with the jury, please see Chapter 11.

credence because they *want* to believe the expert. To a large extent, *how* an opinion is presented can be far more important in communicating to the jury than the scientific or technical basis of the opinion.

## Qualifications

An expert's direct testimony will usually begin with a discussion of her credentials. She should work with counsel to make the testimony about credentials as brief as possible. When explaining credentials to the jury, the expert should stress the credentials that tend to show an expertise in the particular area where she will be testifying. Experts should not fall into the trap of being overly longwinded about their credentials. Doing so runs two major risks. First, the expert may come off as being cocky and self-centered and the jury may hold this against her. Second, and much more importantly, a jury usually has a very limited attention span unless what they are listening to is very interesting. If the jury is only going to pay attention for twenty minutes, an expert doesn't want to spend all of those twenty minutes discussing each and every paper she has published. If she does, the jury won't pay close attention when she gets to the meat of her testimony—her opinions and their bases. Experts should work with retaining counsel to make the qualifications portion of their direct testimony as painless as possible.

## Demeanor

Experts should try to be themselves while on the witness stand. This will make them more relaxed and help them make a better impression on the jury. If an expert makes a good impression on the jurors, they will be more likely to believe him. There is an important exception to this rule. That exception applies to those who are abrasive (for example, cocky and arrogant). An individual with a personality or style of presentation that tends to rub people the wrong way needs to try adopting a different approach when taking the witness stand. It cannot be overemphasized that a witness is less likely to be an effective communicator with the jury if the jury doesn't like him.[7, 8] Having the jury like an expert is generally far more important to his credibility as a witness than are his credentials, awards, and his professional and financial success.

## Looking worried

The successful expert witness won't look worried or anxious. The jurors will pick up on this. If a witness looks worried or nervous, the jurors will ask themselves what he is worried about. The answer to this question is unlikely to enhance one's credibility.

## Confidence

Appearing confident is important. An expert witness should sit up and use good posture. He should maintain eye contact with the jurors, but should not stare at them. Moreover, he needs to appear as though he truly believes in his opinion. If an expert does not appear to believe in his own opinion, he will be unlikely to persuade the jurors to believe it.

---

[7] Think of the political arena. Often, the candidates who get elected are the personable, likeable ones, not the ones with the best resumes or greatest intellect.

[8] See Lindsley Smith, "Juror Assessment of Veracity, Deception, and Credibility." At 8.

# DIRECT EXAMINATION

*Distracting mannerisms*
Expert witnesses should avoid distracting mannerisms, such as gum chewing, hair twisting, hand rubbing, nose picking, beard rubbing, etc. These mannerisms distract from one's effectiveness. When the jurors go back to the jury room, the witness wants them to discuss how impressed they were by him and how his opinion affects the case, not how his mannerisms distracted them. As discussed above, experts should attempt to identify distracting mannerisms prior to testifying. Videotapes of one's prior testimony may help.

*Politeness*
Expert witnesses should be polite, serious, professional, and courteous to everyone in the courtroom. This includes the litigants, judge, jury, attorneys, gallery, and courtroom personnel. The jurors will pick up on this and it will help bolster one's credibility. Expert witnesses should avoid jokes and flippant remarks. These will lessen one's credibility. If, however, something happens in the courtroom to make everyone laugh, including the judge and jury, an expert should laugh along with them. If he doesn't, he'll look like a robot and will lose credibility with the jury.

*Appearing unbiased*
Appearing unbiased is critical. This means avoiding even subtle actions that could imply that an expert is biased. For example, when his testimony is complete, he should leave the courtroom directly. He should not stop to shake hands with his retaining attorney and her client.

*Keeping your mouth shut*
A wise expert will not talk about the case in the hall or bathroom before or after testifying. One never knows who might overhear the conversation. When an expert finishes testifying, he should leave the courthouse. He does not want to be seen hanging around because it may appear that he has a personal interest in the outcome of the case.

*Teach and explain*
The jury is made up of lay people. As such, the expert witness needs to assume that many things need to be explained to them. What seems to be a common term, abbreviation, or concept to an expert can be a mystery to the jury. People like to learn and generally like interesting teachers. An effective expert is one who can teach and thus communicate effectively with the jury.

Experts should use commonly understood terms whenever possible. For example, one should say "collarbone" instead of "clavicle." Using commonly understood terms allows the expert to better communicate with the jury (they can more easily understand what is said), making her a more sympathetic figure in the eyes of the jury (the jury can more readily identify with a person who speaks as they do).

Analogies and examples can be very effective in communicating and explaining complicated opinions to the jury. For example, let's say an expert is trying to explain DNA matching to a jury. A good way to explain DNA matching might be, "DNA is a chemical found in every cell of a person's body. You might call it a chemical 'fingerprint.' Like fingerprints, the odds against any two people having identical DNA are absolutely astronomical, in the order of billions to one. It's nearly impossible." Jurors understand fingerprints and are more likely to remember a testimony with the sound bite of "chemical fingerprint." Counsel can also use the "chemical fingerprint" sound bite from the analogy during her summation. Analogies are a very effective way to explain complicated concepts to a jury. A wise expert plans her analogies and runs them by counsel before she uses them on the witness stand.

Effective experts are likeable and entertaining. Jurors are more likely to pay close attention to entertaining, engaging testimony and more likely to believe experts they like. Boring, arrogant experts are ineffective.

### Address problems head-on during direct examination

Problem areas such as fees, weaknesses in opinions, and skeletons in the closet need to be dealt with during direct examination. Doing so steals the dramatic effect of opposing counsel first bringing up these issues during cross-examination. Addressing problem areas during direct examination also allows the expert to explain away some of the issues and cast them in their most favorable or sympathetic light. Since jurors tend to remember most what occurs at the beginning and end of testimony, problems should be dealt with during the middle of the testimony.

### Demonstrative aids

Experts should strongly consider using visual aids to assist them in giving testimony. If appropriate, one may ask the judge's permission to leave the witness box in order to use the visual aid. Getting out of the witness box has several advantages. First, it gives the jury something more interesting to focus on than a "talking head" in the witness box. Second, an expert will probably be more relaxed, and thus a better witness, when she gets out of the witness box. Finally, by getting out of the witness box, the expert removes a psychological barrier between herself and the jury.

It is important to make sure that everyone on the jury can see the visual aid. An expert witness may consider asking the judge to ask the jurors if they can all see. This serves two purposes. First, to determine whether all the jurors are able to see the visual aid. Second, the jury should like the fact that the expert cares about them. If the jurors feel that the expert cares about them, they may be more likely to pay close attention to her and give her testimony greater credence.

Jurors are becoming more and more visually oriented. Most have grown up with television. Many have grown up with video games, computers, and the Internet. Experts can capitalize upon this by using visual aids to explain their testimony whenever it helps. A picture is worth a thousand words. It also breaks up the monotony of testimony, arguments, and motions, and it provides the jurors with a form of information that they are more likely to pay close attention to and remember when they retire to deliberate.

### Answering counsel's questions

An expert witness should tell the truth. He is under oath. Telling the truth is a legal and ethical duty. After an expert witness presents his testimony on direct examination, he will be subject to cross-examination. Cross-examination is a remarkably effective tool that can be used to expose dishonest experts. An expert witness should not assume that he is more intelligent than the cross-examining lawyer and smarter than the jury and that he can get away with being less than truthful.

Experts should not memorize their testimony. Memorized testimony looks rehearsed or as though words were put into one's mouth by the lawyer. Jurors can pick up on this. Experts should pause before answering counsel's questions. They need to actively listen to the questions and answer the question they are asked, not the question they expected to be asked.

A successful expert explains why she is in a position to provide a valid opinion. She communicates all that she did, the tests she performed, the documents, articles and evidence she reviewed, etc. An opinion is only as good as the facts and work upon which it is based. If the jury sees that an expert has done her homework, she will be a more credible witness.

Long narratives should be avoided. Long narratives are extremely hard for a jury to digest and make expert testimony very boring. The ideal response should be at most three to four sentences. Effective experts get to the point quickly and directly. The art is to communicate to the jury what they need to know, not all the expert knows.

Finally, expert witnesses should direct their answers to the jury, not to the lawyer who is questioning them. They should make eye contact with the jurors and speak clearly and loudly enough to be heard. If there is a microphone on the stand, the witness must speak into it properly. Jurors can't be persuaded to believe an opinion if they cannot hear what a witness has to say. Lastly, an expert should not turn his back on the jury. This is disrespectful and the jurors probably won't be able to hear what the expert has to say.

*Start strong and finish strong*

Jurors remember most what they hear first and what they hear last. As such, a strong start and finish are essential. A good expert should be able to present his opinion and why he is qualified to give it in a memorable, credible way during the first five minutes of the direct examination. Details can be filled in later during the direct examination. Surprise endings are great when telling jokes or stories in a social setting, but they must be avoided when testifying. Effective experts tell the jury where they are going, how they got there, and where they went. They never play "hide the ball."

## 14.4  Conclusion

The key to direct examination is connecting with the jury such that the jury understands, is persuaded by, and remembers the expert's testimony. To connect with the jury, experts should diligently prepare and use the direct testimony testifying techniques described in this chapter.

# Chapter 15  Cross-Examination

## 15.1  Introduction

Cross-examination is one of the most challenging aspects of being an expert witness. Counsel for the opposition will read and study the entire case file and prepare for hours or days for his cross-examination of an expert. To perform well under cross-examination, an expert witness needs to understand cross-examination from the opposing attorney's standpoint, follow the golden rules of testifying under cross-examination, and anticipate the likely areas of inquiry.

## 15.2  Cross-Examination: Opposing Counsel's Goals and Techniques

Generally speaking, opposing counsel will have two major goals during his cross-examination of an expert witness. These are:

- to lessen the credibility of the witness and
- to use the witness, where possible, to bolster his own case.

All trials ultimately boil down to one issue and one issue only. That issue is *credibility*. An expert's opinion is only as strong as her credibility. Opposing counsel will use cross-examination as a vehicle to lessen the expert's credibility. This is most commonly done by attacking an expert's qualifications and expertise, exposing her bias, impeaching her with prior statements or writings, and by challenging her opinions, methodology, facts, and data.

**Example 15.1: Qualifications**
You're not a registered professional engineer, are you?

**Example 15.2: Bias**
Isn't it a fact, Ms. Jones, that you've testified for this defendant as an expert in twelve cases in the last four years?

**Example 15.3: Inconsistency**
That's not what you testified to at deposition, is it?

**Example 15.4: Shoddy investigation**
You never took samples from the accident scene, did you?

Sometimes it may be difficult for opposing counsel to successfully undermine an expert's credibility. Opposing counsel may also feel that attacking an expert witness would not be a good strategic move or may not sit well with the jury. As such, counsel may seek to use the witness's expertise to support his own theory of the case. The most common way this is done is by pointing out the areas in which the witness agrees with the other experts in the case. In many cases, there is quite a large area of agreement. When using this technique, counsel is using the expert to bolster his own case.

**Example 15.5: Using opposing expert to bolster attorney's case**
And you agree, do you not, that the plaintiff will never be able to walk again?

Counsel may also use hypothetical questions. Experts should always remember that their opinions are only as good as the factual assumptions upon which they are based. During cross-examination, counsel may present an alternate set of assumptions and ask if this would change the expert's opinion. It often does. If counsel can then prove the existence of the alternate set of assumptions, he has successfully used the witness to bolster his case.

**Example 15.6: Asking expert to give opinion based on new factual assumptions**
Let's assume for a moment that the velocity data provided to you was false. If the true velocity was 45 mph, would that change your opinion?

It is very important to understand that from the opposing attorney's standpoint, cross-examination is all about control. Controlling the cross-examination allows the attorney to control the information that the jury hears. Control is obtained in two main ways.

- The attorney only asks questions to which he already knows the answer (usually from the discovery process). If the expert gives a surprise answer, he may be impeached with his prior deposition testimony, report, or other material.
- The attorney only asks carefully phrased leading questions to which the expert can only answer "yes" or "no" and never asks for or permits an explanation.

Attorneys are also taught that the best cross-examinations:

- start strong,
- finish strong, and
- are relatively short.

From one trial lawyer's perspective, the ideal cross-examination is one:

1. That to an extent was entertaining, which can be a method of controlling the momentum and maintaining the jury's interest;
2. That to an extent impugned the credibility and/or exposed the adverse witness's true bias or attitude while he/she was on the witness stand;
3. That to an extent destroyed or weakened the adverse witness's observations or the force of his/her harmful testimony, and particularly the opinions or conclusions, if an expert;
4. That to an extent obtained beneficial information or admissions as a predicate for cross-examination of other adverse witnesses and/or supported your theory of the case and/or one of your witnesses (lay or expert) and/or was important for your summation.[1]

---

[1] Bob Gibbins, Advanced Evidence and Discovery Law Course, Chapter K: "Arts and Science of Impeaching Witnesses on Cross-Examination" (Nov. 1995). State Bar of Texas: State Bar of Texas Professional Development CLE Online, Austin: 1997, Section III.

## 15.3  The 17 Golden Rules of Testifying on Cross-Examination
The authors suggest the following while testifying on cross-examination.

*1. An expert witness should tell the truth simply and directly.*
Telling the truth is a legal and ethical duty.  Experts should not be evasive.  If a witness appears evasive, he will lose credibility with the jury.  A good trial lawyer will be persistent and eventually get at the information she seeks.  Evasiveness will only serve to highlight this information to the jury.

> **Example 15.7: Being truthful and non-evasive**
> **Q.** Isn't it true that you earned in excess of $35,000 as an expert witness this year?
> **A.** Yes.
>
> **Comment:** The above response is very effective in that it forces counsel to move on and shows that the expert has nothing to hide. An evasive response of "Well, my accountant keeps those records—I'd have to check with him," would only have prolonged the cross-examination on this point and telegraphed to the jury that the expert has something to hide and that this must be an important point.

*2. An expert witness should stay within his true area of expertise.*
The further a witness strays "out of his sandbox," the more vulnerable he becomes to cross-examination and to successful attacks on his credibility.  Early in the case, an expert should tell retaining counsel which areas he will offer his expert opinion on.  Questions by counsel for either side that attempt to push an expert beyond the area in which he feels comfortable can be answered, "I can't answer that question.  It is beyond my area of expertise."

> **Example 15.8: Just say "no"**
> **Q.** With this level of impairment, she's going to be permanently and totally disabled, isn't she?
> **A.** I can't answer that question.  It is beyond my area of expertise.
>
> **Comment:** Just because an expert is qualified to testify does not mean that the expert is an expert in all areas.  The best experts refuse to be drawn into areas beyond their true areas of expertise.

*3. If an expert doesn't know an answer, the appropriate answer is, "I don't know."*
There is nothing wrong with this response.  Even the most educated people in the world do not know the answer to everything.  An expert witness should not let her ego get in the way of making this response.  She should not be tricked by counsel who asks a series of questions that the expert is forced to answer, "I don't know."  Counsel is just trying to rattle the expert or trying to force her to make a mistake.

> **Example 15.9: "I don't know"**
> **Q.** What was the time of death?
> **A.** I don't know.
>
> **Comment:** The wise expert answers "I don't know" when she doesn't know an answer.

*4. An expert witness should meticulously prepare for cross-examination.*
This includes studying the file in detail, a mock cross-examination with retaining counsel, and preparing in advance answers to the most likely questions the expert will be asked during

cross-examination. Preparation is a crucial key to effectiveness while testifying. For more on preparation, please see Chapter 12.

*5. An expert witness should not argue with counsel.*
Arguing with counsel will detract from an expert's credibility because she will no longer appear to be impartial. However, when appropriate, one can and should disagree with counsel.

**Example 15.10: Expert does not allow himself to be baited into arguing**
**Q.** Do you agree that the cause of the accident was excessive speed?
**A.** No, I do not.

*6. An expert witness should not be arrogant, hostile, or condescending.*
Such behavior can and will destroy rapport with the fact finder or jury. It will thus lessen the expert's persuasiveness.

**Example 15.11: Expert appears hostile**
**Q.** Did you examine the accident scene?
**A.** Counsel, you know very well I was out to the accident scene three times. Why would you even ask a stupid question like that?

**Comment:** The best experts do not lose their cool.[2]

*7. An expert witness should pause before responding to a question.*
This gives the expert time to consider the question carefully. It also gives the witness's retaining attorney an opportunity to object if she chooses to do so. Even so, an expert witness should not overdo this because it can be a distraction and it may affect one's credibility.

**Example 15.12: Overdoing the pauses**
**Q.** Did you graduate from Boston College, sir?
**A.** Well, (pause) yes.

**Comment:** The best experts appear natural and honest answering questions. It does not appear honest or natural to need to pause and think before answering a question as to whether or not you graduated from a particular school.

*8. An expert witness should not exaggerate, speculate, or guess.*
This type of testimony is objectionable and will invite additional cross-examination.

**Example 15.13: Guessing during cross-examination**
**Q.** How far was the car from the intersection when it started to brake?
**A.** I would guess about 110 feet.
**Q.** When you say *guess* and *about*…

---

[2] Consider the confirmation hearings for Supreme Court Justice Samuel Alito in January 2006. At those hearings, the judge was repeatedly accused of being a bigot, unethical, and a lap dog. Alito never lost his cool and the questioning boomeranged on the senators who were trying to stop his confirmation.

**Comment:** There is no place for guesses in expert testimony. Experts should not allow the jury to gain an impression that the expert is a guesser because this could devastate the expert's credibility.

*9. An expert witness should remain cool, calm, and collected.*
If a witness loses his cool, he is likely to blurt out a response that has not been considered carefully.

### Example 15.14: Expert keeps cool
**Q.** How long have you been going to Alcoholics Anonymous?
**A.** Twenty years, and I've kept sober the whole time, I am proud to say.

**Comment:** The best experts understand that certain questions are designed to get them to lose their cool. They don't take the bait.

*10. An expert witness should actively listen to the question.*
The witness should answer the question he was asked, not the question he anticipated or that he should have been asked.

### Example 15.15: Not carefully listening
**Q.** Do you have an opinion as to causation?
**A.** It's causally related.
**Q.** Do you have an opinion?
**A.** Yes.

**Comment:** The expert's inability to carefully listen to the exact question being asked led him to answer the wrong question. It also made his testimony appear rehearsed.

*11. Get all facts and data straight before taking the stand.*
An unprepared witness will lose credibility.

### Example 15.16: Unprepared expert
**Q.** What was the terminal velocity?
**A.** Ah…Ummm…Let me look in my report…Ummm…It's here somewhere….

**Comment:** A well-prepared expert will perform much better on the stand than an unprepared expert.

*12. An expert witness should use accepted methodology.*
If an expert's methodology is suspect, her credibility can be challenged. Opposing counsel may even be able to have her opinion excluded from evidence in its entirety. (For further information, please refer to Chapter 9.)

### Example 15.17: Peer-reviewed studies
**Q.** Can you please cite the peer-reviewed studies which support your opinion?
**A.** I can't think of any.

**Comment:** Employing a reliable methodology denies opposing counsel ammunition to use against the expert.

*13. If interrupted, an expert witness should finish his answers.*
Expert witnesses should assert themselves and not let counsel cut off their answers.

### Example 15.18: Insisting on finishing an answer
**Q.** There were no objective findings of impairment, were there?
**A.** Actually—
**Q.** Doctor, how much are you being paid for your testimony here today?
**A.** You didn't let me answer your previous question. Actually, there were many objective findings of impairment. These included....

**Comment:** Opposing counsel will often try to cut off the expert's answer if that answer is not favorable. The best experts don't let this happen. This expert did a very good job of making sure that he finished his answer.

*14. If questioned about a document, an expert witness should ask to see it.*
An expert witness should never comment on a document without asking to see it. Counsel may very well be mischaracterizing what the document states. Wise experts take the time necessary to read documents carefully before commenting on them.

### Example 15.19: Questioning about a document
**Q.** The 8/1/06 EPA report concluded that the contamination began in 1999. Are you saying that the EPA is wrong and you're right?
**A.** Could I please review the report you are referring to?

*15. An expert witness should not use slang.*
This detracts from one's expertise and one's credibility.

### Example 15.20: Slang diminishes the expert's credibility
**Q.** You never measured the yaw marks again, did you?
**A.** Nope.

*16. Prevention is 95% of the battle.*
The best experts realize that the way to avoid many tough questions on bias, investigations, qualifications, etc. is to deny opposing counsel ammunition to inquire into these areas. For example, to deny counsel questions on past testimony, the expert should try to testify for both plaintiffs and defendants. To prevent questions on methodology, the expert should use an accepted methodology. To prevent questions on qualifications, the expert should only testify in cases where the expert is truly qualified. The easiest questions to answer are the ones that are never asked. Expert witnesses should, wherever possible, deny opposing counsel ammunition.[3]

*17. Be prepared to strike if opposing counsel makes a mistake.*
Opposing counsel usually strives to control the information flowing to the jury by only asking leading questions to which she knows the answers. The idea is to present to the jury

---

[3] For further information on how an expert can bulletproof himself and his opinions, please see Babitsky and Mangraviti, *How to Become a Dangerous Expert Witness* (SEAK 2005).

only facts favorable to that attorney's clients. The best experts seize any mistake provided by an open-ended question by offering devastating facts and explanations.

**Example 15.21: Seizing on the mistake of an open-ended question**
**Q.** Why didn't you become board certified?
**A.** Well, a month before my test I volunteered for the Marines. I was wounded during my third tour in Iraq when a mortar shell hit our hospital while I was operating. I then spent months in rehab getting used to my new prosthesis. I then spent two years in the Peace Corps in Africa treating the AIDS epidemic. I do hope to take the test in the future when circumstances allow.

**Comment:** The opposing counsel in this case would have been better served by asking the narrow leading ("yes" or "no") question, "You're not board certified, are you?" By asking an open-ended question, the lawyer made a mistake that the expert pounced on by giving a powerful explanation that was more than simply, "I haven't had a chance to take the test yet."

## 15.4  What the Expert Will Be Asked

On cross-examination, the expert should anticipate and prepare for intense questioning on the following areas of inquiry.

*1. Qualifications*

Qualifications are relevant to credibility. Typical areas of inquiry regarding qualifications include the following.

**Example 15.22: Education**
**Q.** You do not have a Ph.D. in engineering, do you?

**Example 15.23: Skills**
**Q.** You have never personally performed this procedure, have you?

**Example 15.24: Experience**
**Q.** You haven't performed this procedure in twenty-eight years, have you?

**Example 15.25: Training**
**Q.** You never completed a training course in the use of this software, did you?

**Example 15.26: Knowledge**
**Q.** You really don't know what you're talking about, do you?

**Example 15.27: Mistakes on CV**
**Q.** Do you realize there are 27 mistakes on your CV?

*2. Bias and credibility*

Bias is relevant to credibility. Counsel may try to show that because a witness is biased, her opinions should be discounted. Typical areas of inquiry regarding bias include the following.

**Example 15.28: Expert witness fees**
**Q.** How much are you being paid for your testimony here today?

**Comment:** The artful answer to this question is, "I am being paid for my time, not my testimony. My hourly rate is $350."

**Example 15.29: Expert witness marketing activities**
Q. This is a copy of the ad you placed in *Trial Magazine,* isn't it?

**Example 15.30: Relationship with a party or attorney**
Q. In fact, you've testified on behalf of Attorney Harding six times in the last three years, haven't you?

**Example 15.31: Prior testimony**
Q. You've testified for plaintiffs twenty-eight times in the last four years. Can you name one defendant that you testified for during that time period?

**Example 15.32: Personal and professional writings**
Q. Once again referring to your letter to the editor of the *New York Times,* dated 3/6/06, and I quote, "The tort system is nothing but a sham to keep the trial lawyers rich." Am I reading that correctly?

**Example 15.33: Professional expert**
Q. Isn't it a fact that 75% of your income comes from your work as an expert witness?

**Example 15.34: Ethical violation**
Q. Isn't it true that you were censured by your professional society for giving misleading expert testimony?

**Example 15.35: Web page**
Q. Are you aware that your Web page states that you are an expert in over 42 different areas?

## 3. Challenges to an opinion

Experts can expect counsel to try to undermine their opinions. Typical methods for doing so include the following.

**Example 15.36: Showing that the facts the expert relied upon were inaccurate**
Q. The age you based your opinion on was 48 years. The true age was 58 years, wasn't it?

**Example 15.37: Showing that the facts the expert relied upon were unreliable or biased**
Q. You got all the data you relied on from Attorney Coffone, didn't you?

**Example 15.38: Showing that the expert failed to consider certain key facts**
Q. You never reviewed the geotechnical report from Dr. Siciliano, did you?

**Example 15.39: Presenting the expert with new facts**
Q. If you were to assume that the plaintiff was drunk, would that change your opinion on the proximate causation of this accident?

**Example 15.40: Impeaching the expert's opinion with a prior contrary opinion**
Q. That's not what you testified to at deposition, is it?

**Example 15.41: Impeaching the expert's opinion with a learned treatise**
**Q.** Referring to Smith's text on this subject he quotes….That's contrary to what you did in your investigation, isn't it?

## 15.5  Extent of Cross-Examination

The trial judge will determine the extent of cross-examination.  The judge will consider the relevancy and probative value of the subject matter that the line of questioning explores.  Often, counsel will attempt to impugn an expert's credibility by expanding the cross-examination into areas that are marginally relevant.  Sometimes, the judge will allow questioning into damaging subjects if it is determined that these facts speak to an expert's credibility or bias.  On occasion, the judge may prevent the line of questioning because it is not relevant to the matter of credibility and counsel is simply trying to get unpleasant testimony before the jury.  Other times, the subject matter will be technically relevant, but the judge will not allow the cross-examination because its prejudicial value outweighs its probative value.  However, on many occasions, the judge will allow extensive cross-examination into many facets of one's professional past.  The expert should not count on the judge to limit the cross-examination.  Consider the following examples.  A brief index of the case examples appears first.

### INDEX TO SCOPE OF CROSS-EXAMINATION CASES

### Example 15.42: Unsubstantiated allegations of expert's drug abuse and mental incompetence not allowed during cross-examination

*Perry v. Univ. Hosp. of Cleveland,* 2004 WL 1753169 (Ohio App. 8 Dist. 2004)

The court in this case held improper the cross-examination of an expert witness accusing him of drug abuse and past mental incompetence.  The court stated:

> The trial court permitted Dr. Shah, over Perry's objection, to cross-examine Perry's expert witness, Dr. Cardwell, regarding allegations made against Dr. Cardwell in connection with his departure from a previous employer 18 years prior to the trial.
>
> To counter what he called Dr. Cardwell's mischaracterization, Dr. Shah asked Dr. Cardwell a series of questions implying that Dr. Cardwell's true reason for leaving his former employer was to avoid confronting allegations of drug abuse and mental incompetence. Dr. Cardwell denied the allegations were his reason for leaving his former employer. These allegations were contained solely in the wording of questions put to Dr. Cardwell by Dr. Shah. No evidence was admitted or even offered to substantiate these allegations. In fact, following Dr. Cardwell's denial of [the] truth of these allegations, Dr. Shah failed to provide any connection between the allegations and Dr. Cardwell's expert opinion or his methods used to arrive at his expert opinion. Unproven, unsubstantiated allegations made close in time to Dr. Cardwell's departure from his former employer do not impeach his response that the sole reason he left that employer was his wife's desire to move south.
>
> Dr. Shah argues the fact that "Cardwell admitted the accusations were made confirms counsel's good faith belief that the questioning was proper." Admitting these unsubstantiated accusations "were made" is not equivalent to admitting they are true or that they represent the real motivation for Dr. Cardwell's decision to leave that employer.
>
> Even probative evidence must be excluded "if its probative value is substantially outweighed by the danger of unfair prejudice." Evid.R. 403(A). We find that the trial court abused its discretion in permitting this line of questioning as the record reveals that it produced evidence of meager, if any, probative value that was substantially outweighed by its unfair prejudice. Perry's second assignment of error is sustained. At 5–6.

**Comment:** Although vigorous cross-examination of experts is generally allowed, there are limits. In this case, the court applied the balancing test of evidence (Rule 403) and determined that the danger of unfair prejudice substantially outweighed any probative value of admitting the unsubstantiated allegations.

### Example 15.43: Cross-examination of expert that is harassing and argumentative in tone not allowed

*Gray v. Hoffman-La Roche, Inc.,* 82 Fed.Appx. 639 (C.A.10 Okla. 2003)

The appeals court in this case gave great deference to and upheld the trial court's determination that cross-examination questions to an expert that appeared harassing and argumentative in tone would not be allowed. The court stated:

> Ms. Gray's remaining complaints arise from the trial court's refusal to allow her to ask questions that appear harassing and argumentative in tone. Specifically, Ms. Gray asked Dr. Gudas if she expected the jury to "take this leap" with her, and if Dr. Gudas was curious about whether Accutane "caused pain and death" in the thousands of Accutane users in the MedWatch reports. "The trial court sits in a far better position to resolve disputes over the tone of examination than we do looking at the lifeless pages of a transcript." *United States v. Carter,* 973 F.2d 1509, 1516-17 (10th Cir.1992). We believe the trial court acted within the bounds of its discretion in prohibiting these questions.
>
> In sum, we see no reversible errors in the trial court's rulings pertaining to Ms. Gray's examination of Dr. Gudas. At 7–8.

**Comment:** At trial, a judge is present to protect an expert witness from harassing questions. At deposition, however, this is not the case.

### Example 15.44: Cross-examination based upon records considered but not relied on allowed

*Boucher v. Pennsylvania Hosp.,* 831 A.2d 623 (Pa. Super. 2003)

In this case the court permitted cross-examination of an expert based on a record he had read, but had not relied upon. The court reasoned:

> The scope of cross-examination is within the sound discretion of the trial court, and we will not reverse the trial court's exercise of discretion in absence of an abuse of that discretion. Specifically regarding medical experts, the "scope of cross-examination involving a medical expert includes reports or records which have not been admitted into evidence but which tend to refute that expert's assertion." Collins, 746 A.2d at 618.
>
> On direct examination, Dr. Stavis was asked repeatedly, at various levels of detail, whether there was any evidence of traumatic injury to Rosemary in the "medical records, including the CAT scan films, the MRIs and the reports concerning those," in "any of the records," or in "any of the records, films or reports" that he reviewed. (N.T. Trial, 6/1/01, at 167-73.) He responded that there was no such evidence. *(Id.)* Specifically, he denied that there was any evidence of a cephalohematoma which results from injury to the cranial bone:
>
> > Counsel: What about bleeding in the bone? Apart from being broken, does bone bleed?
> > Dr. Stavis: Well, the bone bleeds, but it bleeds then into the space either above it, the—and then creates a sub—a cephalohematoma if the bleeding is above the brain—above the skull, that's where we showed the—that's where I wrote the periosteum, so if there's bleeding there, it's going to bleed into that space around it, that will be cephalohematoma. If it bleeds on the inside, you get a type of bleeding called epidural hemorrhage, epi meaning above the dura, and in this case it occurs because there's bleeding between the bone and the membrane on the inside of the skull.
> > ***
> > Counsel: With regard to each of the layers we've reviewed so far in the absence of bleeding or other indication, on what you considered to be trauma, sir, if there were sufficient trauma to cause this particular intracranial bleed, do you have an opinion on whether those kinds of bleeds and that kind of injury should be apparent?

Dr. Stavis: I think you've got to have some evidence the trauma occurred from the physical things that are present. Certainly they—the history, but the physical signs that are present should be consistent with a traumatic injury, and that's not the case here. (N.T. Trial, 6/1/01, at 172–74.)

In the face of Dr. Stavis' denial that there was any evidence in the "reports" or "records" of a cephalohematoma, counsel for Appellants attempted to cross-examine him with the report of Dr. Boyko. That report was disclosed to Appellants by Pennsylvania Hospital, apparently in anticipation of Dr. Boyko's testimony at trial. It was, at some point, given to Dr. Stavis, who testified he had seen and considered it. Although in the report, Dr. Boyko's ultimate conclusion that there are "no associated findings to suggest a traumatic etiology" agrees with Dr. Stavis, he nevertheless states that "[t]he subcutaneous tissue overlying the right parietal bone demonstrates swelling consistent with resolving cephalohematoma that often times is seen associated with normal obstetrical delivery." (Report of Orest B. Boyko, M.D., 9/1/00 (R. 438-39) The report thus belies Dr. Stavis' testimony that there were no indications of cephalohematoma in the reports and records he reviewed. In their cross-examination of Dr. Stavis, we conclude that Appellants were entitled to confront Dr. Stavis with this discrepancy as it tends to refute the assertions he made on direct. See *Collins,* 746 A.2d at 617-18. At 629–630.

**Comment:** This expert would have been better off had he been more fully prepared, acknowledged immediately what the contrary record stated, and been prepared to explain why it didn't matter. The value of this fact is magnified for the opposition when the expert fights the point and loses.

### Example 15.45: Scope of physician expert's cross-examination in trial judge's discretion
*Watson ex rel. Watson v. Chapman,* 540 S.E.2d 484 (S.C. App. 2000)
The parents of a child who was born prematurely brought a medical malpractice action against the delivering physician, seeking to recover for permanent injury to the child's lungs. The plaintiffs asserted that the defendant doctor was "addicted to the use of drugs and narcotics to the extent that he was not mentally, emotionally or physically able to have provided competent medical care and attention to [the mother and son]." At 486.

Prior to trial, the trial court rejected the plaintiffs' motion to compel discovery of the defendant's alcohol treatment records because such disclosure would violate federal and state confidentiality statutes. However, the trial court also rejected the defendant's motion in limine to exclude all reference to his alcohol addiction.

**Comment:** Appellate courts are usually extremely hesitant to overturn a trial judge's ruling concerning the scope of cross-examination. As such, the trial judge usually has the last say on what questions can and cannot be asked of the expert witness during cross-examination.

### Example 15.46: In medical malpractice case, questions on what defendant's expert would do in similar circumstances not allowed
*Vititoe v. Lester E. Cox Medical Centers,* 27 S.W.3d 812 (Mo. App. S.Dist. 2000)
Children of a deceased patient brought a malpractice and wrongful death action against a medical center and a doctor. The plaintiffs appealed the judgment in favor of the defendants. The appellate court found, inter alia, that the plaintiffs were not entitled to cross-examine the defendant's medical expert, who was a cardiologist (the defendant was an internist), as to whether internists and cardiologists would prescribe a beta blocker and aspirin following a heart attack.

At issue was the following testimony, which occurred during the plaintiffs' attorney's cross-examination of [the defendant's expert]:

**Q.** If a person has a heart attack similar to what [the plaintiff] has, and we need to be fair, we need to keep this in September of 1995?

# CROSS-EXAMINATION

**A.** Okay.

**Q.** You would order a beta blocker, wouldn't you?

[Defendant's attorney]: Your Honor, I object. It's irrelevant what he would have personally done. It's outside the standard of care for ordinary physicians. This is [the defendant].

The Court: Sustained.

...

**Q.** [By plaintiffs' attorney] At the time of discharge, June 5th, '95, within that time frame, do you agree the standard of care on June 5th, 1995, in the condition such as [the plaintiff] was to prescribe a beta blocker and an aspirin, a very minimum, very minimum?

**A.** A patient like [the plaintiff]?

**Q.** Yes.

**A.** I'd say no.

**Q.** Why?

**A.** Because there's at least three reasons why a very careful internist would not want to use a beta blocker. He'd just had heart failure, he had had bronchial spasm that's what they call wheezing, and he also has diabetes. There's three things that would make, that would make you think twice about using a beta blocker, not that you cannot use it, but that you'd be a little bit hesitant because all three of those conditions have relative, not absolute, relative contraindications.

**Q.** I noticed you kind of qualified that and said an internist. Do you think an internist has a separate standard of care from a cardiologist?

**A.** No, but I think they may be a little bit more cautious than some of the cardiologists that I know who might be a little bit more cavalier and say let's use the beta blocker.

**Q.** So you agree that most cardiologists would say let's use the beta blocker?

[Defendant's attorney]: Again, I object. That's not the standard of care for an internist such as [the defendant].

The Court: Sustained. At 27 S.W.3d at 819.

The plaintiffs argued that the cross-examination should have been allowed because: 1) the defendant had previously testified he did not use a beta blocker because he believed them to have been contraindicated in this case and thus an affirmative answer by the expert would impeach the defendant's testimony, and 2) because an affirmative response would impeach the expert because he had already testified that he believed the defendant treated the plaintiff appropriately. The court rejected these arguments:

> [P]laintiffs' argument is without merit in that plaintiffs' questions did not seek information concerning the requisite standard of care required by members of Dr. Duff's profession. The requisite standard of care is that degree of skill and learning ordinarily exercised under the same or similar circumstances by members of the profession. *Lashmet v. McQueary,* 954 S.W.2d 546, 551 (Mo.App.1997). "[T]he individualized practice or custom of a physician does not constitute the appropriate standard of care." *Allen v. Grebe,* 950 S.W.2d 563, 568 (Mo.App.1997). The questions to which the trial court sustained objections were not relevant to the issue in the case, whether the care [the defendant] rendered was consistent with the degree of skill and learning ordinarily exercised under the same or similar circumstances by members of this profession.[…]The judgment is affirmed. At 820.

## Example 15.47: Cross-examination of design expert allowed after expert "opens the door"
*Phatak v. United Chair Co.,* 756 A.2d 690 (Pa. Super. 2000)

In this products liability case, the plaintiff was injured when her chair tipped forward. She claimed that the chair was defectively designed because the chair legs did not extend to or past the chair's perimeter. At trial, the manufacturer's expert asserted that such a design would have created an "unbelievable" and "unacceptable" hazard. The plaintiff attempted to cross-examine the expert regarding other chairs manufactured by the defendant that did in fact incorporate such a design feature, but this cross-examination was not allowed. The trial court entered judgment for the defendant. On appeal, the court overturned the trial court's decision:

> The question before us, as we see it, is whether an assertion that a design change would make a product "unbelievably hazardous" to other persons enters into the equation of whether the product is "defective" for products liability purposes. We think the answer is yes. Accordingly, by interjecting this factor into the equation in the present case [the manufacturer] "opened the door" and its assertion should have been open to rebuttal, including the introduction of evidence that [the manufacturer], itself, utilized this design feature in certain of its chairs. At 694–95.

**Comment:** When experts volunteer information, bad things happen. In this case, the expert opened the door to letting in a line of damaging evidence.

### Example 15.48: Settled malpractice claim against expert not proper subject of cross-exam to show he "made mistakes in the past"
*Musorofiti v. Vlcek,* 2001 WL 953408 (Conn. App. 2001)
In a tort claim for spinal injuries and TMJ allegedly arising out of an automobile accident, the trial court did not allow the plaintiff to cross-examine the defense medical expert regarding a past malpractice claim against the expert. The appellate court described the relevant fact:

> The defendants filed a disclosure of […] an expert in the area of TMJ dysfunction, who intended to testify as to the plaintiff husband's TMJ injuries. During [the expert's] discovery deposition, he testified that he had a malpractice claim filed against him about ten years ago. That malpractice claim involved a patient with an underlying bone marrow disorder who sought treatment from [the expert]. After treatment, the patient began to bleed and required hospitalization. The patient brought an action against [the expert] for malpractice, and a jury found in favor of the patient in that case. [The expert] appealed and, during the pendency of the appeal, the parties settled.
> [In the present case] the defendants filed a *motion in limine* to preclude questioning at trial about the malpractice claim against [the expert]. The plaintiffs opposed the motion and argued that the line of inquiry regarding the malpractice claim went to the expert's general qualifications as a dentist, that is, "whether he is someone who is fit to give an opinion based upon the fact that he has made mistakes in the past." At the […] hearing on the motion, the court granted the defendants' motion on the grounds that the line of questioning was prejudicial, irrelevant and that a settlement during the appeal did not give rise to any judicially determined liability. We agree with the court's decision to preclude the questioning. At 10.

The court then affirmed the trial court's limitation:

> It was not an abuse of the court's discretion to conclude that a malpractice claim made against [the expert] ten years ago concerning a bleeding complication is not relevant to the credibility of his opinion concerning the cause of the plaintiff husband's TMJ injuries. We previously have allowed cross-examination of an expert relating to a malpractice action where that line of inquiry went to motive and bias; but we know of no authority that any expert who testifies as to his or her qualifications opens the door to an unfettered cross-examination of any malpractice claims made against that expert, however old, that are wholly unrelated to the proposed testimony and serve no purpose but to show that the expert "has made mistakes in the past." At 11.

**Comment:** The law provides protection from unfettered admission at trial of all of the expert's skeletons in the closet.

**Example 15.49: Defense medical expert can be forced on cross-examination to read verbatim medical records of initial treating physician**

*J.E. Merit Constructors, Inc. v. Cooper,* 44 S.W.3d 336 (Ark. 2001)

In this case, a motorist brought a tort action against an employer, alleging that she was injured when an employee drove a bush hog tractor into a ditch, thereby causing a rock to be thrown out from underneath the bush hog and through the motorist's open window, striking her jaw. The trial court entered judgment for the plaintiff, and the employer appealed.

On appeal, the employer argued that it was an error for the trial court to require its expert, on cross-examination, to read verbatim the records of the plaintiff's initial treating doctor. Defense counsel gave the expert medical records to review and asked him to give an independent medical examination concerning the plaintiff's medical problems. The expert disagreed with the treating physician's opinion that the plaintiff suffered from trigeminal neuralgia. During the expert's testimony, the plaintiff asked him to read from the treating physician's records in order to cross-examine him about how the original diagnosis and treatment figured into his medical conclusions. The trial court ruled that because the expert's opinion was so different from those of the plaintiff's other physicians, his credibility and the validity of his report were called into question and that it would be proper for the plaintiff to cross-examine the expert's review of those records.

The appellate court noted that the records were not introduced as part of the plaintiff's case in chief; rather, the plaintiff sought to use the records to cross-examine the expert on the basis of his medical conclusions and to determine his credibility.

> This court has traditionally taken the view that the cross-examiner should be given wide latitude because cross-examination is the means by which to test the truth of the witness's testimony and credibility. At 345.

The court continued:

> Further, the court of appeals, in *Lawhon v. Ayres Corp.,* 67 Ark.App. 66, 992 S.W.2d 162 (1999), held that under Ark. R. Evid. 703, an expert must be allowed to disclose to the trier of fact the factual basis for his opinion because the opinion would otherwise be left unsupported, and the trier of fact would be left with little if any means of evaluating its correctness. *Id.* at 72, 992 S.W.2d 162. Again, it is significant that [the employer] gave [the expert] medical records to aid him in forming an opinion. In utilizing [the treating physician's] records in the cross-examination of [the expert], Plaintiff engaged in valid cross-examination to test the credibility of [the expert's] conclusions, and she also was afforded the opportunity to examine the factual basis for [his] expert opinion. The trial court did not abuse its discretion in permitting this line of questioning. *Id.*

**Comment:** The litigants are usually given fairly wide latitude to cross-examine experts. This expert would have been well advised to have strong, credible, objective reasons why his opinion was so different than the treating doctor's.

**Example 15.50: Admission of expert's list of previous cases not allowed (cumulative), but cross-examination on previous cases allowed**

*Benedict v. Northern Pipeline Const.,* 2001 WL 408776 (Mo. App. W. Dist. 2001)

A pedestrian brought a personal injury action against the defendant pipeline company for injuries she sustained in a fall caused by a sinkhole. The trial court entered judgment for the pedestrian upon a jury award, and the pipeline company appealed.

On appeal, the pipeline company argued that the trial court erred in excluding from evidence a list of cases in which one of the respondent's experts had testified. After extensively questioning the expert about that list, the appellant sought to admit that list into evidence. The respondent objected to the admission of the list on the grounds that it was cumulative and collateral. The trial court sustained the respondent's objection and excluded the list from evidence.

On appeal, the appellant argued that the list was relevant and should have been admitted to impeach the expert's testimony:

> Q: You do a lot of consulting with lawyers or for law firms in Kansas City; is that right?
> A: That's correct. I have been a consultant since about 1975.
> Q: And your role in the cases—it really doesn't matter which side you're on—your role is to deal with numbers?
> A: That's correct.
> Q: In fact, you have testified for the Wallace Saunders firm here?
> A: I have worked for virtually every firm in town, yes.

The pipeline company claimed that it should have been allowed to introduce the list to impeach the expert's testimony that he had testified for Wallace Saunders. However, the appellant was allowed to cross-examine the expert with that document, and the following exchange occurred:

> Q: I'll hand you Defendant's Exhibit No. 160; would you tell the jury what that document is?
> A: It's a list of my cases where I provided testimony in personal injury and commercial litigation cases and anti-trust cases. I keep that for a five-year period.
> Q: Is that a current, complete, and accurate list of all cases over the last five years where you have either given deposition testimony or testified in court similar to what you're doing today?
> A: Right, it is.
> Q: Do you see the name of any of the lawyers from my office on that exhibit?
> A: I work for your firm. I don't testify. I'm hired as a consultant.
> Q: I understand that. Looking at the exhibit, Doctor, doesn't it list the name of the case, when you testified, whether it was a deposition or trial, where you testified, and who the attorney was?
> A: Yes. When I'm retained by your firm, as I said, I'm retained as a consultant as opposed to a testifying expert, which is common with the defense. The burden of proof is with the plaintiff. When I'm hired by the defense, what I'm usually asked to do is evaluate somebody else's report.
> Q: Would you agree with me that over the last five years you have never testified in a case involving our firm or it would be on that list?
> A: That's correct.
> Q: Thank you. Who did you consult with last for our firm?
> A: I probably did about five cases for Frank Saunders this past year.
> Q: You did?
> A: Yes. At 425–26.

The court affirmed the exclusion of the evidence:

> [The pipeline company] has failed to indicate how the admission of the document would further impeach the expert's testimony or how it was prejudiced by the exclusion of the list. Appellant was allowed to cross-examine the expert with the document, and the expert clarified his testimony and unequivocally agreed with [the pipeline company] that he had not testified for Wallace Saunders and had only acted as a consultant for that firm.
>
> This document was clearly cumulative for the purpose that [the pipeline company] sought to introduce it and did not contain any evidence relevant to [the pipeline company's] case in chief…The trial court did not abuse its discretion in excluding this document from evidence. *Id.*

**Comment:** Although the judge can be expected to give wide latitude to the attorneys to cross-examine experts, one limitation that will likely be enforced is the needless presentation of cumulative evidence.

# CROSS-EXAMINATION

**Example 15.51: Professional association's recommendation of discipline for unethical testimony in another case proper subject for cross-examination**

*Wagner v. Georgetown University Medical Center,* 768 A.2d 546 (D.C. 2001)

Plaintiff Wagner awoke from back surgery performed at Georgetown University Medical Center to find herself permanently paralyzed from the waist down. Mrs. Wagner and her husband, Francis Wagner, sued Georgetown and the primary operating surgeon for malpractice. The Superior Court entered judgment on jury verdict for the defendants. The plaintiffs appealed. The Court of Appeals affirmed the judgment, and among other things, held that certain evidence was admissible to impeach the patient's medical expert.

The plaintiffs claimed that the trial court erred in allowing the defendant to impeach the plaintiff's expert physician, Dr. A, with his pending censure by the American Association of Neurological Surgery (AANS) for providing unethical testimony as an expert witness in a prior medical malpractice case.

At trial, during cross-examination of Dr. A, defense counsel asked him if he was a member of the AANS. Plaintiff's counsel, aware of what was coming, immediately asked to approach the bench, where he told the court that a committee of the AANS had recommended discipline against Dr. A based on the complaint of a doctor against whom Dr. A had testified. Plaintiff's counsel objected to cross-examination of Dr. A about that recommendation because the matter was still pending in the AANS and had not been finally resolved. Defense counsel confirmed that he intended to impeach Dr. A with the AANS censure recommendation which, he said, had been adopted and ratified by the full executive committee of the organization. Acknowledging that he did not know the exact status of the recommendation within the AANS, plaintiff's counsel asked for a proffer and a ruling precluding cross-examination. Then, in a brief examination conducted by defense counsel away from the jury:

> Dr. A confirmed that both the Ethics Committee and the "full executive committee" of the AANS had recommended that he be reprimanded for "unethical conduct with regards to providing testimony." Dr. A further testified that he had "one more level of appeal," to the full membership of the AANS. [Plaintiff's counsel] did not elect to examine Dr. A. No one asked the doctor to reveal the nature of the alleged "unethical conduct" or to describe the events that triggered the AANS disciplinary recommendation. At 561–62.

Following this examination, the trial court concluded that the proposed impeachment had a legitimate bearing on Dr. A's credibility and decided to permit the questioning, as well as any explanation that might be offered.

> When his cross examination before the jury resumed, [Dr. A] acknowledged that the AANS ethics and executive committees had recommended that he be censured for "unethical practices in the giving of testimony." He said that he was appealing the censure to the full membership of the AANS. The Wagners did not object to this testimony, and they did not request a limiting instruction. [Dr. A] was questioned no further about the matter. He was never asked about the circumstances which underlay his AANS discipline, and the jury was never told the specific nature of the "unethical practices" in which he allegedly engaged. *Id.*

On appeal, the plaintiffs contended that the trial court abused its discretion in failing to inquire or make findings regarding the factual basis for the impeachment, the relevance of the AANS censure to Dr. A's credibility, and the probative value of the evidence versus the danger of unfair prejudice.

The only reason, however, that the Wagners gave the trial court for resisting the impeachment of [Dr. A] was that the AANS censure was on appeal and not yet final. By itself that reason, though arguably relevant to the court's evaluation of the factual predicate for the impeachment and the danger of unfair prejudice, was insufficient. The Wagners presented no evidence to show that the censure would be reversed on appeal. Even if the censure recommendations of the ethics and executive committees of the AANS were not the last word on the subject, they were a more than sufficient factual predicate for the proposed cross examination of [Dr. A]. [Internal citations omitted.] Similarly, the fact that an appeal was still pending did not without more give rise to a presumption that cross examination about the prior bad act in question would be unfair. At 563.

The court pointed out that the Wagners had a fair chance to be heard and that they presented no evidence that the impeachment of Dr. A was in fact misleading. The court then rejected the challenges to the impeachment.

**Comment:** Expert witnesses are best served by avoiding being disciplined for ethical violations related to testifying.

**Example 15.52: Suspension of expert's privileges not proper subject for cross-examination**
*Liberty Mut. Ins. Co. v. Wolfson,* 773 So.2d 1272 (Fla. App. 4. Dist. 2000)
This was an action by an insured, Wolfson, against his uninsured motorist carrier, Liberty Mutual, seeking coverage for injuries he sustained when an unidentified motorist struck him while he was walking. A jury trial resulted in a verdict in favor of Liberty Mutual, but the trial court granted Wolfson's motion for a new trial. The appellate court affirmed the trial court's granting of a new trial, except with regard to the following expert witness issue.

Wolfson introduced evidence of the extent of his damages through three doctors, one of whom was Dr. G. Just prior to Dr. G's testimony, it came to light that Liberty Mutual's counsel was involved in another case with Dr. G and had learned in that case about a peer review of Dr. G that was underway at the hospital. Wolfson moved to exclude any testimony concerning the peer review. Liberty Mutual argued that the fact that Dr. G's privileges to perform surgeries at certain hospitals had been suspended was relevant to the issue of his competence.

Dr. G explained to the court during a sidebar conference that the peer review process is privileged and he cannot be asked about it. The court responded that if Dr. G was going to testify as an expert in this case, then the issue of suspension was relevant to his qualifications. The doctor explained to the court that during the peer review process, his privileges were temporarily suspended pending review, but they were reinstated at the end of the review. The doctor contended that having to disclose even the temporary suspension of his privileges waived his peer review privilege. The court agreed but ruled that Liberty Mutual certainly had the right to tell the jury that Dr. G's privileges had been suspended because if Wolfson had privileges all over the country, he would certainly wish to point that fact out.

Thereafter, Liberty Mutual's counsel questioned Dr. G about the suspension of his privileges to perform surgery in certain hospitals and, specifically, the peer review process. Dr. G maintained during questioning that information concerning the peer review process was privileged. However, when reminded by the court of its ruling, Dr. G reluctantly testified that his license had been temporarily suspended during the review and then permanently reinstated following the review.

The appellate court found that it was error for the trial court to compel Dr. G to testify about the peer review process, not only because such was an improper attack on his credibility, but also because information about the peer review process is privileged by statute. The court explained:

> The peer review process is a system designed to keep health care costs low by encouraging self-regulation in the medical profession. *See Holly v. Auld,* 450 So.2d 217, 220 (Fla.1984). A limited

guarantee of confidentiality for the information gathered during a peer review is necessary to ensure meaningful review. *Id.* at 220. To that end, the discovery privilege provided in the statute applies not only to medical malpractice actions, but also to "defamation actions arising out of the matters which are the subject of evaluation and review by hospital credentials committees." *Id.* at 221.

Although the peer review privilege is generally confined to malpractice actions and defamation actions arising out of the matters which were the subject of the review, the policy behind the privilege requires courts faced with this issue to tread with caution. Consequently, in order to justify production of material relating to the peer review process in proceedings where the privilege does not expressly apply, one must make a showing of "exceptional necessity" or of "extraordinary circumstances." *See Dade County Med. Ass'n v. Hlis,* 372 So.2d 117, 121 (Fla. 3d DCA 1979).

In the present case, Wolfson sought damages for injuries sustained in an "auto" accident. As in *Hlis,* "no amount of judicial interpretation can render the statute applicable to this case." *Hlis,* 372 So.2d at 119. Nevertheless, absent a showing by Liberty Mutual of exceptional necessity or extraordinary circumstances, which did not occur in the trial below, it was error for the court to allow defense counsel to question Dr. [G] about the suspension of his privileges due to the peer review process. Thus, we affirm the trial court's grant of a new trial, and direct that in future proceedings any reference to the peer review process concerning Dr. [G] not be admitted. At 1274–75.

**Comment:** There are limits to what experts can be asked on cross-examination.

### Example 15.53: Cross-examination on compensation in prior related cases allowed
*Coward v. Owens-Corning Fiberglass Corp.,* 729 A.2d 614 (Pa. Super. 1999)
A group of plaintiffs filed a products liability action against an asbestos manufacturer. The court considered whether an expert physician should have been subjected to cross-examination regarding the amount of money he was paid in other asbestos litigation over the previous twenty years. The court allowed the cross-examination. Cross-examining counsel specifically asked the expert whether that compensation influenced his opinions regarding the case on trial.

**Comment:** Money questions relate to bias and are generally allowed. Experts should answer money questions in a non-evasive, non-defensive manner. Answering money questions evasively or defensively makes it look to the jury that the expert has something to hide or something to be ashamed of. Jurors are sophisticated enough to know that the experts get paid.

### Example 15.54: Article mentioned in textbook chapter bibliography expert co-authored, cross-examination allowed
*Courtney v. Taylor,* 708 N.E.2d 1053 (Ohio App. 1 Dist. 1998)
This was a medical malpractice case filed after physicians failed to diagnose a pulmonary embolism. The court considered whether a physician expert could be cross-examined with a medical journal article. The court found the cross-examination proper because the expert had mentioned the article in the bibliography of a textbook chapter he had co-authored.

**Comment:** Citing authority makes an expert's opinion appear well researched. However, experts should expect to be closely cross-examined on any articles they cite. Experts should, therefore, prepare by studying these articles and be ready to explain to the jury if opposing counsel cherry-picks information from the study in a misleading way.

### Example 15.55: Failure to obtain board certification not admissible where expert was defendant in the case
*Jackson v. Buchanan,* 996 S.W.2d 30 (Ark. 1999)
This was a medical malpractice suit against the defendant expert. The court found that it was improper for him to be cross-examined about his failure to obtain board certification, including his

three failed attempts to pass the exam. The court excluded the evidence because of its prejudicial nature. It feared the jury would consider it evidence of negligence, rather than impeachment material.

**Comment:** The court might have reached a different result in this case had the expert not been the defendant because the danger of unfair prejudice would be much less in that circumstance.

### Example 15.56: Impeachment by statutes and regulations allowed
*Schmidt v. Royer,* 574 N.W.2d 618 (S.D. 1998)
This was a wrongful death action brought by the estate of a truck driver killed in a collision with another truck. The expert, an accident reconstructionist, was to be cross-examined about braking force statutes and regulations and their prescribed methodology. The court found that this was proper because without the cross-examination, the jury would be misled.

**Comment:** An expert should be thoroughly familiar with the relevant statutes, rules, and regulations in her area of expertise. This is especially true if the expert cites statutes and regulations when forming her opinion.

### Example 15.57: Testimony given over 150 times for same insurer, questions allowed
*Brantley v. Sears Roebuck & Co.,* 959 S.W.2d 927 (Mo. App. E.D. 1998)
The plaintiff, a homeowner, sued the seller of a dishwasher, alleging the machine caused a house fire. The court considered whether the fire expert could be cross-examined on the point that he had testified for the same insurer over one hundred and fifty times. The court found the cross-examination proper and allowed it to take place in order for the plaintiff to show bias.

**Comment:** The jurors in this case may not understand fully the technical intricacies of what caused the fire in question. What the jurors will understand, however, is that the expert may have a vested financial interest in keeping the insurance company he is testifying for happy.

### Example 15.58: Questioning on employment status
*Cunningham v. McDonald, Del. Supr.,* 689 A.2d 1190 (De. 1997)
This was a personal injury suit arising out of an automobile accident. The court considered whether the cross-examination of the blood alcohol expert regarding his employment status was proper. The court found that the cross-examination should have been allowed. The court noted that the jury learned that the expert was on paid administrative leave but was never permitted to learn what that meant. The court also deemed it important that the jury learn that the expert's employment status was the subject of pending litigation.

**Comment:** An expert witness should act at all times keeping in mind how his actions might affect his viability as an expert witness. This expert would have been far better off had he avoided whatever circumstances resulted in his being placed on paid administrative leave.

### Example 15.59: Commonality of insurance with the defendant, cross-examination not allowed
*Warren v. Jackson,* 479 S.E.2d 278 (N.C. Ct. App. 1997)
This was a medical malpractice case. The court considered whether the expert physician could be cross-examined regarding the fact that he shared the same medical malpractice carrier as the defendant. The court did not allow the cross-examination. It noted that policyholders in a mutual insurance company have a greater stake in the company than do policyholders in other types of

insurance companies. It then found that the connection was too "attenuated" and that the evidence's prejudicial value outweighed its probative value to the jury.

**Comment:** Note how the court weighed the minimal evidentiary weight of this line of questioning against its prejudicial value when making its ruling of inadmissibility.

### Example 15.60: Commonality of insurance with the defendant, cross-examination not allowed

*Wallace v. Leedhanachoke,* 949 S.W.2d 624 (Ky. Ct. App. 1997)

In this malpractice case, the court considered the very same question it did in the previous case, *Warren.* The court found that the expert could not be cross-examined about the fact that he shared the same medical malpractice carrier as the defendant. The court found no evidence of any connection to the insurance company (i.e., limited insurance pool, fractional ownership interest). It concluded that the mere fact that the expert, as an insured, might experience rising insurance rates in the case of an adverse verdict would be too prejudicial.

### Example 15.61: Report of other expert, cross-examination allowed

*Ratliff v. Schiber Truck Co., Inc.,* 150 F.3d 949 (8th Cir. 1998)

This was a wrongful death suit against a truck driver's employer for his attempts to avoid an unknown wrong-way driver. The court considered whether the accident reconstruction expert could be cross-examined about a report he read before he prepared his own report, although he rejected the conclusion presented in the report. The court allowed the cross-examination because the report in question an accident report prepared by a state trooper—was the type of document accident reconstructionists reasonably rely upon when forming an opinion. "Counsel was free to cross-examine the expert as to all documents he reviewed in establishing his opinion."

**Comment:** Experts should be prepared to be cross-examined on every piece of paper they reviewed prior to forming their opinions. The best experts are ready to explain why they did not rely on certain documents and why they did rely on others.

### Example 15.62: Questions regarding compensation as expert allowed

*Wrobleski v. de Lara,* 727 A.2d 930 (Md. 1999)

In this medical malpractice case, defense counsel questioned one of the plaintiff's medical expert witnesses as to how much money the witness had earned in 1995 from testifying as an expert. The doctor in this case practiced primarily in New York but had testified, mostly for plaintiffs, in fourteen states, ranging from Maine to Louisiana and Illinois. The court allowed inquiry into the expert's income, and stated:

> The allowance of the permitted inquiry, both at the discovery and trial stages, should be tightly controlled by the trial court and limited to its purpose, and not permitted to expand into an unnecessary exposure of matters and data that are personal to the witness and have no real relevance to the credibility of his or her testimony. Second, the fact that an expert witness devotes a significant amount of time to forensic activities or earns a significant portion of income from those activities does not mean that the testimony given by the witness is not honest, accurate, and credible. It is simply a factor that is proper for the trier of fact to know about and consider.

**Example 15.63: Cross-examination allowed on the frequency of the expert's testimony for plaintiffs versus defendants and his annual expert witness income**
*Trower v. Jones,* 520 N.E.2d 297 (Ill. 1988)
*Trower* was a medical malpractice case in which defense counsel was allowed to cross-examine the plaintiff's medical expert as to (1) the frequency with which he testified for plaintiffs rather than defendants, and (2) the annual income he derived from services related to testifying as an expert witness. The witness had testified in over a dozen states on a variety of medical subjects. The court stated:

> Adding to the importance of effective cross-examination is the proliferation of expert "locator" services which, as a practical matter, can help the litigants of either side of most any case find an expert who will help advocate the desired position. As this case helps illustrate, many experts today spend so much of their time testifying throughout the country that they might be deemed not only experts in their field but also experts in the art of being a persuasive witness and in the art of handling cross-examination.

The plaintiff argued that inquiry regarding an expert witness's financial interest should be limited to the remuneration received for testifying (1) in the particular case, (2) for a particular party, or (3) for a particular party's attorney. The court rejected those limitations, noting that "[a] favorable verdict may well help [the witness] establish a 'track record' which, to a professional witness, can be all-important in determining not only the frequency with which [the witness] is asked to testify but also the price which [the witness] can demand for such testimony." The court found wanting the additional arguments that allowing such an inquiry would inject collateral issues into the trial, such as the reasonableness of the fees charged by the witness, and that it would complicate the discovery process by creating conflicts between the need to discover impeachment evidence and various evidentiary privileges, such as the physician-patient privilege. Both of those problems, it held, could be controlled by the trial court and did not suffice to keep relevant information from the jury.

**Comment:** A common question experts face is how much of their testimony is for plaintiffs or defendants. It is wise to try to maintain a balance between the two.

**Example 15.64: Cross-examination on past testimony for other defendants allowed**
*Strain v. Heinssen,* 434 N.W.2d 640 (Iowa 1989)
In this action for medical malpractice, the plaintiff's counsel could cross-examine expert witness doctors concerning the frequency with which they had previously testified on behalf of doctors in other malpractice cases. However, cross-examination concerning the experts' employment by the co-defendant insurance company was improper absent evidence in the record disclosing that the relationship between the witnesses and the defendant's malpractice liability insurance company was closer than that of any other experts or of the insurer calling them in malpractice cases.

**Example 15.65: Significant financial relationship between retaining counsel and expert from numerous case referrals, cross-examination allowed**
*Norfolk & W. R. Co. v. Sonney,* 374 S.E.2d 71 (Va. 1988)
In an action involving a work-related injury to a railroad worker, it was proper for the railroad to show on cross-examination of the plaintiff's doctor the number of injured railroad client referrals the plaintiff's attorney had made to the plaintiff's expert witness.

**Comment:** An expert who has an extraordinarily lucrative financial relationship with retaining counsel will be extremely vulnerable on cross-examination. It is best for experts to diversify their client base and not rely on one or two clients for the majority of their forensic work and income.

**Example 15.66: Compensation question allowed**

*Spino v. John S. Tilley Ladder Co.,* 671 A.2d 726 (Pa. Super. 1996)

In this case, it was proper for the defendant to question the plaintiff's medical expert witness, who was a principal of a forensic consulting company, as to whether he was earning $100,000 a year from that business.

**Comment:** Experts can and will be asked about their forensic income.

**Example 15.67: Involvement in prior medical malpractice action, cross-examination allowed**

*Underhill v. Stephenson,* 756 S.W.2d 459 (Ky. 1988)

In a medical malpractice action, it was proper for the plaintiff to cross-examine the defendant's medical expert regarding the expert's involvement in an unrelated malpractice action. The plaintiff, the court reasoned, had a right to cross-examine the medical expert on "all matters relating to every issue." Evidence to show bias of an expert witness, the court concluded, is relevant.

**Example 15.68: Prior malpractice claims, cross-examination not allowed**

*Wischmeyer v. Schanz,* 536 N.W.2d 760 (Mich. 1995)

In this medical malpractice action, the plaintiff's expert—a surgeon—was properly cross-examined regarding poor surgical results in back surgeries by a technique different from that used by the defendant physician. The expert's competency was before the court and the evidence pertained to his credibility. However, the cross-examination regarding prior medical malpractice claims against the expert that were unrelated was not proper—it was not probative of truthfulness or competency.

**Example 15.69: Suspension from hospital, cross-examination allowed**

*Gasinowski v. Hose,* 897 P.2d 678 (Ariz. App. Div. 1 1994)

Here, the court permitted the cross-examination of an anesthesiologist about his subsequent suspension from the hospital.

**Comment:** The best way to avoid questions like these are to avoid the situations that would engender a suspension. Persons who wish to remain viable as expert witnesses conduct their personal and professional lives with an abundance of caution.

**Example 15.70: Drug addiction, cross-examination allowed**

*Winant v. Carras,* 617 N.Y.S. 2d 487 (A.D. 2 Dept. 1994)

Here, the court permitted counsel for the defense to cross-examine the plaintiff's expert on the issue of alleged drug addiction.

**Example 15.71: Questions on expert's bankruptcy and professional discipline not allowed**

*Ad-Vantage Telephone Directory Consultants, Inc., v. GTE Directories Corporation,* 37 F.3d 1460 (11th Cir. 1994)

In an antitrust and intentional interference with advantageous business relationships case, the plaintiff called a CPA-lawyer for expert testimony about the plaintiff's lost profits. On cross-examination, the defendant's counsel questioned the expert extensively on his methods and calculations. The defendant then moved away from the expert's lost profit estimates and into the expert's past. The personal questioning concerned three events: (1) the expert's bankruptcy several years before trial, (2) the disciplinary proceedings of the state bar and state institute of CPAs against the expert in 1990 and 1991, and (3) his censure by the state board of accountancy in 1969. The court found that the first line of questioning was improper on the ground that, unlike forgery, fraud, and perjury, application for bankruptcy does not show a "disregard for truth that would cast doubt on a witness's veracity." The court also found improper the cross-examination on the second two issues: "Given the absence of any sanctions from the 1990 accusation and the temporal remoteness of the 1969 sanction, we doubt the evidence's relevance. Nonetheless, the evidence—even if relevant—was certainly too weakly probative to survive Rule 403's balancing test."

**Comment:** This case is a good example of an application of Rule 403's balancing test in which cross-examination questions concerning skeletons in the expert's closet were not allowed.

### Example 15.72: Questioning on inflated bill in past case allowed
*Maria R. Navarro De Cosme, et al., v. Hospital Pavia, et al.,* 922 F.2d 926 (1st Cir. 1991)
In this medical malpractice action, the defendant was allowed to cross-examine the plaintiff's medical expert about a case in which the doctor testified under oath that he had submitted an inflated invoice for fees earned as an expert witness. The defendant also questioned the doctor about the suspension of his license as a notary for failure to submit the required reports and about his being a defendant in three medical malpractice cases. The court stated:

> An expert is a person who, due to his training, due to his education, due to his standing in the community, is allowed to come before a court to give an opinion on something after the fact. . . .The person under those circumstances has to come to court and has to submit to the rigor of qualifications which includes not only the technical aspects; but also on . . .his standing in the community and his performance as a physician,. . .all the things that we have been discussing here. I think that these lawyers on the defense side are more than entitled to cover these areas.

**Comment:** Expert witnesses are best served by accurate and transparent billing.

### Example 15.73: Cross-examination not allowed on expert's pending malpractice claims
*Mazzone v. Holmes,* 557 N.E.2d 186 (Ill. App. 1 Dist. 1990)
In this medical malpractice case, the court held that relevancy principles precluded the cross-examination of an expert witness regarding his personal involvement in medical malpractice cases. The cross-examination of the defense medical expert regarding the number of professional negligence cases brought or then pending against him was intended to show interest or bias as the defendant physician's expert. The court noted the "general proposition that parties should have the opportunity to expose the interest or bias of medical experts through cross-examination." The court concluded, however, that such examination should be strictly limited to matters such as "the number of referrals, their frequency, and the financial benefit derived from them."

### Example 15.74: Cross-examination on suspension of expert's privileges at hospital allowed
*Whisenhunt v. Zammit,* 358 S.E.2d 114 (N.C. Ct. App. 1987)
Here a physician testified as an expert for the patient in a professional negligence action alleging the defendant's failure to monitor the effects of prescription medication. The court allowed the cross-examination of the physician regarding his suspension of staff privileges from two separate hospitals. It found the questioning relevant and probative and determined that the question of reasons for the witness's suspension would allow the jury to decide how much weight to give his testimony. The circumstances of the suspension, the court continued, may have also had a bearing on the bias of the witness, which was a proper consideration for the jury.

**Comment:** The best way to avoid these types of questions is for the expert to avoid engaging in activities that may result in having his privileges suspended.

**Example 15.75: Questions regarding expert's nonrenewal of privileges not allowed**
*Kane v. Ryan,* 596 A.2d 562 (D.C. App. 1991)
Here, the court did not allow cross-examination of a patient's medical expert regarding why the expert's privileges at the hospital at which the plaintiff in the medical malpractice action was treated were not renewed. The court found that the evidence had but a remote bearing on possible bias the expert might have had toward the physician being sued as a defendant in the case. During cross-examination, the defendant's attorney inquired as to whether the expert was upset with the subject hospital over the "manner" in which it did not renew her hospital privileges, to which the expert replied the matter was not relevant to the case at issue. The court reasoned that a further exploration of the reasons why the expert's privileges were not renewed would have required a "parade of witnesses on an issue that could have had only a remote bearing on possible bias against" the defendant physician, a doctor who had privileges at the subject hospital but was apparently not among those who had a role in deciding the expert's future.

**Example 15.76: Questions regarding suspension of expert's professional license not allowed**
*Morrow v. Stivers,* 836 S.W.2d 424 (Ky. Ct. App. 1992)
In this medical malpractice action, cross-examination of the medical expert was not allowed. The court determined that the cross-examination into two matters—(1) the expert had had his license suspended for five years because he had passed hepatitis to several patients and (2) the expert could only have transmitted hepatitis through dirty instruments, sexual intercourse, or other exchange of bodily fluids—was improper. It concluded that having hepatitis and thus not practicing for a time did not reflect on the expert's knowledge or ability to testify on matters at hand and that the inflammatory effect of the jury's hearing that the expert may have had sex with patients, although unproved, would have outweighed any probative value it might have had.

## 15.6 Additional Resources

For more detailed coverage of cross-examination of experts, please consult these additional SEAK resources.

Texts:
    *How to Become a Dangerous Expert Witness: Advanced Techniques and Strategies* (2005)
    *Cross-Examination: The Comprehensive Guide for Experts* (2003)
Seminars:
    *How to Become a Dangerous Expert Witness*
    *Advanced Cross-Examination Workshop*
    *Testifying Skills Workshop*
    *Advanced Trick and Difficult Questions Workshop*
    *Advanced Testifying Skills for Experts: The Masters' Program*
DVD Videos:
    *The Most Difficult Questions for Experts: With Answers* (2005)
    *Cross-Examination: How to Be an Effective and Ethical Expert Witness* (2005)

## 15.7 Conclusion

To perform well during cross-examination, an expert should:

- understand the goals and techniques of opposing counsel,
- prepare diligently and anticipate the types of questions he will be asked,
- as much as possible, deny opposing counsel ammunition, and
- follow the 17 golden rules of testifying under cross-examination.

# Chapter 16  What Attorneys and Clients Look for in an Expert

## 16.1  Introduction

Experts who are going to successfully work with and promote themselves to attorneys need to understand what attorneys look for in an expert witness. Attorneys are paid to win. When an attorney goes back to his firm after a trial, he is only asked one question: "Did you win?" The successful attorneys are those who win.

What attorneys look for in expert witnesses are individuals who can help them win. There are many characteristics in an expert that will help an attorney win. These characteristics follow.

- Qualifications
- Credibility
- Availability
- Preparation
- Oral communication skills
- Report writing skills
- Testifying skills
- Demeanor
- Charisma
- Reasonableness
- Assistance to counsel

Attorneys will determine whether experts have the above characteristics in a variety of ways. These include the following.

- Talking to colleagues who have worked for or against the expert in the past.
- Carefully reviewing the expert's CV.
- Trying to get in contact with the expert.
- Listening to the expert's answering machine.
- Interviewing the expert on the phone.
- Reviewing the expert's fee schedule and agreement.
- Conducting due diligence on the expert to verify his credentials.
- Researching the results of the expert's past cases.
- Reviewing the expert's Web site.

## 16.2  Qualifications

An attorney will closely look over an expert's CV to get a feel for the expert's qualifications. As such, drafting a tight, mistake-free, objective, up-to-date, and accurate CV is a must. For more on drafting a CV, please see Chapter 7. Some of the factors the attorney will consider when weighing an expert's qualifications include education, certifications, relevant experience, publications, memberships, and awards.

*Education*

The ideal expert would be educated by a prestigious, well-recognized local institution that is respected by the jurors. Graduation with honors is a plus as is teaching experience. Experts with "missing" education credentials are less desirable unless they excel in other areas.

### Example 16.1: No Ph.D. where opposing expert holds Ph.D.

You are an expert witness who holds an undergraduate degree in your specialty but the opposing expert holds a graduate degree in that specialty. The opposing expert, all other factors being equal, may be given more credibility by the jury.

*Training, licenses, and certification*

The training an expert received, his past and current licenses, and his certifications will be reviewed. The failure to obtain appropriate licenses or certifications may be questioned. Such a failure could lessen the expert's credibility with the jury and make it more difficult for the retaining attorney to persuade the jury.

### Example 16.2: Expert missing key certification

You hold an accounting degree but are not a certified public accountant.

*Practical, real-world experience*

Many attorneys and clients look to see what practical, real-world experience the expert has. Jurors generally find experts with real-world experience to be more believable than "ivory tower" academicians. The more relevant and recent an expert's real-world experience, the more valuable he will be as a witness. "Professional witnesses" who haven't had any recent real-world experience are much less valuable.

### Example 16.3: Qualified by practical experience

An automotive mechanic with twenty years of experience may be more valued in a defective repair case than a retired automotive design engineer with a Ph.D. who never repaired an engine and hasn't worked in the field in ten years.

*Literature published and research projects*

Publication generally brings credibility.[1] An expert who has published in her field or who has been active in research projects may be viewed as more qualified than an expert without these credentials. The most valued experts are often those who "wrote the book." Jurors believe that if an expert wrote the book on a subject, she most likely knows what she is talking about.

### Example 16.4: Expert "wrote the book" on a subject

You recently had a text published entitled *Causation of Catastrophic Failure in Passenger Aircraft*. You will be a very valuable witness in a case where the cause of a passenger airplane crash is at issue.

---

[1] Publication is also an effective way to market oneself as an expert witness because attorneys often locate experts through literature searches.

# WHAT ATTORNEYS AND CLIENTS LOOK FOR IN AN EXPERT

*Professional memberships and affiliations*

Membership in appropriate professional organizations and the additional status of diplomat or fellow also indicate expert qualifications. The lack of such affiliations may be used against an expert to lessen his credibility with the jury. There is one caveat: if the diplomat or fellow status was purchased by simply paying a fee, this can be used against an expert.

**Example 16.5: Expert doesn't belong to relevant professional societies**
**Q.** You don't belong to any professional societies and you haven't worked in the field in seven years. Isn't it a fact that you haven't kept up in this area since your retirement?

*Awards*

An expert who has won legitimate awards in her field is a desirable expert.

**Example 16.6: Awards**
**Q.** Have you won any awards in your field?

## 16.3  Credibility

Credibility is the ultimate issue at every trial. A valuable witness is one who will be credible to the jury. No matter how qualified an expert is, if he is not believed by the jury or fact finder he is of little value to counsel. To get a feel for the expert's credibility, the attorney can be expected to do the following (at a minimum).

- Talk to the expert and get a feel for how the expert presents himself. Does the expert give straight answers? Is he professional? Is he likeable?
- Carefully review the expert's CV. Is there objective evidence (e.g., former Marine officer, elected by peers to a post in a professional organization, etc.) of the expert being respected in his field?
- Talk to colleagues who have used the expert in the past.
- Conduct some due diligence on the expert's credentials such as checking with state licensing boards, schools, and associations. An expert who has exaggerated his credentials is useless and will not be hired.
- Search jury verdict reporters to see how the expert's past cases have turned out. An expert who testified for the defense in a $10,000,000 verdict case might not go over so well with the jury.
- Carefully review the expert's Web site. Are there typos? Unprofessional content? Other baggage?

## 16.4  Availability

An expert, no matter how qualified and credible, is of little value to counsel if she is not available. Experts will be more valuable if they are not too busy and manage to make themselves available for conferences, reviews, testing and examinations, depositions, and trials. Attorneys get to choose who their experts are and many will refuse to work with experts who are difficult to deal with. The expert who does not return inquiry phone calls and e-mails *immediately* telegraphs to attorneys that she may not be readily available. Experts should check their messages and e-mail while on the road and should, ideally, reply to inquiries the same day. This should make a good impression on the inquiring attorney.

Also, since attorneys share information on experts all the time, experts should be just as responsive after they have been hired as they were before they were brought on the case.

## 16.5  Preparation

Peak performance requires proper preparation.  Performing well in a courtroom or deposition is accomplished through perspiration, not inspiration.  Attorneys seek out and highly value experts who are willing (and able) to devote the time necessary to prepare properly.  Proper preparation for deposition and trial involves studying all relevant documents, anticipating the questions that one will be asked, preparing analogies, and pointing out gaps and inconsistencies to counsel.  (More detailed advice on preparation is provided in Chapter 12.)  Attorneys will talk to other attorneys who have used the expert to see if the expert was prepared to testify.

## 16.6  Oral Communication Skills

The main reason an expert is testifying in a case is to proffer an opinion.  This opinion is of little value to counsel unless the expert can communicate it to the jury of lay persons.  This is true even if an individual is the world's leading expert in a particular field.  If the jury cannot understand an expert, does not listen to her, or does not like her, they may not be persuaded by her opinion.  The most sought-after experts are those who are able to explain their testimony to the lay jury in an understandable and memorable fashion.  For detailed information on how to better communicate with a jury, please see Chapters 11 and 14.

A key communication skill is being able to speak easily understood English.  Attorneys will be hesitant to hire any expert witness who speaks with a heavy accent that is difficult for jurors to follow and understand.[2]  As such, potential experts are very well advised to work on minimizing any accents they may have.[3]

## 16.7  Report Writing Skills

Expert witnesses must often draft written reports of their opinions.  The strength of the expert's written report will often affect the settlement value of a case.  Attorneys will seek to hire experts who draft bulletproof reports.  Attorneys may ask prospective experts for examples of reports they have filed in the past or they may obtain these from fellow attorneys.  For detailed information on how to draft a bulletproof expert report, please see Chapter 10.

## 16.8  Testifying Skills

Many attorneys and other clients look for experts who have performed well on the witness stand and at deposition.  This information is learned by communicating with fellow attorneys and researching jury verdicts and settlements.  Counsel then has an idea that the expert will

---

[2] An accent *per se* is not a problem. The problem arises when the accent significantly interferes with the jurors' ability to understand the expert. Many successful experts have accents, including one of the most famous experts of all, Doctor Henry Lee.

[3] You can learn much from a person's outgoing voicemail/answering machine message. Since an expert's verbal communication skills are so crucial to an attorney, experts are well advised to leave a clearly articulated outgoing message on their answering machines/voicemail. If an inquiring attorney hears a message that is not easy to understand, he may cross that expert off his list of potential experts.

perform well on the stand, will be able to communicate effectively, and will not get rattled easily. If an expert has *too much* testifying experience, however, some attorneys will shy away because the opposition may be able to portray him as a professional witness who is nothing more than a hired gun.

**Example 16.7: Too much testifying experience may be a negative**
**Q.** You've testified eighteen times in the last three years. Now, you wouldn't want to say anything that might hurt Attorney Thome's case and jeopardize your lucrative litigation business, would you?

### 16.9  Demeanor and Charisma
If an expert is likeable, he is more likely to be believed by a jury. If, on the other hand, he is gruff, arrogant, or condescending, he is not likely to do well with a jury. Boring experts are of little value. Attorneys prefer and will seek out likeable, charismatic experts and avoid boring or arrogant experts. They will make this determination by talking to the expert on the phone and talking to colleagues who have seen the expert in action in the past.

### 16.10  Reasonableness
Nobody wants to work with a temperamental, difficult, or unreasonable expert. This is especially true if the expert thinks he is smarter and better than everyone else. Counsel will seek out and value experts who are cooperative and not condescending, arrogant, or pompous. Following are some things that could lead an attorney to believe an expert is unreasonable.

- Extraordinarily high fee. If the expert charges 2 or 3 times the average fee in the field, the attorney may not be able to justify paying this and may continue his search for an expert.
- Unfair cancellation fees. For example, an expert who keeps all of the paid-in-advance money for a deposition cancelled more than 14 days in advance.
- Bill padding. If an expert charges for 100 hours to review 100 pages of documents, word will get out that the expert is unreasonable.
- Not being somewhat flexible on setting up times for meetings, depositions, and trial testimony.
- Extraordinary demands regarding incidentals. For example, requiring limousines, demanding housing at a particular five-star hotel, or expecting first-class air travel for short flights.[4]
- Acting as though you are smarter than everyone else involved in the case.
- Not being easily reachable. For example, only being able to reach the expert by setting up an appointment with a gatekeeper or the expert not returning phone calls promptly. Experts are being well paid for their time and they should make themselves available by giving out their cell phone number and home number.

---

[4] Of course, if the case is big enough or the attorney wants the expert enough, he often will agree to an expert's requirements whether he likes them or not.

## 16.11  Assistance to Counsel

The truly valuable expert will be proactive in attempting to educate retaining counsel. Sophisticated experts assist counsel by not only answering the questions asked, but by making valuable suggestions as well.  Suggestions by experts regarding demonstrative aids, questions for depositions, and realistic evaluation of theories, reports, and proposed evidence all make an expert more valuable to counsel.

## 16.12  Conclusion

Attorneys try to win their cases.  Therefore, they look for experts who help them win.  Such an expert is one who is well qualified, can persuade the jury effectively, and holds up well under cross-examination.  Other qualities attorneys look for in a potential expert witness are the willingness to work hard and prepare, availability, charisma, reasonableness, and report writing skills.  Attorneys will evaluate potential experts by talking with their colleagues, closely reviewing the expert's CV, verifying credentials, reviewing reports the expert has written in the past, reviewing the expert's Web page, and by interviewing the expert.

# Chapter 17  How Attorneys Locate and Select Expert Witnesses

## 17.1  Introduction

It is important to understand how attorneys locate and select expert witnesses. Those who understand how attorneys and other clients go about selecting experts for their cases will be in the best position to market themselves as expert witnesses. This chapter discusses the common resources used by counsel and other clients to locate expert witnesses. These include the following.

- Other attorneys
- Experts who opposed the attorney in past cases
- Expert locator and referral services
- Professional and legal associations
- Literature searches
- Certifying agencies
- Universities
- Experts used in the past
- Jury verdict reviews
- Referrals from the client (in-house experts)
- Internet searches
- Expert witness directories
- Advertisements
- Paid online legal research services
- Referrals from other expert witnesses
- Fact witnesses
- Presentations by the witness
- Networking and social acquaintances
- Paralegals

## 17.2  Referrals from Other Attorneys

Lawyers talk to each other all the time, asking for advice and tips on how to handle certain matters. This includes recommendations on expert witnesses. For example, a lawyer undertaking a bad faith case against a certain insurance company will look to a lawyer who has litigated a similar case recently. First, she will look inside her own firm. If that fails, she will contact, usually via e-mail, colleagues in other firms.

### Example 17.1: Intra-office e-mail
To: All Attorneys/Paralegals
Re: Blood Alcohol Expert Needed

I'm defending a new dram shop matter. Anybody know of any good blood alcohol experts they've used or have had used against them?

Experts who have excelled in previous cases are in the best position to be recommended. Being a good expert means being knowledgeable, cooperative, well-prepared, and most importantly, being able to communicate effectively and persuasively at deposition and trial. It does not mean simply telling the retaining attorney what she wants to hear.

When an expert is recommended, the attorney receives a colleague's opinion as to the strengths of an expert witness. This is one of the two main advantages of being recommended.[1] Most other ways of finding experts do not allow attorneys this most important bit of information—how effective the person is as a witness. For example, a literature search may reveal that Ms. Smith is the world's leading expert in a particular area. That same literature search would not, however, say anything about how good a witness Ms. Smith is. For example, counsel wants to know if juries like a witness. Does the witness prepare thoroughly? Can the witness communicate effectively with a lay jury?

## 17.3 Expert Opposed Attorney in Past Case

It is very common for attorneys to seek out experts who have testified *against* their client in a previous matter. One of the greatest compliments an expert can receive is to have the opposing attorneys ask for their business card at the conclusion of a deposition. Experts should treat each time they write a report or testify as an opportunity to showcase their skills and abilities to *all* the attorneys involved in the case.

## 17.4 Expert Locator and Referral Services

Many attorneys turn to expert locator/referral services for assistance. There are several reasons that attorneys may turn to these services. These include the following.

- They are unable to get a recommendation for an expert.
- They do not have the time or inclination to search for an expert by some other means.
- Their first-choice experts have been retained by the opposition.
- Their first-choice experts are unavailable.
- They need an out-of-state expert and can't get a recommendation on an expert in that locale.
- The area of specialty is very narrow (for example, arctic exposure) and there are very few experts in that field.
- They are pressed for time.

Locator and referral services are usually not an attorney's first choice in choosing an expert. There are three main reasons for this. First, they do not get a trusted colleague's opinion as to the effectiveness of the potential expert. Second, there may be a fee involved in using the service, such as a significant mark up of the expert's hourly rate. Finally, the fact that the witness is registered with a referral agency may be brought in front of the jury to show bias.

Although not usually the attorney's first choice, referral services are very commonly used by attorneys to locate and retain experts. They can be especially effective in generating

---

[1] Cost-effectiveness is the other.

business for experts in narrow fields or in a field such as medical malpractice where many qualified experts are reluctant to testify. The sheer number of referral services available is a testament to how much attorneys use these resources. (A list of referral sources is provided in Appendix K.)

## 17.5  Professional and Legal Associations

Counsel looking for a specific type of expert will often contact a particular discipline or profession's association. Many of these associations provide lists of experts and consultants, online membership directories, literature searches, and recommendations. These services may be complimentary to the attorney and may be provided as a free service to the association's members. Experts may contact the professional organizations in which they have memberships to find out if they offer these services. Experts should also make sure to be on the organization's panel of experts. They may also consider joining other relevant professional associations that may have these services. Many attorneys also look to their own local, state, and national professional legal associations that maintain databases of expert witnesses.

## 17.6  Literature Searches

Many lawyers seek out experts who have published texts and articles. They consider such experts to have the credibility inherent in someone who "wrote the book" on a particular topic. Experts who have published in a certain field are very easy to find through computer-based literature searches. Experts who publish articles in legal publications can be found by attorneys when they read the publication. A published expert can expect to be contacted by attorneys who have found her name through literature searches.

## 17.7  Certifying Agencies

Counsel may turn to certifying organizations when searching for experts. For example, the American Board of Independent Medical Examiners (ABIME) lists approximately 1,500 physicians who have passed a rigorous exam and are board certified in their underlying clinical field. Most certifying agencies provide counsel with a directory or list of members for use in selecting experts or have these directories available online. Experts who desire to increase their accessibility to counsel should consider obtaining the appropriate certifications and being listed in the available directories.

There is a note of caution, however, regarding certification. Experts who obtain certifications by purchasing them through diploma mills decrease their value and marketability. By *diploma mill,* the authors mean a certifying agency that has very weak certification standards and is probably most interested in the applicant's money. These facts can be brought out during cross-examination and can harm an expert's credibility.

**Example 17.2: Mail-order "certification"**
**Q.** I see here that you are board certified by the Fictional Board of Forensic Experts?
**A.** Yes.
**Q.** Very impressive.
**A.** Thank you.
**Q.** What requirements did you meet to obtain this board certification?
**A.** The requirements of the board.

**Q.** What were they?
**A.** I forget.
**Q.** Did you take an examination?
**A.** No.
**Q.** Did you complete a specified training program?
**A.** No.
**Q.** You paid your fee and they gave you the certification, didn't they?
**A.** Yes.

**Comment:** Mail-order certification will decrease, not increase, the expert's marketability. Most experts already have very impressive credentials and there is no need to pad these credentials with mail-order degrees.

## 17.8  Universities
Lawyers may try to tap into universities when looking for experts. Professors and other instructors may have increased credibility with a jury. Those experts who act as professors, instructors, or even adjunct instructors at colleges and universities increase their visibility to counsel. Many of the nation's leading experts and consultants have affiliated themselves with colleges and universities. Not only does this help in their being contacted first, it adds a great deal of credibility to their qualifications.

## 17.9  Experts Used in the Past
Attorneys often use experts who have performed well for them in the past.

## 17.10  Jury Verdict Reviews
Settlements and jury verdicts are reported in online and print legal publications. These reports contain the results of the case and often contain the names of the expert witnesses in the case. Counsel will frequently contact experts reported in jury verdict reports when undertaking a new case. Jury verdict reports are another way that being effective in one case can generate additional referrals.

## 17.11  Client Referral of In-House Experts
The client itself is often looked to by counsel when searching for an expert. These in-house experts, usually the employees of the company, are available, experienced, and will testify without additional payment. The impartiality of these in-house experts will often be questioned, however. An individual who is given the opportunity to testify as an expert on behalf of her employer should consider taking it. Testifying for an employer is a good opportunity to gain experience and establish a reputation of being a good expert. Both may be invaluable to someone who later leaves her employer and desires additional expert witness work.

## 17.12  Internet Searches
Attorneys commonly use the Internet to locate expert witnesses. There are many Internet sites of expert witness directories where experts can list themselves. (Appendix N lists some of the more important sites.) These sites may charge the expert or attorney a fee, or they may be free to both. In addition, attorneys may find an expert witness's Web page through search

engines. The Internet is fast and easy to use, and it is a very important tool attorneys use to locate expert witnesses.

## 17.13 Directories

Counsel may use directories and source books to locate experts. Most of these publications require the payment of an annual listing fee for the expert to be listed. Many directories also include an online listing. Directories can be a cost-effective, dignified way for expert witnesses to promote themselves. (Appendix L provides a listing of expert witness directories.)

## 17.14 Advertisements

Many lawyers look in the professional services or classified section of state and national legal publications in their search for experts. (Appendix M lists some representative legal publications.) Many experts find it cost-effective to advertise in these and other state and national legal publications to increase their visibility and to obtain additional expert witness work.

## 17.15 Paid Online Legal Research Services

Attorneys also use paid legal research services to locate expert witnesses. The two most commonly used services are LexisNexis and Westlaw. These databases are quite extensive and can be used to find experts from:

- past cases the expert has testified in,
- past transcripts and reports,
- jury verdict reporters citing the expert, and
- online and print directories of expert witnesses.

## 17.16 Referrals from other Expert Witnesses

Lawyers may contact experts they have used in the past to obtain recommendations on an expert in an allied or even in a different field. For example, a lawyer may call a psychiatrist he has worked with for a recommendation of a psychologist. Experts in a specialty may be willing to refer a colleague for cases when they are unavailable or are conflicted out of a case. It is wise to network with as many experts as possible. This is word-of-mouth marketing at its best.

## 17.17 Fact Witness

Attorneys may ask a fact witness to become their expert witness. The most common example of this is a treating physician. Treating patients who are involved in accidents or workplace injuries can and will lead to expert witness assignments.

## 17.18 Presentations by Witness

Attorneys may hire experts they have heard give presentations at an attorneys' professional association or other venue. Presentations are a great opportunity for an expert to showcase his capabilities because they allow the expert to demonstrate both his knowledge and his presentation skills. Note, however, that opposing counsel will obtain the expert's handout materials to use against the expert during cross-examination.

## 17.19  Networking and Social Acquaintances

Attorneys may hire experts they have become acquainted with socially or whose paths they have crossed professionally.  Experts are well advised to:

- remember to mention to people, especially lawyers, that they do expert witness work, and
- always carry a good supply of business cards.

## 17.20  Paralegals

Experts should recognize that paralegals are often assigned the initial task of compiling a list of experts for counsel.  Paralegals use many of the above techniques for finding experts.  Expert witnesses who wish to grow their practices should therefore not forget to target paralegals in their marketing activity.  This can be done by:

- presenting to paralegal groups,
- publishing in paralegal journals,
- advertising in paralegal journals, and
- networking with paralegals.

## 17.21  How Attorneys Choose Amongst Experts

Often, attorneys will locate more experts than they need in a particular matter.  They will then be in a position where they can choose from amongst these experts the one who they would like to retain.  In making this selection, attorneys consider many factors.  These include the following points.

*Availability*

Does the expert answer his phone and return phone calls?  Is the expert willing to testify?  Does his schedule allow his commitment to the case?  Has he already been hired by another party in the case?

*Reputation as an effective expert*

Does the witness have a reputation as an effective witness?  That is, is this a witness who can persuade the jury and help the attorney win?  This information may only be available if the attorney is able to get a colleague's recommendation on a particular expert or if the attorney has herself used the expert in the past.

*History of past cases*

Was the expert associated with favorable verdicts/settlements in the past?  This can be determined from jury verdict reports and may be relevant to one's ability to persuade and communicate effectively.

*Past reports*

Are the expert's past reports well written? Do they reflect a careful and thorough investigation and lack of bias?

# HOW ATTORNEYS LOCATE AND SELECT EXPERT WITNESSES

*CV*
Are there any missing credentials on the CV? Are there any time gaps, mistakes, or holes in the CV? Does the CV look polished or sloppy? Is there damaging superfluous information on the CV such as a win/loss record of the expert's cases?

*Publication*
Has the expert published? Such experts often carry more credibility with a jury. Has the expert published something inflammatory or controversial? These experts would have baggage and would be less desirable.

*Academic positions*
Experts affiliated with colleges and universities may carry more weight with a jury. The ideal academic position is with a prestigious local university that is likely to be well respected by the jury.

*Perceived ability to communicate and persuade*
In preliminary verbal contacts with the expert (on the phone or in person), did she have good communication skills? Was she likeable and even-tempered or was she pompous and unfocused? Did she appear to have an agenda? Can she explain complicated concepts effectively in laymen's terms? Is she likely to do well in front of a jury?

*Credibility baggage*
Is there anything in the expert's past that can be used against her? Controversial writings? Unprofessional marketing activities? Bias to one side or industry? Is she a "professional" witness who no longer works in the field in question? Was she disqualified in the past? Were there any disciplinary or legal problems? Is there anything on the expert's Web page that will be used by opposing counsel against the expert?

*Geography*
It is less expensive to use an expert who is local to the venue of the litigation. Paying an expert to travel gets very expensive. Jurors may also be more likely to believe a local expert who is "one of them" and not a hired-gun outsider.

*Fees*
This is not the primary consideration, but it will come into play if the fee is too high or too low, or if the case is small. The more at stake in the litigation, the less cost-sensitive the attorney is likely to be. Also, if the fee is too low, the attorney (and jury) may ask, "What's wrong with this expert?"

*Relevant, recent, practical experience*
This plays well with a jury. The more the expert has, the better.

*Easy to work with, reasonable*
This information will be determined from initial contacts and by checking with the attorney's colleagues. Is the expert easy to deal with? Does she return phone calls promptly? Are her retention terms reasonable? Is she pompous and arrogant or have a chip on her shoulder regarding attorneys? Does she do things when she says she's going to do things? (For

example, faxing over a fee agreement and CV promptly.)  Is the expert a good listener or does she constantly interrupt the attorney when talking on the phone?

*Physical appearance*
Counsel is looking for an expert who the jury will like and want to believe.  Does the expert look credible?  Is the expert disheveled or does the expert make an excellent appearance?

*Something that makes the expert unique*
For example, being the winner of a prestigious award, an inventor of a breakthrough device or being a famous person.

*Supply and demand*
The more choices the attorney has, the more picky he can be.  Experts are best advised to try to develop a narrow niche within their specialty where there is little competition.

*Gut instinct*
In the end, the attorney may have more than one very qualified expert to choose from and he may follow his subjective feeling as to who will perform better and be most persuasive.  He may select the expert he likes and with whom he feels most comfortable.

The more an individual can distinguish himself in these areas, the more likely it is that he will be the preferred expert who is consulted and who can command a premium fee for his time.

## 17.22  Conclusion
To properly promote herself, an expert needs to understand how attorneys locate and select expert witnesses.

# Chapter 18  Marketing an Expert Witness Practice

## 18.1  Introduction

Marketing an expert witness practice can be challenging. Experts are faced with the daunting task of marketing their services without compromising their integrity, credibility, professionalism, or reputation. A legitimate concern about marketing activities is how these will play to juries, potential clients, and colleagues.

The type of questioning one can expect to face on cross-examination with regard to marketing efforts will go something like this.

> **Q.** Who first contacted you in regard to this case?
> **A.** Robert Smith.
> **Q.** Doesn't Robert Smith work for National Forensic Science Locator, Inc.?
> **A.** Yes.
> **Q.** And Mr. Smith called you on behalf of NFSL, Inc., did he not?
> **A.** Yes, he did.
> **Q.** Now, NFSL is a service that finds expert witnesses for attorneys, is it not?
> **A.** Yes, it is.
> **Q.** An attorney needs an expert in a field and he calls up NFSL, correct?
> **A.** I would assume so.
> **Q.** And NFSL advertises in various lawyers' publications, does it not?
> **A.** I'm not sure.
> **Q.** Now, sir, you have listed yourself with NFSL as an expert on the topic of arboriculture, have you not?
> **A.** Yes, I have.
> **Q.** That's right before "abortion," is it not?
> **A.** I wouldn't know that.
> **Q.** Here is their brochure. It's right before "abortion," is it not?
> **A.** It appears to be.
> **Q.** Your job here is to help Mr. Babitsky win his case, right?
> **A.** No, I'm here to help the jury.
> **Q.** That's not what your NFSL brochure says. "Our experts will help you win, period." Am I reading that correctly?
> **A.** Well, yes, but...
> **Q.** Do you know where NFSL advertises your services?
> **A.** No.
> **Q.** For all you know it could be on the side of a bus?
> **A.** I don't know.
> **Q.** Did you ever ask?
> **A.** No.
> **Q.** The reason you listed yourself with NFSL is so that you could get more work testifying as an expert witness, is it not?
> **A.** Yes.
> **Q.** Do you think NFSL would recommend you to another attorney in a future case if Mr. Babitsky loses this case?
> **A.** You'd have to ask them.

These types of questions must be kept in mind in reference to each of the marketing methods that will be discussed in this chapter. As more and more experts actively market their forensic practices, the impact of these types of attacks are lessened.

## 18.2  The Three Rules of Marketing

In the authors' opinion, there are three rules of marketing that hold true in most circumstances. These rules are simply:

*1. Nobody can guarantee an expert what will work to market his practice.*
A person who can, with certainty, predict what will work to market a product or service can be compared to a person who can, with certainty, predict the stock market. It just doesn't happen. What a marketing expert can do, however, is look at the ways that similarly situated businesses have successfully sold their products and services. This chapter reviews and explains the techniques that the authors know have worked for experts.

*2. The way to see if something works is to try it.*
The only way to know for certain what will work is to try it. Testing can tell an expert whether direct mail, speaking, writing, or another technique will generate cases.

*3. Track results. Repeat what works. Discontinue what does not work.*
It is essential for an expert to track where her cases come from. The first thing she should ask a new attorney is, "Where did you get my name?" Only through tracking can an expert make an intelligent decision as to which marketing methods work and which do not. An expert should repeat what works and discontinue what doesn't work. For example, if Mr. Lopez wrote a scholarly article for a legal publication and that got him fourteen cases, he should probably try to write more articles for legal publications. On the other hand, if he advertised in a legal publication for two years and got no cases from that ad, that is something he should probably discontinue. A good tracking system will tell an expert that after four years of placing an ad, she received not one new client or piece of business. Thus, it might be time to rethink the notice.

## 18.3  Identify the Target Market

Before undertaking any marketing effort, an expert needs to identify his target market. Asking who one's potential clients are should be the start of any marketing plan. The market for an expert's services will depend upon what services he is willing and able to provide. It will also depend upon the geographic area in which he will seek to market his services. A key to cost-effective marketing is to identify the market with as much precision as possible. For example, if Ms. Browne is a medical malpractice expert, from a marketing standpoint she may be much better off if she speaks at a conference on malpractice for 150 attorneys than if she addresses a general bar association meeting of 1,200 attorneys.

Once an expert identifies her market, the next step involves reaching the market in a cost-effective way. We will discuss the various ways to reach a target market later in this chapter.

## 18.4  The Value of a Client

For each marketing technique that we will discuss, we will stress that the expert needs to do a cost-benefit analysis. The cost of each method will vary by marketing technique and will be a function of the time involved and the out-of-pocket expenditures that must be made. The benefit of a marketing method is a function of how much a client is worth.

Expert witnesses are highly compensated. If an expert charges $350 per hour and bills 50 hours on the average case, each case then generates $17,500. If the average client will retain an expert a total of three times or will refer him to two new clients, then the average client is worth $17,500 x 3 = $52,500. *Since one new client can be extremely valuable, in many cases it makes economic sense to spend substantial time and money to obtain new clients.*

## 18.5  Personal Reputation—Word of Mouth

Most expert witnesses would agree that the most cost-effective, time-efficient, and least offensive marketing method is personal reputation; that is, word of mouth. As former trial lawyers, this point was driven home time and time again to the authors at depositions of experts. All of the lawyers would file in dutifully and then two, three, or more hours of intense questioning of the expert would follow. Each time the expert was prepared, organized, knew the facts and science cold, and testified in a cool, calm, professional manner, the same thing would happen at the conclusion of the deposition. Each lawyer would shake the expert's hand and reach over to the desk and take two to three business cards for future use. This is personal reputation/word-of-mouth marketing in action.

Lawyers constantly communicate with one another and share information. The first stop for a lawyer in search of an expert is usually his colleagues. If an expert does a good job on a case, lawyers will recommend him when asked, "Do you know any experts in the field of…?" Lawyers also frequently discuss the good and bad expert witnesses they have used. It is very common to hear advice such as, "If you ever need a cardiologist, Dr. Davidson, who I deposed last week, was dynamite!" from a colleague.

The lesson is clear. Doing an excellent job on current cases and developing a reputation for professionalism can be an expert's most effective marketing tool. It is also extremely cost-effective in that it costs nothing. If an expert does a good job, lawyers will recommend him to their colleagues and will use him again on other cases.

The converse, however, is also true. If an expert does a poor job on a case, his retaining lawyer is not likely to use him again and the word will spread quickly through the legal community. Attorneys will share information about which experts not to use as readily as they share information about which experts to use. Once the word gets out about an expert, his work can dry up quite quickly.

Word-of-mouth referrals will increase if an expert provides exceptional service. Many long-term relationships with clients are forged not because of lengthy CVs or impressive credentials. Rather, they are due to excellent service and responsiveness by the expert. Most clients look for similar types of things. They want an expert who is prompt, courteous, cooperative, reasonable, and who exceeds expectations.

*Promptness*

An expert who does things promptly—for example, issuing initial oral reports—is highly valued. Trial attorneys face many court-imposed deadlines. The number one reason lawyers get sued for malpractice is for missing deadlines. They appreciate experts who allow them to meet their deadlines.

*Courtesy*

Trial lawyers are involved in an adversarial litigation process. The expert who is courteous to clients and their support staff will tend to stand out and be selected more often than his curt or arrogant counterparts. One comment by a staff member ("Dr. Jones is so nice") may go a long way in forging a long-term relationship with a new client. If a lawyer has a choice between two equally qualified experts, he will retain the expert who is easier to deal with. Trial lawyers deal with big egos all day long. The last thing they want to deal with is an arrogant expert witness.

*Cooperation/availability*

The world-renowned expert who is never available to talk to, who is booked up for six months of appointments, and who is in Europe touring during the summer months is of little value to most clients. Experts who go out of their way to be cooperative and available are highly valued. Going out of one's way to demonstrate cooperation and availability is an excellent marketing technique.

*Reasonableness*

Attorneys prefer to work with reasonable people. Unreasonable attitudes will discourage future referrals and will be publicized by the victimized attorneys. Some common conduct that attorneys may consider unreasonable include a too restrictive nonrefundable deposition cancellation policy and unreasonable expense reimbursement requests (for example, insisting on a limousine for all ground transportation).

*Exceed expectations*

The ability to exceed the client's expectations is perhaps the most important service and marketing technique. When the client is "blown away" by the excellence of a report or recommendation or the research done by the expert, his expectations have been exceeded. This client will place such an expert at the top of the list for future expert witness/consulting work.

***Backlash:*** There is very little backlash potential from word-of-mouth referrals. This is one of its chief advantages.

***Cost-Benefit Analysis:*** Word-of-mouth referrals cost nothing out of pocket. They work very well. Under a cost-benefit analysis, this type of expert witness marketing is always a winner.

## 18.6  Speaking Engagements

Most expert witnesses understand that it is good for business to speak professionally. The idea is that by being seen and recognized, an expert picks up new clients and business. Being a valuable expert is all about one's ability to communicate verbally. If an expert witness can communicate well with juries and judges, she can help an attorney win his case. If she cannot communicate well, all of her expertise and credentials will be of little value to the attorney.

Public speaking is an opportunity to show off one's communications skills. Attorneys seek out and will pay a premium for experts they think will connect with a jury. As such, experts who speak to legal groups should spend as much time preparing the delivery of a talk as they do its content. If an expert can make the topic interesting and easy to understand, the lawyers will rapidly conclude that she would probably make a good witness in front of a jury.

Experts need to be prepared to capitalize on their appearances as speakers. They should bring plenty of business cards in case they are asked for them after the talk. If possible, they should also bring a handout with valuable information that the audience will want to keep. The handout material should contain the expert's contact information. A lawyer can't hire an expert if he can't find her.

To use speaking as an effective marketing tool, the forensic expert should consider:

- to *whom* he will speak,
- *where* he will speak,
- *when* he will speak,
- *what* he will speak about, and most importantly,
- *why,* specifically, he will speak.

### *To whom the expert will speak*
Experts should keep in mind who their target market is when deciding to seek out or accept speaking engagements. To obtain business from attorneys, one needs to contact and speak to local, state, and national bar associates at meetings of lawyers. (See Appendix O for a listing of state and national bar associations.) If, on the other hand, the target market is insurance companies and claims adjusters, one needs to talk to insurance professionals, including claims adjusters' associations and in-house presentations.

It is a common mistake to assume that a bigger audience will provide more clients. In the authors' experience, some of the most effective marketing presentations we ever gave were to small groups of key people. For example, we gave a presentation for a local union group on workers' compensation law. We had only thirty-five attendees. Almost every union person there came for a reason (either they had a case or their friend, who couldn't be there, needed help). We had enough foresight to hand out extra information packets. We received clients and calls for information and help for many years after the presentation. The key wasn't the number of people, but reaching the right people.

These should be an expert's first major considerations: who will attend the presentation, will the audience members be in a position to retain the expert's services, and are the audience members in a position to recommend the expert's services to others? If the answer to these questions is no, then perhaps it is a waste of valuable time to speak to that particular group.

### *Where the expert will speak*
An expert who has to travel from his home base should consider:

- How many days of work will he miss? Traveling over 1,500 miles may require three days—one to get there, one to do the presentation, and one day to get back home. Will the presentation be worth missing three days of work? How many cases would the expert need to generate to make it cost-effective?

- Is the presentation outside of the expert's geographic target market? Does someone who practices in Boston really want to solicit work in San Francisco? Some national presentations may require substantial travel time and effort. Evaluation of the type of exposure one will get is critical when deciding if a speaking engagement will be cost-effective.

In the end, an expert may be better off speaking at a local bar association meeting forty miles from his office than traveling thousands of miles to give national presentations to larger groups.

*When the expert will speak*
A speaker's place in the program may well determine how much exposure and business she picks up. Ideally, one wants to speak as early as possible in the program to the largest group possible. When solicited to speak, an expert should ask the following questions.

1. *When* will I speak? What are the date and time?
2. Will it be a *general session*, a *breakout*, or a *workshop?*
3. *How many* attendees are likely to attend my session?
4. What kind of people are likely to attend my session? For instance, lawyers, adjusters, paralegals?
5. What other sessions will I be up against?

It's important to remember that an expert's exposure will be significantly reduced if she speaks at the same time as a well-known speaker.
Finally, the wise expert knows that a meeting planner wants and needs her to speak. Otherwise the planner would not have called the expert. Therefore, when considering a speaking engagement, one should feel free to request good placement early in the program.

*What the expert will speak about*
What one is asked to speak about is important to determining the cost-benefit of giving the presentation. If the talk an expert is asked to give is already prepared, it will cost him very little time to prepare for the speaking engagement. If, on the other hand, a talk will require considerable preparation time, he should take this into account before deciding if it is worthwhile to agree to give the presentation. In addition, an expert wants to select the topic related most closely to the types of cases he is looking for.

*Why the expert will speak*
It is important for experts to always determine and keep in mind specifically why they are considering speaking. Is it to pick up clients and business? Is it to flesh out a CV? Is it for a nice trip where someone will pick up the airfare? It is wise to consider the cost in terms of time lost from work in determining if the proposed speaking engagement will be cost-effective and makes sense from a business development standpoint.

***Backlash:*** Speaking engagements can and will be used during cross-examination to show an expert's bias. Speaking at well-balanced educational programs will not be a problem. If, however, an expert speaks exclusively at insurance defense conferences or at plaintiff bar association meetings, she can expect to have her impartiality questioned.

### Example 18.1: Expert only presents to trial lawyers

**Q.** I see here on your CV that you do a lot of speaking to groups of lawyers.

**A.** I do speak to groups of lawyers.

**Q.** You've spoken for the Association of Trial Lawyers of America, the Massachusetts Trial Association, the Barnstable County Trial Lawyers' Association, and the New England Trial Lawyers' Association?

**A.** Yes, I have.

**Q.** When was the last time you've spoken to any lawyer's groups that weren't plaintiff's lawyers?

**A.** I don't recall.

**Comment:** This expert could have defused this line of questioning by speaking at some defense lawyer meetings.

Experts should be very careful about what they write in their seminar handouts or handbook materials. Opposing counsel will go to great lengths to obtain these and they can and will be used against the expert during cross-examination. As such, experts should not write anything in their handout materials that they wouldn't want to be questioned about in front of a jury.

***Cost-Benefit Analysis:*** Speaking engagements involve personal contact and can be effective in generating referrals. They offer a very attractive cost-benefit ratio if travel expenses are reimbursed and travel time is kept to a minimum. The cost-benefit ratio is even more attractive if the talk is already "in the can" and does not require substantial preparation time.

## 18.7  Writing Articles

The analysis experts should undertake before agreeing to write articles, book chapters, etc., is similar to the analysis for speaking engagements. Before deciding to spend the time to write an article for publication, one should consider the following carefully.

- *Where* the article will be published.
- *Who* will read it.
- *When* it will be published.
- Whether *contact information* will be provided.
- *Why* the expert will be writing.
- What the potential *backlash* might be.
- Whether writing makes sense after a *cost-benefit analysis.*

*Where will the article be published?*

Before submitting an article for publication, one should consider the publication itself. Is it considered a prestigious peer-reviewed journal? Or is it a publication with few publication requirements that advocates a distinct point of view? There may be a backlash associated with writing only for publications that have slanted views. This could be used against an expert to show bias. The article will generally be more valuable from a marketing standpoint if it is published in a prestigious journal.

*Who will read the article?*

It is helpful to check the circulation and the number of people who actually read the publication. Is it a publication professionals pay to subscribe to or is it sponsored by a grant and mailed free of charge to one or more categories of professionals? Again, the key may not lie only in the number of people who subscribe or read it, but in the specific type of readers. If, for example, Mr. Lee is marketing his services as a reinsurance expert/consultant and the five hundred key reinsurance professionals read an influential journal or newsletter, he might be better off publishing in that journal than in one with five hundred times the circulation. (See Appendix M for a listing of major legal publications.)

At a minimum, one should make sure articles in the publication are indexed in electronic search engines. Many attorneys will search for experts by doing a literature search. Articles are much more valuable from a marketing standpoint if they are electronically indexed.

*When will the article be published?*

To paraphrase Vince Lombardi, "Timing isn't everything, it's the only thing." If an article is published in July or August, when many professionals are on vacation, or if it appears in December when most people are too busy with the holidays to read anything, there will be much less of an impact and interest. If the article is in a peer-reviewed journal, the review process may delay publication. Many editors will hold and save articles for when they are needed to fill in space. An author should attempt to get an agreement in advance for exactly when his article will be published. It is unwise to spend valuable time writing an article that will sit in an editor's file for nine months before she publishes it.

*Contact information*

It is useful to try to insist that the magazine or journal either list the author's phone number, e-mail address, or an easy way to contact him such as the name of his employer. The more difficult it is for the reader to track down an author, the less calls and business he can expect. If they will not list contact information, it may be possible to subtly work into the article information that can be used to find the author (where he lives or works, etc.). Having a personal Web site with the author's name registered in the proper search engines is another good back up.

*Why the expert will write*

An expert needs to identify specifically what she hopes to achieve before she will have any realistic chance of achieving it. Is she trying to beef up her CV? Is she hoping potential clients will see the article and call for consultations and to retain her services? Clearly identifying her goals will force an expert to consider if the article, chapter, or book is a cost-effective marketing method. While there will be little if any out-of-pocket cost, the time it will take to write the article should be factored into one's decision.

**Backlash:** Balancing who one writes for avoids the appearance of partiality and bias. If, on the whole, an expert will not be better off professionally having published in a particular journal or newspaper, why do it? It is also critical to keep in mind that anything an expert writes can and will be used against her during cross-examination. With electronic search engines, attorneys can easily develop a fairly comprehensive list of an individual's publications. These publications can be used against an expert to show bias and to show any inconsistencies with the testimony she provides on the witness stand.

**Example 18.2: Past writing used against expert**

**Q.** You are here giving your unbiased opinion, are you not?

**A.** Of course.

**Q.** In July 2006, in the publication *The Forensic Specialist,* you wrote an article entitled, "Progression of Litigation-related Injury."

**A.** Ahh. Yes.

**Q.** Is this a copy of that article?

**A.** Yes.

**Q.** I direct you to page 3, paragraph 3, the fourth sentence, and I quote, "Of course, it's common knowledge that once an injured person retains a lawyer, his recovery will almost always be delayed." Am I reading that correctly, sir?

**Comment:** Experts are best served by not writing anything that they do not want to be brought in front of a jury.

***Cost-Benefit Analysis:*** As with any marketing effort, a cost-benefit analysis is necessary. Writing can be very time-consuming. It's also important to remember to track referrals. If an expert's tracking reveals that her article generated a number of cases, she should strongly consider spending the time to write more articles.

## 18.8 Writing Texts

An expert who "wrote the book" on a particular topic can become a very highly valued witness. As an example, Mr. Babitsky wrote a book on the legal implications of the American Medical Association's *Guides to the Evaluation of Permanent Impairment*. A few years ago, he was asked to testify in Eagle Pass, Texas, in a case dealing with the *Guides*. Mr. Babitsky lives in Cape Cod. Because he wrote the book and because they wanted him, he was able to arrange a fee whereby he was paid a high portal-to-portal hourly fee from the time he left his house in Cape Cod until the time he returned.

Writing a book makes an expert easy to find. Many attorneys will search for experts by doing a literature search and seeing who comes up on the particular topic in question. Coming up on such a search is great marketing with little or no backlash.

Once an expert has written a book on a topic, this will often open up other opportunities as well. For example, the expert may be invited to write articles for journals or to give presentations. Since the expert has already written a book on the topic, preparing articles and presentations should not be overly time consuming and these articles and presentations may lead to additional cases.

***Backlash:*** Anything written by an expert can and will be used against him during cross-examination. This is especially true of comments that may tend to show bias or comments that can be construed as being inconsistent with the testimony the expert presents on the witness stand.

**Example 18.3: Testimony inconsistent with what is written in expert's book**

**Q.** And you based your opinion, Doctor, partly on the tests that you performed to detect malingering?

**A.** Yes.

**Q.** I have here the book you authored, *Symptom Magnification and Malingering.* Page 189, line 3, and I quote, "Most, if not all, of the tests to detect malingering have serious deficiencies in validity and reliability." Am I reading that correctly?

**Comment:** Experts should expect opposing counsel to pounce on any apparent inconsistencies between what they are testifying to and what they have written in the past.

***Cost-Benefit Analysis:*** When deciding whether to write a book, it is critical to remember that writing a book is a *very* big project. As such, it may be a risky proposition. It is much less costly to "test" whether speaking or writing an article will generate business than to write a book. Of course, depending upon the topic, an author may be able to recoup some or all of the time spent on writing the text through royalties from its sale. As noted above, if an individual "wrote the book" on a particular subject, her time may be worth considerably more to the referring attorney.

## 18.9  Referral Agencies, Locator Services, and Brokers

There are dozens of referral agencies, locator services, and brokers who can help market an expert's services. These organizations vary in geographic scope. Some are local or statewide while many are national. How these organizations get paid also varies. Prior to deciding whether to be listed with one or more of these services, it is necessary to do one's homework. Due diligence is important. Some of the questions the forensic expert needs to ask follow.

*1. How long has the organization been in business?*
Is this a start-up or fly-by-night group? It is critical that attorneys have heard of the organization, that they use it, and that it will be in business in the near future.

*2. How does the organization publicize itself?*
What do copies of their materials look like? Are they professional and classy? Would it be embarrassing to be confronted with them on the witness stand? Are they spending any money to reach clients?

*3. Is there a contract? If so, what does it say?*
One should always read all the fine print. The devil is in the details. Experts who need help should get a lawyer to review the contract.

*4. Is the contract exclusive or nonexclusive?*
In the authors' opinion, it is usually not a good idea to sign an exclusive contract.

*5. What are the financial arrangements?*
Is there a flat fee for listing for a time period (similar to an ad)? Do they surcharge the expert's fee? Do they take a portion of the fee? Who does the billing? Who bears the loss if the client decides to default? When does the expert get paid?

*6. How do they select which expert to offer to the client?*
Is it based upon expertise, experience, a rotating system, or some other criteria?

*7. Do they provide insurance or a hold-harmless agreement if an expert is sued?*

*8. How many times has the organization been sued over the past five years?*
For what were they sued? What were the results?

Many experts we know have had very positive and financially rewarding experiences with referral agencies. The sophisticated forensic expert will, however, exercise caution before signing up with one or more referral agencies, locator services, or brokers. The wise expert understands that his credibility, professionalism, and reputation could be affected adversely by the activities of these agencies. Calling the agency to see how they respond to telephone inquiries and even meeting the people in charge and viewing the premises, personnel, and facility are highly recommended. (See Appendix K for a listing of referral organizations.)

*Backlash:* As can be seen from the first example in this chapter, an affiliation with a referral agency can be used against an expert during cross-examination. One should accept this fact before deciding to sign up with an agency. An expert should also do his homework on the agency to find out if there is anything about the organization that he wouldn't want to be asked about on cross-examination.

*Cost-Benefit Analysis:* Registering with referral agencies usually requires little time and involves little or no out-of-pocket expense. These agencies allow experts to reach potential clients that they could not reach by any other reasonable means. They therefore offer a very attractive cost-benefit ratio, especially for those who possess expertise in a rare area. Attorneys are most likely to use referral agencies for these rare areas of expertise. If, on the other hand, an expert is one of 50,000 chiropractors in the United States, an attorney will probably not have to resort to a referral agency to locate her. The benefit of referral organizations increases if they provide services, such as handling billing, sifting out inappropriate cases, and guaranteeing collections.

## 18.10 One-on-One Meetings

One of the most effective marketing techniques is meeting in-person with potential clients or those responsible for selecting and retaining experts. When using this technique, the potential client will be able to evaluate the expert's ability to communicate and his experience, training, and knowledge in his field. The client will be able to evaluate the type of impression the expert is likely to make on the jury or fact finder. Intangibles, such as whether the expert appears to be credible and likeable, are best learned in face-to-face meetings.

These meetings can also be useful in that they help experts bond with potential clients. During the meeting, the expert has an opportunity to get the potential client to like him. If the client likes the expert, she will be much more likely to retain him.

One of the best ways to set up a meeting with a potential client is to offer to take the client to lunch. Attorneys are hesitant to turn down a free meal, especially if the person who is treating can help them win their next big case. Obviously, no one can take every attorney in the country out to lunch. The key to making the one-on-one meeting technique cost-effective is to narrow down a target market and try to meet with the lawyers who are the best prospects. For example, a tobacco expert should meet with the lawyers doing the tobacco litigation in her geographic area.

The client will use the meeting to try to see if the expert would be useful to her. Specifically, she will look at the following seven points.

*1. Qualifications*
Is the expert truly qualified in the area where he claims expertise?

*2. Credibility*
Is the expert a hired gun? Is testifying all he does?

*3. Track record*
How many cases has the expert been involved in? What were the results?

*4. Ability to communicate*
Would the expert do well in front of a judge and jury?

*5. Availability*
Is the expert available if a case goes to trial, or is he always traveling?

*6. Honesty*
Does the expert "call them as he sees them," or is he biased?

*7. Cost*
Based upon the size of the case, is the expert affordable? Is the expert local such that there will not be large travel costs?

An expert should bring to the meeting his business card, his current CV, and any letters of reference from satisfied clients. He may also want to bring along copies of articles he has written. His goals are to have the attorney remember him and to be able to contact him easily. The expert can also learn, if he asks, about other attorneys who may be interested in his services.

**Cost-Benefit Analysis:** The cost of this marketing technique is very small. It is, therefore, an easy method to test. A support person can set up the meetings. The meetings themselves should take less than an hour and lunch is not an expensive meal. Two additional advantages are immediate feedback and ease of tracking. When meeting one-on-one with someone, an individual can usually get a good idea of whether he is connecting with the other party. Finally, tracking meetings is easy. If an expert gets a case from an attorney he met with, he can probably assume it was a result of that meeting.

### 18.11 Printed Expert Witness Directories
One effective method for marketing services as an expert is to pay to be listed in a printed directory of experts. Directories can be local, state, or national in scope. Some directories are limited as to the type of experts listed (for example, IME physicians, technical experts,

medical experts, experts belonging to a certain association, etc.), while others combine experts from all fields in the same directory. (A listing of print directories is provided in Appendix L.) As in most forms of advertising, experts should ask a number of questions before listing themselves in a print expert witness directory.

- What is the *fee* to be listed and how often is the fee due?
- What is the *circulation* of the directory and is this *guaranteed* in writing?
- Who will *receive* the directory? (Will it be lawyers, insurance companies, etc?)
- What is the *geographic breakdown* of the *circulation* of the directory? (If an expert lives in Maine, is it wise to participate in a directory where 100% of the distribution is on the West Coast?)
- How *large is the directory?* How many pages is it? What is its trim size? If possible, it is a good idea to obtain a past directory to see the quality and feel of the publication.
- How *often* does the directory come out? Is it annual? Semi-annual? When will the expert be listed?
- *What information and how much information will the expert be permitted to list* in the directory? Is the directory arranged alphabetically by specialty, by the name of the expert, geographically, or in some other fashion?
- *What will be the surrounding directory listings?* For example, an arborist may not feel comfortable following an abortion specialist. One can just imagine the cross-examination possibilities.
- *Who has already signed up* for the directory? Who signed up in the past?
- Is the *directory indexed?* If so, how is it indexed? Without an index it may be difficult to find the expert.
- How *long has the publishing company been in existence* and what is their reputation?
- Is there any *guarantee or money-back offer* if one is not satisfied with the results?
- Will there be advertising in the directory? If so, how much will there be and who is likely to advertise?
- Does the print listing also include an online Internet listing?
- Is the print directory searchable on legal databases?

Due diligence on the part of the expert is highly recommended. She should know what she is getting into and make an informed decision as to its likely cost-effectiveness. As with all marketing techniques, experts should take care to track the results so that they can determine if continued listing in a particular directory is cost-effective. As expert witness referrals tend to come in bunches punctuated with droughts, it is usually a good idea to try a directory listing for at least two years before determining whether the listing is working.

***Backlash:*** As with any advertisement, a listing in a directory can be used against an expert on cross-examination in an attempt to show bias. To minimize this risk, the expert needs to be careful where he lists and what his listing actually says. It is critical to avoid any inartful language that could tend to indicate bias.

***Cost-Benefit Analysis:*** Directory listings require a relatively small amount of time to complete. The cost will vary, but will generally be more than recouped with the first referral. Because the out-of-pocket risk and the time commitment are small, directory listings are a good candidate for testing. If an expert has done his due diligence and has a good feel for a particular directory, he should try a listing for a couple of years to give it a fair chance of working. If it works, he has gained a valuable client and the rewards can be great indeed as the client can give repeat business and lead to further word-of-mouth exposure for the expert. If the listing doesn't work, he shouldn't renew it. The losses will be very limited as the time and expense involved in listing in a directory are usually relatively small. Directory listings may have an advantage over advertisements because annual directories usually have a much longer shelf life than daily, weekly, or monthly legal publications.

## 18.12  Classified and Display Advertisements

Many experts advertise for the simple reason that advertising is a simple, time-efficient, and effective way of growing their practices. Other experts choose not to advertise because they are "pound foolish," too busy to accept more cases, or, most commonly, do not want to open themselves up to cross-examination questions concerning their advertisements.

There are two general types of advertising, classified ads and display ads. Each is discussed below. For any advertising to be effective, the publication it is in must reach the target audience of attorneys. Before advertising in a publication, one should verify the total distribution of the publication (how many copies of the ad will get into the marketplace?), whether it is free or paid for (attorneys are more likely to actually read something they had to pay for), the geographical distribution (does it zero-in on attorneys in a region or is it spread from coast to coast?), and the specialty of the attorneys who read it (is it a publication for trial attorneys or is it for all attorneys, many of whom never hire experts?).

After placing an ad, the expert needs to follow up on it by reading the publication in question. It is not uncommon for publishers to make mistakes in typesetting or publishing an ad. If there is a mistake, the expert should inform the publisher immediately. Otherwise, the expert may have difficulty in obtaining a refund.

*Classified advertisements*

Classified advertisements can be a cost-effective way to market services. Classified ads are usually sold by the line or word. To save money, an expert may choose not to repeat the category she is listed under in the classified section. For example, if Dr. Jones is a toxicologist and is listed under "Toxicology," she could probably omit "toxicology" from her advertisement.

The most important factor that will determine whether a classified ad will work is duration. A classified ad must run for a long time if it is to have any reasonable chance of success. This cannot be overemphasized. The authors recommend a two-year minimum to properly test this marketing media. When listing for long periods, an expert should be sure to ask the publisher for any applicable discounts.

A classified ad need *not* be an attention-getter. Basic information is usually sufficient to generate leads. What usually transpires is that an interested attorney will call (or have his paralegal call) every listing in the category. Whether the expert gets the referral will then be up to the strength of his CV and communication skills.[1] The shortness of a classified ad has the added benefit of reducing the potential backlash from advertising. A good classified ad has basic information and may highlight the area that makes an expert stand out in his field.

**Example 18.4: Short and sweet classified advertisement**
Economist. M.I.T. Faculty. Nancy D. Marinelli. 617-555-1234.

*Display advertisements*
Display ads are typical ads found in any publication. They are usually sold by the size of the ad. Since display ads are bigger than classified ads, they can draw more attention. Because display ads are much more expensive than classified ads they are most appropriate for:

- experts who practice in groups,
- experts who cannot get across enough information in a classified ad,
- experts who want to include photographs and other visual information, and
- experts who are willing to pay a premium for additional exposure beyond that which is provided by a classified ad.

There is room for far more information in a display ad than there is in a classified ad. This is a major advantage of display ads over classified ads. It is also, however, a potential *disadvantage* because there is a greater opportunity to include information, claims, or statements inside the display ad that can be used against the expert during cross-examination. As such, the expert should be very careful when drafting her display ads. ***Display ads should not include anything the expert would not want brought up by opposing counsel during cross-examination.***

***Backlash:*** An expert can, and will, be confronted with her advertising on cross-examination. The shorter the ad, the less ammunition the cross-examiner will have. This is another advantage of a short, basic classified advertisement. When confronted with questions concerning whether one advertises, it may be best to answer the question simply and directly. This avoids being evasive and forces counsel to move on.

**Example 18.5: Direct answer to advertisement question**
**Q.** Isn't it a fact that you advertise in *National Law Day?*
**A.** Yes.

**Comment:** This was an effective answer in that the expert did not seem as though he had anything to hide or that he was in any way ashamed. It also forces counsel to move on.

There is nothing unseemly about dignified advertising and there are very few types of professionals who do not advertise. One only needs to pick up any Yellow Pages directory in the country. The largest section of advertisers will probably be for lawyers. To minimize the potential backlash from advertising, the expert should: 1) keep ads short, 2) be

---

[1] Also critical is whether the expert answers his phone and how long it takes him to return a phone inquiry if he doesn't answer his phone.

very careful about what is written in the ads, and 3) maintain balance in *where* the expert advertises (for example, not advertising exclusively in plaintiff's journals or defense journals).

***Cost-Benefit Analysis:*** Display ads cost more than classified ads and take longer to draft and produce. Making the display ad look professional often involves hiring a graphic artist. Classified ads cost much less, the time involved in drafting the ad is small, and the ongoing time commitment is negligible. The cost of a one- or two-year ad may be justified to test whether classified ads will work. Note that publications are sometimes flexible on their published advertising rates, so it's usually a good idea to at least try to negotiate a better price.

      The expert should keep the ad simple and run it for a year or two. He shouldn't waste money by advertising in a publication that doesn't reach his target audience. Also, an expert shouldn't forget to track his referrals by asking contacts how they found out about him. If experts don't track referrals, they'll never know if their ads (or other marketing techniques) worked.

## 18.13 Direct Mail
Direct mail is another way that experts can market their services. (Appendix W provides some sample marketing letters.) There are several points to remember about direct mail.

*1. The most important factor in any direct mail campaign is the mailing list.*
The list is everything. The advantage of direct mail is that an individual can put her material in front of her target audience—if she has the proper list.

*2. Direct mail is expensive and time-consuming.*
Total costs include drafting, designing, printing, mailing, list rental or assembly, postage, and proofing. Depending upon the size of the piece and the volume of the mailing, the final cost could be well over $1 per piece.

*3. Lawyers and other busy professionals usually throw out 99% of the mail they identify as junk mail.*

*4. Direct mail pieces in envelopes usually work the best.*

*5. Direct mail campaigns can be repeated and remain effective.*

*6. Direct mail is a good medium to test new markets.*

*7. Attorneys will save their expert witness direct mail and CVs and file them for the future.*

*8. First-class, personalized, stamped mail in envelopes gets opened the most.*
It's also the most expensive type of direct mail.

***Backlash:*** Anything said in a direct mail piece can and will be used against an expert on cross-examination. To minimize the potential damage, experts should make sure that whatever they write is objective and does not indicate bias. It is also wise to keep it short.

The best designed pieces are 100% objective and professional.[2] If asked whether she markets by direct mail, an expert who does so should defuse the situation by answering "yes." She should not make matters worse by being evasive.

*Cost-Benefit Analysis:* Because of the tremendous time and cost of direct mail campaigns, they are usually not the best option for individual experts.[3] One exception could be, however, extremely personalized and targeted direct mail. This would involve an expert identifying his best target market. For example, the one hundred best, most active medical malpractice attorneys in a particular state in addition to attorneys who have hired the expert in medical malpractice cases in the past. It could be very effective to send each a personalized letter saying, for example, "I am enclosing for your convenience a copy of an article of mine which was recently published in….I have also enclosed an updated CV reflecting this publication and other recent accomplishments." This is professional and gives value to that attorney.

The key here is always the mailing list. A *small, well-targeted* mailing list may very well be cost-effective. Mass mailings, on the other hand, generally aren't cost-effective. An expert should develop and maintain a list of key attorneys. As always, an expert should track referrals, otherwise he'll never know what worked and what didn't. Finally, one shouldn't give up if there isn't an immediate response. Attorneys will often save a direct mail piece for the future when they may need it.[4]

## 18.14  Print Newsletters

The creation, development, and mailing (distribution) of a complimentary newsletter to potential clients can be effective in generating referrals. Because the newsletter is of value to the recipient, it is much more likely to be read than junk mail. It also is professional and may be less susceptible to backlash than a typical direct mail solicitation. Newsletters can be retained as a reference and help reinforce one's expertise. The expert's goal is a well-researched, fully documented, practical, cutting-edge newsletter that leads to the inescapable conclusion that the expert knows her field and should be considered for consultations and retention.

*Backlash:* If a newsletter is designed as a true newsletter, there will be very little backlash. Two areas to look out for are *puff pieces* and controversial issues. Experts should avoid puff pieces that are merely self-promotions. Instead, it is best to stick to real matters of interest to the reader. Also, one must be very careful about writing about controversial issues.

---

[2] "Dear Attorney Jones. I was referred to you by Attorney Tom Smith, whom I met at a recent bar association meeting where I had been invited to speak. Attorney Smith suggested that I send you a copy of my CV, which I have enclosed for your convenience. Please call me if you have any questions, comments, or concerns."

[3] This may be different for a large group of experts. Also, national referral agencies use direct mail to promote their groups of experts cost-effectively.

[4] The authors' business commonly receives responses to mail sent to attorneys many months and sometimes years after the mail has been received.

Anything an expert writes can and will be used against him on the witness stand. This includes opinions expressed in his newsletter.

***Cost-Benefit Analysis:*** The key to making newsletters cost-effective is keeping the time and out-of-pocket expenses down. Both can be controlled by strictly limiting the number of issues written and the number of copies mailed each year. Some recommendations for creating a cost-effective marketing newsletter follow.

*1. Limit the number of pages and the number of issues each year*
Many experts underestimate the time and effort that is required to put together a newsletter. Limiting the newsletter to four pages published four times a year will be enough to achieve marketing goals without overburdening oneself with work.

*2. Make the newsletter useful*
Newsletters that contain puff pieces about degrees the expert has obtained are not retained and, in most cases, are not even read by potential clients. Newsletters that contain breaking stories and practical information are more likely to be read and retained.

*3. Three-hole punch the newsletter*
By three-hole punching a newsletter, the expert encourages the retention of the newsletter in a binder.

*4. Encourage feedback*
By encouraging feedback through the readers' questions, letters, and phone calls, the expert will, in effect, encourage potential clients to contact him.

*5. Distribution*
The key to success will be to create a useful, easy-to-read newsletter distributed to potential clients. The distribution can be by direct mail, handing out at seminars and meetings, by e-mail, or any other way one can get the newsletter into the hands of potential clients.

## 18.15  Online Directories and Listings
There is no shortage of directories that will post the information of expert witnesses on the Internet. A list of online expert witness directories is provided in Appendix L. Online directories can be quite effective in generating new case referrals. Since almost anyone with a computer can start an online expert witness directory, an expert should have answers to the following questions before he lists himself in an online directory.

*1. What is the cost to both the attorney and the expert?*
No cost-benefit analysis can be completed without knowing this. Also, an attorney will be less likely to use the directory if he has to pay to do so.

*2. Do the listings look professional?*
An expert needs to be comfortable with the look and feel of the site and the listings.

*3. How many other experts are listed?*
The more experts the better. This may be counter-intuitive, but attorneys are more likely to use the site if it contains large amounts of experts.

*4. How much information is included?*
Basic information such as name, contact information, the expert's Web page, and areas of expertise should be provided.

*5. What does the directory do to promote its site such that lawyers and paralegals will find it and use it?*
If lawyers cannot find the directory, they won't use it.

*6. How much usage does the site get?*
Ask for statistics on how many times the site is searched per month.

*7. How long has the directory, and the company sponsoring it, been in business?*
Is this a new, speculative venture with no money for promotion?

*8. What is the directory's renewal rate for its listings?*
This gives an idea of the satisfaction of the experts in the directory.

*9. Is there any type of money-back guarantee?*
Does the publisher stand by its product?

*10. When you type in "expert witnesses" in search engines, does the directory show up?*
This provides a gauge of how easy the directory is for attorneys and paralegals to find.

Many professional associations maintain Web site directories of expert witnesses. Experts should check with the societies that they belong to to determine if they maintain an online expert directory and, if so, what the cost of inclusion is. Since attorneys turn to associations to look for experts (see Section 17.5), such listings can be effective. In fact, experts may want to consider joining organizations that maintain online expert witness directories.

***Backlash:*** As with any marketing activity, there can be a potential backlash with listing in online directories. To minimize such a backlash, experts should do the following.

- Carefully word directory listings. Many times, the problem is the wording of the listing. Avoid exaggerations and statements that could indicate bias. For further information on this, please see Chapter 7 on CVs.
- Only list themselves in professional-looking, unbiased directories.

**Example 18.6: "Hired-gun experts"**
**Q.** Is this a copy of your ad on the Web site whose URL is "hiredgunexperts.com"?

**Comment:** Experts should never list themselves, or allow themselves to be listed, on Web sites that appear unprofessional or unbiased.

***Cost-Benefit Analysis:*** Online directory listings including basic information (similar to what would be found in a classified ad) are usually very cost-effective. The listings take very little time to place, are usually inexpensive, and they can be quite effective in getting new cases. The time and expense involved in online listings will increase if the listing is complex with photos, links to documents, streaming audio/video, etc. As with all forms of marketing, experts should experiment and track their referrals to determine what works for them.

## 18.16 E-mails

Experts should not use mass spam e-mail to promote themselves. Use of spam will be counterproductive because it signifies bad judgment, is associated with scams and fraud, and will likely anger the recipients. Targeted, personalized e-mails can, however, be very useful if used to facilitate networking.

> **Example 18.7: Networking e-mail**
> Dear Attorney Jones:
>
> It was very nice meeting you on our recent flight. Attached please find my CV. I have attached it as a PDF file to ease compatibility in case you would like to forward this to colleagues. I hope you had a nice vacation.
>
> Very truly yours,
>
> Joe Expert
> Cell: 555-555-1234
>
> **Comment:** This is a good networking e-mail. It does not say anything that can be used against the expert during cross-examination and it plants the idea in the attorney's head that he should forward the CV to his colleagues. He also provides his cell phone number so that he will be instantly reachable in case there is an inquiry for new business.

> **Example 18.8: Networking e-mail to past client**
> Dear Attorney Jones:
>
> I thought you might be interested in the attached article on head injuries from today's *Wall Street Journal.* I believe those cases were your sub-specialty. Please let me know if you have any questions.
>
> Very truly yours,
>
> Joe Medical Expert, M.D.
> Cell: 555-555-5678
>
> **Comment:** This is another good networking e-mail. The expert witness provides relevant information to a past client and reminds the attorney that he is still around and keeps current.

*Backlash:* Spam e-mail should not be used. Targeted networking e-mails can, however, be quite effective. As long as they are carefully drafted, they should pose few backlash problems.

*Cost-Benefit Analysis:* Networking e-mails can be extremely cost-effective. The out-of-pocket costs are zero and the time involved is minimal. Experts should consider sending networking e-mails as a part of their usual routine.

## 18.17  Electronic Newsletters & Blogs

Many organizations publish their "marketing" newsletters electronically and distribute them via e-mail. The cost advantages over print newsletters are substantial. There are no printing costs, no postage, no mailing costs, and much less cost laying out the design of the newsletter. The drawback to online newsletters is the tendency for recipients to discount any newsletters or advertising they receive free online as "junk mail."

Other people and organizations maintain Weblogs ("blogs") that post relevant information in a particular field. The marketing goals of the electronic newsletter and blog are the same: to help establish the expert's expertise in his field and to help attorneys find the expert.

*Backlash:* As with print newsletters, experts can be cross-examined on anything they have written in their newsletters or blogs. They may also be cross-examined on who receives the newsletter and how the newsletter is sent. Experts should take care in what they write in any newsletter.

*Cost-Benefit Analysis:* Electronic newsletters and blogs can take significant time to write, but they are less expensive to distribute than print newsletters. However, because electronic newsletters are free, they run the risk of being dismissed as spam or thinly disguised sales pitches. They may be deleted without being read.

## 18.18  Web Pages

Experts should consider having a personal Web page. Some advantages Web pages offer include the following.

- They are inexpensive to maintain. Many plans start at $15 per month.
- They result in 24/7 marketing.
- Attorneys will be able to review an expert's qualifications and have access to her contact information at all times.
- Because directory listings and classified ads can contain links to the expert's Web page (which has more detailed information), it can give the expert "more bang for the buck."
- A Web page provides the expert with a professional e-mail address. Rather than using a generic e-mail address like AOL, Yahoo, or Hotmail, a Web site plan generally includes e-mail accounts that represent the Web site (for example, JohnSmith@SmithEngineering.com).

Some experts are daunted by what it takes to create a Web page. They shouldn't be. There are several ways an expert can create a Web site in a cost-effective and time-efficient manner.

- The expert can pay a professional Web site designer to build the site.
- The expert can hire an amateur/freelance designer to build a site.
- Many of the larger Web site hosting companies can build one for a fee.
- The expert can learn to do it herself.

The cost will depend on how many pages the expert would like to have on her site and the complexity of creating those pages. Since the optimum expert witness Web page should be fairly simple, development costs should be relatively low.

Originally, creating and maintaining Web pages was best left to a computer programmer who used HTML (hypertext markup language), the programming code used to create documents on the World Wide Web. This has changed. There are now a variety of tools available so a lay person can create and maintain a Web page without the services of a "Webmaster." Examples of two such products are *Microsoft FrontPage* and *Dreamweaver.*

## Choosing a domain name

Choosing a Web address or domain name is an important decision. It is best to select a domain name that is as short as possible and that is easily recognizable and remembered. It should also be easy to spell. Generally, phonic representations or hyphens make it more difficult for someone trying to remember or find a Web site. For example, "XScash.com" sounds the same as "Excesscash.com" or "Excess-cash.com." Ideally, a Web address should be short, easy to remember, simple to spell, and easily recognizable. It should *not* be something that will embarrass the expert during cross-examination.

Once the expert decides on and registers her domain name, she will need to choose a hosting company for the new Web site. A hosting company posts the Web site on the Internet. Many hosting companies will register the domain name as an added service. Generally, the larger hosting companies have more added features. Many also offer template-based Web site creation tools to help create a professional-looking Web site quickly and easily without using technical programming languages or complicated Web design software. This also allows the expert to keep her site up to date with minimal effort.

## Web site and search engine optimization

Everyone would like to have the top spot on Google or Yahoo. Getting that top spot, or even on the first page, is a difficult task filled with complex algorithms that outsiders rarely understand. The search engines keep the formula top secret.

Web site optimization involves making modifications to a Web site (design, content, page structure, technical structure, and relationship with other Web sites) to make search engines like Google and Yahoo identify the site as highly relevant. The goal is to have your site show up near the top of the search results page.

Below are the basics of Web site and search engine optimization. It is a complicated topic and we cannot go into great depth here. Search engines constantly change the way they rank Web sites. There is no magic formula to getting a high ranking; however, below we outline some general guidelines. The optimization concepts below are current as of the publishing of this text and may change over time. It is best to research this topic if you have further interest in it.

> *1. Copywriting.* This is the actual text on the site. Many feel that it is the most important step in getting a Web site listed high in the search results. Just like a visitor to a site would read the copy on its page to figure out what it offers, search engines do the same. Experts are advised to try to think like their target audience. What would they search for when looking for your Web site? It is very easy to fall

in the trap of coming up with terms you would search for, but what about everyone else? They might use different keywords or phrases.

This text should include the most important keyword phrases and should remain logical and readable. It's important to think of specific keyword phrases rather than keywords. Why? Due to the large amount of competition for general terms in search engines, if keyword phrases are too general it is unlikely that the site will rank well in the search engines. There is a far better chance for a high ranking if the site uses specific phrases where there is less competition. The resulting traffic will be more targeted and therefore should also be high quality. For example, on Google the broad term "expert witness" returns over 28 million results. A more targeted keyword phrase to use would be specific, such as "wastewater discharge expert witness."

*2. Title tag.* This is the text that appears in the top bar of the Web browser. It may be the name of the expert's business or a short description of her specialty. Some Web site design tools automatically generate the title tag. Some Web pages are labeled "Page 1," "Page 2," or "Home Page" in the browser title bar. These are often the result of Web site designers who haven't used their title tag for maximum benefit. An example of a good title tag is: "Morris and Breen, Inc.–Boston Tax Accountants–CPAs in Boston, MA."

*3. Meta tags.* These are computer code information placed in a Web page. They are not intended for users to see. Typically, they provide information to search engines. There are two main types of meta tags: *description tags* and *keyword tags*. Meta tags can be added by a professional programmer or through programs such as Frontpage. Experts should use specific keywords or phrases for the meta tags on their sites.

*4. Link popularity.* This is another major principle that some search engines use to determine a site's relevance. Link popularity is whether Web sites that contain similar content to an expert's site link to her site. Search engines crawl the Web, going from link to link and Web site to Web site, indexing Web pages as they go. Search engines use various link popularity analysis ranking methods, based on the premise that a Web site that is linked to by other sites of similar interest is a relevant site.

*5. An important point.* Do not try to trick the search engines by creating invisible links or overusing keywords. Search engines see this as an attempt to mislead them and may block the expert's site from being listed.

Search engine optimization is a large and growing business. Many companies charge exorbitant fees to optimize a Web site for search engines. Wise experts do their homework before signing up for this type of service.

*Submitting a site to search engines*

After optimizing the Web site, the expert should then submit it to various search engines. Some are currently free (like Google and Yahoo[5]), while others charge a fee. Experts don't necessarily need to submit their sites to be listed with the search engines. If there are enough sites that link to the expert's site, they should find the expert's site eventually. But because it's free to submit a site and it's best to have the site listed as soon as possible, the authors recommend that experts submit their sites. This is a simple process and should take less than 20 minutes.

Usually it takes 4 to 6 weeks to become listed after submitting a Web site to search engines. It may take longer. It's helpful to be patient and to check the search engines to see if the site has been included.

*Web site content*

In designing expert Web pages, the authors suggest that experts follow the advice that "less is more" because anything on an expert's Web site can also be used against the expert during cross-examination. The ideal expert witness Web page should contain:

- an executive summary of who the expert is and what she offers (working in keywords and keyword phrases),
- a *current* CV,
- a recent photo, and
- contact information so the attorneys can find the expert.

The authors suggest that experts who wish to develop their own Web sites review other experts' Web sites. They can then emulate the look and feel of one of the sites that they like.

**Backlash:** *Often, the first place opposing counsel will go to dig up dirt on an expert witness is the expert's Web page. As such, experts need to be very careful about what is written on their Web pages and keep the information there current.* Common Web page problem areas include the following.

1. *Marketing fluff.* Many times, experts employ marketing consultants or Web consultants who typically design Web pages for businesses that sell consumer products to the mass media. These experts may use marketing fluff on the expert's page. Marketing fluff that works in the mass media (such as "Guaranteed results or your money back") is inappropriate on expert witness Web pages. Experts need to carefully proof their Web pages to make sure that no one has included such language without their permission or knowledge.

2. *Out-of-date information on CV.* To avoid this problem, experts should develop a system whereby whenever their offline CV is updated, their online CV is updated as well.

---

[5] At the time of this writing, you can submit Web pages to Google by clicking on "About Google" on the home page and then "Submit your content to Google." For Yahoo, click on "How to suggest a site."

3. *Inconsistencies between the Web page and the expert's CV or report.* A common instance of this is where the Web page lists different areas of expertise than the CV. This needs to be avoided.

4. *Including "content" on the Web site.* Common advice for businesses is to put articles and other "content" on a Web site to encourage visits. Once again, what works for businesses is probably *not* a good idea for experts. Content the expert places on the Web may very well be used against the expert. For example, let's say an expert has a checklist of what needs to be done during an accident reconstruction investigation. How foolish and sloppy would the expert look on cross-examination if he didn't do half of the things on his own checklist?

*Cost-Benefit Analysis:* In general, the cost to have a Web site is less than $350 per year. There are three costs associated with a Web page.

1. The initial cost to launch it. There is an annual fee to reserve the Web site address. *Fees are around $30 per year.*
2. The ongoing monthly hosting charge. This usually relates to the size of the Web site (storage used). Expert Web sites are usually concise, so this can be manageable. *Fees are $10–$25 per month.*
3. The ongoing cost to maintain and update the site. The expert can learn to maintain the site. This can be a fun hobby for those who like technical things. It's also possible to hire a freelance Web designer or hire a professional company to make changes to a site. *Expect to pay at least $100 per hour for any type of technical work.*

Experts should personally review each update to their Web site. Damaging information is often placed on sites by well-intentioned marketing people, programmers, or others who are charged with Web site maintenance.

Because there are many options for each of the three costs associated with a Web page, actual costs will vary. However, for most expert Web pages, these costs can be brought down to a very manageable level, especially if the amount of information on the page is limited.

The benefit of the Web page can only be determined if the expert tracks how many people visit her site, where they come from, and how many of these visitors retain the expert. Many Web hosting services can provide detailed reports of which search terms are used by visitors to the Web site, how many visits there have been to the site, and where those visits came from if they were linked in (e.g., an online directory listing). As always, it is good practice to ask new clients or prospects how they found you.

## 18.19  Online Advertising

*Search marketing*

Generally, online search marketing methods fall in one of two key categories: *natural search* (also called SEO) and *paid search* (also called pay-per-click or PPC).

Natural search is when the search engine lists a Web site in its directory or usual list of results. The bonus to natural search is that once a site is listed, the expert doesn't pay a fee each time someone visits her site. However, getting a search engine to list a Web site high in the results can be difficult (see above).

In a paid search, Web sites pay a fee to the search engine, which then guarantees that the site will be displayed in its sponsored results section for those specifically named terms. These are the sponsored ads that are on the top and right of Google and Yahoo's search results. A company pays a certain amount for a particular keyword phrase and when someone clicks on that phrase, the company is charged a fee to have the visitor sent to their Web site. Fees can range widely depending on the competition for a keyword. The more popular the keyword, the more it will cost to get a top ranking.[6] The fees for a top spot can range from a few cents to $10 for a popular keyword. At one point, the top paid spot on Google for the term "mesothelioma" was $100 per click.

Pay-per-click's strengths are that it is fast and you know exactly what you are going to pay. The expert can budget a daily dollar amount to spend. When that limit is reached, the ad is removed for the rest of the day. Furthermore, the highest bid can have the top ranking almost immediately. The exact costs are predictable and documented in reports provided by the search engines. It is relatively easy to measure the outcomes because pay-per-click tools measure the click-through rates for different terms (i.e., how many times a specific term was clicked and how much the expert paid for them). The downside of pay-per-click is that it may be very costly because the expert pays each time someone clicks on a link to her site.

*Online banner ads*

Banner ads are small graphical advertisements on Web sites. They differ considerably in appearance and subject matter, but they all share a basic function: if you click on them, you are redirected to the advertiser's Web site. Banner ads can display multiple images, including animation. They may also change appearance in other ways. These ads are usually located on the top or sides of Web sites to distinguish them from the site's content.

Expert witnesses sometimes place banner ads on sites that attorneys visit, such as legal publications, legal directories, and online expert witness directories. The cost of this varies. Another cost to factor in for banner ads is the fee of a graphic artist or other professional who designs the ad.

**Backlash:** As with any marketing activities, online advertising may be used against the expert. As such, the expert should, as always, be very careful about both what the ad says and where the expert advertises.

**Example 18.9: Ad on plaintiff's lawyers' Web site**
Q. Are you biased toward plaintiffs?
A. No.
Q. Is this a copy of your ad on the Web site for the New England Association of Trial Lawyers?
A. Yes.
Q. You don't advertise on any Web sites used by defense lawyers, do you?

---

[6] This is yet another reason why it is wise for experts to develop a niche or sub-specialty where there is less competition.

**Comment:** Experts can insulate themselves from these types of attacks by being balanced in where they advertise.

**Example 18.10: "Inexpensive expert witness"**
**Q.** You programmed your ad to come up #1 on Google if someone types in the search term "inexpensive expert witness," is that correct?
**A.** Yes.
**Q.** So the selling point you are trying to get across is that although you may not be any good you sure are cheap?

**Comment:** Experts should carefully review all of their marketing activities by asking the question, "How would this sound and look on cross-examination?"

*Cost-Benefit Analysis:* It is easier to evaluate the benefit of online advertising than print advertising because experts can track how many clicks result from online advertising. An expert can track how many cases he gets from his Web site by asking lawyers how they found him and perhaps by using a "contact" interface on the Web site that tells the expert the e-mail came from his Web site. It is wise to give the Web site time to work. It is also recommended that an expert ask *how* the attorney found his site. Was it from a free search, a paid search, or a link from an online directory?

## 18.20  Additional SEAK Resources
SEAK publishes the print *National Directory of Experts*. Each listing includes a free Internet directory listing. Display advertising is also available. Please see www.seakexperts.com for more information.

## 18.21  Conclusion
There are many different techniques that experts can use to market their services professionally. Experts who wish to increase their business should consider trying one or more of these techniques. They should repeat the techniques that were shown to be cost-effective and discard the others. An expert's marketing activities can and will be used against him on the witness stand. Therefore, all marketing should be conducted professionally, cautiously, and impartially.

# Chapter 19  Fees, Billings, and Collections

## 19.1  Introduction

An expert witness is entitled to be paid a reasonable fee for her time and expertise.[1] The successful expert understands the engagement process, how much to charge, what to charge for, and how and when to collect her fees.

## 19.2  The Engagement Process

Experts should have the key financial terms of their engagement clearly laid out in writing before agreeing to work on a case. (Appendix R contains sample fee schedules, letters, and agreements.) These documents need to specifically cover terms including fees (including cancellation fees), billings, retainers, travel, expenses, and interest for overdue accounts.

*Fees*

This is the hourly rate charged for the expert's time. Many experts charge an increased hourly rate for deposition and trial. Some experts also charge a minimum rate for depositions (for example, two hours) and trial (for example, a half day or four hours). Contingency fee agreements by experts—those that are in whole or in part contingent upon success in a case—are unethical and illegal in most states and should be avoided.

*Billings*

This is how often the client is to be billed—usually every 30 days. Also included are payment terms, also usually 30 days or net 30.

*Retainers*

*1. How much of a retainer is required in order to commence the engagement?* Sophisticated experts require, at a minimum, an initial retainer. The required payment of an initial retainer may help to weed out bad credit risks.

*2. Is the retainer refundable?* The nonrefundable portion of a retainer compensates the expert for those cases in which he is "conflicted out" of other work or for those situations where the case settles after the expert is designated by counsel.

*3. Is the retainer replenishable?* Sophisticated experts ask for a replenishable retainer. A replenishable retainer is where the expert is always paid in advance and will do no further work until the amount of the retainer will cover the anticipated time he will spend on the case. Replenishable retainers eliminate almost all collections problems dealing with fees for an expert's time. Replenishable retainers are also how most attorneys are paid when working on an hourly basis.

*4. When is the retainer applied?* If the expert does not use a replenishable retainer, a fallback technique to help ensure collections is applying the initial retainer only to the final bill on the case. This should result in the expert always having at least some insurance against nonpayment of his fees.

---

[1] As an expert, an individual is paid for her time, not for her testimony.

*Travel*
How does an expert charge for travel? Some experts charge portal-to-portal, especially for local travel. This means that they charge their hourly rate from the moment they leave their office until the moment they return. Some experts charge a flat rate for out-of-state travel (for example, ten times their hourly fee).

*Expenses*
For which out-of-pocket expenses will the expert seek reimbursement? This may include, but is not limited to, photocopying, couriers, research, telephone, and travel expenses.

*Interest*
This is the interest that will be added to overdue accounts. Using a fee letter or agreement will protect experts against troublesome attorneys. There are two reasons for this. First, the document will serve as evidence of what was agreed to. Second, the document will be diagnostic in nature. If the attorney balks at sending a retainer she is an attorney an expert probably does not, from a practice management standpoint, want to get involved with. Sophisticated experts also investigate potential clients to check on their reputation in the legal community. One or two phone calls to fellow experts or attorneys can help avoid problematic engagements.

## 19.3 Setting the Correct Rate
One of the most important decisions an expert needs to make is setting the correct rate for her time. If an expert charges too much, she may price herself out of the market. If she charges too little, she may not seem credible and may be charging less than her true value. In many years of dealing with this issue, the authors have developed two steadfast rules.

*Two rules of fee setting:*
**1. Far more experts undercharge than overcharge.** This is usually the result of inexperience and a psychological hesitancy to charge a rate of hundreds of dollars per hour for the expert's time.
**2. When experts increase their fees, the volume of work they receive increases.** Attorneys are paid to win and seek out the best possible experts. *Many assume that because an expert charges more, she is a better expert.* This assumption results in increased demand for the "best" experts who charge a premium for their services.

There are many factors that affect how much an expert can charge in a certain case. These include the expert's qualifications, his reputation as a witness, his communication skills, the amount at stake in the litigation, the availability of other experts, how much the expert's time is worth objectively, and legal limits to expert fees. (A summary of a recent expert witness fee survey is provided in Appendix X.)

*Qualifications*
The world's leading expert on a particular topic will generally be able to command a higher fee for his time.

### Example 19.1: World's leading experts

Recently, the authors were retained by a client to find the leading experts on a particular type of pharmaceutical. We conducted a world-wide literature search and developed a list of 5 to 7 names. When it came time for these individuals to negotiate fees, they were in a very strong bargaining position. Note also that in huge "life or death" cases (like those currently involving VIOXX) the litigants usually won't be cost-sensitive to what the experts are paid. In such high-stakes litigation the parties' mantra is usually "victory at any cost."

## Reputation as a witness

Someone with the reputation of being a formidable witness will be able to command a higher fee. An expert's value to the attorney is very much determined by how well the expert performs in front of a jury—the people who ultimately decide the case. One's reputation as a witness can be established by word of mouth and through jury verdict reporters. The converse is also true. Someone with a reputation as an ineffective witness will not be able to command a premium fee and might not be offered any work at all.

### Example 19.2: Expert with reputation as formidable witness commands higher fee

In a certain type of toxic tort litigation that the authors used to practice, there was a particular expert witness who usually testified for the defense. The witness was a petite woman in her sixties. Juries *loved* her and she was very effective. Her reputation as a witness was so strong, in fact, that merely naming her as a witness in a case had a substantial effect on its settlement value. As such, she was in a very strong bargaining position regarding her fees.

## Communication skills

If an expert does not yet possess a reputation as being a good witness, attorneys will estimate how well they think he will be able to communicate with and persuade a jury. This will usually be done while the attorney is interviewing the expert during their initial discussions of the case. If the expert can demonstrate that he is a superior communicator and that a jury would probably like him, he will be able to command a higher fee.

### Example 19.3: Communication skills matter

An attorney has done a literature search to locate two or three individuals who have published in a particular field of expertise. The expert that will be in the most demand will be the one who demonstrates the best communication and persuasion skills. In the end, the expert's ability to communicate with and persuade the jury is what makes the expert valuable.

## The amount at stake in the litigation

If a case is worth a significant amount of money, the amount paid for expert witness time will be a minor consideration. For example, in a $2.5 million malpractice case, the top concern of the lawyers will not be whether the experts are paid $400 or $700 per hour. The lawyers want and need to win and will usually be willing to spend whatever it takes to get the expert they need. On the other hand, if a case involves a small amount of money, say a $5,000 property dispute, the attorneys may be very cost-sensitive regarding fees for expert witnesses. There is usually no point in winning a $5,000 case if you run up $7,000 in expert witness fees in the process.

*Availability of other experts*

The rarer an individual's expertise, the higher the fee she will command. If, on the other hand, there is an oversupply of an individual's expertise, she will command a lower fee.

### Example 19.4: Availability of other experts drives down rates

A chiropractor in New York City generally won't be able to command an exceptionally high fee. The reason is simple: there are plenty of other chiropractors in New York City for attorneys to use.

**Comment:** The wise expert makes himself more valuable by:

1. developing a reputation as a skilled witness, and
2. developing a subspecialty or niche expertise that is rare or unique.

### Example 19.5: "Unique" expert charges what he wants

One of the authors is the country's most recognized expert on a particular legal topic. At one point there was a major case in a rural part of the country 2,000 miles from where he lived. He was able to command a high fee and such concessions as portal-to-portal billing for his two-day trip. Why? Under the law of supply and demand, he was the only "supply."

**Comment:** Experts are prudent to establish a niche where there is less competition and the expert can become recognized as the authority in the area.

## How much an expert's time is worth objectively

An expert will command a higher fee for legally related work if she can show that she is forgoing other lucrative work in order to devote time to the case. She will be in a stronger bargaining position with the attorney when it comes time to negotiate her fee because she can point to the income she is forgoing.

### Example 19.6: What the expert's time is worth objectively

**Attorney:** As I understand it, you're looking for $500 per hour for your time. How can you expect me to pay that much?

**Expert:** The microsurgery opportunities I give up and my ongoing overhead demand that I charge $500 per hour.

## Legal limitations

Experts appearing in certain administrative forums may be limited by statute, regulation, or custom as to how much they may be permitted to charge. For example, in workers' compensation cases some states limit the amounts experts can charge. Experts should check with the agencies and/or counsel prior to accepting these assignments. When an opposing party is legally required to pay for the expert's time, for example, in depositions in most jurisdictions, there may be a legal requirement that the expert's fee be reasonable.[2]

### Example 19.7: Flat fee unreasonable, fee reduced to reasonable hourly rate

*Massasoit v. Carter,* 227 F.R.D. 264 (M.D. N.C. 2005)

In this case the expert wanted to charge a flat rate amounting to 8 hours' worth of the expert's time for a deposition that was expected to last two or three hours and would take place in the expert's

---

[2] Fed. R. Civ. Pro. 26(b)(4)(c).

office. The court held such a fee to be unreasonable and reduced it to $250/hour, which is twice the rate the opposing experts were charging. The court stated:

> In the instant case, defendants have not shown a reasonable basis for the expert's $2,000.00 flat rate fee for a deposition at his own office. They state that he blocks out an entire day for a deposition. But that does not explain why he does that for all depositions, even short ones. It appears that their expert does consultation for his business and that if he is not in deposition or trial, or on investigation, he can spend his time reviewing reports. Consequently, in the instant case, the Court does find that a flat rate fee of $2,000.00 for a deposition, which could amount to over $600.00 per hour, is exorbitant. The expert is not like the physician who may have to block out time when he or she could see patients. *Harvey v. Shultz,* No. 99-1217-JTM, 2000 WL 33170885 (D.Kan. Nov.16, 2000)(expert was a physician who lost income because he could not schedule patients during that time). And, even if he were, there is no indication that the expert will lose an entire day's income. The mere fact that defendants' expert and another expert choose to use flat rates does not convince the Court that such a tactic is reasonable. Courts must be on guard against exorbitant expert fees, and retain the ultimate responsibility to keep litigation costs from becoming unreasonable. See *Edin v. Paul Revere Life Ins. Co.,* 188 F.R.D. 543, 547 (D.Ariz.1999).

> Although the Court has rejected the expert's flat rate fee, the Court must determine what a reasonable fee would be. The place to start is by selecting an hourly fee. It appears that defendants' expert charges $250.00 per hour as a general fee for consultation, investigation, and preparation. This is twice what plaintiffs' experts charge. While the differential seems large, plaintiffs have not given the Court sufficient information for the Court to find that $250.00 for a "national" expert is unreasonable. Instead, plaintiffs only rely on the fees charged by their experts. It would have been helpful for plaintiffs to show the fees of experts other than their own, as defendants did. The $250.00 per hour fee amounts to $2,000.00 for an eight-hour deposition. Finally, as defendants point out in their brief, the flat rate fee does not include preparation time, which some courts find to be a reasonable inclusion. *Fleming v. United States,* 205 F.R.D. 188, 190 (W.D.Va.2000). The Court-imposed $250.00 per hour fee does not include the preparation time either. Therefore, the Court will use the $250.00 figure as a base amount

> The next problem is how should the hourly fee be administered. Because depositions can be of an uncertain length, an expert may be called upon to reserve an indefinite amount of time, such as a half-day or a day. In that instance, a party may have to pay for that reservation, whether that time is used or not. This situation particularly arises when the expert, such as a physician, has had to clear his or her schedule and, therefore, will have lost income. *Harvey, supra* (physician required 4-hour minimum when deposition length unspecified). A consultant also has a right to budget his or her time. A review of defendants' documents shows that the expert does spend time traveling and testifying. Therefore, it is only reasonable that, if plaintiffs' wish to take the expert's deposition on an hourly basis, he have a firm schedule. Plaintiffs have stated that they believe that they will only request two to three hours of the expert's time; but the expert has a right to know the approximate time the deposition will take, so that he can adjust his schedule accordingly. Therefore, if plaintiffs wish to depose defendants' expert, they will reserve the number of hours for which they wish to depose the expert, and shall pay a fee of $250.00 per hour for any hour or part of an hour for which the expert is deposed. Any time spent in the deposition less than that reserved because of an abrupt termination shall, nevertheless, be paid by plaintiffs. See *Edin, supra,* at 548.

> IT IS THEREFORE ORDERED that plaintiffs' motion to determine a reasonable expert fee (docket no. 35) pursuant to Fed. Rule Civ. P. 26(b)(4)(C) is granted, and plaintiffs shall reserve the amount of hours for which they wish to depose defendants' expert and pay at a rate of $250.00 per hour for each hour or part of an hour for which the deposition lasts and, in no event, less than $250.00 for the amount of time reserved. At 267–268.

**Comment:** The court noted in this case in footnote #3 as follows:

> The Court notes that defendants' expert charges $3,000.00 per day when the location for the deposition is chosen by counsel. Such a fee has a better chance of being found reasonable because there, the expert may have to reserve an entire day, considering travel time, etc.

Some experts may not have space available in their own offices (usually a home office) appropriate for depositions. This usually has the effect of raising the amount of money that can be charged for depositions as travel time and expense must be factored in.

Note that the court also distinguished the above case of a law enforcement expert with that of a physician who could not schedule patients if he needed to block out a whole day for a deposition.

**Example 19.8: Expert should be paid while lost traveling to deposition, for preparation time, and for waiting for deposition to begin, but travel expenses will not be paid without proof and a flat fee for deposition was unreasonable**

*Mannarino v. U.S.,* 218 F.R.D. 372 (E.D.N.Y. 2003)

In this case the court was forced to address many issues regarding the expert's requested fee, including travel time, preparation time, waiting time, flat fees, and travel expenses. The key portion of the court's opinion is reprinted below:

> In determining the reasonableness of an expert's requested fee, courts weigh the following factors: (1) the witness's area of expertise; (2) the education and training that are required to provide the expert insight that is sought; (3) the prevailing rates for other comparably respected available experts; (4) the nature, quality, and complexity of the discovery responses provided; (5) the cost of living in the particular geographic area; (6) the fee actually being charged by the expert to the party who retained him; and (7) fees traditionally charged by the expert on related matters. See *Mathis v. NYNEX,* 165 F.R.D. 23, 24-25 (E.D.N.Y.1996); *Adams v. Memorial Sloan Kettering Cancer Ctr.,* No. 00 Civ. 9377, 2002 WL 1401979, (S.D.N.Y. June 28, 2002). Additionally, courts consider "any other factor likely to be of assistance to the court in balancing the interests implicated by Rule 26." *Mathis,* 165 F.R.D. at 24-25. As a general rule, "[t]he party seeking reimbursement of deposition fees bears the burden of proving reasonableness....If the parties provide little evidence to support their interpretation of a reasonable rate, the court may use its discretion to determine a reasonable fee." *New York v. Solvent Chem. Co.,* 210 F.R.D. 462, 468 (W.D.N.Y.2002) (citations omitted).
>
> Here, defendant seeks payment of a flat fee of $3,000 and travel expenses of $64. The reasonableness of these requests will be reviewed in turn.
>
> The Flat Fee. Dr. Storace affirms that the $3,000 fee "represents an amount equal to twelve hours at $250/hour." (Storace Aff. ¶ 9.) Although the flat fee does not, by definition, correspond to actual hours expended in connection with a deposition in any particular case, Dr. Storace affirms that the twelve hours assumed by the fee "is based on experience regarding the actual time expended in meeting deposition and court requirements." *(Id.)* He argues, in effect, that the set amount is fair even when he performs fewer than twelve hours' work on a particular case, because he does not charge more than this amount in cases when he performs more than twelve hours' work. *(Id.)* In any event, he affirms that he in fact spent twelve hours in connection with his deposition in this case. *(Id.* ¶ 7.) Dr. Storace avers that he spent four hours attending the deposition as well as traveling to and from it, and an additional eight hours "reviewing the case materials and preparing for the deposition." *(Id.)* Thus, the Government argues, "[i]f plaintiff's attorney had been charged on an hourly basis, based on the hourly fee of $250.00 for twelve hours of work, the fees would still total $3,000.00." (Freeman Ltr. at 3.)
>
> As a flat fee, I find $3,000 unreasonable. Courts expect "some reasonable relationship between the services rendered and the remuneration to which an expert is entitled." *Anthony v. Abbott Labs.,* 106 F.R.D. 461, 464 (D.R.I.1985); see also *Hurst,* 123 F.R.D. at 321 ("[A] reasonable fee should cover the expert's time spent complying with the requested discovery"); *Luddington v. Sec'y of Dep't of Health & Human Servs.,* No. 90-2351V, 1992 WL 206287, at *1 (Cl.Ct. Aug. 5, 1992) (fee requests by expert

witnesses "should be substantiated by a detailed summary of the time and activity records of each expert witness"). By its nature, a flat fee runs counter to this principle. It is simply not reasonable to require parties in every case to pay the same amount regardless of the actual "services rendered" or "time spent complying with the requested discovery." The flat fee charged by Dr. Storace effectively compels parties in relatively simple cases, such as this one, to subsidize parties in complex cases requiring a much greater expenditure of the expert's time. This is unfair, and I therefore find that $3,000 cannot be justified as a flat fee.

In rejecting the flat fee, I note that I am unpersuaded by the fact, offered by the Government, that other clients of Dr. Storace have willingly paid this amount. (Freeman Ltr. at 3; Freeman Decl., Ex. D.) That other parties in other cases have not objected to Dr. Storace's billing scheme has no bearing on whether it is fair to plaintiff in this case. [FN1] Additionally, I note that the fee charged by a different company, Exponent, for an expert in engineering (Freeman Decl., Ex. C)—a fee the Government cites as that of a "comparably respected expert[ ]" (Freeman Ltr. at 3)—does not support the imposition of a flat fee. On the contrary, the bill from Exponent is explicitly based on an hourly rate. (Freeman Decl., Ex. C (invoice showing $2,925 charge for thirteen hours of expert's time at $225 per hour).) That the bottom line of the Exponent bill approximates the amount sought here is purely coincidental, and does not make Dr. Storace's flat fee any more reasonable.

The Government also tries to justify the fee as the product of the hours Dr. Storace actually spent on this case—purported to be twelve—and the hourly rate of $250. (Freeman Ltr. at 3.) Plaintiff does not object to paying a $250 hourly rate, but contends that the twelve hours Dr. Storace claims he spent in connection with the deposition are excessive. (Rosenstock Ltr. at 3-4) (suggesting that Dr. Storace be paid for two hours at the $250 hourly rate).

It is true that when plaintiff first objected to the $3,000 flat fee, Dr. Storace's office offered to bill him at an hourly rate of $375 with a four-hour guaranteed minimum. (Storace Aff. ¶ 4; Rosenstock Ltr. at 2.) Dr. Storace asserts that this rate was contingent upon the deposition's taking place at InterCity, because this supposedly would have limited the disruption of his work schedule. (Storace Aff. ¶ 4.) Plaintiff disputes that any such condition was placed on the rate. (Rosenstock Ltr. at 2.) However, because the deposition did not take place at InterCity, and, more importantly, because Dr. Storace does not seek this hourly rate now, the dispute is irrelevant. In any event, the court notes that, as discussed below, Dr. Storace is being compensated for his travel time and the consequent interruption of his other work.

As mentioned, the deposition lasted approximately one hour and five minutes. Dr. Storace obviously should be fully compensated for this time. Dr. Storace asserts that he also spent approximately eight hours "reviewing the case materials and preparing for the deposition." (Storace Aff. ¶ 7.) Although caselaw supports compensating an expert for preparation time (see, e.g., *Silberman v. Innovation Luggage, Inc.,* No. 01 Civ. 7109, 2002 WL 1870383, at 2 (S.D.N.Y. Aug. 13, 2002)), the court finds eight hours excessive. No one knew in advance that the deposition itself would last only one hour, but counsel for plaintiff did indicate beforehand that she expected it would last only about three hours. (Duffy Ltr. at 1.) Moreover, as plaintiff points out, Dr. Storace had prepared his expert report only a few months prior to the deposition, and he testified that in preparing for the deposition he did not review anything that he had not already reviewed in preparing the report. (Rosenstock Ltr. at 3; Freeman Decl., Ex. F. at 17-18.) Based on these factors, and on the fact that the issues in this case are not complex, I find that four hours of preparation time would have been reasonable. Cf. *Silberman,* 2002 WL 1870383, at *2 (finding eight hours' preparation for six-and-a-half-hour deposition reasonable); *EEOC v. Johnson & Higgins, Inc.,* No. 93 Civ. 5481, 1999 WL 32909, at *2 (S.D.N.Y. Jan. 21, 1999) (finding twenty-three hours' preparation for thirteen-hour deposition excessive, and reducing compensable preparation time to thirteen hours). Dr. Storace is therefore entitled to compensation at his full rate for four hours, plus an hour and five minutes for the time spent at the deposition itself. At the rate of $250 per hour, this comes to $1271.

Travel Time and Expenses. Dr. Storace states that "the total time for the deposition, including the deposition, travel, time lost due to inaccurate directions and time lost due to a disruptive work schedule[,] was four hours." (Storace Aff. ¶ 7.) As mentioned, one hour and five minutes of this time was spent at the deposition itself. It is undisputed that Dr. Storace got lost on his way from his office to

Mr. Rosenstock's office, where the deposition took place. Dr. Storace asserts that he was "repeatedly given inaccurate directions" by Mr. Rosenstock's office. (*Id.* ¶ 5.) Mr. Rosenstock states that his office is easy to find and that Dr. Storace seemed incapable of following directions. (Rosenstock Ltr. at 3.) Dr. Storace's deposition was scheduled for 10 a.m., but because of his lateness, plaintiff's counsel began the deposition of Dr. Meyer at that time. (*Id.* at 2-3.) Upon Dr. Storace's arrival, he was given the choice between waiting until the completion of Dr. Meyer's deposition, and returning at noon, and chose the latter. (*Id.* at 3.)

Regardless of whether plaintiff's attorney's directions or Dr. Storace's navigation skills were responsible for the delay, the fact remains that Dr. Storace was unable to work during the period he was lost. Because Dr. Storace obviously did not intentionally get lost, the court finds that he is entitled to be compensated for this time. In addition, the court finds it somewhat troubling that both Dr. Storace's deposition and Dr. Meyer's were scheduled for the same time. (Rosenstock Ltr. at 2.) It seems reasonable to hold plaintiff responsible for the additional disruption in Dr. Storace's work schedule caused by this "double booking." See *McHale v. Westcott,* 893 F.Supp. 143, 151 (N.D.N.Y.1995) (Pooler, J.) ("[T]he expert certainly should be reimbursed for any time during which he was unavailable to do other work, such as time spent waiting at the deposition").

Plaintiff asserts that, based on his own experience, travel time between his office and Dr. Storace's should not have been more than twenty minutes. (Rosenstock Ltr. at 3.) Dr. Storace does not say how long his initial trip took him, nor does he indicate how long each of the three subsequent trips took. In the absence of any such information from Dr. Storace, the court will accept plaintiff's estimated time for a normal trip between the two offices. The court will also assume that the initial trip, during which Dr. Storace got lost, took twice as long as it otherwise would have. Accordingly, the court finds that Dr. Storace is entitled to compensation for forty minutes for his initial trip to Mr. Rosenstock's office, plus twenty minutes for his first return trip, plus forty minutes for the round trip he made in connection with the rescheduled deposition.

The general rule, which this court follows, is that compensation for travel time should be half the regular hourly amount charged. See, e.g., *Silberman,* 2002 WL 1870383, at *2; *Grdinich v. Bradlees,* 187 F.R.D. 77, 83 (S.D.N.Y.1999). Therefore, Dr. Storace is entitled to $125 per hour for the hour and forty minutes he spent traveling to and from the deposition, or $208.

Dr. Storace also seeks $64 in travel expenses but does not offer any explanation of what these expenses were, much less an itemization thereof or any supporting documentation, such as receipts. Without such guidance, the court cannot assess the reasonableness of the $64 charge. Further, the accuracy of this amount is questionable, given that it was set before any expenses were actually incurred. From his affidavit and the Government's submissions, the only expense the court can fairly assume Dr. Storace incurred is gas. Accordingly, the court finds that Dr. Storace is entitled to only $5 in travel expenses, which represents the court's best guess as to his expenditure on gas.

For the reasons stated above, plaintiff is entitled to reimbursement of $1,271 for Dr. Storace's time spent preparing for and attending his deposition, $208 for Dr. Storace's travel time, and $5 for Dr. Storace's travel expenses. Accordingly, within ten (10) business days of the date of this Order, plaintiff is directed to pay to Dr. Storace $1,484 for the fees and expenses reasonably incurred in connection with Dr. Storace's deposition. SO ORDERED. At 374–377.

**Comment:** This court reaffirmed the expert's right to be paid for travel time, waiting time, and preparation time. All such time is time spent on the case when experts cannot focus on other work. As such, experts should charge for these items.

**Example 19.9: $21,250 fee for three-day deposition unreasonable. Daily minimum reduced to 6 hours. Preparation time limited to 6 hours. Travel costs to be eliminated by having deposition in out-of-state venue that is home to expert**
*Cabana v. Forcier,* 200 F.R.D. 9 (D. Mass. 2001)
A truck driver who worked as an independent contractor brought suit against a truck leasing business and one of its clients, seeking damages for injuries allegedly caused by exposure to hazardous waste.

The defendant sought to depose Dr. Z, Cabana's medical toxicology expert. Dr. Z lived in Maryland, but her deposition was scheduled in Boston. She failed to attend, claiming that she needed compensation in advance. The defendant claimed that it offered to compensate Dr. Z as follows: 1) $325 per hour for deposition time, 2) $975 for each day of travel, and 3) out-of-pocket travel expenses. The defendant further contended that the plaintiff's attorney effectively agreed to that arrangement in the course of correspondence between the parties. The court found that the parties never reached a firm understanding with respect to Dr. Z's compensation.

According to her standard rates, Dr. Z demanded $21,250 for three days of deposition, broken down as follows: 1) $9,000 for 3 days of deposition time ($375 per hour times an 8-hour-per-day minimum); 2) $3,250 for travel ($325 per hour for an estimated 10 hours of travel time); 3) $4,500 overnight fee for 3 nights ($1,500 per night); 4) $4,000 preparation fee; and 5) other expenses (flight tickets, transportation, meals, hotel). The court wrote:

> In determining whether an expert's fee is reasonable, courts have considered the following factors: 1) the expert's area of expertise, 2) the expert's necessary training and education, 3) the prevailing rates for comparable expert witnesses, 4) the nature, quality and complexity of the discovery provided, 5) the cost of living in the relevant community, 6) the fee being charged by the expert to the party who retained him, 7) fees traditionally charged by the expert on related matters, and 8) any other factor likely to be of assistance to the court in balancing the interests implicated by Rule 26. [Citations omitted.] Those factors, however, merely serve to guide the court and [t]he ultimate goal must be to calibrate the balance so that a plaintiff will not be unduly hampered in his/her efforts to attract competent experts, while at the same time, an inquiring defendant will not be unfairly burdened by excessive ransoms which produce windfalls for the plaintiff's experts. 200 F.R.D. at 16.

The court then described the arguments:

> [Defendant] contends that $21,250 is not a "reasonable" fee, noting that it breaks down to $1,180 per hour and an annualized income of over $1 million and that in any event, it should not be paid in advance. Moreover, Defendant asserts that it would not even need to take Dr. [Z]'s deposition if her expert report, submitted pursuant to Fed.R.Civ.P. 26(a)(2)(B), had not been so lacking in citations to supporting authority.
>
> [Plaintiff] responds that the subject fees are simply Dr. [Z]'s standard expert witness fees which are justified because she is a nationally recognized expert in environmental and occupational exposure. Moreover, [Plaintiff's] attorney complains that because he has had to pay Dr. [Z]'s high rates, [Defendant] should as well, especially in light of Cabana's meager financial means. Id.

The court, while accepting the expert's qualifications, found the expert's fees to be "simply unconscionable." Id. It continued:

> Awarding such fees would constitute an abuse of Rule 26(b)(4)(C)...and [the Defendant] should not be held hostage by Cabana's choice of such an expensive expert. Id.

The court then reduced the rate the defendant was required to pay:

> Dr. [Z] will be reimbursed for deposition time at her hourly rate of $375 but her eight hours per day minimum will be reduced to $2,250 (six hours). Dr. [Z] will be reimbursed for preparation time at the rate of $325 per hour, not to exceed a total of six hours of preparation.
>
> This Court is sensitive to Dr. [Z]'s desire to remain in Maryland in order to attend to her patients. Accordingly, the deposition will be taken in Maryland at a time and place mutually agreeable to the parties. [Defendant] will reimburse plaintiff's counsel for his reasonable travel and lodging expenses (but not legal fees) in connection with the taking of Dr. [Z]'s deposition. Id.

**Comment:** The court specifically rejected the argument that the fees were reasonable because the opposing side had to pay them too. Also, to save money, the court ordered the deposition taken in a location where the expert would not have to travel. Finally, note that the court did agree to the $375/hour fee and found that up to six hours of preparation time at $325/hour was reasonable.

### Example 19.10: Preparation time limited to 1 1/2 times length of deposition
*Collins v. Village of Woodridge*, 1999 WL 966455 (N.D. Ill. 1999)
The issue in this case was whether an opposing party can be forced to pay for an opposing expert's time in preparing for a deposition. The court held that it could but that the amount needed to be reasonable, which in this case worked out to one-and-one-half hours of preparation time for every hour of deposition. The court stated:

> Defendants have conceded that they are responsible for the experts' fees during the depositions but object to payment of fees for the experts' preparation time. The amounts involved are significant. Mr. Walton's deposition lasted 8 hours. His preparation time included 20 hours during which he reviewed portions of 53 depositions, 207 exhibits, and his 28 page expert report, as well as 7 hours in which he met with plaintiffs' attorneys. At $125 per hour, the expense for Mr. Walton's preparation time totals $3,375. Dr. Jacobs' deposition lasted 7 hours; his preparation time included 22 1/2 hours, during which he reviewed portions of 42 depositions, as well as voluminous medical and other records and his 11 page expert report. At $350 per hour, the expense for Dr. Jacobs' preparation time totals $7,875.
>
> …The Court believes that the better reading of Rule 26(b)(4)(C)(i) is that the expert's reasonable fees for preparation time are recoverable by the party who tendered the expert. *See Hose v. Chicago and North Western Transportation Co.,* 154 F.R.D. 222, 227-28 (S.D.Iowa 1994); *American Steel Products Corp. v. Penn Central Corp.,* 110 F.R.D. 151, 153 (S.D.N.Y.1986); *Carter-Wallace, Inc. v. Hartz Mountain Industries, Inc.,* 553 F.Supp. 45, 53 (S.D.N.Y.1982) (all ordering party deposing experts to pay reasonable fee for time spent preparing). As noted, the Rule permits recovery for "time spent in responding to discovery under this subdivision." Time spent preparing for a deposition is, literally speaking, time spent in responding to discovery (except where the deposition preparation time actually constitutes *trial* preparation, which we conclude is not the case here given the lengthy lapse of time between the depositions and the trial). And because depositions are the only type of "discovery under this subdivision"--i.e., under Rule 26(b)(4)--it would have been relatively easy for the Rule's drafters to limit recovery to the time actually spent appearing for the deposition if that was what they had intended to do.
>
> It remains for the Court to determine what is "reasonable" in this case. We can certainly imagine cases in which the "reasonable" compensation for deposition preparation time would be zero or a nominal amount. This, however, is not such a case. The amount of material that the experts had reviewed in arriving at their opinions was unusually extensive, and it was entirely reasonable to expect that they would have to re-review significant portions of it in order to be able to answer questions intelligently at their depositions. Moreover, defendants knew in advance that plaintiff planned to seek recovery of the experts' preparation time but made no effort to limit the scope of the depositions, which might have limited the amount of "reasonable" preparation time. On the other hand, defendants requested the depositions promptly after receiving the experts' reports and did not inordinately delay scheduling the depositions. Thus the experts did not need to completely duplicate their earlier work in order to answer questions about their opinions. It is not our intention to allow the experts to seek compensation for reinventing the wheel. Rather, what we believe appropriate is to permit the expert to be compensated by the opposing party for the time reasonably necessary to refresh the expert's memory regarding the material reviewed and the opinions reached.
>
> Weighing these competing considerations, we do not think that a three-to-one ratio of preparation to deposition time is appropriate in terms of the costs that reasonably ought to be shifted to defendants under Rule 26(b)(4)(C). Having reviewed the experts' reports and their listings of the materials that they were required to review, we think that in the particular circumstances of this case, a ratio of one and one-half times the length of the deposition is reasonable. We will therefore order defendants to reimburse plaintiffs for twelve hours of preparation time for Mr. Walton ($1,500 at $125 per hour) and

ten and one-half hours of preparation time for Dr. Jacobs ($3,675 at $350 per hour). These amounts are in addition to the compensation that defendants must pay for the time spent at the depositions themselves: $1,000 for Mr. Walton (8 hours at $125 per hour) and $2,450 for Dr. Jacobs (7 hours at $350 per hour). At 1–4.

**Comment:** The court hinted that its allowance for preparation time might have been greater had the depositions been noticed a longer time after the expert had done his work and released his report.

### Example 19.11: Fee reduced to what expert charged a "friendly" litigator
*Anthony v. Abbott Laboratories,* 106 F.R.D. 461 (D.R.I. 1985)
The plaintiff's medical witness requested a deposition fee of $420 an hour. The defense contested the request on the grounds that the fee was unreasonable. The court held that there must be a reasonable relationship between the services rendered and the amount to which an expert is entitled, then reduced the fee to $250 an hour. The court also found the following factors noteworthy:

1. the expert charged a "friendly" litigant $250 per hour;
2. the expert had little or no discernable overhead;
3. annualization of the requested fee resulted in an exorbitant yearly income; and
4. the requested rate was not merely high, but "astronomical."

**Comment:** Normally, the expert will not be permitted to charge opposing counsel a higher hourly rate than the one he charges retaining counsel.

### Example 19.12: Court cuts deposition fee by more than 50%
*Goldwater v. Postmaster General of the United States,* 136 F.R.D. 337 (D. Conn. 1991)
In this case, a postal employee sued for wrongful termination. During discovery, the defendant deposed the plaintiff's expert, a psychiatrist. The defendant contended that the expert's fee was unreasonable. The court established and applied the criteria that should be considered in determining the reasonableness of an expert's fee:

1. the witness's area of expertise;
2. the education and training required to provide the expert insight sought;
3. the prevailing rates of other comparably qualified experts;
4. the nature, quality, and complexity of the discovery responses provided;
5. the cost of living in the particular geographic area; and
6. any other factor likely to assist the court in balancing Rule 26 interests.

Then, the court found the psychiatrist's fee to be extravagant and reduced it from $450 per hour to $200 per hour.

**Comment:** The court's ruling does not affect how much the expert can charge the retaining party. A prudent expert should have a clause in his retention agreement stating that retaining counsel will reimburse the expert fully for any court-imposed reduction in deposition expenses.

### Example 19.13: Fee reduced to what expert charged retaining counsel
*Jochims v. Isuzu Motors, Ltd.,* 141 F.R.D. 493 (S.D. Iowa 1992)
*Goldwater* was refined in *Jochims v. Isuzu Motors, Ltd.* The case was a products liability action and the plaintiff's main liability expert—a Ph.D.—was an associate professor of mechanical and

aerospace engineering. The expert had been charging the plaintiff between $150 and $250 for activities such as computer modeling and crash avoidance research. However, the expert requested $500 for time spent at deposition. The court in *Jochims* relied on the factors set forth in *Goldwater*, with the exception of the fifth factor, believing that the cost of living in a particular geographic area is not directly relevant to a reasonable fee and is "frequently, at least indirectly, calibrated into prevailing market rates." The court also added the following two factors:

- the fee actually being charged to the party retaining the expert and
- fees traditionally charged by the expert on related matters.

After applying these factors, the court reduced the fee to $250.

**Comment:** Note that the court reduced the fee to no more than what the expert was charging retaining counsel.

### Example 19.14: Court annualizes hourly income to show fee is ridiculous
*Hose v. Chicago & North Western Transportation Co.,* 154 F.R.D. 222 (S.D. Iowa 1994)
The expert, a physician specializing in neurology and disability evaluations, was deposed by the defendant in a Federal Employer's Liability Act action. The expert billed the defendant $800 an hour—in addition to $160 for reviewing medical records. The court declared that neither the expert's background, training, nor the status of his location entitled him to the rate sought. The court multiplied $800 an hour by 40 hours a week to show that the expert would earn $1.6 million a year at $800 an hour. The court then reduced the fees to $400 an hour.

**Comment:** Restating an hourly rate in other terms can be effective on cross-examination as well. For example:

**Q.** That works out to $1.6 million a year?
**Q.** $6,400 a day?
**Q.** Over $13 a minute?
**Q.** Over 22 cents a second?
**Q.** Nice work if you can get it, Doctor.

### Example 19.15: Deposition conducted after hours at expert's office does not disrupt practice, premium fee not warranted
*Hose v. Chicago & North Western Transportation Co.,* 154 F.R.D. 222 (S.D. Iowa 1994)
The deposition in this case was conducted at the offices of the expert after normal business hours. The court found no "disruption" or "inconvenience" to the expert's regular practice, thus a premium fee was not warranted.

**Comment:** A court may consider the inconvenience that a deposition poses upon an expert's professional practice and the losses to the expert stemming from that inconvenience.

### Example 19.16: Court cites fee charged clients who are not attorneys when reducing fee and considers affidavits from comparable witnesses or attorneys
*Dominguez v. Syntex Laboratories, Inc.,* 149 F.R.D. 166 (S.D. Ind. 1993)
The plaintiff's expert, a neurologist specializing in smell and taste disorders, requested $860 an hour for deposition testimony. The court noted that he charged his patients only $94 an hour for office visits, which "presumably" cost more to conduct than a visit with an attorney. The court reduced the expert's deposition fee to $341 an hour.

The defendant's expert witness, a neurologist specializing in smell and taste disorders, was described by the plaintiffs' expert as one of the "gurus" in his field. The defendant's expert provided an affidavit setting forth his maximum fee of $300 per hour, which was $560 per hour less than the rate sought by the plaintiffs' expert witness. The court considered this discrepancy when reducing the plaintiff's fee to $341 an hour.

**Comment:** The court may consider how much the expert charges his patients or professional clients and compare that rate to the rate sought in litigation. A court may also consider affidavits from comparable experts setting forth their standard fees for expert witness services, or counsel can provide the court with an affidavit setting forth the attorney's experience in retaining comparable experts and the fees charged in connection with other litigation.

**Example 19.17: Charging more for videotaped deposition than transcribed deposition "incomprehensible" to court**
*Kirby v. Ahmad,* 63 Ohio Misc. 2d 533, 635 N.E.2d 98 (Ohio Com. Pl. 1994)
In a medical malpractice case, the plaintiff's medical expert, an M.D., set out on his fee schedule fees of $500 per hour for a discovery deposition and $750 per hour for a video deposition. "What rational basis exists for the disparity of the hourly rate between a written deposition and a visual deposition is incomprehensible to this court."

**Example 19.18: Fee reduced for retrieving records because assistant could have performed the task**
*Dominguez v. Syntex Laboratories, Inc.,* 149 F.R.D. 166 (S.D. Ind. 1993)
The court rejected the plaintiff's expert's claim for $460 an hour for retrieving medical records, which he had to perform himself because his records were not computerized and his handwriting was illegible. The court observed that the expert was asking the defendant not to pay for his medical skills but for his personal clerical skills "which are clearly not as good."

**Comment:** When the expert performs a service that did not need to be performed by the expert, the court may set a lower expert witness fee. For example, a court may reduce fees for a service that is clerical in nature.

**Example 19.19: Expert can charge retaining client whatever he wants, but may not charge opposing party unreasonable deposition fees**
*Bowen v. Monahan,* 163 F.R.D. 571 (D. Neb. 1995)
The plaintiff's medical toxicology expert had an extensive and impressive resume. Additionally, he was exclusively employed in his own corporation as an expert witness and consultant in medical toxicology. The court considered his fee unreasonable and reduced the fee by half, stating, "While plaintiff may contract with any expert of plaintiff's choice and, by agreement, that expert may charge unusually high rates for services, the discovery process will not automatically tax such unreasonable fees on the defendant."

**Example 19.20: Court notices little things**
*Bowen v. Monahan,* 163 F.R.D. 571 (D. Neb. 1995)
The plaintiff's medical toxicology expert provided an engagement letter establishing that he required reimbursement for first-class airfare, rather than coach, "time and a half" rates for weekends and holidays, and a mileage rate one and a half times the rate utilized by the IRS. The court reduced the fee by one half.

**Comment:** Often, subtle things most undermine an expert's credibility. Charging 50% more than the IRS rate for mileage, insisting on surcharges for weekend work and first-class air travel may leave the jury with the impression that the expert is only interested in squeezing as much out of the case for himself as possible.

### Example 19.21: Deponent's subjective fears and stress do not support the enhancement of an hourly rate

*U.S. Energy Corp. v. NUKEM, Inc.,* 163 F.R.D. 344 (D. Colo. 1995)
The plaintiff's expert, an attorney, employed a bifurcated fee structure—$170 for support services and $300 per hour for depositions. The defense contended that the upper end of the scale was unreasonable. The reason presented for this structure was that the adversarial nature of depositions, and the resulting stress, justified the higher rate for appearances at depositions. The court rejected this reasoning and reduced the deposition fee to $235 per hour.

**Comment:** The authors suggest that experts employ a single rate for their time, with no different rates for different services. This single rate has several advantages.

- The expert need not explain his different rates.
- Billing is simpler.
- Fee schedules are simpler.
- The expert appears more like a professional and less like a "business."
- The deposition rate will not be reduced for the above reasons.
- The expert will make more money because far more time is usually spent on preparation, investigation, record review, and report drafting than on testifying at deposition and trial.

### Example 19.22: Fee reduced to lowest of expert's hourly rates

*Magee v. The Paul Revere Life Ins. Co.,* 172 F.R.D. 627 (E.D.N.Y. 1997)
In this action, an insured brought suit against a disability insurer for breach of contract by failure to pay benefits. The defendant's expert, a psychologist, was noticed for deposition. The expert sought $250 an hour for preparation time, $350 per hour for travel, and $700 for time spent at the deposition. The court reduced the fees to $250 across the board. The court conceded that the expert was well qualified, but found the fee request unreasonable because he charged the defendant $250 per hour for an examination of the plaintiff, he did not provide evidence of what similar experts charged, and because the plaintiff's experts charged $130 and $250 per hour, while the defendant retained similar experts at $150 and $100 per hour.

**Comment:** This expert might have been better off having a uniform hourly rate of say $350/hour for all time spent on a case.

*Last-minute or "rush" assignments*
When last-minute or "rush and drop everything" assignments are accepted, many experts charge a premium fee. Experts can and do commonly charge 150% of their hourly rates for these last-minute assignments. This is, in most cases, reasonable and will be agreed to by the attorney who doesn't have time to find another willing and able expert.

Many experts have a policy to decline last-minute assignments. These experts realize that the time constraints of such assignments may force them to provide an opinion that has not been thoroughly researched.

*Is the expert listed with a broker or referral service?*
Many expert witness brokers and referral services mark-up the experts' fees to clients significantly. The fact that attorneys still hire an expert despite the mark-up may be an indication that one's fees are too low.

## 19.4  What to Charge for
Not charging for all that they can and should is a common mistake made by many experts. Experts are usually retained by attorneys. There is no reason, therefore, that an expert should not bill a retaining attorney the same way an attorney would bill *him* if the expert had retained the attorney's services. This means charging for the following.

*1. Any and all time spent on the case*
This includes preparation time, portal-to-portal travel time, and time spent on brief telephone conversations. It is helpful for experts to keep a notepad at their side to keep track of all of the time they spend on the case.

*2. Reasonable out-of-pocket expenses*
These include travel expenses, telephone charges, copying expenses, meals, electronic research fees, and all other reasonable out-of-pocket expenses.

*3. Reasonable cancellation fees*
It is important to establish, in writing, reasonable cancellation fees. Such fees will protect an expert from the loss of time for last-minute cancellations of depositions and other testimony. Sophisticated experts charge *reasonable* cancellation fees.

Most attorneys would charge for all their time and expenses if an individual retained their services. There is no reason why an expert shouldn't charge them the same way. What she will charge for should be clearly spelled out in her written retention letter or written fee schedule. This will help prevent any misunderstandings concerning the expert's fees.

## 19.5  Collecting Fees

*Replenishable retainers*
Collecting their fees from attorneys is a common problem faced by many experts. By far the best way to avoid collections problems is to collect the fee up front in the form of a replenishable retainer. This is a common technique employed by many experts. When the retainer is used up, the expert can demand further payment before conducting more work or testifying in the case. The single biggest mistake inexperienced experts make in this area is not requiring prepayment of their replenishable retainer. If counsel is hesitant or reluctant to make these payments, the expert should seriously consider *not* accepting the assignment.

*Out-of-pocket expenses*
The best way to collect out-of-pocket expenses is to have these paid for directly by the retaining attorney in advance of the expert's testimony.

> **Example 19.23: Have attorney put airline tickets on his credit card**
> Your engagement requires taking a commercial airline flight to attend a deposition out of state. Have the attorney charge your airline tickets to his credit card. You will then not have to worry

about your ability to collect for this out-of-pocket expense. You also won't lose any float on the money you fronted for this expense.

*Billings*

*Monthly* itemized bills to counsel are highly recommended. (See Appendix S for model expert bills.) The expert witness bills that frequently go unpaid are those presented for the first time at the conclusion of the assignment or case. If an expert's monthly bills are not paid, he can consider doing no further work on the case until they are satisfied. An expert has much less leverage to collect his billings when he waits to bill until a case concludes.

*Interest*

It is wise to have a written policy that assesses interest on all past-due bills. Charging interest is a good way to discourage slow payment of one's bill.

*Depositions*

In most jurisdictions, the opposing side is responsible for paying the expert a reasonable fee for taking her deposition. Collection difficulties can arise as a result of this arrangement. To avoid such problems, it is best to request payment of the deposition fee up front. Some experts refuse to even schedule a deposition until they have received payment. In cases where the deposition prepayment is used up as a result of the deposition going longer than expected, the expert should, at a minimum, get counsel to agree on the record to pay the expert's hourly rate for the remainder of the deposition within seven business days.

*Legal actions*

When faced with an outstanding bill for services that counsel or the client refuses to pay, the expert has the following legal options.

1. Retain counsel and file suit based upon the contract or bill for services.
2. File a lawsuit in small claims court (if the amount is fairly small).
3. File a complaint with the local bar association or bar fee arbitration board.
4. Walk away from the bill and refuse to work for the client again.

None of the above options is nearly as good as getting paid for one's time in the first place. Prevention is the key. A sophisticated expert uses a replenishable retainer and asks to be paid for depositions up front. At a minimum, she bills monthly and insists that her bills be paid before continuing to work on a case.

## 19.6 Additional Resources

For more detailed coverage of fees, billings, and collections of experts, please consult the SEAK text *National Guide to Expert Witness Fees and Billing Procedures* (2004).

## 19.7 Conclusion

Carefully considered fee setting, billing, and collection policies can greatly enhance an expert's bottom line and save the expert the time and aggravation of trying to collect past-due fees.

# Chapter 20  Expert Witness Liability and Risk Management

## 20.1  Introduction

This chapter provides an in-depth discussion concerning the potential liability of expert witnesses and concludes with risk management advice on how to avoid suffering a loss from being an expert witness.  The law generally affords certain immunities to an expert witness from civil liability stemming from testimony or communications made in the course of litigation.  The law on this subject is somewhat sparse and varies from state to state, but the expert should remember the following general guidelines.

- Expert witnesses are almost always immune from suit for defamation, negligence, and the like from adverse parties.
- There is a continuing trend, however, of allowing the *retaining* "friendly" party to bring negligence claims against the expert.
- Such negligence cases against a friendly expert may be hard to prove as the party may need to prove that but for the expert's negligence, they would have won their case (a trial within a trial requirement).
- Court-appointed experts enjoy greater protections than "hired" experts.
- Experts should always tell the truth.
- Expert witnesses are *not* immune from criminal perjury liability or professional disciplinary actions.

## 20.2  Litigation Privilege and Witness Immunity

Litigation privilege and witness immunity are related—if not quite synonymous— protections.  Both have traditionally protected expert witnesses from civil liability for acts and statements made while serving as experts.  The *litigation privilege* has traditionally shielded trial participants, including expert witnesses and trial consultants, from liability for statements or work product related to a trial.  *Witness immunity* has traditionally shielded expert witnesses from liability for defamation[1] and negligence.[2]  (In this chapter, we will use the terms *privilege* and *immunity* interchangeably.)  The rationale for this legal protection is to encourage witnesses to make full disclosure of all pertinent information, to assuage fears of retribution for giving testimony, and to save courts from an endless spiral of suits brought by parties allegedly injured in trial.[3]

---

[1] The rationale is to encourage frank testimony.

[2] The rationale is that under oath the witness has an obligation to speak the truth.

[3] "Without absolute immunity for their testimony, the objectivity of witnesses might be threatened. If an expert witness could be sued based on her performance in the courtroom, her testimony might be distorted by a desire to avoid a subsequent lawsuit. In addition, holding expert witnesses liable might discourage anyone but a full-time expert from testifying. Only 'professional witnesses' could afford malpractice insurance to protect against such liability." Leslie R. Masterson, "Witness Immunity or Malpractice Liability for Professionals Hired as Experts?" 17 *Rev. Litig.* (1998) 393, 397.

As a result of this immunity, actions for libel, slander, malicious prosecution, negligence, and breach of contract were traditionally of little concern to the expert. However, many courts have begun to carve out exceptions to expert witness immunity for suits against the expert by the retaining party. Even if ultimately vindicated, an expert who is sued and does not carry applicable liability insurance may be faced with large legal bills associated with successfully defending the suit.

### Example 20.1: Restatement's view on witness privilege

The Restatement (Second) of Torts §588 states the general rule that absolute privilege generally applies to statements made in the course of judicial proceedings and acts as a bar to any civil liability:

> A witness is absolutely privileged to publish defamatory matter concerning another in communications preliminary to a proposed judicial proceeding or as a part of a judicial proceeding in which he is testifying, if it has some relation to the proceeding.

**Comment:** The comments of the Restatement emphasize that the privilege does not provide blanket immunity to all statements, and the comments limit the scope of the privilege to statements that have some relation to the proceeding or to a party to the proceeding.

### Example 20.2: Statutory example of litigation privilege

An example of the litigation privilege appears in the California Civil Code §47(b):

> A privileged publication or broadcast is one made:...In any (1) legislative or (2) judicial proceeding, or (3) in any other official proceeding authorized by law, or (4) in the initiation or course of any other proceeding authorized by law and reviewable pursuant to Chapter 2 (commencing with Section 1084) of Title 1 of Part 3 of the Code of Civil Procedure....[4]

## 20.3  Suits Against "Adverse" Experts Generally Barred

Suits by adverse parties against expert witnesses are commonly dismissed on the grounds of witness immunity. The courts generally give expert witnesses broad immunity from lawsuits by adverse parties. This is done so that witnesses are not intimidated from telling the truth

---

[4] Several policies underlie the privilege. First, it affords litigants free access to the courts to secure and defend their rights without fear of harassment by later suits. Second, the courts rely on the privilege to prevent the proliferation of lawsuits after the first one is resolved. Third, the privilege facilitates crucial functions of the trier of fact.

The statutory privilege protects attorneys, judges, jurors, witnesses, and other court personnel from liability arising from publications made during a judicial proceeding. Although originally enacted in the context of defamation actions, the privilege now applies to "any communication, whether or not it amounts to a publication [citations], and all torts except malicious prosecution. [Citations.] Further, it applies to any publication required or permitted by law in the course of a judicial proceeding to achieve the objects of the litigation, even though the publication is made outside the courtroom and no function of the court or its officers is involved. [Citations.]" *Mattco Forge v. Arthur Young & Co.,* 6 Cal. Rptr. 2d 781, 787 (Cal. Ct. App. 1992).

As usually formulated, "the privilege applies to any communication (1) made in judicial or quasi-judicial proceedings; (2) by litigants or other participants authorized by law; (3) to achieve the objects of the litigation; and (4) that have some connection or logical relation to the action. [Citations.]" *Mattco Forge,* 6 Cal. Rptr. 2d 781, 787.

and so that each lawsuit does not create an endless series of retaliatory lawsuits. Please consider the following cases.

### Example 20.3: Claim against adverse expert in arbitration proceeding not allowed
*Gilbert v. Sperbeck,* 126 P.3d 1057 (Alaska 2005)
This was an uninsured motorist benefits arbitration case. The insured sued the psychologist who had testified as an expert witness in arbitration and alleged that the psychologist had conducted a fraudulent independent psychological examination and misrepresented to the arbitrator. The court upheld the dismissal of the claim. It reasoned:

> Gilbert alleges that Dr. Sperbeck conducted a "fraudulent" examination and that he minimized her injuries and mischaracterized her mental state in his deposition. She alleges that the arbitrator relied on Dr. Sperbeck's deposition in resolving issues of credibility and in ultimately deciding for State Farm, and that this decision deprived her of the insurance coverage to which she was entitled.
>
> In *Lythgoe v. Guinn* we held that quasi-judicial immunity barred a lawsuit against a court-appointed expert witness. Dr. Guinn, a psychologist, was appointed in that case "to act as an independent custody investigator" and to make a custody recommendation to the court. Dr. Guinn "served as an 'arm of the court' and performed a function 'integral to the judicial process.'" The mother, a party to the underlying custody dispute, sued Dr. Guinn, alleging negligent and intentional torts during her investigation and in preparing her report. We concluded that "[c]aselaw and policy considerations clearly support the granting of absolute quasi-judicial immunity to Dr. Guinn" as a court-appointed psychologist.
>
> Dr. Sperbeck was hired by a party to the private arbitration and did not serve in a role analogous to an "arm of the court." We therefore look to the principles of witness immunity, rather than quasi-judicial immunity, to determine whether Dr. Sperbeck is immune from liability for his testimony in the arbitration.
>
> Testimony in a judicial proceeding, if pertinent to the matter under inquiry, is absolutely privileged, even if given maliciously or with knowledge of its falsity. "Even defamatory testimony is privileged, and the witness granted immunity, because of the public policy rationale that the privilege leads to more just trials by (1) encouraging more witnesses to come forward and (2) ensuring that witnesses will be more open and honest in testifying."
>
> Gilbert argues that witness immunity applies only to factual, not expert, witnesses. But expert testimony often provides essential help to the finder of fact. In holding that witness immunity barred fraudulent misrepresentation and defamation claims against an opposing expert witness, a federal district court stated that "[t]he overriding concern for disclosure of pertinent and instructive expert opinions before and during medical malpractice actions is no less significant than the clearly-recognized need for all relevant factual evidence during the course of litigation."
>
> Gilbert argues that the truth-encouraging purposes of witness immunity are not furthered by granting immunity to expert witnesses and suggests that additional deterrents from false testimony are necessary because expert witnesses are paid. But we regard the traditional safeguards against untruthful testimony, including the oath or affirmation, the perils of cross-examination, and the threat of perjury prosecution "or other sanctions," as sufficient deterrents.
>
> The same considerations that underlie the application of witness immunity in court proceedings also justify applying the doctrine of witness immunity to the expert testimony given by Dr. Sperbeck in the arbitration matter. As with judicial proceedings, fair and just arbitrations depend on the willingness of witnesses to present relevant evidence in a candid manner. Furthermore, Alaska favors arbitration; this policy would be hampered if arbitration witnesses were not immune from suit to the same extent as litigation witnesses. We assume without deciding here that Dr. Sperbeck was potentially subject to prosecution had he perjured himself during his arbitration deposition; he swore an oath and was subject to cross-examination. And as a licensed psychologist, he was subject to professional discipline. In the context of the adversarial arbitration setting, we regard these deterrents against untruthful testimony by an expert witness as sufficient. We therefore hold that witness immunity bars Gilbert's claims of fraud and misrepresentation against Dr. Sperbeck. At 1059–1060.

**Comment:** In this case the court extended expert witness immunity out of the courtroom and into an arbitration proceeding. The court noted that the expert in the case, although immune from civil suit from the opposing side, was still liable for perjury and professional disciplinary action.

### Example 20.4: Claim against adverse expert not allowed to go forward because expert witness has immunity

*Wilson v. Bernet,* 625 S.E.2d 706 (W.Va. 2005)

In this divorce case the husband sought to sue the wife's expert witness. The court held that no cause of action for tortious interference with a parental or custodial relationship may be maintained against an adverse expert witness based upon his expert testimony and participation in a child custody and visitation proceeding. The court reasoned:

> The reasons given by these tribunals for granting such immunity are varied and include a recognition that "the expert owes no professional duty to the adversary," and the concern that, "unless expert witnesses are entitled to immunity, there will be a loss of objectivity in expert testimony generally," *Bruce,* 113 Wash.2d at 130, 776 P.2d at 670. Other courts have determined that immunity is essential in order that "all witnesses may speak freely without the fear of a reprisal suit for slander," *Moity v. Busch,* 368 So.2d 1134, 1136 (La.Ct.App.1979), and to avoid the potential "chilling effect on free testimony and access to the courts" if suits against adverse expert witnesses were permitted, *Wright v. Yurko,* 446 So.2d 1162, 1164 (Fla.Dist.Ct.App.1984). A further consideration in favor of affording adverse expert witnesses immunity is that "the protected interest [i]s the administration of justice and its objective to uncover the truth," *Marrogi,* 805 So.2d at 1128, and a corresponding concern that if adverse expert witnesses were not granted immunity, they "would always be fearful of subsequent civil suits and would be extremely hesitant or unwilling to testify," *Mattco Forge,* 6 Cal.Rptr.2d at 789, 5 Cal.App.4th at 405 (internal quotations and citation omitted).
>
> However, perhaps the most compelling reason to grant adverse expert witnesses immunity for their testimony and trial participation is the built-in mechanism, in the litigation process, itself, to ascertain the truth and credibility of an adverse witness's testimony.
>
> The law places upon litigants the burden of exposing during trial the bias of witnesses and the falsity of evidence, thereby enhancing the finality of judgments and avoiding an unending roundelay of litigation, an evil far worse than an occasional unfair result....This policy can logically apply, however, only to trial testimony of adverse witnesses.

**Comment:** This case provides a good summary of the law of expert witness liability. That law provides expert witnesses broad protection from tort suits by adverse parties, but far limited protection for suits against experts by the "friendly" parties that retained the expert.

### Example 20.5: Suit against adverse expert for appraisal barred

*Darragh v. Superior Court,* 183 Ariz. 79, 900 P.2d 1215 (Ariz. Ct. App. 1995)

Here, landowners whose land a city was attempting to buy sued the city's expert for undervaluing the land—allegedly as part of a conspiracy to encourage the city to underpay the landowners.

In the underlying case, a city was attempting to buy property in order to redevelop an area. The city hired an expert to prepare written appraisals of the fair market value of the subject properties and to testify as an expert witness at trial if condemnation proceedings became necessary. Owners of a particular piece of property within the designated area rejected the city's offer, which was based upon the expert's appraisals. The city then instituted a condemnation proceeding. The city's expert testified that the land was worth $486,650. The jury disagreed and found the value to be over a million dollars. The property owners then filed a suit against the city and the expert claiming that they conspired to give perjured testimony and submit false and fraudulent documents in an attempt to acquire the owners' property at less than fair market value. The expert asserted immunity from the suit because both his appraisals and subsequent testimony were services rendered while the city was seriously contemplating eminent domain litigation, and thus the services occurred in the course of litigation. The court held that the expert witness had absolute immunity for his testimony at trial and deposition. The court also found that the expert's appraisals were absolutely privileged as communications made in connection with judicial proceedings because, at the time the expert was hired, the city was seriously contemplating litigation.

**Comment:** This court extended expert witness immunity to the expert's work on the case before a lawsuit was even filed because at that time his client "was seriously contemplating litigation."

### Example 20.6: Affidavit of expert is privileged, adverse expert witness cannot be sued
*Bird v. W.C.W.,* 1994 Tex. LEXIS 13, 868 S.W.2d 767 (Tex. 1994)
In this case, a psychologist, Esther Bird, examined a child for signs of sexual abuse. After examining the child, the psychologist concluded that the child had been sexually abused and that the natural father, W.C.W., was the abuser. The psychologist then signed an affidavit reporting these conclusions. The affidavit was filed by the child's mother, B.W., in the family court in an effort to modify child custody and visitation orders. All matters, criminal and civil, predicated upon the assertion that the natural father was a child abuser were eventually dropped. The natural father then sued the psychologist. The issue was whether the psychologist owed a professional duty of care to the natural father to not negligently misdiagnose the condition of the child. In defense, the psychologist asserted that there is no professional duty running to third parties as a matter of law, and regardless, the affidavit asserting the natural father to be the abuser of the child was used as a part of the court litigation process, and consequently, the statement was privileged as a matter of law. The court held that as a matter of law there is no professional duty running from a psychologist to a third party to not negligently misdiagnose a condition of a patient. The court "further reaffirm[ed]" that a statement in an affidavit filed as a part of a court proceeding is privileged.

### Example 20.7: Adverse expert "absolutely immune" from liability
*Lindemann v. Falk,* 1999 Wash. App. LEXIS 85 (Wash. Ct. App. Jan. 19, 1999)
David Lindemann obtained a temporary domestic violence restraining order against Kimi Lindemann, as well as temporary custody of their children, after she assaulted him with a 12-gauge shotgun. Kimi Lindemann's counsel employed Richard Falk, Ed.D., to interview the children and prepare a recommendation for use in the show cause hearing related to that court order. Falk recommended that the children be immediately placed in the residential care of their mother because his interviews with the children allegedly disclosed that they had been inappropriately touched by their father. After Falk's recommendation was given to the court, the children were temporarily placed with their aunt. David Lindemann claims that Falk failed to act in good faith and alienated the affection of his children by preparing that recommendation. David Lindemann's suit against Falk was dismissed upon summary judgment on the basis that Falk is absolutely immune from suit for preparing his recommendation.

### Example 20.8: Adverse expert witness in criminal matter (sentencing) given absolute immunity from suit by convict
*Clark v. Grigson,* 579 S.W.2d 263 (Tex. Civ. App.-Dallas 1978)
Here, a convicted felon sued a psychiatrist who had testified adversely in the punishment stage of the plaintiff's criminal trial. The plaintiff sought damages on the theory that the psychiatrist negligently made an improper diagnosis, which resulted in heavier sentences than the plaintiff would have received if the psychiatrist had made an accurate diagnosis. In support of liability for

expert witness negligence, the plaintiff argued that "improper expert testimony would occur less frequently if experts [were] civilly liable for damages for negligence in reaching the conclusions to which they testify." The court of appeals rejected this argument, finding it "more than counterbalanced" by the policy of affording witnesses absolute immunity in order to encourage unrestrained testimony.

**Example 20.9: Adverse expert's testimony absolutely privileged—suit for intentional libel and slander, intentional infliction of emotional distress, conspiracy to defraud, denial of constitutional due process, and tortious interference dismissed**
*Laub v. Pesikoff,* 979 S.W.2d 689 (Tex. Civ. App. Dist. 1-Houston 1998)
Here, a state court of appeals addressed a party's novel attempt to impose liability upon the opponent's expert witnesses for their affidavit testimony.

*Laub* was a divorce proceeding. Mr. Laub alleged that his wife signed certain documents that conveyed real property and transferred securities to him. Mr. Laub filed a motion requesting the court to uphold these gifts. Mrs. Laub responded by arguing that at the times in question, she did not possess the requisite donative intent to make the alleged gifts. She supported her response with affidavit testimony from her treating psychiatrist and psychologist, who both opined that due to the husband's physical abuse of the wife, she lacked the mental capacity to make the gifts. Soon after the response was filed, Mr. Laub filed a separate lawsuit against both experts, alleging that they had committed intentional libel and slander, intentional infliction of emotional distress, conspiracy to defraud, denial of constitutional due process, and tortious interference. The trial court granted summary judgment in favor of the experts on all theories.

On appeal, the state court of appeals addressed whether Mr. Laub's claims were barred by the judicial communications privilege. The court acknowledged the absolute immunity of parties and witnesses from liability for their testimony in judicial proceedings, noting that "even perjured testimony, made in a judicial proceeding, cannot serve as a basis for a suit in tort." The court also noted a concern for the "full and free disclosure from witnesses unhampered by fear of retaliatory lawsuits."

The *Laub* court held that, regardless of libel, the essence of Mr. Laub's claims against the experts was that he suffered injury as a result of the communication of allegedly false statements during a judicial proceeding. The court found such communications to be absolutely privileged as judicial communications and, therefore, affirmed summary judgment in favor of the experts.

**Example 20.10: Absolute immunity for adverse witness extends to alleged negligence causing death**
*Serchia v. MacMillan,* PICS Case No. 97-0734 (E.D. Pa. March 20, 1997)
A federal judge interpreting Pennsylvania law threw out a medical malpractice claim lodged against a doctor who examined a criminal defendant on behalf of federal prosecutors and said the man was fit to stand trial. The man later died, and his surviving spouse filed a wrongful death suit against the physician.

Ronald Serchia—the decedent—was indicted in 1992 on federal drug charges. His attorney said the proceedings should be delayed because of his health. Serchia's doctor said that because of Ronald's health problems, it would be dangerous for him to endure the stress of a trial.

MacMillan examined Serchia twice in 1993 and testified in September 1993 that while Ronald did have an abdominal aortic aneurysm and high blood pressure, he was fit to stand trial. Proceedings began, and then Ronald Serchia died in May 1994. Serchia's wife sued MacMillan, arguing that he ignored Ronald's medical condition "in order to curry favor" with the government.

The U.S. District Court judge dismissed the suit after concluding that the physician expert witness was absolutely privileged and thus immune from malpractice liability. The judge said that when a person's health is an issue in litigation, the opposing party should be able to "explore" the person's medical condition without fear of being sued at a later date.

"Because [Serchia's] claims for wrongful death and malpractice are based solely on MacMillan's examination of Mr. Serchia in his capacity as the government's expert witness in the criminal proceedings against Mr. Serchia, MacMillan is entitled to immunity in the present action." The judge noted that, although the Pennsylvania Supreme Court had not directly ruled on the issue, it had recognized that that trial participants can't be sued for defamation based on statements they make during litigation. The judge then cited a case in which the Pennsylvania Superior Court had extended immunity beyond defamation.[5]

### Example 20.11: Adverse expert immune to liability

*MacIntyre v. Wilson,* 50 S.W.3d 674 (Tex. App.-Dallas 2001)

This case arose out of a series of lawsuits stemming from plaintiff MacIntyre's severance of a business relationship. After two prior lawsuits (one of which was a malpractice suit against his lawyers), MacIntyre brought this action against his lawyers (again) and witnesses. Among the defendants in this case were Wilson and Fowler, who testified favorably for the defense in the previous malpractice suit. In this suit, among other things, he alleged Fowler, Wilson, *et al.* testified as "legal experts" in the previous malpractice trial and, either negligently or in bad faith, falsely testified that he was precluded from sharing in post-dissolution partnership profits. The trial court granted summary judgment to the defendants, and MacIntyre appealed. The defendants claimed that they were entitled to absolute immunity from suit for their testimony.

The appellate court concluded that absolute immunity bars McIntyre's claims. McIntyre argued that absolute immunity for testifying witnesses was limited to defamation cases, based on his interpretation of the *Bird* case. Alternatively, he argued that, if the immunity applies in all cases, this court should carve out an exception excluding expert witnesses. Regarding the *Bird* case, the court found that *Bird* specifically provides, without limitation, that communications made during the course of judicial proceedings are privileged: "The fact that the case involved defamation-type damages does not so restrict this statement of law; rather, we conclude any analysis was simply made in the context of the specific proceeding." 50 S.W.3d at 683.

The court then explicitly declined to carve out an exception for expert witnesses:

> The policy behind the absolute privilege is to encourage unrestrained access to the courts and full development of the facts in court. It is founded on the theory that the good it accomplishes in protecting the rights of the general public outweighs any wrong or injury which may result to a particular individual. See *Reagan v. Guardian Life Ins. Co.,* 140 Tex. 105, 113, 166 S.W.2d 909, 913 (1942). This policy would not be furthered by carving out an exception for expert witnesses. To the contrary, the intimidating threat of a lawsuit would, in fact, hamper the very purpose for which the privilege was created. *Id.*

---

[5] The judge cited the state Superior Court's decision in *Clodgo v. Bowman,* 601 A.2d 342 (Pa. Super. 1992), in which the court held that a plaintiff couldn't sue a court-appointed doctor for medical malpractice for incorrectly identifying the parent of a child in a custody hearing. The federal judge said the *Clodgo* court determined that while the case involved medical malpractice and not defamation, the traditional privilege against liability should apply. The judge also stated that the *Clodgo* court warned that carving out an exception would create a dangerous precedent, making experts afraid to testify because of potential liability. The federal judge also stated that the fact that the expert in *Clodgo* was court-appointed and MacMillan was testifying on behalf of an adverse party was irrelevant.

## 20.4 Negligence Claims Against "Friendly" Experts

With a notable exception in the state of Washington,[6] there has been a growing trend to *allow* negligence lawsuits against an expert witness by the "friendly" party who retained the expert. This section provides notable case examples, including the $42 million *Mattco Forge* case. The *Mattco Forge* case provides some comfort to experts, however. It held that in order to prevail in a negligence case against an expert witness, the plaintiff must prove that they would have won the case had the expert not been negligent. This so-called "trial within a trial" requirement can be a great burden for a plaintiff to meet. The courts generally allow these lawsuits based on the narrow grounds of negligently forming an opinion (often because of a mathematical error) or negligently abandoning a client. This is far different from allowing a suit against a friendly expert because the party was dissatisfied with testimony based on a thorough and accurate investigation. Please consider the following cases.

> **Example 20.12: "Friendly" expert not immune from suit, but defendant expert witness can only be held liable for harm he is proven to actually have caused**
> *Mattco Forge v. Arthur Young & Co*
> The case *Mattco Forge v. Arthur Young & Co.* made a major impact on expert witness liability for negligence. The court declared that the expert, an accounting firm, was not protected from liability for testifying from negligently prepared data. Mattco Forge was awarded $42 million.
> In *Mattco Forge v. Arthur Young & Co.,* Mattco Forge, a manufacturing company, sued Arthur Young, an accounting firm, for negligently providing accounting services.[7] In the underlying case, Mattco filed a federal civil rights action against General Electric ("GE"), claiming that GE had eliminated Mattco as an approved subcontractor for racial reasons. Mattco hired Arthur Young as a damage consultant and expert witness to assist in calculating lost profits. Among other discovery disputes, GE alleged that Mattco had fabricated documents with the assistance of Arthur Young. Stalled by the discovery disputes, the federal case finally ended before trial in mutual dismissals.[8]
> Mattco subsequently sued Arthur Young, alleging, *inter alia*, for accounting malpractice.[9] Arthur Young moved for summary judgment, raising as a defense a California statute that provided a "litigation privilege."[10] The trial court granted Arthur Young's motion, holding that the statutory litigation privilege barred Mattco's claims as a matter of law. Mattco appealed.
> The court of appeals reversed the summary judgment,[11] refusing to apply the litigation privilege to a "friendly" expert witness. The court reasoned that extending the litigation privilege to protect Arthur Young from professional malpractice would not further the policy of encouraging truthful testimony.[12] In addition, the procedural safeguards that provide a compelling rationale to protect experts from liability are not present when the witness has not testified at trial—she has not

---

[6] See *Bruce v. Byrne-Stevens & Assocs. Engineers, Inc.,* 776 P.2d 666 (Wash. 1989), infra.

[7] See *Mattco Forge,* 60 Cal. Rptr. 2d at 783 (discussing the background of the case).

[8] *Id.*

[9] *Mattco Forge,* 6 Cal. Rptr. 2d at 783.

[10] *Id.* at 787 (citing California Civil Code 47(b) (West 1996), which provides: "A privileged publication or broadcast is one made: ...In any (1) legislative or (2) judicial proceeding or (3) in any other official proceeding authorized by law and reviewable pursuant to Chapter 2 (commencing with Section 1084) of Title 1 of Part 3 of the Code of Civil Procedure....").

[11] *Id.* at 790–791.

[12] *Id.* at 789–790.

sworn an oath, faced the hazard of cross-examination, or the threat of a prosecution for perjury.[13] The court pointed out that the litigation privilege is not "absolute."[14] The court analogized to malpractice suits brought by a party against his former attorney, noting that the litigation privilege does not entirely protect attorneys from suit by a former client.[15]

In order to recover on a claim of expert witness negligence, the plaintiff may be required to prove that the professional's conduct was the cause-in-fact of her injuries. In *Mattco,* Arthur Young argued throughout the trial that in order to prevail on its claim of professional negligence, Mattco had to prove that it would have prevailed in the underlying federal suit against GE.[16] The trial court rejected this approach.[17] In the liability phase of the trial, Mattco merely had to show that Arthur Young had caused Mattco to suffer "harm." Its burden in the damages phase was to prove its case against GE had "value." The jury awarded Mattco $42 million in damages, and Arthur Young appealed.[18]

In this appeal, the main issue was whether the trial court erred in refusing to apply the "suit within a suit" requirement to a claim of accountant malpractice.[19] Mattco, similar to a client who brings a malpractice action against her attorney, complained that it lost its claim against GE due to professional negligence. When an attorney is sued for malpractice relating to the litigation of the underlying suit, the plaintiff must prove that the attorney's conduct was the cause-in-fact of her injury. This burden is called the "suit within a suit" requirement. In effect, two separate lawsuits are tried in the malpractice action. Where the attorney's negligence caused the plaintiff to lose her claim, she must show that she would have prevailed on her claim and the amount that would actually have been collected. Where the attorney's negligence caused the plaintiff to lose a defense in the underlying suit, she must show that the defense was meritorious.

The court of appeals in *Mattco* noted criticism of the suit within a suit requirement, but explained that "it is the most effective safeguard yet devised against speculative and conjectural claims in this era of ever-expanding litigation."[20] The court reversed the award of damages and remanded the case for a new trial. In order to prevail, Mattco would have to establish that but for Arthur Young's negligence, Mattco would have won its case against GE. The court stated that, "Like other defendants in negligence lawsuits, litigation support professionals are only responsible for the losses they cause."[21] Thus, where the alleged negligent conduct results in the plaintiff's loss of the underlying case, the plaintiff is held to the same burden as an attorney who has mishandled litigation.[22]

**Comment:** Under *Mattco Forge,* friendly experts may be sued, but to be held liable, the plaintiff must prove that they would have had a different result in the case "but for" the expert's negligence.

---

[13] *Id.* at 789.

[14] *Id.* at 790.

[15] *Id.* at 789–790.

[16] *Mattco Forge v. Arthur Young & Co.,* 60 Cal. Rptr. 2d 780, 786 (Cal. Ct. App. 1997).

[17] *Id.*

[18] *Id.* at 784.

[19] *Id.* at 784.

[20] *Id.* at 788.

[21] *Id.* at 789.

[22] *Id.*

**Example 20.13: Negligence lawsuit allowed against "friendly" expert for litigation support services**

*Murphy v. A.A. Mathews*, 841 S.W.2d 671 (Mo. 1992)

The Missouri Supreme Court has held that witness immunity does not shield professional experts from negligence claims brought by their former clients. In *Murphy v. A.A. Mathews*,[23] Murphy hired Mathews, as professional engineers, to testify at an arbitration proceeding regarding expenses that arose from construction problems. Mathews testified at the arbitration proceeding, but Murphy was awarded an amount substantially less than his requested compensation. Murphy sued his experts, alleging that Mathews had negligently prepared and documented Murphy's claim. In the malpractice proceeding, Mathews moved to dismiss based on witness immunity.

Mathews asked the court to extend witness immunity, which Missouri courts had traditionally applied to protect witnesses from defamation actions brought by adverse parties to bar malpractice claims against professionals hired to perform litigation support services.[24] Following *James* (Texas) and *Mattco* (California), the Missouri Supreme Court declined to extend witness immunity to protect a privately retained professional who negligently provides pre-trial litigation support services.[25] Experts are not unbiased court servants, but instead sell their professional services for a fee.[26] By their very nature, experts are not objective witnesses, and immunizing their testimony does not further the policies underlying witness immunity.[27]

**Example 20.14: Pennsylvania's exception to witness immunity: "friendly" expert can be sued over mathematical error**

*LLMD of Michigan, Inc. v. Jackson-Cross Co.*, 559 Pa. 297, 740 A.2d 186 (PA 1999)

In this case, the Pennsylvania Supreme Court carved out an exception to the state's long-standing witness immunity principle—that communications that are issued in the regular course of judicial proceedings and that are pertinent and material to the redress or relief sought are immune from civil liability. The underlying case involved an expert witness hired by a plaintiff to calculate and testify regarding his lost profits resulting from a breach of contract. During cross-examination of the plaintiff's expert, defense counsel established that the expert's lost profits calculation contained an error that completely undermined the basis for the damage amount. Because the expert had not calculated the damages himself, he was unable to correct the error and, as a result, the trial judge struck his testimony. The day after the expert's testimony was stricken, the plaintiff accepted a settlement offer of $750,000. Subsequently, the expert provided a corrected computation of lost profits that indicated $2.7 million in damages. The plaintiff then filed a suit against the expert, asserting causes of action for breach of contract and professional malpractice; the expert claimed immunity under the witness immunity doctrine. At 299–301.

---

[23] *Murphy v. A.A. Mathews*, 841 S.W.2d 671 (Mo. 1992).

[24] *Id.* at 674.

[25] *Id.* at 680. The court explained: "Witness immunity is an exception to the general rules of liability. It should not be extended unless its underlying policies require it be so. In Missouri, this immunity generally has been restricted to defamation, defamation-type, or retaliatory cases against adverse witnesses. This narrow restriction is consistent with the historical development of immunity…While witness immunity might properly be expanded in other circumstances, we do not believe that immunity was meant to or should apply to bar a suit against a privately retained professional who negligently provides litigation support services."

[26] *Mathews*, 841 S.W.2d at 681.

[27] *Id.*

Before ruling on the expert's defense, the court reviewed the public policy considerations underlying the judicial and witness immunity doctrines. The court stated:

> The privilege is also extended to parties to afford freedom of access to the courts, to witnesses to encourage their complete and unintimidated testimony in court, and to counsel to enable him to best represent his client's interests. *Id.* at 302.

The court also explained:

> "[A] witness who knows that he might be forced to defend a subsequent lawsuit, and perhaps to pay damages, might be inclined to shade his testimony in favor of the potential plaintiff, to magnify uncertainties, and thus to deprive the fact finder of fact of candid, objective, and undistorted evidence." *Id.* (Quoting *Briscoe v. LaHue*, 460 U.S. 325, 103 S.Ct. 1108, 75 L.Ed.2d 96 (1983).)

The court recognized the continuing significance of these policy concerns, but nonetheless concluded that extending witness immunity to actions arising from the negligent formulation of an opinion would not address them. The court presented its holding:

> The goal of ensuring that the path to truth is unobstructed and the judicial process is protected, by fostering an atmosphere where the expert witness will be forthright and candid in stating his or her opinion, is not advanced by immunizing an expert witness from his or her negligence in formulating that opinion. The judicial process will be enhanced only by requiring that an expert witness render services to the degree of care, skill and proficiency commonly exercised by the ordinarily skillful, careful and prudent members of their profession.
>
> Therefore, we find that the witness immunity doctrine does not bar [the plaintiff's] professional malpractice action against [the expert]. We caution, however, that our holding that the witness immunity doctrine does not preclude claims against an expert witness for professional malpractice has limited application. An expert witness may not be held liable merely because his or her opinion is challenged by another expert or authoritative source. In those circumstances, the judicial process is enhanced by the presentation of different views. Differences of opinion will not suffice to establish liability of an expert witness for professional negligence. *Id.* at 306-07.

The court carefully elucidated the limits of its holding. It stressed that experts were still immune from liability premised on the *substance* of an expert's opinion. Further, the court explained that an expert witness may not be held liable simply because his or her opinion is challenged by another expert or authoritative source. *See id.* Additionally, the court noted that because the sole issue before it was the liability of private experts, its opinion did not address exceptions to the witness immunity doctrine for court-appointed witnesses. *See id.* at 301 n. 4.

**Comment:** This case, as well as the *Mattco Forge* case, involved computational and numerical errors. Experts dealing with "numbers," such as accountants, appraisers, and economists, are particularly vulnerable to the type of error that may lead to a lawsuit by a friendly party. As such, these experts should take extra care to make sure their relevant liability insurance covers their expert witness work.

### Example 20.15: Connecticut "friendly" expert can be sued over allegedly improperly conducted analysis

*Pollock v. Panjabi,* 2000 WL 33408771 (Supr. Ct. Conn. 2000)

This case arose out of a lawsuit by the quadriplegic plaintiff to recover for injuries sustained as a result of police brutality. The plaintiff hired a biomechanics professor, Panjabi, to help determine the cause of the paralysis. Panjabi concluded that an officer's hold on the plaintiff caused the injury. Three times, however, a Canadian trial court barred Panjabi from testifying, finding that the expert had based his conclusion in part on improperly conducted analyses.  Each time the court had granted a continuance in order to allow Panjabi to conduct another experiment with properly functioning equipment.  After the first instance, Panjabi ran the second experiment and provided a report.  However, he refused to testify in court unless he was paid additional money—which he was.  The situation repeated itself, and the plaintiff again paid Panjabi the money.  For a third time, Panjabi appeared in court and underwent voir dire.  At the conclusion of the third and last voir dire, the Canadian judge again ruled that Panjabi's experiments were incorrectly performed and that his reports would be inadmissible at trial.  Ultimately, the plaintiff won a $783,000 verdict.  He then filed the suit in question against Panjabi claiming that the plaintiffs were damaged because of the manner in which the expert rendered services.

The court then considered the applicability of the witness immunity doctrine.  It reviewed the underlying policies of the doctrine and wrote:

> [The] policy reasons undergirding the absolute privilege accorded witnesses are not implicated here. This is not a case in which the right of a witness to speak freely, in or out of court, is involved. While conduct, objects and experiments may have communicative aspects; [citations omitted] the plaintiffs do not complain about what Panjabi said or about anything Cholewicki, who never testified, said or communicated. Rather, the plaintiffs complain of the defendants' failure to perform work, as agreed upon, according to scientific principles as to which there are no competing schools of thought. This is a case where the defendants performed an experiment that turned out to support the thesis of an opposing party. As *Kelley v. Bonney, supra*, 221 Conn. at 567, 606 A.2d 693, suggests, there must be a nexus between the immunity, the fact-finding function of the court and the interest in having witnesses speak freely. That nexus is not implicated by the allegations of the plaintiffs' complaint. 2000 WL 33408771.

The court then denied the defendant's motion to strike:

> The policy on which witness immunity in Connecticut is based—having witnesses speak freely—is not implicated by the allegations of the complaint, which seek to hold the defendants accountable for not doing what they agreed to do. The motion to strike counts one, two and three based on the doctrine of witness immunity, therefore, is denied. *Id.*

**Comment:** This expert was not sued for "saying the wrong thing at trial" when there were competing schools of thought. He was sued for an allegedly improperly conducted analysis in violation of scientific principles. Experts are well advised to conduct careful analyses in forming their opinions.

Note also that this expert witness added insult to injury by insisting on being paid, and thus actually being rewarded, for his mistakes. One wonders whether this insistence factored heavily into making the plaintiff angry enough to sue his own expert witness.

### Example 20.16: "Friendly" expert can be sued in Louisiana for allegedly making erroneous calculations and then abandoning client after error was made known to him
*Marrogi v. Howard,* 805 So.2d 1118 (LA. 2002)

Medical billing records were at issue in the underlying case.  After reviewing the pathology reports, together with a billing and coding schedule for the one fiscal year, the expert Howard provided his client Dr. Marrogi with an affidavit containing Howard's opinion that Tulane should have billed $523,485 for Dr. Marrogi's services during that fiscal year.  In fact, Tulane had billed less than $250,000 for those services, an alleged difference of some $273,485.  Relying on the billing discrepancies identified by Howard in his affidavit, Dr. Marrogi filed a motion to compel Tulane to produce the other four years of its medical records.  At the hearing on the motion to compel, Tulane pointed to numerous mathematical errors in Howard's affidavit, as well as to errors in his assignment of prices to coded services. In light of these errors, the court ordered that Howard submit to a deposition prior to the court's considering the merits of the motion to compel.

At the request of Dr. Marrogi, Howard thereupon prepared and submitted a revised opinion that reduced the amount that Tulane should have billed for Dr. Marrogi's services during the one fiscal year under review to $392,740, rather than the earlier $523,485. Dr. Marrogi furnished a copy of this revised opinion to Tulane. Then, under questioning at the deposition, Howard was forced to admit to having made additional pricing and coding errors in his revised opinion. During a break in the deposition, Howard informed Dr. Marrogi's attorney that he was disgusted by the numerous errors that he had made and that he would neither participate in the remainder of his scheduled deposition nor provide any of the other litigation support that he had contracted to furnish.

Thereafter, Tulane filed a motion for summary judgment, seeking dismissal of Dr. Marrogi's suit. In support of the motion, Tulane submitted Howard's deposition testimony to demonstrate that Dr. Marrogi was unable to produce any credible evidence of underbilling. The Civil District Court, Parish of Orleans, granted the motion and dismissed the suit.

The Louisiana Supreme Court held that witness immunity would not prevent Marrogi from suing Howard. The court stated:

> After reviewing the cases from the courts of our sister states, as well as the applicable policy considerations, we hold that claims in connection with a retained expert's alleged failure to provide competent litigation support services are not barred by the doctrine of witness immunity. The privilege of witness immunity in Louisiana has been applied in defamation and defamation-like cases, as well as retaliation cases against adverse witnesses, expert and otherwise. The policy underlying that rule is that witnesses must be permitted to speak freely and without fear of exposure to vexatious litigation where a search for the truth is before the fact-finder. However, that laudable objective is not advanced by immunizing the incompetence of a party's retained expert witness simply because he or she provides professional services, including testimony, in relation to a judicial proceeding.
>
> We agree that the finder of fact must be able to rely on "candid, objective, and undistorted evidence." *Briscoe v. LaHue,* 460 U.S. at 333, 103 S.Ct. at 1114. However, we do not believe that shielding a client's own professional witness from malpractice liability is necessary to ensure that frank and objective testimony is presented to the fact-finder. A party's retained expert witness, rather than a court-appointed expert, for example, contracts for monetary remuneration with a party to assist in preparing and presenting his case not only in the best light possible but also, surely, in a competent fashion. Thus, the retained expert's function is not only to assist the court or fact-finder in understanding complicated matters, but also to render competent assistance in supporting his client's action against the client's opponent. The *Bruce* court assumed that in the absence of immunity, the expert would be motivated not simply by frankness and objectivity, but by the fear of exposure to civil liability among other considerations. Properly viewed, however, the roles of "hired gun" and servant of the court are not necessarily incompatible. In reality, the expert retained for litigation is hired to present truthful and competent testimony that puts his client's position in the best possible light. The expert witness's oath, the heat of cross-examination, the threat of a perjury prosecution, and, not least, the expert's professional ethics code all serve to limit the feared excesses of an expert subject to malpractice liability. Moreover, the absence of immunity will not only encourage the expert witness to exercise more care in formulating his or her opinion but also protect the litigant from the negligence of an incompetent professional. Given these considerations, witness immunity does not serve an overarching public purpose in barring a client's suit against his own hired professional who deficiently performs agreed upon litigation support services.
>
> The correctness of our view lies in the facts, alleged and established, in the instant case. In this case, defendant Howard, who had allegedly held himself out as an expert in the field of medical billing, got paid to review a set of medical reports and billing records, to make calculations based on this review, and, thereafter, to present his correct calculations and assumptions in court. Instead, the defendant made erroneous calculations and, when that fact was made known to him, he abandoned his

client, rather than continue to assist him in the litigation, and kept the money that he was paid. Clearly then, Dr. Marrogi has made the allegation that the defendant was negligent, not in having a particular opinion, but in formulating his opinion, i.e., the defendant was negligent in performing professional services such as calculations upon which his expert opinion testimony would ultimately be based. That defendant Howard's erroneous calculations were, in this case, presented in an affidavit and in deposition testimony, rather than, say, a written report, does not change our view that an expert witness hired to perform litigation support services, but who performs those services in a negligent manner, cannot hide from civil liability to his client behind the shield of witness immunity.

The benefit to the judicial system in the rule we announce today is a practical one: ridding the system of incompetent experts and ensuring that reliable opinion testimony is presented to the fact-finder. The Washington Supreme Court in *Bruce* speculated that the lack of immunity will result in less truthful expert testimony. With no sanction for incompetent preparation, however, an expert witness is free to prepare and testify without regard to the accuracy of his data or opinion. We do not see how the freedom to testify negligently will result in more truthful expert testimony. Without some overarching purpose, it would be illogical, if not unconscionable, to shield a professional, who is otherwise held to the standards and duties of his or her profession, from liability for his or her malpractice simply because a party to a judicial proceeding has engaged that professional to provide services in relation to the judicial proceeding and that professional testifies by affidavit or deposition. In this case, cross-examination during the deposition succeeded in revealing excesses or inaccuracies in defendant Howard's opinion testimony. The truth-finding function of the judicial system was thus protected. Though defendant Howard contends he is effectively being punished for telling the truth, i.e., confessing to his errors, we see no valid reason why the judicial system should immunize him from liability to his client for his alleged negligence in making calculations and formulating his opinion.

Finally, we see no merit to the argument that witness immunity should apply to expert witnesses because it will otherwise be difficult for the expert's client to prove causation and damages in a suit brought by the client against the expert. Simply because the plaintiff client may have a heavy burden to carry in proving his case does not mean that we should immunize the defendant retained expert from civil liability for his professional negligence or breach of contract.

We therefore answer the question certified to us in the negative: Witness immunity or privilege in Louisiana does not bar a claim against a retained expert witness asserted by a party who in prior litigation retained the expert, which claim arises from the expert's allegedly negligent performance of his agreed upon duties to provide litigation support services. At 1131–1133.

**Comment:** Critical to success as an expert witness is to show up when it is time to testify and to not walk out of your testimony. Note that this expert's problems also arose from a mathematical problem. Experts are well advised to check and recheck their math prior to forming their opinions and to not walk out in the middle of their depositions.

**Example 20.17: Washington court does *not* allow negligence suit against "friendly" expert**
*Bruce v. Byrne-Stevens & Assocs. Engineers, Inc.,* 776 P.2d 666 (Wash. 1989)
In this case, the Washington Supreme Court broadly applied witness immunity to a "friendly" expert witness.

*Bruce* involved an engineer who, as an expert, testified it would cost $10,020 to stabilize the soil on the plaintiff's property. The trial court found in the plaintiff's favor and awarded the plaintiff a judgment for exactly that amount. The actual cost of the repair was twice the amount the expert witness testified to at trial. The plaintiff attempted to sue the expert witness in negligence. The plaintiff contended but for the expert witness's negligent analysis and testimony they would have been awarded the true cost of repair. The court did not agree and held absolute witness immunity barred the suit.

Ultimately, the court was concerned that if immunity was lifted, a witness could testify in a manner that would prevent the potential lawsuit, but would deprive the court of the benefit of candid, unbiased testimony. The court felt that the benefits gained by extending witness immunity were counterbalanced by safeguards inherent in the judicial system. It noted that witness reliability is ensured by oath, cross-examination, and the threat of criminal prosecution for perjury. The court found that those safeguards insured truthful and accurate testimony.

**Comment:** This court did not allow suits against "friendly" expert witnesses for mathematical errors.

### Example 20.18: Suit allowed against friendly expert witness for non-mathematical error where expert knew his opinion was a misrepresentation

*Hart v. Browne,* 163 Cal. Rptr 356 (Cal. App. Dist. 1 1980)
In this case, a patient, Hart, was treated by Dr. Nork. Hart underwent nine operations and eleven hospitalizations. She was unsatisfied with the treatment and retained a lawyer to investigate a medical malpractice case. The attorney retained an expert witness, Dr. Browne, who rendered an opinion that there was no medical malpractice. As a result, the malpractice case was not filed and the statute of limitations ran out. Ms. Hart then sued Dr. Browne. The court rejected Dr. Browne's immunity defense. It then found that the doctor made representations that he knew to be false. The court explained:

> There was abundant testimony that gross malpractice had been committed by Dr. Nork. This subnormal treatment was evident from [Hart's] narrative and her hospital records, both of which were used by [Dr. Browne] in rendering his opinion to appellant's attorneys. [Dr. Browne] enjoyed a reputation as a highly regarded orthopedic surgeon and a teacher of orthopedic surgery at a prestigious medical center. Given the man's reputation and the nature of the information and materials on which he was basing his opinion, the jury could well have inferred that [Dr. Browne] knew his opinion was a misrepresentation. Such a misrepresentation of opinion is actionable when the [expert] holds himself out to be specifically qualified in the area on which he gives the opinion.

**Comment:** Expert witnesses should always tell the truth.

## 20.5 The Expert's Response to Suit by Client—Sue Retaining Counsel for Indemnification

An expert sued by a retaining party may have some recourse in bringing a suit for indemnification against retaining counsel. A California appellate court has let just such a claim go forward.

### Example 20.19: Expert witness allowed to sue retaining counsel for indemnification after expert sued for malpractice

*Forensis Group, Inc. v. Frantz, Townsend & Foldenauer,* 130 Cal.App.4th 14, 29 Cal.Rptr.3d 622 (Cal. App. 4 Dist. 2005)
The experts in this case were sued for malpractice and misrepresenting their credentials after their involvement in a products liability/wrongful death case. They had been retained by the plaintiffs in this matter. The experts settled this case and then sued the plaintiff's lawyers for indemnification, alleging that the lawyers were jointly responsibly for failing to provide them with relevant information and failing to properly rehabilitate the experts at their depositions. The court ruled that this lawsuit was not barred by public policy and remanded the case for trial.

## 20.6 Court-Appointed Experts

Court-appointed experts enjoy absolute immunity from suit in many jurisdictions. However, even a court-appointed expert can be liable for negligence in some circumstances in some jurisdictions. Consider the following cases.

### Example 20.20: Court-appointed expert immune from suit

*Trapp v. State,* 53 P.3d 1128 (Alaska 2002)

This case dealt with whether a court-appointed conservator could be sued. The court stated that:

> The clearest case for quasi-judicial immunity is presented in instances where some aspect of the court's adjudicative responsibility is delegated to another official such as a master or referee. And in Alaska, as well as in almost all other jurisdictions, neutral court-appointed experts are also shielded by absolute quasi-judicial immunity.

### Example 20.21: "A court-appointment is not a talisman for immunity"

*Levine v. Wiss & Co.,* 478 A.2d 397, 398 (N.J. 1984)

In this divorce action, an accountant was hired to evaluate assets. The parties to the divorce agreed, in anticipation of an equitable distribution, that an "impartial expert" would be retained to value the husband's interest in a corporation and that the parties would be bound by the accountant's valuation. The accountant completed his evaluation and submitted a report to the divorce court that estimated the husband's equity interest in the corporation and the company's cash basis income for the four previous years. Before trial, and after receiving the expert's report, the husband and wife reached a pre-trial settlement. This settlement encompassed property, alimony, and child support. Then, both parties jointly moved to vacate the settlement. The trial court denied the motion to vacate and entered a judgment of divorce that incorporated the earlier property settlement.

The husband then brought suit against the accountant, alleging negligence in the valuation of the business. The husband asserted that he was forced to pay his ex-wife an excessive amount because of the incorrect values submitted by the accountant. The accountant argued that he was entitled to immunity because he acted in the role of an arbitrator, he was court-appointed, and his decision regarding valuation was binding. The court rejected this argument. Although the court recognized that arbitrators, like judges, are generally afforded immunity for the consequences of their decisions, the court refused to extend immunity to shield experts performing limited professional services that involved neither testimony nor the exercise of judicial discretion. In contrast to an agreement for arbitration, which generally encompasses the entire controversy between the parties, an appraisal simply resolves the actual cash value of a particular item. The court stated that the:

> defendants were expected to apply their professional accountancy skills....They can appropriately be considered "appraisers"....Consequently, the standards of reasonable care applied to lawyers, doctors, engineers, and other professionals charged with furnishing skilled services for compensation attach with equal force and justification to defendants here.

**Note:** The immunity claimed by the accountant here was based on the notion that arbitrators, because they frequently proceed quasi-judicially, are generally afforded an immunity from liability for the consequences of their decisions or awards that is comparable to that accorded judges. This is why the court discussed whether the accountant was an arbitrator or a professional furnishing skills for compensation. The point of this case can be summed up in the oft-quoted line penned by the judge in *Levine:* "A court-appointment is not a talisman for immunity."

**Comment:** Note again that the basis of the claim that was allowed to go forward dealt with negligence related to numbers (valuing a business).

**Example 20.22: Agreed-upon expert not "court appointed," therefore no immunity**
*Politi v. Tyler,* 751 A.2d 788 (Vt. 2000)
This case arose out of a custody dispute, during which the court ordered forensic evaluation of the children involved. "Forensic evaluation will be done....Counsel to let us know [within] a week who to engage for a forensic evaluation.[…]The evaluation was intended to assist the court in determining the best interests of the child...." At 789.

The defendant, a licensed psychologist, contracted with the plaintiff and her ex-husband to conduct the evaluation, with all fees to be paid equally by the parties. The defendant issued a report and testified about her evaluation and recommendation. The plaintiff and her ex-husband then stipulated to a modified custody agreement. The plaintiff then filed suit against the expert for slander, malpractice, and intentional infliction of emotional distress. She alleged that as a result of the defendant's breach of her duty to professionally perform the forensic evaluation and the defendant's subsequent testimony based on that evaluation, the plaintiff was forced to make the stipulated agreement. The trial court refused to grant the defendant's motion to dismiss the case, rejecting the defendant's immunity claims. She appealed the ruling, making two claims: 1) that she was entitled to judicial immunity and 2) in the alternative, that she was entitled to witness immunity.

The appellate court declined to grant the psychologist judicial immunity. It noted the contractual provision, which provided the parties had requested an evaluation, that the psychologist was being retained by the parties and the psychologist would neither testify nor file her report until all fees were paid in full. It also relied on the fact that the psychologist was not appointed by the trial court; rather, the parties contracted with the psychologist. As a result of this language and the contractual language, the Vermont Supreme Court found the psychologist was acting as an expert witness for the parties and not acting as an arm of the family court. Thus, judicial immunity was not applicable.

The court then moved to the defendant's witness immunity claims. It did not address the protection as it applied to communications made while testifying because the trial court had dismissed the slander and intentional infliction of emotional distress claims. However, it rejected the defendant's assertion that witness immunity should protect her from a malpractice claim:

> [Defendant's argument that] witness immunity should preclude a complaint based on the defendant's actions in conducting a forensic evaluation and preparing a report. Defendant's expansive interpretation of witness immunity would extend the doctrine to nontestimonial acts outside a judicial proceeding. Neither the decision of the United States Supreme Court in *Briscoe* nor the precedents of this Court provide a foundation for doing so. At 792–93.

Furthermore, the defendant asserted that her only duty was to assist the family court in its determination of the best interest of the child in connection with custody and visitation, and that she thus owed no duty of care to the plaintiff. The court rejected this, based on the contractual nature of the relationship between the defendant and the plaintiff:

> Defendant owed whatever duties of care to plaintiff—and, for that matter, plaintiff's ex-husband—the contract provided. See *Peters v. Mindell,* 159 Vt. 424, 429, 620 A.2d 1268, 1271 (1992) ("Accompanying every contract is an implied duty to perform with care, skill, reasonable expedience and faithfulness."). A determination on plaintiff's negligence claims stemming from defendant's alleged breaches of this duty should proceed accordingly. At 793.

**Comment:** This expert was hired by both parties and, by the logic of this decision, was in the unenviable position of being subject to suit by both parties. Since one of the parties is likely to not be fond of the expert's opinions in a situation like this, the expert is uniquely vulnerable to lawsuits. Had the expert been appointed by the court, she likely would have been granted quasi-judicial immunity.

**Example 20.23: Court-appointed psychologist: immunity upheld despite parties splitting psychologist's fees**
*Hathcock v. Barnes,* 25 P.3d 295 (Ok. App. 2001)
The underlying case arose out of a child custody dispute in which the father was accused of sexually abusing his daughters. The trial court appointed Dr. Barnes, a psychologist, to perform psychological evaluations on the family in order to assist the court in making its determination regarding custody and visitation. Before the trial court ruled on the issues of custody and visitation, the father entered into an agreement regarding custody and visitation. The agreement provided the mother would have custody of the children and the father would have supervised visitation with his daughters. Later, the father sought a modification of the decree after new evidence surfaced that the daughters had been abused by a babysitter's minor son. Subsequently, the trial court granted the father permanent custody of his son and unsupervised visitation with his two daughters.

The father then sued the psychologist, alleging negligence, fraud, breach of contract, and intentional infliction of emotional distress. The trial court granted summary judgment for the psychologist based on judicial immunity and the father appealed. The Court of Civil Appeals affirmed the ruling.

On appeal, the plaintiff argued that Dr. Barnes had entered into a contractual agreement. This contract set for the division of payment by the parties for Dr. Barnes's services. The plaintiff argued that the contractual relationship transformed Dr. Barnes into a privately retained (rather than court-appointed) expert. The court replied that the contract expressly stated the purpose of the evaluations was to assist the legal system in determining arrangements that were in the best interests of the children involved and that the psychologist conducting the evaluation was acting as an unbiased, impartial investigator of the family situation. The contract also provided for two methods of payment. However, a provision specified payment must be made before release of the information. The court found that since the trial court had expressly appointed Dr. Barnes and set forth the division of payment, the psychologist was court-appointed. The court found that a psychologist appointed by the court to assist it in making a custody determination performs a function integral to the judicial process. This status entitles the psychologist to immunity from lawsuits arising from this process. 25 P.3d at 297.

The court also rejected the Hathcocks' argument that allowing Dr. Barnes's immunity violated the Hathcocks' rights of due process.

> The jurisdictions which have considered this argument do not agree. Adequate remedies and safeguards, other than civil liability, exist to hold court-appointed psychologists accountable for their actions such as cross-examination, another expert witness to refute the court-appointed psychologist and appellate review. At trial, Mr. Hathcock's attorney vigorously cross-examined and brought to the trial court's attention the alleged deficiencies in the evaluation. Further, Mr. Hathcock was free to present his own expert witness to refute Dr. Barnes' assessment. *Id.* at 297.

**Example 20.24: Court-appointed experts protected absolutely by judicial immunity**
*Hughes v. Long,* 242 F.3d 121 (3d Cir. 2001)
Following a state court child custody dispute, the father, Hughes, brought a federal civil rights and state contract and tort suit against a custody evaluator (a social worker), the psychologist with whom the evaluator consulted and who performed tests on the family members, and the psychologist's supervisor. The father alleged that they falsified results of his evaluation tests,

omitted positive information from their reports and recommendations to the court, withheld data from his expert in defiance of court orders, and testified falsely during custody proceedings.

In the underlying custody case, the court ordered Long, a licensed clinical social worker, to conduct a full custody evaluation. According to the order, Long was to report the results of the psychological evaluations to the court and make any recommendations appropriate to a child custody determination. Although the court appointed Long to conduct the evaluation, Long entered into a private contract with the parties whereby each agreed to pay fifty percent of her fee. After consulting with a psychologist and concluding her evaluation, Long informally told Hughes of her recommendation for custody. Hughes was upset with the recommendation and hired an expert to review the recommendation. He claimed that Long, as well as her supervisor and the psychologist she brought in, refused to hand over records to his experts, destroyed the original data, and fabricated false data.

During the custody hearing, Hughes presented his allegations of fraudulent behavior by Long, the psychologist, and her supervisor. All three testified during the hearing and denied creating false reports, destroying any originals, or intentionally failing to comply with the court's order to release their raw data. In this civil suit against the three evaluators, the trial court granted all three absolute immunity, based on the notion of prosecutorial immunity. Hughes challenged the grant of immunity.

The appellate court, however, affirmed the grant of immunity, but declared that the immunity in question was judicial immunity, rather than prosecutorial, which provided absolute immunity from both federal civil rights claims and state law claims.

The appellate court held that the evaluators "enjoy *judicial* immunity because they acted as 'arms of the court,' similar to a guardian ad litem or a court-appointed doctor or psychologist, a non-judicial person who fulfills a quasi-judicial role at the court's request." 242 F.3d at 129.

In *Hughes,* the plaintiff also asked the federal court to predict that the Pennsylvania Supreme Court would extend the exception to witness immunity announced by the Pennsylvania Supreme Court in *LLMD* to court-appointed experts and causes of action outside of negligence. The federal court stated:

> Given the unique and essential role of court-appointed witnesses, we believe that, if faced with the issue, the Pennsylvania Supreme Court would confine its holding in *LLMD* to privately retained experts sued for professional malpractice. *Id.*

The court based this conclusion largely on the differences between privately retained experts, which were at issue in *LLMD*, and court-appointed experts, which were at issue in *Hughes*. The court stated:

> As we emphasized earlier, court-appointed experts hold a unique role in judicial proceedings. Because they work on behalf of the court rather than any one party, court-appointed experts provide unbiased, neutral information and recommendations and aid the court in its decision-making process. This neutral information is essential to the court, which cannot make necessary observations and gather relevant facts without assistance. Thus, it is crucial to the judicial process that court-appointed witnesses are free to formulate and make recommendations unhindered by the fear of liability. Without such immunity, these "advisors" may be reluctant to assist the court, thereby depriving the court of its *sole* source of neutral information. *Id.* at 130.

The court noted that privately retained experts are compensated and, at some level, are expected to provide a recommendation that favors their client. The court explained, "Although private experts serve an important role and aid the court in 'its path to truth,' they are not neutral 'advisors' to the court and thus should not be subject to the same treatment as court-appointed experts." *Id.* The court went on to note the importance of the contractual relationship between a privately retained expert witness and the client, which obligates the expert to provide services to a certain standard. This relationship does not arise when the expert is court appointed. *See Hughes* at 130–31.

**Comment:** Although a court-appointed expert is generally immune from all civil suits, there can still be serious consequences for malfeasance including criminal prosecution for perjury and, more likely, professional disciplinary action.

## 20.7  Sanction by the Trial Judge

Some trial judges have begun sanctioning expert witnesses. A Georgia judge recently issued an order banning an expert from ever again testifying in his courtroom for giving testimony that was "conflicting, lacking in credibility, and apparently untruthful."[28] This fact would likely be used against the expert in any future case and would probably end his career as a witness.

A trial judge in Massachusetts (in the *Wojcicki* case below) recently assessed monetary sanctions against an expert for intentionally testifying that a fact was true that he did not know was true, misleading the court, and testifying falsely about a telephone conversation that did not exist.

**Example 20.25: Expert sanctioned for $20,305 for providing misleading and false testimony**
*Wojcicki v. Caragher,* 18 Mass.L.Rptr. 581, 2004 WL 3120099 (Mass. Super. 2004)
This case arose after an expert testified for the defense in a medical malpractice case. The plaintiffs requested a new trial based on alleged false testimony by the defense expert. The trial judge awarded monetary sanctions to the plaintiffs from both the defendant and the expert. The court stated:

FINDINGS
A finding of fraud on the court must be shown by clear and convincing evidence. I find that plaintiff has shown by clear and convincing evidence that Dr. Fred Hochberg, an expert witness called by the defendant: 1) intentionally testified at the trial of this case as to the existence of a fact when he did not know whether the fact was true; [FN8] 2) deliberately misled the Court and the jury as to whether he had reviewed the Study data and, in particular, deliberately created the false impression in his trial testimony that he had reviewed the CD-ROM containing the actual data set and that it showed that no cancer patients were included in the Study; and 3) testified falsely at his deposition and in his February 23rd Affidavit that he had had a telephone conversation with Dr. Tilley and that she had provided the information on which his trial testimony was based. [FN9]
FN8. In particular, Dr. Hochberg testified that no patient with cancer was included in the Study. He did not know whether that statement was true. He had made a half-hearted attempt to find out whether a patient like Mrs. Wojcicki "with active cancer" would have been included in the Study by placing phone-calls and sending an e-mail to Drs. Marler and Tilley on the first day of the trial and by asking Mr. Gould on the same day (see 5/19/04 Tr. at 52) whether he should purchase the data set, but he did not obtain an answer to the questions posed in the e-mail, much less an answer to the question whether any patients with cancer were included in the Study.
FN9. Dr. Hochberg also testified at the hearing on May 19, that it was "his memory and belief" that he had spoken with Dr. Tilley and testified that Dr. Tilley was the source of the information to which he testified, a fact that was not true. (5/19/04 Tr. at 39, 42-45, 65-67.) At 8.

---

[28] "Medical Expert Barred from Georgia Court Forever," http://www.amednews.com, December 13, 2004.

I have found no authority directly addressing the issue whether the Court has inherent authority to impose a sanction on a non-party witness. In the unique circumstances of this case, I find that such authority exists. At the hearing on February 23, 2004, the Court stated that it was allowing the motion for a new trial. The Court also stated that she did not find Dr. Hochberg's deposition testimony credible and would issue a written decision on the motion for a new trial. Lastly, the Court stated that if Dr. Hochberg wished to be heard before the decision issued, he would be afforded that opportunity. Counsel for Dr. Hochberg then filed an appearance, issued subpoenas, adduced evidence, and requested further hearings, including a deposition of Dr. Tilley in Charleston, South Carolina, and an evidentiary hearing at which Dr. Hochberg testified. Counsel for the plaintiff continued to provide the balance that is essential to the proper functioning of our adversary system by attending the hearings, examining Dr. Tilley and cross-examining Dr. Hochberg, performing research and preparing memoranda.

In *Avelino-Wright v. Wright, supra,* 51 Mass App Ct. at 5, the Court reiterated that a sanction may be imposed for conduct which obstructs and impedes the orderly course of a legal proceeding. Dr. Hochberg deliberately misled the jury in the first trial testifying that he had knowledge about a fact that was central to the case when he had no such knowledge. He no doubt believed that a patient with Mrs. Wojcicki's medical history would not have been included in the Study, but he testified, without basis, that, as a matter of fact, no cancer patients were included in the Study and deliberately created the false impression that his testimony to that effect was based on his review of the Study data. He compounded this error by falsely testifying that he had had a telephone conversation with Dr. Tilley. He then imposed the burden on Dr. Tilley of proving that she had not had a conversation with him and challenged the credibility of her testimony that she would not have made the statement that he attributed to her. His actions have caused plaintiff to incur attorney's fee and expenses and have wasted valuable judicial resources.

Dr. Hochberg received fair notice of the charges and a reasonable opportunity to be heard. *Beit v. Probate & Family Ct. Dept,* 385 Mass. at 862.

I therefore order as a sanction that Dr. Hochberg pay reasonable costs, including attorneys fees, incurred by plaintiff between February 28, 2004, when counsel for Dr. Hochberg filed an appearance through May 19, 2004, the date of the last hearing, as well as costs that will be incurred by the Office of the Jury Commissioner in connection with the retrial.

FINDINGS AND ORDER AS TO ATTORNEYS FEES AND COSTS

For the reasons stated herein, the plaintiff's motion for a new trial was allowed on February 23, 2004. Applying the factors set forth in *Fontaine v. Ebtec Corp.,* 415 Mass. 309, 324-26 (1993), I find that the appropriate amount of attorneys fees and expenses to be paid by defendant to plaintiff is $56,000, plus expenses in the amount of $12,380. [FN13] I further find that the appropriate sanction to be imposed on Dr. Hochberg is payment of attorneys fees in the amount of $14,770 and expenses in the amount of $2,585. Lastly, I order that Dr. Hochberg pay $2,950 to compensate the Office of the Jury Commissioner for the costs of providing jurors for a second trial. [FN14] I further order that the payments ordered herein shall be made within thirty days of the date this Order enters unless this order has been stayed by the Appeals Court. [FN15]

FN13. I express no opinion as to whether Dr. Caragher has the right to recover these costs and expenses from Dr. Hochberg pursuant to the contract between them. See *Boyes-Bogie v. Horvitz,* 14 Mass. L. Rptr. 208, 2001 WL 1771989 (Mass.Super.2001). If such recovery is available, it would not violate this order.

FN14. According to the Office of the Jury Commissioner, the total cost of providing jurors for the first trial including postage, printing and juror compensation was $2,999.14. Payment shall be made to the "Commonwealth of Massachusetts" and mailed or delivered, along with a copy of this Order to the Administrative Office of the Trial Court, 2 Center Plaza, Boston, MA 02108.

FN15. Proof of timely payment shall be filed with this Court. At 10–11.

**Comment:** The judge was so incensed that she even subtly encouraged the defendant to sue the expert to recover the $68,000 in sanctions the defendant was forced to pay. Experts should never try to mislead a judge or jury. If they do and are caught, their careers as experts will likely come to a rapid and ignominious end.

## 20.8 Defamation

Expert witnesses will usually be protected from defamation liability by immunity. This immunity is provided in order to encourage full and frank disclosure by the expert. Experts need to keep in mind, however, that there is no immunity for communications made outside the context of the lawsuit and that they may be subject to other liability (for example, negligence, professional discipline, and perjury) for making defamatory communications in the context of a lawsuit. Please consider the following cases.

**Example 20.26: Immunity from defamation will be granted only if plaintiff can show the statements were made after a fair and impartial investigation or upon reasonable grounds for belief in their truth**
*Twelker v. Shannon & Wilson, Inc.,* 564 P.2d 1131 (Wash. 1977)
In this case, a soil engineer brought a defamation suit against a fellow soil engineer who allegedly defamed his professional reputation by sending a letter to an insurance company regarding the cause of a landslide. The letter concerned the cause of a landslide that damaged a building completed two months earlier. The insurance company insured the general contractor in charge of the construction of that building and the plaintiff prepared the soil report for the project. Apparently concerned with the possible exposure to the liability of its insured, the insurance company retained the respondent to investigate the slide and issued a statement of its findings with regard to its cause. A three-page report prepared pursuant to that request and forwarded to the insurance company contained the allegedly defamatory remarks.

The defendant prepared his letter following two inspections of the landslide site and a review of various documents, including the plaintiff's soil report, which were pertinent to the construction project. The plaintiff argued that the letter contained several specific false statements regarding the contents of the original soil report, and that those statements concerning the report were made with knowledge of or reckless disregard for their falsity.

The defendant raised the defense of absolute immunity in an attempt to bar the suit. In essence, the court found that the defendant's report was made in the course of judicial or quasi-judicial proceedings, and thus the defendant was eligible for protection. However, the protection was not absolute. The court decided that it was questionable whether the statements were made after a fair and impartial investigation or upon reasonable grounds for belief in their truth. Because of this, the defendant may have abused his privilege and absolute immunity could not extend to protect his statements. The court explained that the privilege of immunity is a judicially created privilege founded upon the belief that the administration of justice requires witnesses in a legal proceeding to be able to discuss their views without fear of a defamation lawsuit. The privilege of absolute witness immunity creates an "extraordinary breadth" of protection and should not be extended absent the existence of compelling public policy justifications. The court remanded the case for a trial on the merits of the suit.

**Comment:** This case provides yet further evidence of the wisdom of experts telling the truth and conducting a fair and impartial investigation.

**Example 20.27: Suit for defamation based on reports filed with probate court not allowed, but suit for negligent diagnosis allowed to go forward**
*James v. Brown,* 637 S.W.2d 914 (Tex. 1982)

In 1982, James sued several doctors who had filed reports with a Texas probate court concerning James's mental competency.

James had been hospitalized for observation. During the course of this observation, she was examined by several doctors who filed reports stating that the plaintiff was not of sound mind, was not competent to handle financial affairs, and was likely to cause injury to herself if she were not restrained.

James later obtained a court order that released her from the hospital's custody. The competency proceeding was then dropped and James sued the doctors who had indicated that she was incompetent. In her complaint, James alleged libel, negligent misdiagnosis, medical malpractice, false imprisonment, and malicious prosecution. Under the libel claim, the Texas court applied witness immunity to the doctors, protecting them from liability for allegedly defamatory statements. The court held that no statements in a judicial proceeding can give rise to a civil action for libel or slander, regardless of negligence or malice as long as the statement has some relation to the proceeding.[29]

However, the court noted that the witness immunity protection does not provide blanket immunity from all civil liability. Specifically, the court stated that James was not precluded from suing the doctors for negligence resulting from their misdiagnoses just because their diagnoses were later communicated to a court in the course of a judicial proceeding.

The court explained, "While the doctors' communications to the court of their diagnoses of [the plaintiff's] mental condition, regardless of how negligently made, cannot serve as the basis for a defamation action, the diagnoses themselves may be actionable on other grounds."

The expert should note that although the court here allowed the suit against the experts for negligent misdiagnosis to proceed, the basis of the suit was a Texas statute that imposed a duty on the psychiatrists to conduct their examinations with the degree of skill ordinarily employed under similar circumstances by similar specialists in the field.

### Example 20.28: Suit against adverse expert witness for trade libel, defamation, and tortious interference with prospective business advantage not allowed to go forward

*Aequitron Medical Inc. v. Joseph P. Dyro, et al.,* No. 96-2187 (E.D.N.Y. 1998)

The plaintiff, a manufacturer of infant heart and breathing monitors, sued the defendant biomechanical engineer for trade libel, defamation, and tortious interference with prospective business advantage. The defendant had testified previously as an expert in two products liability actions involving the plaintiff's monitors.

In its complaint, Aequitron claimed that a videotape of the defendant's test of the monitor was false and misleading because the defendant failed to disclose that he found no defect in an earlier test, that he previously testified that the alarm functioned, and that the device was not returned for factory certification. The plaintiff also alleged that the defendant circulated the videotape in order to get hired as an expert in cases against Aequitron and in other products liability cases.

The U.S. District Court for the Eastern District of New York found that statements by parties and their attorneys are absolutely privileged under any circumstances if they are pertinent to the litigation. "Moreover, and contrary to plaintiff's position, the absolute privilege attaches not only at the hearing or trial phase, but to every step of the proceeding in question, even if it is

---

[29] "A witness is absolutely privileged to publish defamatory matter concerning another in communications preliminary to a proposed judicial proceeding or as a part of a judicial proceeding in which he is testifying, if it has some relation to the proceeding." Restatement (Second) of Torts, section 588 (1981).

preliminary and/or investigatory," the court said.[30] The privilege, the court continued, has been found to extend to letters, settlement offers, statements in a magazine article, and subpoenas. The court added:

> It should also be noted that a retained expert is more than just the average witness, but acts as an agent for the attorney whose reports to the attorney based on information from the client can be subject to attorney-client privilege. Although the videotape was later disclosed to Aequitron's counsel and not subject to any attorney-client privilege . . . the Court finds that a retained expert's role in trial preparation and the privileges accorded to those experts weighs in favor of providing absolute immunity for statements made in the course of those preparations, so long as the statements are pertinent to the ongoing litigation.

**Comment:** Experts involved in high-stakes litigation, especially experts who testify frequently, can expect "scorched earth" tactics from the opposing side. These could include digging into the expert's background, exhaustive *Daubert* challenges, complaints to professional societies and licensing boards and, as in this case, even legal action. Expert witness work, especially work in high-stakes cases, is best performed by someone who is thick skinned and not easily intimidated.

## 20.9  Effect of Immunity upon Professional Disciplinary Action against the Expert

An expert should assume that he will not be able to successfully invoke immunity if his alleged misconduct results in a professional disciplinary proceeding (or proceedings from a society or association of which the expert is a member). In response to a perceived medical malpractice crisis, some medical societies have begun peer reviewing expert testimony[31] and disciplining testimony they consider misleading.[32]

---

[30] The district court cited *Herzfeld & Stern v. Beck*, 175 A.S.2d at 691, 572 N.Y.S.2d at 685 (1st Dep't. 1991) for this proposition.

[31] See, for example, the American Society of General Surgeon's Expert Witness Certification Program Rules:

IV. Review Process of Expert Witness Testimony

The ASGS will establish a Review Panel. An ASGS member may request a review of testimony, by a certified or non-certified expert witness in a case in which they were a party, for accuracy. If the initial review is adverse, the entire panel will review the findings in the case and make recommendations to the ASGS Board of Trustees. If the expert witness in question is a Certified Expert Witness and the testimony is felt to be materially inaccurate, the ASGS Board, at its discretion, may institute the fair hearing due process. If after the fair hearing due process, the testimony is felt to be inaccurate, the ASGS Expert Witness Certification may be withdrawn as well as membership in the ASGS. If the witness is not a certified witness and is not a member of the ASGS, then appropriate state and/or local licensing boards, specialty societies, or legal institutions will be notified of the Review Panel's findings.

[32] Although these rules are all written in a neutral way, the vast majority of all complaints and actions are taken against medical experts who testify for *plaintiffs* in medical malpractice cases. The reason for this is obvious: See *Austin v. American Ass'n of Neurological Surgeons*, 253 F.3d 967 (C.A.7 (Ill.) 2001): "There is no basis for Austin's claim that the Association entertains only complaints against members who testify on behalf of malpractice plaintiffs. What is true is that to date all complaints (but there have been very few) have been against such members; but the reason is at once obvious and innocent. If a member of the Association is sued for malpractice and another member gives testimony for the plaintiff that the defendant believes is irresponsible, it is natural for the defendant to complain to the Association; a fellow member has irresponsibly labeled him negligent. If a member of the

**Example 20.29: Surgeon suspended from voluntary medical society for misleading testimony**
*Austin v. American Ass'n of Neurological Surgeons,* 253 F.3d 967 (C.A.7 (Ill.) 2001)
Donald C. Austin, a neurosurgeon, was suspended for six months by the American Association of Neurological Surgeons, a voluntary association incorporated under Illinois law as a not-for-profit corporation, to which he belonged (he has since resigned). He brought this suit against the Association claiming that he had been suspended in "revenge" for having testified as an expert witness for the plaintiff in a medical malpractice suit brought against another member of the Association, a Dr. Ditmore. Austin argued that the suspension violated Illinois law and sought damages measured by the decline in his expert witness income as a consequence of the suspension. He also sought an injunction expunging the record of the suspension. The complaint was that the Association acted in bad faith because it never disciplines members who testify on behalf of malpractice defendants as distinct from malpractice plaintiffs and that it is against public policy for a professional association to discipline a member on the basis of trial testimony unless the testimony was intentionally false. The court strongly rejected the expert's claim. It found that:

> since Austin plainly had not attempted to sound the opinion of his profession to determine whether a majority of the nation's several thousand neurosurgeons agree with his unorthodox view, there is little doubt that his testimony was irresponsible and that it violated a number of sensible-seeming provisions of the Association's ethical code. These include provisions requiring that a member appearing as an expert witness should testify "prudently," must "identify as such, personal opinions not generally accepted by other neurosurgeons," and should "provide the court with accurate and documentable opinions on the matters at hand.

The court had little sympathy for the expert and even took a parting shot at him:

> We note finally that there is a strong national interest, which we doubt not that Illinois would embrace, in identifying and sanctioning poor-quality physicians and thereby improving the quality of health care. Although Dr. Austin did not treat the malpractice plaintiff for whom he testified, his testimony at her trial was a type of medical service and if the quality of his testimony reflected the quality of his medical judgment, he is probably a poor physician. His discipline by the Association therefore served an important public policy exemplified by the federal Health Care Quality Improvement Act, 42 U.S.C. §§ 11101 et seq., which encourages hospitals to conduct professional review of its staff members and report malpractice to a federal database. As an inducement to the vigorous performance of this reporting function, the Act immunizes hospitals from liability for disciplinary actions they take against staff physicians, provided only that the hospital is acting in good faith. At 974.

**Comment:** After his suspension, the expert's annual income from expert witnessing fell from $220,000 to $77,000. This shows how one "black mark" can be used to show dishonesty and can devastate an expert's testifying "career." Experts who wish to testify in future cases should never exaggerate, embellish, cite references that do not truly support their position, or testify based on an inadequate investigation.

---

Association who testifies for a plaintiff happens to believe that the defendant's expert witness was irresponsible, he is much less likely to complain, because that expert (and fellow member of the Association) has not accused him of negligence or harmed him in his practice or forced him to stand trial or gotten him into trouble with his liability insurer. The asymmetry that Austin points to as evidence of bad faith is thus no evidence of bad faith at all; and he has no other evidence of bad faith." As such, plaintiff's medical malpractice experts are most susceptible to sanction from their professional societies and associations.

**Example 20.30: Psychologist's license suspended for 10 years for expert witness malfeasance (failure to qualify statements, mischaracterization of statements, and failure to verify information): immunity not a defense to disciplinary action**
*Deatherage v. Examining Bd. of Psychology,* 948 P.2d 828 (Wash. 1997)
A state board of psychology (Board) brought disciplinary proceedings against a psychologist, alleging he failed to meet professional ethical standards in work that formed the basis of his expert testimony in several child custody suits. The Board found the psychologist's failure to qualify statements, his mischaracterization of statements, his failure to verify information, and his interpretation of test data were adequate grounds for initiating disciplinary proceedings under state regulations. After an extensive hearing, the Board found that the expert had committed misconduct in three custody evaluations, and suspended his license for ten years. The psychologist sought, and was granted, judicial review of the Board's decision.

The psychologist raised the defense of absolute witness immunity, which, he argued, prevents the Board from initiating disciplinary proceedings against him based upon his work and conduct as an expert witness testifying in a court proceeding. The state supreme court held that absolute witness immunity does not exist in the context of a professional disciplinary proceeding.

**Comment:** For many experts, their professional license is their single most valuable asset. Dishonest experts risk forfeiting this asset and their careers along with it.

## 20.10  Presenting False Evidence

The policies supporting witness immunity for adverse experts are so strongly favored that even a witness who offers perjured testimony may be immune from liability for damages. However, such an expert would still be subject to criminal prosecution and to discipline within his profession (for example, potential loss of an expert's professional license). Consider the following case.

**Example 20.31: Suit against adverse accounting expert for alleged perjurious testimony barred because of expert immunity**
*Carden v. Getzoff,* 190 Cal. App.3d 907, 235 Cal. Rptr. 698 (Mar. 1987)
The plaintiff here sued an expert accounting witness. The underlying case was a marital dissolution between the plaintiff and his wife. The wife's accounting expert allegedly manufactured false evidence in the dissolution action when he prepared a medical practice valuation of the appellant's anesthesiology practice to be used in the negotiation of a settlement agreement. Allegedly, he examined the appellant's anesthesiology practice to determine the goodwill therein and to compare the evaluation of the goodwill found in the appellant's practice to that of "other similar practices" that he had also examined. The plaintiff alleged that those representations were false and that no evaluation was made of the appellant's anesthesiology practice and no comparison was made. Moreover, the plaintiff claimed that the expert misused the process of the court when he testified that he had made an appraisal of the anesthesiology practice based upon an examination of the practice and a comparison of the evaluation of the goodwill of the practice to that of three other comparable anesthesiology medical practices.

The plaintiff then sued the expert. The court dismissed the plaintiff's suit by applying the privilege:

> We in no way condone the alleged perjury. If the allegations in the complaint are true, respondent's conduct is indeed outrageous. However, when there is a good faith intention to bring a suit, even malicious publications "are protected as part of the price paid for affording litigants the utmost freedom of access to the courts." [Citations.] Otherwise, adverse witnesses would always be fearful of subsequent

civil suits and would be extremely hesitant or unwilling to testify. Appellant's potential remedies are to assist in the prosecution of criminal charges; to report any allegations of dereliction to the Board of Accountancy; and to attempt to litigate any claims he might have against his trial attorney.

**Comment:** This is likely to be a good news/bad news situation for the expert in question. The good news is that the civil suit against him has been dismissed. The bad news is that he may face criminal charges or actions against his accounting license.

## 20.11  Changing an Opinion

Experts are expected to tell the truth. Courts have found that experts are not liable to their retaining "friendly" parties if, during the course of a trial, they change their opinions. There is also a strong public policy to support the view that experts should not be liable for breach of contract if they fail to testify as they had originally intended. The courts do not want to sanction an agreement to testify favorably. Consider the following examples.

### Example 20.32: Suit against friendly expert for making concessions on cross-examination and admitting errors barred as "against public policy"

*Panitz v. Behrend,* 632 A.2d 562 (Penn. 1993)

In the underlying case, the expert was retained by a law firm on behalf of clients whom the law firm represented in a personal injury action. On direct examination, the expert testified that the injuries at issue had been caused by formaldehyde. However, on cross-examination, the expert could not explain some inconsistencies in her testimony and admitted that her reasoning was inaccurate. The plaintiffs received an unfavorable verdict, and the law firm refused to pay the expert the balance of her fee. The expert sued to recover her fee, and the law firm counterclaimed alleging gross negligence. The trial court granted the defendant expert's demurrer and dismissed the counterclaim. The law firm appealed.

In refusing to hold the expert liable for her testimony, the appeals court reasoned that "[t]o allow a party to litigation to contract with an expert witness and thereby obligate the witness to testify only in a manner favorable to the party, on threat of civil liability, would be contrary to public policy." The appeals court in this case took the position that "[t]he primary purpose of expert testimony is not to assist one party or another in winning the case but to assist the trier of the facts in understanding complicated matters." The court also stated that an expert witness "will not be subjected to civil liability because he or she in the face of conflicting evidence or during rigorous cross examination, is persuaded that some or all of his or her opinion testimony has been inaccurate." Rather than malpractice liability, the court relied on procedural safeguards, such as judicial discretion on admissibility pursuant to Rule 702, to ensure the reliability of expert testimony.

**Comment:** This suit against the expert came only after he sued the law firm for non-payment of his fee. The suit filed by the expert appeared to be the final action that made the client angry enough to sue. The expert might have been better off writing off the unpaid fee in a situation like this.

### Example 20.33: Expert's duty is to "appear and testify truthfully," expert cannot be contracted to testify a certain way

*Schaffer v. Donegan,* 585 N.E. 2d 854 (Ohio App. 1990)

In this case, the court rejected liability for an expert who changed his testimony during the underlying medical malpractice trial. In the underlying case, the plaintiff brought suit against two surgeons. The plaintiff's expert, another surgeon, reviewed the medical records and agreed to testify that the dentists were negligent and that the negligence caused the plaintiff's injury. On the seventh day of the trial, the expert reported to the plaintiff that he could no longer testify favorably on the issue of liability. He explained that while he was still of the opinion that the two physicians who treated the plaintiff were negligent in failing to diagnose the particular fracture involved, he was no longer able to say that that negligence was the proximate cause of the injuries and losses claimed by the plaintiff. The plaintiff settled the case, then claimed that the expert, by reason of changing his opinion, breached his contract to testify and his duty to provide the other parties to his contract with timely notice of his change of opinion.

The appellate court affirmed the trial court's judgment in favor of the expert. The court recounted the rule: "As a general principle a witness has a duty to appear and testify truthfully concerning his knowledge or belief and a person who violates this duty may be required to respond in damages to the person injured by the violation." It then stated, "We see no liability on the part of [the expert] for changing his opinion on the liability issue if he did so for valid medical reasons as he testified." The court based its opinion on the notion that the plaintiff had no right to expect the witness to say anything but the truth. The contract was for the expert to testify to the truth, thus the expert did not breach it—a contract to testify in a certain way would have been void and unenforceable.

**Comment:** The court here stated that the expert's duty is "to appear and testify truthfully." Hence two crucial rules of expert witness risk management: 1) show up and 2) tell the truth.

### Example 20.34: "Under no circumstances would an agreement to give favorable testimony be sanctioned by the courts"

*Griffith v. Harris,* 116 N.W.2d 133, 136 (Wisc. 1962)

Here, the plaintiff sued a physician for malpractice. While preparing this malpractice case for trial, the plaintiff's attorneys contacted the two defendants, who were both physicians, with the intention of getting them to testify in support of the plaintiff's malpractice case. The plaintiff's attorneys furnished the two doctor-defendants with hospital records on which the malpractice charge was in part based. The hospital records were not sufficient to establish the plaintiff's case without supporting expert medical testimony. The defendants were requested to testify in response to hypothetical questions. They were told that the plaintiff's attorneys would not proceed to trial without supporting expert medical testimony. The defendants took the matter under advisement and subsequently notified the plaintiff's attorneys that they would testify favorably for the plaintiff. Later, the defendants were furnished copies of the proposed hypothetical questions.

Less than 24 hours before they were to be called to testify, the defendants informed the plaintiff's attorneys that they would not testify without a subpoena and, if subpoenaed, they would not testify in any way that would benefit the plaintiff. Because of this latter fact, the defendants were not subpoenaed. They did not appear and testify on behalf of the plaintiff. Because of the absence of favorable expert medical testimony, the plaintiff failed to establish a *prima facie* case of malpractice.

The plaintiff sued the experts for breach of contract. The court found that the essence of the plaintiff's complaint was that the experts broke their contract—not merely to testify, but to testify in the plaintiff's favor. Therefore, the court declared that "under no circumstances would an agreement to give favorable testimony be sanctioned by the courts."

**Comment:** An expert witness's first duty is to the truth, not to the client who pays the expert's bills. Experts should not let clients bully them into testifying in a way they consider untruthful. Obviously, if an expert changes his opinion based on further reflection or new information, this should immediately be communicated to retaining counsel. It is unwise to wait until the eve of trial to deliver this news to retaining counsel.

## 20.12  Spoliation of Evidence

*Spoliation of evidence* is the destruction of relevant evidence by a party or his agent.  The doctrine generally imposes some sanction on the party responsible for the destruction of the evidence.[33]  The law regarding spoliation is vastly different in each jurisdiction.  In some, an expert may face tort liability for negligent, as well as intentional, spoliation.  An expert who loses or destroys key evidence may be sued by the retaining party for breach of contract.  The expert may also face sanctions, such as the exclusion of the expert's testimony or dismissal of the case, for acts of spoliation.  None of these results will help an expert's reputation within the legal community and any of them may very well terminate his career as a witness.

> **Example 20.35: Spoliation cause of action against expert witness by adverse party not recognized, any sanction left to the underlying case**
> *Fletcher v. Dorchester Mut. Ins. Co.,* 437 Mass. 544, 773 N.E.2d 420 (Mass. 2002)
> This case involved a house fire.  The defense's expert removed certain wiring components from the burnt out house and the plaintiff sued the expert for negligent and intentional spoliation of evidence.  The court affirmed the dismissal of the suit and cited the majority rule that such civil suits are not allowed.  The court stated:
>
>> The present appeal requires us to determine whether we should recognize a cause of action in tort for intentional or negligent spoliation of evidence. For the following reasons, we conclude that there is no cause of action for spoliation of evidence and therefore affirm the judgment.
>> 1. Facts and procedural background. On April 4, 1995, five young children were trapped and severely burned in a tragic house fire in Scituate. Three of the children died; the two surviving children sustained permanent injuries. The house was owned by Stephen Littleton, who had leased the premises to the victims' family. In the immediate aftermath of the fire, the owner's insurer, the defendant Dorchester Mutual Insurance Company (Dorchester Mutual), retained an expert to investigate the fire scene. That expert, the defendant Richard Splaine, removed certain wiring components and fixtures from the remains of the building approximately two weeks after the fire.
>> The parents of the children injured and killed in the blaze brought suit against Littleton, alleging that he had failed to maintain the dwelling in a safe and habitable condition.
>> In that underlying tort action, the parents filed a motion for sanctions, alleging that Splaine's removal of the electrical components from the scene had so altered them as to compromise the parents' ability to prove their claims. After an evidentiary hearing on the motion, the judge concluded that the plaintiff parents had "failed to prove that defendant has materially altered, damaged or destroyed any evidence in this case" and therefore denied the motion for sanctions.
>> Meanwhile, the parents had filed the present action against Dorchester Mutual and Splaine, alleging counts of negligence, "negligent spoliation of evidence," and "intentional spoliation of evidence" against each of them.  In support of their negligence claim, the parents alleged that Dorchester Mutual and Splaine were negligent in their "failure to properly preserve and maintain the condition of the subject premises and its components, including the subject electrical circuit and its appurtenant parts when [they] knew or should have known that the condition of said circuit and its appurtenant parts constituted an element vital to the establishment and proof of the cause and origin of the subject fire,"

---

[33] "The most remarkable aspect of the doctrine of spoliation of evidence is that it has been held to be: (1) a cause of action in tort (for either intentional or negligent spoliation of evidence); (2) a defense to recovery; (3) an evidentiary inference or presumption; and (4) a discovery sanction. Furthermore, the doctrine of spoliation of evidence has been held in some jurisdictions to constitute a substantive rule of law, while other courts have held it to be a procedural evidentiary rule." Robert L. Tucker, "The Flexible Doctrine of Spoliation of Evidence: Cause of Action, Defense, Evidentiary Presumption, and Discovery Sanction," 27 *U. Tol. L. Rev.* (1995) 67, 68.

and that they had suffered "irreparable harm" as a result. In separate counts for "negligent spoilation of evidence," the plaintiffs alleged that the defendants "knew, or should have known, that said [electrical] circuit was a relevant piece of causative evidence to potential liability claims" and therefore "owed to the Plaintiffs a duty of care to preserve the fire scene and the subject electrical circuit for prospective civil litigation." The removal of the electrical circuit was allegedly a breach of that duty. Finally, in their counts for "intentional spoilation of evidence," the plaintiffs alleged that the defendants breached that same "duty of care to preserve the property" by removing the electrical circuit "with the purpose of harming the Plaintiffs' prospective actions against [the owner] and others" when they "knew or should have known that harm to the Plaintiffs' prospective claims and lawsuits was substantially certain to follow."

Dorchester Mutual filed a motion to dismiss for failure to state a claim, arguing that Massachusetts does not recognize an action in tort for "spoilation of evidence." The judge agreed, noting that the remedy for spoilation of evidence, if any occurred, would be the imposition of appropriate sanctions in the underlying tort action. Thereafter, Splaine filed his own motion to dismiss, which was allowed on the same ground.

2. Discussion. To date, we have not recognized a cause of action for spoilation of evidence. Most jurisdictions that have considered the issue have declined to recognize such a cause of action. We adhere to that majority view.

A third-party witness may also agree to preserve an item of evidence and thereby enter into an enforceable contract. See *Koplin v. Rosel Well Perforators, Inc.*, 241 Kan. 206, 208, 215, 734 P.2d 1177 (1987) (declining to recognize cause of action for spoilation, but recognizing that duty to preserve evidence may be imposed "by reason of an agreement, contract, statute, or other special circumstance"). Remedies for breach of such an agreement are found in contract law, not in tort law. Again, where the source of a nonparty's duty to preserve evidence is one that already states a cause of action and provides its own remedies, we will not invent a separate, duplicate cause of action in tort.

We have implicitly recognized that persons who are actually involved in litigation (or know that they will likely be involved) have a duty to preserve evidence for use by others who will also be involved in that litigation. Where evidence has been destroyed or altered by persons who are parties to the litigation, or by persons affiliated with a party (in particular, their expert witnesses), and another party's ability to prosecute or defend the claim has been prejudiced as a result, we have held that a judge may exclude evidence to remedy that unfairness. In doing so, we have gone farther than other jurisdictions, many of which address spoilation merely by permitting an adverse inference against the party responsible for the spoilation. See *Kippenhan v. Chaulk Servs., Inc., supra* at 128, 697 N.E.2d 527, citing *Beers v. Bayliner Marine Corp.*, 236 Conn. 769, 775, 675 A.2d 829 (1996). Thus, once "a litigant or its expert knows or reasonably should know that the evidence might be relevant to a possible action," we have imposed a duty to preserve such evidence in the interests of fairness. *Kippenhan v. Chaulk Servs., Inc., supra* at 127, 697 N.E.2d 527.

Again, however, in recognizing such a duty, we simultaneously crafted the remedy for spoilation within the context of the underlying civil action. Sanctions in that action are addressed to the precise unfairness that would otherwise result. Thus, for example, an expert's testimony (or portions thereof) may be excluded so that the expert would not have the unfair advantage of posing as "the only expert with first-hand knowledge" of the item. *Nally v. Volkswagen of Am., Inc., supra* at 198, 539 N.E.2d 1017. Such a sanction "should go no further than to preclude tainted testimony." *Id.* at 199, 539 N.E.2d 1017. The imposition of such a remedy must also take into account the party responsible for the spoilation. Not only do we impose the sanction of excluding testimony, but we do so recognizing that such exclusion of testimony may be dispositive of the ultimate merits of the case, thereby imposing the ultimate sanction on the party responsible for the spoilation. See *Nally v. Volkswagen of Am., Inc., supra* at 195, 199, 539 N.E.2d 1017 (summary judgment for defendant may be appropriate if exclusion of expert testimony prevents plaintiff from making out prima facie case). Of course, if spoilation occurs in violation of a discovery order, various sanctions, including dismissal or judgment by default, may be imposed for that violation. See Mass. R. Civ. P. 37(b)(2), 365 Mass. 797 (1974).

Accordingly, we affirm the dismissal of plaintiffs' claims for spoilation, and leave the plaintiffs to pursue their remedies for the alleged spoilation in the underlying tort actions. At 544–553.

**Comment:** The court here strongly hinted that it would allow a claim for spoliation of evidence based upon breach of a contractual (or other) duty to preserve evidence. Note that the above case involved a suit by the adverse party against the expert witness. The adverse party and the expert had no contractual relationship. The expert did have a contractual relationship with the insurer in the case. Had the expert been sued by the *retaining* party for loss or destruction of evidence, such a suit may have been allowed to go forward on the theory of the expert breaching his retention contract (with an implied or express duty to preserve evidence) with his retaining party.

### Example 20.36: Case lost after spoliation of evidence by expert witness and spoliation instruction to the jury

*Vodusek v. Bayliner Marine Corp.,* 71 F.3d 148 (4th Cir. 1995)

In this products liability suit, a boat exploded, injuring the plaintiff. The plaintiff sued the manufacturer. The plaintiff sought to establish the defendants' liability through the testimony of an expert witness, offered as an expert in marine vessel safety and the causes of fires on vessels. In examining the boat to discover the cause of the explosion and fire, the expert, along with the plaintiff's two sons, employed destructive methods that rendered many portions of the boat useless for examination by the defendants and their experts.

Under the spoliation of evidence rule in this jurisdiction, an adverse inference may be drawn against a party who destroys relevant evidence. The plaintiff argued that she and her expert did not act in bad faith in destroying portions of the boat, but acknowledged that those portions were permanently destroyed as part of the expert's deliberate investigative efforts. While the expert may have decided that the destroyed portions of the boat were not relevant to his theory of the case, that conclusion ignored the possibility that others might have entertained different theories to which destroyed portions might have been relevant. In this case, both the defendants and the district court concluded that the destroyed portions were significant to the effort to explain where and why the boat explosion occurred. The jury was allowed to "draw an inference adverse to the plaintiffs based on the spoliation," and did so. Ultimately, the jury found in favor of the defendants. However, in this instance, the expert did not face civil liability for his spoliation.

**Comment:** This expert should have checked with counsel and received written authorization prior to using destructive methods in his investigation.

### Example 20.37: Destruction of pivotal physical evidence may result in liability

*Gootee v. Lightner,* 274 Cal. Rptr. 697 (Ct. App. 1990)

In this case, the California Court of Appeals held that the protective mantle of a testimonial privilege embraces not only the courtroom testimony of witnesses, but also work product prepared for the testimony of witnesses. Therefore, the failure of a witness to preserve work product generated in preparation for testimony is not subject to the spoliation tort as long as the destruction of the work product does not involve pivotal physical evidence. *Pivotal evidence* consists of evidence that is independently significant, distinct from the witness's report and testimony. Absent this independent significance, third persons such as expert or lay witnesses and adverse parties are immune from spoliation claims.

The *Gootee* court reasoned that considerations, such as access to the courts, encouragement of witnesses to testify truthfully, and finality in litigation would suffer if a witness was exposed to civil litigation "merely because the witness failed to retain every note or paper, generated in anticipation of testifying, which an unhappy litigant surmises would have benefited his cross-examination of the witness."

**Example 20.38: Expert's testimony limited after spoliation of evidence**
*Nally v. Volkswagen of America, Inc.,* 405 Mass. 191, 539 N.E.2d 1017, 1021 (Mass. 1989)
An expert hired by the plaintiff had conducted some tests on parts of an automobile that had been involved in an accident. During the course of the testing, the expert had destroyed those parts. Those parts thus were no longer available for later examination and replicate testing by the defendant. The defendant, in effect, moved to dismiss the case and that motion was allowed in the trial court. On appeal, the Supreme Judicial Court reversed but, in the process, set out the remedy that is to be used in the event of an expert's intentional or negligent spoliation of evidence that is material to a case in which the expert has been hired to testify. The court's explanation is clear:

> We conclude that, in a civil case, where an expert has removed an item of physical evidence and the item has disappeared, or the expert has caused a change in the substance or appearance of such an item in such circumstances that the expert knows or reasonably should know that the item in its original form may be material to litigation, the judge, at the request of a potentially prejudiced litigant, should preclude the expert from testifying as to his or her observations of such items before he or she altered them and as to any opinion based thereon. The rule should be applied without regard for whether the expert's conduct occurred before or after the expert was retained by a party to the litigation. The reason for the rule is the unfair prejudice that may result from allowing an expert deliberately or negligently to put himself or herself in the position of being the only expert with first-hand knowledge of the physical evidence on which the expert opinions as to defects and causation may be grounded. Furthermore, as is possible in this case, the physical items themselves, in the precise condition they were in immediately after an accident, may be far more instructive and persuasive to a jury than oral or photographic descriptions of them. As a matter of sound policy, an expert should not be permitted to intentionally or negligently destroy or dispose of such evidence, and then to substitute his or her own description of it.

**Example 20.39: Expert barred from testifying after spoliation of evidence and his client's case dismissed by judge**
*Patton v. Newmar Corp.,* 538 N.W.2d 116 (Minn. 1995)
The plaintiffs were traveling across California in their motor home when it caught on fire. The driver pulled off the road, and the plaintiffs attempted to get out by way of the passenger side door. While doing so, one of the plaintiffs tripped and allegedly sustained an injury to her back.

After the fire, the vehicle was towed to an auto salvage yard. Six months later, the plaintiffs' counsel retained an expert fire investigator to conduct an examination of what remained of the vehicle. During the course of this investigation, the expert extensively photographed the vehicle and removed and retained several unidentified components.

The plaintiffs commenced this action, alleging that the injuries were the result of the defendant's negligence in its design of what they characterized as a faulty dual fuel system. When the defendant requested to inspect the vehicle, it was informed that the location of the motor home was not known and that the unidentified components removed and retained by the plaintiffs' expert had been lost.

The trial court excluded the expert's testimony and evidence derived from his investigation. As a result, the plaintiffs could not prove their case and the court dismissed the action.

**Comment:** In the above case, the expert's testimony was necessary for the plaintiffs to prevail. When the expert was barred from testifying, the case was dismissed.

**Example 20.40: Testimony barred as sanction for unintentional spoliation**
*Hamann v. Ridge Tool Co.,* 539 N.W.2d 753, 757 (Mich. Ct. App. 1995)
The fifty-year-old plaintiff, an ironworker, broke his knee during a bridge reinforcement project when the cable hoist holding the cable supporting the plaintiff broke. When the hoist handle frame

broke, it shattered into several pieces, three of which were retrieved. One of the plaintiff's experts examined two of the pieces. The plaintiff's attorney then delivered the pieces to another of the plaintiff's experts. While in the custody of this second expert, those pieces were lost. Of the parties' experts, therefore, only the first had the opportunity to examine the pieces. The trial court allowed the plaintiff to offer expert testimony about the evidence. The appellate court reversed that decision, concluding that the trial court erred in permitting the plaintiff to offer testimony about evidence that was lost, even though it was lost unintentionally.

**Example 20.41: Spoliation of evidence does not result in penalty where spoliation caused no harm to adverse party**
*Gentry v. Toyota Motor Corp.*, 471 S.E.2d 485, 488 (Va. 1996)
Here, the Supreme Court of Virginia considered the circumstances under which a party may be sanctioned for spoliation of evidence by that party's expert. The case involved claims arising out of an accident that occurred when one of the plaintiffs lost control of her Toyota truck and crashed into a ravine. The plaintiffs' attorney hired a self-styled sudden acceleration expert who, without receiving authorization from anyone, used a hacksaw to cut into the truck's instrument panel and removed a temperature control cable. At a hearing, Toyota's expert testified that the plaintiffs' expert's conduct had prevented him from evaluating whether the temperature control cable had been involved in causing the accident. The plaintiffs then alleged a new cause of the accident based on the anticipated opinion of a new expert. That new opinion attributed the cause of the crash to a carburetor problem unrelated to the tampered-with temperature control cable. Toyota's expert acknowledged that his evaluation of the plaintiffs' new theory was not affected by anything the plaintiffs' first expert had done to the vehicle.

Nevertheless, the trial court dismissed the case based on the first expert's spoliation of evidence. The Supreme Court reversed and held that, because neither plaintiffs nor their counsel acted in bad faith, and because the first expert's conduct did not prejudice Toyota, the trial court had abused its discretion in dismissing the plaintiffs' action.

## 20.13 Conclusion: Risk Management for Experts

The potential liability of expert witnesses varies from jurisdiction to jurisdiction. To help avoid potential liability, experts should practice sound risk management. There are many techniques that can minimize an expert's exposure to loss as a result of her work as an expert witness. These techniques include the following.

### 1. Testifying honestly
Experts should *always* tell the truth. Truth is a defense to defamation actions. Truthful testimony is not perjurious. If an individual is untruthful, the law may offer her fewer protections from civil liability. Additionally, she could be subject to professional discipline and her reputation can and should suffer.

### 2. Doing one's homework and being competent
Experts should double- and triple-check their data, computations, and conclusions. Many experts get into trouble because of sloppy work. It is best to be careful and do a good job.

### 3. Show up
An expert witness is under a contractual duty to appear to give testimony in the case.

327

*4. Not discussing cases*
Expert immunity is strongest for statements made in court that are relevant to the litigation. It does not apply to statements irrelevant to the litigation.

*5. Maintaining insurance*
Experts should consider maintaining liability insurance against the risks associated with serving as an expert. Even if actual expert civil liability is relatively rare, such insurance will provide peace of mind and will pay the legal costs of defending claims. Experts should check their professional liability policies to see if these cover their expert witness work.

*6. Not destroying, losing, or misplacing evidence*
Experts must be very careful with evidence. They should not use destructive testing techniques unless all counsel and parties approve in writing.[34] In many cases, spoliation of evidence will result in the expert's retaining party losing the case and it may subject the expert to civil liability and negatively affect the expert's reputation.

*7. Calling cases as one sees them*
This is true even if the testimony is unfavorable to the party who retained the expert and contrary to how she originally intended to testify. Honesty and truthfulness are paramount.

*8. Avoiding conflicts of interest*
Experts should not get involved in any cases where there may be a conflict of interest.

*9. Think before suing retaining counsel for nonpayment of fee*
Many claims against experts begin as counterclaims after the expert sues for nonpayment of fees. Before suing a client for nonpayment, experts should consider whether they are vulnerable to countersuit.

*10. Be thoroughly familiar with rules of professional ethics*
Even though an expert witness generally enjoys broad immunity from suits from the opposing parties, there is no immunity that can be claimed when defending professional complaints related to her expert witness work. Please see Chapter 23 for more on ethics.

*11. Avoid being privately retained as an "agreed upon" expert by all parties*
At least one court has held that such experts do not enjoy the quasi-judicial immunity that court-appointed experts enjoy. Additionally, the expert does not enjoy "adverse expert immunity" as the expert is hired by and "friendly" to all sides. The liability is strong in this situation because it is highly likely that one or more parties will not be happy with the expert's opinions and may consider suing.

---

[34] Destructive testing is done frequently, but it is usually coordinated amongst all parties so they have a chance to get involved.

# Chapter 21  Privilege, Work Product, and Expert Discovery

## 21.1  Introduction
Experts who understand privilege, work product, and the limits to expert discovery will be best positioned to communicate with retaining counsel without making unnecessary mistakes.

## 21.2  Attorney-Client Privilege
The attorney-client privilege protects confidential communications between a client and an attorney and the attorney's agents made for the purpose of obtaining legal services or advice from that attorney. *Because an expert is not the retaining attorney's client, the attorney-client privilege generally does not protect communications between the expert and the retaining attorney.* Therefore, experts should assume that any oral or written communication they have with their retaining attorney will be discoverable and can and will be used against them and their clients.

*Attorney-client privilege generally*
The attorney-client privilege is held by the attorney's client.[1] Generally, an attorney has a privilege to refuse to disclose and to prevent any other person from disclosing communications intended to be confidential and made for the purpose of facilitating the rendition of professional legal services to the client.[2] The privilege is designed to encourage full and truthful communication between the client and attorney in order to improve the quality of the advice that a client receives. Only the communication is privileged, not the underlying facts. In essence, the privilege means only that *what a client says* about events to her lawyer is protected, not what the client may know about the events in controversy in the lawsuit.[3]

*The expert and the attorney-client privilege*
Generally, the privilege encompasses confidential communications made to a *representative* of the lawyer; that is, a person employed by the lawyer to assist in the rendition of professional legal services.[4] Thus, a nontestifying expert consultant may fall within the

---

[1] The work-product privilege, in contrast, belongs to the attorney.

[2] The Federal Rules of Evidence do not spell out particular privileges. Rather, Fed. Rule Evid. 501 provides for the application in federal court of federal common law privileges and state law privileges when state law governs the case. Federal common law and every state recognize the attorney-client privilege.

[3] Stanley D. Davis and Thomas D. Beisecker, "Discovering Trial Consultant Work Product: A New Way to Borrow an Adversary's Wits?" 17 *American Journal of Trial Advocacy* (1994) 580, 592.

[4] Jack B. Weinstein and Margaret A. Berger, 2 *Weinstein's Evidence* 503(c)[01](1989) 503–516. An example of the formulation of the privilege appears in what is now known as Supreme Court Standard 503: "A client has a privilege to refuse to disclose and to prevent any other person from disclosing confidential communications made for the purpose of facilitating the rendition of professional legal services to the client."

privilege. An expert hired as a witness who is expected to testify will not be a representative and will be precluded from invoking the privilege.[5] This is because the testifying expert will be presenting evidence rather than assisting the attorney in "render[ing] legal services."[6] However, a nontestifying consulting expert retained to assist counsel may qualify as a representative.

### Example 21.1: Attorney-client privilege does not protect communications between party and testifying expert or between retaining counsel and testifying expert

*Synthes Spine Co., L.P. v. Walden,* 232 F.R.D. 460 (E.D. Pa. 2005)
The court in this case held that attorney-client privilege does not protect communications between a party and his testifying expert nor those between an attorney and his testifying expert. The court stated:

> Plaintiff's expert must disclose the content of all oral communications that plaintiff's expert considered in formulating his opinions as a testifying expert in this case, regardless of whether these oral communications come from plaintiff's counsel or plaintiff itself. The Court sees no principled distinction between the discoverability of oral and written communications that a testifying expert considers in fashioning her opinions. See, e.g., Fed.R.Civ.P. 26(a)(2)(B) (requiring disclosure of "data or other information" considered by testifying expert); *TV-3, Inc. v. Royal Ins. Co. Of Am.,* 193 F.R.D. 490, 492 (S.D.Miss.2000) (requiring disclosure of all documents and oral communications reviewed by experts in connection with formulating opinions, even those ultimately rejected or not relied upon). Nor does the case-law expressly make such a distinction. See, e.g., *B.C.F. Oil Refining, Inc.,* 171 F.R.D. at 67 ("there does not seem to be a principled difference between oral and written communications between an expert and an attorney insofar as discoverability is concerned"); *Karn v. Ingersoll-Rand Co.,* 168 F.R.D. 633, 640 (N.D.Ind.1996); Theodore Banks, 2 Successful Partnering Between Inside and Outside Counsel § 33.34 (noting that "many courts permit discovery of oral communications between a corporation's counsel and their testifying expert"). Consequently, although plaintiff's expert need not disclose the content of privileged communications that plaintiff's expert never considered in formulating his opinion as to damages in the instant case, as such communications would not fall within the scope of Rule 26(a)(2)(B) and therefore would retain their privileged status, plaintiff's expert must nonetheless disclose the content of all oral communications between plaintiff, plaintiff's attorney, and/or plaintiff's expert that plaintiff's expert considered in fashioning his conclusions in this litigation. At 465.

### Example 21.2: Communications between attorney and nontestifying litigation consultant subject to attorney-client privilege

*Baxter Travenol Laboratories, Inc. v. Lemay,* 89 F.R.D. 410 (S.D. Ohio 1981)
In this case, a plaintiff's attorney hired a former associate of the defendant as a litigation consultant. The attorney hired the consultant to aid in an investigation to supply the basis for evaluating the plaintiff's legal rights, including potential litigation. The defendants sought to discover the substance of the conversations between the consultant and the attorney. The court applied the attorney-client privilege to the conversations and held them undiscoverable.

---

[5] Daisy Hurst Floyd, "A 'Delicate and Difficult Task': Balancing the Competing Interests of Federal Rule of Evidence 612, The Work Product Doctrine, and the Attorney-Client Privilege," 44 *Buffalo L. Rev.* (1996) 101.

[6] Another related basis for excluding testifying experts from the definition of representative is that their communications are subject to disclosure at trial and therefore cannot be considered confidential.

### Example 21.3: Communications between lawyer and nontestifying expert subject to attorney-client privilege

*Oines v. State,* 803 P.2d 884 (Alaska App. 1990)

In this criminal prosecution for drunk driving, the defendant's attorney secured a blood alcohol expert regarding blood test results. The court held that the results of the tests performed by the defense expert were privileged. It reasoned that the expert was a representative of the lawyer representing the client, and the results of the blood test were confidential communications between the lawyer and the lawyer's representative. The rationale for this protection in this particular case was to allow the attorney freedom to make an informed judgment regarding the best defense for his client without creating a witness for the state.

### Example 21.4: Privilege applied to expert's environmental audit report

*Olen Properties Corp. v. Sheldahl Inc.,* 1994 W.L. 212135 (C.D. Cal. April 12, 1994)

Here, a company had requested an environmental audit report, which it then provided to its in-house counsel. The court found that the report had been prepared for the purpose of securing an opinion of law, and thus the court applied the attorney-client privilege to the disclosure of the report.

### Example 21.5: Nontestifying expert within the privilege

*Bailey v. Meister Brau, Inc.,* 57 F.R.D. 11 (N.D. Ill. 1972)

In this case, the defendant sought to discover documents. The plaintiff's attorney hired a financial expert to analyze the financial situation of a company. One of the documents was prepared by the plaintiff and summarized discussions between the client, the attorney, and the expert. A second document summarized similar conversations and was prepared by the attorney. A third document, prepared by the plaintiff, contained projections and was read by an accountant retained by the attorney. The court found the privilege to apply to all the documents, based on the principle that confidentiality is not destroyed if a third party privy to the confidential communication is someone hired by the attorney to facilitate the rendition of legal services. The court held that both the expert and the accountant were hired to do so.

## *Waiver*

An adverse party may discover materials within the attorney-client privilege if the privilege is waived. *Waiver* can occur when the client discloses the information in a nonprivileged setting, most often a setting in the presence of a third party. An attorney, as the client's agent, may also waive the privilege for the client by disclosing information in a nonprivileged setting.[7] Such a waiver may take place purposely or inadvertently, although the standards vary from jurisdiction to jurisdiction. Waiver usually occurs when the client or lawyer discloses the confidential communication to someone other than those included within the scope of the privilege. As discussed in the previous section, a consulting expert generally falls within the scope of the privilege, while a testifying expert falls outside. In other words, if the client or the attorney discloses confidential information to a third party who happens to be a consulting expert, there has been no waiver. The same cannot be said for a disclosure to a testifying expert.

---

[7] Many jurisdictions will find that the disclosing attorney, as the client's agent, had implied authority to waive the privilege.

**Example 21.6: Waiver of privilege when expert is designated to testify**
*Multiform Dessicants v. Stanhope Products Co.,* 930 F.Supp. 45 (W.D.N.Y. 1996)
In this patent infringement/validity case, a party designated the attorney who prosecuted the patent as an expert witness. The court held that, by doing so, the party waived any attorney-client or work-product protection from the disclosure of all information pertaining to the subject matter of the expert's opinion.

**Example 21.7: Circulation of memo waives privilege**
*Bituminous Cas. Corp. v. Tonka Corp.,* 140 F.R.D. 381 (D. Minn. 1992)
Here, counsel for the plaintiff copied the plaintiff's environmental consultant on memoranda regarding the environmental consultant's report. The court found the attorney's action to have waived the client's attorney-client privilege regarding the memoranda.

**Example 21.8: Defendant waives privilege**
*Daniels v. Hadley Memorial Hospital,* 68 F.R.D. 583 (D.D.C. 1975)
In this medical malpractice action, the defendant anesthesiologist spoke with an insurance adjuster regarding the claim against her. The adjuster was an agent of the defendant's attorney because he was hired by the attorney to investigate. The adjuster conveyed some of the doctor's statements to the plaintiff's attorney. The plaintiff then sought to depose the agent regarding the defendant's statements. The court found that these statements would have been protected under the attorney-client privilege because the adjuster was a representative of the attorney. However, the defendant waived the privilege by testifying about the statements in her own deposition.

## 21.3 Work Product

Work product is essentially trial preparation material. This includes facts and information "hidden" in the attorney's file and the thought processes—and related notes, drafts, or discussions—of an attorney or a nontestifying expert that lead up to an opinion or a theory. *Core,* or *opinion, work product* refers to analysis, while *fact,* or *ordinary, work product* refers simply to factual information underlying an analysis. The work-product privilege held by the attorney attaches to materials prepared by counsel or *nontestifying* experts in anticipation of litigation and allows them to be discovered only upon a showing of need. The need that the discovering party must show varies and depends upon whether the materials sought are fact or opinion work product. The privilege may be waived.

Generally speaking, there is little protection given to expert witnesses who are expected to testify at trial. Much more protection is given to experts who will not be testifying at trial. Expert witnesses, therefore, should *assume* that any document they create or review and any conversation they have with retaining counsel will be subject to discovery.

The general breakdown of the work-product privilege and the expert discovery rules in the federal courts follows. These rules may be different in state courts.

1. The opinions of and the facts known by an expert retained in anticipation of litigation but not expected to testify (a nontestifying expert) are exempt from discovery unless the other side makes a showing of exceptional circumstances under which it is impracticable for them to obtain facts or opinions on the same subject by other means. Even if this burden is met, the court must still protect against the disclosure of the mental impressions, opinions, or legal theories of the attorney or the expert regarding the litigation (core work product). An opposing party can overcome

the discovery protection afforded nontestifying experts by showing *exceptional circumstances* under which it is impracticable for them to obtain facts or opinions on the same subject by other means.[8] Exceptional circumstance, in the words of one court, means simply a basic lack of ability to discover the equivalent information.[9]

2. Experts who will testify (testifying experts) must disclose opinions, the bases for them, and all information considered in forming them. Some federal courts, however, protect core work product (the attorney's mental impressions and legal theories) considered by testifying experts from discovery. Most federal courts, however, compel discovery of *everything* considered by the testifying expert, whether or not it contains the retaining attorney's mental impressions and legal theories. As such, experts should assume that anything they review or consider will be discoverable.

**Example 21.9: Testifying expert, everything oral or written considered is discoverable (including notes taken at meeting with counsel and conversations with retaining counsel)**
*Synthes Spine Co., L.P. v. Walden,* 232 F.R.D. 460 (E.D. Pa. 2005)
The court resolved the discovery dispute by ordering that everything (oral or written) considered by the testifying expert in this case be produced. The court's opinion provides a good overview of the current trend in the courts toward full disclosure of everything considered by the testifying expert. The court stated:

Defendants seek the production of all information "considered" by plaintiff's damages expert, John Stavros, in fashioning his conclusions in accordance with Federal Rule of Civil Procedure 26(a)(2) ("Rule 26(a)(2)"). Defendants seek this information regardless of its privileged status, arguing that Rule 26(a)(2) trumps or waives any type of privilege against disclosure. (*Id.,* at 8-18).

In response, plaintiff agrees to produce various categories of information that plaintiff's expert reviewed prior to issuing his expert report, subject to the execution of a confidentiality agreement as to several categories of documents. However, plaintiff still refuses to produce three types of information: (a) notes of plaintiff's expert during a September 23, 2005 meeting between plaintiff and plaintiff's in-house counsel, outside counsel, and expert; (b) the content of oral conversations between plaintiff, plaintiff's expert, and/or plaintiff's counsel; and (c) unredacted versions of documents reviewed by plaintiff's expert, including e-mails requesting and/or receiving information from plaintiff and sales charts pre-dating third-party discovery. Plaintiff contends that this information is protected against disclosure by virtue of the core work product privilege and/or the attorney-client privilege. (*Id.,* at 24).
A. Rule 26(a)(2)(B) requires the disclosure of all privileged information considered by a testifying expert.
B. Application
This Court now applies its interpretation of Rule 26(a)(2)(B) to the various documents and information that defendants seek to compel.
1. Materials Furnished to Plaintiff's Expert
The Court finds that plaintiff must disclose all materials, regardless of privilege, that plaintiff's expert generated, reviewed, reflected upon, read, and/or used in formulating his conclusions, even if these materials were ultimately rejected by plaintiff's expert in reaching his opinions. This includes disclosure, in whatever form the expert received them, of materials that plaintiff's counsel supplied to

---

[8] This rule is designed to prevent an opposing party from using the experts of its adversary in an effort to prepare for litigation. *Hartford Fire Ins. Co. v. Pure Air on the Lake, Ltd.,* 154 F.R.D. 202, 207 (N.D. Ind. 1993).
[9] *Eliasen v. Hamilton,* 111 F.R.D. 396 (N.D. Ill. 1986).

plaintiff's expert, including e-mails, summaries of lost sales, summary spreadsheets, pleadings, corporate information, sales charts and breakdowns, time analyses, retainer letters and invoices, and draft expert reports.

2. Expert Notes of the September 23, 2005 Meeting
This Court finds that plaintiff must produce those notes of the September 23, 2005 meeting that plaintiff's expert created in his role as a testifying expert, regardless of whether these notes contain information that falls under the protection of the attorney-client privilege or the work product privilege. These notes may contain information that bears on the credibility of plaintiff's expert, his report, and his trial testimony; and therefore are discoverable pursuant to Rule 26(a)(2)(B) and Rule 26(b)(4). However, in requiring this disclosure, the Court imposes two caveats. First, defendants are not entitled to any notes memorializing conversations unrelated to the instant case. (Noting that participants discussed a wide range of topics in both this case and a number of others). Second, defendants are not entitled to notes that have no relation to the expert's role as a testifying expert on the issue of damages, such as notes unrelated to the subject matter of plaintiff's expert testimony.

3. Oral Communications Between Plaintiff, Plaintiff's Expert, and/or Plaintiff's Counsel
Plaintiff's expert must disclose the content of all oral communications that plaintiff's expert considered in formulating his opinions as a testifying expert in this case, regardless of whether these oral communications come from plaintiff's counsel or plaintiff itself. The Court sees no principled distinction between the discoverability of oral and written communications that a testifying expert considers in fashioning her opinions. Consequently, although plaintiff's expert need not disclose the content of privileged communications that plaintiff's expert never considered in formulating his opinion as to damages in the instant case, as such communications would not fall within the scope of Rule 26(a)(2)(B) and therefore would retain their privileged status, plaintiff's expert must nonetheless disclose the content of all oral communications between plaintiff, plaintiff's attorney, and/or plaintiff's expert that plaintiff's expert considered in fashioning his conclusions in this litigation. At 461–465.

**Comment:** This decision reflects the majority view in the federal courts that everything considered by a testifying expert is discoverable, regardless of whether the information or other data contained the retaining attorney's mental impressions and/or legal theories. Experienced experts (and attorneys) maintain a transparent working relationship and are not concerned about producing their communications as they have nothing to hide. Since the expert's notes are discoverable, even if taken at a private meeting with counsel, experts are well advised to be cognizant of what they are writing in their notes.

### Example 21.10: No privilege attached to material disclosed to or considered by testifying expert
*JB ex rel. Palmer v. ASARCO, Inc.,* 225 F.R.D. 258 (N.D. Okla. 2004)
Any type of work product or other privilege is lost when the material is disclosed to and considered by a testifying expert.

**Comment:** Experts are prudent to assume that anything they review is discoverable and will be made available to opposing parties.

### Example 21.11: Dual-role expert: testifying expert and consultant in same case; ambiguity in expert's role to be resolved in favor of "discoverable"
*In Re Air Crash in Dubrovnik, Croatia,* 2001 WL 777433 (D. Conn. 2001)
This case comprises numerous wrongful death actions, all of which sought damages in connection with the crash of a United States Air Force aircraft in Dubrovnik, Croatia. The plaintiffs, estate representatives, and next of kin to the 34 people killed in the air crash brought these negligence and products liability actions against the defendants, alleging that they designed, manufactured, and sold a defective instrument approach chart that the air crew used.

# PRIVILEGE, WORK PRODUCT, AND EXPERT DISCOVERY

The discovery dispute arose out of the fact that the defendants initially hired an expert as a consultant in late 1997 only to later designate him as their expert witness under Rule 26(a)(2)(B) in September 1999. When the plaintiffs deposed the expert, it became apparent that he had reviewed numerous documents relating to the litigation, and that some of these documents were not identified in his Rule 26 report. The court inspected the documents and ordered some 7,100 to be produced. The defendant contended that 599 of them were privileged work product. The discussion then revolved around which documents the expert reviewed or generated in his consultant role and which documents were reviewed in his role as a testifying expert.

The *Air Crash in Dubrovnik* court considered the 599 contested documents and ordered production of most of them. The court noted that there was ambiguity as to the capacity in which the expert generated or reviewed these materials, and accordingly ordered production. One of the documents included handwritten notes by the expert, which the defendants maintained concerned discovery strategy and evaluation of the defendants' investigation. "That these notes may contain strategy or an evaluation of the defendants' investigation does not, by itself, render them privileged." *Id.* at 5. The court found the existence of the ambiguity to be determinative.

This analysis was repeated for numerous documents. Where the capacity in which the expert reviewed or created the document (testifying or consulting) was ambiguous, the court ordered production. When the distinction was clear, the court applied the work product protection. For example:

> As to documents CAM8571-8574 and CAM8577-8583, the court is persuaded that they were sent to [the expert] by defense counsel asking for [the expert's] "insight" with respect to a letter concerning several witnesses. Accordingly, the court concludes that the required "clear distinction" is present and the defendants need not produce these documents. *Id.* at 6.

Another example appears here:

> The defendants argue that [documents] should remain privileged because [the expert] created these documents to "assist counsel in their search for potential experts" and because they "have absolutely nothing to do with his expert opinions." [T]he court, on reconsideration, agrees with the defendants and concludes that these documents need not be produced. *Id.*

The fact that the expert considered the document before being designated as a testifying witness did not determine the expert's role.

The court also considered several documents that the defendants maintained were opinion work product. The court explained its order to produce these documents:

> The defendants correctly note that defense counsel generated these documents and that they extensively discuss factual information concerning the crash, Air Force procedures, and the flight crew, as well as various aspects of defense strategy. This, however, [does] not mark the end of the court's inquiry. As noted earlier, the court must determine whether these documents relate to the expert statement and were considered by [the expert] in forming his opinion. The defendants do not—and cannot—deny that these documents address topics also contained in [the expert's] expert statement. The subjects covered in these documents include, but are not limited to, the following: information about the crew on the [airplane], various...charts, the flight path of the aircraft, the alleged negligence of the aircraft crew, and a variety of other topics relating to [the expert's] opinion. Even if these documents do represent product, the defendants cannot shield them from discovery after they have been passed on to the testifying expert. *Id.* at 11.

**Comment:** When a consulting expert is later designated to testify, it is prudent for the expert to assume that he may be required to produce all prior documents. Counsel who changes the status of an expert from a consultant to a testifying expert does so at his own peril.

### Example 21.12: The expert's compensation and his "marching orders" can be discovered and the expert cross-examined thereon

*TV-3, Inc. v. Royal Ins. Co. of America,* 193 F.R.D. 490, 491 (S.D. Miss. 2000)
In this case, the defendants requested a protective order relieving them and their expert witnesses from the obligation to respond to certain subpoenas duces tecum directed to their expert witnesses. At issue was whether Rule 26(a)(2) requires that a party produce communications of any kind by and between its attorneys and its testifying experts, regardless of whether a claim of attorney work product would ordinarily protect the communications from disclosure.

The court noted the split in authority on this issue and that the only Mississippi case on point, *Kennedy v. Baptist Memorial Hospital-Booneville, Inc.,* 179 F.R.D. 520 (N.D. Miss. 1998) held that no core attorney work product must ordinarily be divulged by an expert under 26(a)(2)(B) unless special factual circumstances exist. The court then explicitly rejected the *Kennedy* holding and instead adopted the opposite approach that Rule 26, requiring disclosure of material "considered," "allows discovery of all communications between counsel and a retained testifying expert, **even if those communications contain the attorneys' mental impressions or trial strategy or is otherwise protected by the work product privilege**" [emphasis in original]. At 491. The court explained its reasoning:

> We do not imply that this is the case in the present litigation, but only the most naive of experienced lawyers or judges could fail to realize that in our present legal culture money plus the proper "marching orders" will get an "expert" witness who will undertake to prove almost anything....It is most consistent with this trend to say that when an attorney hires an expert both the expert's compensation and his "marching orders" can be discovered and the expert cross-examined thereon. If the lawyer's "marching orders" are reasonable and fair, the lawyer and his client have little to fear. If the orders are in the nature of telling the expert what he is being paid to conclude, appropriate discovery and cross-examination thereon should be the consequence. Such a ruling is most consistent with an effort to keep expert opinion testimony fair, reliable and within the bounds of reason. *Id* at 492.

The court then announced its finding:

> We therefore find that all documents and other communications as described in the subject subpoenas considered by the experts in formulating the opinions the experts are expected to express at trial must be produced to the Plaintiffs. We further interpret the word "considered" as the Court in the *Baxter* case did, that it is intended to encompass: (a) all documents and oral communications relied upon by the experts in formulating their opinions; and (b) all documents and oral communications reviewed by the experts in connection with the formulation of their opinions, but ultimately rejected or not relied upon. *Baxter,* 1993 WL 360674 at 1. We anticipate that that definition will include correspondence and materials from attorneys to the experts which would have been protected by the work product doctrine prior to the 1993 Amendments.
> The undersigned also finds that any material generated by the testifying expert in connection with the subject litigation is not protected and should be produced, so any communications by the expert to the attorneys is discoverable. Also, any documents or communications containing *facts* or factual information about the issues in the lawsuit are not protected by any privilege and must be produced. *Id.*

**Comment:** A key way to attack an expert witness's opinion is to show that the opinion was improperly influenced by retaining counsel. Such attacks can be quite effective because they are likely to be easily understood by the jury.

**Example 21.13: Opinion work product protected: legal theories of retaining attorney to be redacted out**
*Smith v. Transducer Technology, Inc.,* 197 F.R.D. 260 (D. V.I. 2000)
This case fell on the other side of the split regarding opinion work product provided to experts (i.e., that opinion work product is protected from discovery). The court ordered the opinion work product to be redacted before the documents were produced:

> [W]here documents considered by Defendants' experts contain both facts and legal theories of the attorney, Plaintiff is entitled only to discovery of the facts "...where such combinations exist it will be necessary to redact the document so that full disclosure is made of facts presented to the expert and considered in formulating his or her opinion, while protection is accorded the legal theories and the attorney-expert dialectic..." (Citing *Bogosian*, 738 F.2d at 595) At 262.

**Comment:** This is an example of the minority view in federal courts whereby core work product considered by a testifying expert is not discoverable.

**Example 21.14: Substantial need burden not met to compel discovery of work product from nontestifying expert where all underlying factual documents were produced, plaintiff free to conduct own analysis**
*In re Natural Gas Commodities Litigation,* 232 F.R.D. 208 (S.D.N.Y. 2005)
Plaintiffs moved to compel the production of certain documents withheld by the defendants on the basis of attorney-client and/or work product privilege. The requested documents contained analysis of data generated in the course of the defendants' internal investigations related to natural gas trade reporting inaccuracies. The documents were disclosed to government agencies, including the Federal Energy Regulatory Commission, the Commodity Futures Trading Commission, and the United States Department of Justice (collectively, "government agencies"), in connection with investigations of the defendants by the government agencies. The documents were voluntarily produced to the government agencies pursuant to explicit non-waiver agreements. The materials included third-party consultants' analyses and comparisons of the defendants' actual natural gas trades and trades reported to trade publications. The court held that the plaintiffs did not make the required showing of substantial need to compel discovery of the documents in question. It stated:

> Plaintiffs argue that even if Defendants' disclosure of the requested documents did not waive work product privilege, Plaintiffs are entitled to production of the documents because Plaintiffs have shown substantial need for the materials. Pursuant to Fed.R.Civ.P. 26(b)(3), work product privilege may be overcome upon a showing that the party has substantial need for the requested materials in the preparation of the party's case and that the party is unable to obtain the substantial equivalent of the materials by other means without "undue hardship." Fed.R.Civ.P. 26(b)(3). Where, as here, the requested documents contain "mental impressions, conclusions, opinions, or legal theories of an attorney or other representative" (Fed.R.Civ.P. 26(b)(3)), the required showing of substantial need is particularly stringent.
>
> The Court affirms Magistrate Judge Peck's finding that Plaintiffs failed to demonstrate a substantial need for the requested documents. Defendants have produced all of the factual documents underlying the work product analysis provided to the government agencies, with the exception of any documentation underlying the interview memoranda. Therefore, Plaintiffs can perform their own analysis of the trading data. Furthermore, Plaintiffs failed to show substantial need for the interview memoranda. To demonstrate substantial need, a party must demonstrate an inability to obtain equivalent evidence without undue hardship. See *Madanes*, 199 F.R.D. at 150. Plaintiffs have not demonstrated that they would be unable to acquire the data underlying the interview memoranda without undue hardship, as Plaintiffs have not demonstrated why they would not be able to depose the individuals interviewed during the internal investigation. Therefore, the Court concludes that the Plaintiffs have not

made a sufficient showing to overcome work product privilege pursuant to Fed.R.Civ.P. 26(b)(3). At 212–213.

**Comment:** Work product considered or produced by nontestifying expert consultants need only be produced in those rare circumstances where the requesting party is unable to obtain the substantial equivalent of the materials by other means without "undue hardship." The court in this case found that burden not to be met and thus held that the work product need not be produced.

**Example 21.15: Nontestifying expert, circumstances not exceptional, discovery not allowed**
*Hartford Fire Ins. Co. v. Pure Air on the Lake Ltd.,* 154 F.R.D. 202 (N.D. Ind. 1993)
In this litigation arising out of a subsurface collapse that resulted in extensive property damage to a construction site at a generating plant, the defendant sought to discover the reports of the plaintiff's nontestifying engineer expert. The reports contained information on the cause of the cave-in and attendant property damage. The court found that the subject of discovery was the cause of the collapsed pipes and that the defendant had ample opportunity to investigate and evaluate these pipes during the excavation process and, in fact, did undertake an investigation. Thus, the defendant made no showing that it could not discover equivalent information regarding the cause of the pipes' collapse.

**Example 21.16: Circumstances exceptional, discovery allowed from nontestifying expert**
*Delcastor, Inc. v. Vail Assoc., Inc.,* 108 F.R.D. 405 (D. Colo. 1985)
In this case, a mudslide destroyed a construction site. The next day, the defendant's consulting expert was at the site and subsequently prepared a report. The plaintiff's expert was unable to inspect the site until five days later, when the conditions had considerably changed and the conditions of the site immediately after the mudslide could not be reconstructed. The court found exceptional circumstances and ordered the nontestifying expert's report disclosed.

**Comment:** This is an example of the type of situation where the court will order a nontestifying expert consultant's work product produced.

**Example 21.17: Conversation between testifying expert and retaining counsel discoverable**
*BCF Oil Ref., Inc. v. Consolidated Edison Co.,* 171 F.R.D. 57 (S.D.N.Y. 1997)
Here, the court considered a request by the defendant to discover the substance of conversations between a testifying expert and counsel that contained the attorney's mental impressions. The court noted that "data or other information" means documents or conversations, and that an expert could be asked about such conversations at deposition. However, the court held that an attorney's notes recording such conversations, which were never shown to the expert, were not discoverable. The expert could not have "considered" the documents if he never saw them.

**Comment:** Experts should expect to be asked at deposition and trial about their conversations with retaining counsel.

**Example 21.18: Counsel's statements to testifying expert that contained counsel's mental impressions about prior expert were not discoverable**
*Maynard v. Whirlpoool Corp.,* 10 F.R.D. 85 (S.D.W.Va. 1995)
Here, the plaintiffs sought to compel the defendant's expert to respond to deposition questions inquiring about statements defense counsel made to the expert regarding a former expert. The plaintiffs hoped to show that defense counsel was dissatisfied with the former expert. The court found that the conversation was not a document or tangible thing, thus Rule 26(b)(3) was not applicable. It found that the conversation contained counsel's mental impressions and looked to

the common law to determine that these impressions were privileged. The court did not allow the discovery of the conversation.

**Comment:** Although some courts may protect portions of conversations between the expert and retaining counsel from discovery, it is generally a best practice to assume that everything said will be discoverable and act accordingly.

### Example 21.19: Documents in insurance company file were prepared "in anticipation of litigation," thus work product rules applied

*Magee v. Paul Revere Life Ins. Co.,* 172 F.R.D. 627 (E.D.N.Y. 1997)

Here, an insurance company hired a psychiatrist to review a claims file that included correspondence between outside counsel and the claims manager. The expert was designated a testifying expert and the plaintiff sought discovery of several pieces of correspondence that the expert had considered in forming his opinion. The court explained that if a document was prepared exclusively or principally to assist in anticipated or ongoing litigation, then the documents would meet this prong of the work product analysis. However, if the materials were assembled in the ordinary course of business, they are not shielded. The court then noted that this distinction is especially difficult to ascertain in insurance cases. Then it held that the document that was generated after litigation had begun was prepared in anticipation of litigation. The second two documents were created after the claimant's counsel had threatened litigation. The court found that because of this, it was reasonable for defendants to anticipate litigation. Thus, work-product protection was triggered.

**Comment:** Work product applies to documents and tangible things prepared in anticipation of litigation or for trial. Where a lawsuit has been filed there is usually not an issue that the work product was prepared "for trial." Before a lawsuit is filed, however, sometimes the issue arises as to whether the document was prepared "in anticipation of litigation" and thus would be protected from discovery.

### Example 21.20: Example of documents prepared "in anticipation of litigation"

*Logan v. Commercial Union,* 96 F.3d 971 (7th Cir. 1996)

In this case, a plaintiff-insured sued the insurer based upon a denial of coverage. The plaintiff sought to discover documents composed by the insurer relating to the processing and disposition of his claim. The insurer had produced much of the claim file, but withheld several documents that had been created after the plaintiff's claim had been denied on the grounds that they were protected by work-product protection. The court inspected the documents in chambers and found that the work-product doctrine applied. It found that the documents were not only created after the initial claim had been submitted, investigated, and denied, but after the plaintiff filed suit with the state worker's compensation board. Moreover, the court found that the general subject matter of the documents concerned how the insurer planned to defend against the plaintiff's worker's compensation claim. The court noted, however, that "the mere fact that litigation does eventually ensue does not, by itself, cloak materials…with the work product privilege; the privilege is not that broad."

### Example 21.21: Investigation by federal agency sufficient to make documents "in anticipation of litigation"

*Martin v. Monfort, Inc.,* 150 F.R.D. 172 (D. Colo. 1993)

In this case, the Department of Labor sought to compel the discovery of studies conducted by the corporate employer under investigation. Counsel for the corporate employer was contacted by the

Department of Labor concerning the corporate employer's potential violations of the Fair Labor Standards Act. The studies were then conducted. The court found that the work-product privilege protected the documents and that "[i]nvestigation by a federal agency presents more than a remote prospect of future litigation, and provides reasonable grounds for anticipating litigation sufficient to trigger application of the work-product doctrine."

**Example 21.22: Anticipation of litigation: insurance documents**
*Henderson v. Zurn Industries, Inc.,* 131 F.R.D. 560 (S.D. Ind. 1990)
Here, the defendant's employee sued for injuries sustained when a ladder fell on him. The defendant asserted work-product privilege for its insurance company's files regarding the claim at issue. The court found that these documents were privileged because they had been prepared after the insurance company had received a very detailed letter from the plaintiff's attorney regarding settlement negotiations. The letter also contained a threat to file a lawsuit. The court applied privilege to all insurance documents prepared after the receipt of this letter.

**Example 21.23: Documents not prepared in anticipation of litigation**
*Taroli v. General Elec. Co.,* 114 F.R.D. 97 (N.D. Ind. 1987)
Here, the plaintiff brought a products liability action against the manufacturer of a light bulb that exploded and injured the plaintiff. The plaintiff sought to discover documents prepared by the defendant's insurance carrier. These documents contained statements of third parties taken by the carrier and a report prepared by an independent adjusting company at the request of the insurance carrier. The defendant claimed work-product privilege. It asserted that the insurance company had conducted its investigation (and hired the independent adjuster) in anticipation of litigation, because it had received a letter of subrogation and also because the report was prepared after the decision to deny coverage had been made. The court denied the work-product protection. It noted that the mere fact that the plaintiff has consulted an attorney is not enough to trigger a reasonable anticipation of litigation and that a subrogation notice cannot be used to create a work-product privilege in every instance.

**Example 21.24: Not in anticipation of litigation/routine business practice**
*Harper v. Auto-Owners Ins. Co.,* 138 F.R.D. 65 (S.D. Ind. 1991)
The plaintiff-insured sued the defendant after the defendant denied his claim for coverage resulting from a fire that destroyed his business. The plaintiff sought production of several documents produced in relation to his claim. The defendant asserted that all documents related to the claim from the date of the fire were privileged. The insurance company had hired counsel and arson investigators after the fire department's report indicated that the fire was incendiary in origin. The reports of the fire experts and of counsel's examination of the claimant were included in the file. The defendant asserted that the notice of the possibility of arson, based upon the fire department's reports, was in itself a threat of litigation and that all actions taken after that notice were in anticipation of litigation. The court rejected the claim of privilege. It found that the insurer's investigations were a routine business practice, thus they were not motivated because of the anticipation of litigation.

**Example 21.25: Fact work product discoverable at deposition, opinion work product not discoverable**
*Haworth, Inc. v. Herman Miller, Inc.,* 162 F.R.D. 289 (W.D. Mich. 1995)
In this patent infringement action, the defendant deposed the plaintiff's trial expert. Defense counsel asked the expert to testify about discussions he had with plaintiff's counsel regarding the defendant's product manuals. The plaintiff's counsel had provided these manuals to the expert.

The court noted that all factual information considered by an expert must be disclosed in the expert's report. It went on to say that attorneys should no longer be able to make work-product privilege arguments regarding materials containing facts or assemblages of facts because they are obligated to disclose all factual information on their own. The court then discussed which questions regarding the conversations were allowed. If the question tests whether certain facts had not been provided to the expert for his consideration, it would be allowed. The court did not allow questions regarding opinion work product.

### Example 21.26: Majority rule, opinion work product discoverable
*Musselman v. Phillips,* 1997 U.S. Dist. Lexis 16898 (D. Md. Oct. 14, 1997)
In this intentional tort case, the defendant sought production of two letters written by the plaintiff's counsel to expert psychiatrists retained by the plaintiff to testify at trial. The court found that the experts had considered the letters, which contained counsel's mental impressions and legal theories. The court held that when an attorney communicates otherwise protected work product to an expert witness retained for purposes of providing opinion testimony at trial, whether factual in nature or containing the attorney's opinions or impressions, that information is discoverable.

### Example 21.27: Opinion work product discoverable
*Karn v. Rand,* 168 F.R.D. 633 (N.D. Ind. 1996)
In this personal injury action, the defendant sought production of a medical chronology concerning the plaintiff's injury. The chronology was prepared by the plaintiff's attorney's staff and was reviewed by the plaintiff's vocational expert. The defendant also sought production of a letter from the plaintiff's counsel to the plaintiff's liability expert. The court held that "data or other information considered" by the expert means all materials containing work product. Thus, both documents were discoverable. The court noted that this "bright line" rule actually preserved work-product protection because there would be no uncertainty as to what was discoverable. However, the court did mention that oral communication containing work product is not discoverable.

### Example 21.28: Everything considered by the testifying expert is discoverable
*B.C.F. Oil Ref. v. Consolidated Edison Co.,* 171 F.R.D. 57 (S.D.N.Y. 1997)
Here, an oil refiner brought an action against an electric utility and oil transporters, alleging that the utility distributed, and the transporters delivered, contaminated oil to the refinery. The defendants sought production of numerous documents by the plaintiff, which the plaintiff claimed were protected by the work-product privilege. The expert was hired not only to give testimony regarding contamination, but also to assist the plaintiff's counsel with technical issues during the discovery process. The court considered four sets of documents.

The first set of documents was produced by or considered by the expert in his consulting role, rather than his testifying role. Thus, they were not discoverable.

The second set of documents was written by the expert during the preparation of his report and his expert testimony. The court found that all documents, including drafts and memoranda, produced by an expert as he develops his opinions to be presented at trial are discoverable. It ordered production of this set of documents.

The third set of documents contained facts and "assemblages of facts" provided to the expert by counsel. The court found that this factual information did not deserve as much protection as opinion work product and that it was discoverable as "data or other information considered" by the expert.

A fourth set of documents contained the mental impressions and explicit litigation strategies of the plaintiff's counsel. The court held that these were discoverable, relying on the open discovery policies underlying Rule 26 and granting much weight to the 26(a)(2) "data or other information considered" language.

Finally, the court discussed oral communications between the expert and counsel that contained the attorney's mental impressions. The court noted that "data or other information" means documents or conversations, and that an expert could be asked about such conversations at deposition. However, the court held that an attorney's notes recording such conversations, notes that were never shown to the expert, were not discoverable. The expert could not have "considered" the documents if he never saw them.

### Example 21.29: Opinion work product discoverable if it was shared with the testifying expert

*Lamonds v. General Motors Corp.,* 180 F.R.D. 302 (W.D. Va. July 2, 1998)
Here, the plaintiff brought a products liability action against an automobile manufacturer, alleging that a design defect in the automobile caused her to be severely injured in an accident. The defendant sought production of two documents that were created by the plaintiff's legal team and shared with the plaintiff's experts. The court declared that everything "considered" by the experts in forming their opinions was discoverable—in effect, stating that Rule 26(a)2 "trumps" the work-product protection of Rule 26(b)(3). Thus, the court held that the plaintiff must produce the documents, even though they contained opinion work product.

### Example 21.30: Discovery of opinion work product considered by testifying expert not allowed

*Moore v. R.J. Reynolds Tobacco Company,* 194 F.R.D. 659 (S.D. Iowa 2000)
In this case, the defendant requested production of communications between plaintiff's counsel and plaintiff's expert. The plaintiff claimed disclosure of these communications was not required because they were opinion work product, and opinion work product is entitled to immunity even when the attorney for the party claiming immunity discloses the communication to an expert to consider in preparation for testifying.

The court examined the documents to determine whether, and what kind, of work product they contained and whether they were protected under the work-product doctrine. It found that several documents contained opinion work product. The court noted that the Eighth Circuit had not addressed the issue of whether opinion work product is immune from discovery even if shared with an expert witness in preparation for litigation, and it noted the federal split of authority.

The court adopted the *Murphy* reasoning that opinion work product has nearly absolute immunity from discovery, and such work product can be discovered only in very rare and extraordinary circumstances. *Id.* at 664. "This conclusion is bolstered by the persuasive reasoning of those courts holding attorney-opinion materials considered by an expert in preparation for trial are protected from required disclosure." The court then found that the defendants' need to cross-examine experts in this case was not among the very rare and extraordinary circumstances required to establish an exception to the nearly absolute immunity the Eighth Circuit affords to opinion work product.

**Comment:** Attorneys who provide documents to their experts do so at their peril. If these documents are later required to be produced it is the attorney, not the expert, who should be concerned about their production.

## 21.4 Documents Produced by Experts

All written statements prepared by a testifying expert should be assumed to be discoverable. This includes administrative documents, such as time sheets, bills, engagement letters, and fax cover sheets. It bears repeating that experts and their staffs should commit to writing only what is necessary to assist in the preparation of a report or testimony. Retaining counsel will often try to reinforce this by asking an expert not to write a report until the expert has discussed his initial findings with her.

### 21.5 Draft Reports

The law on draft reports is unsettled at best. "The weight of authority is that testifying experts and the attorneys do not share any privileges, it can be persuasively argued that any draft *which is circulated* is discoverable, regardless of its marginalia."[10] (Emphasis added.) At least one court has suggested, *in dicta*, that drafts "prepared solely by the expert while formulating the proper language in which to articulate that experts' own, ultimate opinion arrived at by the expert's own work or those working at the expert's personal direction" might be protected from discovery and need not be preserved by an expert *(Trigon Insurance Company v. United States,* 204 F.R.D. 277, 283 (E.D. Virg. 2001)). At least one federal judge in Northern California has a standing order following *Trigon's* dicta that states that intermediate drafts prepared solely by the testifying expert and not provided or discussed with anyone else need not be produced. These situations should be contrasted with the situations where draft reports are circulated by the expert to retaining counsel or nontestifying experts. These latter types of draft reports will almost always be discoverable because they can be highly probative of any outside influence on the expert's opinions.

Opposing counsel often attempts to obtain these communications through drafts of expert reports that were circulated between the expert and the retaining attorney to shed light on the extent and nature of the attorney's influence on the formation of the expert's opinion. Experts and attorneys can perhaps minimize the discoverability of drafts by communicating over the phone rather than in writing. Then, the expert can answer truthfully that no prior draft ever circulated. Opposing counsel will look for an analysis being removed from the expert's report because the result was not favorable, thus establishing bias and the unreliability—or falsity—of the expert's opinion. She would love for the expert to say to the jury that he "destroyed" previous drafts of the report, which might get the jury wondering why the expert would destroy something that should bolster his testimony. Opposing counsel would also love to see a trail of drafts to show that an expert's opinion was directed by the retaining attorney.

The classic example of overreaching by retaining counsel is the case of *Occulto v. Adamar of New Jersey, Inc.,* 125 FRD 611 (D.N.J. 1989). In this case a draft report surfaced that was *almost* identical to the final report. There was one little problem, however. There was a legend on the top of the draft report that read: "PLEASE HAVE RETYPED ON YOUR OWN STATIONARY. THANK YOU." Not only did the lawyer write the report for the expert, the lawyer couldn't spell "stationery" correctly.

---

[10] Alan B. Rich, Advanced Evidence and Discovery Course, Chapter L: "Discovery of Expert Materials" (Nov. 1996). State Bar of Texas: State Bar of Texas Professional Development CLE Online, Austin.

Kim K. Burke, an environmental lawyer, discusses the discovery of drafts:

> The first risk of alteration is obvious: trial counsel for the other side will ask for all drafts of the report, will focus upon any differences in the text, and will ask why those changes were made. When the testimony is elicited that the attorney was responsible for the change in the document, this will seriously affect the credibility of the expert witness, and his/her independent opinion concerning technical matters. Typically, opposing counsel is baffled when no draft report has been prepared and that counsel would have enough confidence in his or her experts to allow a report to go directly to final. The final reports typically look less lawyer-like, and more like the product of a consultant, which they are. Again, the ability to follow this approach depends upon the trust that the trial attorney has in the experts, and the experts in each other.[11]

Another of the attorney's considerations regarding drafts:

> I am always delighted to have opposing counsel take the opportunity to carefully mark up every draft prepared by an expert so that I can show that the opinions rendered by the expert are not those of the expert, but rather the expert acting as the mouthpiece for the lawyer.[12]

Because a draft report shared with retaining counsel can be easily used against the expert, it is generally a best practice not to circulate draft reports with retaining counsel. It is a better practice to send retaining counsel your final report. If the expert wants to run things by retaining counsel prior to finalizing the report, this is best done on the telephone. If changes need to be made to a written report circulated to counsel because the expert forgot to address an area or had a typo in the report, an addendum to the original report can be sent. The ideal, as always, is complete transparency and truthfulness.

### Example 21.31: Draft reports destroyed prior to deposition

*W.R. Grace and Co.-Conn. V. Zotos International, Inc.,* 2000 WL 1843258 (W.D.N.Y. 2000) The court dealt with a discovery battle that the expert was drawn into after retaining counsel instructed the expert to destroy draft reports prior to deposition. The court stated:

> During the deposition, Barber confirmed the existence of documents in his file which were not produced to Plaintiff, including Defendant's Request for Proposals, the final contract between Plaintiff and Barber for his services, a diary containing notes of Barber's meetings with defense counsel, phone calls, and other work Barber performed on the case, and correspondence and memoranda between Barber and defense counsel after October 1, 1999. Hogan Affidavit, ¶ 5. Additionally, Barber testified that prior drafts of his final report, including written comments to him on the drafts received from Defendant's attorneys had been destroyed two weeks prior to the deposition upon instructions from defense counsel. *Id.* Specifically, Barber testified he had been instructed to discard the drafts in order "not…to confuse things." At 3.

---

[11] Kim K. Burke, "The Use of Experts in Environmental Litigation: A Practitioner's Guide," 25 *N. Ky. L. Rev.* (1997) 111, 136.

[12] Kim K. Burke, "The Use of Experts in Environmental Litigation: A Practitioner's Guide," 25 *N. Ky. L. Rev.* (1997) 111, 136.

Not only was the expert eventually forced to produce his diary entries, but the integrity of his work product was called into question.

> The materials provided for *in camera* review include copies of Barber's draft reports transmitted to Defendant's attorneys via facsimile, on September 28 and 30, 1999, together with Barber's request for the attorneys' comments. On each page of the typewritten texts appear hand written notations, presumably written by one of Defendant's attorneys to whom the drafts were sent for review and comments. Defendant states that only the notes of counsel on the September 30, 1999 draft report were communicated to Barber. Defendant's Memorandum at 20. Defendant also represents that three documents, constituting redrafts of Barber's draft reports, were transmitted from defense counsel to Barber, *id.*, thereby implying they were prepared by counsel to assist Barber in formulating his final report.
> The court's review of the documents shows that although some of the revisions suggested and as redrafted by counsel appear to represent matters of form, others are plainly directed to matters of substance. For example, in the September 30th draft report, the section of the document addressing selection of remedial alternatives was then blank with an "In progress" notation only. However, in the September 30th and October 1st drafts, transmitted from Defendant's attorneys to Barber, the section includes two full paragraphs of text discussing the draft's conclusion that the remedy selected by Plaintiff was not consistent with the National Contingency Plan. Thus, the exchange of documents between counsel and Barber raises an issue of the extent to which Barber's final report represents Barber's own product or that of Defendant's attorneys. At 5.

In the end, the court ordered all of the destroyed material and supporting documents to be produced.

**Comment:** Note that the drafts ordered produced in this case were shared with retaining counsel and thus were highly probative of counsel influencing the expert's opinion. Also note that the expert in this case got in trouble for following retaining counsel's instructions to destroy the draft reports. The experts who will have long careers are generally those who do not blindly follow counsel's instructions when they don't feel right. One technique to deal with any requests from retaining counsel that do not seem ethical is to ask that retaining counsel put the request in writing. This simple request eliminates many potential problems.

### Example 21.32: Buried draft report surfaces

The *Pennsylvania Law Weekly* reported on a case dealing with expert reports. The article[13] deals with an alleged attempt to change a report and then bury the first version. Counsel was alleged to have failed to turn over the first draft of a doctor's report that was unfavorable. He then allegedly had the doctor change his opinion. The draft report came to light when it was inadvertently faxed to defense counsel. The deposition transcript reported in the article reveals the following.

> On direct, Michael M. Badowski, of Margolis Edelstein, questioned Boal about what he believed was the cause of Johnson's injury. "I do not believe [Johnson's low back pain] was related to the car accident but was related to what we call degenerative disc disease of the lumbar spine," he answered. The doctor called this—as well as Johnson's failure to promptly complain of back pain—"the crux of this case."
> On his cross of Boal, Brandes asked, "Any drafts of your report, or you just wrote your report and gave it to defense counsel?"
> "Just wrote it and gave it to him" Boal answered.
> "You wrote in your report on the last page that no one can say that the back injury and the surgery are directly related to the motor vehicle accident due to that few week gap between the date of the

---

[13] "Harrisburg Attorney under Fire over Expert Report," *Pennsylvania Law Weekly,* 8/7/2000.

accident and her first complaint of pain....But it's really not true, there are people who can say it's directly related, right?" asked Brandes. It was then, over objection by Badowski, that Brandes confronted Boal with the earlier report the doctor had written. "You said previously the draft you're telling this jury about was the one and only draft. Doctor, isn't this the first draft of your report you sent to defense counsel, Mr. Kronthat?"

Boal said he did not recall whether he sent the draft to Kronthal, nor did he recall whether he discussed the first draft with Kronthal but said, "I'm sure [Kronthal] pointed out things that would make me think there was something different than my opinion, which would have necessitated writing a second draft."

The Judge was quite upset with counsel due to the fact that the second report had a completely different opinion on causation from the first. The Judge warned counsel as follows:

"That's why we're going through this rather extraordinary proceeding here this morning. You could be criminally prosecuted, given a certain set of facts, for subornation of perjury, criminal conspiracy to be involved in perjury, and perjury as an accomplice. Those are all felonies for which you can spend a substantial portion of your life in a penitentiary."

Counsel's explanation left something to be desired.

"Judge, if there was any intent to bury this report from the beginning...the fact of the matter is it wouldn't have been in our file in the first place. We would have thrown it away," said Banko. "What we've had at all turns in this case, unfortunately, Judge...is really a comedy of errors."

"Oh, this is no comedy," said Clark.

"The allegations are serious, Judge."

"Serious is an understatement...so serious you can be disbarred for this."

**Comment:** It is reasonable to assume that the expert in this case had his credibility seriously and irreparably ruined. Obviously, this expert should not have allowed himself to have been improperly influenced by counsel and should not have been dishonest about the existence of a prior draft report.

### Example 21.33: Draft report and cover letter discoverable

*Krisa v. Equitable Life Insurance Society,* 196 F.R.D. 254 (M.D.Pa. 2000)
The court held:

> Relevant precedent holds that materials prepared by a party's expert are not covered by the attorney work product privilege. Because the conclusion that draft expert reports and other documents prepared by testifying expert witnesses are discoverable is consistent with the policy considerations underlying the attorney work product privilege, Equitable will be required to produce the draft reports and other documents prepared by its experts. Cover letters that do not contain the mental impressions, opinions or conclusions of Equitable's counsel are not covered by the attorney work-product doctrine. Because the cover letters are relevant to an evaluation of what documents were considered by Equitable's experts, Equitable will be required to produce them. At 261.

**Comment:** Experts should assume that all circulated draft reports are discoverable and will surface. When asked about draft reports, they should testify truthfully at all times.

### Example 21.34: Drafts discoverable

*B.C.F. Oil Refin. v. Consolidated Edison Co.,* 171 F.R.D. 57 (S.D.N.Y. 1997)
In this case an oil refiner brought an action against electric utility and oil transporters, alleging that the utility distributed, and the transporters delivered, contaminated oil to the refinery. The defendants sought production of numerous documents by the plaintiff that the plaintiff claimed were protected by the work-product privilege. The expert was hired not only to give testimony regarding contamination, but also to assist the plaintiff's counsel with technical issues during the discovery process. The court considered a set of documents which was written by the expert

during the preparation of his report and his expert testimony. These included drafts. The court found that no work-product protection applied to documents generated by experts in connection with litigation. The court confirmed that this rule applied to all documents, including drafts and memoranda, that experts generate as they develop the opinions they will present at trial. It then ordered the production of the documents.

## 21.6  Document Creation/Retention Policy

The lessons of Watergate, Enron, Martha Stewart, and Arthur Andersen are all the same: "The cover-up is worse than the crime." The same holds true in expert witness work. The jury is not going to understand all of the technical expert witness testimony in the case. What the jury will understand, however, is that a dishonest expert should not be trusted. Experts who discard, destroy, or "misplace" notes, "sticky notes," and draft reports will likely be considered dishonest by the jury. Experts may be best served by following a document retention policy that has them retain everything they create or review while working on the case at hand.

The best way to deal with documents the expert does not want to be produced is to not produce them in the first place. If the expert does not want to produce a draft report, he shouldn't create, and especially circulate, draft reports. In terms of notes, many experts either fail to take notes, take minimal notes, or, at a minimum, they are careful about what they write in their notes. The best experts do not fear questioning about their notes because they have nothing to hide and are careful not to write anything foolish in their notes such as "need to find a way to prove causation" or "opposing expert really qualified," and the like.

There are two types of documents that the authors recommend that experts take care not to retain after the case at hand is fully resolved. These are the expert's report and the expert's deposition transcript. The reason for not retaining these is simple: opposing counsel can request these from the expert in future cases and past testimony and reports can provide enormous amounts of ammunition for opposing counsel.

## 21.7  Financial Information

Opposing counsel will often ask the expert questions relating to the expert's financial records and previous associations with attorneys. They may also attempt to subpoena the expert's financial records. Courts have wide discretion to order disclosure (or protection) of financial records and information during discovery. The scope of discovery allowed into financial matters varies by jurisdiction and the facts of the particular case. In many cases, experts will be able to protect from discovery their gross income and tax returns, but there is no guarantee of this.

**Example 21.35: Discovery of expert's gross income from medical-legal work not allowed**
*Rogers v. U.S. Navy,* 223 F.R.D. 533 (S.D.Cal. 2004)
The government retained board-certified orthopedic surgeon Gregory Schwab, M.D. On June 1, 2004, Dr. Schwab examined the Plaintiff, and on June 24, 2004, the government served Plaintiff's counsel with Dr. Schwab's 28-page report. Plaintiff's counsel, Mr. Wilkinson, was familiar with Dr. Schwab, having retained Dr. Schwab in the recent past as a medical expert in a state court case. Soon after learning that the government had designated Dr. Schwab as its medical expert in this case, Mr. Wilkinson contacted government counsel to discuss Dr. Schwab. Mr. Wilkinson

indicated that he was aware that Dr. Schwab had a policy of not disclosing the particular dollar amount of his income from his entire medical practice as well as from his medical-legal practice. Dr. Schwab agreed to provide estimates of the percentage of his medical practice that involves forensic work versus clinical work, the percentage of his income that is derived from forensic work, the percentage of his forensic practice that is on behalf of plaintiffs versus defendants, the number of forensic evaluations he performs per week, and his hourly billing rate for performing forensic services. In addition, of course, Dr. Schwab agreed to disclose the actual dollar amount that was paid by the government for his services in this case. Dr. Schwab, however, refused to answer any questions seeking to learn his gross annual income earned as a result of forensic work or his gross annual income from all of his combined medical activities. Defendant the United States Navy filed a motion for a protective order seeking to preclude Plaintiff from discovering the amount of total gross income which the government's medical expert, Dr. Schwab, derives from medical-legal work. The court granted the motion. It stated:

> Government counsel points out that if Dr. Schwab is required to testify as to his gross annual income earned as a result of his forensic work, Plaintiff's counsel will easily be able to calculate Dr. Schwab's total gross income based upon Dr. Schwab's disclosure of the percentage of his total practice is forensic versus clinical. The government argues that the information Dr. Schwab has agreed to provide is more than sufficient for Plaintiff to argue financial bias, such that it is not necessary to know the actual dollar amount of Dr. Schwab's forensic work. Plaintiff argues that the actual dollar amount must be disclosed to allow Plaintiff the full opportunity to demonstrate Dr. Schwab's bias and motive to testify in support of the government in this case. Counsel have been unable to resolve this conflict, and this motion followed.

> In this case, the government has agreed to have Dr. Schwab disclose a substantial amount of information regarding the nature of his forensic work. Dr. Schwab will provide estimates of the percentage of his medical practice that involves forensic work versus clinical work, the percentage of his income that is derived from forensic work, the percentage of his forensic practice that is on behalf of plaintiffs versus defendants, the number of forensic evaluations he performs per week, and his hourly billing rate for performing forensic services. Plaintiff will also learn the actual dollar amount that Dr. Schwab has been and will be paid by the government for his services in this case. This should be more than sufficient information to allow Plaintiff to effectively cross-examine Dr. Schwab at the time of trial regarding his opinions and the financial motive or bias that may have influenced those opinions.

> In opposition to the government's motion, Plaintiff's counsel argues that while the Behler decision may be appropriate in run-of-the-mill personal injury cases, this case is "unique" based upon the dramatically unfavorable 28-page opinion rendered by Dr. Schwab. Plaintiff's counsel argues that Dr. Schwab's opinion includes irrelevant information and oversteps the bounds of the expert designation, showing that Dr. Schwab will go to any extent to reach a conclusion supportive of the party that retains his services. Plaintiff's counsel, however, does not explain how he would be unfairly limited in arguing bias unless he learns the actual dollar amount of Dr. Schwab's gross income from forensic work. Plaintiff's counsel does not explain how the information that Dr. Schwab has agreed to provide will be insufficient to show bias and prejudice.

> The Court concludes that Plaintiff's counsel will be more than able to challenge Dr. Schwab's impartiality at the time of trial based upon the information he has been willing to provide without the need to learn the actual dollar amount of Dr. Schwab's annual income. Because Plaintiff does not persuasively explain the need to learn Dr. Schwab's private financial information, the scope of inquiry is properly limited pursuant to Rule 26(b)(2)(iii) and Rule 26(c).

> Conclusion

> For the reasons set forth herein, the government's renewed motion for protective order is GRANTED. Plaintiff's counsel shall not inquire of Dr. Schwab at the time of his deposition regarding the amount of his gross annual income from forensic work. At 535–536.

**Comment:** Experts who would like to keep their financial matters private often limit what they will agree to disclose to those items that the expert in this case agreed to disclose, namely:

- estimates of the percentage of his work that involves forensic work versus clinical work,
- the percentage of his income that is derived from forensic work,
- the percentage of his forensic practice that is on behalf of plaintiffs versus defendants,
- the number of forensic evaluations he performs per week,
- his hourly billing rate for performing forensic services, and
- the actual dollar amount that he has been paid by the government for his services in this case.

If opposing counsel does not agree to these limitations and forces the issue, a protective order may need to be filed (as was done in the above case).

### Example 21.36: Portions of tax returns of IME physician discoverable to show bias, but only after hearing

*Primm v. Isaac, 2002* WL 441448 (Ky. App. 2002)

The court in this case ordered the production of a portion of the expert's tax return from 1998 and stated:

> Finally, we address the issue that specifically pertains to the discoverability of the personal tax records of a non-party to the case. The decision that we render today should not be taken as a blanket authorization for the indiscriminate discovery of such documents. Like all other aspects of discovery, the scope of production is within the discretion of the trial court, but that discretion is not unlimited and should be cautiously exercised on a case-by-case basis after a thorough analysis of the facts and circumstances. In particular, when it comes to personal tax records, the trial court is required to balance the potential invasion of privacy of the individual required to release the documents against the interest and the need of the party seeking to discover those documents. The federal courts have decided that a person has a qualified privilege to the confidentiality of personal tax records. This means that the documents may be discoverable, but only after the trial court has conducted an analysis of the need for the information, its materiality and its relevancy.
>
> The respondent trial court properly considered all those elements. First, the court limited the allowed discovery to 1998. In addition, the court did not order the production of Dr. Primm's entire tax return for 1998, but only the portion that details his medical income. Second, the court conducted several lengthy hearings in which it carefully and actively monitored all facets of the issues presented to it. The court clearly and repeatedly explained the exact nature of the information it wants produced: the total amount of Dr. Primm's medical income for the year 1998 and the percentage of that income derived from performing litigation-related services in 1998. The court also clearly and repeatedly explained that the information is needed because testimony given by Dr. Primm by deposition in previous cases has raised questions as to his bias and the documents sought by Rhodus are relevant to its answer.
>
> During the hearing conducted on August 9, 2001, the court emphasized that it wanted the best evidence of the information needed, but that tax returns did not have to be produced if there exist other documents that would be just as good and credible pieces of evidence as those returns would be. The court suggested that Dr. Primm's billing records, or any record that his office prepares for the surgeon's accountant, might be that type of evidence. However, Dr. Primm's counsel made a number of objections to production of the actual billing records, and proposed to total his 1998 invoices and to produce a statement of the result. The trial court questioned why Dr. Primm could not produce a document that is already in existence and that includes the same information, and it ordered that such a document be produced to it.
>
> During the second hearing, and even after testimony had been adduced from Dr. Primm himself and from his billing records custodian, it became clear that, through "ignorance or resistance," as the

court put it, the best evidence that the court had ordered produced was still not before it. The court expressed its frustration and even implied that Dr. Primm and his counsel were flirting with a contempt citation. The court stated that it would not allow Dr. Primm to hand-pick and prepare his own impeachment evidence and that it intended to enforce its orders until and unless reversed by a higher court.

In view of the circumstances that appear in the record of those hearings, we can conclude that the September 6, 2001, order requiring Dr. Primm to produce a partial tax return, plus other financial documents for 1998, was not arbitrary or capricious nor contrary to any applicable law. Indeed, it appears that the documents the court compelled Dr. Primm to produce may well be the only documents that he cannot reasonably claim to be non-existent or unavailable. Further, those documents being personal to Dr. Primm, it follows that they can only be discovered from him, and it is doubtful that a substantial equivalent could be found by other means.

Finally, we emphasize that the trial court has made no decision regarding the admissibility of the documents. In addition, it incorporated protective language to ensure that the confidentiality of the records will be maintained under seal, with the added prohibition that the information may not be used or disseminated outside the confines of the pending action. At 8.

**Comment:** Production of tax returns is not routine. If tax returns of experts are ultimately ordered to be produced, experts should consider seeking a protective order that prohibits opposing counsel from publicly disclosing the returns. This was done in this case. Another way to potentially make the issue of producing tax returns go away is for retaining counsel to ask opposing counsel to agree to produce the tax returns of *his* experts. Finally, note that the court strongly suggested in this case that had the expert agreed to produce other documents that would have shown the percentage of his income from forensic work, production of the tax returns might not have been necessary.

### Example 21.37: Tax returns and expert's gross income from all sources "overkill" and therefore not discoverable, but expert required to disclose other financial information
*Behler v. Hanlon,* 199 F.R.D. 553 (D. Maryland 2001)
In this dispute over the discoverabilty of an expert's financial records, the magistrate judge held that the expert's tax returns were not discoverable but other financial information was. The court stated:

In the present case, no intellectually honest argument can be made that the information sought by plaintiff regarding Dr. Keehn's activities as a defense expert witness is not relevant to bias/prejudice impeachment, and, therefore, within the scope of discovery permitted by Rule 26(b)(1). However, legitimate issues are raised regarding the extent of the bias discovery sought, the methods of discovery employed, and possible abuses that could occur if the discovery is permitted without a protective order. For example, plaintiff seeks discovery of the total income earned by Dr. Keehn for the last five years, the amount thereof earned providing defense Rule 35 examinations, records relating to the hours spent by Dr. Keehn in this capacity, copies of his tax returns, and a listing of all insurance companies with whom he is affiliated, as well as a listing of all cases in which he has provided expert services. This is overkill. While there may be cases in which an expert's gross income, and the specific amounts thereof earned by providing services as an expert witness, may be discoverable, this should not be ordered routinely, without a showing, absent here, why less intrusive financial information would not suffice. Most people are sensitive about their income, and who knows the details about it. By their very nature, expert witnesses are knowledgeable of information that is scientific, technical, or specialized, generally acquired by long, hard study and experience. When asked to provide expert testimony, they are in a position to request compensation that matches their qualifications, which can seem shockingly high to those not familiar with the costs of modern litigation. Moreover, in the post-*Daubert/Kumho Tire* era, and in light of the Rule 26(a)(2) disclosure requirements and the recent changes to Rules 702 and 703, counsel increasingly are more selective in who they ask to be expert witnesses, knowing that they will be subject to the utmost scrutiny. Those who pass muster likely will be able to command fees commensurate with their skill and experience, which may, to a lay member of the jury, appear exorbitant, when in fact what was charged is the going rate. Rule 26(a)(2)(B) requires disclosure of the compensation received by a retained expert in the particular case at issue, and counsel routinely bring this out during cross-examination when questioning an opposing expert witness. However, permitting routine disclosure of the expert's gross compensation, from all sources—including those unrelated to litigation activities—would provide the jury with little information relevant to a fair assessment of the expert's credibility, while concomitantly introducing the real possibility of creating confusion, distraction and even prejudice. Nor is the trial of a case facilitated if a party sponsoring an expert attempts to draw the possible sting of expert compensation by attempting to prove that what his or her expert charges is within the norm, as this opens the door for collateral issues that could further distract the jury [FN16].

> FN16. Once again, there may be cases where it is appropriate to compel discovery of an expert witness' total compensation, and the portions thereof earned from functioning as an expert witness. There may even be a case where tax returns and other documents relating to expert activities should be compelled as well. However, Rule 26(b)(2) would require a far stronger showing of need than is present in this case, and it is unlikely that such intrusive information would be ordered in routine cases.

Instead, the jury readily should be able to assess possible bias on the part of an expert witness if they are made aware of the total percentage of his or her gross income that is earned from providing expert witness services. Similarly, there is no need for the expert to have to produce his or her tax returns, if the party seeking the discovery has accurate information regarding the percentage of income earned as an expert.

Additionally, while documents relating to all cases within a stated period of time for which an expert was retained are relevant to possible bias impeachment, in this case I do not believe that Dr. Keehn should be required to assemble these records, provided the plaintiff is able to obtain the equivalent information by a more expedient, less costly method. To this end, I will order that Dr. Keehn be produced for questioning at a deposition regarding the information sought by plaintiff. If possible, this deposition will be by telephone, and its scheduling will be expedited. The questioning by plaintiff at the deposition will not last more than 2 hours, provided Dr. Keehn provides complete and unevasive answers to proper questions asked, as is required by Rule 37(a)(3). Further, prior to the deposition, he will make a diligent search of all records in his possession, custody and control, to enable him to provide the following information: (1) The percentage of his gross income earned for each of the preceding five years attributable to performing expert witness services on behalf of insurance companies, and/or attorneys defending personal injury cases; (2) a list of cases in which he has provided such services during the last five years, in sufficient detail to enable the plaintiff to locate the court file, and/or issue a subpoena for it. At a minimum, the name, address and telephone number of the attorney and/or insurance claims representative that engaged Dr. Keehn will be provided; (3) the name of each insurance company for which Dr. Keehn has provided services as an expert witness in personal injury cases, for the preceding ten years.

If, after taking this deposition, plaintiff can demonstrate that additional information is required to enable him to undertake reasonable bias impeachment of Dr. Keehn, he may seek leave from the court to take additional discovery. Further, should the court determine that Dr. Keehn has not provided complete, and unevasive, answers to the discovery herein ordered, or if the court determines that he has not made a good faith, diligent effort to assemble the information for which discovery was ordered, then additional discovery will be ordered, and appropriate sanctions, including not allowing him to testify at trial, if warranted by the level of non-compliance, may be imposed.

Finally, to protect against possible abuse of the sensitive financial information for which discovery has been allowed, it will be subject to a protective order that prohibits dissemination or copying of the information produced for any purpose not directly related to the prosecution of this case, absent the consent of Dr. Keehn, or further order of this Court. This protective order will remain in effect following the conclusion of the pending case, unless withdrawn by order of this Court. At 561–563.

**Comment:** The courts generally recognize the sensitive nature of financial information and may protect against forcing an expert to disclose his tax returns and gross income.

### Example 21.38: Financial records protected, but more general financial information must be produced
*Syken v. Elkins,* 644 So.2d 539 (Fla. Dist. Ct. App. 1994)
Here, the court considered certain discovery orders directing a proposed medical expert in a personal injury action to produce an array of financial records. Specifically, the information sought numerous documents regarding past IMEs performed by the expert. Also, a subpoena duces tecum was issued for all bills generated by the physician as a defense expert examiner to any insurance company or law firm, all journals, ledgers, and 1099 forms pertaining to payments received by the physician during a certain period for examinations performed at the request of any insurance company or law firm.

In setting out guidelines regarding what could be compelled and what could not, the court held that an expert "may be asked to give an approximation of the portion of their professional time or work devoted to service as an expert," but the witness "need not answer how much money he or she earns as an expert or how much the expert's total annual income is." The court's guidelines are helpful as an example of one state's treatment of the issue:

1. The medical expert may be deposed either orally or by written deposition.
2. The expert may be asked as to the pending case, what he or she has been hired to do and what the compensation is to be.
3. The expert may be asked what expert work he or she generally does. Is the work performed for the plaintiffs, defendants, or some percentage of each?
4. The expert may be asked to give an approximation of the portion of their professional time or work devoted to service as an expert. This can be a fair estimate of some reasonable and truthful component of that work, such as hours expended, or percentage of income earned from that source, or the approximate number of IME's that he or she performs in one year. The expert need not answer how much money he or she earns as an expert or how much the expert's total annual income is.
5. The expert may be required to identify specifically each case in which he or she has actually testified, whether by deposition or at trial, going back a reasonable period of time, which is normally three years. A longer period of time may be inquired into under some circumstances.
6. The production of the expert's business records, files, and 1099's may be ordered produced only upon the most unusual or compelling circumstance.
7. The patient's privacy must be observed.
8. An expert may not be compelled to compile or produce nonexistent documents.

The Florida Supreme Court found these factors to strike a reasonable balance between a party's need for information concerning an expert witness's potential bias and the witness's right to be free from burdensome and intrusive production requests.

### Example 21.39: Party's payments to expert discoverable from party
*Allstate Insurance Co. v. Boecher,* 24 Fla. L. Weekly S187 (Fla. April 22, 1999)
The court in this case held that the insured claimant could seek discovery from the party insurer regarding the extent of its relationship with a particular expert. Thus, the claimant could discover how often a particular expert testified on an insurer's behalf and how much money the expert made from his relationship with the insurer.

The alleged victim of an accident sued the defendant, his uninsured motorist carrier. The defendant intended to call an accident reconstruction and injury causation expert in the case. The claimant then propounded interrogatories to the defendant concerning the relationship between the defendant and the expert. The questions sought the identity of cases in which the expert had performed analyses and rendered opinions for the defendant, as well as the fees paid, nationally and in the preceding three years. The trial court overruled the defendant's objections of undue burden because the interrogatories were directed to the party and not to the expert. The appellate court affirmed the ruling, reasoning that the relationship between a particular expert and a party is directly relevant to a party's efforts to demonstrate the witness's bias. Limiting this discovery could potentially undermine the fairness of the trial. As such, the court held that a party may attempt to discover facts known directly by a party concerning the extent of that party's relationship with an expert witness.

**Comment:** Expert witnesses who do a large amount of work for a client can have their credibility easily challenged. The opposition will want to show that the expert would not want to risk such a lucrative relationship by giving an unfavorable opinion.

### Example 21.40: Financial inquiries allowed but court should tightly control and not expand into unnecessary personal matters
*Wrobleski v. de Lara,* 727 A.2d 930 (Md. 1999)
In this medical malpractice case against a gynecologist, the defendant sought the production of numerous financial records from the plaintiff's physician expert. At deposition and at trial, the expert refused to reveal the amount of income he had received from testifying in 1995. The trial court allowed the question but did not force the expert to answer. The jury found for the defendant. On appeal, the court found that the question was proper and that the jury could infer what they wished from the expert's refusal to answer. The court limited its holding, explaining that:

> harassment of expert witnesses through a wholesale rummaging of their personal and financial records under the guise of seeking impeachment evidence is not permitted; rather, the allowance of the permitted inquiry, both at the discovery and trial stages, should be tightly controlled by the trial court and limited to its purpose, and not permitted to expand into an unnecessary exposure of matters and data that are personal to the witness and have no real relevance to the credibility of his or her testimony.

### Example 21.41: Financial records from expert's cases in last 3 years discoverable where expert did not maintain a list of those cases
*Orkin Exterminating Co., Inc. v. Knollwood Properties, Ltd.,* 710 So.2d 697 (Fla. App. 5 Dist. 1998)
Here, a trial court's order requiring an expert witness in a civil trial to provide a list identifying prior cases in which he had testified during the past three years was proper. No list identifying such cases existed. The only documents the expert had that would comply with the order were financial and business records. The expert was required to produce these records.

**Comment:** Experts who wish to be available to testify in federal court should maintain a list of all cases where they have testified by deposition or at trial in the last 4 years. This list is required to be disclosed as part of their report and an expert will not be allowed to testify without producing such a list. Had the expert in the above case maintained such a list, he may not have had to produce the financial records in question.

### Example 21.42: Financial records regarding expert's relationship with party in this case discoverable to show bias
*Rowe v. State Farm Mut. Auto. Ins. Co.,* 670 So.2d 718 (La. App. 3 Cir. 1996)
In this action by insured-plaintiffs against their uninsured/underinsured insurer, the plaintiffs sought production of financial and medical records of the medical expert retained by defense

counsel. They sought the records in order to discover how much work the expert did for the defense counsel and the insurer. The court held that the plaintiffs should have been able to discover those records and that cross-examination alone was not effective to show the expert's possible bias.

### Example 21.43: Income tax returns not discoverable

*Hawkins v. South Plains Intern. Trucks, Inc.,* 139 F.R.D. 679 (D. Colo. 1991)

The plaintiff, a mechanic, sued the manufacturer of a truck after the truck's oil unit's allegedly defective design caused injury to the plaintiff. The plaintiff retained an engineer as a testifying expert witness who would testify to the defective design of the piece of the defendant's truck at issue. The defendant sought to discover the income the expert had received as an expert witness. They sought production of the expert's income tax returns for the previous eleven years. The court applied the two-prong relevancy and compelling need test. The records were relevant to the expert's credibility, but there was no compelling need. The defendant could have obtained the information elsewhere. The court concluded that the plaintiff did not need to produce the records, but would be required to produce information regarding the expert's income at his consulting firm or allow him to be further deposed on the matter.

### Example 21.44: Tax returns not discoverable

*Wacker v. Gehl Company,* 157 F.R.D. 59 (D. Colo. 1994)

In this case, the defendant sought the production of the plaintiff's testifying expert witness's tax records. The request was for a copy of the portions of his tax returns for the past five years reflecting the income he had received in expert consultant and witness matters. The defendant claimed that the information requested might demonstrate the financial interest, bias, or prejudice of the expert. The court found that, although the returns might lead to such information, the request was not "reasonably calculated" to lead to the discovery of such evidence. The court refused to allow such a "fishing expedition," noting that the defendant offered no factual information "whatsoever" that the returns would lead to admissible evidence.

### Example 21.45: Tax returns discoverable

*State ex rel. Creighton v. Jackson,* 879 S.W.2d 639 (Mo. Ct. App. 1994)

Here, the court held that the income tax returns reflecting the income an expert received during the past five years from services as a consultant or witness were within the scope of discovery as impeachment information.

The court discussed the considerations, noting that the trial court should restrict such discovery so that it is no more intrusive than necessary. It went on to say that counsel should never be permitted to "harass, badger and humiliate" the witness with inquiries not strictly necessary to the discovery of matters relevant to professional objectivity. It charged the trial court with the responsibility of delicately balancing privacy interests against the need for accountability. However, the court maintained that the fees earned by an expert witness for testifying in cases bears materially on the witness's credibility and is appropriate impeachment evidence. The trial judge has discretion to allow testimony regarding the amount of annual income derived from employment as an expert witness. Evidence that a witness makes substantial income from testifying illuminates the financial interest that the expert has in giving such testimony.

**Comment:** You never know what a judge will do in a particular case. This judge ordered production of the expert's tax returns. The only way to guarantee that this will not occur is to not agree to be an expert witness.

**Example 21.46: Expert's personal financial records not discoverable**
*In re Doctor's Hosp. of Laredo, Ltd. Partnership,* 2 S.W.3d 504 (Tex. App.-San Antonio 1999)
Here, a medical malpractice action was brought against a hospital regarding a child's birth. The trial court ordered the medical experts' depositions and ordered discovery of the experts' income tax schedules and one expert's calendars. The appellate court held that: (1) the hospital properly redesignated the doctor from a testifying expert to a consulting expert, and thus the trial court abused its discretion in ordering the doctor's deposition, and (2) the new state discovery rules, which provided for the discovery of any bias evidence of testifying witness, did not allow the discovery of personal financial records and appointment books of a nonparty witness.

**Example 21.47: Tax returns not discoverable as such discovery would irreparably violate an expert's privacy**
*Olinger v. Curry,* 926 S.W.2d 832 (Tex. App.-Fort Worth 1996)
In this personal injury action, the plaintiff sought production of the federal tax returns of the defendant's medical expert. The expert admitted in deposition that approximately 90% of his expert consultation services had been provided for defendants, as opposed to personal injury plaintiffs. The court found that the records requested were neither relevant nor reasonably calculated to lead to the discovery of admissible evidence, and therefore the plaintiff was not entitled to discovery of such returns. Otherwise, the court reasoned, such discovery would have irreparably violated the expert witness's privacy.

**Example 21.48: Tax returns not discoverable**
*Young v. Santos,* 611 So.2d 586 (Fla. App. 4 Dist. 1993)
In this case, a physician expert was asked to produce tax records for the last three years. The court found that the federal income tax returns showing the overall income of the expert were not discoverable. It reasoned that the relevant information was the amount of income the physician received from work as an expert consultant or witness, and neither the trial court nor the opposing party had explored less intrusive means of obtaining the information, even though the physician had ignored other attempts at discovery.

**Comment:** Experts who are not evasive about the percentage of their income derived from forensic work, the percentage of work they do for plaintiffs rather than defendants, and the identity of past forensic clients are much less likely to face subpoenas for financial records because opposing counsel will already have the information he is seeking from the financial records.

## 21.8 E-mail
E-mail is discoverable as is anything else considered by or created by the expert.[14] The authors advise that e-mails not be used to communicate with retaining counsel. E-mails are more casual, conversational, and less formal than letters and can easily be used to discredit the expert on the stand.[15] An e-mail might be accidentally deleted, thus opening the expert up to charges of hiding or destroying evidence. E-mails can be forwarded to persons beyond your intended recipient. Finally, e-mails can be sent to the wrong person in an address book,

---

[14] See *Synthes Spine Co., L.P. v. Walden,* 232 F.R.D. 460 (E.D. Pa. 2005).
[15] When G. W. Bush took office in 2001, he decided not to use *any* e-mail the entire time he was in office. The reason was simple. After all the investigations involving his predecessor, he didn't want to have to produce e-mails. You don't have to produce something that doesn't exist.

thus inadvertently revealing confidential information. When an expert needs to communicate with retaining counsel, the preferred method is to pick up the telephone and call her.

## 21.9 Experts Switching Sides

An expert may sometimes have or have had a relationship with one party in a past case, as a past employee or consultant, or even as an expert in the current case and then be hired by another party. Whether an expert will be allowed to testify in such situations is within the discretion of the trial court. The court will generally look to the nature of the past relationship, including if any confidential information relevant to the current litigation was disclosed to the expert in determining whether or not the expert will be allowed to testify. Note that counsel will often contact and retain experts in an effort to "conflict them out" of a case and deny their use to the opposition. Dealing with this form of abuse is covered in Section 24.2. Please consider the following cases.

### Example 21.49: Expert allowed to testify against former client
*Lacroix v. BIC Corp.,* 339 F.Supp.2d 196 (D. Mass. 2004)
This case involved an expert who had served as an expert witness and consultant for the defendant for many years. One year after that relationship ended, the expert was retained to testify against the defendant on an unrelated case. The court allowed the expert to testify because the confidential information the expert gained was not relevant to the current litigation. The court, however, also issued a protective order prohibiting the expert from testifying or utilizing for purposes of the litigation, any information he received during the years of his affiliation with Bic. The court stated:

> Although courts are generally reluctant to disqualify expert witnesses, federal courts have inherent authority to disqualify experts "if necessary to preserve public confidence in the fairness and integrity of the judicial system." *Paul v. Rawlings Sporting Goods,* 123 F.R.D. 271, 278 (S.D.Ohio 1988). Disqualification of an expert is appropriate when a party retains an expert who previously worked for an adversary and received confidential information from the first client. See *Erickson v. Newmar Corp.,* 87 F.3d 298, 300 (9th Cir.1996) (acknowledging that in a "switching sides" case, the "court may grant the original hiring party's motion to disqualify the expert when it is determined that the expert is in possession of confidential information received from the first client."); *Koch Refining Co. v. Boudreaux,* 85 F.3d at 1180 (stating that there is a "clear case for disqualification" when an expert switches sides in the same litigation after receiving confidential information from the adverse party pursuant to its earlier retention).
>
> Although most expert disqualification cases involve a testifying expert, courts employ the same test in determining whether to disqualify a consulting expert. See *Great Lakes Dredge & Dock Co. v. Harnischfeger Corp.,* 734 F.Supp. 334 (N.D.Ill.1990) (denying motion to disqualify expert consultant under the same test used when considering disqualifying a testifying expert finding that there was no "leakage" of information between defendants' experts and plaintiff's expert both of whom worked for the same company.); *Conforti & Eisele, Inc. v. New Jersey,* 170 N.J.Super. 64, 405 A.2d 487 (1979).
>
> To resolve a motion to disqualify an expert in cases other than where an expert has clearly switched sides, the court undertakes a two-step inquiry. The court must determine whether, (1) it was objectively reasonable for the moving party to believe that it had a confidential relationship with the expert; and (2) whether the moving party disclosed confidential information to the expert that is relevant to the current litigation. See *Paul v. Rawlings Sporting Goods Co.,* 123 F.R.D. at 278; *Wang v. Toshiba Corp.,* 762 F.Supp. at 1248. "Affirmative answers to both inquiries compel disqualification." *Id.* However, disqualification may not be warranted even if the expert witness has signed a confidentiality agreement with the adversary. ("[T]here may be situations where, despite the existence of a formal contractual relationship, so little of substance occurs during the course of the relationship that neither the integrity

of the trial process, nor the interests of the party who retained the expert, would be served by blanket disqualification.")

In analyzing the disqualification issue, the court also balances competing policy objectives and considers concerns of fundamental fairness. *Koch Refining Co. v. Boudreaux,* 85 F.3d at 1182. "'The policy objectives favoring disqualification include preventing conflicts of interest and maintaining the integrity of the judicial process.'" *Id.* Policies disfavoring disqualification include "ensuring that parties have access to expert witnesses who possess specialized knowledge and allowing experts to pursue their professional calling."

1. Confidential Relationship

The party seeking disqualification bears the burden of showing that it was reasonable for it to believe that a confidential relationship existed. The Court may consider several factors, including: whether the relationship was one of long standing and involved frequent contacts instead of a single interaction with the expert, whether the expert is to be called as a witness in the underlying case, whether alleged confidential communications were from expert to party or vice-versa, and whether the moving party funded or directed the formation of the opinion to be offered at trial. *Stencel v. Fairchild Corp.,* 174 F.Supp.2d at 1083. "Other factors include whether the parties entered into a formal confidentiality agreement, whether the expert was retained to assist in the litigation, the number of meetings between the expert and the attorneys, whether work product was discussed or documents were provided to the expert, whether the expert was paid a fee, whether the expert was asked to agree not to discuss the case with the opposing parties or counsel, and whether the expert derived any of his specific ideas from work done under the direction of the retaining party." The emphasis "is not on whether the expert was retained per se but whether there was a relationship that would permit the litigant reasonably to expect that any communications would be maintained in confidence."

2. Confidential Information

Confidential information essentially is information "of either particular significance or [that] which can be readily identified as either attorney work product or within the scope of the attorney-client privilege." It could include discussion of the party's "strategy in the litigation, the kinds of experts [the party] expected to retain, [the party's] view of the strengths and weaknesses of each side, the role of each of the [party's] experts to be hired and anticipated defenses." At least one court has concluded that "[c]ommunication based upon technical information as opposed to legal advice is not considered privileged." *Nikkal Indus., Ltd. v. Salton, Inc.,* 689 F.Supp. 187, 191-92 (S.D.N.Y.1988).

Applying this analysis to the facts of this case, I believe that Bic has shown that a sufficient confidential relationship existed between it and Mr. Dembsey concerning Bic's proprietary and confidential information, that is, relating to the manufacturing and design of its products. He is therefore restricted from using or disclosing any information which can be so defined. Additionally, Mr. Dembsey is restricted from communicating any information concerning litigation strategy to which he was exposed during his consultation with Bic. The Agreement signed by Mr. Dembsey before he was retained by Bic requires him to do so, and agreements of this type are generally enforceable. See *Wang v. CFR Associates,* 125 F.R.D. 10, 13 (D.Mass.1989). The relationship between Bic and Mr. Dembsey was significant in that it involved his work as a consultant and as an expert witness over the course of several years.

Notwithstanding the Agreement, there appears to be little or nothing in the way of confidential information relevant to the current litigation to which Mr. Dembsey was exposed. It is undisputed that the parties never communicated on matters of any substance relating to the specifics of this case. It is further undisputed that the last communication between Bic and Mr. Dembsey was in July of 1999, one year before the plaintiff in this case sustained his injury. As in the oft-cited Paul case, Mr. Dembsey did not develop any expertise in the area of fire safety from work done under Bic's direction or using its funds. See *Paul v. Rawlings Sporting Goods Co.,* 123 F.R.D. at 280. Accordingly, I believe that Bic has not disclosed confidential information to Mr. Dembsey that is specific to the current litigation and I will not disqualify him as an expert for the plaintiff.

While Bic has not demonstrated that I should allow its motion to disqualify Mr. Dembsey as an expert witness for the plaintiff, I am compelled to uphold the Agreement with respect to any confidential and proprietary information Mr. Dembsey could have obtained during his relationship with Bic. See

*Wang v. CFR Associates,* 125 F.R.D. at 13. I have the authority, pursuant to Fed.R.Civ.P. 26(c)(7) to prohibit the disclosure of confidential research, development, or commercial information. *Id.* Therefore, I will prohibit Mr. Dembsey from testifying or utilizing for purposes of this litigation, any information he received during the years of his affiliation with Bic. Because of Mr. Dembsey's extensive curriculum vitae in the area of fire science and since no conflict of interest exists with respect to the facts of plaintiff's case, Mr. Dembsey may be an appropriate and useful witness for the plaintiff.

V. Conclusion

1. Defendant Bic Corporation's Motion to Disqualify Plaintiff's Expert, Nicholas Dembsey, Ph.D., (Docket No. 36) is denied, but defendant's motion, in the alternative, to Extend Time for the Completion of His Expert Deposition, is allowed and that deposition shall be completed by September 30, 2004. At 199–202.

**Comment:** The court looked at several factors in determining whether the original party could reasonably assume that its relationship with the expert was confidential. These are:

- whether the relationship was one of long standing and involved frequent contacts instead of a single interaction with the expert,
- whether the expert is to be called as a witness in the underlying case,
- whether alleged confidential communications were from expert to party or vice-versa,
- whether the moving party funded or directed the formation of the opinion to be offered at trial,
- whether the parties entered into a formal confidentiality agreement,
- whether the expert was retained to assist in the litigation,
- the number of meetings between the expert and the attorneys,
- whether work product was discussed or documents were provided to the expert,
- whether the expert was paid a fee,
- whether the expert was asked to agree not to discuss the case with the opposing parties or counsel, and
- whether the expert derived any of his specific ideas from work done under the direction of the retaining party.

This expert was allowed to testify against a client for whom he had done significant work in the past. Practically speaking, however, it will be highly unlikely for the former client to ever hire this expert again. That is something experts should consider before agreeing to testify against a client who has given the expert significant work in the past or against a client (such as a big insurance company) that the expert would like to bring on as a client.

**Example 21.50: Expert allowed to testify despite being previously retained by and paid by other side (court does not want attorneys to be able to lock up all experts)**

*Hewlett-Packard Co. v. EMC Corp.,* 330 F.Supp.2d 1087 (N.D. Cal. 2004)

This was a complicated high-technology patent infringement case where there are presumably not a large number of qualified experts. The court allowed the expert to switch sides where the amount of work he had done for the opposing side was minimal and it was not proven that the expert was provided confidential information relevant to the case at hand. The court was concerned that unscrupulous attorneys not be able to disqualify experts from working for other parties in the case by paying them nominal retainers. The court stated:

Although none of the cases discussed provides binding authority with respect to the precise question at issue here, the reasoning of the cases is sound, and this Court will be guided by it. All of the interests identified—the integrity of the judicial process, avoidance of conflicts of interest, ensuring access to expert witnesses with specialized knowledge, and allowing experts to pursue their professional calling—serve to promote public confidence in the legal system. The Court thus will consider the following questions in deciding whether to disqualify Katz. First, has the moving party demonstrated that it was objectively reasonable for it to conclude that a confidential relationship existed between it and the expert? That is, did the confidential relationship develop into a matter sufficiently substantial to make disqualification or some other judicial remedy appropriate? Second, did the moving party disclose confidential information to the expert during such a confidential relationship that is relevant to the current litigation? Third, will the Court's decision be prejudicial or fundamentally unfair to either of the parties? Fourth, to what extent do the policies of allowing experts to pursue their trade, allowing parties to select their own experts, and preventing parties from creating conflicts solely for the purposes of preventing their adversary from using the services of the expert outweigh the policy of preventing conflicts implicated on the particular facts of the case? Finally, considering all of the above factors together, would disqualification of the expert promote the integrity of the legal process? The moving party bears the burden of proof with respect to each of these factors.

## III. DISCUSSION

First, EMC must demonstrate that it reasonably believed that it had a confidential relationship with Katz. Katz states that he conversed with Dichiara on March 20, 2001 to assess whether he wanted to consult for EMC. It is undisputed that Katz agreed to consult for EMC, signing a confidentiality agreement on April 12, 2001 memorializing their relationship. It clearly was reasonable for EMC to assume that a confidential relationship began on April 12, 2001, and HP does not dispute that such a relationship existed as of that date. EMC thus has met its burden with respect to any confidential disclosures made between April 12, 2001 and July 11, 2002, the date that Katz withdrew from the consulting agreement.

However, EMC has not met its burden with respect to the period prior to April 12, 2001. While it is true that a party may have a reasonable expectation that a confidential relationship exists even absent a formal agreement, EMC has not demonstrated that it had a confidential relationship with Katz prior to the signing of the confidentiality agreement. Katz asserts that he spent only three hours reading six published patents and just one hour (about ten minutes per patent) discussing his impressions of the patents with EMC's counsel. He states that EMC's lawyers did not discuss any litigation strategy and did not disclose their impressions of the patents to him. He represents that, at most, EMC's counsel inquired about his impressions of the validity of the patent claims and that he does not remember discussing litigation strategy or infringement. Although Dichiara states that "[i]t was my understanding that Dr. Katz would hold in confidence all of our discussions and not disclose them without my permission," Dichiara Decl., ¶ 3, Dichiara has provided no evidence contradicting Katz's statements that they did not discuss the accused inventions, the type of evidence needed to prove infringement, and other potential expert witnesses. Moreover, it strains credulity to argue that, only a few weeks after contacting an potential expert witness, EMC's counsel would disclose aspects of its litigation strategy to someone who had not yet signed a confidentiality agreement and that such a conversation could have occurred in the span of a one-hour conversation in which Katz was alleged to have discussed his views of claims in six separate and technically complex patents. The March 20, 2001 conversation appears to have been only an initial discussion, the goal of which was to decide whether EMC wanted to employ Katz and whether Katz wanted to work for EMC. EMC thus has not met its burden of showing that it was objectively reasonable for it to believe that a confidential relationship existed as of March 20, 2001.

Second, EMC must prove that, during a confidential relationship, it disclosed confidential information to Katz that is relevant to the current litigation. As noted above, the parties dispute whether any relevant confidential information was disclosed between April 12, 2001 and July 11, 2002. Katz claims that the only information that he received from EMC during that time was contained in three boxes that he returned to EMC unopened. Although Dichiara contends that he spoke to Katz about the case several times between April 2001 and July 2002, Dichiara notably does not maintain that he discussed anything of substantive importance to the litigation in the course of these conversations, nor does he identify which of the conversations occurred on or after April 12, 2001. Katz states clearly that he initiated all of his telephone conversations with EMC's counsel during that period, that each conversation lasted no more than a few minutes, and that his purpose simply was to inquire about the status the case in light of the fact that EMC had not contacted him except to deliver the three boxes. There is no evidence that Katz was paid any fees other than for his initial four hours of work on March 20, 2001. EMC's characterizations of the discussions that took place during this period are inconsistent with the billing records. EMC has not met its burden of showing disclosure of confidential information.

Additionally, even if, for the sake of argument, the Court accepts EMC's contention that there was a confidential relationship prior to April 12, 2001, EMC has not met its burden of demonstrating that confidential information was communicated to Katz at that time. The only alleged communication during this time period occurred during the March 20, 2001 telephone conversation, which lasted for approximately one hour. Katz asserts that he discussed only his impressions of the validity of the claims of six of EMC's patents. Although, EMC represents that it offered information with respect to its litigation strategy to Katz, it has offered neither specific details of such discussion nor evidence contradicting Katz's version of the events. Just as in Mays, where the court concluded that "[i]n the 60 to 90 minute meeting, it is highly unlikely that there was any detailed or involved discussion concerning litigation strategies, the strengths and weaknesses of each side, the witnesses to be called, the types of experts to be retained and anticipated defenses," Mays, 293 F.Supp.2d at 957, EMC has not explained how it could have disclosed confidential detailed elements of its litigation strategy during such a short conversation in which several patents were discussed.

Finally, to the extent that EMC means to suggest that the very disclosure of which claim terms it thought were important for validity analysis would hint at its litigation strategy, it is noteworthy that the subject matter of the discussion was material contained in publicly available patents. EMC does not develop this point with any specificity. Even assuming that a confidential relationship existed during the March 20, 2001 telephone call, EMC has not met its burden of proving that confidential information was exchanged.

Nor has EMC demonstrated sufficient prejudice to prompt the Court to interfere with HP's interest in successfully litigating this action. At this late stage, the parties have committed to selection of key terms for claim construction and infringement analysis; thus, even if EMC did reveal in the March 20, 2001 conversation which claims it found important to the litigation, no prejudice exists now, given the parties' extensive disclosures in connection with the claim construction process. In contrast, HP clearly would suffer hardship if Katz were disqualified: it relied on Katz's declaration in preparing its claim construction briefs and oral argument. EMC brought the present motion on March 30, 2004, only one week before the claim construction hearing took place.

Policy concerns also weigh in favor of denying the motion. For several reasons, disqualifying Katz under the present circumstances would not serve to promote the integrity of the legal process. First, it is unclear how striking Katz's declaration or refusing to permit HP to rely upon Katz's opinions would impact the Court's consideration of the exceedingly complex legal and factual presentation made by the parties during a two-day claim construction hearing. It is also unclear whether HP will be able to find another suitable expert witness in time for the dispositive motions and trial preparation that will follow the Court's construction of the disputed claims. Second, disqualification, on the facts of this case, would impair Katz's interest in pursuing his trade as an expert witness. It appears that EMC never intended to use Katz's services; for example, during the fifteen-month period that EMC "employed" him, it paid him only two thousand dollars for the initial patent review and telephone conversation. At the same time, according to EMC, Katz should not have been allowed to consult for other litigants. Third, without speculating as to EMC's underlying motivations, the Court notes that if an expert could be disqualified on the facts of this case, parties in other cases might be tempted to create a purported conflict solely for the purpose of preventing their adversaries from using the services of a particular expert. This concern is especially important in high-technology patent infringement cases, in which the courts, as well as the public, rely on experts to explain complicated technologies. Permitting one party to lock up all or most of the best experts might interfere with the proper interpretation of claim language—at task that potentially has preclusive effect with respect to future litigation—as well as fair evaluation of the merits of claims of infringement.

## IV. ORDER
Good cause therefore appearing, IT IS HEREBY ORDERED that the motion is DENIED. At 1092–1098.

**Comment:** This case most likely involved the common expert abuse whereby one side tries to "lock up" the best experts in the field by paying them a nominal retainer. Experts in fields where this is common who wish to avoid being conflicted out of a case should avoid receiving confidential materials from a party unless they are paid up front a non-refundable retainer significant enough to compensate them fairly for their loss of opportunity to work for other parties in the case. One way to avoid being privy to such confidential information is to not open or read documents until the expert receives a signed retainer agreement and the requested non-refundable retainer. See Section 19.5.

**Example 21.51: Member of same firm as plaintiff's original expert allowed to testify as expert for defendant where no disclosure of confidential information has been made by plaintiff's original expert to defense expert**
*Stencel v. Fairchild Corp.,* 174 F.Supp.2d 1080 (C.D. CA 2001)
The plaintiff approached one member of Knobbe, Manens, Olson & Sear ("KMOB"), Craig Summers, to testify as a patent expert. Mr. Summers tentatively agreed to accept the retention, but ultimately withdrew when he discovered a conflict that would prevent him from testifying against the defendant. Later, the defendant retained a different KMOB partner, Thomas Smegal, from a different office of that firm, to testify as a patent expert. Mr. Smegal accepted the assignment and planned to testify for defendant. At issue was whether Mr. Smegal would be allowed to testify for the defendant. The court held that he would be so allowed and stated:

> In the instant case, the issue is not a conflicted attorney but a conflicted expert. Thus, the concerns of loyalty that in large part drive imputed disqualification are absent. In addition, even though the two experts in this case are both employed by KMOB, a proper screen satisfactorily addresses the policy goal of protecting the confidentiality of Clemmer's work product. This screen need not be as restricting as would be appropriate for a conflicted attorney. Likewise, since expert witnesses are hired as individuals and not through firms, the fact that the screen may serve to separate two experts who work in the same organization does not give the Court pause.
>
> An adequate screen is presented here. Summers and Smegal have had no interactions with each other with respect to this matter apart from disclosing that they both were contacted by the parties in this case. Summers also states that he has not disclosed to Smegal any of the potentially confidential information he received from Clemmer during Clemmer's attempt to retain Summers' services. In addition, Summers works in Newport Beach, California, while Smegal works in KMOB's San Francisco office, over five hundred miles distant. Further, Smegal has declared that he has no direct access to any documents Summers may have drafted in this matter, nor will he have such access in the future. Thus, it appears to the Court that plaintiff has not and will not suffer any unfair prejudice it Smegal is permitted to act as Defendant's expert.
>
> The Court finds that Plaintiff had a reasonable expectation that Summers would preserve the confidentiality of his communications and that Clemmer did reveal confidential information to Summers, pursuant to their understanding that such information would remain confidential. However, the fact that Summers would be disqualified is not, in and of itself, sufficient to disqualify all members of KMOB, especially those who are properly screened from any information or documents in Summers' possession. Since no confidential information has been disclosed to Smegal, and steps have been taken to assure that no such information will be disclosed in the future, disqualification of Smegal is unwarranted. At 1087.

**Example 21.52: Doctor disqualified from testifying for defense after previously reviewing medical records for plaintiff along with letter containing confidential information (plaintiff's counsel's mental impressions and trial strategy)**
*Turner v. Thiel,* 553 S.E.2d 765 (VA 2001)
In December 1998, prior to filing a motion for judgment, plaintiff's counsel had a telephone

conversation with Dr. Sanders and asked him to review the plaintiff's potential medical malpractice claim against Thiel. Plaintiff's counsel provided Dr. Sanders with a verbal synopsis of the facts relating to the plaintiff's care and treatment. Dr. Sanders determined he had no conflict of interest and agreed to review any material that plaintiff's counsel would provide to him. Plaintiff's counsel and Sanders also discussed fee arrangements, and Sanders forwarded by facsimile his curriculum vitae to plaintiff's counsel.

Plaintiff's counsel forwarded to Dr. Sanders a letter dated December 16, 1998. The letter, which consisted of two pages, summarized the plaintiff's potential claim against Thiel. Plaintiff's counsel specifically asked Dr. Sanders to "focus" on certain acts of possible medical negligence and issues relating to proximate causation. Plaintiff's counsel enclosed plaintiff's medical records with the letter.

Dr. Sanders reviewed the medical records as requested by plaintiff's counsel. Dr. Sanders and plaintiff's counsel had a telephone conference on January 4, 1999, and Dr. Sanders discussed the care and treatment that Thiel had provided to the plaintiff. Plaintiff's counsel discussed additional information with Dr. Sanders about the plaintiff's case, and plaintiff's counsel generated 12 pages of notes relating to the conversation. At the conclusion of the conversation, Dr. Sanders informed plaintiff's counsel that he was not interested in serving as the plaintiff's expert witness.

Subsequently, Dr. Sanders mailed plaintiff's counsel a bill in the amount of $840.00 for two hours and 20 minutes for reviewing the medical records and participating in the telephone conference. Dr. Sanders was later retained as a defense expert. The court held that he was disqualified from testifying as he had reviewed confidential information from the plaintiff's counsel. It stated:

> We recognize that Sanders stated in his affidavit that he had "no independent recollection of having reviewed this case" and that he did not recall "the specifics of any [telephone] conversation" with the plaintiff's lawyer. However, Sanders' lack of recollection is not relevant to the inquiry whether it was objectively reasonable for plaintiff's counsel to conclude that a confidential relationship existed.
>
> Next, we must consider whether plaintiff's counsel disclosed confidential or privileged information to Sanders. In this context, courts have concluded that the phrase "confidential information" includes discussion of: a party's strategies in litigation, the kinds of experts that the retaining party expected to employ, a party's views of the strengths and weaknesses of each side's case, the role of each of the litigant's expert witnesses to be hired, anticipated defenses, counsel's theory of the case, and counsel's mental impressions. *Koch Refining Co.,* 85 F.3d at 1182; *Mitchell,* 981 P.2d at 176-77.
>
> Upon our *in camera* review of the letter dated December 16, 1998 that plaintiff's counsel forwarded to Sanders, we conclude that the letter contained confidential information because plaintiff's counsel revealed his mental impressions and trial strategies to Sanders. While we recognize that the value of the information that plaintiff's counsel disclosed to Sanders may be debatable, that fact does not negate our conclusion that the letter contains the work product of plaintiff's counsel. Thus, we conclude that plaintiff's counsel disclosed confidential information to Sanders.
>
> We hold that the trial court abused its discretion in refusing to disqualify Sanders as an expert witness. Accordingly, we will reverse the judgment of the circuit court, and we will remand this case for a new trial in which Sanders will not be permitted to testify as an expert witness. At 768–769.

## 21.10  Guidelines for Protecting Unwanted Disclosure of Information

To protect unwanted disclosure of attorney work product, expert work product, and other confidential information, experts should heed the following advice.

- An expert should assume that anything he writes, reviews, or says can and will be used against him and his client.

- An expert should not commit anything to writing that he wouldn't want a jury to see.
- An expert should realize from the outset that any drafts, notes, investigative materials, or correspondence to him are likely to be discovered.
- Experts should be careful when annotating or highlighting materials as these notes will be discoverable and are a legitimate area of inquiry at deposition.
- It is best to avoid circulating draft reports to retaining counsel.
- An expert should be aware that counsel will want to discuss in detail the content of any report before it is committed to writing.
- An expert should not disclose or discuss case information with anyone other than counsel—even an inadvertent disclosure may waive a privilege.
- If unsure about a legal issue the expert should consider consulting with his own legal counsel.

## 21.11  Conclusion

Some legal protection is available to shield documents from discovery. To be safe, however, experts should assume that anything and everything they write or consider will be discoverable. Also, any indication that an expert is being dishonest about the existence of documents can destroy an expert's credibility. Experts should not lose, misplace, or destroy documents they review or create for the case. E-mails, which tend to have a casual tone, should be avoided. Draft reports circulated to retaining counsel can be problematic as well and should be avoided, if possible. Experts should be careful of what they write in their notes. Experts should remember that while it is retaining counsel's job to win the case, it is the expert's job to testify and conduct himself with scrupulous honesty and truthfulness.

# Chapter 22  Communicating with Counsel

## 22.1  Introduction

It is important to be able to communicate effectively and properly with retaining counsel. Communication between counsel and experts is complicated by the differences in technical backgrounds, jargon, and the standards of proof used by each profession. The role of the expert witness is to assist counsel in understanding, evaluating, and if necessary, proving his case. Communication between them must be a two-way street. Both the expert and the attorney need to listen actively and understand clearly what the other person is saying and, in some cases, what they are not saying.

## 22.2  Avoiding Jargon

When experts and attorneys talk to each other, they should avoid technical jargon as much as possible. Use of jargon by either the expert or the attorney may cause unnecessary misunderstandings. An expert should talk to the retaining attorney as she would talk to the jury on direct examination. She should act as a teacher and use analogies and similes. Not only will this help the expert to communicate more clearly with the attorney, it will also demonstrate that she will be an effective witness on the stand. It will also permit her to practice the testimony she may provide during direct examination.

> **Example 22.1: Technical jargon impairs communication**
> **Q. By counsel:** Can you testify to a reasonable degree of scientific certainty that the fire was the result of the arson?
> **A. Expert:** No, because you have not yet provided me with verification of trailers, alligatoring of wood, depth of char, and spalling.
>
> **Comment:** An expert who retaining counsel cannot understand is of little value. The most valuable experts are able to communicate to lay people (jurors, judges, and attorneys).

> **Example 22.2: Legalese not helpful**
> **Q. By expert:** When would you need a written report on this?
> **A. Counsel:** That depends what they do vis à vis Rules 26 and 56 and whether we get a stipulation.
>
> **Comment:** Attorneys will get the most out of their experts if they avoid legalese.

When experts and counsel truly understand what the other party is saying, actual communication has begun.

## 22.3  Discoverability of Communications

*All communications with counsel should be oral unless the expert is asked specifically by his retaining attorney to create a written document.* This rule is followed because the discovery rules may allow the production of any and all written communications between retaining attorneys and experts. The rules governing this possible disclosure vary (see Chapter 21 on confidentiality and work product), but it is best to assume that any and all written communication will be subject to discovery.

Oral communications between an expert and retaining counsel are usually discoverable as well, but the contents of these conversations are subject to the memory of the expert. Some oral communication may be protected from discovery. However, one should assume that any communications between an expert and counsel will be a legitimate area of inquiry at deposition and trial.

**Example 22.3: Asking about conversations with counsel during a break at a deposition**
**Q.** Resuming the deposition of Dr. Jones. Dr. Jones, during our ten-minute break I saw you conferring in private with Attorney Smith. Please tell me everything you said and everything she said.
**A.** We discussed how much longer this deposition might go on and whether or not we'd make it home for game 4 tonight. Then we talked quite a bit about last night's game 3.

**Comment:** Opposing counsel here is trying to get the expert to admit that he was coached by retaining counsel. Experts who do not discuss the case during breaks at deposition insulate themselves from such attacks.

## 22.4  Areas to Cover

The topics that need to be covered between retaining counsel and the expert include the following.

- How the attorney intends to use the expert's testimony
- Conflicts of interest/bias
- Status of the litigation
- Agreement on fees, expenses, and methods of payment
- Initial opinion sought
- Setting reasonable time frames for the completion of the work to be undertaken
- Instructions in scientific principles
- Opinions the expert can express
- Opinions the expert cannot express
- Opinions to be expected by opposing experts
- Demonstrative evidence
- Approval of expert discovery
- Written vs. oral reports

*How the attorney intends to use the expert's testimony*
Prior to accepting an assignment, the expert should discuss with counsel the nature of the case, the parties involved, and how counsel intends to use the expert's testimony. A frank initial discussion will enable the expert to avoid conflicts of interest and cases with which he is uncomfortable. This discussion is the first step in valuable communication between counsel and the expert. As Eric Swan notes:

> It is critical to have an understanding of what the attorney is using your testimony for and how this is used during the litigation. Once you fully understand how the attorney intends to use your expert testimony, then you can clearly communicate with the attorney and provide help

and guidance. You can work together to present the most persuasive and compelling testimony possible given the facts and circumstances of the case.[1]

Of course, experts should avoid going into such detail that includes confidential information from the lawyer until the expert receives back a signed retention agreement and a non-refundable retainer. This will help prevent the expert from being conflicted out of the case.

*Conflicts of interest/bias*

Any potential conflicts of interest or potential bias should be brought to the retaining attorney's attention immediately. Such conflicts could include a financial or personal relationship to an opposing party or lawyer in the case. A potential bias could include a financial or personal relationship to the party or lawyer who is retaining the expert in the case. Experts should not get involved in cases where a potential conflict of interest exists. Bias can and will be brought out before the jury to discredit an expert. An expert should only get involved if he and the retaining attorney feel confident to risk having the expert's credibility challenged due to potential bias.

**Example 22.4: Conflict of interest**
**Q. From expert:** Who is the defendant in the case?
**A.** Smith and Jones, LLP.
**Q.** I'm sorry, I can't get involved. My sister is an equity partner in that firm.

**Example 22.5: Potential bias**
**Q. From expert:** What firm are you with again?
**A.** Robinhood and Coleson.
**Q.** I have to inform you that my niece, Mary Jones, is an associate at your firm and they could use that against me to show bias.

*Status of the litigation*

It is wise to inquire about the status of the litigation or the claim counsel is inquiring about. The case may be:

- contemplated but not yet filed,
- filed without discovery,
- in the initial discovery stage,
- completed with the initial discovery stage and in the process of taking depositions,
- marked ready for trial, or
- scheduled for trial.

A specific understanding of how far the case has proceeded is necessary for an expert to make an informed, intelligent decision regarding whether she wants to get involved in the case. The farther along the case is, the less time one will have to work on the matter.

---

[1] Eric J. Swan, Esq., *Communication with Counsel and Jury.* Handout materials from the SEAK Seventh Annual Expert Witness and Litigation Seminar, Hyannis, Massachusetts (June 18–19, 1998) 200.

Experts who get involved in cases at the last moment should anticipate vigorous cross-examination on this issue. Some experts who are asked to work on a "drop everything" rush basis charge a premium fee in those circumstances. If the expert, due to time constraints, is not able to follow his usual procedures, the expert will be particularly vulnerable on cross-examination.

*Fees*

There must be no misunderstanding about fees, retainers, and expense reimbursements. A written fee schedule or agreement is recommended. (Chapter 19 discusses fees in detail. Model fee schedules and agreements are provided in Appendix R.) To protect oneself from being conflicted out of a case, the expert should neither receive nor review confidential information until he has received a signed fee agreement and a significant non-refundable retainer.

*Initial opinion sought*

After an expert has been retained and has reviewed the available evidence, documents, reports, and studies, he may be asked by counsel for an *initial opinion*. As Harvey Cohen discusses, the expert will usually give counsel one of the following five responses:

> 1. Yes, not only can I be helpful, but I am familiar with the particular issue and will be able to testify on your behalf.
> 2. I need more information and must assess the particular facts in order to reach a conclusion on what I could testify to. At the least, I can help you to put the case into perspective with respect to the scientific issues, show you the strengths and weakness of your case, and help evaluate the opponent's case against you.
> 3. I understand the technical issues, but you should be aware that my position on some of the issues may be contrary to those you would like to prove. Alternatively, I can agree with your theory to some extent, but have some reservations, and if cross-examined on certain issues, I would have to state opinions that may not be helpful. In any event, I can help you in the evaluation of your case and can assist you in understanding both the positive and negative aspects.
> 4. I cannot help you because my position on the issues is completely at odds with your theories.
> 5. I prefer not to get involved because the issues are not in my areas of expertise (or an area in which I do not want to become involved).[2]

Clear communication and full disclosure at this stage are important. Such communication will prevent, or at least help deter, the retaining attorney from pressuring an expert later to testify to more than she may feel truly comfortable with.

*Reasonable timeframes*

The expert should first determine the status of the litigation. Then the expert will want to discuss with counsel a reasonable timeline for the completion of the assignments. Before

---

[2] Harvey Cohen, Ph.D., C.I.H., *Communication with Counsel.* Handout materials from the Sixth Annual SEAK National Expert Witness and Litigation Seminar, Hyannis, MA (June 19–20, 1997) 119–120.

accepting any assignment, the expert should make an honest appraisal of whether she will have the time to do her best work. Counsel who refuses to communicate a timeline or tells the expert "not to worry" should be questioned closely by the expert on realistic timeframes.

The sophisticated expert will refuse assignments in which he is not given adequate time to do a professional job. These experts have a healthy suspicion of such last-minute assignments. Such assignments could result in substandard work with resultant damage to the expert's reputation and potential civil liability. (See Chapter 20 on expert liability and risk management.)

## Instruction on scientific principles

The successful expert instructs counsel on the scientific principles, literature, and its ramifications for the case at hand. The ability of the expert to gather all of the literature and explain it to the attorney so that she truly understands is the key to successful communication in this area. Even attorneys without scientific backgrounds can be educated as to the science involved when they take adequate time to be prepared by the expert. The ability of the expert to make the attorney understand and appreciate the scientific principles, ramifications, nuances, and opposing scientific opinions will often determine the outcome in the case.

## Opinions the expert can express

The opinions the expert can express need to be communicated to the retaining attorney. This should be done orally after the expert has completed the investigation, research, documents review, and other work. A phone call is the preferred method of communication. The expert should communicate:

- the areas on which he will offer opinions,
- the exact parameters of the opinions,
- the degree of scientific certainty and reliability of the opinions, and
- the strengths and weaknesses of the opinions.

It is only after the initial oral report that an expert should create a written report. Such a report should be written *only* if the expert is specifically requested to do so by counsel.

## Opinions the expert cannot express

Equally important is for counsel to know and understand the opinions an expert *cannot* express. Counsel may have a different agenda than an expert. Counsel wants to win. The expert should want to tell the truth and maintain his credibility. If counsel attempts to push, cajole, trick, or intimidate an expert into giving opinions he does not feel comfortable with, the expert should flatly and clearly (but politely, of course) refuse to do so. The expert's role in the case may end, but his reputation will remain intact.

## Opinions by opposing experts

Experts who use their experience and familiarity with opposing experts and provide counsel with their writings, presentations, prior testimony, and likely testimony communicate invaluable information. Frequently the expert, due to her experience and familiarity with the field and other experts, is in an excellent position to offer this assistance to counsel. Experts can also help to prepare counsel to cross-examine and otherwise question the opposing experts' opinions.

*Demonstrative evidence*

*Demonstrative evidence* can be very effective in communicating complex information to a jury or other fact finder. The expert is in an excellent position to recommend to counsel demonstrative evidence, such as charts, videotapes, equipment, and other aids, for use at trial. Likewise, counsel may make similar suggestions to the expert to help her testimony come alive and be memorable for the jury. By working together and communicating with each other, the attorney and the expert can help assure that the expert will be able to communicate properly with the jury.

*Approval of expert discovery*

A sophisticated expert asks to read, approve, and sign-off on all discovery responses or disclosures concerning the expert, her qualifications, opinions, and the factual basis for her opinions. If counsel does not communicate this information to the expert before it is provided to opposing counsel, unnecessary errors can be made. Experts should anticipate being questioned about discovery disclosures at deposition and at trial. A failure of communication between counsel and the expert concerning the discovery process can be a serious mistake with negative consequences.

*Written vs. oral reports*

Experts should communicate with counsel orally to determine if a written report is desired *before* preparing or sending out any reports. It is best to assume that all written reports by experts are discoverable by opposing counsel. It is common practice for experts to orally discuss with counsel their findings and conclusions before preparing any written reports. In addition, it is crucial that experts clearly understand the parameters of the questions to be addressed in any written reports. Additional areas should not be addressed in written reports.

## 22.5 Communications at Deposition and Trial

An expert can generally communicate with counsel prior to deposition or trial or during breaks in these proceedings. Of course, the content of these oral communications is usually a legitimate area of inquiry. An expert is generally not allowed to take a break from either for the specific purpose of consulting with his retaining attorney.

Communication at deposition or trial may, however, still take place. When an objection is made at deposition or at trial, counsel might also be communicating certain key points to an expert. When an objection is made, the expert should immediately stop talking and listen intently to the objection.

> **Example 22.6: Attorney communicates with expert through objection**
> **Counsel:** Objection. Misleading and confusing. He's taking that statement out of context.
> **A.** That's not what I meant. If you read the entire document you can see….

The repetition of certain questions on direct examination may be an attempt to communicate with the expert. One noted trial attorney explains:

> You generally can tell when there is a glitch in communication in court because there are signs of a problem. If the attorney asks you the same or virtually the same question repeatedly there is a problem. Take a step back and try to see why the answer you are providing is not satisfying the attorney. You may want to tell the attorney that you are not sure what he is asking for or getting at. This can force him to rephrase the question so you can learn what the problem may be.[3]

The repeating of a question is a red flag that the expert may have forgotten to include some part of the testimony that he had intended to provide.

**Example 22.7: Follow-up question communicates that the expert forgot to mention examination**

**Q.** What did you base your opinion on, Doctor?

**A.** The history provided by the examinee, the medical records, a review of the depositions, and a review of the relevant medical literature.

**Q.** Anything else?

**A.** Yes, of course. My examination of Ms. Jones on December 3, 1999, and again on February 14, 2000.

## 22.6 Conclusion

Clear and honest communication with counsel is required. Such communication will prevent many potential problems and will enhance the effectiveness of an expert witness. Even so, experts should avoid communicating with counsel in writing unless specifically requested to do so by counsel.

---

[3] Swan, 208.

# Chapter 23  Ethics and the Expert

## 23.1  Introduction

Experts need a full understanding of the moral, legal, and financial reasons for acting in an ethical manner.  If an expert operates unethically, she can be and, in many cases, will be subject to a variety of sanctions including prosecution for perjury, civil suits, monetary sanction by the court, professional discipline, loss of future referrals, and damage to her reputation.  This chapter will identify some of the most common ethical violations by experts and explain how these can be avoided.

## 23.2  Sample Ethical Codes of Professional Groups

In addition to their legal obligations, experts are subject to the ethical standards and codes of conduct of their professional organizations and certifying bodies.  This is a fertile area of cross-examination.  An expert should review the ethical rules governing litigation support with all his relevant organizations.  Experts with multiple affiliations and certifications should take care to know, understand, and comply with all of the applicable standards and codes of conduct they are subject to.  An instructive sampling of relevant standards and codes is provided below.

*Competence and qualifications*

"Engineers shall perform services only in the areas of their competence," and "engineers shall undertake assignments only when qualified by education or experience in the specific technical fields involved."  (NSPE, 2, a)

"A member shall only accept engagements the member can reasonably expect to complete with a high degree of professional competence. If a member lacks the knowledge and/or experience to complete such engagement with a high degree of professional competence, the member is not precluded from performing such engagement. In such instance, the member must take steps necessary to gain such expertise through additional research and/or consultation with other professionals believed to have such knowledge and/or experience prior to completion of such engagement." (NACVA Professional Standards)

"A Certified Fraud Examiner shall, at all times, exhibit the highest level of integrity in the performance of all professional assignments and will accept only assignments for which there is reasonable expectation that the assignment will be completed with professional competence." (Association of Certified Fraud Examiners Code of Professional Ethics)

"Members shall not attempt to obtain personal aggrandizement or business engagements by untruthfully exaggerating, embellishing or otherwise misrepresenting their credentials and/or qualifications." (Forensic Expert Witness Association Code of Ethics)

"A computer professional has a duty to be honest about his or her own qualifications and about any circumstances that might lead to conflicts of interest."  (Association for Computing Machinery (ACM) Code of Conduct, 1.3)

"Engineers shall perform services only in areas of their competence." (American Society of Civil Engineers (ASCE) Code of Ethics, 2)

"ISA members should accept only appraisal assignments that fall within their professional capabilities." (International Society of Appraisers—Code of Ethics and Professional Conduct, Rule 4.07)

"3.4 Appraiser's Obligation to Attain Competency and to Practice Ethically
In order to meet his obligations, the appraiser must be competent in his field. This competency he attains by education, training, study, practice, and experience. He must also recognize, understand, and abide by those ethical principles that are interwoven with and are an essential part of truly professional practice." (American Society of Appraisers, Principles of Appraisal Practice and Code of Ethics)

*Honesty and truthfulness*
"All physicians must...testify honestly." (Code of Medical Ethics: Medical Testimony: Current Opinions of the Council on Ethical and Judicial Affairs of the American Medical Association, Opinion E-9.07)

"A member shall remain objective, apply professional integrity, shall not knowingly misrepresent facts or subrogate judgment to others. The member must not act in a manner that is misleading or fraudulent." (NACVA Professional Standards)

"All traffic collision reconstructionists accredited by ACTAR, therefore, are expected to be honest, impartial, fair and ethical in the services they provide." (The Accident Commission for Traffic Accident Reconstruction Code of Conduct)

"Relate honestly and ethically in all professional relationships." (American College of Occupational and Environmental Medicine (ACOEM) Code of Ethical Conduct)

"A Certified Fraud Examiner will comply with lawful orders of the courts and will testify to matters truthfully and without bias or prejudice." (Association of Certified Fraud Examiners Code of Professional Ethics)

"Engineers in the fulfillment of their professional duties shall avoid deceptive acts." (National Society of Professional Engineers (NSPE) code of ethics for engineers, I, 5)

"Integrity requires a member to be, among other things, honest and candid within the constraints of client confidentiality. Service and the public trust should not be subordinated to personal gain and advantage. Integrity can accommodate the inadvertent error and the honest difference of opinion; it cannot accommodate deceit or subordination of principle." (AICPA Code of Professional Conduct)

"Serve the public, employees, employers, clients and the Society with fidelity, honesty and impartiality." (American Society of Safety Engineers Code of Professional Conduct, 2)

"Honesty is an essential component of trust. Without trust an organization cannot function effectively. The honest computing professional will not make deliberately false or deceptive claims about a system or system design but will instead provide full disclosure of all pertinent system limitations and problems." (ACM, 1.3)

"Engineers shall be guided in all their relations by the highest standards of honesty and integrity." (NSPE, III, 1)

"ACFEI members should not misrepresent or overstate their credentials, education, training, experience, or membership status." (American College of Forensic Examiners Principles of Practice)

"Truthfulness and Candor. (A) In forensic testimony and reports, psychologists testify truthfully, honestly, and candidly and, consistent with applicable legal procedures, describe fairly the bases for their testimony and conclusions. (B) Whenever necessary to avoid misleading, psychologists acknowledge the limits of their data or conclusions." (American Psychological Association: Ethical Principles of Psychologists and Code of Conduct, 7.03)

## Conflicts of interest
"Engineers shall disclose all known or potential conflicts of interest that could influence or appear to influence their judgment or the quality of their services." (NSPE, 4, a)

"To avoid real or perceived conflicts of interest whenever possible, and to disclose them to affected parties when they do exist." (Institute of Electrical and Electronics Engineers—Code of Ethics, 2)

"Conflicts of interest and scientific misconduct, such as fabrication, falsification, and plagiarism, are incompatible with this Code." (The Chemist's Code of Conduct, The American Chemical Society)

"Objectivity is a state of mind, a quality that lends value to a member's services. It is a distinguishing feature of the profession. The principle of objectivity imposes the obligation to be impartial, intellectually honest, and free of conflicts of interest. Independence precludes relationships that may appear to impair a member's objectivity in rendering attestation services." (AICPA Code of Professional Conduct)

"Members shall not permit themselves to be compromised by conflicts of interest or allow the influence of others to override their objectivity." (Forensic Expert Witness Association Code of Ethics)

"Conflict of Interest—ISA members must avoid and withdraw from situations that represent a conflict of interest." (ISA, Rule 4.06)

"Conflict of Interest: Members should avoid conflicts of interest in their professional practices and fully disclose all unavoidable conflicts as they arise." (American Institute of Architects, Code of Ethics 3.2)

## Contingency fees
"Physician testimony must not be influenced by financial compensation; for example, it is unethical for a physician to accept compensation that is contingent upon the outcome of the litigation." (American Medical Association, Code of Medical Ethics: Current Opinions of the

Council on Ethical and Judicial Affairs of the American Medical Association, Opinion E-9.07)

"7.1 Contingent Fees  If an appraiser were to accept an engagement for which the amount of his compensation is contingent upon the amount of an award in a property settlement or a court action where his services are employed; or is contingent upon the amount of a tax reduction obtained by a client where his services are used; or is contingent upon the consummation of the sale or financing of a property in connection with which his services are utilized or is contingent upon his reaching any finding or conclusion specified by his client; then, anyone considering using the results of the appraiser's undertaking might well suspect that these results were biased and self-serving and therefore, invalid. Such suspicion would militate against the establishment and maintenance of trust and confidence in the results of appraisal work, generally; therefore the Society declares that the contracting for or acceptance of any such contingent fee is unethical and unprofessional." (American Society of Appraisers, Principles of Appraisal Practice and Code of Ethics)

"No engagement shall be undertaken on a contingent fee basis."  (American Society of Questioned Document Examiners, Code of Ethics, Rule 7)

"Contingent Fees. A member shall not perform a valuation engagement which results in the expression of a Conclusion of Value, as defined in §3.2, for a contingent fee." (NACVA Professional Standards)

*Confidentiality*
"To treat information received from a client as confidential; and when a matter has already been undertaken, to refuse to perform any services for any person whose interests are opposed to those of the original client, except by express consent of all concerned, or where required by established administrative procedure or by law." (ASQDE Code of Ethics, Rule 3)

"A member shall not disclose any confidential client information to a third party without first obtaining the express consent of the client, unless required to do so by competent legal authority." (NACVA Professional Standards)

"A Certified Fraud Examiner shall not reveal any confidential information obtained during a professional engagement without proper authorization." (Association of Certified Fraud Examiners Code of Professional Ethics).

"When a legal claim pertains to a patient the physician has treated, the physician must hold the patient's medical interests paramount, including the confidentiality of the patient's health information, unless the physician is authorized or legally compelled to disclose the information." (American Medical Association, Code of Medical Ethics: Current Opinions of the Council on Ethical and Judicial Affairs of the American Medical Association, Opinion E-9.07)

"Article 7, sec 2.d Unacceptable Conduct. Conviction, judgment or sanction by a court having jurisdiction for any act of breach of confidentiality." (The Accident Commission for Traffic Accident Reconstruction Code of Conduct)

"Chemists should serve clients faithfully and incorruptibly, respect confidentiality, advise honestly, and charge fairly." (The Chemist's Code of Conduct, The American Chemical Society)

"Members shall respect the confidentiality of information acquired during the performance of their service(s) and shall not disclose to a third party any confidential or proprietary information without appropriate and specific authority." (Forensic Expert Witness Association Code of Ethics)

"Confidentiality—ISA members shall maintain the confidentiality of their relationship with the client regarding the property that is being appraised. The ISA members shall safeguard all appraisal reports and documents from unauthorized scrutiny and/or seizure, unless legally required to make such disclosure." (ISA, Rule 4.00)

"Confidentiality: Members should safeguard the trust placed in them by their clients." (American Institute of Architects, Code of Ethics and Professional Conduct, Ethical Standard, 3.4)

"Keep confidential all individual medical information, releasing such information only when required by law or overriding public health considerations, or to other physicians according to accepted medical practice, or to others at the request of the individual." (ACOEM, 5)

"The principle of honesty extends to issues of confidentiality of information whenever one has made an explicit promise to honor confidentiality or, implicitly, when private information not directly related to the performance of one's duties becomes available. The ethical concern is to respect all obligations of confidentiality to employers, clients, and users unless discharged from such obligations by requirements of the law or other principles of this Code." (ACM, 1.8)

*Impartiality*
"2.2 Objective Character of the Results of an Appraisal Undertaking
The primary objective of a monetary appraisal, is determination of a numerical result, either as a range or most probable point magnitude—the dollar amount of a value, the dollar amount of an estimated cost, the dollar amount of an estimated earning power. This numerical result is objective and unrelated to the desires, wishes, or needs of the client who engages the appraiser to perform the work. The amount of this figure is as independent of what someone desires it to be as a physicist's measurement of the melting point of lead or an accountant's statement of the amount of net profits of a corporation. All the principles of appraisal ethics stem from this central fact." (American Society of Appraisers, Principles of Appraisal Practice and Code of Ethics)

"When physicians choose to provide expert testimony, they should...be committed to evaluating cases objectively and to providing an independent opinion." (American Medical

Association, Code of Medical Ethics: Current Opinions of the Council on Ethical and Judicial Affairs of the American Medical Association, Opinion E-9.07)

"Members shall not permit themselves to be compromised by conflicts of interest or allow the influence of others to override their objectivity." (Forensic Expert Witness Association Code of Ethics)

"To act at all times both in and out of court in an absolutely impartial manner and to do nothing that would imply partisanship or any interest in the case except the proof of the facts and their correct interpretation." (ASQDE, 5)

"ACFEI and its members are to remain completely objective and use their ability to serve justice by making an accurate determination of the facts involved." (American College of Forensic Examiners Principles of Practice)

"Being honest and impartial and serving with fidelity the public, their employers and clients." (ASCE, 2)

*Reports, investigations, and opinions*
"Engineers shall be objective and truthful in professional reports, statements or testimony. They shall include all relevant and pertinent information in such reports, statements or testimony, which should bear the date indicating when it was current." (NSPE, 3a)

"Article 7, sec 2.b Unacceptable Conduct. Conviction, judgment or sanction by a court, administrative board or professional licensure review board relating to falsification or spoliation of evidence intended for, or reasonably deemed to be intended for, use in a legal matter." (The Accident Commission for Traffic Accident Reconstruction Code of Conduct)

"Members shall expeditiously perform forensic services with due care, competence, and diligence only in the fields of their expertise. Members shall utilize standards and controls to provide services in a professional and scientific manner, and in doing so shall conduct objective examinations and analysis and be truthful in reports, statements and testimony." (Forensic Expert Witness Association Code of Ethics)

"A Certified Fraud Examiner, in conducting examinations, will obtain evidence or other documentation to establish a reasonable basis for any opinion rendered. No opinion shall be expressed regarding the guilt or innocence of any person or party…A Certified Fraud Examiner will reveal all material matters discovered during the course of an examination which, if omitted, could cause a distortion of the facts." (Association of Certified Fraud Examiners Code of Professional Ethics)

"A member must exercise due professional care in the performance of services, including completing sufficient research and obtaining adequate documentation…A member shall obtain sufficient relevant data to afford a reasonable basis for conclusions, recommendations or positions relating to any service rendered." (NACVA Professional Standards)

"Integrity also requires a member to observe the principles of objectivity and independence and of due care." (AICPA Code of Professional Conduct)

"To render an opinion or conclusion strictly in accordance with the physical evidence in the document, and only to the extent justified by the facts. To admit frankly that certain questions cannot be answered because of the nature of the problem, the lack of material, or insufficient opportunity for examination." (ASQDE, 4)

"4.3 Appraiser's Obligation Relative to Giving Testimony
When an appraiser is engaged by one of the parties in a controversy, it is unethical for the appraiser to suppress any facts, data, or opinions which are adverse to the case his client is trying to establish; or to overemphasize any facts, data, or opinions which are favorable to his client's case; or in any other particulars to become an advocate. It is the appraiser's obligation to present the data, analysis, and value without bias, regardless of the effect of such unbiased presentation on his client's case." (American Society of Appraisers, Principles of Appraisal Practice and Code of Ethics)

"4.4 Appraiser's Obligation to Document Appraisal Testimony
When a member accepts employment to make an appraisal, or to testify as to value of property before a court of law or other judicial or quasi-judicial forums, the appraiser shall, before testifying, complete an adequate written appraisal report, or have complete documentation and substantiation available in his files." (American Society of Appraisers, Principles of Appraisal Practice and Code of Ethics)

## 23.3 Lawyers' Ethical Obligations

The lawyers involved in a case are subject to their profession's ethical rules. Sophisticated experts understand not only their own legal and ethical obligations but those of counsel who has retained them and those who will cross-examine them as well. Unfortunately, experts may be subjected to intense pressure by counsel to reach the result that counsel desires. Knowledge of lawyers' legal and ethical obligations gives experts valuable information, which can and should be used to help them stand their ethical ground.

The ethical obligations of lawyers are controlled by their state rules of professional conduct or code of professional responsibility. The American Bar Association's model rules of professional conduct, which have been adopted by the majority of states provides:

### Rule 3.1 Meritorious Claims and Contentions
A lawyer shall not bring or defend a proceeding, or assert or controvert an issue therein, unless there is a basis in law and fact for doing so that is not frivolous, which includes a good faith argument for an extension, modification or reversal of existing law. A lawyer for the defendant in a criminal proceeding, or the respondent in a proceeding that could result in incarceration, may nevertheless so defend the proceeding as to require that every element of the case be established.

### Rule 3.2 Expediting Litigation
A lawyer shall make reasonable efforts to expedite litigation consistent with the interests of the client.

## Rule 3.3 Candor Toward the Tribunal

(a) A lawyer shall not knowingly:

(1) make a false statement of fact or law to a tribunal or fail to correct a false statement of material fact or law previously made to the tribunal by the lawyer;

(2) fail to disclose to the tribunal legal authority in the controlling jurisdiction known to the lawyer to be directly adverse to the position of the client and not disclosed by opposing counsel; or

(3) offer evidence that the lawyer knows to be false. If a lawyer, the lawyer's client, or a witness called by the lawyer, has offered material evidence and the lawyer comes to know of its falsity, the lawyer shall take reasonable remedial measures, including, if necessary, disclosure to the tribunal. A lawyer may refuse to offer evidence, other than the testimony of a defendant in a criminal matter, that the lawyer reasonably believes is false.

(b) A lawyer who represents a client in an adjudicative proceeding and who knows that a person intends to engage, is engaging or has engaged in criminal or fraudulent conduct related to the proceeding shall take reasonable remedial measures, including, if necessary, disclosure to the tribunal.

(c) The duties stated in paragraphs (a) and (b) continue to the conclusion of the proceeding, and apply even if compliance requires disclosure of information otherwise protected by Rule 1.6.

(d) In an ex parte proceeding, a lawyer shall inform the tribunal of all material facts known to the lawyer that will enable the tribunal to make an informed decision, whether or not the facts are adverse.

## Rule 3.4 Fairness to Opposing Party and Counsel

A lawyer shall not:

(a) unlawfully obstruct another party's access to evidence or unlawfully alter, destroy or conceal a document or other material having potential evidentiary value. A lawyer shall not counsel or assist another person to do any such act;

(b) falsify evidence, counsel or assist a witness to testify falsely, or offer an inducement to a witness that is prohibited by law;

(c) knowingly disobey an obligation under the rules of a tribunal except for an open refusal based on an assertion that no valid obligation exists;

(d) in pretrial procedure, make a frivolous discovery request or fail to make reasonably diligent effort to comply with a legally proper discovery request by an opposing party;

(e) in trial, allude to any matter that the lawyer does not reasonably believe is relevant or that will not be supported by admissible evidence, assert personal knowledge of facts in issue except when testifying as a witness, or state a personal opinion as to the justness of a cause, the credibility of a witness, the culpability of a civil litigant or the guilt or innocence of an accused; or

(f) request a person other than a client to refrain from voluntarily giving relevant information to another party unless:

(1) the person is a relative or an employee or other agent of a client; and

(2) the lawyer reasonably believes that the person's interests will not be adversely affected by refraining from giving such information.

**Rule 3.5 Impartiality and Decorum of the Tribunal**

A lawyer shall not:

(a) seek to influence a judge, juror, prospective juror or other official by means prohibited by law;

(b) communicate ex parte with such a person during the proceeding unless authorized to do so by law or court order;

(c) communicate with a juror or prospective juror after discharge of the jury if:

(1) the communication is prohibited by law or court order;

(2) the juror has made known to the lawyer a desire not to communicate; or

(3) the communication involves misrepresentation, coercion, duress or harassment; or

(d) engage in conduct intended to disrupt a tribunal.

…

**Rule 8.4 Misconduct**

It is professional misconduct for a lawyer to:

(a) violate or attempt to violate the Rules of Professional Conduct, knowingly assist or induce another to do so, or do so through the acts of another;

(b) commit a criminal act that reflects adversely on the lawyer's honesty, trustworthiness or fitness as a lawyer in other respects;

(c) engage in conduct involving dishonesty, fraud, deceit or misrepresentation;

(d) engage in conduct that is prejudicial to the administration of justice;

(e) state or imply an ability to influence improperly a government agency or official or to achieve results by means that violate the Rules of Professional Conduct or other law; or

(f) knowingly assist a judge or judicial officer in conduct that is a violation of applicable rules of judicial conduct or other law.

The exact rules that govern the conduct of attorneys vary from state to state. (As an example, see the rules that govern Massachusetts attorneys in Appendix Y.) The thread that binds all ethical rules governing attorneys is honesty. If an expert feels that she is being asked or pressured to provide false testimony, she should strongly consider discretely reminding the attorney that she is aware of the ethical rules that the attorney is subject to and that she would never provide false testimony, reports, or data. If the expert still feels that she is under pressure to provide dishonest testimony, reports, or data, it may be time to end the relationship with the attorney in question.

## 23.4 Common Ethical Violations by Expert Witnesses

Harold Feder notes that the most common ethical violations committed by experts include:

- Outright false data
- Investigation not done
- Data altered
- Conditional engagement undertaken
- False testimony
- Intentional ignoring of available data
- Recanting prior contra positions
- Assignment beyond competence
- Accepting unauthorized attorney influence

- Inadequate support or time to complete assignment
- Conclusion reached before research
- Conflicts of interest[1]

Other ethical violations include *trimming* (smoothing irregularities to make data look accurate and precise), *cooking* (retaining only those results that fit the theory and discarding others), and *forging* (inventing research data).[2]

## 23.5  Results of Expert's Dishonesty on Litigation in Question

Experts who testify dishonestly can be subject to criminal, civil, and professional legal action. Dishonest expert testimony may also result in the setting aside of the verdict in the case in which the expert testified.

**Example 23.1: New trial granted after expert's perjury was discovered**
*Trapp v. American Trading & Production Corp.,* 414 N.Y.S.2d 11 (1st Dept., 1979)
In an action by a seaman to recover damages for personal injuries, alleging unseaworthiness and common law negligence, the jury verdict in the plaintiff's favor was properly set aside by the trial judge and a new trial was properly granted on the ground of newly discovered evidence. Such evidence being that one of the plaintiff's expert witnesses lied about his academic and occupational qualifications, where the trial judge thought perjury so infected the verdict as to require the verdict to be set aside in the interests of justice.

In giving his qualifications, the expert lied. He said that he held a Bachelor of Science degree in mechanical engineering from Brown University; that he held a Master of Science degree in electrical engineering from the University of California; that he had taken advanced studies at Rensselaer Polytechnic Institute and Old Dominion University; that he had served for twenty-two years in the United States Navy achieving the rank of captain; that he had commanded destroyers, cruisers and ultimately the aircraft carrier *Saratoga*; that he held a master's license in the merchant marine for unlimited tonnage on all oceans; that he had sailed in the merchant marine for about seven years principally as chief officer and master; that he had been a marine surveyor, as vice-president in charge of the Norfolk office of Fraser Marine Surveyors, a company of which he and apparently his brother were part owners.

On the motion for a new trial on the ground of newly discovered evidence, it was conclusively established that these qualifications were wholly false; that he held no degrees, graduate or undergraduate; that he had not completed his freshman year in college; that although he was a "member of the Navy" for twenty-five years, he served on active duty for only nine years; that the highest rank he ever held was chief warrant officer; that he had never reached the rank of captain or commanded the *Saratoga*; that he holds no licenses in the merchant marine, master or even third mate; and that he has no connection with his brother's marine surveying firm and has no business connection with his brother, although without authority he apparently uses his brother's name on his letterhead.

**Comment:** This case reminds one of the movie *Catch Me If You Can*, where the protagonist impersonated an airline pilot, a doctor, and a lawyer. Such cases involving expert witnesses are actually more common than one would think—they are reported fairly frequently in the press.

---

[1] Harold A. Feder, *Shepard's Expert and Scientific Evidence Quarterly,* 2, no. 4 (Spring 1995) 7–10.
[2] Steven Babitsky and James J. Mangraviti, Jr., *How to Excel at Cross-Examination: Techniques for Experts That Work* (Falmouth, MA: SEAK, Inc. 1997) 14.

**Example 23.2: Jury verdict reversed after false testimony by plaintiff's expert**
*Oxendine v. Merrell Dow Pharmaceuticals, Inc.,* 563 A.2d 330 (Dist. Col. App. 1989)
In a products liability case, the plaintiff's expert testified that (1) he was presently, on May 3 and May 11, 1983, a member of the Wayne State University Medical School faculty, when, in fact, he had submitted a letter of resignation from Wayne State dated April 24, 1983, to the Dean of the University, which the Dean accepted on April 29, 1983; (2) he was, at the time of the trial, Chairman of the Formulary Committee at Children's Hospital, a hospital affiliated with the Wayne State Medical School, when, in fact, he had ceased in January 1982 to be Chairman, and in March 1982 to be a member of the committee; (3) he was presently responsible for a fully staffed laboratory at Children's Hospital that conducted ongoing research at his request and direction, even though he had no laboratory assigned solely to him for the two years prior to his testimony and had conducted no research projects at any laboratory during that time; (4) he was presently responsible for the care and treatment of patients, even though after his resignation he had no such responsibilities; and (5) he was a Professor of Pharmacology and Toxicology at the Wayne State Medical School, when no such faculty rank existed and his correct title was Professor of Pediatrics and Pharmacology.

Judge Wolf also found that Dr. Done implied at trial that he was an expert in teratology (the study of birth defects and malformations) and epidemiology (the study of disease incidence and control in a population), but he later stated at the evidentiary hearing that he was not an expert in those entire fields. The trial judge reversed a jury verdict in the plaintiff's favor solely because of the expert's false testimony, although the jury verdict was later reinstated.

**Example 23.3: New trial awarded to criminal defendant after false testimony by expert witness for prosecution**
*State v. DeFronzo,* 394 N.E.2d 1027, 1034 (Ohio Ct. App. 1978)
The state's expert, a police laboratory technician, testified at the defendant's trial for drug possession, possession of an illegal firearm, and falsifying prescriptions. He purported to qualify himself as an expert in drug analysis by stating under oath that (1) he had a four-year bachelor's degree in Pharmacy from the University of Toledo (when he did not); (2) he had a license from the Drug Enforcement Administration that allowed him to analyze and test controlled substances and drugs (when, in fact, nowhere in the expert's personnel file was there a license from the Drug Enforcement Administration, nor was any such license produced at any hearing); (3) that he had received certain on-the-job training (when the training he had received was from various police captains who served as heads of the crime laboratory); (4) he had attended various state and federal seminars regarding the analysis of drugs (when, in fact, he did not attend any state seminars conducted by the Ohio Bureau of Criminal Identification and Investigation, nor did he produce any evidence that he attended any federal drug seminars).

Moreover, the expert testified that he had analyzed the substance found in the foil packet and determined that cocaine was present. In a later hearing, a civilian crime lab technician testified that the expert related to him that he, the expert, had not performed the drug analysis in the Nicholas DeFronzo case, but that a local doctor made the analysis. The expert testified that he attended the FBI Academy on the subject of handwriting, as well as BCI-sponsored handwriting analysis seminars. He did not. Based upon this, and other, false testimony, the court awarded a new trial.

**Example 23.4: New trial granted where expert misrepresented credentials**
*Herington v. Smith,* 485 N.E.2d 500 (Ill. App. 4 Dist. 1985)
The plaintiff won a negligence action for personal injury arising out of an auto accident, but the damages fell far short of the plaintiff's medical costs. Later it was learned that the defendant's

expert witness, a chiropractor, had lied under oath concerning his credentials, and the plaintiff requested a new trial. The expert was presented to the court and the jury as a licensed chiropractor and a licensed medical doctor. He testified that he had graduated from the University of Iowa in 1966, when in fact he graduated from Upper Iowa University in 1979. He testified that he received an M.D. degree from the University of Santo Domingo, when, in fact, he had an M.D. from the Universidad Cetec in the Dominican Republic. Finally, he testified he was licensed to practice medicine in the state of Florida, when, in fact, his only Florida certificate relates to homeopathic medicine. The court granted the plaintiff a new trial, based upon a rule that mandates where perjured testimony so permeates the process as to constitute a fraud upon the court, false testimony by a material witness may alone be sufficient to warrant a new trial.

**Comment:** Experts should never lie or exaggerate about their credentials or anything else.

### Example 23.5: Mix-up in document production
*Peteet, et al. v. Dow Chemical Co.,* 868 F.2d 1428 (5th Cir. 1989)
In a products liability action, the plaintiffs' expert, a toxicologist, testified that the product at issue, a herbicide, caused the plaintiff's death. The defendant claimed that the expert testified falsely at trial about knowing a man named Joseph Moss. Before the expert's deposition, his assistants collected three boxes of medical records regarding this case for the deposition. In one box of documents, the medical records of Mr. Moss, another of the expert's patients, were mistakenly included. The defendant's counsel noticed the error and asked the expert what records he relied upon in forming his opinion that the herbicide caused the plaintiff's cancer. The doctor expansively responded that he had relied upon all the documents in the room, and the defense counsel marked all the records as exhibit number 2. At trial, counsel produced exhibit 2 and asked the expert if he had relied on those records. The expert apparently became confused when he saw the Moss records contained in exhibit 2 and stated that he did not know Joseph Moss. This testimony was false because Moss was a patient of the expert.

   Counsel admitted that he realized during the deposition that the expert's assistants had mistakenly included Moss's medical records, which had nothing to do with the plaintiffs' case, and was simply trying to show that the expert made a mistake. The expert reiterated that his opinion was based on the plaintiff's medical records. The court found that this "false" testimony could not have affected the jury's decision and refused to overturn the defense verdict based on this "false" testimony.

**Comment:** Problems can occur when the expert does not personally supervise her production of documents or does not ensure that a highly competent person does so. Irrelevant documents dealing with other cases and containing confidential information should not be produced.

## 23.6 Avoiding Ethical Violations
The sophisticated expert takes the following steps to avoid potential ethical violations.

*Experts should tell the truth simply and directly.*
Honesty is *always* the best policy. Honesty is a legal, ethical, and moral duty.

*An expert should conduct an honest and complete investigation.*
Experts should not cook, trim, ignore, or forge data. They should review all available material prior to offering an opinion.

# ETHICS AND THE EXPERT

*Experts should not accept assignments outside of their area of competence.*
This is a disservice to everyone involved in the case, including the expert. Experts should not let counsel push them into areas outside of their true area of expertise and should never hold themselves out to be what they are not. Such conduct is unethical and short-sighted. Expert opinions will usually be examined under cross-examination and a lack of true expertise will probably be exposed publicly.

*An expert should undertake assignments only when she is able to perform them in a professional and timely manner.*
An expert should not take an assignment if she does not have time to consider her opinion carefully and to review all of the relevant information.

*Experts should not serve in cases where there is a potential conflict of interest.*
If an expert is subject to a real or perceived conflict of interest that might bias her opinion, the expert should decline to serve in the case. Examples are direct or indirect financial interest in the case or testifying against a former or current employer or client.

*Experts should maintain confidentiality.*
This is not only good ethics, it is also good business. If word ever gets out that an expert disclosed confidential information improperly, her days of being retained as an expert witness will come to a close rapidly.

*Experts should act with impartiality at all times.*
An expert is not an advocate. An expert should call cases as she sees them and avoid advocacy. The attorneys, not the experts, are the advocates.

*It is important to be objective and truthful in all reports, testimony, and statements.*

*A wise expert provides opinions based upon the evidence and a reasonable degree of scientific certainty.*
In most civil cases, an expert's opinion must be based upon a "reasonable degree of scientific or medical certainty." In other words, it is more likely than not that the expert's opinion is valid. An expert is not required to say more, but if she gives an opinion based on less than this minimal threshold, it will be found to be legally insufficient.

*Experts should avoid contingent fees.*
These are not only unethical, but they may open an expert up to a potentially devastating cross-examination.

*Experts should always act with integrity, competence, and moral, professional, and scientific responsibility.*
Whenever in doubt, an expert should take the high road. The case at hand may soon end, but an expert's reputation will stay with her for the rest of her life. One should not risk damaging one's reputation.

*Request written instruction from retaining counsel when one suspects retaining counsel wants the expert to do something unethical.*

Experts should ask for written instructions from the retaining attorney when they suspect that they are being asked to do something unethical. Attorneys may try to push experts into unethical behavior, such as modifying a report. When faced with such pressure, the expert should consider asking the retaining attorney to put his request in writing and to send it to the expert. This should end the pressure very quickly.

## 23.7  Conclusion

Experts should be aware of their ethical obligations and conduct themselves in an ethical manner at all times. Experts also need to be aware of the ethical obligations of attorneys. It may sometimes be prudent to remind attorneys of their ethical obligation of candor.

# Chapter 24  Handling Abuse

## 24.1  Introduction

Expert witnesses are commonly subjected to various forms of abuse.  The purpose of this chapter is to identify the most common of these forms of abuse and to provide practical advice on how to deal with the abuse.

## 24.2  The Most Common Forms of Abuse

The most common forms of abuse are reviewed below.

*Abuse 1. Pirating an expert's name and reputation*

In this form of abuse, counsel, without first contacting the expert, settles or attempts to settle the case based on the expert's reputation.  In effect, the lawyer is misappropriating the expert's name and reputation.  This may be done in a purposeful attempt to avoid having to pay an expert's fee.  It usually involves the situation where the attorney discloses the name of an expert witness to opposing counsel without the expert's knowledge or permission.  This may also be done because the lawyer would like to deny the other parties in the case the opportunity to retain the expert but does not want to spend the time and money necessary to contact her.

> **Example 24.1: Expert disclosed as an expert without consent or even notification**
> You are a highly regarded lead paint expert.  In a lead paint poisoning case, defense counsel discloses your name as an expert who will testify.  Subsequently, the case settles on favorable terms.  You are never notified of any of this, are never retained, and are never compensated.

This type of action by counsel may violate the rules of professional conduct of lawyers that prohibit attorneys from engaging in dishonest behavior.  If faced with this situation, an expert could report the potential misconduct of the attorney to opposing counsel, the judge, or the state organization responsible for disciplining attorneys.  Alternatively, the expert could bill the attorney for the use of his name and bring suit if the attorney does not pay. The problem with each of these courses of action is that the expert would first need to detect the fact that his name is being used without his consent.  Even in today's computer age, however, this is not easily done.

> **Example 24.2: Expert sues attorney for defamation after dispute over the expert being designated without permission, but loses**
> *Solomon v. Molligan,* 2002 WL 31623604 (Cal. App. 2 Dist. 2002)
> Kenneth A. Solomon, Ph.D., the chief scientist for (and the sole owner of) the Institute of Risk & Safety Analyses, sometimes served as an expert witness.  His "retention agreement" provided, among other things, that the "[f]ee for naming expert without sending file is $2,000; this policy is strictly enforced."
> In April 1999, Solomon learned that his deposition had been noticed by defense counsel in a case entitled *Wiedershine v. American Golf Corporation.* It seems that Lingaraj Bahinipaty, the lawyer representing Wiedershine, had designated Solomon as one of the plaintiff's experts—notwithstanding that Solomon had not been retained and had not agreed to testify. Relying on the provision in his retainer agreement, Solomon contacted Bahinipaty and demanded $2,000. When Bahinipaty refused to pay, Solomon sued him in small claims court. To settle that dispute,

Bahinipaty gave Solomon a check for $2,000 drawn on his client's account (or an account of the client's relative); a note on the face of the check says it was "for dismissal." At some point, Wiedershine retained a new lawyer, Rene J. Molligan.

In April 2000, Solomon learned he had again been designated as an expert for the plaintiff in the Wiedershine case, this time by Molligan. Solomon, who claimed he had not been retained, communicated his objection to Molligan. Molligan, in turn, demanded that Solomon return the $2,000 he had received "in settlement of the Small Claims action" or agree to serve as Wiedershine's expert and apply the $2,000 to his fee. Solomon declined. On May 25, Molligan faxed the following letter to Solomon at his Institute:

> I'll make this short and to the point. Unless you immediately return to Bernice Wiedershine $2,000 for payment by her to you in connection with services never rendered to her by you, I will file the enclosed lawsuit for breach of contract, embezzlement, fraud, etc.
>
> After speaking to you several times at length about this matter, on April 15, 2000 I signed a retainer agreement on behalf of plaintiff that you sent to me memorializing our agreement that the $2,000 already paid to you by plaintiff would be applied toward this case. This was, in your opinion, a better result than returning the entire amount to plaintiff.
>
> Thereafter, and pursuant to your agreement to be retained as an expert, I designated you on behalf of plaintiff, Bernice Wiedershine. Note: You faxed your CV and retainer agreement on 4-15-00 for this purpose which I signed and returned the same date.
>
> Several days before designating you as plaintiff's expert, we discussed at length a possible conflict of interest as alleged by John Higgins who claims to have had repeated discussions with you regarding this case as well as your possible retention by defendants in this matter. You repeatedly denied any such conversation(s) with Mr. Higgins and agreed to be telephonically available for a conference call with me and Mr. Higgins on 4-28-00 to discuss any potential conflicts.
>
> Unfortunately, Mr. Higgins refused to participate in any such discussion, preferring instead to bring a motion to exclude you as plaintiff's expert.
>
> Adding insult to injury, you actually signed a declaration that you had not been retained as plaintiff's expert. As you are well aware, Mrs. Wiedershine has already been sufficiently victimized by her former lawyer who has cost the Wiedershines thousands of dollars. Now you, her own expert, hang her out to dry just three weeks before trial. Adding further insult to injury, you have cast a black cloud over my integrity as the lawyer who signed the expert designation. As a member of the Board of Governors for the Consumer Attorney's Association of Los Angeles, whose business you actively solicit, it is my duty to inform the members of your utterly reprehensible business practices.
>
> Please make the $2,000 check payable to Leonard and Bernice Wiedershine and mail it immediately to my office via overnight delivery. If this money is not received by Tuesday, May 30, 2000, I will file the enclosed complaint on Wednesday, May 31, 2000.

The proposed complaint (alleging breach of contract, fraud, embezzlement, and other tortious conduct) was faxed to Solomon along with the quoted letter, without any "precautions to ensure the materials would be received and read only by" Solomon. As a result, the fax "was published to and reviewed by at least four other persons" employed at the Institute.

Concerned about Molligan's threat to inform other lawyers about his "utterly reprehensible business practices," Solomon went to three lawyers "who were an important source of business referrals" and showed them the letter in an effort to "protect his business and reputation," and to "explain, deny and refute [Molligan's] devastating and false allegations." According to Solomon, Molligan never intended to file her complaint but intended only to use it and her letter as "a tactical ploy to negotiate a bargain."

On May 30, Solomon sued Molligan and Wiedershine for defamation. The court dismissed the expert's suit since Molligan's statements were privileged and even awarded Molligan the costs of her appeal, including attorney's fees.

**Comment:** Note that in this case the expert *was* able to obtain a settlement for his full demand of $2,000 in his small claims action against plaintiff's first counsel for designating him as an expert witness without his permission. In this regard, the expert was successful in "fighting back."

## Abuse 2. Nonpayment or slow payment of fee

In this form of abuse, counsel retains an expert and then delays or never pays his fee. This is an all too common form of abuse. When retained by the defense, insurance companies often pay for the expert witness fees. Unfortunately, it is common for insurance companies to be very slow in paying expert bills. When retained by plaintiffs, plaintiff's counsel often advance the fees of expert witnesses out of their own pockets. Many plaintiff's attorneys would like to avoid taking the risk that their client will be unable to pay them back.

***The foolproof way to avoid this type of abuse is to get paid in advance with the use of a replenishable retainer.*** A replenishable retainer is how an attorney would charge you if you hired him and thus attorneys are not in a position to complain about such an arrangement. (For a complete discussion of fees, billings, and collections, please refer to Chapter 19.)

## Abuse 3. Missing records or information

Here counsel of the party retaining the expert intentionally fails to send the expert crucial records, notes, studies, or other underlying data. Counsel, or the client, then pushes the expert for a report or opinion based on the incomplete or limited information provided.

This type of action by counsel may violate the rules of professional conduct of lawyers that prohibit attorneys from engaging in dishonest behavior and presenting false testimony before a court. An expert should remind the attorney of this fact and demand that he be provided with complete documentation. He should refuse to issue an opinion or report until given access to the missing information. Failure to do so can result in damage to one's professional reputation, credibility, and viability as an expert in future cases. If an expert suspects game-playing, he should ask counsel to verify in writing that the expert has been provided with all the records. In any event, experts should always be prepared to state that their opinions are based upon the information they had available to them and if they are presented with additional information they may or may not change their opinions.

## Abuse 4. Pushing the expert outside his area of expertise

Here retaining counsel asks, cajoles, or demands that the expert testify on matters outside his true area of expertise. This usually happens after the expert has been retained and is working on the case for some time. It happens for two reasons. First, counsel may have been too lazy or not had time to locate and retain another expert. More commonly, counsel is trying to save money by, in effect, getting two experts for the price of one.

### Example 24.3: "Oh, by the way"

You are an orthopedic surgeon who has been retained by the plaintiff in a broken leg case. On the way into the courtroom, the retaining attorney states to you, "Oh, by the way, I'll also need you to causally relate her depression to the broken leg."

**Comment:** Many potential problems can be avoided by the expert simply saying "no" to retaining counsel. Here the expert could respond "I'm not qualified to give that opinion and if you ask me that question on the stand, that's what I'll have to tell the jury."

Experts should not be tricked, cajoled, or forced into testifying in areas that are outside their true areas of expertise and in which they do not feel comfortable. Experts who allow themselves to be pushed beyond their true area of expertise are likely to get destroyed on cross-examination. This won't do the expert or the retaining attorney any good.

If an expert is pushed into testifying beyond her area of expertise, she can tell counsel, "I am not an expert in that area and I will so testify if you pose those questions to me." If pushed on the stand, one can simply reply, "That's outside my area of expertise and I don't have an opinion on it." The solution to this common form of abuse is to "just say no."

*Abuse 5. Unrealistic time demands*

Here counsel or the client asks that the expert "drop everything" and work up a preliminary report or opinion quickly. The expert is frequently either intentionally (to save money) or unintentionally (due to poor planning or late notice) given inadequate time to assimilate the facts and documents, conduct research, and operate in a professional manner consistent with her standard procedures.

**Example 24.4: Rush assignment**
You are an engineer. An attorney calls you up and asks for your report and opinion regarding a particular surface where a slip and fall took place. He states, "And I'll need your signed affidavit in the form of an expert report in 48 hours because I have to file an opposition to a motion for summary judgment."

**Comment:** It is wise to find out up-front what the timelines for any assignment are. An expert should either refuse to take a rush assignment or charge a premium for assignments requiring her to put other work aside and redo her schedule.

Many people do not like to say no. Unfortunately, when one is not given adequate time to do a professional job, saying no is probably the best course of action. Last-minute assignments will likely result in substandard work and resultant damage to an expert's reputation. If an expert feels that he can do a professional job in the time frame allowed, he should consider charging a premium fee. This is only fair because he was given a "drop everything" assignment. Counsel is unlikely to refuse because she may not be able to find another expert in time.

*Abuse 6. Tying preliminary opinion to being retained*

Counsel may inquire directly or indirectly as to what an expert's opinion is likely to be before she retains and pays the expert. Frequently, counsel will give the expert a version of the facts and ask, "What do you think?" The implication is clear—if the expert supports the lawyer's position, he will be retained. If he doesn't, he won't.

**Example 24.5: "What do you think?"**
"Yes, Doctor, I represent the plaintiff in a case where there was a broken ankle and the issue in question is the long-term impairment likely to be resultant thereto. What do you think?"

**Comment:** Prudent experts do not give preliminary opinions based on incomplete information.

If an expert does not have enough information to form a very preliminary opinion, he should say so. Failure to do so could box him into a corner that may be difficult to get out of later on. When faced with a situation like this, an expert should tell counsel that, based upon the amount of material she would like the expert to review, he can get her a preliminary opinion in *x* hours, and to please send over a non-refundable retainer for that amount of work. If counsel refuses to send the records and check it could be an indication that counsel is not looking for an honest opinion, but is rather looking for an expert who will "play ball."

*Abuse 7. Refusal to prepare the expert for deposition or trial*
While almost all of the abuse at deposition and trial takes place at the hands of opposing counsel, a failure or refusal to prepare the expert is abuse or neglect by counsel who has retained that expert. The typical last-minute hurried meeting is usually the result of counsel who has been too busy to focus properly on the case or who is trying to save money.

In all but routine, simple, or small cases, an expert should insist that counsel have an in-depth pre-testimony (deposition or trial) conference with her. In this conference, counsel should brief the expert fully on the issues, on the status of the litigation, on the discovery, conduct mock examinations, and be prepared to answer any and all questions the expert may have. It is in everybody's best interest that the expert be briefed fully and that her testimony goes well.

*Abuse 8. Providing an uncomfortable environment for deposition*
Opposing counsel may try to make an expert uncomfortable at deposition in an attempt to distract or break her concentration. The theory here is that if counsel can make the expert uncomfortable enough, she will say anything to get out of the room.

**Example 24.6: Deposition environment like a secret police interrogation**
A deposition that is held in a small, poorly lit, poorly ventilated room with no writing surfaces and hard, uncomfortable chairs is part of this tactic. The room is kept at a temperature of 80 degrees. You are forced to sit facing bright sun and there are no blinds on the window.

**Comment:** Most judges would probably agree that it is unreasonable to be subjected to the conditions described above. The expert in this situation should firmly request that the situation be remedied. If this is not done the expert can consider terminating the deposition and requesting a protective order from the court.

The expert can ask, and, if necessary, demand that she be made comfortable while being deposed. Experts need not be subject to uncomfortable situations for depositions that drone on endlessly. If the request is not complied with, the expert should make sure that it is repeated on the record (that is, recorded on the deposition transcript by the stenographer). The expert should state on the record that she will be forced to terminate the deposition if she is not provided with a comfortable setting. It is wise to specify on the record what is wrong with the setting. If an expert chooses to terminate the deposition, she should make sure that a protective order from the court is filed for promptly.

This abuse can also be avoided by asking that the deposition be scheduled in the expert's own office. There is a potential downside to this, however, because having a deposition in the expert's office subjects the expert to informal discovery. In addition, an expert is likely to prepare less thoroughly for an "on-site" deposition and be more distracted and less focused when in his own office.

*Abuse 9. Repetitive questioning at deposition*
Here counsel tries to get under the expert's skin by deliberately asking the same questions over and over again. Counsel will attempt to get the expert to "blow up" or to change his answer. In a lengthy deposition, this may be part of the overall strategy of trying to break the expert's will by wearing him down.

**Example 24.7: Successfully getting the expert to "lose it"**
**Q.** Is the plaintiff's condition causally related?
**A.** Where the hell do you get off? You've asked me that question seven times already. No. No. Noooooooo. All you plaintiff's attorneys are the same. Nothing but damn scheisters. They need to pass tort reform and get rid of the whole lot of you bastards.

**Comment:** The best experts never let repetitive questions annoy them. Repetitive questions are best dealt with by repetitive answers. Such answers may even get counsel to blow up.

Counsel is granted great leeway with regard to cross-examination of the expert at deposition. Additionally, there is no judge present to cut off repetitive questioning. Thus, the expert will be best served by exercising tireless patience and politeness and just answering the questions. Repetitive questions should not get under the expert's skin, especially because he is being paid by the hour—usually by opposing counsel. Once counsel realizes the expert's answers are not changing and he is not getting flustered, she will usually move on and drop this tactic. If she doesn't, it will cost her dearly as she is usually paying for the opposing expert's time at a deposition.

Also keep in mind that many jurisdictions limit the length of depositions. For example, in Federal Court, depositions are limited to one day with no more than seven hours of testimony.[1] Some states have even shorter limits. When attorneys ask repetitive questions at time-limited depositions they are in effect running the clock out on themselves.

*Abuse 10. Threats of counsel for failing to answer improper questions at deposition*
Counsel will attempt to get the expert to answer improper questions (for example, a question asked in bad faith to annoy, embarrass, or oppress the expert) by threatening to go to the judge and seek a contempt finding and sanctions, such as court costs and legal fees.

**Example 24.8: Improper threats at depositions**
You are asked at deposition about the financial details of your divorce that occurred seventeen years previously and alleged marital infidelity. This was ten years before you were retained as an expert in your very first case. You refuse to answer and counsel threatens you with sanctions.

---

[1] FRCP 32(d)(2).

**Comment:** Experts who know their rights do not succumb to improper threats at depositions. Retaining counsel could intervene and argue it out. If not, the expert could state, "If you insist on a response to this question, which appears designed simply to embarrass and oppress me, I will be forced to terminate this deposition and seek a protective order and sanctions against you, Counselor." Such a response may have the effect of calling counsel's bluff.

It is important to understand that judges are never happy to be bothered with these types of discovery disputes. An expert should not be bullied into answering questions that he knows or strongly suspects to be improper. Although the expert's retaining counsel is not the expert's lawyer, she will frequently pose objections and assist by instructing the expert not to answer. While these objections are technically incorrect, they usually will resolve the matter. In the rare instance when the expert is left alone to deal with this abuse, he can terminate the deposition and seek a protective order (or threaten to do so).

## Abuse 11. Lack of breaks at deposition

This form of abuse involves counsel keeping the deposition questioning going for hours without permitting any breaks. It is designed to wear down the expert so that she will begin to provide answers that have not been considered carefully.

### Example 24.9: Breaks not given

You are questioned for five hours at deposition. After every hour of questioning you ask for a five-minute break to stretch. All of these requests are refused.

The break schedule (including for lunch) is probably best addressed in advance by agreement of all the lawyers. Such an agreement will eliminate almost all problems with a lack of breaks. It also frees the expert from looking at his watch as retaining counsel can point out when it is time for a break. The expert should ask retaining counsel to arrange the break schedule at the beginning of the deposition. If you have particular need for more frequent breaks (say for a back problem), let counsel know in advance.

If an expert needs an unscheduled break, he can and should ask for one. Remember, however, that anything that the expert discusses with retaining counsel or with opposing counsel during a break can and often will be brought up when the deposition resumes. If counsel unreasonably refuses to grant breaks during a lengthy deposition, the expert should make the record clear and simply take a break. Alternately, the expert could terminate the deposition and seek a protective order.

## Abuse 12. Harassing questions at deposition

Counsel may attempt to intimidate, distract, or break an expert's will by asking a series of harassing questions at deposition.

### Example 24.10: Harassing question at deposition

Have you had any homosexual sexual relationships in your life?

Counsel is not permitted to ask bad faith questions that are designed to unreasonably annoy, embarrass, or oppress experts.[2] Counsel is, however, given a good amount of latitude

---

[2] Fed. R. Civ. Pro. 30(d)(3).

in asking questions at deposition. In *Gasinowski v. Hose*, 897 p.2d 678 (Ariz. App. Div. 1 1994), the court permitted the cross-examination of an anesthesiologist about his subsequent suspension from the hospital. In the case of *Winant v. Carras*, 617 N.Y.S. 2d 487 (A.D. 2 Dept. 1994), the court permitted counsel for the defense to cross-examine the plaintiff's expert on the issue of alleged drug addiction. The courts have gone as far as permitting counsel to inspect the personnel files of a retired Los Angeles police officer who was testifying as an expert witness. See *Michael v. Gates*, 45 Cal.Rptr. 163 (Cal. App. 1995).

If counsel who retained the expert does not put a stop to the harassment, the expert should warn opposing counsel about his actions on the record: "Note for the record that counsel is harassing me and if it continues, I will have no alternative but to terminate the deposition and seek a protective order." If the harassment continues, the expert can consider terminating the deposition and seeking a protective order from the judge. The judge will most likely find in the expert's favor if the question was in no way relevant to credibility. If the question was relevant to the expert's credibility (which is always a legitimate issue in a case), then the expert will be more likely to lose before the judge. The losing party may be subject to sanctions.

*Abuse 13. Hostile personal attacks at deposition*
Here the attorney crosses the line with sarcastic, hostile, or profane remarks.

**Example 24.11: Ethnic slur**
So how many other wops do they have on faculty at Harvard?

**Comment:** Counsel is permitted to conduct pointed and aggressive questioning at depositions. However, no judge would consider an ethnic slur to be proper.

If an expert is sure that counsel has crossed the line, such as with a vulgarity or an ethnic, professional, or gender slur, the expert should warn counsel on the record. If the behavior continues, it is best to terminate the deposition and seek the protection of the judge through a motion for a protective order.

*Abuse 14. Nonpayment of deposition fees*
Under the Federal Rules of Civil Procedure, the party seeking to depose an expert is liable for his reasonable fees.[3] Under this form of abuse, counsel will schedule the deposition and not arrange for payment of the expert.

Experts should ask to be paid prior to the deposition. Failure to do this may result in collection problems. If the deposition goes longer than was estimated (which is not uncommon) sophisticated experts have counsel agree on the record (recorded by the stenographer) to make the additional payments required, ask for the check then and there, or

---

[3] Fed. R. Civ. Pro. 26(b)(4)(c) states: "Unless manifest injustice would result, (i) the court shall require that the party seeking discovery pay the expert a reasonable fee for time spent in responding to discovery under this subdivision; and (ii) with respect to discovery obtained under subdivision (b)(4)(B) of this rule the court shall require the party seeking discovery to pay the other party a fair portion of the fees and expenses reasonably incurred by the latter party in obtaining facts and opinions from the expert."

ask for the deposition to be continued until additional payment is received. Some experts also require in their fee agreements that retaining counsel pay for all deposition fees. Retaining counsel can then worry about chasing opposing counsel for reimbursement.

*Abuse 15. Wasting the time of the expert at deposition*
There are three ways that this is commonly done. These are:

- dragging on the deposition with endless questions,
- canceling the deposition on short notice, or
- requiring the expert to travel substantial distances.

An expert can counteract this abuse by charging by the hour (including travel time) and requiring a nonrefundable retainer in the event of the last-minute cancellation of a deposition. When counsel realizes that she is being charged for all of the expert's lost time, the wasted-time problem often resolves itself quickly. If counsel would like to ask endless questions, an expert should let her because the expert is being paid for his time by the hour.

*Abuse 16. Abusive questioning at trial*
Counsel may ask a series of difficult, pointed, or embarrassing questions at trial.

**Example 24.12: Pointed cross-examination question**
Isn't it a fact that your professional license was suspended seven years ago?

**Comment:** Expert witnessing is not an endeavor for the thin skinned. Pointed questions are allowed at trial. At trial, as opposed to at deposition, a judge is present. If counsel crosses the line at trial, retaining counsel may object and the judge may act to limit the questioning.

Unfortunately, counsel is given a good deal of latitude in asking relevant questions about credibility. Many pointed questions will be relevant to an expert's credibility. The only surefire way to avoid being asked tough questions on the stand is to choose not to become involved in expert witness work in the first place.

Some questions do, however, cross the line. In these instances, it will be up to the attorney who retained the expert to object. The judge (who is present, unlike at a deposition) will then be able to rule on the objection and either direct the expert to answer or will sustain the objection and force counsel to move on.

Retaining lawyers can also protect their experts from certain lines of questioning at trial by filing a *motion in limine* before the expert testifies. If this motion is granted, the other lawyers will be precluded from asking the expert questions regarding whatever was covered under the motion in limine. Motions in limine are a good technique to remove the uncertainty of how a judge will rule on an evidentiary matter that is expected to come up at trial. (Chapter 4 provides a further explanation of motions in limine.)

**Example 24.13: Circumstance where a motion in limine might be requested**
You had a nervous breakdown after the death of your teenage son in an auto accident ten years ago. This included a suicide attempt and a 4-week hospitalization at a mental health facility. You could request retaining counsel to file a motion in limine so that opposing counsel can't ask, "Have you ever been confined to a mental hospital?"

*Abuse 17. Trying to "steal" the expert's opinion by calling him as a fact witness and then asking his opinion*

This is where the expert may have some independent factual knowledge relevant to the case, but has not been retained as an expert witness. A common example of this is an injured person's treating physician. An attorney may attempt to subpoena such a witness as a fact witness (who is not entitled to more than a nominal fee for her time) and then ask the witness questions that call for an opinion. When subpoenaed as fact witnesses under these circumstances, experts can take one of two courses of action. If the expert is willing to testify, she should firmly ask the attorney for her usual and customary expert witness fee and state that if the fee is not provided no opinions will be testified to. In the vast majority of cases this will resolve the problem because the lawyer would not want to put "an unhappy expert" on the stand. In most cases, a non-retained expert cannot be legally forced to provide an opinion, which puts the non-retained expert in a strong position when requesting a fee. For example, Federal Rule of Civil Procedure 45(c)(3)(B)(ii) states that:

> If a subpoena requires disclosure of an unretained expert's opinion or information not describing specific events or occurrences in dispute and resulting from the expert's study made not at the request of any party the court may, to protect a person subject to or affected by the subpoena, quash or modify the subpoena or, if the party in whose behalf the subpoena is issued shows a substantial need for the testimony or material that cannot be otherwise met without undue hardship and assures that the person to whom the subpoena is addressed will be reasonably compensated, the court may order appearance or production only upon specified conditions.

This rule was enacted to protect the intellectual property of non-retained expert witnesses.

If the expert does not want to get involved in the litigation (for example, if he would be testifying against a friend or former employer), he can hire an attorney and attempt to quash the subpoena. The likely result is that the expert will not have to provide any opinions but will have to relate any relevant factual knowledge. Please consider the following cases.

### Example 24.14: Unretained expert could not be compelled to give expert testimony
*Nesvig v. Nesvig,* 2006 WL 787955 (N.D. 2006)

Richard Nesvig argued that the district court erred in quashing a subpoena issued to his own expert witness, Wendell Herman. At the second trial, Wendell Herman was subpoenaed by Richard Nesvig to serve as his expert witness on the issue of damages for Gordon Nesvig's failure to invest Richard Nesvig's funds prudently. Herman, a vice president and senior trust administrator at Wells Fargo Bank, had testified at the first trial as an expert witness; however, sometime before the second trial in October 2004, Herman's employer, Wells Fargo, informed him that he would not be allowed to testify at the second trial because of corporate policy. Herman communicated this in correspondence to Richard Nesvig's attorney as early as June 2004. Herman had previously refused compensation for his expert testimony in the first trial and continued to refuse to accept any payment. The court held that the expert could not be compelled to testify. It stated:

> N.D.R.Civ.P. 45(c)(4)(iv), addresses the subpoenaing of unretained experts, and states:
>
> > On timely motion, the court by which a subpoena was issued shall quash or modify a subpoena that
> > ....

(iv) requires disclosure of an unretained expert's opinion or information not describing specific events or occurrences in dispute and resulting from the expert's study made not at the request of any party.

We have often said that where a state rule is adopted from a federal rule, we may consider the federal courts' interpretation of the federal rule as persuasive authority for construing our state rule.

The language of Rule 45(c)(3)(B)(ii), Fed.R.Civ.P., which is identical to N.D.R.Civ.P. 45(c)(4)(iv), was adopted to address a growing problem of the use of subpoenas to compel the giving of evidence and information by unretained experts, and to provide appropriate protection for the intellectual property of non-party witnesses. The advisory committee notes to Fed.R.Civ.P. 45(c)(3)(B)(ii) reflect the concern of the drafters that the subpoena power could be used to deprive expert witnesses of the opportunity to bargain for the value of their services:

Clause (c)(3)(B)(ii) provides appropriate protection for the intellectual property of the non-party witness; it does not apply to the expert retained by a party, where information is subject to the provisions of Rule 26(b)(4). A growing problem has been the use of subpoenas to compel the giving of evidence and information by unretained experts. Experts are not exempt from the duty to give evidence, even if they cannot be compelled to prepare themselves to give effective testimony, but compulsion to give evidence may threaten the intellectual property of experts denied the opportunity to bargain for the value of their services. Arguably the compulsion to testify can be regarded as a "taking" of intellectual property. The rule establishes the right of such persons to withhold their expertise, at least unless the party seeking it makes the kind of showing required for a conditional denial of a motion to quash as provided in the final sentence of subparagraph (c)(3)(B); that requirement is the same as that necessary to secure work product under Rule 26(b)(3) and gives assurance of reasonable compensation. Fed.R.Civ.P. 45(c)(3)(B)(ii), Advisory Committee Notes (citations omitted).

Thus, the party seeking the compelled testimony must show a substantial need for the testimony or material which cannot be otherwise met without undue hardship, and the party must assure reasonable compensation to the person to whom the subpoena is addressed. *Id.* The advisory committee notes also provide the following factors to guide a court in whether to exercise its discretion to compel testimony of an unretained expert:

[T]he degree to which the expert is being called because of his knowledge of facts relevant to the case rather than in order to give opinion testimony; the difference between testifying to a previously formed or expressed opinion and forming a new one; the possibility that, for other reasons, the witness is a unique expert; the extent to which the calling party is able to show the unlikelihood that any comparable witness will willingly testify; and the degree to which the witness is able to show that he has been oppressed by having to continually testify.

Here, in quashing the subpoena, the district court held it could not compel Herman to appear and provide expert testimony because he was an unretained expert. It is important to note that Richard Nesvig was not seeking to compel the testimony of an opposing party's expert, but rather his own expert. During oral argument to this Court, Richard Nesvig conceded he sought to call Herman only as an expert witness, not as a fact witness. An asserted purpose of Herman's testimony was to give an analysis of the hypothetical projected earnings for the money held by Gordon Nesvig for Richard Nesvig from December 1993 to August 1998.

Although Herman testified at the first trial in this case, he refused any compensation and was ultimately prevented by his employer from testifying in the second trial. The district court determined for an expert to be "retained" the expert must receive some type of consideration, payment, or reward.

Richard Nesvig knew as early as four months before the second trial that Herman would not testify at that trial. Yet, on the eve of trial, the district court concluded Richard Nesvig acted to his own detriment in failing to secure a different expert witness or to seek an extension from the court to find another expert. Additionally, Richard Nesvig did not make a sufficient showing to the district court establishing Herman's testimony was of such a unique nature that another witness could not have been procured. Although it quashed the subpoena, the district court did attempt to ameliorate the situation by permitting Richard Nesvig to read Herman's testimony from the first trial to the jury in the second trial.

Based upon our review of the record, we conclude the district court reached its decision through a rational mental process and did not act in an arbitrary, unreasonable, or unconscionable manner. We therefore hold the district court did not abuse its discretion in quashing the subpoena for Herman to testify at the second trial. At 2–4.

**Comment:** The court here cites the Advisory Committee Notes to Federal Rule of Civil Procedure 45(c)(3)(B)(ii) in determining the factors when judging whether to compel expert testimony in a particular case. The factors cited are:

- [T]he degree to which the expert is being called because of his knowledge of facts relevant to the case rather than in order to give opinion testimony;
- the difference between testifying to a previously formed or expressed opinion and forming a new one;
- the possibility that, for other reasons, the witness is a unique expert;
- the extent to which the calling party is able to show the unlikelihood that any comparable witness will willingly testify; and
- the degree to which the witness is able to show that he has been oppressed by having to continually testify.

**Example 24.15: To compel an expert to testify involuntarily, a party must not only show a compelling need for the testimony but also present a plan of reasonable compensation**
*Carney-Hayes v. Northwest Wisconsin Home Care, Inc.,* 284 Wis.2d 56, 699 N.W.2d 524 (Wis. 2005)
The plaintiff sued Northwest, alleging that one of its employees, Kathy Avery, negligently provided emergency nursing treatment. Carney-Hayes now sought to compel expert opinion testimony regarding the applicable standards of care from three unwilling witnesses—Avery, Cheryl Fontaine, and Jodene Verbracken. All three played a role in Northwest's treatment of Carney-Hayes, but only Avery was a named defendant. All three refused to answer certain questions posed at their depositions. Carney-Hayes filed motions asking the circuit court to compel the three witnesses to testify on these standard of care questions. The court took the opportunity to clarify the rules regarding compelling expert witnesses in these circumstances. It stated:

We take this opportunity to reaffirm our holdings in *Alt* and *Glenn* and to clarify the duties and privileges of medical witnesses in a medical malpractice case. (1) A medical witness must testify about her own conduct relevant to the case, including her observations and her thought processes, her treatment of the patient, why she took or did not take certain actions, what institutional rules she believed applied to her conduct, and her training and education pertaining to the relevant subject. (2) Subject to the compelling need exception recognized in *Alt* and *Glenn,* a medical witness who is unwilling to testify as an expert cannot be forced to give her opinion of the standard of care applicable to another person or her opinion of the treatment provided by another person. Unless a medical witness who is unwilling to testify as an expert is alleged to have caused injury to the plaintiff by her medical negligence, the witness is not required to give her opinion on the standard of care governing her own conduct. (3) A medical witness who is alleged to have caused injury to the plaintiff by her medical negligence may be required to give her opinion on the standard of care governing her own conduct. A witness in this category may be a party defendant. However, no medical witness may be named a party defendant for the purpose of eliciting the witness's expert opinion. The circuit court may assess whether there is a reasonable basis for naming a medical witness as a party defendant. The court should assure that any medical witness from whom expert opinion is required is qualified to testify as an expert, pursuant to Wis. Stat. § 907.02. The court may employ evidentiary rules, including §§ 904.02, 904.03, and 906.11 to maintain the focus of a medical malpractice trial on whether the defendant conformed to the standard of care, not whether the defendant performed well as an expert witness. At 529.

We conclude that a witness's privilege to refuse to provide expert testimony is inherent in Wis. Stat. § 907.06. Any other result would be inconsistent and fly in the face of logic. *Alt*, 224 Wis.2d at 86, 589 N.W.2d 21.The existence of the privilege recognized in *Alt* is not revolutionary. We note that a similar privilege has been recognized in several other jurisdictions. See, e.g., *Young v. United States,* 181 F.R.D. 344, 346 (W.D.Texas 1997) ("In the absence of a statute to the contrary, a professional witness may not generally be compelled to testify as an expert at the request of a private litigant, as such testimony is a matter of contract or bargain."); *Agnew v. Parks,* 172 Cal.App.2d 756, 343 P.2d 118, 123 (1959) (treating physician must testify regarding facts learned during examination and treatment of patient, but cannot be compelled to give expert opinion of standard of care or of treatment provided by another); *Mason v. Robinson,* 340 N.W.2d 236, 242-43 (Iowa 1983) (expert witness is free to refuse to provide opinion testimony absent a "compelling necessity" for the testimony); *Commonwealth v. Vitello,* 367 Mass. 224, 327 N.E.2d 819, 827 (1975) ("[A] party may not by summons compel the involuntary testimony of an expert witness solely for the expertise he may bring to the trial, and in the absence of any personal knowledge on his part related to the issues before the judge and the jury"); *Klabunde v. Stanley,* 384 Mich. 276, 181 N.W.2d 918, 921 (1970) ("By definition, an expert is one who gives opinion testimony, and not testimony concerning 'relevant facts.' He has a property right in his opinion and cannot be made to divulge it in answer to a subpoena."); *Stanton v. Rushmore,* 112 N.J.L. 115, 169 A. 721 (E. & A.1934) (expert may be compelled to give factual testimony but not expert opinion); *People ex rel. Kraushaar Bros. & Co. v. Thorpe,* 296 N.Y. 223, 72 N.E.2d 165, 166 (1947) (real estate expert could be compelled to give testimony as to what he had seen on the premises in question, but could not be compelled to testify as to his expert opinion); *Penn. Co. for Ins. on Lives & Granting Annuities v. City of Philadelphia,* 262 Pa. 439, 105 A. 630, 630 (1918) ("The process of the courts may always be invoked to require witnesses to appear and testify to any facts within their knowledge; but no private litigant has a right to ask them to go beyond that [and give expert testimony]"); *Owens v. Silvia,* 838 A.2d 881, 901-02 (R.I.2003) ("Absent extraordinary circumstances ... a non-party expert cannot be compelled to give opinion testimony against his or her will.") (citing *Sousa v. Chaset,* 519 A.2d 1132, 1136 (R.I.1987)). Generally, these courts have determined that the privilege is rooted in the common law.

Having recognized a privilege inherent in the statute, the court sought to define its scope. After considering the alternatives, the court adopted the test the Iowa Supreme Court articulated in *Mason v. Robinson,* 340 N.W.2d 236 (Iowa 1983). Under that test, absent a showing of compelling circumstances by the party seeking the testimony, a witness cannot be compelled to testify as an expert. *Alt,* 224 Wis.2d at 89, 589 N.W.2d 21. If there are a number of people in a given field of expertise with similar knowledge, each capable of rendering an expert opinion on a particular question, then any one expert's opinion is not unique or "irreplaceable," and there is no compelling need for a particular expert's testimony. *Id.* at 89, 589 N.W.2d 21.

To compel an expert to testify involuntarily, a party must not only show a compelling need for the testimony but also present a plan of reasonable compensation. *Id.* The unwilling expert may only be compelled to give existing opinions and may not be asked to undertake additional preparation. *Id.; Glenn,* 269 Wis.2d 575, 676 N.W.2d 413.

**Comment:** Note that experts can be forced to testify as fact witnesses if they have some relevant knowledge, such as being a treating physician.

## 24.3 Fighting Back

In some cases, counsel has been sanctioned for abusing an expert witness. In others, retaining counsel have successfully sued. Consider the following examples.

**Example 24.16: Law firm sues expert for fraudulent billing, expert countersues and wins**
*Murray & Murray, Co., L.P.A. v. Brugger,* Slip Copy, 2005 WL 2415979 (Ohio App. 6 Dist. 2005)

A law firm brought action against an expert witness, alleging breach of contract and fraud, and the expert counterclaimed for breach of contract. On March 5, 2002, Murray and Brugger entered into a written contract for services to be performed by Brugger as an expert witness in an electric shock fatality case (the *"Haar* case"). The contract stated that Brugger would provide engineering consulting services, including investigation and possible testimony at trial as an expert witness. In exchange for these services, Murray would pay Brugger an hourly rate of $140 plus expenses according to a schedule set forth in the contract.

Brugger was hired for two reasons: (1) to determine if the height of the electrical line that caused the fatality was in violation of the applicable safety codes, and (2) to determine if the warning sign on the truck used by the decedent was adequate to prevent such an electric shock fatality. The contract specified, however, that it was understood that Brugger was "an independent professional consultant."

Murray's complaint alleged breach of contract and fraud. Brugger's counterclaim also alleged breach of contract. On the breach of contract claims, the lower court held that Murray and Brugger entered into a valid and enforceable contract for services, that Brugger promised to perform certain work for Murray, that Brugger did perform that work, and that Murray promised to pay for that work. The court further held that Brugger billed Murray for the work performed through three invoices, the third of which remained unpaid. As to the first and second invoices, the court held that if Murray disputed their contents it should not have paid the bills and that Murray's payment of those bills constituted a waiver of any defects in them. As to the third invoice, the court held that Brugger performed the work as required under the contract and that Murray had not paid him for that work. Accordingly, the court held that Murray breached the contract, that Brugger did not breach the contract, and awarded Brugger $1,464 on his counterclaim.

On the fraud claim, the court first noted that Murray claimed Brugger damaged the *Haar* case by failing to provide information or providing the wrong information. Brugger countered that the information he provided was correct and that Murray did not like it because it was not helpful to the case against one of the defendants in the *Haar* case. The court held that the parties' disagreement was simply a disagreement among experts, not an intentional wrongdoing, and that Murray had failed to prove the elements of fraud. The court therefore held that Murray's claim failed on the merits. The appeals court affirmed the trial court's ruling in favor of the expert, but reversed the attorney's fees that the expert had been awarded.

**Comment:** When sued by his former client, this expert chose to fight back by filing a counterclaim and won. The expert was awarded his attorney's fees, although this award was later reversed on appeal. Experts can fight back and win.

**Example 24.17: Expert sues for unpaid fees, retaining counsel countersues for $400,000 for misrepresenting credentials, case settles in expert's favor for $23,100**
*Bennett v. Lacy,* 2003 WL 22945637 (Tex.App.-Houston [14 Dist.] 2003)

On March 6, 2002, Lacy sued Bennett. In his original petition, Lacy alleged he was a professional engineer employed by Abacus. In 1997, Bennett, an attorney, retained him as an expert witness in Jennie Drain, Individually, and as Administratrix of the Estate of Joe D. Drain v. Galveston County, No. G-97-316, in the United States District Court for the Southern District of Texas, Galveston Division, involving the fatal shooting of Joe Drain by a Galveston County Constable. Bennett retained Lacy to perform an analysis of the shooting, including bullet trajectory and ballistic analysis. Lacy prepared a report dated January 28, 1998, on which he spent over 100 hours, incurring expenses in investigation, analysis, and preparation. Lacy alleged that Bennet had partially paid him, but a balance of $16,440.80 remained, which Bennett refused to pay. Accordingly, Lacy brought suit on a sworn account and asserted a claim for breach of contract.

Bennett filed a motion for change of venue, contingent answer, counterclaim for fraud, and request for disclosure. Bennett alleged that Lacy advertised his services as an expert in a legal publication. Bennett spoke to Lacy about an excessive force case involving a man who shot his wife and then when he attempted to surrender, "[a] constable then shot him dead." Lacy assured Bennett that he was a highly qualified expert in the area of police shootings. After deposing Lacy, Galveston County moved to disqualify him. The federal magistrate ruled that Lacy was not qualified to testify on the topic of police shootings or any other type of shooting. The magistrate's ruling occurred after the deadline to designate experts had passed, leaving Bennett without a shooting expert in the excessive force action. Bennett lost the case. Bennett alleged that Lacy's misrepresentation of his qualifications was intentional and he would not have retained Lacy had he known that Lacy was not qualified to testify as an expert on police shootings. Bennett sought $400,000—the amount to compensate him for the loss of a fee in a case he claims he would have won if Lacy had not lied to him, plus punitive damages.

On December 9, 2002, the trial court ordered the parties to mediation. According to the trial court's order on the mediation fee signed March 21, 2003, the case was mediated on March 20, 2003. On April 3, 2003, an "Agreed Final Judgment" was signed by the trial court, ordering that Lacy recover from Bennett $23,100 and that Bennett take nothing on his counterclaim against Lacy.

**Comment:** Suit was brought against the expert witness in the case only after the expert had sued for his unpaid bills. Many claims against experts are actually counterclaims after experts sue for unpaid bills. In a case like this where there was a bad result (the expert was found not qualified and the case was dismissed), the expert should carefully consider whether he wants to bring suit against retaining counsel because such a suit may well invite a counterclaim (as happened here).

### Example 24.18: Attorney publicly reprimanded and suspended for 6 months for being uncivil and trying to humiliate an expert witness during cross-examination
*In re Petition for Disciplinary Action against James Malcolm Williams, Attorney at Law of the State of Minnesota,* 414 N.W.2d 394 (Minn. 1987)
This action for disciplinary action arose out of a fraud case against a lending institution and its attorney. The plaintiff cross-examined the defendant attorney's expert witness, the former chief justice of the Minnesota Supreme Court, who was testifying as an expert for the defendant on the standard of care required of an attorney. The plaintiff's counsel converted a proper inquiry regarding "the real party in interest status of liability insurers in personal injury litigation where the insurer retains counsel to represent the insured" into a false personal attack on the witness. Excerpts follow.

> WILLIAMS: Well, Mr. Sheran, you regularly appeared before the juries as a defense lawyer and told the juries that you were representing an individual when in truth and fact you were representing an insurance company, isn't that true?
> OPPOSING COUNSEL: Argumentative, your honor.
> COURT: Objection sustained.
> SHERAN: It is an untrue statement in addition.
> WILLIAMS: Well, don't you think that a juror would want to know whether or not you were representing an insurance company as well as a client who you were professing to represent?

OPPOSING COUNSEL: Same objection, your honor.

COURT: Objection sustained.

WILLIAMS: And yet you went through case after case for a number of years as a former FBI agent, knowingly misrepresenting to the juries time and time again that you were representing an individual when in truth in fact you were representing insurance companies in those cases?

SHERAN: That statement is false and scandalous.

\* \* \*

WILLIAMS: Didn't you, on several occasions, while you were on the court rule that if in fact a jury was told that there was an insurance company involved behind the defense lawyer, that you would take that jury verdict away from the plaintiff and send it back for a new trial because you felt that the jury is not entitled to know the truth about who in fact was being represented in the lawsuit?

OPPOSING COUNSEL: I object, your honor, but I would ask the witness to be permitted to answer.

\* \* \*

SHERAN: The statement is inaccurate and it is scandalous.

The trial court chastised the attorney and stated, in *Sievert v. First National Bank in Lakefield*, 358 N.W.2d 409 (Minn. App. 1984): "[I]t is not in keeping with the role of the advocate to try to humiliate a witness for self-gratification" (at 416). Similarly, the court that disciplined the attorney stated: "[Attorney] asserts he has a right, indeed an obligation, to represent his clients vigorously, aggressively, and zealously. To be vigorous, however, does not mean to be disruptively argumentative; to be aggressive is not a license to ignore the rules of evidence and decorum; and to be zealous is not to be uncivil." The attorney was publicly reprimanded and suspended for 6 months.

**Comment:** One suspects that the fact that the victimized witness in this case was a former chief justice of the State Supreme Court may have had something to do with the attorney being disciplined.

### Example 24.19: Attorney disbarred after being obnoxious to an expert witness (and for other ethical violations)

*In the Matter of Lester T. Vincenti,* 704 A.2d 927 (N.J. 1998)

An attorney was disbarred for repeated ethics violations. One of these occurred during the course of a proceeding to terminate parental rights of the natural mother of a minor for whom the attorney acted as a guardian at law. Selected treatment of the witnesses follows:

Attorney's treatment of the State's witnesses was equally obnoxious. He was abusive and tried to intimidate the witnesses, with some success. [Attorney] personally attacked the witnesses during his unreasonably long and confrontational cross-examinations. He called the witnesses insulting names and belittled the credentials of the expert witnesses.

Dr. Douglas Haymaker, a psychologist, treated J.D.'s son, A.R.S. During cross-examination, when Haymaker did not immediately answer [attorney]'s question, [attorney] snapped:

Do you want time to think about it, Doctor? Because I mean there seems to be a habit in this case of witnesses who don't know what to say to simply sit there and think and come up with some cockamamie response to a very serious question. Now I'd like you to answer the question without thinking about it ad nauseam for the next five minutes.

[Attorney] harassed Haymaker by asking him irrelevant questions, such as whether he was an aficionado of pornography, a militarist and whether he believed in military solutions to political problems. When Haymaker testified that a statement made by A.R.S. could not necessarily be attributed to his foster mother, [attorney] sarcastically asked, "Oh, it could have come from the froggies or the horsies or some other non-living thing, is that right?" [Attorney] also accused Haymaker of having a highly selective memory and of being "in cahoots" with the foster parents.

In reply to one of [attorney]'s questions, Haymaker used the word "assume," prompting [attorney] to interrupt him:

A. I assume, I assume it was a work similar—

Q. No, don't make assumptions, I mean that's all you've done so far is make assumptions and speculations and give us your opinions and conclusions. I'm not interested in your opinions and conclusions, speculations or assumptions, Doctor. I'm interested in having you search your memory, think if you can come up with what was stupid, et cetera. Make your best effort, Doctor. It's only a year ago. As a matter of fact, it's not even a year ago. It's eight months ago. That's not such a long time ago. Tell us. I challenge you to tell us.

[Attorney]'s comments were particularly inappropriate because he previously had demanded that Haymaker express his opinions and conclusions.

During the trial, [attorney] referred to Haymaker as a "liar," "so-called psychologist," "busy body do-gooder" and "so-called therapist." He belittled Haymaker's therapy sessions with A.R.S. as "your so-called game therapy, play therapy so-called." [Attorney] accused Haymaker of condoning violence, insults to women, pornography and brutality.

Another witness called by DYFS was a social worker. At the request of James Valenti, law guardian for A.R.S., the social worker conducted a bonding evaluation to address the issue of where A.R.S. should reside permanently. The social worker, too, was the victim of harassment and intimidation by [attorney]. At the ethics hearing, the social worker testified as follows about [attorney]'s courtroom behavior:

A. The thrust of his questions as I experienced them had less to do with the content than with an attempt to demean me, to ridicule me. I felt the nature of his cross-examination was highly personalized and had very little to do with the content or with trying to uncover the truth of the issues. For example, in the voir dire, he took a tremendous amount of time asking me what specific courses I had taken when I was in graduate school. At the time that I testified, I had—it had been fifteen years since I completed my doctorate and over twenty years since I completed my Masters degree. He wanted to know the specific names of the courses I had taken. I said I couldn't remember the specific names, but I could talk about the kinds of courses I took and how they were related to the work that I was doing. He ridiculed me for the fact that I could not remember the course name and went over that over and over again.

[Attorney] also made insinuations about the social worker's sexual orientation. He suggested that she inappropriately touched his client, J.D., during a bonding-evaluation session with J.D. and A.R.S. [Attorney] attached significance to the fact that the social worker used purple paper for taking notes in her office, despite her explanation that it was the easiest color for her eyes. [Attorney] even said that he would bring in an expert to talk about the meaning of using purple paper. [Attorney] also used sashaying and other body language to question her sexuality.

In addition, [attorney] took the social worker's notes from her during her testimony. He then toyed with her, refusing to return the notes. When she asked Judge Hanifan to instruct [attorney] to return the notes, [attorney] berated the judge for talking to the witness.

Unfortunately for the social worker, the conclusion of the A.R.S. trial did not signal the end of [attorney]'s harassment toward her. About six months after the trial ended, she and Dr. Hagovsky, another witness who had testified in the A.R.S. matter, were invited to participate at a conference sponsored by the Association of Trial Lawyers of America. There was no connection between the trial and the conference. However, in a letter to Cary B. Cheifetz, the conference coordinator, [attorney] contended that the social worker and Hagovsky held "Nazi views" and suggested that it would be helpful if [attorney] attended the conference to denounce them. Although the letter could not be introduced into evidence because Cheifetz discarded it after receiving it, both Cheifetz and the social worker testified at the ethics hearing about the contents of the letter. While [attorney] complained that the letter was not produced, he did not deny having sent it.

**Comment:** While on the witness stand, it is usually a good sign (from the expert's perspective) when the attorney is obnoxious. This usually means that the attorney has lost his cool and has little of substance left to inquire about. The jury is also likely to be offended by the attorney's behavior.

**Example 24.20: Attorney suspended for insulting expert**
*Florida v. Schaub,* 618 So.2d 202 (Fla. 1993)
A prosecutor was suspended for thirty days after he insulted the defense expert, elicited irrelevant information from the expert, and expressed his own derogatory opinions of the expert's field.

**Example 24.21: Expert sues law firm for abuse of process and wins $50,000,000**
*In the case of Lexecon v. Milberg Weiss[4]*
A Chicago-based economic consulting firm filed an abuse of process suit against a well-known law firm. One of the chief allegations in the suit was that an attorney at the defendant law firm sued an expert/consultant at Lexecon because he wanted to "put the little fucker out of business." The expert/consultant and the attorney had done battle in several previous high-profile cases. At the conclusion of the trial, the jury awarded the plaintiff expert/consulting firm $45 million. While the jury was out considering punitive damages, the defendant law firm settled the case for $50 million. The law firm had reportedly earned $679 million in profits since 1988.

## 24.4  Conclusion

Experts may be subject to various form of abuse. They should know how to deal with each in a professional, constructive manner.

---

[4] See Karen Donovan, "Milberg Weiss' $50M Mistake," *National Law Journal,* April 26, 1999 at A1. See also Richard B. Schmitt, "Milberg Weiss Agrees to Pay $50 Million to Settle Lexecon Case," *Wall Street Journal,* April 14, 1999, at B17. The firm had represented a class of plaintiffs who had lost savings in a savings and loan failure. The suit named numerous defendants, one of which was the consulting firm Lexecon. The firm also named a principal at the consulting firm in the suit—this same principal had testified as an expert previously against the law firm's clients. Lexecon later filed the abuse of process lawsuit, alleging that the law firm used the legal process to drive the expert out of business. The chairman of the federal jury that heard the abuse of process suit said, "The biggest single factor for us was that they went after [the expert] personally."

# Appendix A  CV Quality Control Checklist

The expert's CV is often the first place opposing counsel looks to gather information for deposition, trials, and cross-examination purposes. Preparation, attention to detail, accuracy, and precision can help the expert avoid unnecessary difficulty.

## Accuracy
\_\_ Was your CV 100% accurate when written?
\_\_ Has anything changed since your CV was written?
\_\_ Was your CV 100% accurate when presented to counsel?
\_\_ No exaggerations on awards received?

## Typos
\_\_ CV proofed by yourself _and_ another competent person
\_\_ Voice recognition software (which commonly generates mistakes) not used

## Timeline and Gaps
\_\_ Have you listed your inclusive dates of work, education, and other activities?
\_\_ Do you have gaps in your CV timeline?

## Contact Information
\_\_ Have you listed contact information where you are readily reachable?

## Prior CVs
\_\_ Are your prior CVs consistent with your current one?
\_\_ Are there material changes, omissions, or alterations that open lines of inquiry?

## Web Page
\_\_ Is the CV 100% consistent with the information on your Web page?

## Multiple CVs
\_\_ Do you have more than one current CV?
\_\_ Are your multiple CVs prepared and used for different clients?

## Professional Societies and Certifications
\_\_ Are the affiliations listed current?
\_\_ Have you included relevant dates?
\_\_ Have you removed those organizations in which you merely paid a fee and obtained the credentials?

## Writings
\_\_ Are the dates, titles, and claims to authorship accurate?
\_\_ Have you listed co-authors?
\_\_ Have you exaggerated the importance of the publication or your role in it?
\_\_ Have you cited the publication with sufficient specificity?
\_\_ Do these match what shows up on a computer-generated literature search?

## Areas of Expertise
\_\_ Do you list so many areas of expertise on your CV that it will be difficult for anyone to believe that you truly are an expert in all of these areas?

## Self-Serving Comments
__ Have you made self-serving comments that can be taken out of context and used to cross-examine you?
__ Change subjective language (e.g., "nationally known") into objective language (e.g., listing presentations made to national groups).

## Previous Cases
__ Do you list the cases you have worked on and how they turned out?
__ Should you consider removing these from your CV?

## Printing
__ Do you print your CV on a high-quality paper?

## Attorneys Worked With
__ Do you list the attorneys you have worked with/for?
__ Should you consider removing these from your CV?

## Identity Theft Prevention
__ Do you have your Social Security number and date of birth on your CV?
__ Should you consider removing these from your CV?

## Updates
__ Do you have a system to make sure your CV is accurately updated when necessary?

## Dating
__ Is your CV dated so that it is easy to update and keep current?

## Extraneous Information
__ Has this been removed from your CV (e.g., political associations, hobbies, etc.)?

# Appendix B  Report Quality Control Checklist

__ Has a written report been expressly requested by counsel at this time?
__ Have you covered all the issues counsel wanted addressed?
__ Have you avoided covering any issues counsel did not want addressed?
__ Is your report dated?
__ Have you had the report proofed for spelling and grammar mistakes by a competent person and have you proofed it?
__ Have you numbered the report's pages?
__ Have you included a cover page and table of contents?
__ Have you included color digital photographs?
__ Have you listed, with a precise description of each, all the documents you have reviewed?
__ Have you stated your qualifications accurately and objectively?
__ Have you resisted sharing draft versions of your report with retaining counsel?
__ Have you removed any inappropriate or extraneous remarks from your report?
__ Have you specified upon which facts, data, standards, and information your opinions are based?
__ Is the tone of the report formal?
__ Have you formatted the report with subheadings for ease of reading?
__ Opinions
    __ When did you form your opinion?
    __ Upon what underlying facts and data is your opinion based?
    __ What are your opinions?
    __ Have you stated that you may have additional opinions if additional material is provided?
    __ Are your opinions expressed in a legally sufficient manner?
    __ Are your opinions expressed in a confident manner?
    __ Do you cite authority in support of your opinion?
    __ Do you document a reliable methodology upon which your opinion is based?
    __ Have you only opined in areas in which you are qualified to do so?
__ Have you included a summary of conclusions and opinions?
__ Have you included appropriate appendices?
    __ Correspondence
    __ Copies of documents
    __ Photos
    __ Charts
    __ Test results
    __ Drawings
    __ Underlying data
    __ Codes
    __ Records
    __ Ordinances
    __ Statutes
    __ Licenses
    __ Permits
    __ Other documentary material

__ Does your report comply with the Federal Rules of Civil Procedure Rule 26 2(B) and contain the following?

    __ A complete statement of all opinions to be expressed by the expert

    __ The basis and reasons for the expert's opinions

    __ The data or information considered by the witness in forming the opinions

    __ Any exhibits to be used as a summary of or support for the opinions

    __ The qualifications of the witness, including a list of all publications in the preceding ten years

    __ The compensation to be paid for the study and testimony

    __ A list of any other cases in which the witness has testified as an expert (at trial or in deposition) within the preceding four years

    __ Do you avoid?

        __ Guessing

        __ Boilerplate language

        __ Absolute words

        __ The passive tense

        __ Hedge words

        __ "Friendly" language directed at retaining counsel

        __ Pronouns

        __ Legal terms

        __ Run-on sentences

# Appendix C  Deposition Areas of Inquiry

Experts should prepare for deposition with their retaining counsel.  An understanding of the common areas of inquiry is helpful.

## Subpoena Duces Tecum
__ Have you received a subpoena?
__ What were you requested to produce?
__ Is the material in your file?
__ Do you have copies of the materials?
__ Have you produced all of the material subpoenaed?
__ Have you removed anything from the file?

## General Background Information
__ Name
__ Date of birth
__ Where you were born and raised
__ Your home and professional addresses

## CV
__ Is it correct and accurate?
__ Do you have copies for the attorneys and stenographer?
__ Do you use any other versions of your CV?

## Educational Background
__ What schools have you attended?
__ What were your major areas of study?
__ What degrees did you obtain?
__ What are the dates for your attendance and degrees?
__ What additional training courses have you attended?
__ What continuing education courses have you attended in the past ten years?
__ Have you been the subject of any disciplinary actions?
__ Have your licenses ever been suspended or revoked?
__ What were your grades?
__ What did you do between any gaps in your education?

## Relationship with Counsel
__ What is your personal/financial relationship with counsel who has retained you in this case?

## Employment
__ What were the dates of each position?
__ Why did you leave each?
__ What are all the positions you have held?
__ What were your titles?
__ What were your duties at each position?
__ What did you do during gaps in your CV?

## Teaching at Schools
\_\_ Have you taught at any educational facility?
\_\_ Where and when did you teach?  What was taught?

## Teaching at Seminars
\_\_ Have you been on the faculty of any seminars, conferences, or workshops?
\_\_ What did you speak on?
\_\_ Were there outlines, course materials, or other handout materials?

## Fees
\_\_ How much have you been paid to date in this case?
\_\_ What is your hourly rate?
\_\_ Do you have any outstanding bills in the case?
\_\_ How much do you expect to bill in the future in the case?

## Forensic Income
\_\_ Who are your major clients?
\_\_ How much income did you obtain for forensic work in the past three years?
\_\_ What percentage of your professional time is devoted to forensic work?
\_\_ What percentage of your income is from forensic work?

## Bias
\_\_ Do you have any biases in this case?
\_\_ Are you impartial?
\_\_ Do you have a direct or indirect financial interest in the case?
\_\_ Are you a friend or relative of an attorney/party?

## Witness Experience
\_\_ How often do you testify?
\_\_ What percentage for plaintiffs?  Defendants?

## Publications
\_\_ State all of the articles, chapters, books, reviews, abstracts, and other writings that you have had published.
\_\_ When and where were these published?
\_\_ Have any of your writings not been accepted for publication?  Specify.

## Organizations
\_\_ Of what professional organizations and societies are you a member?
\_\_ What is your status in the organization(s)?
\_\_ Have you ever paid a fee to obtain additional credentials?

## Involvement in Case
\_\_ When were you first contacted concerning this case?
\_\_ By whom were you contacted?
\_\_ How were you contacted: Phone, letter, e-mail, other?

## Acceptance of Case
\_\_ When did you accept this case?

# DEPOSITION AREAS OF INQUIRY

**What materials or records were you provided?  By whom and when were they provided?**
__ Correspondence (including e-mails)
__ Reports
__ Messages
__ Transcripts
__ Notes
__ Computer files
__ Police reports
__ Investigative reports
__ Medical and hospital records
__ Literature
Tables
__ Standards
__ Contracts
__ Photographs
__ Videotapes
__ Other materials

**Pleadings**
__ Which of the pleadings have you read in this case?
   __ Complaint
   __ Answer
   __ Interrogatories
   __ Deposition Transcripts
   __ Motions
   __ Other

**Research**
__ What research did you do prior to forming your opinions?

**Authorities**
__ What do you recognize as authoritative in your field?
   __ Books
   __ Treatises
   __ Articles
   __ Journals
   __ Other experts
   __ Others

**Site Inspection**
__ Have you visited the site of the accident?
   __ When?
   __ With whom?
   __ Did you take or have you taken:
      __ Sketches?
      __ Photos?
      __ Videotapes?
      __ Any other depictions of the site?

## Standards of Care
__ What is your understanding of the standard of care in this case?
__ From what are they derived?

## Standards
__ What are the industry standards in this case?
__ From what are they derived?

## Work You Have Done in this Case
__ Records and documents reviewed: Which ones and when?
__ Examination of the product: When and what was done?
__ Testing: What was done, when was it done, and what were the results?
__ Is all of this work reflected on your bills and invoices?
__ What additional work do you anticipate doing prior to the trial?

## Help
__ Who helped you form your opinion in this case?

## Retaining Counsel
__ Describe all communications.
__ Describe conversations held during breaks.

## Notes
__ What do notations you have made on records mean?
__ Please explain the other notes you have made.

## Reports
__ When drafted?
__ Drafts shared with retaining counsel?

## Equipment
__ What equipment did you use in this case? Who were the manufacturer and calibrator? How was the equipment used?

## Answers to Interrogatories
__ Do you agree with retaining party's answers to interrogatories?

## Computers
__ What computers did you use to test or formulate your opinion? How did you use them?

## Demonstrative Aids
__ Have you produced or used, or do you intend to produce or use, any of the following demonstrative aids at the trial? If so, specify:
   __ Graphs
   __ Charts
   __ Models
   __ Illustrations
   __ Computer animation
   __ Other

# DEPOSITION AREAS OF INQUIRY

## Methodology
__ Has your theory been tested?
__ Has your theory been subjected to peer review?
__ What is the known error rate?
__ To what degree is your theory accepted in the relevant professional community?
__ Was your theory developed outside of the context of litigation?

## Opinions
__ What are the facts and assumptions upon which your opinions are based?
__ What are the opinions you will be testifying to?
__ What is the methodology employed in reaching the opinion?
__ What areas will you not be offering opinions on?

## Concluding Remarks
__ Have you stated all of your conclusions and opinions in this case?

# Appendix D  Areas of Inquiry during Cross-Examination

Experts need to be effective when questioned by opposing counsel during cross-examination. Anticipating the areas of likely inquiry and preparing accordingly will increase an expert's effectiveness.  The following outline describes some of the most important lines of inquiry opposing counsel may follow.

## Initial Consultation
___ When you were first contacted
___ By whom you were contacted
___ When you were retained
___ What you were requested to do

## Qualifications
___ Accuracy of CV
___ Misleading information on CV
___ Knowledge
___ Skill
___ Education/degrees/licenses or lack thereof
___ Training
___ Extensive areas of expertise listed in CV, suggesting expert is expert in everything
___ Self-serving characterizations in CV
___ Memberships in societies
___ Awards
___ Practical experience
    ___ Recentness of experience
    ___ Relevancy of experience
___ Credibility
___ Marketing activities
___ Relationship to retaining party or attorney
___ Affiliation with an insurance company
___ Conversations with retaining attorney
___ Indirect monetary interest
___ Prior testimony
___ Professional presentations
___ Professional and personal writings
___ Professional errors or miscues by expert
___ Information on Web page

## Opinions
___ Documents and pleadings reviewed
___ Validity of underlying facts
___ Validity of underlying assumptions
___ Conflicts with opinions of other experts
___ Notes on documents
___ Information expert failed to review

\_\_ Time spent forming opinion
\_\_ Sources of information
\_\_ Reports of other experts reviewed
\_\_ Your opinion's foundation
\_\_ Reliance on tests not personally performed
\_\_ Reliance on other experts' records
\_\_ Reliance on self-reported history
\_\_ Omitted facts
\_\_ When you formed your opinions
\_\_ Opinions you will be offering
\_\_ Opinions you will not be offering
\_\_ Prior contrary opinions

## Fees and Billing
\_\_ Hourly rate
\_\_ Amount billed to date
\_\_ Amount anticipate billing
\_\_ Amount paid in prior cases by client

## Forensic Work
\_\_ Percentage of your time spent on forensic work
\_\_ Amount for plaintiffs
\_\_ Amount for defendants
\_\_ Percentage of your total income derived from forensic work
\_\_ Consulting work where not retained to testify
\_\_ Marketing activity, including Web pages

## Bias
\_\_ Impartiality
\_\_ Inflexibility
\_\_ Personal/social relationship with party/attorney
\_\_ Professional witness
\_\_ Advocate
\_\_ Fees and compensation
\_\_ Direct or indirect financial interest in the case

## Reports
\_\_ Dates of reports
\_\_ Oral vs. written
\_\_ Revisions
\_\_ Information in report
\_\_ Inaccuracy in reports
\_\_ Preliminary vs. final
    \_\_ Additions, alterations, corrections
    \_\_ Prior drafts

## Tests Performed
\_\_ When, where, at whose request
\_\_ Results

# AREAS OF INQUIRY DURING CROSS-EXAMINATION

__ Equipment used
__ Similarity of conditions
__ Photos, videos, or sketches taken
__ Tests not performed
__ Accuracy of calculations, tests

## Visit to Accident Scene
__ When and at whose request
__ Similarity of conditions
__ What was done during visit

## Skeletons in Closet
__ Professional discipline
__ Loss of job
__ Failing certification exams
__ Criminal convictions
__ Suspension/revocation of licenses
__ Testimony rejected by other courts or administrative agencies
__ Findings of being not qualified to testify
__ Prior professional or testifying mistakes

## Subpoenas
__ Fully complied with subpoena
__ Removed documents from your file

## Learned Treatises
__ Which texts, treatises, and articles are authoritative
__ Contrary statements in treatises

## Prior Testimony
__ One-sidedness
__ Inconsistencies (impeachment with prior testimony)

## Legal Standards
__ Degree of probability required
__ Standards of practice
__ Pertinent statutes, rules, regulations, and codes

## *Daubert* Issues
__ Has your technique or theory been tested?
__ Has your technique or theory been subject to peer review and publication?
__ The known or potential rate of error of the technique or theory
__ The existence of standards and controls
__ The degree to which the technique or theory has been generally accepted by the scientific community
__ Theory developed "for litigation only"

# Appendix E  Complaint

COMMONWEALTH OF MASSACHUSETTS   SUPERIOR COURT

NORFOLK, SS:         No.  06-00447

| | |
|---|---|
| CHARLES SMITH; PATRICIA SMITH;    ) | |
| and KATELYN SMITH, KYLE SMITH,   ) | |
| and MATTHEW SMITH, Minors by Their  ) | |
| Mother and Next Friend, PATRICIA SMITH, ) | |
| Plaintiffs           ) | |

               )    <u>COMPLAINT</u>

VS.               )

               )

ABC CONSTRUCTION CO., INC.,    )

Defendant

## PARTIES

1. The Plaintiff, Charles Smith, is an adult individual and is a resident of Jackson, Rhode Island.

2. The Plaintiff, Patricia Smith, is an adult individual who at all times relevant has been the lawful spouse of Charles Smith, and is a resident of Jackson, Rhode Island.

3. The Plaintiffs Katelyn Smith, Kyle Smith and Matthew Smith are minor children of Charles Smith; are residents of Jackson, Rhode Island; and are represented in this action by their mother and next friend Patricia Smith.

4. The Defendant, ABC Construction Co., Inc., is a business corporation, duly organized under the laws of the Commonwealth of Massachusetts, having the powers and purposes, *inter alia,* of developing real property and buildings thereon; and has a locus in Milton, Norfolk County, Massachusetts.

## DECLARATION OF FACTS

5. On or about February 24, 2005, the Defendant ABC Construction Co., Inc., was the owner of certain real property in Wilder, Norfolk County, Massachusetts, being known as 10 Maple Drive, in the Wilder Farms subdivision.

6. On or about February 24, 1988, the Defendant was then engaged as general contractor for the construction of a dwelling house on the property at 10 Maple Drive, Wilder, Massachusetts.

7. The Defendant had a subcontract with ACME Construction Company, of Fairfield, Massachusetts, in effect as of February 24, 2005, to furnish carpentry services for the construction of the dwelling at 10 Maple Drive.

8. The Plaintiff, Charles Smith, was an employee of ACME Construction Company as of February 24, 2005; and was employed by said company as a carpenter.

9. On or about February 24, 2005, the Plaintiff Charles Smith was lawfully on the Defendant's premises at 10 Maple Drive, for the purpose of acting within the scope of his employment with ACME Construction Company, to provide carpentry services to Defendant on said property.

10. While on said premises on February 24, 2005, the Plaintiff Charles Smith was at all times exercising due care for his personal safety.

11. While on Defendant's premises on February 24, 2005, the Plaintiff did step upon a plywood covering placed over a floor opening, which cover was not properly constructed or adequately secured;

and as a result the Plaintiff Charles Smith did then and there fall through the floor opening sustaining severe personal injuries.

12. The injuries sustained by Plaintiff from such fall on February 24, 2005, include a herniated lumbar disc which has required surgery. By reason of such injury, Plaintiff has suffered such pain and will suffer such pain in future.

13. By reason of such injury, Plaintiff has suffered loss of bodily function and disability, with consequent loss of earning capacity which is in excess of $44,800 at present; and such disability with loss of earning capacity continues and will continue in future.

14. By reason of such injury, Plaintiff has incurred reasonable medical expenses to date in excess of $10,000.00 and Plaintiff continues to require medical care and will require further medical care in the future.

15. By reason of such injury, Plaintiff Charles Smith has also suffered the loss of the ability to enjoy life and to attend to daily activities, and such loss continues and will continue in future.

16. By reason of the physical and mental injuries sustained by Charles Smith, the Plaintiff Patricia Smith has suffered loss of her husband's full care, society, companionship, service, comfort and spousal consortium, and she has been damaged thereby; and Plaintiff Patricia Smith continues to suffer such loss and will suffer such loss in future.

17. By reason of the physical and mental injuries sustained by Charles Smith, the minor Plaintiffs Katelyn Smith, Kyle Smith and Matthew Smith, have suffered loss of their father's full care, society, companionship, service, comfort and parental consortium, and they have been damaged thereby; and said minor Plaintiffs continue to suffer such loss and will suffer such loss in future.

18. The proximate cause of the injury, loss and damage sustained by the Plaintiffs was the negligence and lack of due care of Defendant, ABC Construction Co., Inc., in the following particulars.

a) The Defendant did cause to exist on its premises an unreasonably dangerous and defective condition, i.e., the improperly constructed floor hole covering;

b) The Defendant did, by failure to reasonably inspect its premises, suffer or permit the unreasonably dangerous and defective condition to remain on its premises;

c) The Defendant failed to provide adequate warnings or other safeguards to prevent injury to persons such as Plaintiff from the unreasonably dangerous and defective condition on its property; and

d) The Defendant failed to take reasonable action to correct the dangerous and defective condition existing on its property.

## COUNT I: CHARLES SMITH, PERSONAL INJURY

19. By reason of the matters stated in Paragraphs 1 to 18, above, the Defendant ABC Construction Co., Inc., is liable for its negligence to the Plaintiff Charles Smith, for damages to compensate for his injury and loss, to include pain and suffering, lost earning capacity and medical expense, as stated above.

## COUNT II: PATRICIA SMITH, LOSS OF SPOUSAL CONSORTIUM

20. By reason of the matters stated in Paragraphs 1 to 18 above, the Defendant ABC Construction Co., Inc., is liable for its negligence to the Plaintiff Patricia Smith, for damages to compensate for her injury and loss, to include loss of spousal consortium, as stated above.

## COUNT III: KATELYN SMITH, LOSS OF PARENTAL CONSORTIUM

21. By reason of the matters stated in Paragraphs 1 to 18 above, the Defendant ABC Construction Co., Inc., is liable for its negligence to the minor Plaintiff Katelyn Smith, by her mother and next friend Patricia Smith, for damages to compensate for her injury and loss, to include loss of parental consortium as stated above.

# COMPLAINT

## COUNT IV: KYLE SMITH, LOSS OF PARENTAL CONSORTIUM

22. By reason of the matters stated in Paragraphs 1 to 18 above, the Defendant ABC Construction Co., Inc., is liable for its negligence to the minor Plaintiff Kyle Smith, by his mother and next friend Patricia Smith, for damages to compensate for his injury and loss, to include loss of parental consortium, as stated above.

## COUNT V: MATTHEW SMITH, LOSS OF PARENTAL CONSORTIUM

23. By reason of the matters stated in Paragraphs 1 to 18 above, the Defendant ABC Construction Co., Inc., is liable for its negligence to the minor Plaintiff Matthew Smith, by his mother and next friend Patricia Smith, for damages to compensate for his injury and loss, to include loss of parental consortium, as stated above.

WHEREFORE, Plaintiffs demand relief as follows:

**First**, Judgment for Plaintiff Charles Smith, on Count I above, for damages to include $44,800 for lost earning capacity to date, and such further amounts as may be determined by the jury for continuing and future lost earning capacity; to include $10,000 for medical expense incurred to date, and such further amounts to be determined by the jury for continuing and future medical expense; to include damages to be determined by the jury to compensate Plaintiff in full for his physical and mental pain and suffering, and loss of ability to enjoy life and attend to daily activities; plus interest and costs of the action.

**Second**, Judgment for Plaintiff Patricia Smith, on Count II above, for damages in an amount to be determined by the jury to compensate for her past, present and future loss of spousal consortium; plus interest and costs of the action.

**Third**, Judgment for Plaintiff Katelyn Smith, on Count III above, for damages in an amount to be determined by the jury to compensate for her past, present and future loss of parental consortium; plus interest and costs of action.

**Fourth**, Judgment for Plaintiff Kyle Smith, on Count IV above, for damages in an amount to be determined by the jury, to compensate for his past, present and future loss of parental consortium; plus interest and costs of the action.

**Fifth**, Judgment for Plaintiff Matthew Smith, on Count V above, for damages in an amount to be determined by the jury, to compensate for his past, present and future loss of parental consortium; plus interest and cost of the action.

**Sixth**, Judgment for such other relief as the Court may be empowered to grant Plaintiffs for the loss.

## PLAINTIFFS DEMAND JURY TRIAL ON ALL ISSUES.

For the Plaintiffs,
by their Attorney,

_____

Daniel P. Larsen
Hamlin, Rose, Larsen & Nicholson
Box 111, 20 Doyle Road
Fraser Lake, MA 01234
(000) 555-1111
BBO #987654

Dated: February 12, 2006

421

# Appendix F  Answer

COMMONWEALTH OF MASSACHUSETTS

NORFOLK, SS.

SUPERIOR COURT DEPARTMENT
CIVIL ACTION NO. 06-00447

```
*****************************************
CHARLES SMITH; and              *
KATELYN SMITH, KYLE             *
SMITH, and MATTHEW              *
SMITH, Minors by Their          *
Mother and Next Friend,         *
PATRICIA SMITH,                 *   ANSWER AND JURY CLAIM
     Plaintiffs                 *   OF THE DEFANDANT,
                                *   ABC CONSTRUCTION CO.,
VS.                             *   TO THE PLAINTIFFS'
                                *   AMENDED COMPLAINT
                                *
ABC CONSTRUCTION CO., INC.,     *
   Defendant and Third-         *
   Party Plaintiff              *
                                *
                                *
VS.                             *
                                *
ACME CONSTRUCTION COMPANY,      *
INC. and 123 CONCRETE, INC.     *
Third-Party Defendants          *
*****************************************
```

## FIRST DEFENSE

The Complaint of the Plaintiff fails to state a claim against the defendant upon which relief can be granted.

## SECOND DEFENSE

Now comes the Defendant, ABC Construction Co., Inc., and responds to the allegations in the Plaintiff's Complaint, paragraph by paragraph, as follows:

1.  The Defendant admits the allegations contained in paragraph 1 of the Plaintiff's Complaint.
2.  The Defendant admits the allegations contained in paragraph 2 of the Plaintiff's Complaint.
3.  The defendant, ABC Construction Co., Inc. does admit that it is a business corporation duly organized under the laws of the Commonwealth of Massachusetts, but suggests that it has greater powers than suggested in paragraph 3 and admits it has a locus of business in Newberry, Massachusetts. Therefore, the defendant admits part of paragraph 3 and denies a part of paragraph 3, as stated in its response.
4.  The Defendant alleges that it is without knowledge or information sufficient to form a belief as to the truth of the allegations contained in paragraph 4 of the Plaintiff's Complaint.

5.  The Defendant denies the allegations contained in paragraph 5 of the Plaintiff's Complaint.
6.  The Defendant denies the allegations contained in paragraph 6 of the Plaintiff's Complaint.
7.  The Defendant denies the allegations contained in paragraph 7 of the Plaintiff's Complaint.
8.  The Defendant alleges that it is without knowledge or information sufficient to form a belief as to the truth of the allegations contained in paragraph 8 of the Plaintiff's Complaint.
9.  The Defendant alleges that it is without knowledge or information sufficient to form a belief as to the truth of the allegations contained in paragraph 9 of the Plaintiff's Complaint.
10. The Defendant alleges that it is without knowledge or information sufficient to form a belief as to the truth of the allegations contained in paragraph 10 of the Plaintiff's Complaint.
11. The Defendant alleges that it is without knowledge or information sufficient to form a belief as to the truth of the allegations contained in paragraph 11 of the Plaintiff's Complaint.
12. The Defendant alleges that it is without knowledge or information sufficient to form a belief as to the truth of the allegations contained in paragraph 12 of the Plaintiff's Complaint.
13. The Defendant alleges that it is without knowledge or information sufficient to form a belief as to the truth of the allegations contained in paragraph 13 of the Plaintiff's Complaint.
14. The Defendant alleges that it is without knowledge or information sufficient to form a belief as to the truth of the allegations contained in paragraph 14 of the Plaintiff's Complaint.
15. The Defendant denies the allegations contained in paragraph 15 of the Plaintiff's Complaint.
16. The Defendant denies the allegations contained in paragraph 16 of the Plaintiff's Complaint.
17. The Defendant denies the allegations contained in paragraph 17 of the Plaintiff's Complaint.
18. The Defendant denies the allegations contained in paragraph 18 of the Plaintiff's Complaint.
19. The Defendant denies the allegations contained in paragraph 19 of the Plaintiff's Complaint.
20. The Defendant denies the allegations contained in paragraph 20 of the Plaintiff's Complaint.
21. The Defendant denies the allegations contained in paragraph 21 of the Plaintiff's Complaint.
22. The Defendant alleges that it is without knowledge or information sufficient to form a belief as to the truth of the allegations contained in paragraph 22 of the Plaintiff's complaint.

## COUNT I

23. The Defendant denies the allegations contained in paragraph 23 of the Plaintiff's Complaint.

## COUNT II

24. The Defendant denies the allegations contained in paragraph 24 of the Plaintiff's Complaint.

## COUNT III

25. The Defendant denies the allegations contained in paragraph 25 of the Plaintiff's Complaint.

## COUNT IV

26. The Defendant denies the allegations contained in paragraph 26 of the Plaintiff's Complaint.

### THIRD DEFENSE

The defendant says that if the plaintiffs suffered damages as alleged in the Plaintiff's Complaint, such damages were caused by someone or something for whose conduct the defendant was not responsible.

### FOURTH DEFENSE

The plaintiffs are barred from recovery because this action has not been brought within the time allowed by the appropriate statue of the Massachusetts General Laws.

### FIFTH DEFENSE

The defendant says that at the time and place alleged in the Plaintiff's Complaint, the plaintiff so carelessly and negligently conducted himself so that he, by his own negligence, contributed directly and proximately to his own alleged injuries and damages.

# ANSWER

### SIXTH DEFENSE

The defendant says that the negligence of the plaintiff was as great or greater than the alleged negligence of the defendant and that such negligence of the plaintiff contributed to his damages and that, therefore, the plaintiff is barred from recovery under M.G.L., C. 231, Sec. 85 as amended.

### SEVENTH DEFENSE

The defendant says that the plaintiff is guilty of contributory negligence and that damages, if any, recovered by the plaintiff should be reduced in proportion to the negligence of the plaintiff in accordance with M.G.L., C. 231, Sec 85 as amended.

### EIGHTH DEFENSE

The defendant says further that the plaintiffs have no standing to sue the defendant in tort.

### NINTII DEFENSE

The defendant says that the alleged incident resulted from dangers, the risk of which the plaintiff assumed.

### TENTH DEFENSE

The defendant says that the plaintiffs have suffered no damages as a result of the alleged accident.

### ELEVENTH DEFENSE

The defendant denies that any agents, servants or employees of his business were involved in any incident at the time and place alleged, as a result of which the plaintiff claims damages.

### TWELFTH DEFENSE

The defendant says that at the time and place alleged in the Plaintiff's Complaint, the plaintiff was on the premises of the defendant without the permission or consent of the defendant, and was a trespasser.

### THIRTEENTH DEFENSE

By way of affirmative defense, the defendant states that the plaintiffs are prohibited from making any claim against the defendant pursuant to General Laws, Ch. 152, as amended, and, therefore, the claims of the plaintiffs are barred.

WHEREFORE, the defendant requests this Honorable Court to dismiss the Plaintiff's Complaint and to award the defendant reasonable costs and attorney's fees for the defense of this action.

THE DEFENDANT DEMANDS TRIAL BY JURY ON ALL ISSUES.

By the Attorney for the Defendant,

_____

Ronald A. Patton, Jr., Esquire
PATTON, DESOTO & HALL, P.C.
1 Inverness Place
Hillsborough, MA 23456
555-9999
BBO No. 777777

Dated: _____

## CERTIFICATE OF SERVICE

I, Ronald A. Patton, Jr., Attorney for the defendant in the foregoing action, do hereby certify that I have, this day, served a copy of the foregoing:

**ANSWER AND JURY CLAIM OF THE DEFENDANT, ABC CONSTRUCTION CO., INC. TO THE PLAINTIFFS' AMENDED COMPLAINT.**

to the attorneys of record by mailing same postage prepaid to:

Daniel P. Larsen, Esq.
Hamlin, Rose, Larsen & Nicholson
P.O. Box 111, 20 Doyle Road.
Fraser Lake, MA 01234
BBO #987654
(000)555-1111

Loren DeMol, Esq.
Michael A. Bruce, Jr., Esq.
Law Offices of Michael A. Bruce, Jr.
222 Benton Ave.
Baileys, MA 22666
(000) 555-8844

Richard Logan, Esq.
Logan, Coens, and Richey
100 Randolph Street
P.O. Box 789
Boston, MA 02000
(000) 555-4567

Ronald A. Patton, Jr., Esquire
PATTON, DESOTO & HALL, P.C.
1 Inverness Place
Hillsborough, MA 23456
555-9999
BBO No. 777777

Dated: _____

# Appendix G  Answers to Interrogatories

COMMONWEALTH OF MASSACHUSETTS

NORFOLK, SS.

SUPERIOR COURT DEPARTMENT
CIVIL ACTION NO. 06-00447

```
*********************************************
```

CHARLES SMITH; PATRICIA       *
SMITH; and KATELYN SMITH,     *
KYLE SMITH, and MATTHEW     *
SMITH, Minors by Their          *
Mother and Next Friend,        *
PATRICIA SMITH,             *
PLAINTIFF, CHARLES SMITH'S   *
Plaintiffs                  *

                         *   ANSWERS TO DEFENDANT'S
                         *   INTERROGATORIES

VS.                        *
                       *
ABC CONSTRUCTION CO., INC.,   *
Defendant                 *

```
*********************************************
```

Q. 1. Please identify yourself by stating your full name, date of birth, social security number, residence, employer, business address, occupation and, if married, the name of your spouse.

A. 1. Charles Smith; 4/6/58; 012-34-4567; 27 Harbor Road, Jackson, RI; Unemployed; Not applicable; Framing Carpenter/Disabled; Patricia Smith.

Q. 2. Please describe in full detail how the alleged accident occurred, stating what you saw, heard, did and what happened to you in order in which the events took place.

A. 2. We returned to the job site at 10 Maple Drive in Wilder, Massachusetts, on the morning of February 24, 2005. I went over to the area of the cellar hole opening that we had covered with plywood laid down on framing timbers and I saw it had been covered over with plastic since we were there the previous week. I went over to remove the plastic sheet and I stepped on the plywood covering the hole. When I stepped on the plywood my foot went through and I fell 3 feet or so when I got hung up on a steel center beam which was below the opening. I came down on to this steel beam with my back and my right shoulder making contact.

Q. 3. Please state the exact hour, day and date and when the alleged accident occurred.

A. 3. The accident occurred on February 24, 2005, at about 7:00 A.M.

Q. 4. Please give a complete description of the injuries you received as a result of the alleged accident.

A. 4. As a result of this accident I suffered a herniated disc in my lower back with right leg pains resulting from the sciatic nerve. This has been diagnosed as herniated nucleus pulposis at L5-S1, with sciatica.

Q. 5. Please give a complete description of the injuries which you believe to be permanent as a result of the alleged accident.

A. 5. I believe the injury of herniated disc with residual back pain and sciatic pain as described in answer to question 4 permanent. I have suffered symptoms continuously from the date of the accident through the present by reason of such injuries.

Q. 6. If, as a result of any injuries received with regard to this alleged accident, you received medical and/or other treatment, state:

a. The name and address of any and all persons or institutions from which you received such medical or other treatment;

b. The number of treatments so received, setting forth as accurately as possible, all dates of treatment and a description of said treatments;

c. The number and description of treatments received at a doctor's office or institution and the number at your home; and

d. An itemized account of all expenses incurred for the above referred to treatments.

A. 6. My medical treatment has included the following:

<u>V.A. Hospital</u>
Epworth, RI

|  |  |  |
|------|-----------|--------|
| 2/25/05 | Orthopedic Clinic, X-ray | $ 127.00 |
| 3/1/05 | Orthopedic Clinic | 127.00 |
| 4/20/05 | Orthopedic Clinic | 127.00 |
| 5/4/05 | Orthopedic Clinic, X-ray | 127.00 |
| 6/29/05 | Orthopedic Clinic | 127.00 |
| 7/5-7/8/05 | Inpatient: CT and Myelogram | 1,419.00 |
| 7/27/05 | Orthopedic Clinic | 127.00 |
| 8/22-8/26/05 | Inpatient Care | 1,892.00 |
| 8/29-9/3/05 | Inpatient: Disc Surgery | 3,055.00 |
| 9/19/05 | Orthopedic Follow-up | 127.00 |
| 10/17/05 | Orthopedic Clinic | 110.00 |
| 11/28/05 | Orthopedic Clinic | 110.00 |
| 12/5-12/10/05 | Inpatient: CAT Scan, Myelogram | 2,415.00 |
| 8/14/05 | Orthopedic Clinic | 110.00 |
| 10/4/05 | Orthopedic Clinic | 116.00 |
| 10/6/05 | Physical Therapy | 116.00 |
| 10/11/05 | Physical Therapy | 116.00 |
| 10/16/05 | Physical Therapy | 116.00 |
| 10/20/05 | Physical Therapy | 116.00 |
| 10/23/05 | Physical Therapy | 116.00 |

# ANSWERS TO INTERROGATORIES

| 10/25/05 | Physical Therapy | 116.00 |
| 11/1/05 | Physical Therapy | 116.00 |
| 11/3/05 | Physical Therapy | 116.00 |
| 1/11/06 | Orthopedic Clinic, X-ray | 116.00 |

More detailed information is contained on my medical records, copies of which are being provided to Defendant in response to request for production of documents.

Q. 7. a. Please state the dates between which you were confined to your home as a result of the alleged accident;

b. Please state the dates between which you were confined to your bed as a result;

c. Please state the dates between which you were absent from work as a result of the alleged accident.

A. 7. a. After seeing the doctor on February 25, 2005, I went home and stayed home for one week. On March 1, 2005, I went out again, to see the doctor.

Following this visit, I went back to work for a period of weeks between March 5, 2005, and April 15, 2005. I worked only a few days each week, and I missed many days due to back pain. I did not keep a record of these days. I last worked on April 15, 2005. On those days that I missed, I was confined to home, at bed rest.

After seeing the doctor on April 20, 2005, I stayed home at bed rest for 2 weeks, and I have remained at home since that time. Gradually, I have increased my ability to get out of the house, to where I now can be up and about from one to two hours per day. The remainder of the time, I am still confined to home, with frequent bed rest.

b. I was confined to bed, at home from February 25, 2005, after seeing the doctor, to March 3, 2005. I was confined to bed at home, on doctor's orders, from April 20, 2005, through May 3, 2005. I was confined to bed, in hospital, from July 5, 2005, to July 8, 2005. I was confined to bed at home from July 9, 2005, to July 27, 2005, when I returned to the doctor. I remained at bedrest, at home, from July 28, 2005, to August 21, 2005. I remained at bedrest, in hospital, from August 22, 2005, to August 26, 2005, to August 28, 2005. I remained at bedrest, in hospital, from August 29, 2005, through September 3, 2005. I remained at bedrest, at home, from September 4, 2005, to September 19, 2005, when I returned to the doctor. I remained at bedrest, at home, from September 20, 2005, to October 17, 2005, when I returned to the doctor. I remained at bedrest at home, on doctor's orders, from October 18, 2005, to November 28, 2005, when I saw the doctor again. I was confined to bedrest, in hospital, from December 5, 2005, through December 10, 2005.

At all other times, from and after April 20, 2005, I have remained sedentary, spending most of my time at home sitting or reclining, with gradual increase in my ability to get up and about.

c. I have been out of work, as follows:

February 25, 2005 through March 4, 2005; and April 18, 2005, to present.

Also, I missed several days between March 5, 2005, and April 15, 2005, but I have not record of these days.

Q. 8. Describe fully and in complete detail any illnesses, injuries, diseases, defects or operations which you may have or suffered from:

a. within five years prior to the date of the alleged accident;

b. at any time subsequent to the date of the alleged accident; and

c. at any time after the date of the alleged accident not caused by or arising from the same, setting forth the dates upon which each of the above was had or suffered from.

A. 8. a. With the exception of the occasional cold or flu, I had no illness, injuries, diseases, defects or operations within 5 years prior to February 24, 2005. In 1979, while serving in the Army, I injured my back, and since that time, over the years, I did experience occasional backaches, for which I was treated at the VA Hospital Orthopedic Clinic. Also, in 1987 or 1988, I experienced some ankle swelling, but I do not know of any accident or injury that caused the swelling.

b. With the exception only of the occasional cold or flu, and the residual affects and/or treatment for the injury I sustained on February 24, 2005, I have had no further illness, injuries, diseases, defects or operations since that time.

c. With the exception only of the occasional cold or flu, and the residual affects and/or treatment for the injury I sustained on February 24, 2005, I have had no further illness, injuries, diseases, defects or operations since that time.

Q. 9. State the name and residence, business address, occupation, and specialty of each person you expect may be called by you as an expert witness at the trial of this action, setting forth:

a. the subject matter in detail on which each such person may be expected to testify;

b. in detail, the substance of all facts about which each such person may be expected to testify; and

c. in detail, the contents of all opinions to which each such person may be expected to testify.

A. 9.    Patrick McDonald, M.D.
         15 Kildeer Blvd.
         Providence, RI 02907

(a) Dr. McDonald will be asked to testify as to Charles Smith's injuries, including diagnosis, causation, prognosis, symptomology, loss of function and disability.

(b) Dr. McDonald will testify as to the following facts and opinions.

REPORTED HISTORY: The patient is a 48-year-old male who had been employed for three and a half years of Acme Construction as a carpenter prior to his injury. The injury occurred on February 24, 2005 at about 10:00 A.M. He fell through an opening in the floor, falling about four feet and landing diagonally across a metal beam. He struck his lower back and injured his upper back and shoulder as well. He was able with some difficulty to sit and wait out the rest of the day. He did very little work. Since it was a Friday, he went home.

The following Monday because of increasing pain, he was seen at the VA Hospital. He was evaluated over a period of months. He did not improve and, in fact, he began developing right leg pain for which he underwent a lumbar laminectory by Dr. Lynne in August of 2005. He says the numbness and some of the pain in his right leg improved briefly after that but then his low back pain became more severe and his right leg pain returned. He is now using crutches for stability. He has physical therapy ongoing three times a week and he sees the VA people back about every three months.

Current Complaints: He has basically pain which is quite extreme in his low back, into both groins and into his right leg down to the ankle. He denies any pain on the left side. He is able to drive a car but does so only rarely. He is anxious to try and get better but is also concerned that another operation may not help him anymore than the first.

PAST MEDICAL HISTORY: Medications: Percocet, Tylenol No. 3 and Motrin. Medical problems: None. He smokes one half pack of cigarettes a day for 20 years. He admits to no alcohol use. Surgical history is for tonsils and adenoids and lumbar laminectomy.

PHYSICAL EXAMINATION: On examination, he is 6'1" tall and weighs 230 pounds. He is able to move with an antalgic gait around the room. There seems to be some weakness on dorsiflexion on the right side compared to the left. His EHL on the right is slightly weak as well. His reflexes are 1+ Achilles tendon and patella tendon. Straight-leg raising sitting is negative on the left side to about 60 degrees.

On the right side, it is positive at about 40 degrees sitting with pain down the right lower extremity below the knee. When he is recumbent, I can get the right leg only up to about 20 degrees before again he has right radicular type of pain. On the left side, I can get it to about 40 degrees before he has significant low back pain. He has a well-healed incision in the lumbar spine which is about two inches in length which is minimally tender to palpatin. SI joints are slightly tender but the sciatic notch on the right is exquisitely tender compared to the left side.

Forward bending of the lumbar spine is perhaps 20 degrees at best, and extension is neutral. Lateral flexion is about 3 degrees at best and rotation is really not possible.

DIAGNOSIS: Status-post herniated lumbar disc with chronic low back pain and radicular pain, right lower extremity, suggestive or recurrent disc.

ASSESSMENT: It is Dr. McDonald's opinion that the patient's injury occurred acutely as a result of his job on February 24, 2005.

Based on examination of 6/22/06, it is Dr. McDonald's opinion that Plaintiff is not capable of returning to his regular work. He is capable of minimal sedentary work.

Dr. McDonald concurs with the need for aggressive therapy, also for the evaluation for facet blocks and work up to see if the patient has indeed another fragment of disc where he is in need of further surgery would be appropriate as well.

Dr. Danes would concur that there is a functional overlay here which is almost expected given a two year history of out of work with significant back injury.

 (c) The bases of Dr. McDonald's opinions include the history taken from Plaintiff and the observations made during examination on June 22, 2006.

<u>Steven Danes, M.D.</u>

(a) Dr. Danes will be asked to testify as to Charles Smith's injuries, including diagnosis, causation, prognosis, symptomology, loss of function and disability.

(b) Dr. Danes will testify as to the following facts and opinion:

REPORTED HISTORY: The patient was seen on November 3, 2005 and on January 23, 2006. Patient is 41-year-old male who worked as a framing carpenter for ACME Construction for about two and a half years. He sustained an injury to his low back on February 24, 2005, when he was on the deck of a building and walked onto a piece of plywood covering a fireplace opening which gave way. He fell approximately two feet backwards and his back hit a steel center beam. He was unable to hold himself from fall further by grabbing the beam.

He was initially seen at the Veterans Administration Hospital and was subsequently seen in the orthopedic clinic there by Dr. Lynne. He underwent lumbar spine surgery on August 31, 2005. Post-operatively, he states that he continued to have symptoms.
Interval History: The patient states that his right leg numbness and deadness have resolved approximately 90 percent. However, he continues to have severe low back pain and some difficulty with the right lower extremity. He has been to physical therapy for about two weeks but could not tolerate the therapeutic regimen.

Complaints are of persistent severe pain in the low back with difficulty moving at all out of a recliner chair or bed. He states that he spends most of his day lying or sitting in a recliner chair or in his bed and has used two crutches for ambulation, having progressed to two canes, and having the feeling of instability and increasing back pain. He takes two Percocet every six hours, 800 milligrams of Ibuprofen every six hours and two Soma tablets every six to eight hours.

Post-operatively, the patient did undergo a myelogram and CT Scan. He remains under the care of Dr. Lynne. A second operation is under consideration.

PAST HISTORY: The patient denies any interval injury since last seen or since his injury of February 24, 2005. Past history is positive for some low back pain with his work. He never had leg pain or missed any work because of this.

PHYSICAL EXAMINATION: Height is 6'1" tall and weight is 235 pounds. Patient enters the building and the exam room with two crutches and a very slow and cautions gait, limping on the right lower extremity. He has a two inch mid-line lumbar scar and tenderness over the scar.
There is no paraspinous spasm although he does withdraw on palpation of his scar. Lumbar range of motion is quite limited with 30 degrees of flexion, 15 degrees of left and right side bending and 5 degrees of extension. Deep-tendon reflexes are trace at the knees bilaterally and absent at the right ankle and trace at the left ankle. Sensation is preserved to light touch in the lower extremities. Motor testing shows 5/5 strength of extensor hallucis longus, tibialis anterior and quadriceps bilaterally.

The sciatic stretch tests on the right in the seated position is positive for his radiating pain as well as in the supine position. However, the sciatic stretch test is aggravated by knee flexion. Also of note is a positive patella tilt sign with complaints of low back pain aggravation by manipulation of the right patella. This is indicative of significant non-anatomic pain. He also has a slightly positive axial compression test.

# ANSWERS TO INTERROGATORIES

DIAGNOSIS: Severe back pain and status post failed lumbar disc surgery.

ASSESSMENT: The onset of this patient's problem was the injury at work as stated above.

A subsequent course and failure to improve stems from that original injury.

The patient does show objective signs of limitation of lumbar motion and decreased right ankle jerk. He is not capable of regular or light work at this time.

In addition, he shows significant overlay of psychophysiological pain experienced as demonstrated by exacerbation of his pain by knee flexion and patella tilt sign.

Prognosis is extremely guarded given his progress to date.

(c) The bases of Dr. Danes's opinions include the history taken from Plaintiff and the observations made during examinations on November 3, 2005, and January 23, 2006.

Q. 10. State whether or not there were any witnesses to the alleged accident and, if so, state the name and address of all such witnesses other than the parties involved in this suit.

A. 10. Yes, there were witnesses present. They include:

John Williams, 900 Correy Street, Pawtucket, RI.
Karl Amons, 416 Kaspar Lane, Pawtucket, RI.
Thomas Andrews, 40 W. School Rd., Pawtucket, RI.

Q. 11. State what, if any, you consumed by way of any alcoholic beverages or drugs for a period of 24 hours prior to this accident, setting forth in detail where same were consumed, the type of alcohol or drugs, the amounts thereof consumed by you, and at what time intervals.

A. 11. I had no alcohol nor any medications or drugs within 24 hours prior to this accident.

Q. 12. Give an itemized statement of all monetary loss sustained by you as a result of the alleged accident.

A. 12. My economic loss to date is as follows:

Medical Expense:

V.A. Hospital
2/25/05 to present. As itemized at No. 6, above: $11,506.00

Lost Earning Capacity:
Total disability from 4/15/05 to present: $57,640.00; 131 weeks at $440

Both medical expense and lost earning capacity continue to accrue, and these sums are expected to increase accordingly through the date of trial.

Q. 13. Please state in detail and as fully as possible, all conversations or the substance thereof that any defendant had with you or others in your presence concerning the alleged accident, stating as accurately as you are able, what was said by each.

A. 13. I do not recall any conversations with ABC Construction Company, Inc. Nor do I recall any conversations with ABC's owner, individually.

Q. 14. State with reference to the time of the alleged accident, the occupation in which you were engaged, setting forth the name of your employer, the particular capacity in which you were employed, and the wages, salary or profit you were receiving at that time.

A. 14. At the time of this accident I was employed by ACME Construction Company Inc. I was employed as a framing carpenter. I was earning $11.00 an hour, and I was averaging 40 hours a week.

Q. 15. If as a result of this accident you have received compensation from workers' compensation or other insurer, please identify the insurer and state the amounts received on a weekly basis and/or lump sum basis.

A. 15.
a. Workers' Compensation, Goode Insurance Co. $213.84 per week.

b. Other insurance: Social Security Disability, Title II: $171 per month

Q. 16. If you allege that the occurrence resulted in whole or in part from a defective condition involving the defendant's equipment or premises, please:

a. describe the alleged defective condition in complete detail;

b. state how long to your knowledge the alleged defective condition had existed prior to the alleged occurrence;

c. state whether or not you had observed or otherwise become aware of the alleged defective condition prior to the alleged occurrence.

A. 16. a. The defective condition consisted of a makeshift covering over the floor hole which was not properly secured by nailing and/or cross bracing. This consisted solely of half inch plywood laid across the opening. There were two sheets of plywood which were laid side-by-side over the hole and were not lapped over each other. This plywood was not adequate to support the weight of a 210-pound adult male. Additionally, the plywood was covered by plastic sheeting which obscured the edges of the plywood where it lapped over the perimeter of the hole, so I could not see that the 2x4 cross bracing had been removed.

b. The condition existed at least 24–48 hours to the best of my knowledge and information.

c. No. I was unaware of the defective condition prior to the accident. I was aware that when the ACME crew for whom I was working left the job site approximately one week earlier, we left the floor opening properly covered by laying 2x4's on the flat across the floor opening and then covering it with half-inch plywood which was nailed through to the decking.

Q. 17. Please give the date and time of day when you first saw the defect or defective condition in existence.

A. 17. I first became aware of the defective condition when my foot went through and I fell into the hole.

# ANSWERS TO INTERROGATORIES

Q. 18. If you claim that the negligence of any person or persons, including the defendant, contributed to cause the alleged occurrence, please state their names and the manner in which each contributed to cause the alleged occurrence.

A. 18. The negligence of ABC Construction Co., Inc. (Defendant) arose in two contexts:

(a) as owner and party in control of the premises at 10 Maple Drive, Wilder, MA; and

(b) as general contractor, in charge of all construction activities at that location.

The specific negligent conduct of Defendant included:

(a) As owner or party in control of the premises, Defendant was negligent in failing to maintain the premises in a reasonably safe condition for lawful visitors by creating or permitting to exist an unreasonably dangerous and defective condition: i.e., an inadequately and improperly covered floor opening on the premises.

(b) as general contractor, Defendant was negligent in creating or permitting to exist on premises under construction an unreasonably dangerous and defective condition: i.e., an inadequately and improperly covered floor opening.

Also, as general contractor, Defendant failed to warn of the dangerous and defective condition.

Also, as general contractor, Defendant failed to designate suitable, competent persons to inspect the premises for safety hazards, such as the improperly covered floor opening.

Also, as general contractor, Defendant failed to assign to a suitable and competent person the task of covering or otherwise guarding the floor opening in a proper manner after Defendant's employees last used the floor opening for access to the basement, prior to the morning of February 24, 2005.

There may be others whose negligence contributed to my injury, to include other contractors on the site during the week prior to February 24, 2005, who had occasion to use the floor opening to the cellar and who may have been directly responsible for not covering the floor opening in a proper manner. Plaintiff's discovery, still unanswered by Defendant, seeks the names of any such other parties as may exist. In any event, as general contractor, Defendant was ultimately responsible for overall safety on this job site, even if the dangerous and defective condition had been directly created by such others.

Q. 19. Please describe the weather at the time of the alleged occurrence and during the 24 hours prior to the alleged occurrence, including whether it was clear, cloudy, raining lightly or sprinkling, raining hard, sleeting, snowing or otherwise, and whether or not there was an accumulation of any type of precipitation around the area of the occurrence.

A. 19. The weather was cold and clear.

Q. 20. Please state fully and in complete detail all that the defendant did or failed to do which in any way caused or contributed to cause the alleged occurrence, including every act or omission of the defendant which you allege constitutes negligence.

A. 20. See answer to Question 18, above, and Question 23, below.

435

Q. 21. Please identify by name, title, and business address the person with whom you dealt as being the person responsible for, in charge of or supervising the performance of your work on behalf of the owner of the premises at which you were performing your work at the time of the alleged accident.

A. 21. My work was supervised by Mr. Thomas Andrews as president and principal of ACME Construction Company Inc. Mr. Andrews did not supervise the performance of my work as a servant of the owner of the premises but was, on my information, an independent contractor.

Q. 22. If on the day of the alleged accident you were part of a work crew or group, please identify each member of the crew or group by name and residential and business address stating the identity of the person in charge of or in the position as the supervisor of the group and whether any of such persons were present at the time and place of the accident and witnessed the accident.

A. 22. The work crew consisted of the following individuals:

John Williams, 900 Correy Street, Pawtucket, RI.
Karl Amons, 416 Kaspar Lane, Pawtucket, RI.
Thomas Andrews, 40 W. School Rd., Pawtucket, RI, Supervisor.

Q. 23. If you claim that the defendant in any way violated any trade standards, safety standards, state, local or federal governmental regulations in the production or construction of the dwelling house at which the accident occurred, please state:

a. the exact standard which it is claimed that the defendant violated and the respect in which the standard was violated;

b. how and in what manner this violation caused or contributed to cause the alleged occurrence.

A. 23. (a) Defendant, as general contractor, violated the following provisions:

Mass. Division of Industrial Safety
Prevention of Accidents in Construction Operations
411 CMR 10.00 (Effective 1/1/78)

| | |
|---|---|
| 10.03 (1) | Protection of Health & Safety |
| 10.03 (5) | Requirements of Competence |
| 10.03 (7) | Safety Inspections |
| 10.04 (6) | Falling Hazards |
| (a) | Prevention; and |
| (b) | Floor Security |

Current regulations, 454 CMR 10.00, became effective on 7/8/2005, after Plaintiff's accident, and therefore Defendant's violations arose under the previous regulations at 441 CMR 10.00.

OSHA Safety & Health Standards
Construction Industry Standards
29 U.S.C. Part 1926
Subpart C
Sect. 1926.20 Contractor Requirements for Accident Prevention

Subpart G
Sect. 1926.200   (b)      Danger signs

# ANSWERS TO INTERROGATORIES

      (c)      Caution signs

Subpart M
Sect. 1926.500 (9) (b) (8), and (f) (5) (ii) Floor hole guards

      (b)      These violations caused or contributed to the accident as follows:

Mass. DIS Violations
(1) 441 CMR 10.04 (6) (a) required that every hold or opening in any floor through which a person may fall shall have all exposed sides guarded by a barrier sufficient to prevent falls. This was not done at 10 Maple Drive. If Defendant had complied with this section, Plaintiff would not have fallen through the floor opening.

(2) 441 CMR 10.04 (6) (c) required that when floor openings are covered by solid temporary construction, such cover shall be properly anchored to prevent accidental displacement. When ACME left the site a week before the accident, they had left the floor opening secured in compliance with this section, by laying 2x4s across the opening and then nailing plywood onto the 2x4s and through to the decking. This cover was removed when Defendant's employees or others used the floor opening to gain access to the cellar when the concrete floor was poured. This cover was replaced by loose sheets of 1/2 in. plywood laid across the opening, with no timber supports and no nailing, in violation of 10.04 (6) (c). When Plaintiff stepped on the unsecured 1/2 in. plywood, this was not adequate to support his weight, and he fell through the hole. If Defendant had complied with 10.04 (6)(c), the accident would have been prevented.

(3) 441 CMR 10.03 (5) required that the general contractor designate a person of suitable competence to perform in all work. Defendant permitted an incompetent person or persons to perform the task of covering the cellar hole opening after the basement floor was poured.

Also, if Defendant had arranged for daily inspections on the site, Defendant did not designate a person of suitable competence to perform such inspections.

Had a competent person been designated to cover the floor hole after the basement floor was poured, or had a competent person been designated to inspect the site, this accident could have been prevented.

(4) 441 CMR 10.03 (1) (a) required that all work sites be so arranged as to provide reasonable and adequate protection for the safety of employees and others. And 441 CMR 10.03 (1) (b) provided that it is the responsibility of both owners and contractors to provide for such safety. Defendant, both as owner and as general contractor, violated this section by causing or permitting to exist on the job site a dangerous and defective condition, which consisted of an inadequately constructed floor-hole cover. And this was compounded by Defendant's causing or permitting to exist a plastic sheet which covered and obscured the hazardous condition.

OSHA Violations
29 U.S.C. Part 1926
(1) Subpart C, sect. 1926.20 (b) (1), provides that it is an employer's responsibility to initiate and maintain safety programs on a job site. And sect. 1926.20 (b) (2) provides that this must include frequent and regular inspections. If a competent inspection had been performed at 10 Maple Drive, the accident would have been prevented, where the unsecured and inadequate floor hole cover was a hazard to employees.

(2)  Subpart G, Sect. 1926.200 (b) requires that danger signs be posted at dangerous locations on a job site, and Sect. 1926.200 (c) requires that caution signs be posted where potential hazards exist. If, for any valid reason, it was not possible to re-secure the floor hole cover with adequate cross bracing and nailing down, then such danger or hazard should have been signaled by the placement of an appropriate sign. Had such sign been posted, Plaintiff would have been alerted to the fact that the solid floor hole covering had been replaced by an inadequate cover, and this accident could have been prevented. Instead of providing such warning, Defendant caused or permitted to exist a plastic sheet over the floor hole cover, which obscured the hazard.

(3)  Subpart M. Sect. 1926.500 (b) (8) provides that floor holes into which a person may fall must be guarded by either a railing and toe board, or a floor hole cover of standard strength and construction that is secured against accidental displacement. When ACME left the job site a week before the accident, they left the floor hole covered with a secure cover, in compliance with this section. When Plaintiff returned on February 24, 1988, the secure cover had been removed, and it was replaced with one that was of less than standard construction and which was not secured properly. If the floor hole had been properly covered after Defendant's employees or others had worked on the cellar floor, this accident would have been prevented.

Q. 24.  Please describe any and all written or oral warnings or instructions given to you in relation to the defect, its existence or use, giving the name and address of each person who gave each such warning or instruction.

A. 24.  None.

Subscribed on pain of perjury this 6th day of November, 2006
Charles Smith

# Appendix H  Request for the Production of Documents

COMMONWEALTH OF MASSACHUSETTS

NORFOLK, SS.

SUPERIOR COURT DEPARTMENT
CIVIL ACTION NO. 05-00447

```
****************************************
CHARLES SMITH; PATRICIA SMITH;        *
and KATELYN SMITH, KYLE SMITH,        *
and MATTHEW SMITH, Minors by Their    *
Mother and Next Friend, PATRICIA SMITH, *   REQUEST OF THE DEFENDANT
    Plaintiffs                        *   FOR THE PRODUCTION OF
                                      *   DOCUMENTS UNDER RULE 34
VS.                                   *   TO THE PLAINTIFF,
                                      *   CHARLES SMITH
                                      *
ABC CONSTRUCTION CO., INC.            *
    Defendant                         *
****************************************
```

Now comes the defendant, ABC Construction Co., Inc. in the above entitled action through its attorney and pursuant to Rule 34 of the Massachusetts Rules of Civil Procedure, requests that the plaintiff, Charles Smith, produce and permit the said defendant to inspect, copy, and/or photograph all documents and things in the possession, custody, or control of the plaintiff, or any agent of the plaintiff, other than writing, documents, and tangible things prepared in anticipation of litigation or for trial, which embody, refer to, or relate in any way to the subjects listed below.

The said defendant requests that these documents and things herein requested be produced at the law firm of PATTON, DESOTO & HALL, P.C., 61 Inverness Place, Hillsborough, Massachusetts 22222, on or before the 30th day after service of this request, except that compliance with this request may be made by mailing copies of said documents to the defendant's attorney, but mail, postage prepaid, such mailings to be postmarked prior to the 30th day following service of this request.

NOTE: With respect to the hospital records, signed hospital authorization slips will suffice.

## REQUESTS

1. Any and all hospital and medical records and reports regarding the injuries and damages and treatments thereof, received by the plaintiff with reference to the injuries alleged to have been sustained by the plaintiff in his Complaint.
2. True copies on the plaintiff's and Patricia Smith's Federal income tax returns for the years 2002 through 2005, and copies of all forms W-2 received by the plaintiff for those years.
3. Full and complete records of any and all hospitals and other medical facilities at which the plaintiff was examined and/or treated in the past five-year period prior to the date of the alleged accident.
4. All employers' written confirmation or verification of the time and/or earnings lost as result of the accident.
5. Any and all written or documentary evidence which relates to the issue of the plaintiff's damage.
6. All signed and/or unsigned statements made by the defendant which are in the possession of the plaintiff or under his control and which relate directly or indirectly to any subject which is the basis of this complaint.

7. Any and all photographs in the possession, control and custody of the plaintiff relating in any way to the accident alleged in the plaintiff's Complaint and amended Complaint, including all photographs showing the scene of the alleged accident, showing that the injuries sustained by the plaintiff or any effect thereof, and photographs of the scene of the accident and any components or parts of the equipment or dwelling house which caused the accident alleged in the plaintiff's Complaint.

8. Any and all written or other documentary evidence relating to the issue of the defendant's liability.

9. And all written or other documentary evidence which tends to exonerate or exculpate the defendant.

10. Any and all written or other documentary evidence which tends to show that the conduct by act or omission of some third person or persons caused or contributed to the happening of the event or injuries which form the subject matter of this complaint.

11. Any and all photographs which the plaintiffs intend to offer at the time of trial.

12. Any and all documentary evidence which the plaintiffs intend to offer at the time of trial.

13. All financial records, bills, invoices or other such documents relating to amounts charged to or expended by or on behalf of the plaintiff as a result of the occurrence referred to in the plaintiff's Complaint.

14. All employment records of the plaintiff including, but without being limited to the names and addresses of all employers the records of the dates lost from work for any reason whatsoever, and the employment income loss during the period of time commencing five years before the date of the occurrence alleged in the plaintiff's Complaint and amended Complaint up to and including the present day.

15. Copies of any and all written statements, signed or unsigned, of any and all witnesses to the accident and/or copies of all verbatim written transcripts of any and all statements of such witnesses taken on a recording device prior to the filing of the suit herein, which are in the possession, custody or control of the plaintiff or the plaintiff's attorney.

16. Copies of all written statements, signed or unsigned, of any and all witnesses to the subject of the plaintiff's alleged allegations of both liability and/or damages from the incident as alleged in the plaintiff's Complaint and/or copies of all verbatim written transcripts of any and all statements of such witnesses taken on a recording device prior to the filing of this suit herein which are in the possession, custody or control of the plaintiff or the plaintiff's attorney.

17. Copies of all accident reports made by the plaintiff which relate to the accident alleged in the plaintiff's Complaint and amended Complaint.

18. If the plaintiff applied for or received workers' compensation as a result of the accident, which is the subject of the plaintiff's Complaint, the entire file maintained by the workers' compensation carrier with respect to the loss.

19. Each investigation report relating to the accident which is the subject of the plaintiff's Complaint and which was prepared by any agency, bureau or commission of the Federal government, or any state, local or municipal government.

By the Attorney for the Defendant,

_____

Ronald A. Patton, Jr., Esquire
PATTON, DESOTO & HALL, P.C.
1 Inverness Place
Hillsborough, MA 23456
BBO No. 777777

Dated: _____

# Appendix I  Sample Schedule from Subpoena Duces Tecum

SCHEDULE A.

You are requested to bring with you any and all materials of the following descriptions which (a) you referred to in preparing your report of November 28, 2006; and/or (b) to which you may refer in giving testimony at trial.

1. Notes prepared by you in the course of your inspection of the 480DM screener and/or in the course of your research.

2. Diagrams, blueprints, plans, drawings and sketches.

3. Graphs and/or charts.

4. Records and reports from other persons or entities.

5. Photographs, films and/or videotapes.

6. Deposition excerpts to which you referred in preparing your report.

7. Governmental regulations, including OSHA.

8. Published standards of any industrial or professional associations, including ANSI and ASME.

9. Non-published written standards from any industrial or professional source.

10. Product brochures and/or manuals.

11. Written or transcribed statements of any person.

12. Treatises and/or publications.

13. Test results and survey reports.

14. Physical objects, to include without limitation any exemplar wrenches used by you in performing any test or experiment on the 480DM screener and any instruments used by you in performing any such test or experiment.

# Appendix J  Deposition Transcript

The following is a sample (partial) deposition transcript of an automotive glass expert. Note that the tone of the deposition is collegial and not contentious. The deposition demonstrates many features of a typical expert witness deposition including the following.

- Introductory questions
- The questions are open-ended and designed to elicit information
- Review of the expert's CV after determining that it is the latest CV
- Background questions focus on the specific topic (glass) that the expert is testifying on in the case at hand
- Exhaustive questioning follows on everything the expert has reviewed to form his opinion in the case at hand
- Detailed questioning on the testing the expert performed
- Questions on the documents relied upon by the expert
- Questions on the expert's opinions
- Questions on exhibits the expert plans on using at trial

(By agreement of counsel, the certification, sealing, and filing of the deposition were waived, and all objections except as to the form of the question were reserved to the time of trial.)

- - -

JOHN A. SMITH, PhD, PE, after having been first duly sworn, was examined and testified as follows:

### Identity of witness

**Q.** Would you give your full name and spell your last name, please?
**A.** It's John Albert Smith. S as in Sam, M I T H.
**Q.** And it's Dr. Smith , right?
**A.** Yes, sir.
**Q.** What is your doctoral degree in?
**A.** It's in mechanical engineering dash engineering mechanics.

### Preliminary matters

**Q.** May I call you, from time to time, John? Do you have a problem with that?
**A.** Not at all.
**Q.** It's easier than saying Dr. Smith over and over. Have you had your deposition taken before, Dr. Smith?
**A.** I have.
**Q.** Then you generally know the rules we're about to go over, but let me just go over my own sort of housekeeping rules. First, we have a court reporter here today. As a consequence of that, everything you say and everything the lawyers say will end up on a written record. Do you understand that?
**A.** Yes.
**Q.** The court reporter is not allowed to interpret any nods or gestures you may give, so every answer you give has to be a complete verbal answer such as yes or no. Do you understand?
**A.** I do.
**Q.** If you don't understand one of my questions, ask me to repeat it or rephrase it and I'll do that for you. Fair enough?
**A.** Fair enough.

**Q.** If, however, you answer one of my questions, I'll assume that you understood it and are answering it accordingly. Fair enough?

**A.** Fair enough.

**Q.** Don't guess, don't speculate. If you don't know the answer to my question, tell me that. I'll either rephrase it or ask a different question. Last, but not least, and this is very important, we're sort of on a relatively narrow table here, and we always need to remember we're not at the dining room table where the goal is to talk over all the other people in the family or all the other people at the table. Always try to let me finish my question before you try to answer. Okay?

**A.** Okay.

**Q.** And I will always try, but can't guarantee that I will always succeed, at letting you finish your answer before I ask my next question. Okay?

**A.** We'll have a friendly deposition.

**Q.** Yes. That will make it easier for the court reporter, too, because she'll only have to listen to one of us at a time rather than having two conversations going at one time.

**A.** We won't play cross-fire.

MR. MARTIN: I'm going to mark as Exhibit No. 1 a copy of the notice of deposition. Actually, it's the second re-notice, which only differs from the previous notices by virtue of the place and time when we rescheduled it to today. (A Defendants' Second Re-Notice of Deposition was marked Exhibit-1 for identification.)

BY MR. MARTIN:

**Q.** I'll ask you if you've seen this or an earlier version of this deposition notice prior to today (indicating).

**A.** Yes, sir.

### *Subpoenaed documents*

**Q.** Have you reviewed that duces tecum prior to today—

**A.** Yes.

**Q.**—what I call on here Exhibit A? You've done that before?

**A.** Yes, sir.

**Q.** Have you searched your files and brought everything to the deposition today upon which you're relying for your opinions in this case?

**A.** Yes, largely. There's one thing I wanted to bring for this case which was Ford discovery, 1988 Aerostar testing. I spoke to an attorney who said that's protected, so I'll meet with him tomorrow and talk to him about it because it was my impression it was not.

**Q.** So you did not bring a Ford document on an Aerostar?

**A.** Right. It's a whole document of the test regimen and then a videotape which is on a disk, actually, of the impacts.

**Q.** So it's a test document and a video?

**A.** Yes, sir.

**Q.** What model year Aerostar?

**A.** 1988.

**Q.** What kind of a test is it?

**A.** I want to be general here—

**Q.** I understand that.

**A.**—I don't want to get into legal trouble.

**Q.** I don't want you to violate the protective order, but if you can, tell me what kind of test it was. I won't ask you what the results were, but if you can, tell me the kind of test it was. If you, in your own mind, can make a judgment as to whether or not you think that would keep you on the right side of the protective order, then please answer.

**A.** Yes, it is an impact test of a Hybrid III side-impact dummy into a high-g sled with a door on it and bilaminate glass. Richard Morrison said that this has been in the glass collection for years which makes me think it's unprotected, but that's in dispute.

**Q.** Who is Richard Morrison?

**A.** He is a retired Ford employee who does significant amounts of expert witnessing for defense attorneys regarding glass.

**Q.** He's a defense witness?

**A.** He is.

**Q.** Is he a witness who testified in the Garcia case in Texas recently?

**A.** I believe so. I had already busted camp by the time they had their expert.

**Q.** I'm sorry?

**A.** I had already left by the time—after my testimony was called for.

**Q.** By the time Ford began putting on its witnesses?

**A.** Right, and I haven't seen trial transcripts, but I think that's a pretty reasonable assumption here.

**Q.** And Richard Morrison, although a defense witness, is someone you correspond with or talk with, at least, from time to time?

**A.** Yes.

**Q.** And he advised you that he thought that this document was subject to a protective order?

**A.** No, an attorney, Pat Ardis, told me that.

**Q.** Pat Ardis out of Memphis?

**A.** Yes, sir.

**Q.** Did Richard Morrison say anything with respect to whether he thought the document was protected?

**A.** He said that it has been in the glass collection for years, and it's my understanding that everything in the glass collection is unprotected, but I'm not a lawyer, so I have to be careful about what I say.

**Q.** When you say "in the glass collection," you mean a Ford glass collection of documents?

**A.** Yes. Ford has a generic glass collection of documents.

MR. ZAJAC: Is that different from Ford.com or part of it?

THE WITNESS: I don't know; I haven't been on that. Stuff just magically appears in my mailbox and I get it.

BY MR. MARTIN:

**Q.** The question you've been waiting for: Have you taken anything out of your file prior to attending the deposition today?

**A.** No, only those things which we have discussed that I do not rely upon that are used by other members of my firm so I didn't have to tote them to Philadelphia.

**Q.** How about this Ford document, was it once in your file and then pulled out because of the question about it?

**A.** It was in my library, it wasn't in this particular file.

**Q.** Aside from that Ford document that you had considered putting into your file for this case is there anything else upon which you are relying for your opinions in this case that you haven't brought with you today?

**A.** The only other thing that I wish I had brought is some popular literature write-ups of the Ford—not Ford, but Volvo rollovers of the XC-90.

**Q.** These are write-ups you've seen where?

**A.** They're on the internet, they're in Wards Auto Week, just, as I said, popular literature, not technical literature. That's not as authoritative, I don't think, as internal documents and such, but I will get those to you because we have, as one of our items, a Volvo rollover movie, and this is the only thing that I have that documents that at this point.

**Q.** So you are relying on some documentation pertaining to a rollover or rollovers of a Volvo XC-90 for your opinions in this case?

**A.** Yes.

**Q.** What you have available to you somewhere are some popular literature documents pertaining to that?

**A.** Right, and what they say in the popular literature is it was at 30 miles an hour, there was only crease denting, and the doors still opened. That's about the extent of it. Then they extol the virtues of the vehicle.

**Q.** And that's all you have in your library or back at your office?

**A.** That's right. I don't have any internal Volvo discovery documents or things.

**Q.** I would like you to then supply to Mr. Zajac—you can perhaps have someone in your office fax it to him tomorrow—these pages that you're relying on, or if you're back in the office tomorrow you can fax it to him.

**A.** Can I get it next week? Is that too late?

**Q.** Today is Thursday. If you can get it to him by Monday, that would be helpful.

**A.** I can do Monday. I'm not going to be back in the office tomorrow.

**Q.** Or you can get it directly to the court reporter. We can make arrangements to do that.

MR. MARTIN: We're going to mark as Exhibit No. 2 Volvo popular literature items. (Volvo Popular Literature Items were scheduled to be marked, upon receipt, Exhibit-2 for identification.)

BY MR. MARTIN:

**Q.** You told me you do not have any testing on the XC-90; in other words, you have no test reports or materials actually prepared by Volvo regarding the XC-90?

**A.** Right, nothing with the Volvo letterhead on it that comes to mind. I will go back and ransack my office for the stuff and give you everything I have.

**Q.** So you are relying on that for your opinions in this case, these popular literature items?

**A.** Yes.

**Q.** Have you, at any time, seen test reports or video prepared by Volvo or any entity under Volvo's direction pertaining to rollover or 216 or other testing on the XC-90?

**A.** Yes.

**Q.** You have?

**A.** Yes.

**Q.** What were the circumstances of your having seen that?

**A.** I pulled them off of the internet. Since this is their vehicle being dolly rolled over, it's unthinkable that somebody else staged this. This has got to be at their facility.

**Q.** So you've seen dolly rollover testing of a Volvo XC-90 which you have taken off the internet?

**A.** Yes, kind of a low-resolution movie.

**Q.** Like an mpeg kind of movie?

**A.** Exactly.

**Q.** What website did you pull that off of?

**A.** I don't have that in front of me.

**Q.** Did you see test results, that is, test document with data plots and such things like that, information from accelerometers and such, on this XC-90?

**A.** Not yet.

**Q.** You have not seen that yet?

**A.** Right. I'm sure that information is available somewhere, but I have not seen that yet.

**Q.** So you have not seen test documentation?

**A.** Right, I've only seen the results that are kind of a macro of observations, which windows broke and do the doors still open.

**Q.** What was your understanding of the test procedure that Volvo followed when it rolled this XC-90?

**A.** 1996 test. The video and the write-ups of it. In the popular literature? Right, the guns and ammo version of SAE correctly.

**Q.** Did the video you've seen show the vehicle move through this whole sequence until it came to rest?

**A.** Yes.

**Q.** You were able to view the vehicle as it came to rest?

**A.** Yes.

**Q.** When the vehicle came to rest, were any of the side windows, side glazing, broken?

**A.** Yes.

**Q.** Which ones?

**A.** I believe only the passenger front window was broken.

**Q.** So the passenger front door window?

**A.** Yes.

**Q.** What direction roll was it; was it a driver's side or passenger's side leading rollover?

**A.** Passenger's side.

MR. ZAJAC: We downloaded it, just in case you want to ask him any questions about what it shows.

MR. MARTIN: Can you burn that to a CD on this laptop, should be able but to do something in CD?

BY MR. MARTIN:

**Q.** So the passenger front side window broke. And it' s a passenger side leading roll?

**A.** Yes, sir.

**Q.** What is your understanding of the composition of the side windows or at least that right front passenger side window?

**A.** From my observation, I think it is tempered glass, but I am not sure.

**Q.** You're not sure?

**A.** Right. As I say, I don't have the internal write-up on this giving all the test specs.

**Q.** Did you have any understanding as to what Volvo was using for side window glazing aside from your view of this video?

**A.** No. Wait a minute. I do have a listing of vehicles that use different types of glass, in particular, which ones use laminated side glass, and the Volvo XC-90 had laminated side glass in 2003 and 2004 as a package option. That's about my extent of the knowledge of what glass they were using in that vehicle.

**Q.** So what you have information on is that laminated side glass is available as an option in the 2003, 2004 model years?

**A.** Yes, sir.

**Q.** What model year was this vehicle in the video?

**A.** I don't recall.

**Q.** Have you attempted to analyze the video in any way to determine if, in fact, the side glazing is laminated or tempered glass?

**A.** Yes.

**Q.** What have you done?

**A.** I just looked at it, and it appears that when it broke, it completely evacuated the porthole, so I would say that it's probably tempered glass.

**Q.** We've talked about the windows. Did any other windows on this vehicle break out?

**A.** I believe the windshield is cracked as well, but that's it.

**Q.** How many times did the vehicle roll?

**A.** Three and one-quarter.

**Q.** So it came to rest on what side?

**A.** Passenger.

**Q.** Did any of the doors open?

**A.** As I recall from reading the popular literature, all the doors still opened after the test.

**Q.** They were openable after the crash?

**A.** That's right. You could see trim getting torn off the vehicle as it's running along, including the mirrors and roof rack, I believe, but none of the doors opened. The hood stayed shut.

**Q.** So all the doors remained latched during the crash?

**A.** Yes, sir.

**Q.** And your understanding is that all of the doors were openable after the crash?

**A.** Yes.

**Q.** Were you able to analyze the roof deformation, if any?

**A.** Yes.

**Q.** What was your analysis?

**A.** Very minor, crease denting, it said in the write-up, and if the doors still open, that's a good indication that it did well. The windshield did not tear out. Most of the glass did not break, so this is, as I understand it, typical XC-90 rollover performance.

**Q.** Did you perform any comparisons as between the deformed roof of this XC-90 that was rolled over and an undeformed XC-90 roof?

**A.** No, that's not really possible from that video.

**Q.** We had gotten into that because we talked about materials that you wished you had brought to the deposition, and you're going to provide us with this popular literature item and we'll talk later on about whether we can download this video to a CD and mark it as an exhibit. Is there anything else that you wish you had brought to the deposition that you did not bring?

**A.** Nothing else comes to mind.

### *CV Questions*

**Q.** Let's find in here your CV. I think you brought that with you today?

**A.** Yes, I just printed one up the other day. That should be late March.

**Q.** It says February 24, 2005.

**A.** Didn't I hand you one?

**Q.** It was in your book here (indicating).

**A.** If I can see it—maybe I didn't update the date there. That often happens. It's not an automatic update. This is the most up-to-date. It says 02/24, but as I say, that date in the upper right-hand corner doesn't automatically update the way I think it should, so if I update it, it won't change that.

MR. MARTIN: I have marked that as Exhibit-3. (A Curriculum Vitae was marked Exhibit-3 for identification.)

BY MR. MARTIN:

**Q.** Would it be fair to say that this is a copy of your most recent CV?

**A.** Yes, sir.

**Q.** Your CV includes your areas of expertise, your education, your licenses, your professional history, your affiliations, publications, courses taught, continuing education, presentations, research contracts awarded. Is that pretty much a summary of what is in your CV?

**A.** Yes.

**Q.** We have not met before, so I do need to talk to you a little bit about your background. First of all, when did you receive your bachelor's degree?

**A.** 1986.

**Q.** You got that from Michigan Technological University?

**A.** Yes.

**Q.** That was in mechanical engineering?

**A.** Yes.

**Q.** Were there any areas of concentration you had for your bachelor's?

**A.** Yes, in vibrations.

**Q.** After you got your bachelor's degree, did you then immediately go on to obtain an MS degree or did you work for a while?

**A.** I worked for a long time.

**Q.** It looks like in 1986 you went into the Army as an ordnance officer?

**A.** Yes, sir, a butter bar.

**Q.** What is that?

**A.** A butter bar, second lieutenant.

**Q.** Are you still in the Army?

**A.** I am.

**Q.** As a reserve?

**A.** Yes, I'm a reserve ordnance major.

**Q.** So you've been in the Army, either in the regular Army or reserves, since '86?

**A.** Nineteen years. One more.

**Q.** Did you spend four years in the regular Army then?

**A.** Yes, sir.

**Q.** And you didn't get discharged, you went into the reserves in 1990?

**A.** Right, I had an active-duty discharge and then accepted a reserve commission. That's the way that works.

**Q.** So you've been in the reserves about 15 years then?

**A.** I have.

**Q.** But in 1990, you went to work for a company called Ring Screw Works in Troy, Michigan?

**A.** Yes.

**Q.** You were a manufacturing engineer there. What did Ring Screw Works do, what sort of work?

**A.** They provided specialty fasteners for the automotive industry. If you open up the hood on your car and see a bolt and in the center there's a little circle and then all the stuff saying what grade of bolt it is, that will tell you that they made it.

**Q.** What was your job there besides manufacturing engineer?

**A.** I would install new plant equipment, design tooling, keep the plant running.

**Q.** How large a company was Ring Screw Works at that time?

**A.** They employed something like 1200 people in the various divisions, I think.

**Q.** You continued working for them until 1993; is that correct?

**A.** Right through the end of the year.

**Q.** When did you begin your studies at GMI?

**A.** I started that, I think, in '92 part time at night, then when I left Ring I had six months to finish on my master's degree so I just did it as a full-time graduate student and full-time lab instructor.

**Q.** Just so the record is clear, what is GMI?

**A.** GMI is now Kettering University, and it's the former General Motors Institute. It's a technical school in Flint, Michigan that really caters to the automotive industry.

**Q.** Did you travel to Flint for your classes or do it by correspondence?

**A.** They were only nine miles from my house. It was great. I just went to campus.

**Q.** You did eventually get an MS degree from GMI in 1994—

**A.** Yes, sir.

**Q.**—correct? That's in manufacturing systems engineering?

**A.** Yes it.

**Q.** What does that mean?

**A.** That is somewhat like industrial engineering. It centers on statistics and manufacturing processes and ergonomics and plant work flow, so it really had more to do with my job at Ring Screw Works than any other degree I could have taken.

**Q.** While you were at Michigan Technological University for your mechanical engineering degree, did you have any formal education in the area of glazing or glass?

**A.** At Michigan Tech, I took course work in materials science which covered glass, and it may have talked about automobile glass as a composite of the windshield. I remember we talked about tempered glass, how that worked, so some.

**Q.** Were there any courses dedicated to the issues relating to glazing or glass?

**A.** I don't believe so, not in my department.

**Q.** Or that you took?

**A.** There was a materials science department there that may have had a glass class, but I didn't take that.

**Q.** I just want to confirm whether you took a glass class as compared to a class that had some componentry related to glass. Did you?

**A.** No.

**Q.** How about when you were at GMI, did you take any classes that were dedicated to the study of glazing or automotive glass or other kind of glass?

**A.** No.

**Q.** Then you went on to start a degree, a Ph.D. degree, going back to Michigan Technological University; is that correct?

**A.** Yes.

**Q.** You received your Ph.D. in 1998?

**A.** I did.

**Q.** That is in what field?

**A.** It's officially mechanical engineering dash engineering mechanics. I did my dissertation modeling the high-temperature, high-strain rate response of tool steels, so it was materials science and engineering mechanics based.

**Q.** Can you summarize what your concentration was in your Ph.D. program?

**A.** It was primarily manufacturing and engineering mechanics.

**Q.** Did you have any course work specifically dedicated to glazing or glass in your Ph.D. program?

**A.** No.

**Q.** Did you have any courses that touched on or included glazing or glass in your Ph.D. program?

**A.** Not that I recall.

**Q.** After you got your Ph.D., did you then move to the Iowa State University?

**A.** I did.

**Q.** And you were a temporary assistant professor there?

**A.** Yes.

**Q.** For one year?

**A.** Yes.

**Q.** Then what was your next job assignment?

**A.** Then I went to the University of Arkansas.

**Q.** In 1999, I see something here about a forensic engineer job at Hall Engineering in Ames, Iowa?

**A.** Yes.

**Q.** What was that?

**A.** At Iowa State University, I had a nine-month appointment, so that left the summer open before I got the tenure track job at University of Arkansas, so this was like a summer job for a professor.

**Q.** What sorts of things did you do as a forensic engineer at Hall Engineering?

**A.** I did discovery summations, I did research into codes and standards, and product performance and testing.

**Q.** How large a company was Hall Engineering?

**A.** It was Dr. Hall, his wife, a technician which was a student, the quarterback of the Iowa State Cyclones, as a matter of fact, and me and one staff engineer.

**Q.** And Dr. Hall, what is his first name?

**A.** I think it's Joe, but I'm not sure.

**Q.** Was he a retained expert in litigation?

**A.** I think so.

**Q.** So you did assistant kind of work to him, looking at discovery, organizing files, summarizing things, and things of that nature?

**A.** Yes.

**Q.** That was a three-month job?

**A.** Yes.

**Q.** Then from there, you went on to get a job in the mechanical engineering department at the University of Arkansas?

**A.** I did.

**Q.** You were there for how long; how long have you been at the University of Arkansas? Are you still there?

**A.** I'm there as an adjunct.

**Q.** Initially, you went as a full-time assistant professor?

**A.** I did.

**Q.** How long a period of time were you there full time, that is, at the University of Arkansas?

**A.** Through the end of 2002.

**Q.** What happened at the end of 2002 that changed your status?

**A.** My son went to school, and it cost so much that I decided I had to get another job and so I became full time at Renfroe Engineering.

**Q.** Prior to 2002, did you have any association with Renfroe Engineering?

**A.** Yes.

**Q.** When did you first associate with Renfroe Engineering?

**A.** The year 2000, if I recall correctly.

**Q.** And that was part-time work with Renfroe?

**A.** Yes.

**Q.** Give me an estimate of how many hours you would have worked a month for Renfroe in, say 2000, on average. It can be a ballpark number.

**A.** Sure. When I started, it was small, so three or four that first year.

**Q.** Three or four hours?

**A.** Three or four hours a week or a month. It was not much, just a few jobs that year, very low. It gradually increased. In '01 it was more; in '02 it was more. When I was at the university, I was only working ten hours a week on average consulting. Being a professor took up most of my time.

**Q.** In 2002, what month did you go full time with Renfroe?

**A.** December 16.

**Q.** Of 2002?

**A.** Yes. The academic year had ended and I was picked up.

**Q.** So you've been with Renfroe for about two and a quarter years full time?

**A.** Yes, sir.

**Q.** In that period of time up until December 16, 2002 when you went full time with Renfroe, what sorts of jobs did you work on at Renfroe in all those times when you were part time?

**A.** It was material failure or accident reconstruction.

**Q.** What sorts of material failure?

**A.** Things like—his practice is mostly cars, so the first case I had that actually went to deposition was on a seat track failure of a GM product.

**Q.** So one case would certainly have included seat tracking. What other sorts of material failure cases did you work on?

**A.** When I was just starting out, we were doing insurance cases, too, so I looked at a failed ice machine, I looked at an overhead crane assembly, I've looked at a leaking roof, just all sorts of kind of everyday things, we need some engineer with a technical background to look at.

**Q.** In that period 2000 to 2002, did you ever have any cases where you were studying glazing?

**A.** At least one.

**Q.** In that period of 2000 to 2002?

**A.** Yes, sir.

**Q.** What kind of a case was that?

**A.** The first glass case I ever had was in August of 2002, an untripped, friction-induced rollover of a Ford Explorer with a belted occupant. She was partially ejected and received life-altering injuries.

**Q.** So you worked on a Ford Explorer rollover case. What was your assignment in that case?

**A.** To research the crashworthiness of the vehicle.

**Q.** Including what component parts?

**A.** It's open-ended, certainly. The attorney says are there any crashworthiness defects for this vehicle. Generally, in a rollover, it quickly gets down to the roof and the glass.

**Q.** So did you, in fact, analyze the roof and the glass in that first Explorer case?

**A.** Yes.

**Q.** Did you testify in that case?

**A.** I have given a deposition, but it has not gone to court.

**Q.** What's the name of the case?

**A.** *Travis versus Ford.*

**Q.** Where is it located, if you remember?

**A.** Texas.

**Q.** Who is the plaintiff?

**A.** Ted B. Lyon, L-y-o-n.

**Q.** Did you offer any opinions with respect to the roof performance of that Explorer?

**A.** I don't believe so. The injuries didn't come from roof crush excepting for the fact that there was a flexure in the roof and door frames that caused the tempered glass to break out.

**Q.** Did you offer opinions with respect to glazing?

**A.** I did.

**Q.** What were your opinions with respect to glazing?

**A.** That the glazing was not designed to retain the occupant in the event of a rollover and it was defective.

**Q.** What occupant was at issue in that Explorer case?

**A.** The driver.

**Q.** Was the driver ejected?

**A.** Partially ejected.

**Q.** Was the driver wearing a seat belt?

**A.** Yes, she was.

# DEPOSITION TRANSCRIPT

**Q.** Was she partially ejected out the driver's window?

**A.** Yes.

**Q.** What was the driver's window composed of?

**A.** Three-point-eight millimeter tempered soda-lime glass. It's way at the end (indicating).

**Q.** I see.

**A.** Rather surprisingly.

**Q.** The case is called Travis?

**A.** Yes.

**Q.** I see it. You gave a deposition in Travis in—

**A.** Last month.

**Q.**—February of 2005; is that correct?

**A.** Yes. I don't get it either, why it took so long, but there you have it.

**Q.** But you were retained in that case in 2002?

**A.** Yes, in August, or before. That's when I looked at the vehicle. I don't recall the date we were retained.

**Q.** Prior to working on the glazing aspect of the Travis case, what specific work had you done with respect to the study of glazing? This would be prior to your retention in the Travis case in 2002.

**A.** As far as glazing goes, I have taught materials science since 1997, and materials science comprises four major areas: metals; ceramics, which glass is a ceramic; polymers, which the windshield has a polymer inner layer; and composites, which are mixtures of the other two, and laminated glass is a composite. So I have taught about these things, I know the material properties, I know about design, I taught design classes, and I had used automotive examples in the past, talking about how the windshield behaves, done demonstrations with glass. I used to take my students to the gaffers' guild and we'd see how a good gob of glass would perform.

**Q.** Prior to your retention in the Travis case, had you ever designed any automotive glass?

**A.** No.

**Q.** Had you ever been involved in the manufacture of any automotive glass?

**A.** No.

**Q.** Had you ever consulted with any automotive glass manufacturer about automotive glass? This is all prior to your retention in the Travis case.

**A.** I had not.

**Q.** Had you ever consulted with any auto company with respect to automotive glazing prior to your retention in the Travis case?

**A.** No.

**Q.** But you had taught materials science?

**A.** Materials science and design, and manufacturing, too.

**Q.** What specific research had you done prior to your retention in the Travis case on automotive glazing? This is specific research in automotive glazing prior to your retention in the Travis case.

**A.** Only the basics that I would use as examples in class, knowing how a windshield is bonded to a vehicle, using urethane, knowing that the materials of windshields and knowing how glass is tempered, which is actually pretty cool.

**Q.** So you had done some research with respect to the tempering of glass and with the bonding of windshields?

**A.** Yeah, I was familiar with these things. As I say, I had given them as examples, but to answer your question more fully as far as reading what the federal standards are and such, no, I hadn't done that.

**Q.** Was there any specific research you had done prior to your retention in the Travis case comparing the type of glazing used in automotive products, say, over the last 40 or 50 years?

**A.** No.

**Q.** Had you done any research comparing the type of glazing that, say, a Ford or a General Motors vehicle or a Toyota vehicle would have used in, say, the 1960s or '70s, '80s, or '90s prior to your retention in the Travis case?

**A.** No.

### Other case work as an expert witness

**Q.** Now, since your retention in the Travis case, have you been retained in other cases where you've been asked to analyze the properties of automotive glazing?

**A.** Yes.

**Q.** What I'm going to do, John, just to sort of get this done in somewhat of an efficient way, because we have listed cases here, I won't explore with you cases where you have not been disclosed or anything of that nature, but I'd like you to take a look at this list of prior testimony and tell me which of these cases, if you can, involve glazing, where you've been retained to offer glazing—

**A.** Sure.

**Q.** Put a check next to them.

**A.** The first one, I made an error. If it's a big mark, you'll know.

**Q.** The little mark is next to what case?

**A.** The first one the list, Miller versus Ford. That wasn't a glass case. I have one on here which is a glass case which is an aquarium. I'll put that to the side.

MR. ZAJAC: Off the record.

MR. MARTIN: This is Exhibit No. 4. (A List of Principle Testimony was marked Exhibit-4 for identification.)

MR. MARTIN: We're back on the record now.

BY MR. MARTIN:

**Q.** You've made some marks on Exhibit No. 4 which identify those cases where you have been retained to offer opinions with respect to glazing; would that be fair?

**A.** Yes.

**Q.** The first one that you have marked is a case called Anderson versus Ford. What kind of vehicle was that?

**A.** It was a Ford Explorer.

**Q.** Your deposition date in that case was in May of 2004?

**A.** Yes, sir.

**Q.** When were you retained in Anderson, if you can recall?

**A.** I don't recall.

**Q.** Was it sometime after 2002?

**A.** Yes.

**Q.** Would it be fair to say that all the cases in which you've been retained to offer glazing opinions with the exception of Travis were after 2002?

**A.** I think so.

**Q.** Since 2002, you've been asked to offer opinions in about 12—

**A.** There are a bunch of repeats in there.

**Q.** I was about to say 12, but then I see in some cases you've been deposed more than once and you've given trial testimony and such, so give me a ballpark number on the number of cases where you've testified with respect to glazing issues.

**A.** I'd say ten.

# DEPOSITION TRANSCRIPT

*Research and education on topic at issue*

**Q.** What I'd like to explore with you for a moment is what specifically have you done by way of research, training, education, formal education on the subject of automotive glazing since taking the Travis case.

MR. ZAJAC: Objection to the form.

BY MR. MARTIN:

**Q.** You can answer.

**A.** The first thing I did in the Travis case was I started looking at the pertinent federal regulations.

**Q.** You started reading federal regulations?

**A.** Yes.

**Q.** What is or are the pertinent federal regulations pertaining to glazing?

**A.** The FMVSS 205, automotive glazing.

**Q.** The FMVSS 205, in other words, you read the standard?

**A.** I did.

**Q.** Did you read the history of FMVSS 205? In other words, did you go all the way back to the time when FMVSS 205 was being considered and implemented to get an overview of what went into the making of FMVSS 205 and how it was amended, if at all, over the course of the years in which it has been in place?

**A.** I read as much historical background as I found. I haven't found any of the internal deliberations of the regulatory agency. All these records are going to be somewhat incomplete.

**Q.** Where did you get the historical background on FMVSS 205?

**A.** What I found was available in the literature from the SAE group and other sources, and ones that were pertinent to the 205 that I could find. I did include in my glazing references.

**Q.** So you found some literature in SAE pertaining to 205?

**A.** I found things about glass. Whether it talked directly about 205, I'm not sure.

**Q.** So in addition to learning about FMVSS 205 to prepare yourself to be trained, educated, perform research on automotive glazing, since 2002 what have you done?

**A.** I have also—I read the 205; I read the ANSI Z2621 which is referenced by the 205; I've read other pertinent federal standards like 208 standards to get a better feel for the government regulatory process because as an engineer, you often don't care what the laws are, that's not your area. I've read the majority of the papers, I believe, published by the SAE and then other journals. I've read some of the popular literature—

**Q.** Before we go into the popular literature, do you have a list of the SAE papers that you have reviewed?

**A.** I don't. Did you get a copy of our glazing references? It may be on the way or you may have it. It will be in there. If you don't have it, I'll give you a copy.

**Q.** You didn't bring a copy with you today?

**A.** I might have, now that I think about it. I did. This is a current copy of our glazing references, which includes most everything that's ever been in there. We recently culled out some papers that we just didn't reference that I read. When I started compiling that, I put in everything I ever read. That's not useful (indicating).

**Q.** So what you provided me, and which we will mark as Exhibit-5, is a Renfroe Engineering list of automotive glazing technical references?

**A.** Yes. That is a document that I have prepared and maintained. (Automotive Glazing Technical References were marked Exhibit-5 for identification.)

BY MR. MARTIN:

**Q.** I take it you have reviewed all of these articles?

**A.** I've read them all at least once, many several times.

**Q.** We got to this by my asking you what you had reviewed, and you said some SAE papers. Are all those SAE papers identified in here (indicating)?

**A.** Yes, sir.

**Q.** And other technical papers are identified in here?

**A.** Yes.

**Q.** You were going on to talk about popular literature. Are those items identified in Exhibit No. 5 as well?

**A.** Yes, a few of them are. I don't know if the Volvo ones are in there, but as I said, Wards's Auto Week will put out something, or there's a particular reference called a primer on automotive glazing which is already — that's listed in there.

**Q.** Have you taken any courses on automotive glazing since your retention in the Travis case?

**A.** I have.

**Q.** Who taught that course?

**A.** Sid Herliczech.

**Q.** You might want to spell that for the

**A.** H-e-r-l-i-c-z-e-c-h, just like it sounds.

**Q.** When did you take that course, Steve?

**A.** Last year.

**Q.** In 2004?

**A.** I did.

**Q.** It was a two-day seminar?

**A.** It was, in Troy, Michigan, which we're all familiar with.

**Q.** Who sponsored that seminar?

**A.** The Society of Automotive Engineers.

**Q.** SAE?

**A.** Yes.

**Q.** Aside from that single course, two-day seminar that you took on—was that on automotive glazing or was it just on glazing?

**A.** It was on automotive glazing.

**Q.** Aside from that single seminar that you've mentioned, have you taken any other courses or seminars on automotive glazing since your retention in the Travis case?

**A.** Can I see my resume?

**Q.** Sure (indicating).

**A.** No, I haven't.

**Q.** Now, we've talked about what you've read and what courses you've taken on automotive glazing since your retention in the Travis case?

**A.** Yes. I've read also—and I don't think have it listed in there, a number of glass textbooks that are exceedingly detailed and dry. I read those.

**Q.** Are they listed in this technical reference paper?

**A.** No. They tend to be what are the atomic reactions, precipitates, bonding structure, devitrification.

**Q.** Is there any particular glass book that you have found particularly authoritative and that you would rely on for your opinions in this case?

**A.** No.

**Q.** What else have you done with respect to training or education on glazing since your retention in the Travis case?

**A.** I have spoken to other glass experts.

**Q.** Such as who?

**A.** Such as Sid Herliczech. During the breaks, I would talk to him about what my understanding of this was.

**Q.** How many times did you speak with Mr. Herliczech?

**A.** I don't know.

**Q.** Was this all in the context of this two-day seminar?

**A.** Yes.

**Q.** Did you ever consult with him on any other occasion?

**A.** No.

**Q.** Have you spoken with any other glass experts?

**A.** Yes.

**Q.** Such as who?

**A.** I've spoken to Hank Chamberlain.

**Q.** Who is Hank Chamberlain?

**A.** He is the president of Allied Glass Experts up in Kansas City.

**Q.** Is he a retained expert in cases?

**A.** I believe he has testified. I haven't seen his full resume.

**Q.** What is his company's name?

**A.** Allied Glass Experts.

**Q.** What city are they in?

**A.** Kansas City, Kansas.

**Q.** Who else have you spoken to?

**A.** Herb Yudenfriend.

**Q.** Can you spell that?

**A.** H-e-r-b Y-u-d-e-n-f-r-i-e-n-d.

**Q.** What was the purpose of that conversation?

**A.** Since he has been working on this stuff since the '50s, I wanted to talk with him about my understanding of this and see if he had any insights that I was missing.

**Q.** What does he do for a living?

**A.** He does some litigation consulting, and he owns glass installation firms and film application. He has worked in the glass industry, as I say, since the '50s. He is the grandfather of all this stuff.

**Q.** Have you spoken with or consulted with any other persons aside from the ones you've mentioned here?

**A.** Richard Morrison.

**Q.** Richard Morrison from Ford?

### Testing

**A.** Yes. He was critical of my testing, so I asked him if he would review my test protocol before I did the next set of tests. He politely declined.

MR. ZAJAC: Is that the on the record somewhere?

THE WITNESS: No, it isn't.

MR. ZAJAC: It is now.

THE WITNESS: It was an unfair question.

BY MR. MARTIN:

**Q.** Mr. Morrison was critical of testing you had conducted on one occasion or more than one occasion?

**A.** Yeah, I had one set of testing that's been applied for the peer-reviewed literature, and he had some criticisms.

**Q.** What were his criticisms?

**A.** He said that my use of a blunt impactor constructed of a bowling ball was not realistic. He said that the chamois that I used should have been wet. He didn't like the angle of incidence of the bowling ball against the glass. I don't think he liked the weight of it, either. Perhaps that's not all of it, but it's most of it.

**Q.** In summary, and to make sure I got it all there, your understanding of Mr. Morrison's criticisms of your testing of glazing is that your use of a blunt impactor was not realistic?

**A.** Right. He didn't like the choice of material.

**Q.** And the angle that you used to impact the glass was improper?

**A.** Yes.

**Q.** He felt you needed to use a wet chamois versus a dry chamois, I take it?

**A.** Yes.

**Q.** And that the weight you had selected for the impactor was inappropriate?

**A.** Yes. And also, just to be complete, I don't think he liked the location of impact either.

**Q.** That is where you were impacting the glazing?

**A.** Yes. And, of course, I don't want to speak for him, but that's my recollection.

**Q.** This was testing that you conducted on what?

**A.** We took a 2003 Lincoln Navigator driver's door and impacted it repeated times with a blunt impactor at normal incidence to test the retention capability of tempered and laminated glass.

**Q.** Did Mr. Morrison also criticize the speed?

**A.** Not that I recall. He may have.

**Q.** We'll come back and talk about your testing later. Have we talked about all the persons with whom you have spoken or consulted about glazing since your retention in the Travis case?

**A.** I've also spoken to Dr. Anthony Sances and Dr. Dennis Shanahan, and Dr. Joe Burton.

**Q.** Dr. Anthony Sances, he is not a glazing expert, is he?

**A.** He has glazing expertise. He has published at least three papers on glass and he has done experimentation of Hybrid III impacts into glass, so I wouldn't say he is an expert, but he has expertise, he has knowledge.

**Q.** Joe Burton, do you consider him a glazing expert?

**A.** No. He is a physician.

**Q.** What is Shanahan's first name?

**A.** Dennis.

**Q.** What is Dennis Shanahan's expertise?

**A.** He does injury causation.

**Q.** Is he a glazing expert?

**A.** No, but when he was in the United States Army, he did numerous traffic accident investigations and saw real, actual interactions of people with windshield glass.

**Q.** So of those three that you just mentioned Sances, Shanahan, and Burton, only, to your knowledge, does Sances claim a glazing expertise to some extent? I'm asking you about your knowledge.

**A.** Yes. I don't think they would market themselves as glass experts.

**Q.** Including Sances?

**A.** Right, including Sances, but they do have knowledge. They're educated guys.

**Q.** Have we now talked about all the persons with whom you have consulted or talked to about glazing since your retention in the Travis case?

**A.** Yes.

**Q.** Have you, since your retention in the Travis case, consulted for any automotive companies with respect to automotive glazing?

**A.** I have not.

**Q.** Have you consulted—and this is all since your retention in the Travis case—have you consulted with any automotive glazing companies about automotive glazing?

**A.** No.

**Q.** Have you designed any automotive glazing?

**A.** Yes.

**Q.** Since your retention in the Travis case?

**A.** Yes, for my own vehicles.

**Q.** I think I know what you are talking about. You've taken some laminate and you've applied it to the interior of OEM glazing of your own car and cars in your family; is that correct?

**A.** Yes, I applied an antishatter film, so I would agree this is the lowest level of design that you can do, but I did it and there you have it.

**Q.** Let's explore that for a moment. When in time did you apply this antishatter film to these car windows, when was the first time you did this?

**A.** We did this all in the summer of last year, I believe in August, if I recall correctly.

**Q.** In August of 2004?

**A.** Right. We put it in one vehicle, then the next, then the next in my family, got them all taken care of.

**Q.** You had been involved in the Travis case for nearly two years at that point, but the first time you applied antishatter film to your own car windows was in August of 2004?

**A.** Yes.

**Q.** Did you, yourself, apply this antishatter film to your car windows?

**A.** Not in the initial ones, no. I paid a tint shop to do it.

**Q.** So you went to a tint shop to do the first one or two of these vehicles?

**A.** Three.

**Q.** We're talking about your car, your wife's car, and what else?

**A.** My son's car.

**Q.** What's the name of that tint shop that you went to?

**A.** I don't recall, but I can get it to you if you need it.

**Q.** Is it near your home town?

**A.** Yes.

**Q.** In Arkansas?

**A.** It is. It was the most convenient, highly recommended shop.

MR. MARTIN: In the deposition transcript, since Dr. Smith is going to read and sign, let's leave a blank for the name of that tint shop:

BY MR. MARTIN:

**Q.** When you do your review, if you would, just make that correction. It's the simplest way to do it.

**A.** I've never done that before. I think that's a great idea.

**Q.** So you went to a tint shop to get this antishatter film. Did you, before or during the course of this process, talk with these folks about the properties of this antishatter film?

**A.** Yes.

**Q.** What were you told?

**A.** I was given an online source where I could download the properties, and I got that on a sheet, a PDF document of the tensile strength of the film.

**Q.** Do you have that sheet or document which was a PDF that identifies the properties of this antishatter film?

**A.** We had three boxes of stuff sent here, and two of them made it yesterday and one should be here during the deposition, and it should be in that document.

**Q.** We'll mark as Exhibit-6, even if it doesn't get here today, this PDF document. You say you got this from this tint shop?

**A.** I got it online.

**Q.** What was the source?

**A.** I don't know. It was from the vendor, the wholesaler or manufacturer who put this out.

**Q.** What's the name of the manufacturer?

**A.** I don't recall.

**Q.** What was your understanding of the properties of this antishatter film?

**A.** It's 4 mils thick, it had a tear strength of over 100 pounds per linear inch, and that seemed to me to be a sufficient strength based upon my knowledge of impacts.

**Q.** We're going to talk about your testing later on, but just so we can be efficient here, have you ever performed any impactor testing on a vehicle window which had this antishatter film that you've just described to me applied?

**A.** Not impact in the classic sense, but I have done a pushout test.

**Q.** So you've done a pushout test?

**A.** Yes.

**Q.** But you have not done an impactor test?

**A.** That's correct.

**Q.** Do you have an impactor test in mind to do in the future?

**A.** We considered it, but it's on the burner.

**Q.** So if we wanted to compare the results of an impactor test on this Navigator driver's door window using your impactor in all the ways that you set it up with another window which had this antishatter film applied that you've gotten the properties on, we have no way of doing that, correct? We can't compare those two; is that correct?

**A.** Not at this time.

*Testing performed*

**Q.** What is the pushout test that you did on this window with the antishatter film?

**A.** My son's '95 Buick LeSabre had this material applied to all the windows. He went on a camping trip, and when he came back to the parking lot, his left rear window was broken, for an unknown reason. There was no hole in it. A bird hit it or something. So we decided that that window had to be replaced, obviously, and I told him to drive the vehicle down from Rolla to Prairie Grove, Arkansas, and that took about a month. So he had the vehicle in use with the shattered tempered glass that was only retained by this film, then he drove it the 200-odd miles, and it survived. I made a fixturing device, test fixture, such that I could press a styrofoam head form into the geometric center of the glass and measured the force that it took to push it out of the seals.

**Q.** What was the weight, size, etc., of that styrofoam head form?

**A.** It was a wig head that you probably have seen, so it was about a pound.

**Q.** So you used a wig head form?

**A.** Yes, one made out of polystyrene, probably cost three bucks through the mail.

**Q.** Estimate the weight for me.

**A.** A pound.

**Q.** One pound in weight?

**A.** Yes.

**Q.** Estimate the diameter.

**A.** The size of a head, so 8, 9 inches, 10.

**Q.** How did you conduct this pushout test?

**A.** We took two rods so they would telescope, and on the male side of the one rod --sorry, the female side, we put a slot in it so that when the other side was telescoping, you'd have a little window that you could see the end of it. This male side had a block of wood on it, and I could lean that up against a closed door. Then I had the rod going to the head form to the geometric center of the other door with the broken glass—are you with me—so it could push. The way I extended the rods was I put a heavy-duty scale hooked onto the end that I could see through the window and I pulled on it, and I was reading it as it was pushing the glass out of the seals.

**Q.** What did you ultimately read on the scale?

**A.** Eighty pounds. So we didn't, like previous tests or other tests, we didn't take the door out, mount it horizontally, put the head form in the middle of it and stack weights. That was way too much trouble.

**Q.** Did you document this pushout test in any manner?

**A.** We did.

**Q.** Did you photograph it?

**A.** Yes.

**Q.** Did you bring that material with you today?

**A.** I shipped it. It's not here yet.

**Q.** So that's something else that you're relying on that we're not seeing here so far; is that correct?

**A.** Yes. We should have that and you should be able to get copies of that. We've written up internal glazing reports on the various activities that we've undergone.

**Q.** We'll mark as Exhibit-7 your pushout test results that have not yet arrived here.

**A.** Yes, and we have a whole binder of our internal glazing reports that you can see. You may want to make that whole binder just Exhibit-7.

**Q.** We'll see what we do with that. This wig head form was about a pound?

**A.** Yes.

**Q.** How much does a human head weigh?

**A.** I think a human head weighs around 10 pounds.

**Q.** What's the basis for that?

**A.** That's just from my discussion with people. I'm not sure I've ever sliced one off and weighed it.

**Q.** Have you ever done any research as to the weight of an average head on, say, a fiftieth percentile male?

**A.** No. I don't know what that is.

**Q.** So aside from discussions with people as to what the weight of a head might be, you've not done any independent research as to what the weight of a head would be?

**A.** That's right.

**Q.** What was the basis for selecting 80 pounds of push with this 1-pound head form?

**A.** I was pushing on it, and the weight just came out to be whatever it came out to be. I was pulling on the scale, causing the rod to telescope, smashing this styrofoam head into the center of the glass, and I was about at the limit of my capacity.

**Q.** What was the scientific basis for going to 80 pounds or stopping at some other number or just going to the limits of your capacity?

**A.** I wanted to know how much force it would take applied to the geometric center in order to cause separation from the seals.

**Q.** Why did you select that number versus, say, 150 pounds of force or 300 pounds of force or 20 pound of force?

**A.** I did do 20 pounds of force, but the window didn't go out, so I kept increasing the weight slowly, slowly until it pushed out, so the window chose the pounds.

**Q.** Sorry?

**A.** The window chose 80 pounds.

**Q.** So at 80 pounds, what happened to the window?

**A.** Then the window had deformed sufficiently to pull itself out of the surrounding channel. We have a picture of that in the report.

**Q.** This window was previously cracked?

**A.** It was. It's tempered glass, so it's broken all over into countless pieces.

**Q.** Is there a reason why you have not done, up until now, an impactor test utilizing, say, that LeSabre door mounted with tempered glass covered with antishatter film?

**A.** No particular reason other than the usual, time and money.

### Testing not performed

**Q.** Wouldn't you think it would be important to compare the properties of such a piece of glass with the 2003 Navigator driver's door glass that you have tested with the impactor?

**A.** I'd like to do that, but as I say, I just haven't gotten to that. That will probably happen this year.

**Q.** But in point of fact, you can't compare the performance of one to the other; is that correct?

**A.** I can't, not based on testing, not at this time.

**Q.** Aside from applying antishatter film to car windows which you've said in the broadest accepts is the design of glazing, is there any other glazing that you've designed since your retention in the Travis case?

**A.** No.

**Q.** Have you ever taken this particular design in the broadest sense of this antishatter film on glazing to any automotive glazing company and said this might be something you'd be interested in considering for sale?

**A.** No. It already is for sale.

**Q.** Not by an automotive glazing company, is it?

**A.** Well, yes.

**Q.** Aside from the tint shop?

**A.** That's correct.

**Q.** Have you ever taken that glazing that you've designed with the antishatter material film to an automotive company such as a Ford or General Motors or Toyota with the purpose of seeing if they had an interest in testing this, marketing it, etc.?

**A.** No.

### Summary question with catchall to elicit any missing information

**Q.** We've been generally looking at the training and preparation you had in the areas of glazing since your retention in the Travis case. We've talked about your reading, we've talked about your course, we've talked about persons with whom you have conferred, we've talked about this glazing that you have installed in your family's vehicles. What other preparation have you done to make yourself knowledgeable with respect to automotive glazing since your retention in the Travis case?

**A.** I've done other tests. It would be much easier to have that book in front of us. Perhaps we can shelve this until then.

MR. ZAJAC: We can take a break and see if it's here.

BY MR. MARTIN:

**Q.** Certainly, we've been going awhile, but when you say "other tests," let's get that on the record. What other tests are we talking about?

**A.** I have done some—I talked about the pushout test. We haven't talked in detail about the testing...

**Q.** The impactor testing?

**A.** The impactor testing. And I just recently have done some testing with a sunroof. That report hasn't been sent. That's still a work in progress.

**Q.** So you've done other testing. We've talked about the pushout testing, and we haven't talked about the impactor testing on the 2003 Navigator glass, and then you've done sunroof testing on what kind of a vehicle?

# DEPOSITION TRANSCRIPT

**A.** That was a Ford Explorer.

**Q.** Is there any other testing that you've done since your retention in the Travis case?

**A.** I think that's it.

*Five-minute break*

MR. MARTIN: Let's take that break and come back in about five minutes or so.

(Recess.)

BY MR. MARTIN:

**Q.** So of all the testing that we discussed today so far, the only testing that you are relying on is what is set forth in Tab Six, correct?

**A.** Tab Six and Tab Three.

**Q.** Tab Three being?

**A.** The pushout test on my son's window with the bilaminate.

**Q.** I thought we had covered that and you said that you weren't relying on that.

**A.** I thought I said I was.

**Q.** My memory may not be precise. Are you relying on that for your opinions in this case?

**A.** I think I said modestly that you can see how this keeps the glass fragments in the window portal and provides some ejection mitigation properties. I don't plan on bringing it up at trial, if that helps.

*Opinions*

**Q.** What opinions are you offering with respect to the testing that is set forth in Tab Six?

**A.** There are a couple of things. First of all, using this blunt head form impactor, we found we can get three times the energy absorption with the laminated than we could with tempered, so I could drop it from three times higher. The second thing is that the laminated glass will take multiple impacts without losing the integrity of the PVB. It takes a lot of impacts with broken glass in order to start developing a hole in there. We didn't know is the glass going to break, is a sharp edge on the plastic going to cut it and it will just go through the next impact. You just don't know until you try it. The third thing we get is that our HIC values are very consistent with what other people have seen that with this seven-mile-per-hour impact, 15 milliseconds, that you're not approaching a thousand whatsoever. The last thing was that in this apples-to-apples comparison of this chamois being dropped into tempered versus laminated, for this test, the laceration was not of real concern.

**Q.** Let's try to go through those opinions that are based on the testing in Tab Six so I understand it. Those are opinions, I take it, that you would be offering at trial in this case?

**A.** Yes.

**Q.** The first opinion is that there is three times the energy absorption seen in laminated glass that you've tested in this testing at Tab Six versus the tempered glass that you have tested in Tab Six. Did I say that generally correctly?

**A.** Yes.

**Q.** What is the energy absorption value for the tempered glass? Can you give me a value for that?

**A.** Yes, I can. If I take an average value of this, it's about 10 inches, which is just under a foot times 20 pounds, so that would be 200 inch-pounds.

**Q.** Point out to me where you're getting that from.

**A.** Energy is the product of force times distance. So if I'm dropping a 20-pound device from 10 inches, I just multiply those two together and I get energy.

**Q.** I understand that part. I just want to know what page you're working on.

**A.** I'm on this first one. That's about 10 inches average times 20, 200.

**Q.** So you're on the first page of the Excel spreadsheet?

**A.** Right. I don't have an exact value. In fact, I guess I should back it off to the one where it didn't fracture. Here it went to ten and three-eighths (indicating). The other one—something less than 200.

**Q.** Let's compare the energy absorption for the laminated glass and tell me where you're getting that.

**A.** That's hard to do an exact apples-to-apples analysis because the failure mechanisms are different, but if I say that at a seven-mile-per-hour impact, here I have a 25-inch drop height times 20 pounds, that's 500 compared to something under 200 before.

**Q.** Show me where you're getting that.

**A.** This one, it went 25 inches, so times 20 pounds is 500. If I look at this one here, I have 30 inches and it survives, so 600 (indicating).

**Q.** So 5 to 600 inch-pounds?

**A.** Yes. Rough numbers, three times.

**Q.** When you say "energy absorption," do we take that to mean that in neither instance has the glass cracked or broken?

**A.** No, I'm not saying that.

**Q.** But for the tempered glass you're saying that, correct?

**A.** Right.

**Q.** But for the laminated glass, we're conceding that it's going to be cracked but not pushed through?

**A.** Right. You'll have to get new glass but it has kept your head form inside the envelope.

**Q.** Tell me at that 5 to 600-inch-pound point, going back to this chart that we looked at at the beginning of this paper, L1, 2, and 3, tell me where approximately we're seeing 5 to 600 inch-pounds.

**A.** It doesn't say that in this table. You have to back that out.

**Q.** That's what I'd like you to do, back that out for me if you can.

**A.** From this you're going to see less of a difference in velocity than you are from drop height because kinetic energy is proportional to the square of velocity but to height alone, so I would just go back to here and just do the math again. This table is based upon this chart (indicating).

**Q.** Can you tell me at what point we have 5 to 600 inch-pounds of energy seen in the laminated glass?

**A.** Yeah.

**Q.** What is it?

**A.** Let me give you a line item on this. The test occurred 10/28/04, so this is L2 data, file name L2 underscore 25A. There's a drop height of 25 inches with a 20-pound impactor, so that is 500 inch-pounds of energy absorbed, but that is not exactly an apples-to-apples comparison because it already absorbed four more major impacts, so something like another 2000 inch-pounds of energy have already been absorbed by this panel. So when you say it will absorb three times as much, that's really understating the case.

*Paper submitted for publication*

**Q.** You've written this up in a paper. Has this paper been published?

**A.** No.

**Q.** This is an internal report?

**A.** That's an internal report that's right there.

**Q.** Have you sought to publish these results anywhere?

**A.** Yes.

**Q.** Has it been accepted for publication anywhere?

**A.** Not yet.

**Q.** Where have you sought to have it published?

**A.** The ASME biomedical or biomechanical engineering conference this summer in Colorado. We have not been told one way or the other on the paper's status.

**Q.** When did you make the application to have them accept the paper?

**A.** At least two months ago. It's been a long time.

**Q.** What, in your experience, if you know, how long do they typically take to accept a paper?

**A.** Three months, four months.

**Q.** So you don't know yet whether they will accept the paper?

**A.** That's right.

**Q.** Do you know what the process is for them to accept the paper? Do they send it out to other reviewers to see if the scientific method that is employed is sound, for instance?

MR. ZAJAC: Objection as to form.

THE WITNESS: That's the process. The organizers of the conference have separate symposiums where they have symposia organizers who will receive the papers, and then the methodology that they use to analyze this usually includes peer review, and it may be a blind process, maybe not. I don't know the exact details of this particular symposium.

BY MR. MARTIN:

**Q.** But your understanding is that your paper would be reviewed by individuals who are your peers?

**A.** Yes.

**Q.** And those peers would, in your knowledge, review the paper to see if it was prepared in an accurate and scientific manner?

MR. ZAJAC: Objection to form.

THE WITNESS: That's the way it's supposed to occur.

BY MR. MARTIN:

**Q.** The second opinion you offered — I may not have written this down correctly – is something like the laminated glass will take multiple impacts before breaking out. Did I get that down essentially correct?

**A.** Yeah, before pulling out of the seals, it will retain its integrity sufficiently to provide occupant retention.

**Q.** Did you measure how much deflection there was resident in the laminated glass after each impact, in other words, before the pushout occurred, whether or not the laminated glass was bowed out, for instance, and if so, by how much of a distance?

**A.** No, we didn't measure that.

**Q.** Did you make any observations by way of photographs or video as to the condition of the glass relative to the plane of the door and to the glass in its unbroken condition after each run?

**A.** There are photographs. I'm not sure we went exactly with the plane. It's hard to do that with the plane of the door because it's not planar, it's curved.

**Q.** I'm trying to determine whether the plane of this window is in the exact or a different position than its OEM position after each impact.

**A.** After each impact, we ensure—no, wait a minute. We are not—we are making sure that the bottom is in the same position so that the bottom stays fixed.

**Q.** By the bottom you mean the top of the door rail?

**A.** By the regulator magnet, because that's a fixed point. Around the seals of the glass, we didn't do anything with that. It is changing shape. In one of the comments it says you are getting a bowl shape made from this.

**Q.** So the glass is changing shape, it's becoming more of a bowl shape after each impact?

**A.** Yes.

**Q.** If we look at photographs, are we going to see that or not?

**A.** I think so. I haven't checked for that specifically.

**Q.** Is that bowl shape measured in each instance after each run?

**A.** No.

**Q.** So you can't tell me as we sit here today whether after the first run we're out a millimeter, after the third run we're out 20 millimeters in the geometric center of the glass?

**A.** Right, I can't tell you that, but I can say that for the drop heights we did measure from the center of the bowl to the impactor so that as it changed its shape, we were accounting for the change in velocity. We weren't going to its nominal position, we were going to its actual position.

**Q.** You'd agree with me that if the glass is bowing out and one's head is in contact with the glass as it's bowing out, one's head would be beyond the plane of the door frame, correct, in a rollover event?

**A.** Yes.

**Q.** The third opinion goes to HIC values. You said something like the HIC values are very consistent with what others have seen, that is, less than one thousand HICs. Did I get that essentially correct?

**A.** Yes.

**Q.** What did you mean by that?

**A.** As you know, the HIC is an integration of the impact acceleration curve.

**Q.** First of all, what does the term HIC mean?

**A.** Head impact criteria.

**Q.** And where does that come from?

**A.** It comes from the biomechanics world where they realized that force has a time element with respect to injury—I'm sorry, acceleration has a time impact with respect to injury.

**Q.** Were you measuring HIC values on this head form in each of these runs?

**A.** No, we were measuring accelerations, and then you have to manipulate the data to get the HIC.

**Q.** Let's do this first: Did you manipulate the data to get the HIC in those runs that involve the tempered glass?

**A.** I did not.

**Q.** Do you know if it was done?

**A.** It was done.

**Q.** But you don't have that?

**A.** Right. As you'll notice, there are a lot of names on this paper because we had different areas. I was overall test and occupant containment. Kerry Allen did the HIC and Mark Martin and Jeff Evans did laceration.

**Q.** Do you know whether the HIC values with the tempered glass were less than a thousand?

**A.** Yes.

**Q.** Were they?

**A.** We never had a HIC value go above 250.

**Q.** Including with the tempered glass?

**A.** Right.

**Q.** What was the highest HIC value that you had for the laminated glazing, if you can pick it out?

**A.** Just about 200.

**Q.** What was the highest HIC value that you had for the tempered glazing?

**A.** Without the glass breaking, we had something on the order of 70, but then we got over 101, over 200 when the glass breaks because it has that stored elastic energy and it jiggers the ball, and I'm not sure that's good data.

**Q.** The fourth opinion is laceration. I suppose that is relative to the laminated glazing, just not of a real concern?

**A.** Right, on either one.

**Q.** With respect to either tempered glass or laminated glass?

**A.** That's correct.

**Q.** Explain what you mean by that.

**A.** What we did was we looked at the chamois laceration scale—I didn't, but we, corporately, did. We found that for the six impacts that we were just getting, you know, some moderate punctures on one of the laminated sheets and then everything else was just little bits of abrasion damage at most, that if you look into the inner chamois it's virtually undamaged, so repeated impacts weren't causing significant laceration damage.

**Q.** Are there any other opinions that you're offering with respect to the testing that is included in Tab Six? I just want to keep it narrowly focused there for a moment.

**A.** I believe that's it.

**Q.** Have we now talked about all the testing that you have been involved with or are relying upon for your opinions in this case?

**A.** Yes.

### *Questions about documents brought to deposition*

**Q.** What else do you have that you brought with you today?

**A.** I have this; you can have it (indicating). That is what I had written in a report prior and I just updated it based on current discovery.

MR. MARTIN: This is 23, an updated version of your January report.

(Automotive Glazing Technical Synopsis - GM Extract was marked Exhibit-23 for identification.)

THE WITNESS: Yes, it's got one or two more things in it.

BY MR. MARTIN:

**Q.** What else?

**A.** This is just a paper. I don't know why it's out. It's been referenced in the reports.

**Q.** Just read the name of the paper in so we have it clear.

**A.** Occupant Protection, Review of Energy Absorbing Devices by Jeffrey P. Hill. I'll bring it again next time. I'd just as soon put it back in the file.

**Q.** Fine. What is this, John (indicating)?

**A.** These are notes. You asked me for stuff on Mondays.

**Q.** I'll let you keep that then. What's in the rest of that pile there?

**A.** Just the 216 test.

MR. MARTIN: Let's mark that, two versions to Eric, both by fax and FedEx. We're going to mark those binders. (A No. 216 Test Report was marked Exhibit-24 for identification.)

THE WITNESS: Those are all the GM things.

BY MR. MARTIN:

**Q.** They are two binders of this, right?

**A.** Yeah. They're just in date order. It makes it much easier to work with.

MR. MARTIN: Let's mark as Exhibit-25 a binder that contains protected documents produced by General Motors, then we'll mark as Exhibit-26 a second binder of documents produced by General Motors.

(Binder Entitled Automotive Glass Documents was marked Exhibit-25.)

(Binder Entitled Automotive Glass Documents was marked Exhibit-26.)

BY MR. MARTIN:

**Q.** What is in here?

**A.** These are just papers given as part of 18 the references. We had that, like, 85 different references.

**Q.** That's in your reference list?

**A.** Yeah. These are then printed out.

**Q.** If you bring this back, the next time if we have particular questions on those, we can go over that.

**A.** There are roof crush ones and glazing ones.

## *Catchall on opinions*

**Q.** Is there any other opinion that you're offering with respect to this analysis you've just conducted?

**A.** No.

**Q.** Do we now have all your opinions in final form?

**A.** Yes.

**Q.** You've offered me all of your opinions that you expect to offer at the time of trial?

**A.** Yes.

## *Exhibits to be used at trial*

**Q.** We sort of got off on a tangent with this when I asked the question are there any exhibits and such that you plan to use at the time of trial, and that's when we got to Exhibit-33, so let me go back there and ask are there any other exhibits or things that you expect to use at the time of trial beyond photographs and potentially what we see here in Exhibit-33?

MR. ZAJAC: Objection as to form. We do reserve our right to create demonstrative exhibits before trial.

MR. MARTIN: I understand that. I'm just asking the witness if he has any exhibits he plans to offer at the time of trial.

THE WITNESS: Absolutely.

**A.** An XC-90 roof. I will bring in the subject roof.

**Q.** You won't remove the roof from the subject vehicle?

**A.** Exactly; I won't do that. I'll bring an exemplar roof.

**Q.** Such as the one we see in the photographs that you have presented today?

**A.** Yes.

**Q.** Anything else? The XC-90 roof, did you say?

**A.** Yes.

**Q.** Anything else?

**A.** That's exhaustive. I'm done.

MR. MARTIN: I have no further questions at this time.

MR. ZAJAC: That's it.

(Witness excused.)

# Appendix K  Referral Organizations

**A & B Forensics/TALIG Corp.**
2707 Kings Forest Dr.
Kingwood, TX 77339
Phone: (888) 824-0518
*www.talig.com*

**AMFS, Inc.**
2640 Telegraph Ave.
Berkeley, CA 94704
Phone: (800) 275-8903
*www.amfs.com*

**Association of Scientific
Advisors**
16161 Ventura Blvd., Ste. 215
Encino, CA 91436
Phone (818) 784-1800
*www.asaexperts.com*

**Benchmark Medical
Consultants**
10423 Old Placerville Rd., #100
Sacramento, CA 95827
Phone: (800) 458-1261
*www.benchmarkadmin.com*

**CECON Group, Inc.**
242 N. James St., #202
Wilmington, DE 19804
Phone: (888) 263-8000
*www.cecon.com*

**Chatham Group**
101 First St., #477
Los Altos, CA 94022
Phone: (650) 948-1243
*www.chathamlaw.com*

**Consolidated Consultants Co.**
289 Church Ave.
Chula Vista, CA 91910
Phone: (800) 683-9847
*www.freereferral.com*

**Diligence, Inc.**
21241 Ventura Blvd., Ste. 250
Woodland Hills, CA 91364-2121
Phone: (800) 809-8210
*www.diligenceinc.com*

**DJS Associates, Inc.**
1603 Old York Rd.
Abington, PA 19001
Phone: (800) 332-6273
*www.forensicdjs.com*

**Expert Medical Witnesses, Inc.**
85 Logan Blvd.
Altoona, PA 16602
Phone: (888) 944-8456
*www.expertmedicalwitnesses.com*

**Expert Resources, Inc.**
1225 East Samuel Ave., Ste. B
Peoria Heights, IL 61616-6455
Phone: (800) 383-4857
*www.expertresources.com*

**Expertwitness.com**
1902 Central Dr.
Bedford, TX 76021
Phone: (877) 837-9736
*www.expertwitness.com*

**Expert Witness & Consultant
Group**
4601 Hunting Hound Ln.
Marietta, GA 30062-6339
Phone: (770) 587-0740
*www.ew-cg.com*

**Forensic Expert Advisors Inc.**
PO Box 1829
Big Bear Lake, CA 92315
Phone: (800) 584-8178
*www.forensic-experts.com*

**ForensisGroup**
Gateway Towers
3452 East Foothill Blvd., #1160
Pasadena, CA 91107-3160
Phone: (800) 555-5422
*www.forensisgroup.com*

**FTI Teklicon**
3031 Tisch Way, #1010
San Jose, CA 95128-2533
Phone: (800) 926-8972
*www.teklicon.com*

**IMS ExpertServices**
4400 Bayou Blvd., Ste. 6
Pensacola, FL 32503
Phone: (877) 838-8464
*www.ims-expertservices.com*

**Legal Expert Network**
11 East Wheeling St.
Baltimore, MD 21230
Phone: (800) 597-5371
*www.expertnetwork.com*

**Lexpert Research Services**
PO Box 4362
Malibu, CA 90264
Phone: (310) 589-5546
*www.lexpertresearch.com*

**Medco Associates, Inc.**
1603 Olympus Dr.
Austin, TX 78733
Phone: (800) 341-6461
*www.medcoassociates.com*

**Medical Advisors/Technical
Network Consulting Service**
5215 B Militia Hill Rd.
Plymouth Meeting, PA 19462
Phone: (800) 355-1329
*www.techmedexperts.com*

**Medical Consultant Services,
Inc.**
2377 West Foothill Blvd., Ste. 9
Upland, CA 91786
Phone: (909) 946-0350
*www.expertsatmcs.com*

**MedicoLegal Consultants**
11041 Santa Monica Blvd., #719
Los Angeles, CA 90025
Phone: (888) 661-3593
*www.mlegal.com*

**Medico-Legal Information
Services**
140 East Division Rd., Ste. B-1
Oak Ridge, TN 37830-6900
Phone: (865) 482-6600
*www.medicolegalexperts.com*

**Medical Review Foundation**
120 Beulah Rd., NE, Ste. 200
Vienna, VA 22180
Phone: (800) 336-0332
*www.malpracticeexperts.com*

**Med-Witness Ltd.**
8123 North Tripp Ave.
Skokie, IL 60076
Phone: (847) 673-4422
*www.medwitness.com*

**New England Medical Legal Consultants, Inc.**
1507 Post Rd.
Warwick, RI 02888
Phone: (800) 583-0088
*www.nemlc.com*

**Premier Legal Experts, LLC**
PO Box 401
Annapolis, MD 21404
Phone: (410) 530-1135
*www.premierlegalexperts.com*

**Pro/Consul**
1945 Palo Verde Ave., Ste. 200
Long Beach, CA 90815-3443

Phone: (800) 392-1119
*www.pro-consul.com*

**PsyBar LLC**
5151 Edina Industrial Blvd., #675
Minneapolis, MN 55439
Phone: (952) 285-9000
*www.psybar.com*

**Registered Nurse Experts, Inc.**
14421 SW 93rd Ave.
Miami, FL 33176
Phone: (800) 759-6938
*www.rnexperts.com*

**Rieback Medical-Legal Consultants**
772 NW 100th Terrace
Fort Lauderdale, FL 33324
Phone: (954) 472-1825
*www.medicalexpert.com*

**Round Table Group**
980 N. Michigan Ave.,14th Floor
Chicago, IL 60611
Phone: (312) 635-7877
*www.roundtablegroup.com*

**Silicon Valley Expert Witness Group Inc.**
2570 W. El Camino Real,
Ste. 650
Mountain View, CA 94040
Phone: (650) 917-0700
*www.svewg.com*

**Summit Professional Resources, LLC**
486 Schooley's Mountain Rd.
Building 2A, Ste. #11
Hackettstown, NJ 07840-4000
Phone: (908) 852-9008
*www.summitresources.com*

**TASA**
1166 DeKalb Pike
Blue Bell, PA 19422-1853
Phone: (800) 523-2319
*www.tasanet.com*

**Technical Assistance Bureau, Inc.**
11469 Olive Blvd., #108
St. Louis, MO 63141
Phone: (800) 260-8174
*www.tabexperts.com*

Also, it is very important to explore the professional organizations within your field or relating to your field. Many of these maintain referral networks or provide referral services to their members.

# Appendix L  Expert Witness Directories

**Accident Reconstruction Network**
118 Lake St. South, Ste. G
Kirkland, WA 98033
Phone: (866) 223-4984
www.accidentreconstruction.com
*Online directory.*

**AELE-Americans for Effective Law Enforcement**
841 W. Touhy Ave.
Park Ridge, IL 60068-3351
Phone: (847) 685-0700
www.aele.org
*Online directory.*

**American Academy of Forensic Psychology**
Phone: (800) 255-7792
www.abfp.com

**American Academy of Forensic Sciences**
410 North 21st St.
Colorado Springs, CO 80904
Phone: (719) 636-1100
www.aafs.org
*6,000 members. Online directory, searchable by members only.*

**American Board of Forensic Document Examiners**
7887 San Felipe, Ste. 122
Houston, TX 77063
Phone: (713) 784-9537
www.abfde.org
*Online directory.*

**American Board of Vocational Experts**
3540 Soquel Ave, Ste. A
Santa Cruz, CA 95062
(831) 464-4890
www.abve.net
*Online directory.*

**American College of Forensic Examiners**
2750 East Sunshine St.
Springfield, MO 65804
Phone: (800) 423-9737
www.acfei.com
*Online directory.*

**American Lawyer Media**
101 Madison Ave.
New York, NY 10016
Phone: (888) 809-0133
www.almexperts.com
*Online and regional print directories. Listing starts at $550. Circulation: 10,000-20,000*

**American Society of Appraisers**
555 Herndon Parkway, Ste. 125
Herndon, VA 20170
Phone: (703) 478-2228
www.appraisers.org
*Online directory.*

**ASTM-American Society of Testing and Materials**
100 Barr Harbor Dr.
PO Box C700
West Conshohocken, PA 19428
Phone: (610) 832-9585
www.astm.org
*Online consultants directory. Listing fee is $125.*

**ATLA–Association of Trial Lawyers of America**
1050 31st St., NW
Washington, DC 20007
Phone: (800) 344-3023
www.atla.org
*ATLA Exchange, online experts database searchable by members only. Publishes Trial Magazine.*

**Best's Directory of Recommended Expert Service Providers**
A.M. Best Company, Inc.
PO Box 828806
Philadelphia, PA 19182-8806
Phone: (908) 439-2200
www.ambest.com
*Both print and online.*

**Ca-Experts.com**
2154 Hastings Court, Ste. 101
Santa Rosa, CA 95405-8377
Phone: (707) 577-0100
www.ca-experts.com
*Online directory of CA. Listing fee is $99.*

**Calif-legal.com**
California Legal, LLC 174 West Foothill Blvd., #209
Monrovia, CA 91016
Phone: (800) 939-1088
www.calif-legal.com
*Online directory of California experts. Listing fees start at $199.*

**Claims Providers of America**
National Expert Witness Directory
PO Box 270529
San Diego, CA 92198-0529
Phone: (800) 735-6660
www.national-experts.com
*Both print and online. Circulation of 10,000 copies. Listing fees start at $265.*

**Defense Research Institute (DRI)**
150 North Michigan Ave., #300
Chicago, IL 60601
Phone: (312) 698-6218
www.dri.org
*Online directory, searchable by DRI members only.*

**Exify, LLC**
8140 Burnet Rd., #215
Austin, TX 78757
Phone: (512) 699-6487
www.exify.com
*Online directory. Listing fees start at $265.*

**Expert Witness Network**
201 US Route One, PMB 215
Scarborough, ME 04074
Phone: (207) 885-1555
www.witness.net
*Online directory. Searchable by members only. Listing fees start at $199.*

**Expert4law**
261 S. Figueroa St., #300
Los Angeles, CA 90012
Phone: (213) 896-6470
www.expert4law.org
*Online directory. Listing fees start at $300.*

# THE A–Z GUIDE TO EXPERT WITNESSING

**Expertpages.com**
PO Box 1739
Sausalito, CA 94966-1739
Phone: (800) 487-5342
www.expertpages.com
*Online directory. Starts at $295.*

**Experts.com**
2800 W. March Lane, #340
Stockton, CA 95219
Phone: (866) 239-7378
www.experts.com
*Online directory. Starts at $250.*

**Findlaw.com**
610 Opperman Dr.
Eagan, MN 55123
Phone: (888) 346-3529
www.findlaw.com
*Online directory.*

**Forensic Expert Witness Association**
2402 Vista Nobleza
Newport Beach, CA 92660
Phone: (888) 322-3231
www.forensic.org
*Online and print. 400 CA experts.*

**Hieros Gamos, Inc.**
333 Clay St., Ste. 4490
Houston, TX 77002
Phone: (832) 553-7488
www.hg.org
*Online directory. Starts at $195.*

**IEEE-USA Consultants Database**
1828 L St., N.W., Ste. 1202
Washington, DC 20036-5104
Phone: (202) 785-0017
www.ieeeusa.org
*Online. Listing fees start at $235.*

**Institute of Transportation Engineers**
1099 14th St., NW, #300 West
Washington, DC 20005
Phone: (202) 289-0222
www.ite.org

**JurisPro**
703 Pier Ave., Ste. B213
Hermosa Beach, CA 90254
Phone: (888) 905-4040

www.jurispro.com
*Online directory. $349 fee.*

**JurisSolutions**
550 Old Country Rd., Ste. 407
Hicksville, NY 11801
Phone: (877) 935-8750
www.jurissolutions.com
*Online directory. Starts at $199.*

**LawFirmPro**
PO Box 101
Lakeville, NY 14480
www.lawfirmpro.com
*Online directory.*

**Lawinfo.com**
1782 La Costa Meadows Dr.
Ste. 100
San Marcos, CA 92078
Phone: (800) 397-3743
www.lawinfo.com
*Online directory.*

**Lawsonline.com**
330 First St. SE, Ste. A
Cedar Rapids, IA 52401
Phone: (800) 529-5121
www.lawsonline.com
*Online directory. Starts at $350.*

**Lawyers Weekly**
41 West St.
Boston, MA 02111
Phone: (800) 444-5297
www.lawyersweekly.com

**Martindale-Hubbell**
121 Chanlon Rd.
New Providence, NJ 07974
Phone: (800) 526-4902
www.martindale.com
*Online and print directory.
Listing fees start at $780.*

**MoreLaw.com**
406 S. Boulder, Ste. 460
Tulsa, OK 74103
Phone: (888) 354-4529
www.morelaw.com

**National Academy of Forensic Engineers**
174 Brady Ave.
Hawthorne, NY 10532

Phone: (866) 623-3674
www.nafe.org

**Northern California Register of Experts and Consultants**
The Bar Assoc. of San Francisco
465 California St., #1100
San Francisco, CA 94104
Phone: (415) 782-8927
www.sfbar.org
*600 experts. Print and online.
Listing fees start at $300.*

**Professional & Technical Consultants Association**
543 Vista Mar Ave.
Pacifica, CA 94044
Phone: (800) 747-2822
www.patca.org
*Online consultants directory.
Listing fees start at $395.*

**Rominger Legal**
PO Box 1148
Carlisle, PA 17013
Phone: (888) 240-8143
www.romingerlegal.com
*Online directory.*

**SEAK, Inc.**
SEAK National Directory of Experts
PO Box 729
Falmouth, MA 02541
www.seakexperts.com
*Print and online. Circulation of 50,000 copies. Fees start at $295.*

**Southern California Directory of Experts & Consultants**
LA County Bar Association
PO Box 55020
Los Angeles, CA 90055
Phone: (213) 896-6470
www.lacba.org
*Print and online. Starts at $350.*

**Witnesssearch.com**
PO Box 69
New York, NY 10108-0069
Phone: (631) 806-5192
www.witnesssearch.com
*Online directory. $69 fee.*

# Appendix M  Legal Journals and Other Publications

Experts may advertise in or submit articles to the following publications.

**American Lawyer Media**
www.americanlawyer.com
105 Madison Ave
New York, NY 10016
Phone: (212) 545-6194

American Lawyer Media publishes numerous journals, magazines, and newsletters for the legal community, including:

*Accounting and Financial Planning for Law Firms*
*The American Lawyer*
*The Bankruptcy Strategist*
*Business Crimes Bulletin*
*CalLaw*
*Commercial Leasing Law & Strategy*
*The Corporate Compliance & Regulatory Newsletter*
*Corporate Counsel*
*The Corporate Counselor*
*Daily Business Review (FL)*
*Daily Report (GA)*
*e-Commerce Law & Strategy*
*e-Discovery Law & Strategy*
*Employment Law Strategist*
*Entertainment Law & Finance*
*The Insurance Coverage Law Bulletin*
*The Intellectual Property Strategist*

*IP Law & Business*
*Law Firm Partnership & Benefits Report*
*Law Firm, Inc.*
*Law Technology News*
*Legal Intelligencer (PA)*
*Legal Times (DC)*
*LJN's Bioethics Legal Review*
*LJN's Equipment Leasing Newsletter*
*The Matrimonial Strategist*
*Medical Malpractice Law & Strategy*
*Minority Law Journal*
*National Law Journal*
*New Jersey Law Journal*
*Pennsylvania Law Weekly*
*Small Firm Business*
*Texas Lawyer*

**DRI – Defense Research Institute**
*For The Defense*
150 North Michigan Ave, #300
Chicago, IL 60601
Phone: (312) 795-1101
www.dri.org

**ATLA – American Trial Lawyers Association**
*Trial Magazine*
1050 31st Street, NW
Washington, DC 20007
Phone: (800) 344-3023
www.atla.org

## Legal Newspapers Published by Lawyers Weekly

41 West Street
Boston MA 02111-1233
(800) 444-5297
www.lawyersweekly.com

**National Newspaper**
*Lawyers Weekly USA*

**State Newspapers**
*Massachusetts Lawyers Weekly*
*Michigan Lawyers Weekly*
*Missouri Lawyers Weekly*
*North Carolina Lawyers Weekly*

*Rhode Island Lawyers Weekly*
*South Carolina Lawyers Weekly*
*Virginia Lawyers Weekly*

**Medical Law Reports**
*Massachusetts Medical Law Report*
*Michigan Medical Law Report*
*Missouri Medical Law Report*
*Virginia Medical Law Report*

## National Legal Journals

**American Bar Association**
www.abajournal.com
321 N. Clark St., 15th Floor
Chicago, IL 60610
Phone: (800) 285-2221

The American Bar Association (ABA) publishes numerous journals, magazines, and newsletters for the legal community, including:

*ABA in Brief*
*ABA Journal*
*Administrative & Regulatory Law News*
*Administrative Law Section*
*Antitrust Law Journal*
*Antitrust Law Section*
*Antitrust Magazine*
*Antitrust Law Section*
*Bar Leader Magazine*
*BIFOCAL (Commission on Legal Problems of the Elderly)*
*Bound for Home*

*Commission on Homelessness & Poverty*
*The Brief (Tort & Insurance Practice Section)*
*Business Law Section*
*Business Law Today*
*The Business Lawyer (Business Law Section)*
*Child CourtWorks (Center on Children and the Law)*
*Dispute Resolution Magazine*
*Entertainment and Sports Lawyer*
*Family Advocate*
*Family Law Quarterly*
*Franchise Law Journal*
*Human Rights*
*Jurimetrics*
*National Security Law Report*
*Probate & Property Magazine (Real Property, Probate and Trust Law Section)*
*Public Contract Law Journal*
*Real Property, Probate and Trust Law Journal*
*The Tax Lawyer*
*Tort & Insurance Law Journal*

## State Bar Journals

**Alabama State Bar**
*The Alabama Lawyer*
415 Dexter Avenue
Montgomery, AL 36101
Phone: 334-269-1515
www.alabar.org

**Arizona State Bar**
*Arizona Attorney*
111 West Monroe, Suite 1800
Phoenix, AZ 85003-1742
Phone: 602-252-4804
www.azbar.org

**Arkansas State Bar**
*The Arkansas Lawyer*
400 West Markham
Little Rock, AR 72201
Phone: 800-609-5668
Email: arkbar1@swbell.net
www.arkbar.com

**Boston Bar Association**
*Boston Bar Journal*
16 Beacon Street
Boston, MA 02108
Phone: 617-742-0615
www.bostonbar.org

**Colorado Bar Association**
*The Colorado Lawyer*
1900 Grant St., Suite 900
Denver, CO 80203
Phone: 303-860-1115
www.cobar.org

**District of Columbia Bar**
*Washington Lawyer*
1250 H Street, NW, 6th Floor
Washington, DC 20005-5937
Phone: 202-737-4700
www.dcbar.org

**Federal Bar Association**
*Federal Bar News and Journal*
2215 M Street, NW
Washington, DC 20037
Phone: 202-785-1614
www.fedbar.org

**Florida Bar Association**
*The Florida Bar Journal*
651 E. Jefferson Street
Tallahassee, FL 32399-2300
Phone: 850-561-5600
www.flabar.org

**Georgia Bar Association**
*Georgia State Bar*
104 Marietta St. NW, Ste. 100
Atlanta, GA 30303
Phone: 404-527-8700
www.gabar.org

**Hawaii Bar Association**
*Hawaii Bar Journal*
1132 Bishop Street, Suite 906
Honolulu, HI 96813
Phone: 808-537-1868
Email: lshiraishi@hsba.org
www.hsba.org

**Illinois State Bar Association**
*Illinois Bar Journal*
424 S. Second Street
Springfield, IL 62701
Phone: 217-525-1760
www.illinoisbar.org

**Indiana State Bar Association**
*Res Gestae*
230 East Ohio Street, 4th Floor
Indianapolis, IN 46204-2199
Phone: 800-266-2581
www.inbar.org

# LEGAL JOURNALS AND OTHER PUBLICATIONS

**Kansas Bar Association**
*The Journal of the Kansas Bar*
1200 SW Harrison
Topeka, KS 66612-1806
Phone: 785-234-5696
Email: info@ksbar.org
www.ksbar.org

**Kentucky Bar Association**
*Kentucky Bench and Bar*
514 West Main Street
Frankfort, KY 40601-1883
Phone: 502-564-3795
www.kybar.org

**Los Angeles County Bar Association**
*Los Angeles Lawyer*
261 S. Figueroa Street, Ste 300
Los Angeles, CA 90012
Phone: 213-627-2727
www.lacba.org

**Louisiana State Bar Association**
*Louisiana Bar Journal*
601 St. Charles Avenue
New Orleans, LA 70130-3404
Phone: 504-566-1600
Email: lsbainfo@lsba.org
www.lsba.org

**Maryland Bar Association**
*Maryland Bar Journal*
520 W Fayette Street
Baltimore, MD 21201
Phone: 410-685-7878
800-492-1964
Email: msba@msba.org
www.msba.org

**Michigan Bar Association**
*Michigan Bar Journal*
306 Townsend Street
Lansing, MI 48933-2083
Phone: 800-968-1442
www.michbar.org

**New Hampshire Bar Association**
*New Hampshire Bar News*
112 Pleasant St.
Concord, NH 03301
Phone: 603-224-6942
Fax: 603-224-2910
Email: NHBAinfo@nhbar.org
hwww.nhbar.org

**New York State Bar Association**
*New York State Bar Journal*
One Elk Street
Albany, NY 12207
Phone: 518-463-3200
www.nysba.org

**North Carolina State Bar**
*North Carolina State Bar Quarterly*
8000 Weston Pkwy.
PO Box 3688
Cary, NC 27519
Phone: 919-677-0561
Email: ncba@ncbar.org
www.ncbar.org

**Oklahoma Bar Association**
*Oklahoma Bar Journal*
1901 N. Lincoln Blvd.
PO Box 53036
Oklahoma City, OK 73152
Phone: 405-416-7000
Email: web@okbar.org
www.okbar.org

**Orange County Bar Association**
*Orange County Bar Association Bulletin*
PO Box 17777
Irvine, CA 92623-7777
Phone: 949-440-6700
www.ocbar.org

**Pennsylvania Bar Association**
*The Pennsylvania Lawyer*
100 South Street, PO Box 186
Harrisburg, PA 17108-0186
Phone: 717-238-6715
Email: info@pabar.org
www.pabar.org

**Tennessee Bar Association**
*Tennessee Bar Journal*
221 Fourth Avenue North,
Suite 400
Nashville, TN 37219-2198
Phone: 615-383-7421
Email: email@tnbar.org
www.tba.org

**Texas Bar Association**
*Texas Bar Journal*
1414 Colorado PO Box 12487
Austin, TX 78711
Phone: 512-463-1463
800-204-2222
Email: jsirman@texasbar.com
www.texasbar.com

**Virginia Bar Association**
*The Virginia Bar Association Journal*
707 E. Main Street, Suite 1500
Richmond, VA 23219-2800
Phone: 804-775-0500
www.vsb.org

**Washington Bar Association**
*Washington State Bar News*
2101 Fourth Avenue, Suite 400
Seattle, WA 98121-2330
Phone: 206-443-9722
800-945-9722
Email: questions@wsba.org
www.wsba.org

**Wisconsin Bar Association**
The Wisconsin Lawyer
5302 Eastpark Blvd.
PO Box 7158
Madison, WI 53708-7158
Phone: 800-728-7788
www.wisbar.org

## Legal Newsletters by Specialty

**Agricultural Law**
Agricultural Law
Agricultural Law Digest
Agricultural Law Update

**Architects and Engineers**
Codes & Standards
The Last Word

**Aviation**
The Air and Space Lawyer
Air Safety Week

**Bar Associations**
Agricultural Law
The Air and Space Lawyer
Construction Law
Education Law
Elder Law
Elder Law News
Environmental Law News
Environmental Mineral &
  Natural Resources Law
  Section Newsletter
Family Law
Franchise Lawyer
Health Care Lawyer
Health Law Journal
Health Law News
The Health Lawyer
Indian Law News
Intellectual Property Law
Intellectual Property Law
  Newsletter
Labor and Employment Law
Mental and Physical Disability
  Law Reporter
Product, Trust, Property &
  Death Tax Newsletter
Traffic Laws and Courts
Trusts and Estates
Workers' Compensation Law

**Biotechnology**
Biotech Law Weekly
Biotech Watch
Biotechnology Law Report

**Building Codes**
Building Safety Bulletin

**Casinos**
Entertainment Industry
  Litigation Reporter
Gaming Law Review

**Cemeteries**
Reasonable Efforts

**Civil Rights**
Prison Legal News

**Computers and Automation**
Computer Law Association
  Bulletin
Computer Law Reporter
Computer Technology Law
  Report
Cybercrime Law Report
Cyberspace Lawyer
E-Commerce Law & Strategy

**Construction Law**
The Construction Lawyer

**Consumer Finance**
Consumer Financial Services
  Law Report

**Criminal Justice**
Correctional Law Reporter
Corrections Digest
Death Row U.S.A. Reporter

**Disability Law**
Accommodating Disabilities
  Newsletter
American with Disabilities
  Newsletter
Disability Compliance Bulletin
Disability Litigation Reporter
Mental and Physical Disability
  Law Reporter

**Discrimination**
Employment Discrimination
  Law Update
Sexual Harassment Litigation
  Reporter

**Drunk Driving**
Drinking/Driving Law Letter
DWI Journal: Law & Science
Impaired Driving Update

**Elder Law**
Elder Law Report
Elder Law Weekly

**Energy**
The Environment & Energy
  Daily
Utilities Industry Litigation
  Reporter

**Environmental Law**
Business and the Environment
The Digest of Environmental
  Law
National Wetlands Newsletter

**Estate Planning**
The Estate Law and Planning
  Digest

**Fires**
Fire Code Inspections Law
  Bulletin
Fire Control Digest
Fire Findings

**Food, Drugs, Cosmetics**
Biotechnology Law Report
Drug Industry Daily
Medicine & Law Weekly
Pharmacy Today

**Forests**
Forest Landowner

**Gun Control**
Gun Industry Litigation
  Reporter
Swift & Certain

**Hazardous Substances**
Toxics Law Daily
Toxics Law Reporter

**Healthcare**
Cancer Law Weekly
Emergency Department
  Liability Alert
Health Law Bulletin
Health Law Digest
Hospital Liability & Litigation
  Alert
Medical Liability Alert
Medical Liability Monitor
Medical Malpractice Law &
  Strategy
Ob/Gyn Liability Alert

**Highways**
Highway & Vehicle/Safety
  Report

**Horses**
Equine Law & Business
  Newsletter

# LEGAL JOURNALS AND OTHER PUBLICATIONS

**Insurance**
Defense Law Journal
Fire Findings
Insurance Bad Faith Litigation
  Reporter
The Insurance Coverage Law
  Bulletin
Insurance Law & Litigation
  Week

**Intellectual Property**
The Intellectual Property
  Strategist
The IP Litigator

**Labor and Employment**
Employment Law Strategist
Employment Practices Liability
  Consultant
Employment Practices
  Newsletter
Employment Practices Update
Personnel Practice Pointers

**Licensing**
Professional Licensing Report

**Malpractice**
Professional Liability Reporter

**Marriage and Divorce**
Divorce Litigation

**Mines and Mining**
Mine Safety and Health News
Mining Week

**Mortgages**
Inside Mortgages Compliance

**Motor Vehicles**
Between the Lines
Highway and Vehicle

Safe Ride News

**Nursing**
Nursing Law's Regan Report

**Nursing Homes**
Elder Law Weekly
Housing for Seniors Report
Nursing Home Law &
  Litigation Report
Nursing Law's Regan Report

**Occupational Safety**
BNA's SafetyNet
Inside OSHA
Occupational Safety & Health
  Daily

**Patents**
Patent, Trademark & Copyright
  Daily

**Police**
Law Enforcement Liability
  Reporter
Police Misconduct and
  Civil Rights Law Report

**Products Liability**
Asbestos Litigation Reporter
Product Liability Daily
Product Safety & Liability
  Reporter
Products Liability Advisor
Products Liability Law &
  Litigation Report

**Schools**
Legal Notes for Education
Maintaining Safe Schools
School Law Bulletin

**Securities**
The Corporate Counsel
Corporate Governance Report

**Security**
Security Law Newsletter
Security Letter
Transport Security Advisor
  Newsletter

**Social Security**
The NOSSCR Forum
Social Security Practice
  Advisory

**Special Education**
The Special Educator

**Sports**
Sports and Entertainment Law
  News
The Sport, Parks and
  Recreation Law Reporter

**Torts**
Commercial Damages Reporter
Toxics Law Reporter

**Transportation**
Safe Ride News
The Transportation Lawyer

**Trial Practice**
The Advocate

**Valuation**
Shannon Pratt's Business
  Valuation Update
Valuation

**Zoning Law**
Municipal Lawyer
Zoning Bulletin
Zoning Practice

# Appendix N  Forensic Organizations

**Accident Reconstruction Network**
www.accidentreconstruction.com

**American Academy of Forensic Psychology**
www.abfp.com

**American Academy of Forensic Sciences**
www.aafs.org

**American Academy of Psychiatry and Law**
www.aapl.org

**American Association of Legal Nurse Consultants**
www.aalnc.org

**American Board of Criminalistics**
www.criminalistics.com

**American Board of Forensic Anthropology**
www.csuchico.edu/anth/ABFA/

**American Board of Forensic Document Examiners**
www.abfde.org

**American Board of Forensic Odontology**
www.abfo.org/

**American Board of Forensic Psychology**
www.abfp.com

**American Board of Forensic Toxicology**
www.abft.org

**American Board of Vocational Experts**
www.abve.net

**American College of Forensic Examiners**
www.acfe.com

**American Society of Appraisers**
www.appraisers.org

**American Society of Questioned Document Examiners**
www.asqde.org

**American Society of Testing and Materials**
www.astm.org

**Americans for Effective Law Enforcement**
www.aele.org

**Association for Crime Scene Reconstruction**
www.acsr.org

**Association of Certified Fraud Examiners**
www.acfe.com

**Association of Firearm and Tool Mark Examiners**
www.afte.org

**Expert Communications**
www.expertcommunications.com

**Forensic Expert Witness Association**
www.forensic.org

**High Technology Crime Investigation Association**
www.htcia.org

**IEEE-USA Consultants Database**
www.ieeeusa.org

**Institute of Transportation Engineers**
www.ite.org

**International Association for Identification**
www.theiai.org

**International Association for Property and Evidence**
www.iape.org

**International Association of Arson Investigators**
www.firearson.com

**International Association of Forensic Nurses**
www.forensicnurse.org

**International Association of Forensic Toxicologists**
www.tiaft.org

**International Crime Scene Investigators Association**
www.icsia.com

**International Organization for Standardization**
www.iso.ch

**International Society of Explosives Engineers**
www.isee.org

**National Academy of Forensic Engineers**
www.nafe.org

**National Academy of Sciences**
www.nas.edu

**National Association of Certified Valuation Consultants**
www.nacva.com

**National Association of Forensic Economics**
www.nafe.net

**National Committee for Clinical Laboratory Standards**
www.nccls.org

**National Institute of Standards and Technology**
www.nist.gov

**Occupational Safety and Health Administration**
www.osha.gov

**Professional and Technical Consultants Association**
www.patca.org

**SEAK, Inc.**
www.seak.com

**Society of Forensic Engineers and Scientists**
www.forensic-society.org

**Society of Forensic Toxicologists**
www.soft-tox.org

**Southeastern Association of Forensic Document Examiners**
www.safde.org

# Appendix O  Bar Associations and Other Legal Associations

## National Bar Associations

**American Agricultural Law Association**
PO Box 2025
Eugene, OR 97402-2025
Phone: (541) 485-1090
Fax: (541) 302-1958
www.aglaw-assn.org

**American Bar Association**
750 N. Lake Shore Dr.
Chicago, IL 60611
Phone: (312) 988-5000
Email: askaba@abanct.org
Link: www.abanet.org

**American Immigration Lawyers Association**
918 F St., NW
Washington, DC 20004-1400
Phone: (202) 216-2400
Fax: (202) 783-7853
www.aila.org

**American Intellectual Property Law Association**
2001 Jefferson Davis Highway, Ste. 203
Arlington, Virginia 22202
Phone: (703) 415-0780
Fax: (703) 415-0786
www.aipla.org

**Association of Corporate Counsel**
1025 Connecticut Ave. NW, #200
Washington, DC 20036-5425
Phone: (202) 293-4103
www.acca.com

**Association of Trial Lawyers of America**
1050 31st St., NW
Washington, DC 20007
Phone: (800) 424-2725
www.atla.org

**Black Entertainment & Sports Lawyers Association**
7961 Eastern Ave., Ste. 303
Silver Spring, MD 20910
Phone: (301) 248-1818
Fax: (301) 248-0700
www.besla.org

**Defense Research Institute**
150 N. Michigan Ave., Ste. 300
Chicago, IL 60601
Phone: (312) 795-1101
Fax: (312) 795-0747
www.dri.org

**Federal Bar Association**
2215 M St., NW
Washington, DC 20037
Phone: (202) 785-1614
Fax: (202) 785-1568
www.fedbar.org

**Federation of Defense & Corporate Counsel**
11812-A North 56th St.
Tampa, FL 33617
Phone: (813) 983-0022
Fax: (813) 988-5837
www.thefederation.org

**Hispanic National Bar Assoc.**
8201 Greensboro Dr., Ste. 300
McLean, VA 22102
Phone: (703) 610-9038
Fax: (703) 610-9005
www.hnba.com

**International Association of Defense Counsel**
One North Franklin, Ste. 1205
Chicago, IL 60606
Phone: (312) 368-1494
Fax: (312) 368-1854
www.iadclaw.org

**National Academy of Elder Law Attorneys**
1604 North Country Club Rd.
Tucson, Arizona 85716
Phone: (520) 881-4005
Fax: (520) 325-7925
www.naela.com

**National Asian Pacific American Bar Association**
1341 G St., NW, 5th Floor
Washington, DC 20005
Phone: (202) 626-7693
Fax: (202) 628-6327
www.napaba.org

**National Bar Association**
1225 W St. NW
Washington, DC 20001-4217
Phone: (202) 842-3900
www.nationalbar.org

**National Lawyers Association**
City Center Square
PO Box 26005
Kansas City, MO 64196
Phone: (816) 471-2994
Fax: (816) 471-2995
www.nla.org

## Additional National Associations

ALI-ABA Committee on Continuing Prof. Education

American Association of Law Libraries

American College of Trust and Estate Counsel

American Corporate Counsel Association

The American Inns of Court Foundation

American Judicature Society

American Society of Corporate Secretaries

Association for Continuing Legal Education

Association of Federal Defense Attorneys

Association of Legal Administrators

Commercial Law League of America

Corporate Bar Association

CyberSpace Bar Association

Federal Magistrate Judges Association

First Amendment Lawyers Association

National Asian Pacific American Bar Association

National Association for Public Interest Law

National Association of Bond Lawyers

National Association of College and University Attorneys

National Association of Legal Assistants

National Association of Legal Secretaries

National Association of Patent Practitioners

National Employment Lawyers Association

National Federation of Paralegal Associations

National Health Lawyers Association

National Organization of Bar Counsel

## State Bar Associations

**ALABAMA**
**Alabama Bar Association**
415 Dexter Ave.
Montgomery, AL 36101
Phone: (334) 269-1515
www.alabar.org

**Alabama Defense Lawyers Association**
www.adla.org

**Alabama Trial Lawyers Association**
www.atla.net
Phone: (334) 262-4974
Fax: (334) 262-1452

**ALASKA**
**Alaska Bar Association**
PO Box 100279
Anchorage, AK 99510-0279
Phone: (907) 272-7469
Fax: (907) 272-2932
Email: info@alaskabar.org
www.alaskabar.org

**Alaska Trial Lawyers Association**
www.alaskatriallawyers.org
Phone: (907) 258-4040
Fax: (907) 258-8751

**ARIZONA**
**Arizona Bar Association**
111 West Monroe, Ste. 1800
Phoenix, AZ 85003-1742
Phone: (602) 252-4804
www.azbar.org

**Arizona Trial Lawyers Association**
www.aztla.org
Phone: (602) 235-9356
Fax: (602) 235-9331

**ARKANSAS**
**Arkansas Bar Association**
400 West Markham
Little Rock, AR 72201
Phone: (800) 609-5668
Email: arkbar1@swbell.net
www.arkbar.com

**Arkansas Trial Lawyers Association**
www.arktla.org
Phone: (501) 376-2852
Fax: (501) 372-0951

**CALIFORNIA**
**Association of Defense Council of Northern California**
www.adcnc.org

California Bar Association
180 Howard St.
San Francisco, CA 94105
Phone: (415) 538-2000
Email: feedback@calbar.ca.gov
www.calbar.ca.gov

**Consumer Attorneys Association of Los Angeles**
www.caala.org
Phone: (213) 487-1212
Fax: (213) 487-1224

**Consumer Attorneys of California**
www.caoc.com
Phone: (916) 442-6902
Fax: (916) 442-7734

**Consumer Attorneys of Orange County**
www.octla.org
Phone: (949) 916-9577
Fax: (949) 215-2222

**Consumer Attorneys of San Diego**
www.casd.org
Phone: (619) 696-1166
Fax: (619) 696-1294

**Consumer Attorneys of San Francisco**
www.sftla.org
Phone: (415) 956-6401
Fax: (415) 956-6680

**San Francisco Trial Lawyers Association**
www.sftla.org
Phone: (415) 956-6401
Fax: (415) 956-6680

## COLORADO
**Colorado Bar Association**
1900 Grant St., Ste. 900
Denver, CO 80203
Phone: (303) 860-1115
Email: comments@cobar.org
www.cobar.org

**Colorado Trial Lawyers Association**
www.ctlanet.org
Phone: (303) 831-1192
Fax: (303) 831-0111

## CONNECTICUT
**Connecticut Bar Association**
30 Bank St., PO Box 350
New Britain, CT 06050-0350
Phone: (860) 223-4400
Email: ctbar@ctbar.org
www.ctbar.org

**Connecticut Trial Lawyers Association**
www.cttriallawyers.org
Phone: (860) 522-4345
Fax: (860) 522-1027

## DELAWARE
**Delaware Bar Association**
301 North Market St.
Wilmington, DE 19801
Phone: (302) 658-5279
www.dsba.org

**Delaware Trial Lawyers Association**
www.dtla.org
Phone: (302) 421-2801
Fax: (302) 421-2803

## DISTRICT OF COLUMBIA
**District of Columbia Bar Association**
1250 H St. NW, Sixth Floor
Washington D.C., 20005-5937
Phone: (202) 737-4700
www.dcbar.org

**Trial Lawyers Association of Metro Washington DC**
www.tla-dc.org
Phone: (202) 659-3532
Fax: (202) 775 9010

## FLORIDA
**Academy of Florida Trial Lawyers**
www.aftl.org
Phone: (850) 224-9403
Fax: (850) 224-4254

**Florida Bar Association**
651 E Jefferson St.
Tallahassee, FL 32399-2300
Phone: (850) 561-5600
www.flabar.org

**Florida Defense Lawyers Association**
www.fdla.org

## GEORGIA
**Georgia Bar Association**
104 Marietta St. NW, Ste. 100
Atlanta, GA 30303
Phone: (404) 527-8700
www.gabar.org

**Georgia Defense Lawyers Association**
www.gdla.org

**Georgia Trial Lawyers Association**
www.gtla.org
Phone: (404) 522-8487
Fax: (404) 522-3705

## HAWAII
**Consumer Lawyers of Hawaii**
www.clh.org
Phone: (808) 599-2769
Fax: (808) 599-2859

**Hawaii Bar Association**
1132 Bishop St., Ste. 906
Honolulu, HI 96813
Phone: (808) 537-1868
Email: lshiraishi@hsba.org
www.hsba.org

## IDAHO
**Idaho Bar Association**
PO Box 895
Boise, ID 83701
Phone: (208) 334-4500
www2.state.id.us

**Idaho Trial Lawyers Association**
www.itla.org
Phone: (208) 345-1890
Fax: (208) 345-1894

## ILLINOIS
**Illinois Association of Defense Trial Counsel**
www.iadtc.org

**Illinois Bar Association**
424 S Second St.
Springfield, IL 62701
Phone: (217) 525-1760
www.illinoisbar.org

**Illinois Trial Lawyers Association**
www.iltla.com
Phone: (217) 789-0755
Fax: (217) 789-0810

## INDIANA
**Indiana Bar Association**
230 East Ohio St., 4th Floor
Indianapolis, IN 46204-2199
Phone: (317) 639-5465/(800) 266-2581
Email: isbaadmin@inbar.org
www.inbar.org

**Indiana Trial Lawyers Association**
www.i-t-l-a.org
Phone: (317) 634-8841
Fax: (317) 634-4898

## IOWA
**Iowa Bar Association**
521 East Locust St., 3rd Floor
Des Moines, IA 50309-1939
Phone: (515) 243-3179
Email: isba@iowabar.org
www.iowabar.org

**Iowa Trial Lawyers Association**
www.iowatla.org
Phone: (515) 280-7366
Fax: (515) 280-3745

## KANSAS
**Kansas Association of Defense Counsel**
www.kadc.org

**Kansas Bar Association**
1200 SW Harrison
Topeka, KS 66612-1806
Phone: (785) 234-5696
Email: info@ksbar.org
www.ksbar.org

**Kansas Trial Lawyers Association**
www.ktla.org
Phone: (785) 232-7756
Fax: (785) 232-7730

## KENTUCKY
**Kentucky Academy of Trial Lawyers**
www.kata.org
Phone: (502) 339-8890
Fax: (502) 339-1780

**Kentucky Bar Association**
514 West Main St.
Frankfort, KY 40601-1883
Phone: (502) 564-3795
www.kybar.org

## LOUISIANA
**Louisiana Bar Association**
601 St. Charles Ave.
New Orleans, LA 70130-3404
Phone: (504) 566-1600
Email: lsbainfo@lsba.org
www.lsba.org

**Louisiana Trial Lawyers Association**
www.ltla.org
Phone: (225) 383-5554
Fax: (225) 387-1993

## MAINE
**Maine Bar Association**
PO Box 788
Augusta , ME 04332-1788
Phone: (207) 622-7523
www.mainebar.org

**Maine Trial Lawyers Association**
Phone: (207) 623-2661
Fax: (207) 621-0118

## MARYLAND
**Maryland Bar Association**
520 W Fayette St.
Baltimore, MD 21201
Phone: (410) 685-7878
(800) 492-1964
Email: msba@msba.org
www.msba.org

**Maryland Trial Lawyers Association**
www.mdtriallawyers.com
Phone: (410) 539-4336
Fax: (410) 783-5981

## MASSACHUSETTS
**Massachusetts Academy of Trial Attorneys**
www.massacademy.com
Phone: (617) 248-5858
Fax: (617) 248-8701

**Massachusetts Bar Association**
20 West St.
Boston, MA 02111
Phone: (617) 338-0500
www.massbar.org

## MICHIGAN
**Michigan Bar Association**
306 Townsend St.
Lansing, MI 48933-2083
Phone: (800) 968-1442
www.michbar.org

**Michigan Defense Trial Counsel**
www.mdtc.org

**Michigan Trial Lawyers Association**
www.mtla.net
Phone: (517) 321-3073
Fax: (517) 321-4694

## MINNESOTA
**Minnesota Bar Association**
600 Nicollet Mall, Ste. 380
Minneapolis, MN 55402
Phone: (800) 882-6722
Email: jfenner@statebar.gen.mn.us
www.mnbar.org

**Minnesota Defense Lawyers Association**
www.mdla.org

**Minnesota Trial Lawyers Association**
www.mntla.com
Phone: (612) 375-1707
Fax: (612) 334-3142

## MISSISSIPPI
**Mississippi Bar Association**
643 North State St., PO Box 2168
Jackson, MS 39225
Phone: (601) 948-4471
www.msbar.org

**Mississippi Trial Lawyers Association**
www.mstla.com
Phone: (601) 948-8631Fax: (601) 948-8633

## MISSOURI
**Missouri Association of Trial Attorneys**
www.matanet.org
Phone: (573) 635-5215
Fax: (573) 634-6282

**Missouri Bar Association**
PO Box 119
Jefferson City, MO 65102
Phone: (573) 635-4128
www.mobar.org

## MONTANA
**Montana Bar Association**
The Power Block
7 West 6th Ave., Ste. 2B
PO Box 577
Helena, MT 59624
Phone: (406) 442-7660
Email: mailbox@montanabar.org
www.montanabar.org

**Montana Trial Lawyers Association**
www.monttla.com
Phone: (406) 443-3124
Fax: (406) 449-6943

## NEBRASKA
**Nebraska Association of Trial Attorneys**
www.nebraskatrial.com
Phone: (402) 435-5526
Fax: (402) 435-5547

# BAR ASSOCIATIONS AND OTHER LEGAL ASSOCIATIONS

**Nebraska Bar Association**
635 South 14th St., PO Box 81809
Lincoln, NE 68501
Phone: (402) 475-7091
Email: sclinch@nebar.com
www.nebar.com

## NEVADA
**Nevada Bar Association**
600 E. Charleston Blvd.
Las Vegas, NV 89104
Phone: (702) 382-2200
Email: marcm@nvbar.org
www.nvbar.org

**Nevada Trial Lawyers
Association**
www.ntla.org
Phone: (775) 883-3577
Fax: (775) 883-5372

## NEW HAMPSHIRE
**New Hampshire Bar Association**
112 Pleasant St.
Concord, NH 03301
Phone: (603) 224-6942
Fax: (603) 224-2910
Email: NHBAinfo@nhbar.org
hwww.nhbar.org

**New Hampshire Trial Lawyers
Association**
www.nhtla.org
Phone: (603) 224-7077
Fax: (603) 224-3256

## NEW JERSEY
**New Jersey Bar Association**
New Jersey Law Center One
Constitution Square
New Brunswick, NJ 08901-1520
Phone: (732) 249-5000
www.njsba.com

**New Jersey Defense Association**
www.njdefenseassoc.com

**New Jersey Trial Lawyers
Association**
www.atlanj.org
Phone: (609) 396-0096
Fax: (609) 396-2463

## NEW MEXICO
**New Mexico Bar Association**
5121 Masthead NE, PO Box 25883
Albuquerque, NM 87125
Phone: (505) 797-6000
Email: sbnm@nmbar.org
www.nmbar.org

**New Mexico Trial Lawyers
Association**
www.nmtla.org
Phone: (505) 243-6003
Fax: (505) 243-6099

## NEW YORK
**New York Bar Association**
One Elk St.
Albany, NY 12207
Phone: (518) 463-3200
www.nysba.org

**New York Criminal & Civil
Courts Bar Association**
30 Vesey St., Ste. 1400
New York, New York 10007
Phone: (212) 766-4030
www.nycccba.org

**New York State Trial Lawyers
Association**
www.nystla.org
Phone: (212) 349-5890
Fax: (212) 608-2310

## NORTH CAROLINA
**North Carolina Academy of Trial
Lawyers**
www.ncatl.org
Phone: (919) 832-1413
Fax: (919) 832-6361

**North Carolina Association of
Defense Attorneys**
www.ncada.org

**North Carolina Bar Association**
8000 Weston Parkway
PO Box 3688
Cary, NC 27519
Phone: (919) 677-0561
Email: ncba@ncbar.org
www.ncbar.org

## NORTH DAKOTA
**North Dakota Bar Association**
515 1/2 E. Broadway, Ste. 101
Bismarck, ND 58502
Phone: (701) 155-1404
Email: info@sband.org
www.sband.org

**North Dakota Trial Lawyers
Association**
www.ndtla.com
Phone: (701) 663-3916
Fax: (701) 663-3917

## OHIO
**Ohio Academy of Trial Lawyers**
www.oatlaw.org
Phone: (614) 341-6800
Fax: (614) 341-6810

**Ohio Bar Association**
1700 Lake Shore Dr.
Columbus, OH 43204
Phone: (614) 487-2050
(800) 282-6556
Email: osba@ohiobar.org
www.ohiobar.org

## OKLAHOMA
**Oklahoma Bar Association**
1901 N. Lincoln Blvd.
PO Box 53036
Oklahoma City, OK 73152-3036
Phone: (405) 416-7000
Email: web@okbar.org
www.okbar.org

**Oklahoma Trial Lawyers
Association**
www.otla.org
Phone: (405) 525-8044
Fax: (405) 528-2431

## OREGON
**Oregon Bar Association**
5200 SW Meadows Rd.
Lake Oswego, OR 97035
Phone: (503) 620-0222
Email: info@osbar.org
www.osbar.org

**Oregon Trial Lawyers
Association**
www.oregontriallawyers.org
Phone: (503) 223-5587
Fax: (503) 223-4101

**PENNSYLVANIA**
**Pennsylvania Bar Association**
100 South St., PO Box 186
Harrisburg, PA 17108-0186
Phone: (717) 238-6715
Email: info@pabar.org
www.pabar.org

**Pennsylvania Defense Institute**
www.padefense.org

**Pennsylvania Trial Lawyers Association**
www.patla.org
Phone: (215) 546-6451
Fax: (215) 546-5430

**Philadelphia Trial Lawyers Association**
www.philatla.org
Phone: (215) 732-2256
Fax: (215) 732-7637

**RHODE ISLAND**
**Rhode Island Bar Association**
115 Cedar St.
Providence, RI 02903
Phone: (401) 421-5740
Email: info@ribar.com
www.ribar.com

**Rhode Island Trial Lawyers Association**
www.ritla.org
Phone: (401) 273-8820
Fax: (401) 521-3350

**SOUTH CAROLINA**
**South Carolina Bar Association**
950 Taylor St.
Columbia, SC 29202
Phone: (803) 799-6653
Email: scbar-info@scbar.org
www.scbar.org

**South Carolina Defense Trial Attorneys**
www.scdtaa.com

**South Carolina Trial Lawyers Association**
www.sctla.org
Phone: (803) 799-5097
Fax: (803) 799-1041

**SOUTH DAKOTA**
**South Dakota Bar Association**
222 East Capitol Ave.
Pierre, SD 57501-2596
Phone: (800) 952-2333
Email: webmaster@sdbar.org
www.sdbar.org

**South Dakota Defense Lawyers Association**
www.sddla.com

**South Dakota Trial Lawyers Association**
www.sdtla.org
Phone: (605) 224-9292
Fax: (605) 945-1204

**TENNESSEE**
**Tennessee Bar Association**
221 Fourth Ave. N, Ste. 400
Nashville, TN 37219-2198
Phone: (615) 383-7421
Email: email@tnbar.org
www.tba.org

**Tennessee Trial Lawyers Association**
www.ttla.org
Phone: (615) 329-3000
Fax: (615) 329-8131

**TEXAS**
**Texas Association of Defense Counsel**
www.tadc.org

**Texas Bar Association**
1414 Colorado
PO Box 12487
Austin, TX 78711
Phone: (800) 204-2222
Email: jsirman@texasbar.com
www.texasbar.com

**Texas Trial Lawyers Association**
www.ttla.com
Phone: (512) 476-3852
Fax: (512) 473-2411

**UTAH**
**Utah Bar Association**
645 South 200 East
Salt Lake City, UT 84111
Phone: (801) 531-9077
Email: licensing@utahbar.org
www.utahbar.org

**Utah Trial Lawyers Association**
www.utla.org
Phone: (801) 531-7514
Fax: (801) 531-1207

**VERMONT**
**Vermont Bar Association**
35-37 Court St.
PO Box 100
Montpelier, VT 05601-0100
Phone: (802) 223-2020
www.vtbar.org

**Vermont Trial Lawyers Association**
www.vtla.org
Phone: (802) 223-0501
Fax: (802) 223-4880

**VIRGINIA**
**Virginia Association of Defense Attorneys**
www.vada.org

**Virginia Bar Association**
707 E. Main St., Ste. 1500
Richmond, VA 23219-2800
Phone: (804) 775-0500
www.vsb.org

**Virginia Trial Lawyers Association**
www.vtla.com
Phone: (804) 343-1143
Fax: (804) 343-7124

**WASHINGTON**
**Washington Bar Association**
2101 Fourth Ave., Ste. 400
Seattle, WA 98121-2330
Phone: (206) 443-9722/
(800) 945-9722
Email: questions@wsba.org
www.wsba.org

**Washington Defense Trial Lawyers Association**
www.wdtl.org

**Washington State Trial Lawyers Association**
www.wstla.org
Phone: (206) 464-1011
Fax: (206) 464-0703

# BAR ASSOCIATIONS AND OTHER LEGAL ASSOCIATIONS

## WEST VIRGINIA

**West Virginia Bar Association**
2006 Kanawha Blvd., East
Charleston, WV 25133-2204
Phone: (304) 558-2456
Email: webmaster@wvbar.org
www.wvbar.org

**West Virginia Defense Trial Counsel**
www.dtcwv.org

**West Virginia Trial Lawyers Association**
www.wvtla.org
Phone: (304) 344-0692
Fax: (304) 343-7926

## WISCONSIN

**Wisconsin Academy of Trial Lawyers**
www.watl.org
Phone: (608) 257-5741
Fax: (608) 255-9285

**Wisconsin Bar Association**
5302 Eastpark Blvd., PO Box 7158
Madison, WI 53708-7158
Phone: (800) 728-7788
www.wisbar.org

## WYOMING

**Wyoming Bar Association**
500 Randall Ave.
PO Box 109
Cheyenne, WY 82003-0109
Phone: (307) 632-9061
www.wyomingbar.org

**Wyoming Trial Lawyers Association**
www.wytla.org
Phone: (307) 635-0820
Fax: (307) 634-5331

# Appendix P  Federal Rules of Evidence

## ARTICLE I. GENERAL PROVISIONS

**Rule 101. Scope**

These rules govern proceedings in the courts of the United States and before United States bankruptcy judges and United States magistrate judges, to the extent and with the exceptions stated in rule 1101.

**Rule 102. Purpose and Construction**

These rules shall be construed to secure fairness in administration, elimination of unjustifiable expense and delay, and promotion of growth and development of the law of evidence to the end that the truth may be ascertained and proceedings justly determined.

**Rule 103. Rulings on Evidence**

(a) Effect of erroneous ruling.

Error may not be predicated upon a ruling which admits or excludes evidence unless a substantial right of the party is affected, and

(1) Objection. - In case the ruling is one admitting evidence, a timely objection or motion to strike appears of record, stating the specific ground of objection, if the specific ground was not apparent from the context; or

(2) Offer of proof. - In case the ruling is one excluding evidence, the substance of the evidence was made known to the court by offer or was apparent from the context within which questions were asked. Once the court makes a definitive ruling on the record admitting or excluding evidence, either at or before trial, a party need not renew an objection or offer of proof to preserve a claim of error for appeal.

(b) Record of offer and ruling

The court may add any other or further statement which shows the character of the evidence, the form in which it was offered, the objection made, and the ruling thereon. It may direct the making of an offer in question and answer form.

(c) Hearing of jury

In jury cases, proceedings shall be conducted, to the extent practicable, so as to prevent inadmissible evidence from being suggested to the jury by any means, such as making statements or offers of proof or asking questions in the hearing of the jury.

(d) Plain error

Nothing in this rule precludes taking notice of plain errors affecting substantial rights although they were not brought to the attention of the court.

## Rule 104. Preliminary Questions

(a) Questions of admissibility generally.

Preliminary questions concerning the qualification of a person to be a witness, the existence of a privilege, or the admissibility of evidence shall be determined by the court, subject to the provisions of subdivision (b). In making its determination it is not bound by the rules of evidence except those with respect to privileges.

(b) Relevancy conditioned on fact.

When the relevancy of evidence depends upon the fulfillment of a condition of fact, the court shall admit it upon, or subject to, the introduction of evidence sufficient to support a finding of the fulfillment of the condition.

(c) Hearing of jury.

Hearings on the admissibility of confessions shall in all cases be conducted out of the hearing of the jury. Hearings on other preliminary matters shall be so conducted when the interests of justice require, or when an accused is a witness and so requests.

(d) Testimony by accused.

The accused does not, by testifying upon a preliminary matter, become subject to cross-examination as to other issues in the case.

(e) Weight and credibility.

This rule does not limit the right of a party to introduce before the jury evidence relevant to weight or credibility.

## Rule 105. Limited Admissibility

When evidence which is admissible as to one party or for one purpose but not admissible as to another party or for another purpose is admitted, the court, upon request, shall restrict the evidence to its proper scope and instruct the jury accordingly.

## Rule 106. Remainder of or Related Writings or Recorded Statements

When a writing or recorded statement or part thereof is introduced by a party, an adverse party may require the introduction at that time of any other part or any other writing or recorded statement which ought in fairness to be considered contemporaneously with it.

## ARTICLE II. JUDICIAL NOTICE
### Rule 201. Judicial Notice of Adjudicative Facts
(a) Scope of rule.

This rule governs only judicial notice of adjudicative facts.

(b) Kinds of facts.

A judicially noticed fact must be one not subject to reasonable dispute in that it is either (1) generally known within the territorial jurisdiction of the trial court or (2) capable of accurate and ready determination by resort to sources whose accuracy cannot reasonably be questioned.

(c) When discretionary.

A court may take judicial notice, whether requested or not.

(d) When mandatory.

A court shall take judicial notice if requested by a party and supplied with the necessary information.

(e) Opportunity to be heard.

A party is entitled upon timely request to an opportunity to be heard as to the propriety of taking judicial notice and the tenor of the matter noticed. In the absence of prior notification, the request may be made after judicial notice has been taken.

(f) Time of taking notice.

Judicial notice may be taken at any stage of the proceeding.

(g) Instructing jury.

In a civil action or proceeding, the court shall instruct the jury to accept as conclusive any fact judicially noticed. In a criminal case, the court shall instruct the jury that it may, but is not required to, accept as conclusive any fact judicially noticed.

## ARTICLE III. PRESUMPTIONS IN CIVIL ACTIONS AND PROCEEDINGS
### Rule 301. Presumptions in General Civil Actions and Proceedings
In all civil actions and proceedings not otherwise provided for by Act of Congress or by these rules, a presumption imposes on the party against whom it is directed the burden of going forward with evidence to rebut or meet the presumption, but does not shift to such party the burden of proof in the sense of the risk of nonpersuasion, which remains throughout the trial upon the party on whom it was originally cast.

### Rule 302. Applicability of State Law in Civil Actions and Proceedings
In civil actions and proceedings, the effect of a presumption respecting a fact which is an element of a claim or defense as to which State law supplies the rule of decision is determined in accordance with State law.

## ARTICLE IV. RELEVANCY AND ITS LIMITS
### Rule 401. Definition of "Relevant Evidence"
"Relevant evidence" means evidence having any tendency to make the existence of any fact that is of consequence to the determination of the action more probable or less probable than it would be without the evidence.

### Rule 402. Relevant Evidence Generally Admissible; Irrelevant Evidence Inadmissible
All relevant evidence is admissible, except as otherwise provided by the Constitution of the United States, by Act of Congress, by these rules, or by other rules prescribed by the Supreme Court pursuant to statutory authority. Evidence which is not relevant is not admissible.

### Rule 403. Exclusion of Relevant Evidence on Grounds of Prejudice, Confusion, or Waste of Time
Although relevant, evidence may be excluded if its probative value is substantially outweighed by the danger of unfair prejudice, confusion of the issues, or misleading the jury, or by considerations of undue delay, waste of time, or needless presentation of cumulative evidence.

### Rule 404. Character Evidence Not Admissible To Prove Conduct; Exceptions; Other Crimes
(a) Character evidence generally

Evidence of a person's character or a trait of character is not admissible for the purpose of proving action in conformity therewith on a particular occasion, except:

(1) Character of accused - Evidence of a pertinent trait of character offered by an accused, or by the prosecution to rebut the same, or if evidence of a trait of character of the alleged victim of the crime is offered by an accused and admitted under Rule 404 (a)(2), evidence of the same trait of character of the accused offered by the prosecution;

(2) Character of alleged victim - Evidence of a pertinent trait of character of the alleged victim of the crime offered by an accused, or by the prosecution to rebut the same, or evidence of a character trait of peacefulness of the alleged victim offered by the prosecution in a homicide case to rebut evidence that the alleged victim was the first aggressor;

(3) Character of witness - Evidence of the character of a witness, as provided in rules 607, 608, and 609.

(b) Other crimes, wrongs, or acts

Evidence of other crimes, wrongs, or acts is not admissible to prove the character of a person in order to show action in conformity therewith. It may, however, be admissible for other purposes, such as proof of motive, opportunity, intent, preparation, plan, knowledge, identity, or absence of mistake or accident, provided that upon request by the accused, the prosecution in a criminal case shall provide reasonable notice in advance of trial, or during trial if the court excuses pretrial notice on good cause shown, of the general nature of any such evidence it intends to introduce at trial.

## Rule 405. Methods of Proving Character

(a) Reputation or opinion.

In all cases in which evidence of character or a trait of character of a person is admissible, proof may be made by testimony as to reputation or by testimony in the form of an opinion. On cross-examination, inquiry is allowable into relevant specific instances of conduct.

(b) Specific instances of conduct.

In cases in which character or a trait of character of a person is an essential element of a charge, claim, or defense, proof may also be made of specific instances of that person's conduct.

## Rule 406. Habit; Routine Practice

Evidence of the habit of a person or of the routine practice of an organization, whether corroborated or not and regardless of the presence of eyewitnesses, is relevant to prove that the conduct of the person or organization on a particular occasion was in conformity with the habit or routine practice.

## Rule 407. Subsequent Remedial Measures

When, after an injury or harm allegedly caused by an event, measures are taken that, if taken previously, would have made the injury or harm less likely to occur, evidence of the subsequent measures is not admissible to prove negligence, culpable conduct, a defect in a product, a defect in a product's design, or a need for a warning or instruction. This rule does not require the exclusion of evidence of subsequent measures when offered for another purpose, such as proving ownership, control, or feasibility of precautionary measures, if controverted, or impeachment.

## Rule 408. Compromise and Offers to Compromise

Evidence of (1) furnishing or offering or promising to furnish, or (2) accepting or offering or promising to accept, a valuable consideration in compromising or attempting to compromise a claim which was disputed as to either validity or amount, is not admissible to prove liability for or invalidity of the claim or its amount. Evidence of conduct or statements made in compromise negotiations is likewise not admissible. This rule does not require the exclusion of any evidence otherwise discoverable merely because it is presented in the course of compromise negotiations. This rule also does not require exclusion when the evidence is offered for another purpose, such as proving bias or prejudice of a witness, negativing a contention of undue delay, or proving an effort to obstruct a criminal investigation or prosecution.

**Rule 409. Payment of Medical and Similar Expenses**

**Rule 410. Inadmissibility of Pleas, Plea Discussions, and Related Statements**

Except as otherwise provided in this rule, evidence of the following is not, in any civil or criminal proceeding, admissible against the defendant who made the plea or was a participant in the plea discussions:

(1) a plea of guilty which was later withdrawn;

(2) a plea of nolo contendere;

(3) any statement made in the course of any proceedings under Rule 11 of the Federal Rules of Criminal Procedure or comparable state procedure regarding either of the foregoing pleas; or

(4) any statement made in the course of plea discussions with an attorney for the prosecuting authority which do not result in a plea of guilty or which result in a plea of guilty later withdrawn.

However, such a statement is admissible (i) in any proceeding wherein another statement made in the course of the same plea or plea discussions has been introduced and the statement ought in fairness be considered contemporaneously with it, or (ii) in a criminal proceeding for perjury or false statement if the statement was made by the defendant under oath, on the record and in the presence of counsel.

**Rule 411. Liability Insurance**

Evidence that a person was or was not insured against liability is not admissible upon the issue whether the person acted negligently or otherwise wrongfully. This rule does not require the exclusion of evidence of insurance against liability when offered for another purpose, such as proof of agency, ownership, or control, or bias or prejudice of a witness.

**Rule 412. Sex Offense Cases; Relevance of Alleged Victim's Past Sexual Behavior or Alleged Sexual Predisposition**

(a) Evidence generally inadmissible.

The following evidence is not admissible in any civil or criminal proceeding involving alleged sexual misconduct except as provided in subdivisions (b) and (c):

(1) Evidence offered to prove that any alleged victim engaged in other sexual behavior.

(2) Evidence offered to prove any alleged victim's sexual predisposition.

(b) Exceptions.

(1) In a criminal case, the following evidence is admissible, if otherwise admissible under these rules:

(A) evidence of specific instances of sexual behavior by the alleged victim offered to prove that a person other than the accused was the source of semen, injury, or other physical evidence;

(B) evidence of specific instances of sexual behavior by the alleged victim with respect to the person accused of the sexual misconduct offered by the accused to prove consent or by the prosecution; and

(C) evidence the exclusion of which would violate the constitutional rights of the defendant.

(2) In a civil case, evidence offered to prove the sexual behavior or sexual predisposition of any alleged victim is admissible if it is otherwise admissible under these rules and its probative value substantially outweighs the danger of harm to any victim and of unfair prejudice to any party. Evidence of an alleged victim's reputation is admissible only if it has been placed in controversy by the alleged victim.

(c) Procedure to determine admissibility.

(1) A party intending to offer evidence under subdivision (b) must --

(A) file a written motion at least 14 days before trial specifically describing the evidence and stating the purpose for which it is offered unless the court, for good cause requires a different time for filing or permits filing during trial; and

(B) serve the motion on all parties and notify the alleged victim or, when appropriate, the alleged victim's guardian or representative.

(2) Before admitting evidence under this rule the court must conduct a hearing in camera and afford the victim and parties a right to attend and be heard. The motion, related papers, and the record of the hearing must be sealed and remain under seal unless the court orders otherwise.

## Rule 413. Evidence of Similar Crimes in Sexual Assault Cases

(a) In a criminal case in which the defendant is accused of an offense of sexual assault, evidence of the defendant's commission of another offense or offenses of sexual assault is admissible, and may be considered for its bearing on any matter to which it is relevant.

(b) In a case in which the Government intends to offer evidence under this rule, the attorney for the Government shall disclose the evidence to the defendant, including statements of witnesses or a summary of the substance of any testimony that is expected to be offered, at least fifteen days before the scheduled date of trial or at such later time as the court may allow for good cause.

(c) This rule shall not be construed to limit the admission or consideration of evidence under any other rule.

(d) For purposes of this rule and Rule 415, "offense of sexual assault" means a crime under Federal law or the law of a State (as defined in section 513 of title 18, United States Code) that involved--

(1) any conduct proscribed by chapter 109A of title 18, United States Code;

(2) contact, without consent, between any part of the defendant's body or an object and the genitals or anus of another person;

(3) contact, without consent, between the genitals or anus of the defendant and any part of another person's body;

(4) deriving sexual pleasure or gratification from the infliction of death, bodily injury, or physical pain on another person; or

(5) an attempt or conspiracy to engage in conduct described in paragraphs (1)-(4).

## Rule 414. Evidence of Similar Crimes in Child Molestation Cases

(a) In a criminal case in which the defendant is accused of an offense of child molestation, evidence of the defendant's commission of another offense or offenses of child molestation is admissible, and may be considered for its bearing on any matter to which it is relevant.

(b) In a case in which the Government intends to offer evidence under this rule, the attorney for the Government shall disclose the evidence to the defendant, including statements of witnesses or a summary of the substance of any testimony that is expected to be offered, at least fifteen days before the scheduled date of trial or at such later time as the court may allow for good cause.

(c) This rule shall not be construed to limit the admission or consideration of evidence under any other rule.

(d) For purposes of this rule and Rule 415, "child" means a person below the age of fourteen, and "offense of child molestation" means a crime under Federal law or the law of a State (as defined in section 513 of title 18, United States Code) that involved--

(1) any conduct proscribed by chapter 109A of title 18, United States Code, that was committed in relation to a child;

(2) any conduct proscribed by chapter 110 of title 18, United States Code;

(3) contact between any part of the defendant's body or an object and the genitals or anus of a child;

(4) contact between the genitals or anus of the defendant and any part of the body of a child;

(5) deriving sexual pleasure or gratification from the infliction of death, bodily injury, or physical pain on a child; or

(6) an attempt or conspiracy to engage in conduct described in paragraphs (1)-(5).

## Rule 415. Evidence of Similar Acts in Civil Cases Concerning Sexual Assault or Child Molestation

(a) In a civil case in which a claim for damages or other relief is predicated on a party's alleged commission of conduct constituting an offense of sexual assault or child molestation, evidence of that party's commission of another offense or offenses of sexual assault or child molestation is admissible and may be considered as provided in Rule 413 and Rule 414 of these rules.

(b) A party who intends to offer evidence under this Rule shall disclose the evidence to the party against whom it will be offered, including statements of witnesses or a summary of the substance of any testimony that is expected to be offered, at least fifteen days before the scheduled date of trial or at such later time as the court may allow for good cause.

(c) This rule shall not be construed to limit the admission or consideration of evidence under any other rule.

## ARTICLE V. PRIVILEGES

### Rule 501. General Rule

Except as otherwise required by the Constitution of the United States or provided by Act of Congress or in rules prescribed by the Supreme Court pursuant to statutory authority, the privilege of a witness, person, government, State, or political subdivision thereof shall be governed by the principles of the common law as they may be interpreted by the courts of the United States in the light of reason and experience. However, in civil actions and proceedings, with respect to an element of a claim or defense as to which State law supplies the rule of decision, the privilege of a witness, person, government, State, or political subdivision thereof shall be determined in accordance with State law.

## ARTICLE VI. WITNESSES

### Rule 601. General Rule of Competency

Every person is competent to be a witness except as otherwise provided in these rules. However, in civil actions and proceedings, with respect to an element of a claim or defense as to which State law supplies the rule of decision, the competency of a witness shall be determined in accordance with State law.

### Rule 602. Lack of Personal Knowledge

A witness may not testify to a matter unless evidence is introduced sufficient to support a finding that the witness has personal knowledge of the matter. Evidence to prove personal knowledge may, but need not, consist of the witness' own testimony. This rule is subject to the provisions of rule 703, relating to opinion testimony by expert witnesses.

### Rule 603. Oath or Affirmation

Before testifying, every witness shall be required to declare that the witness will testify truthfully, by oath or affirmation administered in a form calculated to awaken the witness' conscience and impress the witness' mind with the duty to do so.

### Rule 604. Interpreters

An interpreter is subject to the provisions of these rules relating to qualification as an expert and the administration of an oath or affirmation to make a true translation.

### Rule 605. Competency of Judge as Witness

The judge presiding at the trial may not testify in that trial as a witness. No objection need be made in order to preserve the point.

### Rule 606. Competency of Juror as Witness

(a) At the trial.

A member of the jury may not testify as a witness before that jury in the trial of the case in which the juror is sitting. If the juror is called so to testify, the opposing party shall be afforded an opportunity to object out of the presence of the jury.

(b) Inquiry into validity of verdict or indictment.

Upon an inquiry into the validity of a verdict or indictment, a juror may not testify as to any matter or statement occurring during the course of the jury's deliberations or to the effect of anything upon that or any other juror's mind or emotions as influencing the juror to assent to or dissent from the verdict or indictment or concerning the juror's mental processes in connection therewith, except that a juror may testify on the question whether extraneous prejudicial information was improperly brought to the jury's attention or whether any outside influence was improperly brought to bear upon any juror. Nor may a juror's affidavit or evidence of any statement by the juror concerning a matter about which the juror would be precluded from testifying be received for these purposes.

## Rule 607. Who May Impeach

The credibility of a witness may be attacked by any party, including the party calling the witness.

## Rule 608. Evidence of Character and Conduct of Witness

(a) Opinion and reputation evidence of character.

The credibility of a witness may be attacked or supported by evidence in the form of opinion or reputation, but subject to these limitations: (1) the evidence may refer only to character for truthfulness or untruthfulness, and (2) evidence of truthful character is admissible only after the character of the witness for truthfulness has been attacked by opinion or reputation evidence or otherwise.

(b) Specific instances of conduct.

Specific instances of the conduct of a witness, for the purpose of attacking or supporting the witness' character for truthfulness, other than conviction of crime as provided in rule 609, may not be proved by extrinsic evidence. They may, however, in the discretion of the court, if probative of truthfulness or untruthfulness, be inquired into on cross-examination of the witness (1) concerning the witness' character for truthfulness or untruthfulness, or (2) concerning the character for truthfulness or untruthfulness of another witness as to which character the witness being cross-examined has testified. The giving of testimony, whether by an accused or by any other witness, does not operate as a waiver of the accused's or the witness' privilege against self-incrimination when examined with respect to matters that relate only to character for truthfulness.

## Rule 609. Impeachment by Evidence of Conviction of Crime

(a) General rule.

For the purpose of attacking the credibility of a witness,

(1) evidence that a witness other than an accused has been convicted of a crime shall be admitted, subject to Rule 403, if the crime was punishable by death or imprisonment in excess of one year under the law under which the witness was convicted, and evidence that an accused has been convicted of such a crime shall be admitted if the court determines that the probative value of admitting this evidence outweighs its prejudicial effect to the accused; and

(2) evidence that any witness has been convicted of a crime shall be admitted if it involved dishonesty or false statement, regardless of the punishment.

(b) Time limit.

Evidence of a conviction under this rule is not admissible if a period of more than ten years has elapsed since the date of the conviction or of the release of the witness from the confinement imposed for that conviction, whichever is the later date, unless the court determines, in the interests of justice, that the probative value of the conviction supported by specific facts and circumstances substantially outweighs its prejudicial effect. However, evidence of a conviction more than 10 years old as calculated herein, is not admissible unless the proponent gives to the adverse party sufficient advance written notice of intent to use such evidence to provide the adverse party with a fair opportunity to contest the use of such evidence.

(c) Effect of pardon, annulment, or certificate of rehabilitation.

Evidence of a conviction is not admissible under this rule if (1) the conviction has been the subject of a pardon, annulment, certificate of rehabilitation, or other equivalent procedure based on a finding of the rehabilitation of the person convicted, and that person has not been convicted of a subsequent crime which was punishable by death or imprisonment in excess of one year, or (2) the conviction has been the subject of a pardon, annulment, or other equivalent procedure based on a finding of innocence.

(d) Juvenile adjudications.

Evidence of juvenile adjudications is generally not admissible under this rule. The court may, however, in a criminal case allow evidence of a juvenile adjudication of a witness other than the accused if conviction of the offense would be admissible to attack the credibility of an adult and the court is satisfied that admission in evidence is necessary for a fair determination of the issue of guilt or innocence.

(e) Pendency of appeal.

The pendency of an appeal therefrom does not render evidence of a conviction inadmissible. Evidence of the pendency of an appeal is admissible.

## Rule 610. Religious Beliefs or Opinions

Evidence of the beliefs or opinions of a witness on matters of religion is not admissible for the purpose of showing that by reason of their nature the witness' credibility is impaired or enhanced.

## Rule 611. Mode and Order of Interrogation and Presentation

(a) Control by court.

The court shall exercise reasonable control over the mode and order of interrogating witnesses and presenting evidence so as to (1) make the interrogation and presentation effective for the ascertainment of the truth, (2) avoid needless consumption of time, and (3) protect witnesses from harassment or undue embarrassment.

(b) Scope of cross-examination.

Cross-examination should be limited to the subject matter of the direct examination and matters affecting the credibility of the witness. The court may, in the exercise of discretion, permit inquiry into additional matters as if on direct examination.

(c) Leading questions.

Leading questions should not be used on the direct examination of a witness except as may be necessary to develop the witness' testimony. Ordinarily leading questions should be permitted on cross-examination. When a party calls a hostile witness, an adverse party, or a witness identified with an adverse party, interrogation may be by leading questions.

## Rule 612. Writing Used to Refresh Memory

Except as otherwise provided in criminal proceedings by section 3500 of title 18, United States Code, if a witness uses a writing to refresh memory for the purpose of testifying, either--

(1) while testifying, or

(2) before testifying, if the court in its discretion determines it is necessary in the interests of justice, an adverse party is entitled to have the writing produced at the hearing, to inspect it, to cross-examine the witness thereon, and to introduce in evidence those portions which relate to the testimony of the witness. If it is claimed that the writing contains matters not related to the subject matter of the testimony the court shall examine the writing in camera, excise any portions not so related, and order delivery of the remainder to the party entitled thereto. Any portion withheld over objections shall be preserved and made available to the appellate court in the event of an appeal. If a writing is not produced or delivered pursuant to order under this rule, the court shall make any order justice requires, except that in criminal cases when the prosecution elects not to comply, the order shall be one striking the testimony or, if the court in its discretion determines that the interests of justice so require, declaring a mistrial.

## Rule 613. Prior Statements of Witnesses

(a) Examining witness concerning prior statement.

In examining a witness concerning a prior statement made by the witness, whether written or not, the statement need not be shown nor its contents disclosed to the witness at that time, but on request the same shall be shown or disclosed to opposing counsel.

(b) Extrinsic evidence of prior inconsistent statement of witness.

Extrinsic evidence of a prior inconsistent statement by a witness is not admissible unless the witness is afforded an opportunity to explain or deny the same and the opposite party is afforded an opportunity to interrogate the witness thereon, or the interests of justice otherwise require. This provision does not apply to admissions of a party-opponent as defined in rule 801(d)(2).

## Rule 614. Calling and Interrogation of Witnesses by Court

(a) Calling by court.

The court may, on its own motion or at the suggestion of a party, call witnesses, and all parties are entitled to cross-examine witnesses thus called.

(b) Interrogation by court.

The court may interrogate witnesses, whether called by itself or by a party.

(c) Objections.

Objections to the calling of witnesses by the court or to interrogation by it may be made at the time or at the next available opportunity when the jury is not present.

## Rule 615. Exclusion of Witnesses

At the request of a party the court shall order witnesses excluded so that they cannot hear the testimony of other witnesses, and it may make the order of its own motion. This rule does not authorize exclusion of (1) a party who is a natural person, or (2) an officer or employee of a party which is not a natural person designated as its representative by its attorney, or (3) a person whose presence is shown by a party to be essential to the presentation of the party's cause, or (4) a person authorized by statute to be present.

## ARTICLE VII. OPINIONS AND EXPERT TESTIMONY

## Rule 701. Opinion Testimony by Lay Witnesses

If the witness is not testifying as an expert, the witness' testimony in the form of opinions or inferences is limited to those opinions or inferences which are (a) rationally based on the perception of the witness, and (b) helpful to a clear understanding of the witness' testimony or the determination of a fact in issue, and (c) not based on scientific, technical, or other specialized knowledge within the scope of Rule 702.

## Rule 702. Testimony by Experts

If scientific, technical, or other specialized knowledge will assist the trier of fact to understand the evidence or to determine a fact in issue, a witness qualified as an expert by knowledge, skill, experience, training, or education, may testify thereto in the form of an opinion or otherwise, if (1) the testimony is based upon sufficient facts or data, (2) the testimony is the product of reliable principles and methods, and (3) the witness has applied the principles and methods reliably to the facts of the case.

## Rule 703. Bases of Opinion Testimony by Experts

The facts or data in the particular case upon which an expert bases an opinion or inference may be those perceived by or made known to the expert at or before the hearing. If of a type reasonably relied upon by experts in the particular field in forming opinions or inferences upon the subject, the facts or data need not be admissible in evidence in order for the opinion or inference to be admitted. Facts or data that are otherwise inadmissible shall not be disclosed to the jury by the proponent of the opinion or inference unless the court determines that their probative value in assisting the jury to evaluate the expert's opinion substantially outweighs their prejudicial effect.

## Rule 704. Opinion on Ultimate Issue

(a) Except as provided in subdivision (b), testimony in the form of an opinion or inference otherwise admissible is not objectionable because it embraces an ultimate issue to be decided by the trier of fact.

(b) No expert witness testifying with respect to the mental state or condition of a defendant in a criminal case may state an opinion or inference as to whether the defendant did or did not have the mental state or condition constituting an element of the crime charged or of a defense thereto. Such ultimate issues are matters for the trier of fact alone.

**Rule 705. Disclosure of Facts or Data Underlying Expert Opinion**

The expert may testify in terms of opinion or inference and give reasons therefor without first testifying to the underlying facts or data, unless the court requires otherwise. The expert may in any event be required to disclose the underlying facts or data on cross-examination.

**Rule 706. Court Appointed Experts**

(a) Appointment.

The court may on its own motion or on the motion of any party enter an order to show cause why expert witnesses should not be appointed, and may request the parties to submit nominations. The court may appoint any expert witnesses agreed upon by the parties, and may appoint expert witnesses of its own selection. An expert witness shall not be appointed by the court unless the witness consents to act. A witness so appointed shall be informed of the witness' duties by the court in writing, a copy of which shall be filed with the clerk, or at a conference in which the parties shall have opportunity to participate. A witness so appointed shall advise the parties of the witness' findings, if any; the witness' deposition may be taken by any party; and the witness may be called to testify by the court or any party. The witness shall be subject to cross-examination by each party, including a party calling the witness.

(b) Compensation.

Expert witnesses so appointed are entitled to reasonable compensation in whatever sum the court may allow. The compensation thus fixed is payable from funds which may be provided by law in criminal cases and civil actions and proceedings involving just compensation under the fifth amendment. In other civil actions and proceedings the compensation shall be paid by the parties in such proportion and at such time as the court directs, and thereafter charged in like manner as other costs.

(c) Disclosure of appointment.

In the exercise of its discretion, the court may authorize disclosure to the jury of the fact that the court appointed the expert witness.

(d) Parties' experts of own selection.

Nothing in this rule limits the parties in calling expert witnesses of their own selection.

**ARTICLE VIII. HEARSAY**

**Rule 801. Definitions**

The following definitions apply under this article:

(a) Statement.

A "statement" is (1) an oral or written assertion or (2) nonverbal conduct of a person, if it is intended by the person as an assertion.

(b) Declarant.

A "declarant" is a person who makes a statement.

(c) Hearsay.

"Hearsay" is a statement, other than one made by the declarant while testifying at the trial or hearing, offered in evidence to prove the truth of the matter asserted.

(d) Statements which are not hearsay.

A statement is not hearsay if--

(1) Prior statement by witness. The declarant testifies at the trial or hearing and is subject to cross-examination concerning the statement, and the statement is (A) inconsistent with the declarant's testimony, and was given under oath subject to the penalty of perjury at a trial, hearing, or other proceeding, or in a deposition, or (B) consistent with the declarant's testimony and is offered to rebut an express or implied charge against the declarant of recent fabrication or improper influence or motive, or (C) one of identification of a person made after perceiving the person; or

(2) Admission by party-opponent. The statement is offered against a party and is

(A) the party's own statement, in either an individual or a representative capacity or

(B) a statement of which the party has manifested an adoption or belief in its truth, or

(C) a statement by a person authorized by the party to make a statement concerning the subject, or
(D) a statement by the party's agent or servant concerning a matter within the scope of the agency or employment, made during the existence of the relationship, or
(E) a statement by a coconspirator of a party during the course and in furtherance of the conspiracy. The contents of the statement shall be considered but are not alone sufficient to establish the declarant's authority under subdivision (C), the agency or employment relationship and scope thereof under subdivision (D), or the existence of the conspiracy and the participation therein of the declarant and the party against whom the statement is offered under subdivision (E).

## Rule 802. Hearsay Rule

Hearsay is not admissible except as provided by these rules or by other rules prescribed by the Supreme Court pursuant to statutory authority or by Act of Congress.

## Rule 803. Hearsay Exceptions; Availability of Declarant Immaterial

The following are not excluded by the hearsay rule, even though the declarant is available as a witness:

(1) Present sense impression. A statement describing or explaining an event or condition made while the declarant was perceiving the event or condition, or immediately thereafter.

(2) Excited utterance. A statement relating to a startling event or condition made while the declarant was under the stress of excitement caused by the event or condition.

(3) Then existing mental, emotional, or physical condition. A statement of the declarant's then existing state of mind, emotion, sensation, or physical condition (such as intent, plan, motive, design, mental feeling, pain, and bodily health), but not including a statement of memory or belief to prove the fact remembered or believed unless it relates to the execution, revocation, identification, or terms of declarant's will.

(4) Statements for purposes of medical diagnosis or treatment. Statements made for purposes of medical diagnosis or treatment and describing medical history, or past or present symptoms, pain, or sensations, or the inception or general character of the cause or external source thereof insofar as reasonably pertinent to diagnosis or treatment.

(5) Recorded recollection. A memorandum or record concerning a matter about which a witness once had knowledge but now has insufficient recollection to enable the witness to testify fully and accurately, shown to have been made or adopted by the witness when the matter was fresh in the witness' memory and to reflect that knowledge correctly. If admitted, the memorandum or record may be read into evidence but may not itself be received as an exhibit unless offered by an adverse party.

(6) Records of regularly conducted activity. A memorandum, report, record, or data compilation, in any form, of acts, events, conditions, opinions, or diagnoses, made at or near the time by, or from information transmitted by, a person with knowledge, if kept in the course of a regularly conducted business activity, and if it was the regular practice of that business activity to make the memorandum, report, record or data compilation, all as shown by the testimony of the custodian or other qualified witness, or by certification that complies with Rule 902(11), Rule 902(12), or a statute permitting certification, unless the source of information or the method or circumstances of preparation indicate lack of trustworthiness. The term "business" as used in this paragraph includes business, institution, association, profession, occupation, and calling of every kind, whether or not conducted for profit.

(7) Absence of entry in records kept in accordance with the provisions of paragraph (6). Evidence that a matter is not included in the memoranda reports, records, or data compilations, in any form, kept in accordance with the provisions of paragraph (6), to prove the nonoccurrence or nonexistence of the matter, if the matter was of a kind of which a memorandum, report, record, or data compilation was regularly made and preserved, unless the sources of information or other circumstances indicate lack of trustworthiness.

(8) Public records and reports. Records, reports, statements, or data compilations, in any form, of public offices or agencies, setting forth (A) the activities of the office or agency, or (B) matters

observed pursuant to duty imposed by law as to which matters there was a duty to report, excluding, however, in criminal cases matters observed by police officers and other law enforcement personnel, or (C) in civil actions and proceedings and against the Government in criminal cases, factual findings resulting from an investigation made pursuant to authority granted by law, unless the sources of information or other circumstances indicate lack of trustworthiness.

(9) Records of vital statistics. Records or data compilations, in any form, of births, fetal deaths, deaths, or marriages, if the report thereof was made to a public office pursuant to requirements of law.

(10) Absence of public record or entry. To prove the absence of a record, report, statement, or data compilation, in any form, or the nonoccurrence or nonexistence of a matter of which a record, report, statement, or data compilation, in any form, was regularly made and preserved by a public office or agency, evidence in the form of a certification in accordance with rule 902, or testimony, that diligent search failed to disclose the record, report, statement, or data compilation, or entry.

(11) Records of religious organizations. Statements of births, marriages, divorces, deaths, legitimacy, ancestry, relationship by blood or marriage, or other similar facts of personal or family history, contained in a regularly kept record of a religious organization.

(12) Marriage, baptismal, and similar certificates. Statements of fact contained in a certificate that the maker performed a marriage or other ceremony or administered a sacrament, made by a clergyman, public official, or other person authorized by the rules or practices of a religious organization or by law to perform the act certified, and purporting to have been issued at the time of the act or within a reasonable time thereafter.

(13) Family records. Statements of fact concerning personal or family history contained in family Bibles, genealogies, charts, engravings on rings, inscriptions on family portraits, engravings on urns, crypts, or tombstones, or the like.

(14) Records of documents affecting an interest in property. The record of a document purporting to establish or affect an interest in property, as proof of the content of the original recorded document and its execution and delivery by each person by whom it purports to have been executed, if the record is a record of a public office and an applicable statute authorizes the recording of documents of that kind in that office.

(15) Statements in documents affecting an interest in property. A statement contained in a document purporting to establish or affect an interest in property if the matter stated was relevant to the purpose of the document, unless dealings with the property since the document was made have been inconsistent with the truth of the statement or the purport of the document.

(16) Statements in ancient documents. Statements in a document in existence twenty years or more the authenticity of which is established.

(17) Market reports, commercial publications. Market quotations, tabulations, lists, directories, or other published compilations, generally used and relied upon by the public or by persons in particular occupations.

(18) Learned treatises. To the extent called to the attention of an expert witness upon cross-examination or relied upon by the expert witness in direct examination, statements contained in published treatises, periodicals, or pamphlets on a subject of history, medicine, or other science or art, established as a reliable authority by the testimony or admission of the witness or by other expert testimony or by judicial notice. If admitted, the statements may be read into evidence but may not be received as exhibits.

(19) Reputation concerning personal or family history. Reputation among members of a person's family by blood, adoption, or marriage, or among a person's associates, or in the community, concerning a person's birth, adoption, marriage, divorce, death, legitimacy, relationship by blood, adoption, or marriage, ancestry, or other similar fact of personal or family history.

(20) Reputation concerning boundaries or general history. Reputation in a community, arising before the controversy, as to boundaries of or customs affecting lands in the community, and reputation as to events of general history important to the community or State or nation in which located.

(21) Reputation as to character. Reputation of a person's character among associates or in the community.

(22) Judgment of previous conviction. Evidence of a final judgment, entered after a trial or upon a plea of guilty (but not upon a plea of nolo contendere), adjudging a person guilty of a crime punishable by death or imprisonment in excess of one year, to prove any fact essential to sustain the judgment, but not including, when offered by the Government in a criminal prosecution for purposes other than impeachment, judgments against persons other than the accused. The pendency of an appeal may be shown but does not affect admissibility.

(23) Judgment as to personal, family or general history, or boundaries. Judgments as proof of matters of personal, family or general history, or boundaries, essential to the judgment, if the same would be provable by evidence of reputation.

## Rule 804. Hearsay Exceptions; Declarant Unavailable

(a) Definition of unavailability.

"Unavailability as a witness" includes situations in which the declarant--

(1) is exempted by ruling of the court on the ground of privilege from testifying concerning the subject matter of the declarant's statement; or

(2) persists in refusing to testify concerning the subject matter of the declarant's statement despite an order of the court to do so; or

(3) testifies to a lack of memory of the subject matter of the declarant's statement; or

(4) is unable to be present or to testify at the hearing because of death or then existing physical or mental illness or infirmity; or

(5) is absent from the hearing and the proponent of a statement has been unable to procure the declarant's attendance (or in the case of a hearsay exception under subdivision (b)(2), (3), or (4), the declarant's attendance or testimony) by process or other reasonable means.

A declarant is not unavailable as a witness if exemption, refusal, claim of lack of memory, inability, or absence is due to the procurement or wrongdoing of the proponent of a statement for the purpose of preventing the witness from attending or testifying.

(b) Hearsay exceptions.

The following are not excluded by the hearsay rule if the declarant is unavailable as a witness:

(1) Former testimony. Testimony given as a witness at another hearing of the same or a different proceeding, or in a deposition taken in compliance with law in the course of the same or another proceeding, if the party against whom the testimony is now offered, or, in a civil action or proceeding, a predecessor in interest, had an opportunity and similar motive to develop the testimony by direct, cross, or redirect examination.

(2) Statement under belief of impending death. In a prosecution for homicide or in a civil action or proceeding, a statement made by a declarant while believing that the declarant's death was imminent, concerning the cause or circumstances of what the declarant believed to be impending death.

(3) Statement against interest. A statement which was at the time of its making so far contrary to the declarant's pecuniary or proprietary interest, or so far tended to subject the declarant to civil or criminal liability, or to render invalid a claim by the declarant against another, that a reasonable person in the declarant's position would not have made the statement unless believing it to be true. A statement tending to expose the declarant to criminal liability and offered to exculpate the accused is not admissible unless corroborating circumstances clearly indicate the trustworthiness of the statement.

(4) Statement of personal or family history. (A) A statement concerning the declarant's own birth, adoption, marriage, divorce, legitimacy, relationship by blood, adoption, or marriage, ancestry, or other

similar fact of personal or family history, even though declarant had no means of acquiring personal knowledge of the matter stated; or (B) a statement concerning the foregoing matters, and death also, of another person, if the declarant was related to the other by blood, adoption, or marriage or was so intimately associated with the other's family as to be likely to have accurate information concerning the matter declared.

(5) [Other exceptions.][Transferred to Rule 807]

(6) Forfeiture by wrongdoing. A statement offered against a party that has engaged or acquiesced in wrongdoing that was intended to, and did, procure the unavailability of the declarant as a witness.

## Rule 805. Hearsay Within Hearsay

Hearsay included within hearsay is not excluded under the hearsay rule if each part of the combined statements conforms with an exception to the hearsay rule provided in these rules.

## Rule 806. Attacking and Supporting Credibility of Declarant

When a hearsay statement, or a statement defined in Rule 801(d)(2)(C), (D), or (E), has been admitted in evidence, the credibility of the declarant may be attacked, and if attacked may be supported, by any evidence which would be admissible for those purposes if declarant had testified as a witness. Evidence of a statement or conduct by the declarant at any time, inconsistent with the declarant's hearsay statement, is not subject to any requirement that the declarant may have been afforded an opportunity to deny or explain. If the party against whom a hearsay statement has been admitted calls the declarant as a witness, the party is entitled to examine the declarant on the statement as if under cross-examination.

## Rule 807. Residual Exception

A statement not specifically covered by Rule 803 or 804 but having equivalent circumstantial guarantees of trustworthiness, is not excluded by the hearsay rule, if the court determines that (A) the statement is offered as evidence of a material fact; (B) the statement is more probative on the point for which it is offered than any other evidence which the proponent can procure through reasonable efforts; and (C) the general purposes of these rules and the interests of justice will best be served by admission of the statement into evidence. However, a statement may not be admitted under this exception unless the proponent of it makes known to the adverse party sufficiently in advance of the trial or hearing to provide the adverse party with a fair opportunity to prepare to meet it, the proponent's intention to offer the statement and the particulars of it, including the name and address of the declarant.

## ARTICLE IX. AUTHENTICATION AND IDENTIFICATION

## Rule 901. Requirement of Authentication or Identification

(a) General provision.

The requirement of authentication or identification as a condition precedent to admissibility is satisfied by evidence sufficient to support a finding that the matter in question is what its proponent claims.

(b) Illustrations.

By way of illustration only, and not by way of limitation, the following are examples of authentication or identification conforming with the requirements of this rule:

(1) Testimony of witness with knowledge. Testimony that a matter is what it is claimed to be.

(2) Nonexpert opinion on handwriting. Nonexpert opinion as to the genuineness of handwriting, based upon familiarity not acquired for purposes of the litigation.

(3) Comparison by trier or expert witness. Comparison by the trier of fact or by expert witnesses with specimens which have been authenticated.

(4) Distinctive characteristics and the like. Appearance, contents, substance, internal patterns, or other distinctive characteristics, taken in conjunction with circumstances.

(5) Voice identification. Identification of a voice, whether heard firsthand or through mechanical or electronic transmission or recording, by opinion based upon hearing the voice at any time under circumstances connecting it with the alleged speaker.

(6) Telephone conversations. Telephone conversations, by evidence that a call was made to the number assigned at the time by the telephone company to a particular person or business, if (A) in the case of a person, circumstances, including self-identification, show the person answering to be the one called, or (B) in the case of a business, the call was made to a place of business and the conversation related to business reasonably transacted over the telephone.

(7) Public records or reports. Evidence that a writing authorized by law to be recorded or filed and in fact recorded or filed in a public office, or a purported public record, report, statement, or data compilation, in any form, is from the public office where items of this nature are kept.

(8) Ancient documents or data compilation. Evidence that a document or data compilation, in any form, (A) is in such condition as to create no suspicion concerning its authenticity, (B) was in a place where it, if authentic, would likely be, and (C) has been in existence 20 years or more at the time it is offered.

(9) Process or system. Evidence describing a process or system used to produce a result and showing that the process or system produces an accurate result.

(10) Methods provided by statute or rule. Any method of authentication or identification provided by Act of Congress or by other rules prescribed by the Supreme Court pursuant to statutory authority.

## Rule 902. Self-authentication

Extrinsic evidence of authenticity as a condition precedent to admissibility is not required with respect to the following:

(1) Domestic public documents under seal. A document bearing a seal purporting to be that of the United States, or of any State, district, Commonwealth, territory, or insular possession thereof, or the Panama Canal Zone, or the Trust Territory of the Pacific Islands, or of a political subdivision, department, officer, or agency thereof, and a signature purporting to be an attestation or execution.

(2) Domestic public documents not under seal. A document purporting to bear the signature in the official capacity of an officer or employee of any entity included in paragraph (1) hereof, having no seal, if a public officer having a seal and having official duties in the district or political subdivision of the officer or employee certifies under seal that the signer has the official capacity and that the signature is genuine.

(3) Foreign public documents. A document purporting to be executed or attested in an official capacity by a person authorized by the laws of a foreign country to make the execution or attestation, and accompanied by a final certification as to the genuineness of the signature and official position (A) of the executing or attesting person, or (B) of any foreign official whose certificate of genuineness of signature and official position relates to the execution or attestation or is in a chain of certificates of genuineness of signature and official position relating to the execution or attestation. A final certification may be made by a secretary of an embassy or legation, consul general, consul, vice consul, or consular agent of the United States, or a diplomatic or consular official of the foreign country assigned or accredited to the United States. If reasonable opportunity has been given to all parties to investigate the authenticity and accuracy of official documents, the court may, for good cause shown, order that they be treated as presumptively authentic without final certification or permit them to be evidenced by an attested summary with or without final certification.

(4) Certified copies of public records. A copy of an official record or report or entry therein, or of a document authorized by law to be recorded or filed and actually recorded or filed in a public office, including data compilations in any form, certified as correct by the custodian or other person authorized to make the certification, by certificate complying with paragraph (1), (2), or (3) of this rule or complying with any Act of Congress or rule prescribed by the Supreme Court pursuant to statutory authority.

(5) Official publications. Books, pamphlets, or other publications purporting to be issued by public authority.

(6) Newspapers and periodicals. Printed materials purporting to be newspapers or periodicals.

(7) Trade inscriptions and the like. Inscriptions, signs, tags, or labels purporting to have been affixed in the course of business and indicating ownership, control, or origin.

(8) Acknowledged documents. Documents accompanied by a certificate of acknowledgment executed in the manner provided by law by a notary public or other officer authorized by law to take acknowledgments.

(9) Commercial paper and related documents. Commercial paper, signatures thereon, and documents relating thereto to the extent provided by general commercial law.

(10) Presumptions under Acts of Congress. Any signature, document, or other matter declared by Act of Congress to be presumptively or prima facie genuine or authentic.

(11) Certified domestic records of regularly conducted activity. The original or a duplicate of a domestic record of regularly conducted activity that would be admissible under Rule 803(6) if accompanied by a written declaration of its custodian or other qualified person, in a manner complying with any Act of Congress or rule prescribed by the Supreme Court pursuant to statutory authority, certifying that the record:

(A) was made at or near the time of the occurrence of the matters set forth by, or from information transmitted by, a person with knowledge of those matters;

(B) was kept in the course of the regularly conducted activity; and

(C) was made by the regularly conducted activity as a regular practice.

A party intending to offer a record into evidence under this paragraph must provide written notice of that intention to all adverse parties, and must make the record and declaration available for inspection sufficiently in advance of their offer into evidence to provide an adverse party with a fair opportunity to challenge them.

(12) Certified foreign records of regularly conducted activity. In a civil case, the original or a duplicate of a foreign record of regularly conducted activity that would be admissible under Rule 803(6) if accompanied by a written declaration by its custodian or other qualified person certifying that the record:

(A) was made at or near the time of the occurrence of the matters set forth by, or from information transmitted by, a person with knowledge of those matters;

(B) was kept in the course of the regularly conducted activity; and

(C) was made by the regularly conducted activity as a regular practice.

The declaration must be signed in a manner that, if falsely made, would subject the maker to criminal penalty under the laws of the country where the declaration is signed. A party intending to offer a record into evidence under this paragraph must provide written notice of that intention to all adverse parties, and must make the record and declaration available for inspection sufficiently in advance of their offer into evidence to provide an adverse party with a fair opportunity to challenge them.

## Rule 903. Subscribing Witness' Testimony Unnecessary

The testimony of a subscribing witness is not necessary to authenticate a writing unless required by the laws of the jurisdiction whose laws govern the validity of the writing.

## ARTICLE X. CONTENTS OF WRITINGS, RECORDINGS, AND PHOTOGRAPHS

## Rule 1001. Definitions

For purposes of this article the following definitions are applicable:

(1) Writings and recordings. "Writings" and "recordings" consist of letters, words, or numbers, or their equivalent, set down by handwriting, typewriting, printing, photostating, photographing, magnetic impulse, mechanical or electronic recording, or other form of data compilation.

(2) Photographs. "Photographs" include still photographs, X-ray films, video tapes, and motion pictures.

(3) Original. An "original" of a writing or recording is the writing or recording itself or any counterpart intended to have the same effect by a person executing or issuing it. An "original" of a photograph

includes the negative or any print therefrom. If data are stored in a computer or similar device, any printout or other output readable by sight, shown to reflect the data accurately, is an "original".

(4) Duplicate. A "duplicate" is a counterpart produced by the same impression as the original, or from the same matrix, or by means of photography, including enlargements and miniatures, or by mechanical or electronic re-recording, or by chemical reproduction, or by other equivalent techniques which accurately reproduces the original.

## Rule 1002. Requirement of Original

To prove the content of a writing, recording, or photograph, the original writing, recording, or photograph is required, except as otherwise provided in these rules or by Act of Congress.

## Rule 1003. Admissibility of Duplicates

A duplicate is admissible to the same extent as an original unless (1) a genuine question is raised as to the authenticity of the original or (2) in the circumstances it would be unfair to admit the duplicate in lieu of the original.

## Rule 1004. Admissibility of Other Evidence of Contents

The original is not required, and other evidence of the contents of a writing, recording, or photograph is admissible if--

(1) Originals lost or destroyed. All originals are lost or have been destroyed, unless the proponent lost or destroyed them in bad faith; or

(2) Original not obtainable. No original can be obtained by any available judicial process or procedure; or

(3) Original in possession of opponent. At a time when an original was under the control of the party against whom offered, that party was put on notice, by the pleadings or otherwise, that the contents would be a subject of proof at the hearing, and that party does not produce the original at the hearing; or

(4) Collateral matters. The writing, recording, or photograph is not closely related to a controlling issue.

## Rule 1005. Public Records

The contents of an official record, or of a document authorized to be recorded or filed and actually recorded or filed, including data compilations in any form, if otherwise admissible, may be proved by copy, certified as correct in accordance with rule 902 or testified to be correct by a witness who has compared it with the original. If a copy which complies with the foregoing cannot be obtained by the exercise of reasonable diligence, then other evidence of the contents may be given.

## Rule 1006. Summaries

The contents of voluminous writings, recordings, or photographs which cannot conveniently be examined in court may be presented in the form of a chart, summary, or calculation. The originals, or duplicates, shall be made available for examination or copying, or both, by other parties at reasonable time and place. The court may order that they be produced in court.

## Rule 1007. Testimony or Written Admission of Party

Contents of writings, recordings, or photographs may be proved by the testimony or deposition of the party against whom offered or by that party's written admission, without accounting for the nonproduction of the original.

## Rule 1008. Functions of Court and Jury

When the admissibility of other evidence of contents of writings, recordings, or photographs under these rules depends upon the fulfillment of a condition of fact, the question whether the condition has been fulfilled is ordinarily for the court to determine in accordance with the provisions of rule 104. However, when an issue is raised (a) whether the asserted writing ever existed, or (b) whether another writing, recording, or photograph produced at the trial is the original, or (c) whether other evidence of contents correctly reflects the contents, the issue is for the trier of fact to determine as in the case of other issues of fact.

## ARTICLE XI: MISCELLANEOUS RULES
### Rule 1101. Applicability of Rules

(a) Courts and judges.

These rules apply to the United States district courts, the District Court of Guam, the District Court of the Virgin Islands, the District Court for the Northern Mariana Islands, the United States courts of appeals, the United States Claims Court, and to the United States bankruptcy judges and United States magistrate judges, in the actions, cases, and proceedings and to the extent hereinafter set forth. The terms "judge" and "court" in these rules include United States bankruptcy judges and United States magistrate judges.

(b) Proceedings generally.

These rules apply generally to civil actions and proceedings, including admiralty and maritime cases, to criminal cases and proceedings, to contempt proceedings except those in which the court may act summarily, and to proceedings and cases under title 11, United States Code.

(c) Rule of privilege.

The rule with respect to privileges applies at all stages of all actions, cases, and proceedings.

(d) Rules inapplicable.

The rules (other than with respect to privileges) do not apply in the following situations:

(1) Preliminary questions of fact. The determination of questions of fact preliminary to admissibility of evidence when the issue is to be determined by the court under rule 104.

(2) Grand jury. Proceedings before grand juries.

(3) Miscellaneous proceedings. Proceedings for extradition or rendition; preliminary examinations in criminal cases; sentencing, or granting or revoking probation; issuance of warrants for arrest, criminal summonses, and search warrants; and proceedings with respect to release on bail or otherwise.

(e) Rules applicable in part.

In the following proceedings these rules apply to the extent that matters of evidence are not provided for in the statutes which govern procedure therein or in other rules prescribed by the Supreme Court pursuant to statutory authority: the trial of misdemeanors and other petty offenses before United States magistrate judge; review of agency actions when the facts are subject to trail de novo under section 706(2)(F) of title 5, United States Code; review of orders of the Secretary of Agriculture under section 2 of the Act entitled "An Act to authorize association of producers of agricultural products" approved February 18, 1922 (7 U.S.C. 292), and under section 6 and 7(c) of the Perishable Agricultural Commodities Act, 1930 (7 U.S.C. 499f, 499g(c)); naturalization and revocation of naturalization under sections 310 - 318 of the Immigration and Nationality Act (8 U.S.C. 1421 - 1429); prize proceedings in admiralty under sections 7651 - 7681 of title 10, United States Code; review of orders of the Secretary of the Interior under section 2 of the Act entitled "An Act authorizing associations of producers of aquatic products" approved June 25, 1934 (15 U.S.C. 522); review of orders of petroleum control boards under section 5 of the Act entitled "An act to regulate interstate and foreign commerce in petroleum and its products by prohibiting the shipment in such commerce of petroleum and its products produced in violation of State law, and for other purposes", approved February 22, 1935 (15 U.S.C. 715d); actions for fines, penalties, or forfeitures under part V of title IV of the Tariff Act of 1930 (19 U.S.C. 1581 - 1624), or under the Anti-Smuggling Act (19 U.S.C. 1701 - 1711); criminal libel for condemnation, exclusion of imports, or other proceedings under the Federal Food, Drug, and Cosmetic Act (21 U.S.C. 301 - 392); disputes between seamen under sections 4079, 4080, and 4081 of the Revised Statutes (22 U.S.C. 256 - 258); habeas corpus under sections 2241 - 2254 of title 28, United States Code; motions to vacate, set aside or correct sentence under section 2255 of title 28, United States Code; actions for penalties for refusal to transport destitute seamen under section 4578 of the

Revised Statutes (46 U.S.C. 679); actions against the United States under the Act entitled "An Act authorizing suits against the United States in admiralty for damage caused by and salvage service rendered to public vessels belonging to the United States, and for other purposes", approved March 3, 1925 (46 U.S.C. 781 - 790), as implemented by section 7730 of title 10, United States Code.

**Rule 1102. Amendments**

Amendments to the Federal Rules of Evidence may be made as provided in section 2072 of title 28 of the United States Code.

**Rule 1103. Title**

These rules may be known and cited as the Federal Rules of Evidence.

# Appendix Q  Select Federal Rules of Civil Procedure

**Rule 1. - Scope and Purpose of Rules**
These rules govern the procedure in the United States district courts in all suits of a civil nature whether cognizable as cases at law or in equity or in admiralty, with the exceptions stated in Rule 81. They shall be construed and administered to secure the just, speedy, and inexpensive determination of every action.

**Rule 16. Pretrial Conferences; Scheduling; Management**
(a) Pretrial Conferences; Objectives.
In any action, the court may in its discretion direct the attorneys for the parties and any unrepresented parties to appear before it for a conference or conferences before trial for such purposes as
(1) expediting the disposition of the action;
(2) establishing early and continuing control so that the case will not be protracted because of lack of management;
(3) discouraging wasteful pretrial activities;
(4) improving the quality of the trial through more thorough preparation, and;
(5) facilitating the settlement of the case.
(b) Scheduling and Planning.
Except in categories of actions exempted by district court rule as inappropriate, the district judge, or a magistrate judge when authorized by district court rule, shall, after receiving the report from the parties under Rule 26(f) or after consulting with the attorneys for the parties and any unrepresented parties by a scheduling conference, telephone, mail, or other suitable means, enter a scheduling order that limits the time
(1) to join other parties and to amend the pleadings;
(2) to file motions; and
(3) to complete discovery.
The scheduling order may also include
(4) modifications of the times for disclosures under Rules 26(a) and 26(e)(1) and of the extent of discovery to be permitted;
(5) the date or dates for conferences before trial, a final pretrial conference, and trial; and
(6) any other matters appropriate in the circumstances of the case.
The order shall issue as soon as practicable but in any event within 90 days after the appearance of a defendant and within 120 days after the complaint has been served on a defendant. A schedule shall not be modified except upon a showing of good cause and by leave of the district judge or, when authorized by local rule, by a magistrate judge.
(c) Subjects for Consideration at Pretrial Conferences.
At any conference under this rule consideration may be given, and the court may take appropriate action, with respect to
(1) the formulation and simplification of the issues, including the elimination of frivolous claims or defenses;
(2) the necessity or desirability of amendments to the pleadings;
(3) the possibility of obtaining admissions of fact and of documents which will avoid unnecessary proof, stipulations regarding the authenticity of documents, and advance rulings from the court on the admissibility of evidence;
(4) the avoidance of unnecessary proof and of cumulative evidence, and limitations or restrictions on the use of testimony under Rule 702 of the Federal Rules of Evidence;

(5) the appropriateness and timing of summary adjudication under Rule 56;

(6) the control and scheduling of discovery, including orders affecting disclosures and discovery pursuant to Rule 26 and Rules 27 through 37;

(7) the identification of witnesses and documents, the need and schedule for filing and exchanging pretrial briefs, and the date or dates for further conferences and for trial;

(8) the advisability of referring matters to a magistrate judge or master;

(9) settlement and the use of special procedures to assist in resolving the dispute when authorized by statute or local rule;

(10) the form and substance of the pretrial order;

(11) the disposition of pending motions;

(12) the need for adopting special procedures for managing potentially difficult or protracted actions that may involve complex issues, multiple parties, difficult legal questions, or unusual proof problems;

(13) an order for a separate trial pursuant to Rule 42(b) with respect to a claim, counterclaim, cross-claim, or third-party claim, or with respect to any particular issue in the case;

(14) an order directing a party or parties to present evidence early in the trial with respect to a manageable issue that could, on the evidence, be the basis for a judgment as a matter of law under Rule 50(a) or a judgment on partial findings under Rule 52(c);

(15) an order establishing a reasonable limit on the time allowed for presenting evidence; and

(16) such other matters as may facilitate the just, speedy, and inexpensive disposition of the action.

At least one of the attorneys for each party participating in any conference before trial shall have authority to enter into stipulations and to make admissions regarding all matters that the participants may reasonably anticipate may be discussed. If appropriate, the court may require that a party or its representatives be present or reasonably available by telephone in order to consider possible settlement of the dispute.

(d) Final Pretrial Conference.

Any final pretrial conference shall be held as close to the time of trial as reasonable under the circumstances. The participants at any such conference shall formulate a plan for trial, including a program for facilitating the admission of evidence. The conference shall be attended by at least one of the attorneys who will conduct the trial for each of the parties and by any unrepresented parties.

(e) Pretrial Orders.

After any conference held pursuant to this rule, an order shall be entered reciting the action taken. This order shall control the subsequent course of the action unless modified by a subsequent order. The order following a final pretrial conference shall be modified only to prevent manifest injustice.

(f) Sanctions.

If a party or party's attorney fails to obey a scheduling or pretrial order, or if no appearance is made on behalf of a party at a scheduling or pretrial conference, or if a party or party's attorney is substantially unprepared to participate in the conference, or if a party or party's attorney fails to participate in good faith, the judge, upon motion or the judge's own initiative, may make such orders with regard thereto as are just, and among others any of the orders provided in Rule 37(b)(2)(B), (C), (D). In lieu of or in addition to any other sanction, the judge shall require the party or the attorney representing the party or both to pay the reasonable expenses incurred because of any noncompliance with this rule, including attorney's fees, unless the judge finds that the noncompliance was substantially justified or that other circumstances make an award of expenses unjust.

### Rule 26. General Provisions Governing Discovery; Duty of Disclosure

(a) Required Disclosures; Methods to Discover Additional Matter.

(1) Initial Disclosures.

# SELECT FEDERAL RULES OF CIVIL PROCEDURE

Except in categories of proceedings specified in Rule 26(a)(1)(E), or to the extent otherwise stipulated or directed by order, a party must, without awaiting a discovery request, provide to other parties:

(A) the name and, if known, the address and telephone number of each individual likely to have discoverable information that the disclosing party may use to support its claims or defenses, unless solely for impeachment, identifying the subjects of the information;

(B) a copy of, or a description by category and location of, all documents, data compilations, and tangible things that are in the possession, custody, or control of the party and that the disclosing party may use to support its claims or defenses, unless solely for impeachment;

(C) a computation of any category of damages claimed by the disclosing party, making available for inspection and copying as under Rule 34 the documents or other evidentiary material, not privileged or protected from disclosure, on which such computation is based, including materials bearing on the nature and extent of injuries suffered; and

(D) for inspection and copying as under Rule 34 any insurance agreement under which any person carrying on an insurance business may be liable to satisfy part or all of a judgment which may be entered in the action or to indemnify or reimburse for payments made to satisfy the judgment.

(E) The following categories of proceedings are exempt from initial disclosure under Rule 26(a)(1):

(i) an action for review on an administrative record;

(ii) a petition for habeas corpus or other proceeding to challenge a criminal conviction or sentence;

(iii) an action brought without counsel by a person in custody of the United States, a state, or a state subdivision;

(iv) an action to enforce or quash an administrative summons or subpoena;

(v) an action by the United States to recover benefit payments;

(vi) an action by the United States to collect on a student loan guaranteed by the United States;

(vii) a proceeding ancillary to proceedings in other courts; and

(viii) an action to enforce an arbitration award.

These disclosures must be made at or within 14 days after the Rule 26(f) conference unless a different time is set by stipulation or court order, or unless a party objects during the conference that initial disclosures are not appropriate in the circumstances of the action and states the objection in the Rule 26(f) discovery plan. In ruling on the objection, the court must determine what disclosures - if any - are to be made, and set the time for disclosure. Any party first served or otherwise joined after the Rule 26(f) conference must make these disclosures within 30 days after being served or joined unless a different time is set by stipulation or court order. A party must make its initial disclosures based on the information then reasonably available to it and is not excused from making its disclosures because it has not fully completed its investigation of the case or because it challenges the sufficiency of another party's disclosures or because another party has not made its disclosures.

(2) Disclosure of Expert Testimony.

(A) In addition to the disclosures required by paragraph (1), a party shall disclose to other parties the identity of any person who may be used at trial to present evidence under Rules 702, 703, or 705 of the Federal Rules of Evidence.

(B) Except as otherwise stipulated or directed by the court, this disclosure shall, with respect to a witness who is retained or specially employed to provide expert testimony in the case or whose duties as an employee of the party regularly involve giving expert testimony, be accompanied by a written report prepared and signed by the witness. The report shall contain a complete statement of all opinions to be expressed and the basis and reasons therefor; the data or other information considered by the witness in forming the opinions; any exhibits to be used as a summary of or support for the opinions; the qualifications of the witness, including a list of all publications authored by the witness within the preceding ten years; the compensation to be paid for the study and testimony; and a listing of any other cases in which the witness has testified as an expert at trial or by deposition within the preceding four years.

(C) These disclosures shall be made at the times and in the sequence directed by the court. In the absence of other directions from the court or stipulation by the parties, the disclosures shall be made at least 90 days before the trial date or the date the case is to be ready for trial or, if the evidence is intended solely to contradict or rebut evidence on the same subject matter identified by another party under paragraph (2)(B), within 30 days after the disclosure made by the other party. The parties shall supplement these disclosures when required under subdivision (e)(1).

(3) Pretrial Disclosures.

In addition to the disclosures required by Rule 26(a)(1) and (2), a party must provide to other parties and promptly file with the court the following information regarding the evidence that it may present at trial other than solely for impeachment:

(A) the name and, if not previously provided, the address and telephone number of each witness, separately identifying those whom the party expects to present and those whom the party may call if the need arises;

(B) the designation of those witnesses whose testimony is expected to be presented by means of a deposition and, if not taken stenographically, a transcript of the pertinent portions of the deposition testimony; and

(C) an appropriate identification of each document or other exhibit, including summaries of other evidence, separately identifying those which the party expects to offer and those which the party may offer if the need arises.

Unless otherwise directed by the court, these disclosures must be made at least 30 days before trial. Within 14 days thereafter, unless a different time is specified by the court, a party may serve and promptly file a list disclosing (i) any objections to the use under Rule 32(a) of a deposition designated by another party under Rule 26(a)(3)(B), and (ii) any objection, together with the grounds therefor, that may be made to the admissibility of materials identified under Rule 26(a)(3)(C). Objections not so disclosed, other than objections under Rules 402 and 403 of the Federal Rules of Evidence, are waived unless excused by the court for good cause.

(4) Form of Disclosures; Filing.

Unless the court orders otherwise, all disclosures under Rules 26(a)(1) through (3) must be made in writing, signed, and served.

(5) Methods to Discover Additional Matter.

Parties may obtain discovery by one or more of the following methods: depositions upon oral examination or written questions; written interrogatories; production of documents or things or permission to enter upon land or other property under Rule 34 or 45(a)(1)(C), for inspection and other purposes; physical and mental examinations; and requests for admission.

(b) Discovery Scope and Limits.

Unless otherwise limited by order of the court in accordance with these rules, the scope of discovery is as follows:

(1) In General.

Parties may obtain discovery regarding any matter, not privileged, that is relevant to the claim or defense of any party, including the existence, description, nature, custody, condition, and location of any books, documents, or other tangible things and the identity and location of persons having knowledge of any discoverable matter. For good cause, the court may order discovery of any matter relevant to the subject matter involved in the action. Relevant information need not be admissible at the trial if the discovery appears reasonably calculated to lead to the discovery of admissible evidence. All discovery is subject to the limitations imposed by Rule 26(b)(2)(i), (ii), and (iii).

(2) Limitations.

By order, the court may alter the limits in these rules on the number of depositions and interrogatories or the length of depositions under Rule 30. By order or local rule, the court may also limit the number of requests under Rule 36. The frequency or extent of use of the discovery methods otherwise permitted under these rules and by any local rule shall be limited by the court if it determines that: (i) the discovery sought is unreasonably cumulative or duplicative, or is obtainable from some other source that is more convenient, less burdensome, or less expensive; (ii) the party seeking discovery has had ample opportunity by discovery in the action to obtain the information sought; or (iii) the burden or expense of the proposed discovery outweighs its likely benefit, taking into account the needs of the case, the amount in controversy, the parties' resources, the importance of the issues at stake in the litigation, and the importance of the proposed discovery in resolving the issues. The court may act upon its own initiative after reasonable notice or pursuant to a motion under Rule 26(c).

(3) Trial Preparation: Materials.

Subject to the provisions of subdivision (b)(4) of this rule, a party may obtain discovery of documents and tangible things otherwise discoverable under subdivision (b)(1) of this rule and prepared in anticipation of litigation or for trial by or for another party or by or for that other party's representative (including the other party's attorney, consultant, surety, indemnitor, insurer, or agent) only upon a showing that the party seeking discovery has substantial need of the materials in the preparation of the party's case and that the party is unable without undue hardship to obtain the substantial equivalent of the materials by other means. In ordering discovery of such materials when the required showing has been made, the court shall protect against disclosure of the mental impressions, conclusions, opinions, or legal theories of an attorney or other representative of a party concerning the litigation.

A party may obtain without the required showing a statement concerning the action or its subject matter previously made by that party. Upon request, a person not a party may obtain without the required showing a statement concerning the action or its subject matter previously made by that person. If the request is refused, the person may move for a court order. The provisions of Rule 37(a)(4) apply to the award of expenses incurred in relation to the motion. For purposes of this paragraph, a statement previously made is (A) a written statement signed or otherwise adopted or approved by the person making it, or (B) a stenographic, mechanical, electrical, or other recording, or a transcription thereof, which is a substantially verbatim recital of an oral statement by the person making it and contemporaneously recorded.

(4) Trial Preparation: Experts.

(A) A party may depose any person who has been identified as an expert whose opinions may be presented at trial. If a report from the expert is required under subdivision (a)(2)(B), the deposition shall not be conducted until after the report is provided.

(B) A party may, through interrogatories or by deposition, discover facts known or opinions held by an expert who has been retained or specially employed by another party in anticipation of litigation or preparation for trial and who is not expected to be called as a witness at trial, only as provided in Rule 35(b) or upon a showing of exceptional circumstances under which it is impracticable for the party seeking discovery to obtain facts or opinions on the same subject by other means.

(C) Unless manifest injustice would result, (i) the court shall require that the party seeking discovery pay the expert a reasonable fee for time spent in responding to discovery under this subdivision; and (ii) with respect to discovery obtained under subdivision (b)(4)(B) of this rule the court shall require the party seeking discovery to pay the other party a fair portion of the fees and expenses reasonably incurred by the latter party in obtaining facts and opinions from the expert.

(5) Claims of Privilege or Protection of Trial Preparation Materials.

When a party withholds information otherwise discoverable under these rules by claiming that it is privileged or subject to protection as trial preparation material, the party shall make the claim expressly and shall describe the nature of the documents, communications, or things not produced or disclosed in a manner that, without revealing information itself privileged or protected, will enable other parties to assess the applicability of the privilege or protection.

(c) Protective Orders.

Upon motion by a party or by the person from whom discovery is sought, accompanied by a certification that the movant has in good faith conferred or attempted to confer with other affected parties in an effort to resolve the dispute without court action, and for good cause shown, the court in which the action is pending or alternatively, on matters relating to a deposition, the court in the district where the deposition is to be taken may make any order which justice requires to protect a party or person from annoyance, embarrassment, oppression, or undue burden or expense, including one or more of the following:

(1) that the disclosure or discovery not be had;

(2) that the disclosure or discovery may be had only on specified terms and conditions, including a designation of the time or place;

(3) that the discovery may be had only by a method of discovery other than that selected by the party seeking discovery;

(4) that certain matters not be inquired into, or that the scope of the disclosure or discovery be limited to certain matters;

(5) that discovery be conducted with no one present except persons designated by the court;

(6) that a deposition, after being sealed, be opened only by order of the court;

(7) that a trade secret or other confidential research, development, or commercial information not be revealed or be revealed only in a designated way; and

(8) that the parties simultaneously file specified documents or information enclosed in sealed envelopes to be opened as directed by the court.

If the motion for a protective order is denied in whole or in part, the court may, on such terms and conditions as are just, order that any party or other person provide or permit discovery. The provisions of Rule 37(a)(4) apply to the award of expenses incurred in relation to the motion.

(d) Timing and Sequence of Discovery.

Except in categories of proceedings exempted from initial disclosure under Rule 26(a)(1)(E), or when authorized under these rules or by order or agreement of the parties, a party may not seek discovery from any source before the parties have conferred as required by Rule 26(f). Unless the court upon motion, for the convenience of parties and witnesses and in the interests of justice, orders otherwise, methods of discovery may be used in any sequence, and the fact that a party is conducting discovery, whether by deposition or otherwise, does not operate to delay any other party's discovery.

(e) Supplementation of Disclosures and Responses.

A party who has made a disclosure under subdivision (a) or responded to a request for discovery with a disclosure or response is under a duty to supplement or correct the disclosure or response to include information thereafter acquired if ordered by the court or in the following circumstances:

(1) A party is under a duty to supplement at appropriate intervals its disclosures under subdivision (a) if the party learns that in some material respect the information disclosed is incomplete or incorrect and if the additional or corrective information has not otherwise been made known to the other parties during the discovery process or in writing. With respect to testimony of an expert from whom a report is required under subdivision (a)(2)(B) the duty extends both to information contained in the report and to information provided through a deposition of the expert, and any additions or other changes to this information shall be disclosed by the time the party's disclosures under Rule 26(a)(3) are due.

(2) A party is under a duty seasonably to amend a prior response to an interrogatory, request for production, or request for admission if the party learns that the response is in some material respect

incomplete or incorrect and if the additional or corrective information has not otherwise been made known to the other parties during the discovery process or in writing.

(f) Meeting of Parties; Planning for Discovery.

Except in categories of proceedings exempted from initial disclosure under Rule 26(a)(1)(E) or when otherwise ordered, the parties must, as soon as practicable and in any event at least 21 days before a scheduling conference is held or a scheduling order is due under Rule 16(b), confer to consider the nature and basis of their claims and defenses and the possibilities for a prompt settlement or resolution of the case, to make or arrange for the disclosures required by Rule 26(a)(1), and to develop a proposed discovery plan that indicates the parties' views and proposals concerning:

(1) what changes should be made in the timing, form, or requirement for disclosures under Rule 26(a), including a statement as to when disclosures under Rule 26(a)(1) were made or will be made;

(2) the subjects on which discovery may be needed, when discovery should be completed, and whether discovery should be conducted in phases or be limited to or focused upon particular issues;

(3) what changes should be made in the limitations on discovery imposed under these rules or by local rule, and what other limitations should be imposed; and

(4) any other orders that should be entered by the court under Rule 26(c) or under Rule 16(b) and (c).

The attorneys of record and all unrepresented parties that have appeared in the case are jointly responsible for arranging the conference, for attempting in good faith to agree on the proposed discovery plan, and for submitting to the court within 14 days after the conference a written report outlining the plan. A court may order that the parties or attorneys attend the conference in person. If necessary to comply with its expedited schedule for Rule 16(b) conferences, a court may by local rule (i) require that the conference between the parties occur fewer than 21 days before the scheduling conference is held or a scheduling order is due under Rule 16(b), and (ii) require that the written report outlining the discovery plan be filed fewer than 14 days after the conference between the parties, or excuse the parties from submitting a written report and permit them to report orally on their discovery plan at the Rule 16(b) conference.

(g) Signing of Disclosures, Discovery Requests, Responses, and Objections.

(1) Every disclosure made pursuant to subdivision (a)(1) or subdivision (a)(3) shall be signed by at least one attorney of record in the attorney's individual name, whose address shall be stated. An unrepresented party shall sign the disclosure and state the party's address. The signature of the attorney or party constitutes a certification that to the best of the signer's knowledge, information, and belief, formed after a reasonable inquiry, the disclosure is complete and correct as of the time it is made.

(2) Every discovery request, response, or objection made by a party represented by an attorney shall be signed by at least one attorney of record in the attorney's individual name, whose address shall be stated. An unrepresented party shall sign the request, response, or objection and state the party's address. The signature of the attorney or party constitutes a certification that to the best of the signer's knowledge, information, and belief, formed after a reasonable inquiry, the request, response, or objection is:

(A) consistent with these rules and warranted by existing law or a good faith argument for the extension, modification, or reversal of existing law;

(B) not interposed for any improper purpose, such as to harass or to cause unnecessary delay or needless increase in the cost of litigation; and

(C) not unreasonable or unduly burdensome or expensive, given the needs of the case, the discovery already had in the case, the amount in controversy, and the importance of the issues at stake in the litigation.

If a request, response, or objection is not signed, it shall be stricken unless it is signed promptly after the omission is called to the attention of the party making the request, response, or objection, and a party shall not be obligated to take any action with respect to it until it is signed.

(3) If without substantial justification a certification is made in violation of the rule, the court, upon motion or upon its own initiative, shall impose upon the person who made the certification, the party on whose behalf the disclosure, request, response, or objection is made, or both, an appropriate sanction, which may include an order to pay the amount of the reasonable expenses incurred because of the violation, including a reasonable attorney's fee.

## Rule 29. Stipulations Regarding Discovery Procedure

Unless otherwise directed by the court, the parties may by written stipulation (1) provide that depositions may be taken before any person, at any time or place, upon any notice, and in any manner and when so taken may be used like other depositions, and (2) modify other procedures governing or limitations placed upon discovery, except that stipulations extending the time provided in Rules 33, 34, and 36 for responses to discovery may, if they would interfere with any time set for completion of discovery, for hearing of a motion, or for trial, be made only with the approval of the court.

## Rule 30. Deposition Upon Oral Examination

(a) When Depositions May Be Taken; When Leave Required.

(1) A party may take the testimony of any person, including a party, by deposition upon oral examination without leave of court except as provided in paragraph (2). The attendance of witnesses may be compelled by subpoena as provided in Rule 45.

(2) A party must obtain leave of court, which shall be granted to the extent consistent with the principles stated in Rule 26(b)(2), if the person to be examined is confined in prison or if, without the written stipulation of the parties.

(A) a proposed deposition would result in more than ten depositions being taken under this rule or Rule 31 by the plaintiffs, or by the defendants, or by third-party defendants;

(B) the person to be examined already has been deposed in the case; or

(C) a party seeks to take a deposition before the time specified in Rule 26(d) unless the notice contains a certification, with supporting facts, that the person to be examined is expected to leave the United States and be unavailable for examination in this country unless deposed before that time.

(b) Notice of Examination: General Requirements; Method of Recording; Production of Documents and Things; Deposition of Organization; Deposition by Telephone.

(1) A party desiring to take the deposition of any person upon oral examination shall give reasonable notice in writing to every other party to the action. The notice shall state the time and place for taking the deposition and the name and address of each person to be examined, if known, and, if the name is not known, a general description sufficient to identify the person or the particular class or group to which the person belongs. If a subpoena duces tecum is to be served on the person to be examined, the designation of the materials to be produced as set forth in the subpoena shall be attached to, or included in, the notice.

(2) The party taking the deposition shall state in the notice the method by which the testimony shall be recorded. Unless the court orders otherwise, it may be recorded by sound, sound-and-visual, or stenographic means, and the party taking the deposition shall bear the cost of the recording. Any party may arrange for a transcription to be made from the recording of a deposition taken by nonstenographic means.

(3) With prior notice to the deponent and other parties, any party may designate another method to record the deponent's testimony in addition to the method specified by the person taking the deposition. The additional record or transcript shall be made at that party's expense unless the court otherwise orders.

(4) Unless otherwise agreed by the parties, a deposition shall be conducted before an officer appointed or designated under Rule 28 and shall begin with a statement on the record by the officer that includes

# SELECT FEDERAL RULES OF CIVIL PROCEDURE

(A) the officer's name and business address; (B) the date, time and place of the deposition; (C) the name of the deponent; (D) the administration of the oath or affirmation to the deponent; and (E) an identification of all persons present. If the deposition is recorded other than stenographically, the officer shall repeat items (A) through (C) at the beginning of each unit of recorded tape or other recording medium. The appearance or demeanor of deponents or attorneys shall not be distorted through camera or sound-recording techniques. At the end of the deposition, the officer shall state on the record that the deposition is complete and shall set forth any stipulations made by counsel concerning the custody of the transcript or recording and the exhibits, or concerning other pertinent matters.

(5) The notice to a party deponent may be accompanied by a request made in compliance with Rule 34 for the production of documents and tangible things at the taking of the deposition. The procedure of Rule 34 shall apply to the request.

(6) A party may in the party's notice and in a subpoena name as the deponent a public or private corporation or a partnership or association or governmental agency and describe with reasonable particularity the matters on which examination is requested. In that event, the organization so named shall designate one or more officers, directors, or managing agents, or other persons who consent to testify on its behalf, and may set forth, for each person designated, the matters on which the person will testify. A subpoena shall advise a non-party organization of its duty to make such a designation. The persons so designated shall testify as to matters known or reasonably available to the organization. This subdivision (b)(6) does not preclude taking a deposition by any other procedure authorized in these rules.

(7) The parties may stipulate in writing or the court may upon motion order that a deposition be taken by telephone or other remote electronic means. For the purposes of this rule and Rules 28(a), 37(a)(1), and 37(b)(1), a deposition taken by such means is taken in the district and at the place where the deponent is to answer questions.

(c) Examination and Cross-Examination; Record of Examination; Oath; Objections
Examination and cross-examination of witnesses may proceed as permitted at the trial under the provisions of the Federal Rules of Evidence except Rules 103 and 615. The officer before whom the deposition is to be taken shall put the witness on oath or affirmation and shall personally, or by someone acting under the officer's direction and in the officer's presence, record the testimony of the witness. The testimony shall be taken stenographically or recorded by any other method authorized by subdivision (b)(2) of this rule. All objections made at the time of the examination to the qualifications of the officer taking the deposition, to the manner of taking it, to the evidence presented, to the conduct of any party, or to any other aspect of the proceedings shall be noted by the officer upon the record of the deposition; but the examination shall proceed, with the testimony being taken subject to the objections. In lieu of participating in the oral examination, parties may serve written questions in a sealed envelope on the party taking the deposition and the party taking the deposition shall transmit them to the officer, who shall propound them to the witness and record the answers verbatim.

(d) Schedule and Duration; Motion to Terminate or Limit Examination.

(1) Any objection during a deposition must be stated concisely and in a non-argumentative and non-suggestive manner. A person may instruct a deponent not to answer only when necessary to preserve a privilege, to enforce a limitation directed by the court, or to present a motion under Rule 30(d)(4).

(2) Unless otherwise authorized by the court or stipulated by the parties, a deposition is limited to one day of seven hours. The court must allow additional time consistent with Rule 26(b)(2) if needed for a fair examination of the deponent or if the deponent or another person, or other circumstance, impedes or delays the examination.

(3) If the court finds that any impediment, delay, or other conduct has frustrated the fair examination of the deponent, it may impose upon the persons responsible an appropriate sanction, including the reasonable costs and attorney's fees incurred by any parties as a result thereof.

(4) At any time during a deposition, on motion of a party or of the deponent and upon a showing that the examination is being conducted in bad faith or in such manner as unreasonably to annoy, embarrass, or oppress the deponent or party, the court in which the action is pending or the court in the district where the deposition is being taken may order the officer conducting the examination to cease forthwith from taking the deposition, or may limit the scope and manner of the taking of the deposition as provided in Rule 26(c). If the order made terminates the examination, it may be resumed thereafter only upon the order of the court in which the action is pending. Upon demand of the objecting party or deponent, the taking of the deposition must be suspended for the time necessary to make a motion for an order. The provisions of Rule 37(a)(4) apply to the award of expenses incurred in relation to the motion.

(e) Review by Witness; Changes; Signing.

If requested by the deponent or a party before completion of the deposition, the deponent shall have 30 days after being notified by the officer that the transcript or recording is available in which to review the transcript or recording and, if there are changes in form or substance, to sign a statement reciting such changes and the reasons given by the deponent for making them. The officer shall indicate in the certificate prescribed by subdivision (f)(1) whether any review was requested and, if so, shall append any changes made by the deponent during the period allowed.

(f) Certification and Filing by Officer; Exhibits; Copies; Notices of Filing.

(1) The officer must certify that the witness was duly sworn by the officer and that the deposition is a true record of the testimony given by the witness. This certificate must be in writing and accompany the record of the deposition. Unless otherwise ordered by the court, the officer must securely seal the deposition in an envelope or package indorsed with the title of the action and marked "Deposition of [here insert name of witness]" and must promptly send it to the attorney who arranged for the transcript or recording, who must store it under conditions that will protect it against loss, destruction, tampering, or deterioration. Documents and things produced for inspection during the examination of the witness must, upon the request of a party, be marked for identification and annexed to the deposition and may be inspected and copied by any party, except that if the person producing the materials desires to retain them the person may (A) offer copies to be marked for identification and annexed to the deposition and to serve thereafter as originals if the person affords to all parties fair opportunity to verify the copies by comparison with the originals, or (B) offer the originals to be marked for identification, after giving to each party an opportunity to inspect and copy them, in which event the materials may then be used in the same manner as if annexed to the deposition. Any party may move for an order that the original be annexed to and returned with the deposition to the court, pending final disposition of the case.

(2) Unless otherwise ordered by the court or agreed by the parties, the officer shall retain stenographic notes of any deposition taken stenographically or a copy of the recording of any deposition taken by another method. Upon payment of reasonable charges therefor, the officer shall furnish a copy of the transcript or other recording of the deposition to any party or to the deponent.

(3) The party taking the deposition shall give prompt notice of its filing to all other parties.

(g) Failure to Attend or to Serve Subpoena; Expenses.

(1) If the party giving the notice of the taking of a deposition fails to attend and proceed therewith and another party attends in person or by attorney pursuant to the notice, the court may order the party giving the notice to pay to such other party the reasonable expenses incurred by that party and that party's attorney in attending, including reasonable attorney's fees.

(2) If the party giving the notice of the taking of a deposition of a witness fails to serve a subpoena upon the witness and the witness because of such failure does not attend, and if another party attends in

person or by attorney because that party expects the deposition of that witness to be taken, the court may order the party giving the notice to pay to such other party the reasonable expenses incurred by that party and that party's attorney in attending, including reasonable attorney's fees.

## Rule 33. Interrogatories to Parties

(a) Availability.

Without leave of court or written stipulation, any party may serve upon any other party written interrogatories, not exceeding 25 in number including all discrete subparts, to be answered by the party served or, if the party served is a public or private corporation or a partnership or association or governmental agency, by any officer or agent, who shall furnish such information as is available to the party. Leave to serve additional interrogatories shall be granted to the extent consistent with the principles of Rule 26(b)(2). Without leave of court or written stipulation, interrogatories may not be served before the time specified in Rule 26(d).

(b) Answers and Objections.

(1) Each interrogatory shall be answered separately and fully in writing under oath, unless it is objected to, in which event the objecting party shall state the reasons for objection and shall answer to the extent the interrogatory is not objectionable.

(2) The answers are to be signed by the person making them, and the objections signed by the attorney making them.

(3) The party upon whom the interrogatories have been served shall serve a copy of the answers, and objections if any, within 30 days after the service of the interrogatories. A shorter or longer time may be directed by the court or, in the absence of such an order, agreed to in writing by the parties subject to Rule 29.

(4) All grounds for an objection to an interrogatory shall be stated with specificity. Any ground not stated in a timely objection is waived unless the party's failure to object is excused by the court for good cause shown.

(5) The party submitting the interrogatories may move for an order under Rule 37(a) with respect to any objection to or other failure to answer an interrogatory.

(c) Scope; Use at Trial.

Interrogatories may relate to any matters which can be inquired into under Rule 26(b)(1), and the answers may be used to the extent permitted by the rules of evidence.

An interrogatory otherwise proper is not necessarily objectionable merely because an answer to the interrogatory involves an opinion or contention that relates to fact or the application of law to fact, but the court may order that such an interrogatory need not be answered until after designated discovery has been completed or until a pre-trial conference or other later time.

(d) Option to Produce Business Records.

Where the answer to an interrogatory may be derived or ascertained from the business records of the party upon whom the interrogatory has been served or from an examination, audit or inspection of such business records, including a compilation, abstract or summary thereof, and the burden of deriving or ascertaining the answer is substantially the same for the party serving the interrogatory as for the party served, it is a sufficient answer to such interrogatory to specify the records from which the answer may be derived or ascertained and to afford to the party serving the interrogatory reasonable opportunity to examine, audit or inspect such records and to make copies, compilations, abstracts or summaries. A specification shall be in sufficient detail to permit the interrogating party to locate and to identify, as readily as can the party served, the records from which the answer may be ascertained.

## Rule 34. Production of Documents and Things and Entry Upon Land for Inspection and Other Purposes
(a) Scope.

Any party may serve on any other party a request (1) to produce and permit the party making the request, or someone acting on the requestor's behalf, to inspect and copy, any designated documents (including writings, drawings, graphs, charts, photographs, phonorecords, and other data compilations from which information can be obtained, translated, if necessary, by the respondent through detection devices into reasonably usable form), or to inspect and copy, test, or sample any tangible things which constitute or contain matters within the scope of Rule 26(b) and which are in the possession, custody or control of the party upon whom the request is served; or (2) to permit entry upon designated land or other property in the possession or control of the party upon whom the request is served for the purpose of inspection and measuring, surveying, photographing, testing, or sampling the property or any designated object or operation thereon, within the scope of Rule 26(b).

(b) Procedure.

The request shall set forth, either by individual item or by category, the items to be inspected, and describe each with reasonable particularity. The request shall specify a reasonable time, place, and manner of making the inspection and performing the related acts. Without leave of court or written stipulation, a request may not be served before the time specified in Rule 26(d).

The party upon whom the request is served shall serve a written response within 30 days after the service of the request. A shorter or longer time may be directed by the court or, in the absence of such an order, agreed to in writing by the parties, subject to Rule 29. The response shall state, with respect to each item or category, that inspection and related activities will be permitted as requested, unless the request is objected to, in which event the reasons for the objection shall be stated. If objection is made to part of an item or category, the part shall be specified and inspection permitted of the remaining parts. The party submitting the request may move for an order under Rule 37(a) with respect to any objection to or other failure to respond to the request or any part thereof, or any failure to permit inspection as requested.

A party who produces documents for inspection shall produce them as they are kept in the usual course of business or shall organize and label them to correspond with the categories in the request.

(c) Persons Not Parties.

A person not a party to the action may be compelled to produce documents and things or to submit to an inspection as provided in Rule 45.

## Rule 35. Physical and Mental Examination of Persons
(a) Order for Examination.

When the mental or physical condition (including the blood group) of a party or of a person in the custody or under the legal control of a party, is in controversy, the court in which the action is pending may order the party to submit to a physical or mental examination by a suitably licensed or certified examiner or to produce for examination the person in the party's custody or legal control. The order may be made only on motion for good cause shown and upon notice to the person to be examined and to all parties and shall specify the time, place, manner, conditions, and scope of the examination and the person or persons by whom it is to be made.

(b) Report of Examiner.

(1) If requested by the party against whom an order is made under Rule 35(a) or the person examined, the party causing the examination to be made shall deliver to the requesting party a copy of the detailed written report of the examiner setting out the examiner's findings, including results of all tests made, diagnoses and conclusions, together with like reports of all earlier examinations of the same condition. After delivery the party causing the examination shall be entitled upon request to receive from the party

against whom the order is made a like report of any examination, previously or thereafter made, of the same condition, unless, in the case of a report of examination of a person not a party, the party shows that the party is unable to obtain it. The court on motion may make an order against a party requiring delivery of a report on such terms as are just, and if an examiner fails or refuses to make a report the court may exclude the examiner's testimony if offered at trial.

(2) By requesting and obtaining a report of the examination so ordered or by taking the deposition of the examiner, the party examined waives any privilege the party may have in that action or any other involving the same controversy, regarding the testimony of every other person who has examined or may thereafter examine the party in respect of the same mental or physical condition.

(3) This subdivision applies to examinations made by agreement of the parties, unless the agreement expressly provides otherwise. This subdivision does not preclude discovery of a report of an examiner or the taking of a deposition of the examiner in accordance with the provisions of any other rule.

(c) Definitions.

For the purpose of this rule, a psychologist is a psychologist licensed or certified by a State or the District of Columbia.

### Rule 37. Failure to Make or Cooperate in Discovery; Sanctions

(a) Motion for Order Compelling Disclosure or Discovery.

A party, upon reasonable notice to other parties and all persons affected thereby, may apply for an order compelling disclosure or discovery as follows:

(1) Appropriate Court.

An application for an order to a party shall be made to the court in which the action is pending. An application for an order to a person who is not a party shall be made to the court in the district where the discovery is being, or is to be, taken.

(2) Motion.

(A) If a party fails to make a disclosure required by Rule 26(a), any other party may move to compel disclosure and for appropriate sanctions. The motion must include a certification that the movant has in good faith conferred or attempted to confer with the party not making the disclosure in an effort to secure the disclosure without court action.

(B) If a deponent fails to answer a question propounded or submitted under Rules 30 or 31, or a corporation or other entity fails to make a designation under Rule 30(b)(6) or 31(a), or a party fails to answer an interrogatory submitted under Rule 33, or if a party, in response to a request for inspection submitted under Rule 34, fails to respond that inspection will be permitted as requested or fails to permit inspection as requested, the discovering party may move for an order compelling answer, or a designation, or an order compelling inspection in accordance with the request. The motion must include a certification that the movant has in good faith conferred or attempted to confer with the person or party failing to make the discovery in an effort to secure the information or material without court action. When taking a deposition on oral examination, the proponent of the question may complete or adjourn the examination before applying for an order.

(3) Evasive or Incomplete Disclosure, Answer, or Response.

For purposes of this subdivision an evasive or incomplete disclosure, answer, or response is to be treated as a failure to disclose, answer, or respond.

(4) Expenses and Sanctions.

(A) If the motion is granted or if the disclosure or requested discovery is provided after the motion was filed, the court shall, after affording an opportunity to be heard, require the party or deponent whose conduct necessitated the motion or the party or attorney advising such conduct or both of them to pay to the moving party the reasonable expenses incurred in making the motion, including attorney's fees, unless the court finds that the motion was filed without the movant's first making a good faith effort to obtain the disclosure or discovery without court action, or that the opposing party's nondisclosure, response, or objection was substantially justified, or that other circumstances make an award of expenses unjust.

(B) If the motion is denied, the court may enter any protective order authorized under Rule 26(c) and shall, after affording an opportunity to be heard, require the moving party or the attorney filing the motion or both of them to pay to the party or deponent who opposed the motion the reasonable expenses incurred in opposing the motion, including attorney's fees, unless the court finds that the making of the motion was substantially justified or that other circumstances make an award of expenses unjust.

(C) If the motion is granted in part and denied in part, the court may enter any protective order authorized under Rule 26(c) and may, after affording an opportunity to be heard, apportion the reasonable expenses incurred in relation to the motion among the parties and persons in a just manner.

(b) Failure to comply with order.

(1) Sanctions by Court in District Where Deposition is Taken.

If a deponent fails to be sworn or to answer a question after being directed to do so by the court in the district in which the deposition is being taken, the failure may be considered a contempt of that court.

(2) Sanctions by Court in Which Action Is Pending.

If a party or an officer, director, or managing agent of a party or a person designated under Rule 30(b)(6) or 31(a) to testify on behalf of a party fails to obey an order to provide or permit discovery, including an order made under subdivision (a) of this rule or Rule 35, or if a party fails to obey an order entered under Rule 26(f), the court in which the action is pending may make such orders in regard to the failure as are just, and among others the following:

(A) An order that the matters regarding which the order was made or any other designated facts shall be taken to be established for the purposes of the action in accordance with the claim of the party obtaining the order;

(B) An order refusing to allow the disobedient party to support or oppose designated claims or defenses, or prohibiting that party from introducing designated matters in evidence;

(C) An order striking out pleadings or parts thereof, or staying further proceedings until the order is obeyed, or dismissing the action or proceeding or any part thereof, or rendering a judgment by default against the disobedient party;

(D) In lieu of any of the foregoing orders or in addition thereto, an order treating as a contempt of court the failure to obey any orders except an order to submit to a physical or mental examination;

(E) Where a party has failed to comply with an order under Rule 35(a) requiring that party to produce another for cxamination, such orders as are listed in paragraphs (A), (B), and (C) of this subdivision, unless the party failing to comply shows that that party is unable to produce such person for examination.

In lieu of any of the foregoing orders or in addition thereto, the court shall require the party failing to obey the order or the attorney advising that party or both to pay the reasonable expenses, including attorney's fees, caused by the failure, unless the court finds that the failure was substantially justified or that other circumstances make an award of expenses unjust.

(c) Failure to Disclose; False or Misleading Disclosure; Refusal to Admit.

(1) A party that without substantial justification fails to disclose information required by Rule 26(a) or 26(e)(1), or to amend a prior response to discovery as required by Rule 26(e)(2), is not, unless such failure is harmless, permitted to use as evidence at a trial, at a hearing, or on a motion any witness or information not so disclosed. In addition to or in lieu of this sanction, the court, on motion and after affording an opportunity to be heard, may impose other appropriate sanctions. In addition to requiring payment of reasonable expenses, including attorney's fees, caused by the failure, these sanctions may

include any of the actions authorized under Rule 37(b)(2)(A), (B), and (C) and may include informing the jury of the failure to make the disclosure.

(2) If a party fails to admit the genuineness of any document or the truth of any matter as requested under Rule 36, and if the party requesting the admissions thereafter proves the genuineness of the document or the truth of the matter, the requesting party may apply to the court for an order requiring the other party to pay the reasonable expenses incurred in making that proof, including reasonable attorney's fees. The court shall make the order unless it finds that (A) the request was held objectionable pursuant to Rule 36(a), or (B) the admission sought was of no substantial importance, or (C) the party failing to admit had reasonable ground to believe that the party might prevail on the matter, or (D) there was other good reason for the failure to admit.

(d) Failure of Party to Attend at Own Deposition or Serve Answers to Interrogatories or Respond to Request for Inspection.

If a party or an officer, director, or managing agent of a party or a person designated under Rule 30(b)(6) or 31(a) to testify on behalf of a party fails (1) to appear before the officer who is to take the deposition, after being served with a proper notice, or (2) to serve answers or objections to interrogatories submitted under Rule 33, after proper service of the interrogatories, or (3) to serve a written response to a request for inspection submitted under Rule 34, after proper service of the request, the court in which the action is pending on motion may make such orders in regard to the failure as are just, and among others it may take any action authorized under subparagraphs (A), (B), and (C) of subdivision (b)(2) of this rule. Any motion specifying a failure under clause (2) or (3) of this subdivision shall include a certification that the movant has in good faith conferred or attempted to confer with the party failing to answer or respond in an effort to obtain such answer or response without court action. In lieu of any order or in addition thereto, the court shall require the party failing to act or the attorney advising that party or both to pay the reasonable expenses, including attorney's fees, caused by the failure unless the court finds that the failure was substantially justified or that other circumstances make an award of expenses unjust.

The failure to act described in this subdivision may not be excused on the ground that the discovery sought is objectionable unless the party failing to act has a pending motion for a protective order as provided by Rule 26(c).

(e) [Abrogated]

(f) [Repealed]

(g) Failure to Participate in the Framing of a Discovery Plan.

If a party or a party's attorney fails to participate in the development and submission of a proposed discovery plan as required by Rule 26(f), the court may, after opportunity for hearing, require such party or attorney to pay to any other party the reasonable expenses, including attorney's fees, caused by the failure.

## Rule 45. Subpoena

(a) Form; Issuance.

(1) Every subpoena shall

(A) state the name of the court from which it is issued; and

(B) state the title of the action, the name of the court in which it is pending, and its civil action number; and

(C) command each person to whom it is directed to attend and give testimony or to produce and permit inspection and copying of designated books, documents or tangible things in the possession, custody or control of that person, or to permit inspection of premises, at a time and place therein specified; and

(D) set forth the text of subdivisions (c) and (d) of this rule. A command to produce evidence or to permit inspection may be joined with a command to appear at trial or hearing or at deposition, or may be issued separately.

(2) A subpoena must issue as follows:

(A) for attendance at a trial or hearing, in the name of the court for the district where the trial or hearing is to be held;

(B) for attendance at a deposition, in the name of the court for the district where the deposition is to be taken, stating the method for recording the testimony; and

(C) for the production and inspection, if separate from a subpoena commanding a person's attendance, in the name of the court for the district where the production or inspection is to be made.

(3) The clerk shall issue a subpoena, signed but otherwise in blank, to a party requesting it, who shall complete it before service. An attorney as officer of the court may also issue and sign a subpoena on behalf of

(A) a court in which the attorney is authorized to practice; or

(B) a court for a district in which a deposition or production is compelled by the subpoena, if the deposition or production pertains to an action pending in a court in which the attorney is authorized to practice.

(b) Service.

(1) A subpoena may be served by any person who is not a party and is not less than 18 years of age. Service of a subpoena upon a person named therein shall be made by delivering a copy thereof to such person and, if the person's attendance is commanded, by tendering to that person the fees for one day's attendance and the mileage allowed by law. When the subpoena is issued on behalf of the United States or an officer or agency thereof, fees and mileage need not be tendered. Prior notice of any commanded production of documents and things or inspection of premises before trial shall be served on each party in the manner prescribed by Rule 5(b).

(2) Subject to the provisions of clause (ii) of subparagraph (c)(3)(A) of this rule, a subpoena may be served at any place within the district of the court by which it is issued, or at any place without the district that is within 100 miles of the place of the deposition, hearing, trial, production, or inspection specified in the subpoena or at any place within the state where a state statute or rule of court permits service of a subpoena issued by a state court of general jurisdiction sitting in the place of the deposition, hearing, trial, production, or inspection specified in the subpoena. When a statute of the United States provides therefor, the court upon proper application and cause shown may authorize the service of a subpoena at any other place. A subpoena directed to a witness in a foreign country who is a national or resident of the United States shall issue under the circumstances and in the manner and be served as provided in Title 28, U.S.C. § 1783.

(3) Proof of service when necessary shall be made by filing with the clerk of the court by which the subpoena is issued a statement of the date and manner of service and of the names of the persons served, certified by the person who made the service.

(c) Protection of Persons Subject to Subpoenas.

(1) A party or an attorney responsible for the issuance and service of a subpoena shall take reasonable steps to avoid imposing undue burden or expense on a person subject to that subpoena. The court on behalf of which the subpoena was issued shall enforce this duty and impose upon the party or attorney in breach of this duty an appropriate sanction, which may include, but is not limited to, lost earnings and a reasonable attorney's fee.

(2) (A) A person commanded to produce and permit inspection and copying of designated books, papers, documents or tangible things, or inspection of premises need not appear in person at the place of production or inspection unless commanded to appear for deposition, hearing or trial.

(B) Subject to paragraph (d)(2) of this rule, a person commanded to produce and permit inspection and copying may, within 14 days after service of the subpoena or before the time specified for compliance if such time is less than 14 days after service, serve upon the party or attorney designated in the subpoena written objection to inspection or copying of any or all of the designated materials or of the premises. If objection is made, the party serving the subpoena shall not be entitled to inspect and copy the materials or inspect the premises except pursuant to an order of the court by which the subpoena was issued. If objection has been made, the party serving the subpoena may, upon notice to the person commanded to produce, move at any time for an order to compel the production. Such an order to compel production shall protect any person who is not a party or an officer of a party from significant expense resulting from the inspection and copying commanded.

(3) (A) On timely motion, the court by which a subpoena was issued shall quash or modify the subpoena if it

(i) fails to allow reasonable time for compliance;

(ii) requires a person who is not a party or an officer of a party to travel to a place more than 100 miles from the place where that person resides, is employed or regularly transacts business in person, except that, subject to the provisions of clause (c)(3)(B)(iii) of this rule, such a person may in order to attend trial be commanded to travel from any such place within the state in which the trial is held, or

(iii) requires disclosure of privileged or other protected matter and no exception or waiver applies, or

(iv) subjects a person to undue burden.

(B) If a subpoena

(i) requires disclosure of a trade secret or other confidential research, development, or commercial information, or

(ii) requires disclosure of an unretained expert's opinion or information not describing specific events or occurrences in dispute and resulting from the expert's study made not at the request of any party, or

(iii) requires a person who is not a party or an officer of a party to incur substantial expense to travel more than 100 miles to attend trial, the court may, to protect a person subject to or affected by the subpoena, quash or modify the subpoena or, if the party in whose behalf the subpoena is issued shows a substantial need for the testimony or material that cannot be otherwise met without undue hardship and assures that the person to whom the subpoena is addressed will be reasonably compensated, the court may order appearance or production only upon specified conditions.

(d) Duties in Responding to Subpoena.

(1) A person responding to a subpoena to produce documents shall produce them as they are kept in the usual course of business or shall organize and label them to correspond with the categories in the demand.

(2) When information subject to a subpoena is withheld on a claim that it is privileged or subject to protection as trial preparation materials, the claim shall be made expressly and shall be supported by a description of the nature of the documents, communications, or things not produced that is sufficient to enable the demanding party to contest the claim.

(e) Contempt.

Failure by any person without adequate excuse to obey a subpoena served upon that person may be deemed a contempt of the court from which the subpoena issued. An adequate cause for failure to obey exists when a subpoena purports to require a non-party to attend or produce at a place not within the limits provided by clause (ii) of subparagraph (c)(3)(A).

**Rule 50. Judgment as a Matter of Law in Jury Trials; Alternative Motion for New Trial; Conditional Rulings**

(a) Judgment as a Matter of Law.

(1) If during a trial by jury a party has been fully heard on an issue and there is no legally sufficient evidentiary basis for a reasonable jury to find for that party on that issue, the court may determine the issue against that party and may grant a motion for judgment as a matter of law against that party with respect to a claim or defense that cannot under the controlling law be maintained or defeated without a favorable finding on that issue.

(2) Motions for judgment as a matter of law may be made at any time before submission of the case to the jury. Such a motion shall specify the judgment sought and the law and the facts on which the moving party is entitled to the judgment.

(b) Renewing Motion for Judgment After Trial; Alternative Motion for New Trial; Conditional Rulings.

If, for any reason, the court does not grant a motion for judgment as a matter of law made at the close of all the evidence, the court is considered to have submitted the action to the jury subject to the court's later deciding the legal questions raised by the motion. The movant may renew its request for judgment as a matter of law by filing a motion no later than 10 days after entry of judgment -- and may alternatively request a new trial or join a motion for a new trial under Rule 59. In ruling on a renewed motion, the court may:

(1) if a verdict was returned:

(A) allow the judgment to stand,

(B) order a new trial, or

(C) direct entry of judgment as a matter of law; or

(2) if no verdict was returned:

(A) order a new trial, or

(B) direct entry of judgment as a matter of law.

(c) Granting Renewed Motion for Judgment as a Matter of Law; Conditional Rulings; New Trial Motion.

(1) If the renewed motion for judgment as a matter of law is granted, the court shall also rule on the motion for a new trial, if any, by determining whether it should be granted if the judgment is thereafter vacated or reversed, and shall specify the grounds for granting or denying the motion for the new trial. If the motion for a new trial is thus conditionally granted, the order thereon does not affect the finality of the judgment. In case the motion for a new trial has been conditionally granted and the judgment is reversed on appeal, the new trial shall proceed unless the appellate court has otherwise ordered. In case the motion for a new trial has been conditionally denied, the appellee on appeal may assert error in that denial; and if the judgment is reversed on appeal, subsequent proceedings shall be in accordance with the order of the appellate court.

(2) Any motion for a new trial under Rule 59 by a party against whom judgment as a matter of law is rendered shall be filed no later than 10 days after entry of the judgment.

(d) Same: Denial of Motion for Judgment as a Matter of Law.

If the motion for judgment as a matter of law is denied, the party who prevailed on that motion may, as appellee, assert grounds entitling the party to a new trial in the event the appellate court concludes that the trial court erred in denying the motion for judgment. If the appellate court reverses the judgment, nothing in this rule precludes it from determining that the appellee is entitled to a new trial, or from directing the trial court to determine whether a new trial shall be granted.

# SELECT FEDERAL RULES OF CIVIL PROCEDURE

## Rule 56. Summary Judgment

**(a) For Claimant.**

A party seeking to recover upon a claim, counterclaim, or cross-claim or to obtain a declaratory judgment may, at any time after the expiration of 20 days from the commencement of the action or after service of a motion for summary judgment by the adverse party, move with or without supporting affidavits for a summary judgment in the party's favor upon all or any part thereof.

**(b) For Defending Party.**

A party against whom a claim, counterclaim, or cross-claim is asserted or a declaratory judgment is sought may, at any time, move with or without supporting affidavits for a summary judgment in the party's favor as to all or any part thereof.

**(c) Motion and Proceedings Thereon.**

The motion shall be served at least 10 days before the time fixed for the hearing. The adverse party prior to the day of hearing may serve opposing affidavits. The judgment sought shall be rendered forthwith if the pleadings, depositions, answers to interrogatories, and admissions on file, together with the affidavits, if any, show that there is no genuine issue as to any material fact and that the moving party is entitled to a judgment as a matter of law. A summary judgment, interlocutory in character, may be rendered on the issue of liability alone although there is a genuine issue as to the amount of damages.

**(d) Case Not Fully Adjudicated on Motion.**

If on motion under this rule judgment is not rendered upon the whole case or for all the relief asked and a trial is necessary, the court at the hearing of the motion, by examining the pleadings and the evidence before it and by interrogating counsel, shall if practicable ascertain what material facts exist without substantial controversy and what material facts are actually and in good faith controverted. It shall thereupon make an order specifying the facts that appear without substantial controversy, including the extent to which the amount of damages or other relief is not in controversy, and directing such further proceedings in the action as are just. Upon the trial of the action the facts so specified shall be deemed established, and the trial shall be conducted accordingly.

**(e) Form of Affidavits; Further Testimony; Defense Required.**

Supporting and opposing affidavits shall be made on personal knowledge, shall set forth such facts as would be admissible in evidence, and shall show affirmatively that the affiant is competent to testify to the matters stated therein. Sworn or certified copies of all papers or parts thereof referred to in an affidavit shall be attached thereto or served therewith. The court may permit affidavits to be supplemented or opposed by depositions, answers to interrogatories, or further affidavits. When a motion for summary judgment is made and supported as provided in this rule, an adverse party may not rest upon the mere allegations or denials of the adverse party's pleading, but the adverse party's response, by affidavits or as otherwise provided in this rule, must set forth specific facts showing that there is a genuine issue for trial. If the adverse party does not so respond, summary judgment, if appropriate, shall be entered against the adverse party.

**(f) When Affidavits are Unavailable.**

Should it appear from the affidavits of a party opposing the motion that the party cannot for reasons stated present by affidavit facts essential to justify the party's opposition, the court may refuse the application for judgment or may order a continuance to permit affidavits to be obtained or depositions to be taken or discovery to be had or may make such other order as is just.

**(g) Affidavits Made in Bad Faith.**

Should it appear to the satisfaction of the court at any time that any of the affidavits presented pursuant to this rule are presented in bad faith or solely for the purpose of delay, the court shall forthwith order the party employing them to pay to the other party the amount of the reasonable expenses which the filing of the affidavits caused the other party to incur, including reasonable attorney's fees, and any offending party or attorney may be adjudged guilty of contempt.

## Rule 59. New Trials; Amendment of Judgments

(a) Grounds.

A new trial may be granted to all or any of the parties and on all or part of the issues (1) in an action in which there has been a trial by jury, for any of the reasons for which new trials have heretofore been granted in actions at law in the courts of the United States; and (2) in an action tried without a jury, for any of the reasons for which rehearings have heretofore been granted in suits in equity in the courts of the United States. On a motion for a new trial in an action tried without a jury, the court may open the judgment if one has been entered, take additional testimony, amend findings of fact and conclusions of law or make new findings and conclusions, and direct the entry of a new judgment.

(b) Time for Motion.

Any motion for a new trial shall be filed no later than 10 days after entry of the judgment.

(c) Time for Serving Affidavits.

When a motion for new trial is based upon affidavits, they shall be filed with the motion. The opposing party has 10 days after service to file opposing affidavits, but that period may be extended for up to 20 days, either by the court for good cause or by the parties' written stipulation. The court may permit reply affidavits.

(d) On Initiative of Court.

No later than 10 days after entry of judgment the court, on its own, may order a new trial for any reason that would justify granting one on a party's motion. After giving the parties notice and an opportunity to be heard, the court may grant a timely motion for a new trial for a reason not stated in the motion. When granting a new trial on its own initiative or for a reason not stated in a motion, the court shall specify the grounds in its order.

(e) Motion to Alter or Amend a Judgment.

Any motion to alter or amend a judgment shall be filed no later than 10 days after entry of the judgment.

## Rule 60. Relief from Judgment or Order

(a) Clerical Mistakes.

Clerical mistakes in judgments, orders or other parts of the record and errors therein arising from oversight or omission may be corrected by the court at any time of its own initiative or on the motion of any party and after such notice, if any, as the court orders. During the pendency of an appeal, such mistakes may be so corrected before the appeal is docketed in the appellate court, and thereafter while the appeal is pending may be so corrected with leave of the appellate court.

(b) Mistakes; Inadvertence; Excusable Neglect; Newly Discovered Evidence; Fraud, Etc.

On motion and upon such terms as are just, the court may relieve a party or a party's legal representative from a final judgment, order, or proceeding for the following reasons: (1) mistake, inadvertence, surprise, or excusable neglect; (2) newly discovered evidence which by due diligence could not have been discovered in time to move for a new trial under Rule 59(b); (3) fraud (whether heretofore denominated intrinsic or extrinsic), misrepresentation, or other misconduct of an adverse party; (4) the judgment is void; (5) the judgment has been satisfied, released, or discharged, or a prior judgment upon which it is based has been reversed or otherwise vacated, or it is no longer equitable that the judgment should have prospective application; or (6) any other reason justifying relief from the operation of the judgment. The motion shall be made within a reasonable time, and for reasons (1), (2), and (3) not more than one year after the judgment, order, or proceeding was entered or taken. A motion under this subdivision (b) does not affect the finality of a judgment or suspend its operation. This rule does not limit the power of a court to entertain an independent action to relieve a party from a judgment, order, or proceeding, or to grant relief to a defendant not actually personally notified as provided in Title 28, U.S.C., § 1655, or to set aside a judgment for fraud upon the court. Writs of coram nobis, coram vobis, audita querela, and bills of review and bills in the nature of a bill of review, are abolished, and the procedure for obtaining any relief from a judgment shall be by motion as prescribed in these rules or by an independent action.

### Rule 61. Harmless Error
No error in either the admission or the exclusion of evidence and no error or defect in any ruling or order or in anything done or omitted by the court or by any of the parties is ground for granting a new trial or for setting aside a verdict or for vacating, modifying, or otherwise disturbing a judgment or order, unless refusal to take such action appears to the court inconsistent with substantial justice. The court at every stage of the proceeding must disregard any error or defect in the proceeding which does not affect the substantial rights of the parties.

# Appendix R  Model Fee Schedules and Agreements

SCHEDULE OF FEES AND CONDITIONS

A.      Expert consulting time (report preparation, analysis, consultations, telephone conferences, interviews, inspection, photography, research, review of materials, testing, preparation, including travel (portal to portal)) will be billed at a rate of $xxx.00 per hour plus expenses.  Any time related to the case or project which is beyond the scope of an initial telephone interview of the consultant may be considered billable time.

B.      A minimum **retainer of $xxx.00** will be required **in advance** for all work for un-established accounts and the retainer will be credited against the final bill.  A retainer is required prior to any work being initiated.

C.      Estimates of time anticipated to be spent will be gladly provided upon request.

D.      Upon presentation of reports, any balance due must be paid.  Past due invoices shall be charged interest at the rate of 1.5% per month (annual rate of 18%).  Prepayment is required for deposition and court testimony.  All invoices are due when rendered.

E.      Depositions and travel time are charged at an hourly rate of $xxx.00 plus expenses (minimum 10 hours).  An advance payment of (10) hours, $xxxx, is required, at least five working days prior to the deposition, which is credited towards the total bill.  Billing is made for preparation time, travel time, expenses incurred, time being deposed, waiting time, and time expended to read and correct transcript if required.  Cancellation of a scheduled deposition, with less than 48 hours notice, shall result in a minimum billing of two hours.

F.      Court room testimony time, travel time and court room waiting time will be charged as a minimum of 10 hours for the first day ($xxxx).  (Testimony fee will normally include one hour of telephone preparation time.)  Cancellation of court room testimony at less than 48 hours notice will result in a minimum billing of 2 hours.  Cancellation of court room testimony at less than 24 hours notice will result in a minimum billing of 4 hours.  Same-day cancellation will result in a full-day fee of $xxxx

G.      Scheduled air time over two hours and thirty minutes (2:30 minutes) one way shall be business class.  If business class is not available, such travel shall be first class.

H.      Reasonable and customary expenses for photography, travel, air fare, photograph enlargements, etc. may be billed in addition to hourly rates.  Estimates of expenses anticipated to be spent will be gladly provided upon request.

I.      Checks can be made payable to _____.  Taxpayer ID number is 123-45-6789.

# RETAINER AGREEMENT FOR PROFESSIONAL EXPERT ANALYSIS AND TESTIMONY SERVICES

**Regarding:**

Made by and between:

and

This AGREEMENT, dated the _____ of _____ 2006, incorporating the following:

**1.0 General Scope of Services:** Services may include, but are not limited to, the following: a visit to and examination of the site of the case; photography at the site; review of related documents; telephone consultations; meetings; research; analysis; preparation of written draft preliminary and final reports; assistance in formulating discovery inquiries; preparation of exhibits and demonstrative evidence; testimony at trials, arbitrations, mediations and depositions; assistance during the testimony of others.

**2.0 Compensation:** Compensation to firm shall be as follows:

**2.1 Preparatory Work:** For time spent preparing for the case, including site visit(s), document review, research, analysis, report preparation, trial preparation and travel time: **$XXX per hour.**

**2.2 Testimony:** For time spent testifying, awaiting testimony, assisting in the testimony of others, and for travel to and from the testimony location: **$XXX per hour.** Out-of-state testimony will be charged at a one-day (8-hour) minimum, which will include travel time. Deposition testimony and assistance during the testimony of others will be charged at a 4-hour minimum, which may include travel time.

**2.3 Reimbursable Expenses:** Extraordinary out-of-pocket costs related to the case, such as travel, photography, printing and trial exhibits, shall be reimbursable at cost.

**2.4 Billing:** Billing will be on a monthly billing cycle, except at times where extraordinary costs necessitate interim billing. Fees will be billed against retainers received. Payments are due upon receipt of the bill. Bills not paid within 30 days will incur a 1.5% monthly service charge.

**3.0 Retainers:** Retainers are due and payable in advance as follows:

**3.1 Initial Retainer:** A minimum fee/retainer in the amount of **$XXXXX is due** and payable upon execution. This retainer is non-refundable.

**3.2 Report Retainer:** Due and payable in advance of submission of any preliminary or final report: **$XXX**. If this work is cancelled, the unexpended portion of this retainer shall be refundable.

# MODEL FEE SCHEDULES AND AGREEMENTS

**3.3 Testimony Retainer:** Due and payable in advance of testimony: for testimony in Philadelphia: **$XXXX**; for testimony out of Philadelphia: **$XXXX.** If testimony is cancelled, the unexpended portion of this retainer shall be refundable. Retainer payments for testimony in depositions will not be accepted from opposing attorneys. Law Firm is responsible for the retainer payment.

**4.0 Balance Due:** All outstanding fees shall be paid in full prior to the initiation of reports and prior to testimony.

**5.0 Fees Paid by Third Parties:** Law Firm is responsible for the payment of all fees. If a Third Party, such as an insurance carrier, is designated to pay fees directly to firm, the Third Party shall be identified by name, address, and telephone number herein below:

_____

_____

Law Firm shall instruct the Third Party to identify the name of the case for which compensation is being made, when payment is made.

**6.0 Increase in hourly rates:** Due to inflation or other cost-of-living increases, hourly rates may increase slightly annually. Two months advance notice of any increase will be provided.

**7.0 Referral or Assignment:** If the Law Firm refers or assigns the subject case to another Attorney, Written Notice shall be provided to _____. All outstanding Fees and Reimbursements shall be made at the time of the Notice. If Law Firm retains a direct participating interest in the case, this Agreement will remain in effect.

**8.0 Miscellaneous Provisions:**

**8.1 Representation:** Law Firm's Signee of this Agreement represents that he/she is representing the Law Firm and its obligations under this Agreement.

**8.2 Pennsylvania Law:** This Agreement shall be governed and construed in accordance with the laws of the Commonwealth of Pennsylvania.

**8.3 Termination:** Either party may terminate this Agreement for cause, or in the event that the subject case has been resolved. Written Notice of the Termination or resolution of the subject case, shall be made by the terminating party to the other. All outstanding fees and reimbursements shall be made at Termination.

**9.0 Agreed by the Parties Below:** on the date set forth above:

# THE A–Z GUIDE TO EXPERT WITNESSING

## Standard Contract of Agreement (a)

1. In consideration of his agreeing (b) to serve as consultant/expert (c) to the undersigned, _____ shall be reimbursed for all time spent on the case, including portal-to-portal local travel (d), at a rate of $XXX per hour plus expenses; $XXXX per hour for depositions, with 2 hours fee ($XXXX) due three business days in advance as a condition for scheduling the deposition (e), and the same due for cancellations that occur less than 72 hours in advance (f); and $XXX per hour for trial. Examinees who fail to appear for their duly scheduled independent medical examination incur a charge of two hours ($XXXX); rescheduling is at mutual convenience. (g)

2. For out-of-state travel, the rate of payment shall be $XXXX per day and $XXXX per half day (four hours or fraction thereof) plus all expenses, including travel by first-class conveyance (h) and appropriate lodging if needed. Before such travel is undertaken, and as a condition for its being undertaken, a retainer of $XXXX specific to this travel is expected three business days in advance (i); any existing balance shall also have been paid three business days before departure. PLEASE NOTE: because of vacation scheduling, _____ will be unavailable for testimony in person during the month of August. (j)

3. Payment in a timely (k) manner, made out to _____by name (l), is the sole responsibility of the retaining attorney or insurer (m), irrespective of case outcome (n) or defaulted appearances. Overdue accounts may accrue interest at 6% p.a., prorated (o). Failure to comply may void this agreement (p), leaving the retaining attorney or insurer individually liable for any unpaid balance. This agreement may be terminated by either party upon notice, and such termination shall relieve each party of any assumed or implied obligations other than payment of any balance due (q). _____'s FID# is 12-3456789.

4. A non-refundable replenishable retainer (r) of $ _____ is required before commencement of work on the case, as an advance against which initial expenses are billed (s).

5. The retaining attorney is expected to furnish all relevant documents and materials as they are obtained and to provide all requested documents, materials and examinations as discovery rules permit (t). For out-of-state evaluation or testimony the retaining attorney shall ensure in advance that any licensing problems or conflicts about expert function in that state have been satisfactorily resolved. The retaining attorney understands that my forensic work on the case is not the practice of medicine. (u)

6. Signature below indicates agreement with all (v) these terms; please return one copy to _____.

Signed,

_____

Attorney or firm representative as individual and on behalf of firm (Signatory shall have the power to bind the law firm with regard to this contract.) (w)

Date,

NB: Please send all case materials, legal documents, fees or communications to: (Address)

# MODEL FEE SCHEDULES AND AGREEMENTS

Annotations

(a, b) "Contract" "agreement" and "consideration" are trigger words that signal to attorneys that this a formal contract.

(c) You are initially retained only as a consultant; whether you become an expert depends on your taking the case as meritorious and the attorney accepting you as an expert witness (that is, for deposition or trial). You may remain as a consulting witness, advising the attorney.

(d) To cut through nit-picking, travel time starts when you leave your home or office for court and stops when you return, hence, portal to portal.

(e) It is best to lock in depositions in this manner since you spend a lot of time preparing and clearing space in your schedule.

(f) Cancellations should be paid for if not noticed in advance; you can set your own timing per your schedule.

(g) No-shows of examinees for independent medical examinations are a scheduling bane; this holds the attorney accountable for reminding or even transporting the examinee.

(h) First-class tickets allow you to 1) spread out with the case on the plane and 2) more importantly, reschedule a flight without charges if, as often occurs, the exact time of your appearance shifts repeatedly or unexpectedly.

(i) For unexplained reasons, attorneys are sometimes slow to reimburse travel expenses for deposition, interview or trial. Since you will be investing a considerable amount in travel costs, a secondary retainer is advised. This clause holds the attorney responsible for the considerable cost outlay of travel.

(j) If you know your vacation schedule in advance, declare it; everyone benefits as to scheduling. This allows the attorney to ask for continuance or rescheduling; or to take video depositions if you won't be around; or even, to hire another expert.

(k) You have the right to request timely payment, to prevent excess balance build-up. If the retaining party is relentlessly slow, you may decide to withdraw. Other clauses (l, p, q) address squaring the balances before major steps in the sequence.

(l) If you are the sole proprietor or a member of a group practice or corporation, make that clear so that you do not waste a lot of time swapping checks between payees.

(m) Some attorneys, dunned for appropriately earned fees, will throw up their hands in mock exasperation and say, "You are right, Doc, but what can I do? That client just won't honor his/her obligations." Make it clear that you do not work for the client. The attorney or the insurer (in some civil defense cases) is the responsible party. Working for the client, moreover, can constitute a bias or the appearance of an unethical contingency fee arrangement.

(n) That is, your fee is non-contingent, as it should ethically be. A case decision that goes against your retaining attorney is not grounds for non-payment for your time.

(o) This is a standard rate of interest on overdue accounts, and an incentive to timely payment.

(p) You must be free to withdraw from the case if the contract is breached; this makes the attorney agree to that possibility.

(q) As in the previous clause, your withdrawal does not mean that you may not be paid for the work already done.

(r) On rare occasions attorneys may attempt to tie up (legally bind) an expert by retaining him/her on paper to prevent the other side from using him/her. Such attorneys may pay the retainer, making you ineligible to work for the other side; give you no work to do; and, after settling the case, in part because of the threat of your participation, ask for the retainer back since you did not work. You have been sandbagged, at no cost to the attorney but at lost time and income to you. Making the retainer non-refundable pulls for seriousness and tends to eliminate these shenanigans.

(s) The retainer is not only a means of establishing the contract, but an actual advance against the initial expenses.  When this is used up, it may be replenished with a second retainer; some experts simply submit additional invoices.

(t) This protects you against the effects of withheld documents by your attorney; you have put the attorney on notice that you want it all.  Anything less may require adjustment of the opinion.

(u) This does not come up often but attempts may be made to disqualify you in a state in which you are not licensed; states vary widely on this.  This clause makes it the attorney's problem.

(v) A small word, but one that prevents attorney selection of only some terms to agree with.

(w) This protects you if the paralegal signs or if the main attorney on the case changes or leaves the law firm; this clause means the contract remains valid even if the original signer is gone.

# MODEL FEE SCHEDULES AND AGREEMENTS

## EXPERT FEES

$xxx.00 per hour for all services *except* appearance (or video in lieu of appearance) for trial or arbitration.

$xxx.00 per hour for videotaped testimony meant for use at trial.

$xxxx.00 half day and $xxxx.00 full day (or part thereof beyond half day) for trial/arbitration appearance.

$xxx.00 portal-to-portal travel time for any service requiring travel. Travel and hotel accommodations, when necessary, to be arranged and paid for by retaining attorney.

**$xxxx.00 (4-hour) retainer to accompany the initial set of documents to be reviewed.**

Subsequently, should I become the *designated* Emergency Medicine Expert on the case in question, I will require a $xxxx.00 "tail-end" retainer which will be held for application to the last fee-for-service payment due at the conclusion of the case.

**Comment:** I am a Professional Corporation (P.C.).
All fees should be paid to:

XXXXXXXXXXXX
Federal Tax ID #12-3456789

## Expert Fee Agreement

1. You, as the hiring attorney, are my client. You are responsible for the payment of all fees as outlined below, regardless of what third parties are involved or the outcome of the case.

2. My current fee for all medical legal activities is **$xxx.00** per hour. This includes medical records review, review of depositions, literature searches, consultation time, preparation for deposition and trial testimony, oral or written reports, all travel time (billed as portal to portal), deposition and trial testimony or any miscellaneous task as requested by client. All payments should be made to _____, M.D., and mailed to my home address as above. My Social Security number is 123-45-6789

3. A retainer fee of **$xxxx.00** is required prior to commencing any work on a case. This retainer will be kept until the case is completed and will be applied to the final billing statement. This retainer represents the minimum fees to be paid for review of any case. If the retainer is in excess of the final bill, the difference will be refunded to the client unless total case fees are less than $xxxx.00.

4. Billing will occur approximately monthly depending upon services provided. Payment of each bill is expected within 30 days of the date of the statement. Accounts over 30 days will be charged interest of 10% per month.

5. All out-of-the-area travel which requires an overnight stay is billed at $xxxx per day. If I must cancel an entire office day to provide requested services, my fees are also $xxxx per day.

6. If I am scheduled for a consultation, deposition, or court testimony and the case is settled or delayed, my fees for the time away from my practice remain the same. Clients can avoid charges for events requiring rescheduling or cancellation by notifying me at least one week in advance of the scheduled event.

7. Travel and actual expenses reasonably and necessarily incurred (such as meals, lodging, ground transportation, etc.) will be billed to the client at cost and copies of bills will be attached to all invoices. Travel by auto will be billed at $0.xx per mile. Business class or first class air travel is expected on all flights over one hour duration.

8. Fees for deposition shall be paid prior to the start based upon the anticipated length of the examination with a two-hour minimum fee. Balances due, if any, shall be paid within 10 days of the deposition. If the opposing attorney is designated to pay deposition costs and fails to pay them, the client will be responsible for the bill.

9. After a case is closed or settled, fees are not available for retrospective negotiation and cannot be linked in any way to the outcome of the case. Any contingency fees are unacceptable and unethical.

10. _____ reserves the right to suspend all work and refuse delivery of further services or reports until outstanding balances over 30 days old are paid in full.

11. If the client violates the terms of this contract, client is responsible for all legal fees and court costs associated with resolution of the dispute.

# MODEL FEE SCHEDULES AND AGREEMENTS

I acknowledge that I have read the above contract and terms of payment to _____ for all services related to expert medical review. I agree that all of the above fees and terms are acceptable. I understand that my firm is responsible for the payment of all fees as described above. By signing this agreement and enclosing the retainer fee of $xxxx.00, I have engaged the medical legal services of _____ for the case noted below.


_____
Attorney Signature                                      Date

# Appendix S  Model Bills

September 19, 2006

John Attorney
555 Deer Park Lane
Suite 123
New York, NY  10038

RE:  Mary Jones  vs. ABC Company, Inc.
     Date of Accident:  5/10/05
     CIV Number:   96-4354 (BSJ)

**INVOICE NO.  1-2059.1**        **IRS  Identification Number:  12-345-6789**

SERVICES RENDERED:

| | |
|---|---|
| -06/20/06:Generate case file | 0.1 hrs. |
| -07/14/06:Review documents | 1.3 hrs. |
| -07/15/06:Review documents | 3.6 hrs. |
| -08/26/06:Review documents | 1.3 hrs. |
| -08/28/06:Review documents | 0.6 hrs. |
| -08/29/06:Review documents | 2.1 hrs. |
| -08/30/06:Review documents; outline report | 1.0 hrs. |
| -09/01/06:Write report | 4.0 hrs. |
| -09/02/06:Write report | 3.5 hrs. |
| -09/03/06:Write report | 2.1 hrs. |
| -09/05/06:Edit/type report | 0.6 hrs. |
| -09/08/06:T/C's with Attorneys Hobbes & Ally | 0.3 hrs. N/C |
| -09/08/06:Further revise and fax report | 0.3 hrs. |
| -09/10/06:Three T/C's with Attorney Ally | 1.0 hrs. |
| -09/11/06:Revise report | 1.3 hrs. |
| -09/15/06:T/C with Karen Cho | 0.2 hrs. N/C |
| -09/17/06:T/C's with Attorney Ally; revise report | 0.6 hrs. N/C |
| -09/17/06:Letter to Attorney Hobbes | 0.2 hrs. N/C |
| -09/19/06:Review and sign reports | 0.1 hrs. N/C |

**TOTAL DUE:**        **$3,990.00**

---

**INVOICE NO.:**        **IRS Identification Number:** 12-345-6789

---

RETAINER FOR CONSULTING SERVICES          $1,250.00

**TOTAL DUE:**          **$1,250.00**

NOTE: We will bill against the retainer. We will refund or invoice additionally depending on the time and cost expended.

     Work will begin on receipt of retainer.

# MODEL BILLS

June 3, 2006

RE:_____

Dear Mr. _____:

      This bill is for professional services rendered by _____ as follows:

1.     Onsite inspection, September 10, 2005, physical measurements, photography, including travel time (Washington, DC)            9.5 hrs.

| | |
|---|---|
| 11:30 AM-1:30 PM | Travel from West Islip to LaGuardia Airport |
| 1:30 PM-2:30 PM | NYC to Washington, DC air travel |
| 2:30 PM-5:00 PM | Onsite inspection, physical measurements, photography |
| 5:00 PM-6:30 PM | Travel to Washington National Airport |
| 6:30 PM-7:30 PM | Washington National Airport to LaGuardia Airport |
| 7:30 PM-9:00 PM | LaGuardia Airport to West Islip |

2.     Review of materials provided           .5 hrs.
3.     Research and review of codes and standards      1.0 hrs.
4.     Research Kennedy Western University, review of expert report and telephone conferences    (Actual 3.00 hrs.)    1.5 hrs.
5.     Draft Report preparation, case analysis, standby until settlement (Actual 6.00 hrs.)       4.0 hrs.

| | |
|---|---|
| TOTAL: | 16.5 hrs |
| 16.5 hrs. @ $220.00 = | $3,630.00 |
| 35 Black & white photographs @ $7.00 ea. | |
| (time lapse and flash) | $ 245.00 |
| Color photographs | $ 21.00 |
| Travel expenses (mileage, airport parking) | $ 38.00 |
| Airline Travel Expenses (copy of invoice attached) | $ 306.50 |
| TOTAL: | $4,240.50 |
| Less Retainers ($750 initial, $1600 inspection) | ($2,350.00) |
| **BALANCE DUE:** | **$1,890.50** |

**SS#:** 012-34-5678

Ernest Lawyer, Esq.
Ketchum & Cheatum, LLP
1800 Tall Building, Suite 720
Philadelphia, PA  19000

April 30, 2006
For Period: 03/26/06-04/29/06

RE:  Good Guy v. Bad Guy, Inc.

| Date | Service | Hours | Rate | Amount |
|------|---------|-------|------|--------|
| 4/15/06 | telephone correspondence, review documents | 0.5 | $225 | $112.5 |
| 4/15/06 | review documents, supp. report | 3.5 | $225 | $787.5 |
| 4/19/06 | written correspondence | 0.75 | $225 | $168.75 |
| 4/22/06 | testimony at trial | 3 | $325 | $975 |
| 4/22/06 | travel, trial prep. | 6 | $225 | $1350 |
| 4/23/06 | travel, trial prep. | 6 | $225 | $1350 |
| 4/23/06 | testimony at trial | 2 | $325 | $650 |
| 4/24/06 | trial prep. | 1 | $225 | $225 |
| 4/26/06 | travel, trial prep. | 6 | $225 | $1350 |

**Terms:  Net Due Upon Receipt**

**EXPERT Tax ID #123-45-6789**          **BILLED THIS MONTH:  $9,243.75**

# MODEL BILLS

Ernest Lawyer, Esq.
Ketchum & Cheatum, LLP
1800 Tall Building, Suite 720
Philadelphia, PA  19000

**4/30/06**

**Total Amount Due: $17,956.25**

| Date | Summary of Bills, Payments, & Fin. Charges | Amount | Balance |
|------|--------------------------------------------|--------|---------|
| 03/31/06 | Balance Forward | | $412.50 |
| | **Good Guy v. Bad Guy, Inc.** | | |
| 04/09/06 | Inv. #155 | $10,800.00 | $11,212.50 |
| 04/24/06 | PMT #3534 | $- 2,500.00 | $ 8,712.50 |
| 04/30/06 | Inv. #165 | $ 9,243.75 | $17,956.25 |

| Current | 1-30 Days Past Due | 31-60 Days Past Due | 61-90 Days Past Due | Over 90 Days Past Due | Total Amount Due |
|---------|--------------------|--------------------|--------------------|----------------------|------------------|
| $9,243.75 | $8,712.50 | 0.00 | 0.00 | 0.00 | $17,956.25 |

547

# Appendix T  Model CVs

**Harold J. Bursztajn, M.D.**

## CURRICULUM VITAE

PERSONAL INFORMATION
- Born November 18, 1950, Lodz, Poland
- Married
- Tax ID #123-45-6789

EDUCATION
- 1968: Diploma, Eastside High School, Paterson, NJ
- 1972: A.B. Princeton University, Princeton, NJ
- 1977: M.D. Harvard Medical School, Boston, MA

POSTDOCTORAL TRAINING
- Internships and Residencies:
  - *1977-1978: *Resident in Pediatrics*, Children's Hospital Medical Center
  - *1979-1982: *Resident in Psychiatry*, Massachusetts Mental Health Center
  - *1981-1982: *Chief Resident*, Program in Psychiatry and the Law, Massachusetts Mental Health Center
- Fellowships and Other Education:
  - *1975-1976: *Special Fellow*, Department of Preventive and Social Medicine, Harvard Medical School
  - *1978-1980: *Research Fellow*, Division of Family Medicine and Primary Care, Harvard Medical School
  - *1981: *Special Student*, Harvard Law School
  - *1981: *Candidate*, Boston Psychoanalytic Institute
  - *1989: *Advanced Candidate*, Boston Psychoanalytic Institute

LICENSURE AND CERTIFICATION
- 1978: Massachusetts, #43038
- 1982: New Hampshire, #6572
- 1984: American Board of Psychiatry and Neurology, #26278
- 1994: American Board of Psychiatry and Neurology Added Qualifications in Forensic Psychiatry, #38

ACADEMIC APPOINTMENTS
- 1982-1984: *Clinical Instructor*, Department of Psychiatry, Harvard Medical School
- 1984-1990: *Assistant Clinical Professor*, Department of Psychiatry, Harvard Medical School
- 1990-: *Associate Clinical Professor*, Department of Psychiatry, Harvard Medical School

HOSPITAL APPOINTMENTS
- 1978-1979: Metropolitan State Hospital, Waltham, MA
- 1979-1982: Massachusetts General Hospital, Boston, MA
- 1982-1986: Hampstead Hospital, Hampstead, NH

- 1985-: Massachusetts Mental Health Center, Boston, MA
- 1986-: Mount Auburn Hospital, Cambridge, MA
- 1989-: Beth Israel Hospital, Boston, MA

## OTHER PROFESSIONAL POSITIONS AND MAJOR VISITING APPOINTMENTS
- 1968-1972: *Health Consultant*, Model Cities Program, Paterson, NJ
- 1978-1979: *Acting Medical Director*, Concord Unit, Metropolitan State Hospital
- 1983-: *Co-Director*, Program in Psychiatry and the Law of Harvard Medical School Department at the Massachusetts Mental Health Center
- 1985 (July): *Acting Medical Director*, Hampstead Hospital, Hampstead, NH
- 1994-: *Consultant,* National Institutes of Health, Bethesda, M.D.

## AWARDS AND HONORS
- 1968-1972: *University Scholar*, Princeton University
- 1972: *Phi Beta Kappa*
- 1972: *magna cum laude,* Department of Philosophy, Princeton University
- 1977: *cum laude* Honors Thesis, Harvard Medical School
- 1981: *Co-winner*, Solomon Award, Massachusetts Mental Health Center
- 1983: *Second Place*, Solomon Award, Massachusetts Mental Health Center
- 1998: *Honorary mention*, Article: Medical Negligence and Informed Consent in the Managed Care Era, The American College of Physician Executives

## COMMITTEE ASSIGNMENTS
- 1972-1977: Recruiter, socioeconomically disadvantaged students, Harvard Medical School
- 1974-1976: Harvard Medical School Admissions Committee, Subcommittee II, student member
- 1974-1977: Boston Alumni School Committee of Princeton University
- 1982-1986: Hampstead Hospital, Peer Review Committee
- 1984: International Advisory Committee, International Congress on Psychiatry, Law and Ethics, Israel
- 1988-: Campaign for the Third Century Committee, Harvard Medical School
- 1988-1989: Harvard Medical School Admissions Committee, Subcommittee II, faculty member
- 1988-1989: Ethics Committee, Mount Auburn Hospital
- 1990-: Committee on Institute Analysis, Boston Psychoanalytic Institute
- 1990-: Massachusetts Board of Registration, Medicine, Consultant and Supervisor
- 1991-: Charter Supporter, United States Holocaust Memorial Hospital
- 1996-: Rappeport Fellowship Committee, American Academy of Psychiatry & the Law
- 1997-: Subtaskforce on Competency to Stand Trial. American Academy of Psychiatry and the Law
- 1998-: Advisory and Expert Panel Member, State Justice Institute (SJI) Benchbook Project on Psychiatric and Psychological Evidence. American Bar Association
- 1999-: Advisory Board, The International Center for Health Concerns
- 1999-: Gender Issues Committee, American Academy of Psychiatry & the Law

## MEMBERSHIPS, OFFICES, AND COMMITTEE ASSIGNMENTS IN SOCIETIES
- 1972-: Phi Beta Kappa
- 1975-: The Hastings Center Institute and Society, Ethics and the Life Sciences; Associate member
- 1976-: Society for Health and Human Values
- 1979-: Society for Medical Decision Making
- 1980-: American Academy of Psychiatry and the Law

- 1981-: American Society of Law and Medicine
- 1981-: American Psychiatric Association
- 1984-: American Psychoanalytic Association
- 1994-: American Academy of Forensic Sciences
- 1995-: American College of Physician Executives
- 1997-: The Academy of Experts
- 1997-: American Hospital Association
- 1998-: Physicians for Human Rights

## MAJOR RESEARCH INTERESTS

1. Psychiatry, medical decision making, ethics, and the law
2. Informed consent and risk management
3. Trauma and the life cycle
4. Forensic neuropsychiatric evaluation of disability and diminished capacity

## PRINCIPAL CLINICAL, HOSPITAL SERVICE RESPONSIBILITIES AND PROFESSIONAL ACTIVITY

- Presently: Private Practice, Cambridge, MA
  Consultant to attorneys and institutions
- *Co-Director*, Program in Psychiatry and the Law of Harvard Medical School Department at the Massachusetts Mental Health Center

## TEACHING EXPERIENCE

- 1982-1983: Psychiatric Decision-Making Seminar - Harvard Medical School Core
- 1982-: Psychiatry, the Law, and the Practice of Medicine; North House Seminar 113, Harvard University
- 1982-: Ethics Rounds, Massachusetts Mental Health Center, New England Deaconess Hospital, Mount Auburn Hospital
- 1983-: Program in Psychiatry and the Law Research Seminar, Massachusetts Mental Health Center, Co-Director
- 1991-: Extension Division, Boston Psychoanalytic Institute-Clinical Ethics, Risk Management, and the Psychoanalytic Perspective

## EDITORIAL

- 1988-: Editorial Board-Adult Development, Book Review Board of the American Journal of Psychotherapy
- Occasional Article, Book and Video Reviewer:
    * American Academy of Psychiatry and the Law
    * American Journal of Psychiatry
    * Archives of Internal Medicine
    * Bioscience
    * Boston Psychoanalytic Society Newsletter
    * Contemporary Psychiatry
    * The Forensic Examiner
    * General Hospital Psychiatry
    * Hospital and Community Psychiatry
    * Journal of Child and Adolescent Psychopharmacology
    * Journal of Clinical Ethics
    * Journal of Health Politics, Policy and Law

* Medical Decision Making
* Merloyd Lawrence Books: Addison-Wesley
* New England Journal of Medicine
* Oxford Medical Publications
* Patient Care
* Routledge, Chapman & Hall: Methuen Inc.

BIBLIOGRAPHY
Original Reports
1. Bursztajn HJ. The role of a training protocol in formulating patient instructions as to terminal care choices. J Med Educ. 1977; 52:347-348.
2. Bursztajn HJ, Hamm RM. Medical maxims: two views of science. Yale J Biol Med. 1979; 52:483-486.
3. Bursztajn HJ, Hamm RM. The clinical utility of utility assessment. Med Decision Making. 1982; 2:162-165.
4. Wulsin LR, Bursztajn HJ, Gutheil TG. Unexpected clinical features of the Tarasoff decision: the therapeutic alliance and the "duty to warn." Am J Psychiatry. 1983; 140:601-603.
5. Gutheil TG, Bursztajn HJ, Hamm RM, Brodsky A. Subjective data and suicide assessment in the light of recent legal developments. Part I: Malpractice prevention and the use of subjective data. Int J Law Psychiatry. 1983; 6:317-329.
6. Bursztajn HJ, Gutheil TG, Hamm RM, Brodsky A. Subjective data and suicide assessment in the light of recent legal developments. Part II: Clinical uses of legal standards in the interpretation of subjective data. Int J Law Psychiatry. 1983; 6:331-350.
7. Gutheil TG, Bursztajn HJ, Brodsky A. Malpractice prevention through the sharing of uncertainty: informed consent and the therapeutic alliance. N Engl J Med. 1984; 311:49-51. Reprinted in 'Grand Rounds on Medical Malpractice' article 3.2, p.131-133.
8. Bursztajn HJ, Hamm RM, Gutheil TG, Brodsky A. The decision-analytic approach to medical malpractice law: formal proposals and informal syntheses. Med Decision Making. 1984; 4:401-414.
9. Hamm RM, Clark JA, Bursztajn HJ. Psychiatrists' thorny judgments: describing and improving decision-making processes. Med Decision Making. 1984; 4:425-447.
10. Bursztajn HJ, Barsky AJ. Facilitating patient acceptance of a psychiatric referral. Arch Intern Med. 1985; 145:73-75.
11. Bursztajn HJ. More law and less protection: "critogenesis," "legal iatrogenesis," and medical decision-making. J Geriat Psychiatry. 1985; 18:143-153.
12. Bursztajn HJ, Gutheil TG, Mills M, Hamm RM, Brodsky A. Process analysis of judges' commitment decisions: a preliminary empirical study. Am J Psychiatry. 1986; 143:170-174.
13. Gutheil TG, Bursztajn HJ, Brodsky A. The multidimensional assessment of dangerousness: competence assessment in patient care and liability prevention. Bull Am Acad Psychiatry Law. 1986; 14:123-129.
14. Bursztajn HJ, Gutheil TG, Warren MJ, Brodsky A. Depression, self-love, time, and the "right" to suicide. Gen Hospital Psychiatry. 1986; 8:91-95.
15. Bursztajn HJ. Ethicogenesis. Gen Hospital Psychiatry. 1986; 8:422-424.
16. Gutheil TG, Bursztajn HJ. Clinicians' guidelines for assessing and presenting subtle forms of patient incompetence in legal settings. Am J Psychiatry. 1986; 143:1020-1023.
17. Pavlo AM, Bursztajn HJ, Gutheil TG, Levi LM. Weighing religious beliefs in determining competence. Hospital and Community Psychiatry. 1987; 38:350-352.
18. Pavlo AM, Bursztajn HJ, Gutheil TG. Christian Science and competence to make treatment choices: clinical challenges in assessing values. Int J Law Psychiatry. 1987; 395-401.

19. Gutheil TG, Bursztajn HJ, Kaplan AN, Brodsky A. Participation in competency assessment and treatment decisions: the role of a psychiatrist-attorney team. Mental Physical Disabilities Law Reporter. 1987; 11:446-449.

20. Bursztajn HJ, Gutheil TG, Hamm RM, Brodsky A, Mills M. Parens Patriae considerations in the commitment process. Psychiatric Quart. 1988; 59:3:165-181.

21. Bursztajn HJ, Gutheil TG, Brodsky A, Swagerty E. Magical thinking, suicide, and malpractice litigation. Bull Am Acad Psychiatry Law, 1988; 16:369-376.

22. Bursztajn HJ, Harding HP, Gutheil TG, Brodsky A. Beyond cognition: the role of disordered affective states in impairing competence to consent to treatment. Bull Am Acad Psychiatry Law. 1991; 19:383-388.

23. Bursztajn HJ, Chanowitz B, Kaplan E, Gutheil TG, Hamm RM, Alexander V. Medical and judicial perceptions of the risks associated with use of antipsychotic medication. Bull Am Acad Psychiatry Law. 1991; 19:271-275.

24. Bursztajn HJ, Chanowitz B, Gutheil TG, Hamm RM. Micro-effects of language on risk perception in drug prescribing behavior. Bull Am Acad Psychiatry Law. 1992; 20:59-66.

25. Deaton RJS, Illingworth PML, Bursztajn HJ. Unanswered questions about the criminalization of therapist-patient sex. Am J Psychotherapy. 1992; 46:526-531.

26. Bursztajn HJ. From PSDA to PTSD: The patient self-determination act and post-traumatic stress disorder. J Clinical Ethics. 1993; 4:71-74.9

27. Pitman RK, Orr SP, Bursztajn HJ. Vinal v. New England Telephone: admission of PTSD psychophysiologic test results in a civil trial. AAPL Newsletter. 1993; 18(3): 67-69.

28. Bursztajn HJ, Scherr AE, Brodsky A. The rebirth of forensic psychiatry in light of recent historical trends in criminal responsibility. Psychiat Clinics N Am. 1994; 17:611-635.

29. Bursztajn HJ, Brodsky A. Authenticity and autonomy in the managed care era: forensic psychiatric perspectives. J Clinical Ethics. 1994; 5:237-242.

30. Bursztajn HJ, Brodsky A. Clear, convincing, and authentic advance directives in the context of managed care? J Clinical Ethics. 1994; 5:364-366.

31. Bursztajn HJ. Reflections on my father's experience with doctors during the Shoah (1939-1945). J Clinical Ethics. 1996; 7:100-102.

32. Bursztajn HJ, Brodsky A. A new resource for managing malpractice risks in managed care. Archives of Internal Medicine. 1996; 156:2057-2063.

33. Bursztajn HJ, Saunders LS, Brodsky A. Medical negligence and informed consent in the managed care era. Health Lawyer. 1997; 9(5): 14-17.

34. Bursztajn HJ, Hamm RM, Gutheil TG. Beyond the black letter of the law: an empirical study of a judge's decision-making process in civil commitment hearings. Bull Am Acad Psychiatry Law. 1997; 25:79-94.

35. Bursztajn HJ, Brodsky A. Ethical and legal dimensions of benzodiazepine prescription. Psychiatric Annals. 1998; 28(3): 121-128.

36. Bursztajn HJ, Gutheil TG, Brodsky A. Ethics and the triage model in managed care hospital psychiatry. Psychiatric Times. 1998; 15(9): 33-40.

37. Bursztajn HJ, Sobel R. Accountability without health care data banks. Health Affairs. 1998; 17(6): 252-253.

38. Bursztajn HJ. Melatonin therapy: from benzodiazepine-dependent insomnia to authenticity and autonomy. Archives of Internal Medicine. 1999; 159 (20): 2393-2395.

39. Bursztajn HJ, Brodsky A. Captive patients, captive doctors: clinical dilemmas and interventions in caring for patients in managed health care. General Hospital Psychiatry. 1999, 21., 239-248.

40. Bursztajn HJ, Berman S. What is in a neuropsychiatric diagnosis? Evidence-Based Mental Health. In Press.

## Book Chapters

1. Feinbloom RI, Bursztajn HJ, Hamm RM, Brodsky A. Bringing the family into family practice. In: Brazelton TB, Vaughn VC III, eds. The family: Setting Priorities. New York: Science and Medicine Publishing Co, 1979; 169-179.

2. Bursztajn HJ, Hamm RM, Gutheil TG. The technological target: involving the patient in clinical choices. In: Reiser SJ, Anbar M, eds. The Machine at the Bedside: Strategies for Using Technology in Patient Care. Cambridge, England: Cambridge University Press, 1984; 177-191.

3. Bursztajn HJ, Gutheil TG, Cummins B. Legal issues in inpatient psychiatry. In: Sederer LI, ed. Inpatient Psychiatry. 2d ed, Baltimore: Williams and Wilkins, 1986; 338-356.

4. Bursztajn HJ, Gutheil TG, Cummins B. Legal issues in inpatient psychiatry. In: Sederer LI, ed. Inpatient Psychiatry. 3d ed., Baltimore: Williams and Wilkins, 1991; 379-406.

5. Bursztajn HJ, Hamm RM, Brodsky A, Alexander V, Levi L. Probability, decision analysis, and conscious gambling. In: Gutheil TG, Bursztajn HJ, Brodsky A, Alexander V, eds. Decision making in psychiatry and the law. Baltimore: Williams & Wilkins, 1991; 37-52.

6. Bursztajn HJ, Hamm RM, Brodsky A, Gutheil TG, Alexander V. Subjective assessment in clinical decision making and malpractice liability. In: Gutheil TG, Bursztajn HJ, Brodsky A, Alexander V, eds. Decision Making in Psychiatry and the Law. Baltimore: Williams & Wilkins, 1991; 53-68.

7. Bursztajn HJ, Gutheil TG, Brodsky A. Affective disorders, competence, and decision-making. In: Gutheil TG, Bursztajn HJ, Brodsky A, Alexander V, eds. Decision Making in Psychiatry and the Law. Baltimore: Williams & Wilkins, 1991; 153-170.

8. Gutheil TG, Bursztajn HJ, Brodsky A, Alexander V. Managing uncertainty: the therapeutic alliance, informed consent, and liability. In: Gutheil TG, Bursztajn HJ, Brodsky A, Alexander V, eds. Decision Making in Psychiatry and the Law. Baltimore: Williams & Wilkins, 1991; 69-88.

9. Alexander V, Bursztajn HJ, Brodsky A, Hamm RM, Gutheil TG, Levi L. Involuntary commitment. In: Gutheil TG, Bursztajn HJ, Brodsky A, Alexander V, eds. Decision Making in Psychiatry and the Law. Baltimore: Williams & Wilkins, 1991; 89-112.

10. Kaplan E, Bursztajn HJ, Alexander V, Hamm RM, Brodsky A, Barnard D, Kaplan AN. Making treatment decisions. In: Gutheil TG, Bursztajn HJ, Brodsky A, Alexander V, eds. Decision Making in Psychiatry and the Law. Baltimore: Williams & Wilkins, 1991; 113-132.

11. Alexander V, Bursztajn HJ, Brodsky A, Gutheil TG. Deciding for others; autonomy and protection in tension. In: Gutheil TG, Bursztajn HJ, Brodsky A, Alexander V, eds. Decision Making in Psychiatry and the Law. Baltimore: Williams & Wilkins, 1991; 133-152.

12. Warren M, Commons ML, Gutheil TG, Swagerty EL, Bursztajn HJ, Brodsky A. Suicide, magical thinking, and liability. In: Gutheil TG, Bursztajn HJ, Brodsky A, Alexander V, eds. Decision Making in Psychiatry and the Law. Baltimore: Williams & Wilkins, 1991; 189-208.

13. Hauser MJ, Commons ML, Bursztajn HJ, Gutheil TG. Fear of malpractice liability and its role in clinical decision-making. In: Gutheil TG, Bursztajn HJ, Brodsky A, Alexander V, eds. Decision Making in Psychiatry and the Law. Baltimore: Williams & Wilkins, 1991; 209-226.

14. Canning S, Hauser MJ, Gutheil TG, Bursztajn HJ. Communications in psychiatric practice: Decision-making and the use of the telephone. In: Gutheil TG, Bursztajn HJ, Brodsky A, Alexander V, eds. Decision Making in Psychiatry and the Law. Baltimore: Williams & Wilkins, 1991; 227-238.

15. Commons ML, Sonnert G, Gutheil TG, Bursztajn HJ. Ethics and decisions about suicide. In: Gutheil TG, Bursztajn HJ, Brodsky A, Alexander V, eds. Decision Making in Psychiatry and the Law. Baltimore: Williams & Wilkins, 1991; 239-256.

16. Deaton RJS, Colenda CC, Bursztajn HJ. Medical-legal issues. In: Stoudemire A, Fogel BS, eds. Psychiatric Care of the Medical Patient. New York: Oxford University Press, 1993; 929-938.

17. Deaton R, Bursztajn HJ. Antipsychotic medication: regulation through the right to refuse. In: Schwartz HI, ed. Psychiatric Practice Under Fire. Washington, DC: American Psychiatric Press, Inc., 1994; 85-101.
18. Bursztajn HJ. One axiom and eight corollaries for managing legal issues in an inpatient psychiatric setting. In: Docherty JP, ed. Inpatient Psychiatry in the 1990s. San Francisco: Jossey-Bass Publishers, 1994; 95-107.
19. Bursztajn HJ, Brodsky A. Competence and insanity. In: Jacobson JL, Jacobson AM, eds. Psychiatric Secrets. Philadelphia: Hanley & Belfus, Inc., 1996; 501-515.
20. Bursztajn HJ, Brodsky A. Patients who sue and clinicians who are sued in the managed-care era. In: Lifson LE, Simon RI, eds. The Mental Health Practitioner and the Law. Cambridge, MA: Harvard University Press, 1998; 237-249.
21. Bursztajn HJ, Brodsky A. Ethical and effective testimony during direct examination and cross-examination post-Daubert. In: Lifson LE, Simon RI, eds. The Mental Health Practitioner and the Law. Cambridge, MA: Harvard University Press, 1998; 262-280.
22. Bursztajn HJ. Responses to a defective managed care product: medical negligence, lack of informed consent, and choicelessness. In: 2000 Wiley Expert Witness Update. New York: Aspen Law Business/Panel Publishers, 2000; 239-264.

Books
1. Reiser SJ, Bursztajn HJ, Gutheil TG, Appelbaum PS. Divided Staffs, Divided Selves: A Case Approach to Mental Health Ethics. Cambridge, England: Cambridge University Press, 1987.
2. Bursztajn HJ, Feinbloom RI, Hamm RM, Brodsky A. Medical Choices, Medical Chances: How Patients, Families, and Physicians Can Cope With Uncertainty. New York: Delacorte, 1981; New York: Routledge, Chapman & Hall, 1990.
3. Gutheil TG, Bursztajn HJ, Brodsky A, Alexander V, eds. Decision Making in Psychiatry and the Law. Baltimore: Williams & Wilkins, 1991.

COURSE CO-DIRECTOR AND FACULTY
Harvard Medical School, Department of Continuing Education and Massachusetts Mental Health Center:
    "Ethical Issues in Clinical Practice," September 1990
    "Sex Between Clinicians and Patients: Clinical, Legal and Medico-Legal Perspectives," September 1990
    "Malpractice Prevention for the 1990s: An Update on the Issues and Practical Approaches," January 1991
    "The Clinician in Court: A Survival Guide," January 1992
    "Dangers and Pitfalls of Forensic Practice," January 1992
    "Liability Prevention for Medical and Surgical Practitioners: Trends and Update," January, 1993.
    "Doctors and Nurses in Court: A Basic Survival Guide," January, 1993.
    "Malpractice in the 1990s: Trends and Update," February, 1993.
    "The Clinician in Court: A Survival Guide," February, 1993.
    Massachusetts Bar Association, Continuing Legal Education Course:
    "Nuts and Bolts of Using Medical Experts at Trial," November 1990

FACULTY
Harvard Medical School, Department of Continuing Education and Massachusetts Mental Health Center:
"Intensive Diagnostic Interviewing," 1990-

RECENT PRESENTATIONS

1. "Prevention of Violence and Suicide by the High Risk Patient," Mount Auburn Hospital Grand Rounds, Cambridge, MA, September 15, 1992.

2. "Malpractice Prevention," Brookside Hospital Grand Rounds, Nashua, New Hampshire, March 15, 1993.

3. "Post-Traumatic Stress Disorder in the Courtroom," Panel, American Psychiatric Association, San Francisco, California, May 26, 1993.

4. "Psychiatry Issues," Medical Malpractice Seminar for Office of Legal Education, Executive Office for United States Attorneys, Salt Lake City, Utah, July 1993.

5. "Liability for Sexual Misconduct of Government Providers," with Thomas G. Gutheil, M.D., Workshop, Office of Legal Education, Executive Office for United States Attorneys, Salt Lake City, Utah, July 13, 1993.

6. "Competency to Confess to a Criminal Act," American Academy of Forensic Sciences, Boston, Massachusetts, 1993.

7. "Malpractice Prevention in High Risk Doctor-Patient Encounters," Lawrence General Hospital, Lawrence, Massachusetts, January 18, 1994.

8. "Forensic Psychiatric Assessment of Mental Damages," Discussant, Panel, American Psychiatric Association, Philadelphia, Pennsylvania, May 24, 1994.

9. "What is Forensic Psychiatry?: A Guide for Judges." New Hampshire Bar Association Meeting, January 27, 1995.

10. "Diminished Capacity in the Criminal Justice System." Seventh Annual Bridgewater State Hospital Conference, April 7, 1995.

11. "Fact vs. Expert Witness." Workshop, The Clinician in Court: A Survival Guide, Harvard Medical School Department of Continuing Education, April 8, 1995.

12. "Medical Choices, Managed Care and Uncertainty." Medical Staff Conference, Emerson Hospital, Concord, MA, June 9, 1995.

13. "Behavioral Strategies for Malpractice Prevention in a Managed Care Era." Medical Grand Rounds, Marlborough Hospital, Marlborough, MA, November 30, 1995.

14. "Violence Against Attorneys, Judges, and Litigants in the Family Law Courtroom." Boston Bar Association, Family Law Section, December 1995.

15. "Violence in the Courtroom." Annual Conference of Massachusetts Probate and Family Court Judges, Stockbridge, MA, May 10, 1996.

16. "How to be an Ethical and Effective Medical Witness, Post-Daubert." National Expert Witness and Litigation Seminar, Hyannis, MA, June 20, 1996.

17. "Effective and Ethical Testimony for Mental Health Professionals." Testifying and Consulting Experts, San Francisco, CA, September 1996.

18. "Being an Ethical and Effective Medical Expert." Testifying and Consulting Experts, San Francisco, CA, September 1996.

19. "Dimensions of a Forensic Psychiatric Home Page." American Academy of Psychiatry and the Law, San Juan, Puerto Rico, October 1996.

20. "From the Shoah to Managed Health: What One Forensic Psychiatrist has Learned about Clinical Ethics." YIVO Institute and New School for Social Research, New York, NY, November 1996.

21. "Preventing Malpractice Litigation in Managed Health Care Settings." Harvard Medical School Department of Continuing Education, November 22, 1996.

22. "Ethical and Effective Testimony for Physicians Accused of Malpractice." Harvard Medical School Department of Continuing Education, November 23, 1996.

23. "Ethical and Decision Making Issues in Primary Care Medicine in a Managed Care Context." Vermont Technical College, Vermont Ethics Network, February 10, 1997.

24. "Surreptitious LSD Administration: Ethical, Toxicologic and Psychiatric Impact on Product Liability Issues." American Academy of Forensic Sciences, February 19, 1997.

25. "Medical Historical Perspectives Regarding Managed Care and Medical Necessity: True and False." Chairman of Symposium on Ethical Issues in Managed Health Care. American Psychiatric Association Annual Meeting, San Diego, CA, May 19, 1997

26. "Medical Necessity, Managed Health Care Denial of Benefits, and the Nuremberg Code." Panel: "Medical Ethics: Who Gets the Care?" Moderator: Professor Uwe E. Reinhardt, Ph.D., Princeton University 250th Anniversary Symposium, Princeton, NJ, May 29, 1997.

27. "Capital Punishment in the Mcveigh Case." BBC World Services. Cambridge, MA, June 13, 1997.

28. "Managed Health Care: Protecting the Quality of Care in the Clinic and the Courtroom." Saints Memorial Medical Center, Lowell, MA, July 9, 1997.

29. "Why Do They Do It? Motivation of Violent Criminals." National Association of Legal Secretaries Annual Meeting and Educational Conference, Boston, MA, July 26, 1997.

30. "Substituting Alliance for Alienation: Supporting the Human Side in Changing Health Care." Advanced Risk Management Seminar, New England Health Care Assembly, Falmouth, MA, July 28, 1997.

31. "High Risk Patients and Families in Chronic Illness Situations." Physicians' Meeting, Spaulding Rehabilitation Hospital, Boston, MA, October 8, 1997.

32. "Protecting Yourself from Potential Litigation from Employees and Patients." Harvard School of Public Health conference: "Leadership in Evolving Health Care Systems." Boston, MA, November 4, 1997.

33. "Forensic Psychiatry and Brain Imaging." Harvard Medical School, Advanced Workshop, "Liability Prevention" postgraduate course, Boston, MA, November 22, 1997.

34. "Sexual Harassment Post Daubert." Presidential Panel, American Academy of Forensic Sciences, San Francisco, CA, February, 1998.

35. "Exploring the Consequences of a National Health Care Data Base: Cyberspace Medicine." Harvard Law School Berkman Center: "Privacy and Cyber/Spaces: Government Databanks and Identification. Medical and Other Instances," Cambridge, MA, May 13, 1998.

36. "Values in the Physician Patient Managed Health Care Relationship." American Psychiatric Association Annual Meeting, Toronto, Canada, June 1, 1998.

37. "Employment Disability and Accommodation Dilemmas." American Psychiatric Association Annual Meeting, Toronto, Canada, June 4, 1998.

38. "Sexual Misconduct in Managed Health Care Settings." Boston Psychoanalytic Society and Institute: "Sexual Misconduct by Psychotherapists, other Health Care Professionals, and Clergy: Prevention and Treatment of Boundary Violations by Professionals." Chestnut Hill, MA, October 4, 1998.

39. "Boundary Violations: How are they defined in the patient-physician relationship?" Massachusetts Medical Society, Waltham, MA, October 7, 1998.

40. "Risk Management: How to reduce medical malpractice suits," Sheraton-Newton Hotel, October 10-11, 1998.

41. "Post-Daubert Sexual Harassment Expert," 1998 Annual Meeting Program, American Academy of Psychiatry and the Law, New Orleans, Louisiana, October 22, 1998.

42. "Functional Brain Imaging and Criminal Behavior," with Lisa Acosta, BA, 1998 Annual Meeting Program, American Academy of Psychiatry and the Law, New Orleans, Louisiana, October 23, 1998.

43. "Protecting Yourself from Potential Litigation from Employees and Patients." Harvard School of Public Health: "Leadership in Evolving Health Care Systems." Boston, MA, November 4, 1998.

44. "Ethical and Legal Issues in Managed Health Care." Mount Auburn Hospital, Cambridge, MA, November 11, 1998.

45. "Ethical & Technical Effects of Daubert on Expert's Opinions." Harvard Medical School: "The Mental Health Clinician in Court: A Survival Guide." Boston, MA, November 21, 1998.
46. "Managed Care, Standards of Care & Informed Consent: How to Present Your Medical Opinion." Harvard Medical School: "Medical and Surgical Practitioners in Court: A Survival Guide." Boston, MA, November 21, 1998.
47. "When am I Going To Be Sued: How Can Physicians, Lawyers, and Surgeons Prevent Malpractice, Sexual Misconduct, and Employee Litigation." Lawrence General Hospital, Lawrence, MA, January 13, 1999.
48. "Forensic Psychiatry and Brain Imaging Testimony Post-Daubert." New England School of Law: "Criminal and Civil Issues Concerning the Mentally Ill: Lawyers, Courts & Mental Health Professionals." Boston, MA, January 1999.
49. "An Essential Guide to Ethical and Effective Conflict Resolution via an Objective Expert's Deposition." SEAK Inc. "National Medical Witness Summit." Fort Lauderdale, FL, February 20-21, 1999.
50. "Boundary Violations: How to Avoid the Slippery Slope." The Massachusetts Medical Society. Holyoke, MA, March 10, 1999.
51. "Clinical Responses to Managed Health Care." American Psychiatric Association, Washington, D.C., May 18, 1999.
52. "Beyond the Court Appointed Custody Expert Post-Daubert." American Psychological Association Convention: " Abusive Practices in Divorce Cases: Clinical, Legal and Ethical Dilemmas." Boston, MA, August 23, 1999.
53. "Clinical Ethics and Shared Decision-Making with Patients and Their Families." Healthcare Educational and Research Fund and Saratoga Hospital, Saratoga, NY, September 18, 1999
54. "Working with High-Risk Patients and Families to Turn Alienation into Patient Loyalty." Healthcare Educational and Research Fund and Saratoga Hospital, Saratoga, NY, September 18, 1999
55. "Brain Imaging and Child Development." Watertown Public School, Watertown, MA, November 4, 1999.
56. "Premises Liability: Ethical and Effective Psychological and Psychiatric Evaluation Post-Daubert." ICLE, Atlanta, Georgia, November 5, 1999.

POPULAR PUBLICATIONS
1. Gutheil TG, Bursztajn HJ, Brodsky A. Liability prevention through informed consent with some new approaches for the clinician. Risk Management Foundation Forum. 1986; 7:8-9.
2. Bursztajn HJ. Flight: the eloquence of silence. Harvard Medical Alumni Bulletin. 1989; 62:3:45-47.
3. Bursztajn HJ. The phobic in court. Lawyers Weekly, December 7, 1992.
4. Bursztajn HJ. The role of a forensic psychiatrist in legal proceedings. Journal of the Massachusetts Academy of Trial Attorneys, Vol. 1, No. 2, October, 1993.
5. Bursztajn HJ. New developments in the role of Post-Traumatic Stress Disorder in civil and criminal law. Journal of the Massachusetts Academy of Trial Attorneys, Vol. 1, No. 3, January, 1994.
6. Bursztajn HJ. Traumatic memories as evidence: true or false? Journal of the Massachusetts Academy of Trial Attorneys, March 15, 1994.
7. Bursztajn HJ. The role of the forensic psychiatrist in civil proceedings. (New Hampshire) Trial Bar News 16, Summer 1994:84-86.
8. Bursztajn HJ. Psychiatric experts in victim litigation. Crime Victims' Litigation Quarterly, Vol. 2, No. 1, February 1995.
9. Bursztajn HJ. Supervisory negligence litigation in context. Journal of the Massachusetts Academy of Trial Attorneys, Vol. 2, No. 2, October, 1994.

10. Bursztajn HJ, Saunders LS, Brodsky A. National certification for forensic psychiatrists: A preview of the post-*Daubert* expert. Journal of the Massachusetts Academy of Trial Attorneys, Vol. 2, No. 4, April, 1995.

11. Saunders LS, Bursztajn HJ, Brodsky A. Recovered memory and managed care: HB 236's post-*Daubert* "science" junket. Trial Bar News 17, Spring 1995:27-37.

12. Bursztajn HJ, Joshi PT, Sutherland SM, Tomb DA (Article Consultants). Recognizing posttraumatic stress. Patient Care, March 30, 1995.

13. Bursztajn HJ, Hilliard JT. Violence Against Attorneys and Judges: Protecting Yourself Before and After a Threat. Journal of the Massachusetts Academy of Trial Attorneys, July, 1995.

14. Bursztajn HJ, Saunders LS, Brodsky A. Daubert without prejudice: Achieving relevance and reliability without randomness. J Mass Acad Trial Attys, January 1996:54-58.

15. Bursztajn HJ, Saunders LS, Brodsky A. Keeping a jury involved during a long trial. Criminal Justice, Vol. 11, 1997:8-9.

16. Bursztajn, HJ. Criminalizing doctor-assisted suicide isn't a cure. The Boston Globe, January 9, 1997.

17. Bursztajn HJ, Brodsky A. Responsibility without scapegoating. Health Decisions, A Publication of The Vermont Ethics Network, May 1997.

18. Bernstine EG, Bursztajn HJ, Wilkens J. Effective use of scientific evidence: lessons from the Simpson trial. J Mass Acad Trial Attys. Winter 1997:22-28.

19. Bernstine EG, Bursztajn, HJ, Wilkens J. Emotional justice: further lessons from the Simpson trial. Journal of the Massachusetts Academy of Trial Attorneys. Spring 1997: 18-26.

20. Bursztajn HJ. Preventing neo-nazi cult violence in our schools. Jewishfamily.com. 1999.

LETTERS TO THE EDITOR

1. Bursztajn HJ. Efficacy research and psychodynamic psychiatry. Am J Psychiatry. 1991; 148:817-818.

2. Bursztajn HJ. Competency to make a will. Am J Psychiatry. 1992; 149:10:1415.

3. Bursztajn HJ. Protecting Patients from clinician-patient sexual contact. Am J Psychiatry. 1992; 149:9:1276.

4. Bursztajn HJ. An overview of sexual harassment. Am J Psychiatry. 1995; 152:3:478.

5. Bursztajn HJ. Psychotherapist versus expert witness. Am J Psychiatry. 1998; 155:2:307.

6. Bursztajn HJ. Recovered Memories. Psychiatric Services. 1998; 49:5:699-700.

7. Bursztajn HJ. On the goals of the Freud Library of Congress Museum Exhibition. New York Times Magazine. November 1, 1998:Section 6:20.

RECENT BOOK REVIEWS

1. Bursztajn HJ. Managing Care, Not Dollars: The Continuum of Mental Health Services. Am J Psychiatry. 1998; 155:7:985.

2. Bursztajn HJ. Managing Managed Care. Am J Psychiatry. 1999; 156:1:148.

## QUALIFICATIONS OF
## DAVID A. DODGE, C.S.P.

**P.O. Box 600, Standish, ME   04084**                **Phone 207-642-5459**
**e-mail:  penhome@mix-net.net**                          **Fax   207-642-2506**

### EXPERIENCE

| | |
|---|---|
| 1986 to Present | Safety and Forensic Consulting |
| | Safety Consultant. Accident analysis in the areas of safety, worker/machinery accidents, products liability and boiler pressure failure and design. |
| | Loss Control Consultant to many insurance companies performing risk evaluation and accident investigation. |
| 1984 to 1986 | Medical and Technical Consultants |
| | Same safety consultations as described above. |
| | Establishment of products and employee safety programs for industry. |
| 1982 to 1983 | Authorized National Board Inspector for General Electric's South Portland, Maine, facility monitoring the quality control of pressure vessels for the nuclear power plant industry. Technical Safety Consultant and Authorized Inspector to the Energy Testing Laboratory of Maine. |
| 1976 to 1981 | Safety Consultant/Manager for Commercial Union Insurance Company in the State of Maine, responsibilities included Bath Iron Works, Great Northern Paper Company, and Scott Paper Company. |
| 1975 to 1976 | Safety Consultant/Manager for Commercial Union Insurance Company, Syracuse, New York.  Established and monitored safety program of Standard Brands, Inc., construction project including over 75 subcontractors. |
| 1974 to 1975 | High Pressure Boiler Design, Riley Stoker Corp., Worcester, Massachusetts. |
| 1971 to 1973 | Safety Consultant for Commercial Union Insurance Company, accident investigation and safety inspection, Boston, Massachusetts. |

### EDUCATION

Maine Maritime Academy, Castine, Maine. Graduated: 1971
B.S. Marine Engineering

Industrial Safety
Northeastern University, Boston, Massachusetts

National Board/A.S.M.E. High Pressure Boiler and Pressure Boiler and Pressure Vessel Welded Repair

Ohio Arson School
Columbus, Ohio

Industrial Safety
University of Massachusetts, Amherst, Massachusetts

Industrial Safety
Syracuse University, Syracuse, New York

Annual Education Requirements for Certified Safety Professional Certification

# MODEL CVS

## TECHNICAL ACCOMPLISHMENTS

- Certified Safety Professional Test Question Examiner
- American Nat'l Standard Institute Committee Member - Lock Out/Tag Out Safety Standard (Z244)
- Formulation of User and Installation Manuals and Labeling for Fundamental Energies, Inc., to comply with Consumer Product Safety Commission regulations
- Technical Safety Consultant and Authorized Inspector to the Energy Testing Laboratory of Maine
- Authorized National Board Inspector for General Electric's South Portland, Maine, Facility monitoring the quality control of pressure vessels for the nuclear power plant industry
- Author of the paper "Product Safety and Liability Prevention"
- Author of the book Safety Manual for Municipalities
- Authored Safety Manual for the State of Maine Correctional Woodworking Program
- Authored Safety Manual for the State of Maine
- Authored Safety Procedures for the State of New Hampshire, Department of Transportation
- Lecturer, "Confined Space Entry", University of Southern Maine
- Lecturer, "Hazardous Materials Recognition", University of Southern Maine
- Developed and taught "Product Safety", University of Southern Maine
- Developed instructions and warnings for Prestone, Inc.

## PROFESSIONAL CERTIFICATIONS AND MEMBERSHIPS

- Certified Safety Professional. (Designations in Products Safety, Safety Management and Comprehensive Safety Aspects)
- Registered Professional Engineer (P.E.), Massachusetts
- Associate in Risk Management (A.R.M.)
- Member, American Society of Safety Engineering
- Member, Maine Safety Council
- Formerly Commissioned, National Board of Boiler and Pressure Vessel Inspectors
- Former U.S. Coast Guard Licensee, Third Assistant Engineer
- Third Class Engineer, State of Maine
- Former Certified Boiler and Pressure Vessel Inspector; Maine, Massachusetts, and New York
- Member, International Association of Arson Investigators
- Crane Inspections and Certification Bureau - Inspection Certification
- Former Member, Maine State Occupational Safety and Health Board
- Former Member, Energy Testing Laboratory of Maine, Board of Directors

# Appendix U  Model Forensic Reports

(Note: The attachments and appendices referenced in the reports have not been included.)

IN THE UNITED STATES DISTRICT COURT
FOR THE SOUTHERN DISTRICT OF TEXAS
LINCOLN DIVISION


| | |
|---|---|
| LYNN STEPHENS,<br>Plaintiff | *<br>*<br>* |
| vs. | * CIVIL ACTION H-94-4168<br>*<br>* |
| THE CITY OF LINCOLN, ET AL.,<br>Defendants | *<br>* |

## PRELIMINARY
## REPORT OF MELVIN L. TUCKER

### QUALIFICATIONS

My name is Melvin L. Tucker and I retired as the Chief of Police of Tallahassee, Florida, on December 31, 1993, where I had served from October 15, 1979. During a twenty-five year law enforcement career I served as a Chief of Police in four cities, in three states and as an Agent for the Federal Bureau of Investigation.

I served as the Chairman of the North Carolina Criminal Justice Education and Training Council from 1977 until 1979, and as Vice-Chairman of the Florida Criminal Justice Standards and Training Commission from 1981 until 1984.

I served as an adjunct faculty member in criminal justice at Western Carolina University, Florida State University, Florida A&M University, and other institutions.

I have held several law enforcement certifications, including the advanced certificate from the State of North Carolina. I currently hold a Florida Law Enforcement Certificate and a Board Certificate from the National Academy of Police Specialists.

I completed my bachelors degree at the University of South Florida, Tampa, Florida and my masters degree at Appalachian State University, Boone, North Carolina. I have authored over twenty articles that have been published in public administration and criminal justice professional journals. (See CV attached)

I have served as a consultant and expert witness on numerous matters relating to police practices. I have published, conducted training, and taught in the areas of law enforcement standards, policies, issues, and training requirements.

My expert witness testimony has been evenly divided between plaintiff and defense.

I am familiar with the issues involved with women in policing, having managed a department which, in 1993, was 18% female. I have supervised investigations into allegations of sexual harassment and have disciplined officers as a result of sustained complaints of sexual harassment. During my career I frequently observed the phenomenon known commonly in the field of law enforcement as the "code of silence" or the "blue curtain" and have been called upon to testify, as a consultant, concerning this phenomenon before a grand jury investigating corruption in a municipal police department.

My fee for the analysis in this case is $2,500.00 which is my standard fee for this type of work.

EXPERT TESTIMONY
I have provided deposition or trial testimony in the following cases in the past four years:

1.  Marceline Lasater, et al
v.
City of Tyler, Texas, et al

2.  Margaret A. Georgiadis
v.
Amneal Corporation and David Petroski
Marion County, Florida

3.  Ken Hall
v.
City of Sarasota, Florida Police Dept., et al

4.  Frederick E. Hendricks
v.
State of Florida DHS&MV
Volusia County, Florida

5.  Wayne Howell
v.
Carolina Beach, N.C.

6.  James R. Sasser
v.
Tallahassee Police Department

7.  Sidney Herlich
v.
Lake Worth Florida Police Department

8.  Wyner
v.
DeWald, et al
West Palm Beach, Florida

9.  Gaila Triggs
v.
Park Inn International, et al
Lee County, Florida

10.  Dave M. Mathewson
v.
Florida Game & Fresh Water Fish Commission

11.  Stalvey
v.
City of Waycross, Georgia

12.  Claude Jones
v.
City of Douglas, Georgia

13.  Steven L. Shephard
v.
City of Folly Beach, South Carolina, et al

14.  Larry Gabbard
v.
Eastern Airlines, Inc.
Alachua County, Florida

15.  Thomas R. Zutell And John Kale
v.
Ralph A. Dahlstrom, Jr.
Gainesville, Florida

16.  Styles
v.
Tallahassee Housing Authority

17.  Kastogianis
v.
Pillsbury and Burger King
West Palm Beach, Florida

18.  Kirkland
v.
Gadsden County Sheriff's Department
Quincy, Florida

# MODEL FORENSIC REPORTS

MATERIALS REVIEWED

I reviewed the following materials in developing my opinion(s) in this case:

1. Plaintiff's First Amended Complaint;
2. Defendants' Answers;
3. The Sexual Harassment Policies for the Lincoln Police Department before and after Officer Stephens's charge of sexual harassment;
4. A transcript of the deposition of Leigh Anne Smith;
5. A transcript of the deposition of Mary Johnston;
6. A transcript of the deposition of William Thomas;
7. The Lincoln Police Department Internal Affairs Division investigation in this case;
8. The personnel file of Plaintiff Lynn Stephens;
9. The personnel file of Defendant George Johnston;
10. The personnel file of defendant William Thomas; and
11. Lincoln Police Department General Orders (numbers 200-25, 300-8, 200-8,200-3 and 300-14).

The materials that I comprehensively reviewed in this case are materials that are typically relied upon by consultants and experts in analyzing law enforcement issues.

BRIEF SUMMARY OF DISPOSITIVE FACTS

The following facts have been obtained from documentation provided by counsel and I have relied upon them in consideration of this case:

Lynn Stephens was employed with the City of Lincoln Police Department in May, 1986. In August, 1989 she was assigned to the Lincoln Police Department Mounted Patrol Unit of the Special Operations Division where her immediate supervisors were Sergeant George Johnston and Lieutenant William Thomas.

During her tenure with the Mounted Patrol Officer Stephens was frequently subjected to acts and statements from both Johnston and Thomas which constituted sexual harassment.

In February, 1993 Sergeant Johnston put his hands on Officer Stephens's shoulders and kissed her on her right ear. She immediately relayed her shock and disgust to Sergeant Johnston in the presence of another employee who witnessed the event. Officer Stephens did not report these incidents to Lieutenant Thomas (Johnston's supervisor) as she was experiencing the same type of conduct from him and had no confidence he would take corrective action.

In May, 1993 an allegation of race discrimination in the Mounted Patrol Unit was made by Officer Jon Turner. During an investigation into the complaint of Officer Turner, the conduct of Johnston and Thomas regarding the sexual harassment of Officer Stephens came to light and was also investigated. The following violations were sustained against Lieutenant Thomas:

1. Improper conduct and behavior (urinating and lowering pants in public);
2. Interfering in cases or operations (for attempting to intimidate a witness);
3. Insubordination (for failing to follow a direct order to not interfere with the investigation);
4. Sexual harassment (for improper acts or statements to Officer Stephens);
5. Respect for fellow employees (for acts or statements made in front of employees of the Mounted Patrol Unit); and
6. Truthfulness(for denying allegations that were witnessed and confirmed by more than one employee).

The following violations were sustained against Sergeant Johnston:

1. Sexual harassment (for acts and statements made to Officer Stephens);
2. Respect for fellow employees (for conduct toward Officer Stephens and Officer Karen Larsen); and
3. Truthfulness (for denying allegations made that were witnessed and confirmed by more than one employee).

Sergeant Johnston and Lieutenant Thomas were each suspended for ninety days without pay and transferred out of the Mounted Patrol Unit for their misconduct. This action was less than the Administrative Disciplinary Committee, convened by the Lincoln Police Department, recommended to the Chief of Police (demotion to Sergeant for Thomas and demotion to patrol officer for Johnston in addition to transfer and suspension).

Because of her complaint against two fellow officers (breaking the code of silence) Officer Stephens was subjected to "blackballing" by some of her fellow employees in the Mounted Patrol and retaliation efforts by Thomas, Johnston, and his wife Mary Johnston. As one example of "blackballing" Sergeant Patrick Foley held a roll call session in the lobby at the Mounted Patrol Units quarters while Officer Stephens was waiting in the roll call room. Before this time roll call had never been held in the lobby. (Leigh Anne Smith deposition pages 50 & 51)

Because of her complaint against two fellow officers Officer Stephens was subjected to retaliation by George Johnston, Mary Johnston, and William Thomas. As an example, Mary Johnston conducted a three week investigation of Officer Stephens (including video-taping Stephens at her off-duty employment) with the knowledge of her husband, George Johnston. (Mary Johnston deposition page 60)

Opinion(s)

The basis and reasons for my opinion(s) are premised upon my education, training, experience, knowledge of law enforcement standards, analysis and study in the field, through consulting professional literature, through seminars, and the facts of the case presented and the materials reviewed. My opinion(s) are based upon a synthesis of the above.

I presently hold the following preliminary opinion(s) to a reasonable degree of professional certainty:

1. As a result of the failure of the supervisors of the Lincoln Police Department and its Chief to enforce its own directive, General Order 200-8 (Supervisor's Responsibilities), Officer Lynn Stephens was subjected to a violation of the law (sexual harassment) by Sergeant George Johnston and Lieutenant William Thomas while she was assigned as an officer in the Mounted Patrol Unit under the immediate supervision of Sergeant Johnston and the unit command of Lieutenant William Thomas.

2. Chief Tim Duncan's failure to insure the Lincoln Police Department's own directive system was followed (General Order 200-3 titled INVESTIGATION OF ALLEGED MISCONDUCT BY OFFICERS) in the investigation into the sexual harassment of Officer Stephens (that all complaints of serious misconduct be investigated by the Internal Affairs Division as a Class 1 complaint) sent a message to the employees of the Lincoln Police Department that sexual harassment is not considered a serious act of misconduct.

3. Chief Tim Duncan's decision to suspend for ninety days and to transfer Johnston and Thomas, but not to demote Johnston and Thomas as the Departments' Administrative Disciplinary Committee had recommended, re-enforced the message already sent to the employees of the Lincoln Police Department that sexual harassment allegations would not be treated as seriously by the administration of the department as their Directives require or their employees (membership of Administrative Disciplinary Committee) expected.

# MODEL FORENSIC REPORTS

Chief Duncan's failure to terminate Thomas when another complaint was sustained against him after he returned to work from his ninety day suspension (as Chief Duncan had warned Thomas he would do) and the Department's performance evaluation of Thomas (very good) during the time period of his suspension again re-enforced this message.

By neglecting to reflect the disciplinary actions taken against Lieutenant Thomas on Thomas performance evaluation that covered the time period in which he was suspended for sexually harassing Officer Stephens, Chief Duncan and the supervisors of the Lincoln Police Department failed to insure General Order 300-8 (Performance Evaluations) was followed and properly enforced.

By failing to provide counseling (corrective action) for Thomas and Johnston, in addition to the ninety day suspension (punishment), about their misconduct in the sexual harassment of Officer Stephens, as required by General Order 300-8, Chief Duncan and the Lincoln Police Department placed female employees in the divisions where Thomas and Johnston were transferred to possible risk of sexual harassment.

4. Chief Duncan's failure to take decisive, clear, and visible action as to the Department's values when it became apparent that Officer Stephens was being subjected to "blackballing" and "retaliation" sent a message to the employees of the Lincoln Police Department that the custom and policy of the Department would continue to be the "code of silence" and officers who file complaints against other officers will not be supported by the leadership of the department.

5. The phenomenon known as "code of silence" or blue curtain" in the field of law enforcement has been recognized and discussed in criminal justice literature over the past quarter century. The "code of silence" is known to thrive if the leadership of the department does not make it clear, by policy and practice, that the value statement of the organization is to rebuke the few miscreants whose conduct falls below standards and to support the majority of officers who are doing their jobs effectively and lawfully.

6. That the "code of silence" existed in the Lincoln Police Department during the time when Officer Stephens was being sexually harassed and subjected to retaliation for her complaint against fellow officers is not only evidenced by the testimony of witnesses such as Leigh Anne Smith (deposition page 39 of volume 1 and page 14 of volume 2) wherein she stated that "she has experienced it herself" but is also evidenced by the Lincoln Police Department's own official documents (Page 17 of the Investigative Summary of Stephens Sexual Harassment Complaint) wherein it is stated "Mounted Patrol was considered a highly desirable assignment and the reluctance of some witnesses to "rock the boat" was understandable". This statement clearly supports the contention that to tell the truth may cost you the loss of assignment to a desirable job.

Further evidence that the "code of silence" was a custom and policy of the Lincoln Police Department is the fact that no officer, employee, or supervisor in the Mounted Patrol Unit came forward after Sergeant George Johnston warned all officers at a roll call session, after the investigation into the race discrimination and sexual harassment allegations had begun, to "stick together and they can't get any of us" and to "stick to your story no matter what happens" (Leigh Anne Smith deposition page 33) even though his conduct was in violation of Lincoln Police Department General Order 200-8 titled SUPERVISORS' RESPONSIBILITIES.

I may have additional opinions and reasoning depending upon the review of additional materials and what is asked of me at trial.

Respectfully Submitted,

Melvin L. Tucker

**Dr. David W. Richardson, D.O.**
**111 E. Main St., Suite 201**
**Coastal City, FL 12345**

October 3, 1995

Mary Smith, Esq.
Smith, Thomas, and Hart
600 Constitution Avenue
Suite 1200
Coastal City, FL 12345

RE: Amy Garson (File No. 98-4512)

This workers' compensation case involves a back injury. The examinee has not yet reached maximum medical improvement and recommendations are made as to her clinical management. The physician is unable to conclude that the totality of the examinee's difficulties are causally related to the reported injury.

This 33-year-old, right-handed woman was referred for an independent medical evaluation by the above client. The IME process was explained to the examinee, and she understands that no patient/treating physician relationship exists and that a report will be sent to the requesting client. History was provided by the examinee, who was a cooperative, fair to good historian and completed the questionnaire. She was driven 3½ hours to the appointment by her sister and arrived on time. Her sister waited in the reception area. The patient reported that the long ride aggravated her back.

The client provided clinical records of Jean Loren, M.D. Coastal Imaging; and Betsy Coens, RPT. No records prior to May 15, 1995 or subsequent to September 13, 1995 were available for review. Significant missing records included those of pre-existing status.

To ensure accuracy, the clinical synopsis was reviewed in the presence of the examinee. The issues requested in the referral are addressed in the Conclusions.

## HISTORY

**Pre-existing Status**
Ms. Garson admits to a low back injury in 1990, when she was pregnant. She was bending forward to remove a food tray from the lower level of a cart. She suffered low back strain, for which she received short-term treatment. She was out of work for 8 months; however, most of this was due to her pregnancy and a death in the family. She indicates that after several weeks her low back improved. Subsequently she noticed "on and off lameness," especially "if I overdid it." However, she denies any significant episodes requiring her to miss time from work.
She states that prior to the injury of May 1995 she was not experiencing significant problems.

**Injury**
She reports that on May 2, 1995 she was transferring a client from bed to walker and then wheelchair. The client had gotten up to the walker but started to fall. Ms. Garson was able to help her into the wheelchair, but had to bear her full weight. She felt something "pull" across her low back. She

continued working that shift and didn't feel too bad; however, by the end of the shift she had mildly increased low back pain. The following day her pain was worse. She had difficulty continuing her job, and called her family physician for an appointment.

## Initial Clinical Encounter
She was seen on May 15, 1995 by Jean Loren, M.D.. The patient presented complaining of low back pain but also indicated the left side of the abdomen was bothering her, near the site of a hernia repair. The doctor refers to "on and off 3 weeks." It is not clear if this is in regard to the hernia site or the low back pain. She recommended the patient remain out of work for rest, but due to financial constraints the patient could not do so, and they finally agreed to reduce her to four days per week. However, she did remain on her usual activities.

## Clinical Synopsis
Within a couple of weeks she began experiencing increasing pain to the right buttocks, radiating to the leg intermittently. She states this went as far as the ankle but was not associated with paresthesias, bladder or bowel dysfunction, and there was no pain with valsalva. She was referred to physical therapy and attended twice, but there was no insurance reimbursement so she discontinued. Because the patient is living in Canada she has Canadian Medicare, and in early July this coverage began paying for her physical therapy. She returned to treatments twice a week, consisting of ultrasound, hot packs, and stretching exercises. She continues attending physical therapy one to two times per week, but has not received instruction or progressive exercises. She continues receiving passive modalities. She does some stretching at home on a nightly basis.

At this point she doesn't feel that her symptoms are particularly improved. She remains under the care of Dr. Loren and has not seen other providers for consultation or assessment.

## Clinical Management Summary
### Health Care Providers
Jean Loren, M.D. is identified as the primary treating doctor. The last appointment was September 5, 1995 and the next is scheduled for October 4, 1995. Dr. Loren is also her primary care physician.

## Evaluation Summary
X-ray, LS spine, June 9, 1995: "Some disc space narrowing at L4-5 but no other significant findings . . . and . . . little if any degenerative changes. There is only a minimal curvature of the spine convex to the right." Films were reviewed and there appeared to be no sign of spondylolysis or spondylolisthesis. Disc space appeared well-maintained. I do not agree with the radiologist's impression that there was narrowing at L4-5. If there is narrowing here, it certainly is minimal.

## Treatment Summary
Physical therapy:        As noted above.
Medications:             Currently Flexeril 10 mg up to three times per day. She consistently takes this in the evening, but finds it causes too much drowsiness when she works. She previously used Darvocet but has discontinued it because it made her sick.

Other: Currently none; previously heat, ice, and walking.

## Current Status

The examinee's major concern is whether she will improve. She feels she has remained the same. The pain is located primarily in the low back with occasional radiation to the right posterior buttocks, posterolateral thigh, into the lateral calf as far as the ankle, and is described as aching in the low back and at times burning in the buttocks. There are no left lower extremity symptoms.

Aggravating Factors:          Almost all activities.

Relieving Factors: Doing nothing.

The pain is nearly constant (present 50-80% of the time). On a scale from 0 (no pain) to 10 (excruciating pain), initially it was a 9. During the past month it averaged a 7, with a low of 6 and a high of 9. Today the pain is an 8.

She denies any history of paresthesias/numbness or tingling, and weakness in the leg or foot. She notes occasional morning stiffness in the lower back "if I do to[o] much" the previous day. She has no history of headaches. She admits to depression, but states this is primarily related to other personal stresses not her back. There is no history of suicidal ideation. She admits to secondary insomnia due to low back pain. There has been no history of increased pain with coughing, sneezing, or bowel movement.

## Functional Status

She estimates she can sit or walk for a maximum of 30 minutes at a time and stand for up to 20 minutes, but she is not sure how much she can lift. She reports major difficulties sweeping, vacuuming, and driving a car. She indicates minor problems lifting a gallon of milk or a light bag of groceries, bending, pulling or pushing, climbing stairs, and kneeling. She is unsure about her ability to lift heavy weights and heavy bags of groceries, reach above shoulder level, and climb ladders. Her most difficult tasks are sweeping, vacuuming, and riding for long distances in a car.

## Occupational History

At the time of the injury the examinee had been employed by Elder Care Nursing Home since April 1988. She was working full-time (38-75 hours a week) as a CNA. According to the description provided by the examinee, this involved caring for the residents. The physical demands included sitting or standing for up to half an hour at a time, walking for up to 5 hours, repetitive use of the hands, frequent lifting, and awkward positioning. The heaviest object she usually had to lift was a resident.

She previously worked as a cashier in a grocery store and in a fish factory. She is a high school graduate and has a current driver's license.

The examinee was "not put out of work but cut back from a 5 day . . . to a 4 day work week" since May 15, 1995.

## Social History

The examinee has been married for 8 years but is currently separated. She has three children living with her, ages 4, 8, and 12. During the day she rests, watches TV, cleans house (she is unable to do heavy chores), and works as described above. She briefly describes an average day as follows: "I get up [at 4:30 AM] and get ready for work. Then I get my 3 children ready for school. Then I go to work. Then I come home, change and rest for a while. Then I do housework, cook supper, do laundry. Get kids ready for bed. Watch T.V. Then I get ready and go to bed [at 8:00]." She reports having no specific hobbies.

She has smoked one pack of cigarettes a day for 11 years, for an 11 pack-year history. She drinks approximately 2 alcoholic beverages per week, and denies having had any problems with alcohol or other drugs. She consumes 5 caffeinated beverages per day. She does have health insurance.

## Past Medical History

| | |
|---|---|
| Unrelated surgery: | Tonsillectomy, C-section, exploratory surgery, tubal ligation. |
| Other hospitalizations: | Noncontributory. |
| Drug allergies: | None. |
| Unrelated medications: | None. |
| Review of systems: | Positive for fatigue. |
| Family history: | Positive for grandparents with arthritis. |

## PHYSICAL EXAMINATION

### Observations

The examinee is a white female who appeared healthy. She reported her weight as 186 lbs. and her height as 5 ft. 6 in.

### Behavioral Examination

The examinee was pleasant, cooperative, and attentive. Her affect was normal and she maintained eye contact. She appeared comfortable during the interview and exam, sitting continuously for 20 minutes. No behavioral dysfunction or non-physiologic findings were observed.

### Structural Examination

In the standing neutral position cervical, thoracic, and lumbar curves were well-maintained. Gait was normal, with no antalgia. She was able to heel and toe walk, and demonstrated normal balance.

Examination focused on the low back and lower extremities.

Brief inspection of the upper quarter indicated normal range of the cervical spine and bilateral shoulders, as well as elbows, wrists, and digits. There was no pain to palpation throughout the shoulder girdle or upper thoracic paraspinal regions. DTRs were 2/4 at the Johnstonps, brachioradialis, and triceps.

### Low Back Examination

There were no surgical scars. There was no generalized tenderness. Tenderness was reported at the lumbosacral junction, primarily on the right SI region extending to the sciatic notch and piriformis area. There was no significant pain at the coccyx or left gluteal area.

| Lumbar Motion (degrees) | Normal | Angle |
|---|---|---|
| Flexion forward | 60 | 60 |
| Extension backward | 25 | 28 |
| Right lateral flexion | 25 | 24 |
| Left lateral flexion | 25 | 24 |

Lumbar motion was normal. Range of motion measurements were made with an inclinometer. Sacroiliac testing was positive on the right. Somatic dysfunction was identified at the right sacroiliac joint. There was pain reported at the right piriformis region with palpation.

Lower Extremity Neurologic Examination
Patellar reflexes were +2/4 L, +2/4 R; Achilles were +2/4 L, +2/4 R.

Manual muscle strength testing throughout the bilateral lower extremities disclosed no focal areas of weakness. There was no gross evidence of atrophy. To gross inspection there appeared to be slight calf atrophy on the left (unaffected) side compared to the right. There is no history of trauma to the left leg, and no dysfunction.

Sensory examination with sharp/soft discrimination was normal throughout all dermatomes. Straight-leg raising was negative seated and supine on the left. On the right the patient noted increased minor back discomfort at 90° seated and at about 75° supine; however, there was associated hamstring tension.

There was full and symmetric hip motion bilaterally. There was normal knee motion bilaterally, with no signs of crepitus or instability.

Palpation and inspection were unremarkable.

## PAIN STATUS INVENTORIES

### Pain Drawing
The examinee completed a pain drawing (enclosed), using symbols to describe sensations. This drawing received a normal score.

### Pain Disability Index
The Pain Disability Index uses rating scales to measure the extent of perceived disability in seven areas of life. The results are as follows:

| Area | Perceived Disability |
|---|---|
| Family/home responsibilities | 70% |
| Recreation | 70% |
| Social activity | 70% |
| Occupation | 70% |
| Sexual activity | 80% |
| Self-care | 70% |
| Life-support activities | 50% |

The total score is 48 out of a possible 70, for a total index of 69% (a high level of perceived disability).

### McGill Pain Questionnaire
The examinee completed the McGill Pain Questionnaire (Short Form), rating 15 pain descriptors on a scale from 0 (none) to 3 (severe). The sum of eleven sensory descriptors was 8, averaging 0.7. The sum of four affective descriptors was 6, averaging 1.5. The total of all descriptors was 14. The descriptors were primarily affective, suggesting an exaggerating pain patient. The overall pain intensity was rated at 3 (distressing) on a scale of 0-5.

### Multidimensional Pain Inventory
The results of the University of Pittsburgh School of Medicine Multidimensional Pain Inventory were computer analyzed. The examinee rated the impact of the pain in several areas on a 0-6 scale. The

report (appended) gives scores and statistical analysis, along with a graphic representation of the results compared with a control group.

This profile is classified as that of a dysfunctional individual. Compared with the control group, these individuals report a higher severity of pain, greater interference with their lives, a higher degree of psychological distress, a lower perceived ability to control their lives, and lower activity levels. They are labeled dysfunctional because the pain has affected a broad range of their functioning.

## CES-D
The Center for Epidemiologic Studies Depressed Mood Scale was administered. The examinee scored 35, suggesting a depressed mood.

## Oswestry Function Test
Her score on the Oswestry Function Test was 25 out of a possible 50 (50th percentile), indicating a perception of severe disability.

## CONCLUSIONS
### Diagnoses
1.      Low back pain (724.2).
        1.1.    Sciatica, right side.
        1.2.    Somatic dysfunction, right sacroiliac and piriformis area.
        1.3.    Doubt radiculopathy.
2.      Obesity (278.0)/Deconditioning (728.2).
3.      Tobacco use (305.1).
4.      Nonrestorative sleep disorder.
5.      Probable depression.

Ms. Garson was pleasant and cooperative with today's evaluation. Her physical findings would support a chronic low back problem, primarily localized to the right sacroiliac and sciatic region. It appears that piriformis spasm and sacroiliac somatic dysfunction are contributing to sciatica, causing low back pain. Despite the subjective complaints, over all her physical findings are relatively mild. She continues to work 30 hours per week in a fairly demanding job, and maintains her household with three young children as a single parent.

The patient achieved an elevated score on the CES-D test. While this test cannot diagnose depression, certainly the results suggest a depressed mood and she may in fact be clinically depressed. This does not appear related to her low back injury.

## Causation
Based upon the available information, to a reasonable degree of medical certainty, there is a possible causal relationship between the current complaints and the occupational injury reported. More likely than not her ongoing complaints are due to a combination of cumulative work trauma, obesity, Deconditioning, and lack of appropriate rest during her "off" time. I would rate all of these factors as equally contributory to her condition.

## Prognosis
Prognosis would seem good to excellent considering her apparent high motivation level.

## Maximum Medical Improvement

Maximum medical improvement (MMI) is defined as the date after which further recovery and restoration of function can no longer be anticipated, based upon reasonable medical probability. She has not reached MMI.

## Work Capacity

This examinee has at least a moderate to heavy work capacity as defined in the *Dictionary of Occupational Titles*, U.S. Department of Labor. Moderate work is defined as exerting up to 50 lbs. of force occasionally and/or up to 20 lbs. of force frequently and/or up to 10 lbs. of force constantly to move objects. Heavy work is defined as exerting up to 100 lbs. of force occasionally and/or up to 50 lbs. of force frequently and/or up to 20 lbs. of force constantly to move objects.

The examinee can work part- to full-time, 4-5 days a week. She should alternate between sitting and standing based upon comfort. She can lift up to 45-50 lbs. occasionally and up to 20-25 lbs. frequently, depending upon the circumstances. Factors include the height of the lift, the distance from the body, and the bulk. She may have greater capabilities, particularly with conditioning. She can occasionally bend and twist.

In my opinion she is capable of continuing to perform her current job at her current capacity. I would expect her capacity to increase as her symptoms improve. Please see recommendations.

I would be pleased to review any written functional job descriptions or videotapes of jobs, to make arrangements to view work being considered, and/or to discuss any issues concerning work capability or the return to work process.

## Appropriateness of Care

Her care has been consistent with the usual standards of care for this problem.

## Recommendations

Diagnostic

I think the primary problem is sciatica related to musculoligamentous irritation. I would recommend ruling out nerve impingement through an EMG/nerve conduction study. I think this would provide more information and be more cost-effective than an MRI. It will probably require the services of a neurologist. I am not sure if there is one in her immediate area; if not, she could obtain this at Neurology Associates in Presque Isle, or might have to travel to Bangor.

Therapeutic

She seems to have chronic irritability at the right SI joint as well as piriformis area. This should be an area of focus by the physical therapist. The examinee seems to be following a fairly simple routine of low back exercises, and while these might be somewhat beneficial, a more specific program aimed at the piriformis area would probably be more beneficial.

The examinee also might be a candidate for osteopathic manipulative therapy of 4-6 visits. The goal of this treatment would be to increase mobilization of the sacroiliac and piriformis area, helping to speed recovery.

She should be encouraged to lose weight and quit smoking.

The patient notes poor sleep. This may be contributing to her poor recovery. I would suggest a trial of low-dose tricyclic antidepressant medication to treat this; in fact, increasing this medication to therapeutic levels for depression might be beneficial as well.

The above analysis is based upon the subjective complaints, the history given by the examinee, the medical records and tests provided, the results of pain status inventories, and the physical findings. It is assumed that the material provided is correct. If more information becomes available at a later date, an additional report may be requested. Such information may or may not change the opinions rendered in this evaluation.

The examiner's opinions are based upon reasonable medical probability and are totally independent of the requesting agent. Medicine is both an art and a science, and although an individual may appear to be fit for return to duty, there is no guarantee that the person will not be reinjured or suffer additional injury. If applicable, employers should follow the process established in the Americans with Disabilities Act, Title 1. Comments on appropriateness of care are professional opinions based upon the specifics of this case, and should not be generalized to the involved providers or disciplines. The opinions expressed do not constitute a recommendation that specific claims or administrative functions be made or enforced.

Thank you for asking me to see this examinee in consultation. If you have any further questions, please do not hesitate to contact me.

Respectfully submitted,


David W. Richardson, DO
Occupational Medicine

DWR/ge
Enclosures:        Work Capacity Report

cc:                Jean Loren, M.D.

# Appendix V  Model Consulting Agreement

This Agreement is made effective as of _____, by and between <Client Organization>, of <Client Address>, _____, ___ _____, and Consultant, of <Consultant address>, _____, ___ _____.

In this Agreement, the party who is contracting to receive services shall be referred to as "Client," and the party who will be providing the services shall be referred to as "Consultant."

Consultant has a background in medicine and is willing to provide services to Client based on this background.

Client desires to have services provided by Consultant.

Therefore, the parties agree as follows:

**1. DESCRIPTION OF SERVICES.** Beginning on _____, Consultant will provide the following services (collectively, the "Services"): review of medical files, answering specific medical questions asked by client, meeting individually with claims adjusters to provide medical advice on cases, participating in case conferences, and providing medical training to staff.

**2. PERFORMANCE OF SERVICES.** The manner in which the Services are to be performed and the specific hours to be worked by Consultant shall be determined by Consultant. Client will rely on Consultant to work as many hours as may be reasonably necessary to fulfill Consultant's obligations under this Agreement.

**3. PAYMENT.** Client will pay a fee of $_____ per hour to Consultant for the Services. This fee shall be payable monthly, no later than the first day of the month following the period during which the Services were performed. Upon termination of this Agreement, payments under this paragraph shall cease; provided, however, that Consultant shall be entitled to payments for periods or partial periods that occurred prior to the date of termination and for which Consultant has not yet been paid.

**4. EXPENSE REIMBURSEMENT.** Consultant shall be entitled to reimbursement from Client for all reasonable expenses, including but not limited to, travel, telephone, fax, and photocopying expense.

**5. NEW PROJECT APPROVAL.** Consultant and Client recognize that Consultant's Services will include working on various projects for Client. Consultant shall obtain the approval of Client prior to the commencement of a new project.

**6. TERM/TERMINATION.** This Agreement shall be effective for a period of one year and shall automatically renew for successive terms of the same duration, unless either party provides 60 days written notice to the other party prior to the termination of the applicable initial term or renewal term.

**7. RELATIONSHIP OF PARTIES.** It is understood by the parties that Consultant is an independent contractor with respect to Client, and not an employee of Client. Client will not provide fringe benefits, including health insurance benefits, paid vacation, or any other employee benefit, for the benefit of Consultant.

**8. DISCLOSURE.** Consultant is required to disclose any outside activities or interests, including ownership or participation in the development of prior inventions, that conflict or may conflict with the best interests of Client. Prompt disclosure is required under this paragraph if the activity or interest is related, directly or indirectly, to any activity that Consultant may be involved with on behalf of Client.

**9. INJURIES.** Consultant acknowledges Consultant's obligation to obtain appropriate insurance coverage for the benefit of Consultant (and Consultant's employees, if any). Consultant waives any rights to recovery from Client for any injuries that Consultant (and/or Consultant's employees) may sustain while performing services under this Agreement and that are a result of the negligence of Consultant or Consultant's employees.

**10. INDEMNIFICATION.** Client agrees to indemnify and hold Consultant harmless from all claims, losses, expenses, and fees including attorney fees, costs, and judgments that may be asserted against Consultant that result from the acts or omissions of Client, Client's employees, if any, and Client's agents.

**11. ASSIGNMENT.** Consultant's obligations under this Agreement may not be assigned or transferred to any other person, firm, or corporation without the prior written consent of Client.

**12. CONFIDENTIALITY.** Client recognizes that Consultant has and will have the following information:

- products
- future plans
- business affairs
- process information
- trade secrets
- technical information
- customer lists
- product design information

and other proprietary information (collectively, "Information") which are valuable, special, and unique assets of Client and need to be protected from improper disclosure. In consideration for the disclosure of the Information, Consultant agrees that Consultant will not at any time or in any manner, either directly or indirectly, use any Information for Consultant's own benefit, or divulge, disclose, or communicate in any manner any Information to any third party without the prior written consent of Client. Consultant will protect the Information and treat it as strictly confidential. A violation of this paragraph shall be a material violation of this Agreement.

**13. RETURN OF RECORDS.** Upon termination of this Agreement, Consultant shall deliver all records, notes, data, memoranda, models, and equipment of any nature that are in Consultant's possession or under Consultant's control and that are Client's property or relate to Client's business.

**14. NOTICES.** All notices required or permitted under this Agreement shall be in writing and shall be deemed delivered when delivered in person or deposited in the United States mail, postage prepaid, addressed as follows:

# MODEL CONSULTING AGREEMENT

IF for Client:

&lt;Client Organization&gt;
&lt;Client Address&gt;

IF for Consultant:

&lt;Consultant&gt;
&lt;Consultant Address&gt;

Such address may be changed from time to time by either party by providing written notice to the other in the manner set forth above.

**15. ENTIRE AGREEMENT.** This Agreement contains the entire agreement of the parties and there are no other promises or conditions in any other agreement whether oral or written. This Agreement supersedes any prior written or oral agreements between the parties.

**16. AMENDMENT.** This Agreement may be modified or amended if the amendment is made in writing and is signed by both parties.

**17. SEVERABILITY.** If any provision of this Agreement shall be held to be invalid or unenforceable for any reason, the remaining provisions shall continue to be valid and enforceable. If a court finds that any provision of this Agreement is invalid or unenforceable, but that by limiting such provision it would become valid and enforceable, then such provision shall be deemed to be written, construed, and enforced as so limited.

**18. WAIVER OF CONTRACTUAL RIGHT.** The failure of either party to enforce any provision of this Agreement shall not be construed as a waiver or limitation of that party's right to subsequently enforce and compel strict compliance with every provision of this Agreement.

**19. APPLICABLE LAW.** This Agreement shall be governed by the laws of the State of

_____ .


Party receiving services:
&lt;Client Organization&gt;

By: _____


Party providing services:
&lt;Consultant&gt;

By: _____

# Appendix W  Model Marketing Letters

(Note:  Each of the following letters can be adapted as e-mail correspondence.)


[Date]


Steven Babitsky, Esq.
13 Falmouth Heights Road
Falmouth, MA  02540

Dear Attorney Babitsky,

Enclosed is a recent article of mine which appeared in <u>Forensic Accident Investigations.</u>  I thought that it might be of interest to you.

If you have any questions on the article, machine guarding, or our services in the fields of product liability cases, slip and fall, vehicular accident reconstruction, and other personal injury cases, please feel free to call upon me.

Thank you.

Sincerely,


John M. Nichols, PE, CSP, BCFE

P.S.:    For additional information and my CV, see my Web site: www.jnichols.com.

[Date]


Steven Babitsky, Esq.
13 Falmouth Heights Road
Falmouth, MA  02540

Dear Attorney Babitsky,

Your colleague, Jim Mangraviti, Esq., advised me that I should write to you.  I met Jim at a recent meeting of the Barnstable County Bar Association, where I gave a presentation on symptom magnification.

The purpose of this letter is to advise you of our capabilities in performing independent medical evaluations.  We understand the challenges you face in clarifying issues associated with injuries and illness.  I have received special training in the performance of independent medical evaluations and have the knowledge, skills and abilities to assist you and your clients.

We can assist you by:

> Providing comprehensive independent medical evaluations responding to your specific issues,
> Clarifying the specific diagnoses associated with a case,
> Assessing causation, to a reasonable degree of medical probability,
> Evaluating maximal medical improvement and permanent impairment,
> Specifying medical restrictions and suggesting appropriate modified duties,
> Assessing appropriateness of care,
> Offering recommendations when requested,
> Preparing a thorough written report, and
> Being available for depositions and testimony, if needed.

My curriculum vitae and a sample report are enclosed.  Please call me if you have any questions or comments.

Sincerely yours,


Joseph Banks, M.D.

# MODEL MARKETING LETTERS

[Date]

Steven Babitsky, Esq.
13 Falmouth Heights Road
Falmouth, MA  02540

Dear Attorney Babitsky,

When your firm needs a forensic psychiatrist—who are you going to call?

I am a board certified, Harvard-trained psychiatrist who testifies on behalf of both plaintiffs and defendants.

I am available to offer assistance in the following areas:

> Criminal cases
> Personal injury
> Custody cases
> Medical malpractice
> Workers' compensation
> Testamentary capacity

A sample written opinion and curriculum vitae will be furnished upon request.

I have enclosed a Rolodex card for your convenience.

Thank you.

Sincerely,

Raymond R. Robinson, M.D.

P.S.:     For additional information, see my Web site: www.rrrmd.com

# Appendix X  Fee Survey

The following is a brief summary of a detailed fee survey completed by 1,030 experts from June to December 2003. For complete results, including results by specialty and state, and a summary of each survey filled out by the experts, please see *2004 SEAK, Inc. National Guide to Expert Witness Fees and Billing Procedures* (SEAK 2004).

|  | High | Low | Average | Median |
|---|---|---|---|---|
| **In-court Testimony (hourly)** | $7,500 | $75 | $385 | $300 |
| **File Review/Prep (hourly)** | $1,000 | $0 | $254 | $240 |
| **Depositions (hourly)** | $3,000 | $0 | $353 | $300 |

**Some other results of the SEAK fee survey:**

- Expert fees vary significantly by state and specialty
- 73% of experts collect an up-front retainer
- 46% of experts use a written fee agreement
- 45% of experts are in the medical field, 55% are non-medical
- 46% of experts had collection problems with retaining counsel in the previous 5 years
- 58% of experts have a minimum charge for depositions and trials
- 45% of experts have a cancellation fee for depositions and trial testimony cancelled without sufficient notice

# Appendix Y  Attorneys' Rules of Ethics

Because of their role in society and their close involvement in the administration of law, lawyers are subject to special standards, regulations, and liabilities. Sometimes called legal ethics, sometimes professional responsibility, the topic is perhaps most comprehensively described as the law governing lawyers.

Because lawyers are admitted to practice by states this topic is largely one of state law. However, because federal courts and federal agencies set their own practice rules, the topic has a federal component, too.

Rules of professional conduct are often promulgated by the state bar, which has a division dedicated to attorney ethical oversight. Attorneys can be disciplined by the state bar for violation of these rules—discipline usually ranges from an admonition to disbarment. In some jurisdictions, these rules are also incorporated into the codified law, or the codified law has separate provisions governing professional conduct. Violation of these laws may result in civil or criminal penalty.

For rules in specific jurisdictions, as well as decisions handed down by the body in each respective jurisdiction responsible for attorney discipline, begin your research at the following two sites:

**www.law.cornell.edu/ethics/**
**www.legalethics.com**

The American Bar Association has published a collection of Model Rules of Professional Conduct (Model Rules). Over the years, many jurisdictions have adopted rules of professional conduct similar to—and often identical to—these model rules. Moreover, the rules in states that have not adopted the Model Rules are quite similar in language and concept to the Model Rules.

As an example, we have reprinted Rule 3:07 of the Massachusetts Canons of Ethics and Disciplinary Rules Regulating the Practice of Law. This contains the Massachusetts Rules of Professional Conduct. All lawyers admitted to practice in Massachusetts are bound by these Rules of Professional Conduct, which have been adopted by the Massachusetts Supreme Judicial Court. The purpose of the Rules is to set forth minimum ethical standards for the practice of law. It is the responsibility of the Board of Bar Overseers and the Office of the Bar Counsel (administrative agencies in Massachusetts created by the Supreme Judicial Court) to see that the Rules of Professional Conduct are observed.

In order for a lawyer to be found to have committed misconduct, it must be shown that his or her acts have violated the Rules of Professional Conduct. Charges of misconduct must be supported by the facts.

## RULE 3:07
## MASSACHUSETTS RULES OF PROFESSIONAL CONDUCT*

*Including amendments through 7/1/05.

### Index to the Rules

# ATTORNEYS' RULES OF ETHICS

## PREAMBLE: A LAWYER'S RESPONSIBILITIES

A lawyer is a representative of clients, an officer of the legal system, and a public citizen having special responsibility for the quality of justice.

1. As a representative of clients, a lawyer performs various functions. As advisor, a lawyer provides a client with an informed understanding of the client's legal rights and obligations and explains their practical implications. As advocate, a lawyer zealously asserts the client's position under the rules of the adversary system. As negotiator, a lawyer seeks a result advantageous to the client but consistent with requirements of honest dealing with others. A lawyer acts as evaluator by examining a client's legal affairs and reporting about them to the client or to others.

2. In all professional functions a lawyer should be competent, prompt, and diligent. A lawyer should maintain communication with a client concerning the representation. A lawyer should keep in confidence information relating to representation of a client except so far as disclosure is required or permitted by the Rules of Professional Conduct or other law.

3. A lawyer's conduct should conform to the requirements of the law, both in professional service to clients and in the lawyer's business and personal affairs. A lawyer should use the law's procedures only for legitimate purposes and not to harass or intimidate others. A lawyer should demonstrate respect for the legal system and for those who serve it, including judges, other lawyers, and public officials. While it is a lawyer's duty, when necessary, to challenge the rectitude of official action, it is also a lawyer's duty to uphold legal process.

4. As a public citizen, a lawyer should seek improvement of the law, the administration of justice, and the quality of service rendered by the legal profession. As a member of a learned profession, a lawyer should cultivate knowledge of the law beyond its use for clients, employ that knowledge in reform of the law, and work to strengthen legal education. A lawyer should be mindful of deficiencies in the administration of justice and of the fact that the poor, and sometimes persons who are not poor, cannot afford adequate legal assistance, and should therefore devote professional time and civic influence in their behalf. A lawyer should aid the legal profession in pursuing these objectives and should help the bar regulate itself in the public interest.

5. Many of a lawyer's professional responsibilities are prescribed in the Rules of Professional Conduct, as well as in substantive and procedural law. However, a lawyer is also guided by personal conscience and the approbation of professional peers. A lawyer should strive to attain the highest level of skill, to improve the law and the legal profession, and to exemplify the legal profession's ideals of public service.

6. A lawyer's responsibilities as a representative of clients, an officer of the legal system, and a public citizen are usually harmonious. Thus, when an opposing party is well represented, a lawyer can be a zealous advocate on behalf of a client and at the same time assume that justice is being done. So also, a lawyer can be sure that preserving client confidences ordinarily serves the public interest because people are more likely to seek legal advice, and thereby heed their legal obligations, when they know their communications will be private.

7. In the nature of law practice, however, conflicting responsibilities are encountered. Virtually all difficult ethical problems arise from conflict between a lawyer's responsibilities to clients, to the legal system, and to the lawyer's own interest in remaining an upright person while earning a satisfactory living. The Rules of Professional Conduct prescribe terms for resolving such conflicts. Within the framework of these Rules, many difficult issues of professional discretion can arise. Such issues must be resolved through the exercise of sensitive professional and moral judgment guided by the basic principles underlying the Rules.

8. The legal profession is largely self-governing. Although other professions also have been granted powers of self-government, the legal profession is unique in this respect because of the close relationship between the profession and the processes of government and law enforcement. This

connection is manifested in the fact that ultimate authority over the legal profession is vested largely in the courts.

9. To the extent that lawyers meet the obligations of their professional calling, the occasion for government regulation is obviated. Self-regulation also helps maintain the legal profession's independence from government domination. An independent legal profession is an important force in preserving government under law, for abuse of legal authority is more readily challenged by a profession whose members are not dependent on government for the right to practice.

10. The legal profession's relative autonomy carries with it special responsibilities of self-government. The profession has a responsibility to assure that its regulations are conceived in the public interest and not in furtherance of parochial or self-interested concerns of the bar. Every lawyer is responsible for observance of the Rules of Professional Conduct. A lawyer should also aid in securing their observance by other lawyers. Neglect of these responsibilities compromises the independence of the profession and the public interest which it serves.

11. Lawyers play a vital role in the preservation of society. The fulfillment of this role requires an understanding by lawyers of their relationship to our legal system. The Rules of Professional Conduct, when properly applied, serve to define that relationship.

## RULE 1.1 COMPETENCE

A lawyer shall provide competent representation to a client. Competent representation requires the legal knowledge, skill, thoroughness, and preparation reasonably necessary for the representation.

## RULE 1.2 SCOPE OF REPRESENTATION

(a) A lawyer shall seek the lawful objectives of his or her client through reasonably available means permitted by law and these rules. A lawyer does not violate this rule, however, by acceding to reasonable requests of opposing counsel which do not prejudice the rights of his or her client, by being punctual in fulfilling all professional commitments, by avoiding offensive tactics, or by treating with courtesy and consideration all persons involved in the legal process. A lawyer shall abide by a client's decision whether to accept an offer of settlement of a matter. In a criminal case, the lawyer shall abide by the client's decision, after consultation with the lawyer, as to a plea to be entered, whether to waive jury trial, and whether the client will testify.

(b) A lawyer's representation of a client, including representation by appointment, does not constitute an endorsement of the client's political, economic, social, or moral views or activities.

(c) A lawyer may limit the objectives of the representation if the client consents after consultation.

(d) A lawyer shall not counsel a client to engage, or assist a client, in conduct that the lawyer knows is criminal or fraudulent, but a lawyer may discuss the legal consequences of any proposed course of conduct with a client and may counsel or assist a client to make a good faith effort to determine the validity, scope, meaning, or application of the law.

(e) When a lawyer knows that a client expects assistance not permitted by the rules of professional conduct or other law, the lawyer shall consult with the client regarding the relevant limitations on the lawyer's conduct.

## RULE 1.3 DILIGENCE

A lawyer shall act with reasonable diligence and promptness in representing a client. The lawyer should represent a client zealously within the bounds of the law.

## RULE 1.4 COMMUNICATION

(a) A lawyer shall keep a client reasonably informed about the status of a matter and promptly comply with reasonable requests for information.

(b) A lawyer shall explain a matter to the extent reasonably necessary to permit the client to make informed decisions regarding the representation.

## RULE 1.5 FEES

(a) A lawyer shall not enter into an agreement for, charge, or collect an illegal or clearly excessive fee. The factors to be considered in determining whether a fee is clearly excessive include the following:

(1) the time and labor required, the novelty and difficulty of the questions involved, and the skill requisite to perform the legal service properly;

(2) the likelihood, if apparent to the client, that the acceptance of the particular employment will preclude other employment by the lawyer;

(3) the fee customarily charged in the locality for similar legal services;

(4) the amount involved and the results obtained;

(5) the time limitations imposed by the client or by the circumstances;

(6) the nature and length of the professional relationship with the client;

(7) the experience, reputation, and ability of the lawyer or lawyers performing the services; and

(8) whether the fee is fixed or contingent.

(b) When the lawyer has not regularly represented the client, the basis or rate of the fee shall be communicated to the client, preferably in writing, before or within a reasonable time after commencing the representation.

(c) A fee may be contingent on the outcome of the matter for which the service is rendered, except in a matter in which a contingent fee is prohibited by paragraph (d) or other law. Except for contingent fee arrangements concerning the collection of commercial accounts and of insurance company subrogation claims, a contingent fee agreement shall be in writing and signed in duplicate by both the lawyer and the client within a reasonable time after the making of the agreement. One such copy (and proof that the duplicate copy has been delivered or mailed to the client) shall be retained by the lawyer for a period of seven years after the conclusion of the contingent fee matter. The writing shall state:

(1) the name and address of each client;

(2) the name and address of the lawyer or lawyers to be retained;

(3) the nature of the claim, controversy, and other matters with reference to which the services are to be performed;

(4) the contingency upon which compensation to be paid, and whether and to what extent the client is to be liable to pay compensation otherwise than from amounts collected for him or her by the lawyer;

(5) the method by which the fee is to be determined, including the percentage or percentages that shall accrue to the lawyer out of amounts collected, and unless the parties otherwise agree in writing, that the lawyer shall be entitled to the greater of (i) the amount of any attorney's fees awarded by the court or included in the settlement or (ii) the percentage or other formula applied to the recovery amount not including such attorney's fees; and

(6) the method by which litigation and other expenses are to be deducted from the recovery and whether such expenses are to be deducted before or after the contingent fee is calculated.

Upon conclusion of a contingent fee matter for which a writing is required under this paragraph, the lawyer shall provide the client with a written statement stating the outcome of the matter and, if there is a recovery, showing the remittance to the client and the method of its determination.

(d) A lawyer shall not enter into an arrangement for, charge, or collect:

(1) any fee in a domestic relations matter, the payment or amount of which is contingent upon the securing of a divorce or upon the amount of alimony or support, or property settlement in lieu thereof; or

(2) a contingent fee for representing a defendant in a criminal case.

(e) A division of a fee between lawyers who are not in the same firm may be made only if, after informing the client that a division of fees will be made, the client consents to the joint participation and the total fee is reasonable. This limitation does not prohibit payment to a former partner or associate pursuant to a separation or retirement agreement.

(f) The following form of contingent fee agreement may be used to satisfy the requirements of paragraph (c). The authorization of this form shall not prevent the use of other forms consistent with this rule.

CONTINGENT FEE AGREEMENT

To be Executed in Duplicate

Date:_____, 19__

The Client _____

(Name) (Street & Number) (City or Town)

retains the Lawyer_____

(Name) (Street & Number) (City or Town)

to perform the legal services mentioned in paragraph (1) below. The lawyer agrees to perform them faithfully and with due diligence.

(1) The claim, controversy, and other matters with reference to which the services are to be performed are:

(2) The contingency upon which compensation is to be paid is:

(3) The client is not to be liable to pay compensation or court costs and expenses of litigation otherwise than from amounts collected for the client by the lawyer, except as follows:

(4) Compensation (including that of any associated counsel) to be paid to the lawyer by the client on the foregoing contingency shall be the following percentage of the (gross) (net) [indicate which] amount collected. [Here insert the percentages to be charged in the event of collection. These may be on a flat rate basis or in a descending scale in relation to amount collected.] The percentage shall be applied to the amount of the recovery not including any attorney's fees awarded by a court or included in a settlement. The lawyer's compensation shall be such attorney's fees or the amount determined by the percentage calculation described above, whichever is greater. [Modify the last two sentences as appropriate if the parties agree on some other basis for calculation.]

This agreement and its performance are subject to Rule 1.5 of the Rules of Professional Conduct adopted by the Massachusetts Supreme Judicial Court.

WE EACH HAVE READ THE ABOVE AGREEMENT BEFORE SIGNING IT.

Witnesses to signatures

(To client) _____

(Signature of Client)

(To lawyer)_____

(Signature of Lawyer)

(If more space is needed separate sheets may be attached and initialed.)

## RULE 1.6 CONFIDENTIALITY OF INFORMATION

(a) A lawyer shall not reveal confidential information relating to representation of a client unless the client consents after consultation, except for disclosures that are impliedly authorized in order to carry out the representation, and except as stated in paragraph (b).

(b) A lawyer may reveal, and to the extent required by Rule 3.3, Rule 4.1(b), or Rule 8.3 must reveal, such information:

(1) to prevent the commission of a criminal or fraudulent act that the lawyer reasonably believes is likely to result in death or substantial bodily harm, or in substantial injury to the financial interests or property of another, or to prevent the wrongful execution or incarceration of another;

(2) to the extent the lawyer reasonably believes necessary to establish a claim or defense on behalf of the lawyer in a controversy between the lawyer and the client, to establish a defense to a criminal charge or civil claim against the lawyer based upon conduct in which the client was involved, or to respond to allegations in any proceeding concerning the lawyer's representation of the client;

(3) to the extent the lawyer reasonably believes necessary to rectify client fraud in which the lawyer's services have been used, subject to Rule 3.3 (e);

(4) when permitted under these rules or required by law or court order.

(c) A lawyer participating in a lawyer assistance program, as hereinafter defined, shall treat the person so assisted as a client for the purposes of this rule. Lawyer assistance means assistance provided to a lawyer, judge, other legal professional, or law student by a lawyer participating in an organized nonprofit effort to provide assistance in the form of (a) counseling as to practice matters (which shall not include counseling a law student in a law school clinical program) or (b) education as to personal health matters, such as the treatment and rehabilitation from a mental, emotional, or psychological disorder, alcoholism, substance abuse, or other addiction, or both. A lawyer named in an order of the Supreme Judicial Court or the Board of Bar Overseers concerning the monitoring or terms of probation of another attorney shall treat that other attorney as a client for the purposes of this rule. Any lawyer participating in a lawyer assistance program may require a person acting under the lawyer's supervision or control to sign a nondisclosure form approved by the Supreme Judicial Court. Nothing in this paragraph (c) shall require a bar association-sponsored ethics advisory committee, the Office of Bar Counsel, or any other governmental agency advising on questions of professional responsibility to treat persons so assisted as clients for the purpose of this rule.

# ATTORNEYS' RULES OF ETHICS

## RULE 1.7 CONFLICT OF INTEREST: GENERAL RULE

(a) A lawyer shall not represent a client if the representation of that client will be directly adverse to another client, unless:

(1) the lawyer reasonably believes the representation will not adversely affect the relationship with the other client; and

(2) each client consents after consultation.

(b) A lawyer shall not represent a client if the representation of that client may be materially limited by the lawyer's responsibilities to another client or to a third person, or by the lawyer's own interests, unless:

(1) the lawyer reasonably believes the representation will not be adversely affected; and

(2) the client consents after consultation. When representation of multiple clients in a single matter is undertaken, the consultation shall include explanation of the implications of the common representation and the advantages and risks involved.

## RULE 1.8 CONFLICT OF INTEREST: PROHIBITED TRANSACTIONS

(a) A lawyer shall not enter into a business transaction with a client or knowingly acquire an ownership, possessory, security, or other pecuniary interest adverse to a client unless:

(1) the transaction and terms on which the lawyer acquires the interest are fair and reasonable to the client and are fully disclosed and transmitted in writing to the client in a manner which can be reasonably understood by the client;

(2) the client is given a reasonable opportunity to seek the advice of independent counsel in the transaction; and

(3) the client consents in writing thereto.

(b) A lawyer shall not use confidential information relating to representation of a client to the disadvantage of the client or for the lawyer's advantage or the advantage of a third person, unless the client consents after consultation, except as Rule 1.6 or Rule 3.3 would permit or require.

(c) A lawyer shall not prepare an instrument giving the lawyer or a person related to the lawyer as parent, child, sibling, or spouse any substantial gift from a client, including a testamentary gift, except where the client is related to the donee.

(d) Prior to the conclusion of representation of a client, a lawyer shall not make or negotiate an agreement giving the lawyer literary or media rights to a portrayal or account based in substantial part on information relating to the representation.

(e) A lawyer shall not provide financial assistance to a client in connection with pending or contemplated litigation, except that:

(1) a lawyer may advance court costs and expenses of litigation, the repayment of which may be contingent on the outcome of the matter; and

(2) a lawyer representing an indigent client may pay court costs and expenses of litigation on behalf of the client.

(f) A lawyer shall not accept compensation for representing a client from one other than the client unless:

(1) the client consents after consultation;

(2) there is no interference with the lawyer's independence of professional judgment or with the client-lawyer relationship; and

(3) information relating to representation of a client is protected as required by Rule 1.6.

(g) A lawyer who represents two or more clients shall not participate in making an aggregate settlement of the claims of or against the clients, or in a criminal case an aggregated agreement as to guilty or nolo contendere pleas, unless each client consents after consultation, including disclosure of the existence and nature of all the claims or pleas involved and of the participation of each person in the settlement.

(h) A lawyer shall not make an agreement prospectively limiting the lawyer's liability to a client for malpractice unless permitted by law and the client is independently represented in making the agreement, or settle a claim for such liability with an unrepresented client or former client without first advising that person in writing that independent representation is appropriate in connection therewith.

(i) A lawyer related to another lawyer as parent, child, sibling, or spouse shall not represent a client in a representation directly adverse to a person whom the lawyer knows is represented by the other lawyer except upon consent by the client after consultation regarding the relationship.

(j) A lawyer shall not acquire a proprietary interest in the cause of action or subject matter of litigation the lawyer is conducting for a client, except that the lawyer may:

(1) acquire a lien granted by law to secure the lawyer's fee or expenses; and

(2) contract with a client for a reasonable contingent fee in a civil case.

## RULE 1.9 CONFLICT OF INTEREST: FORMER CLIENT

(a) A lawyer who has formerly represented a client in a matter shall not thereafter represent another person in the same or a substantially related matter in which that person's interests are materially adverse to the interests of the former client unless the former client consents after consultation.

(b) A lawyer shall not knowingly represent a person in the same or a substantially related matter in which a firm with which the lawyer formerly was associated had previously represented a client

(1) whose interests are materially adverse to that person; and

(2) about whom the lawyer had acquired information protected by Rules 1.6 and 1.9(c) that is material to the matter, unless the former client consents after consultation.

(c) A lawyer who has formerly represented a client in a matter or whose present or former firm has formerly represented a client in a matter shall not thereafter, unless the former client consents after consultation:

(1) use confidential information relating to the representation to the disadvantage of the former client, to the lawyer's advantage, or to the advantage of a third person, except as Rule 1.6, Rule 3.3, or Rule 4.1 would permit or require with respect to a client; or

(2) reveal confidential information relating to the representation except as Rule 1.6 or Rule 3.3 would permit or require with respect to a client.

## RULE 1.10 IMPUTED DISQUALIFICATION: GENERAL RULE

(a) While lawyers are associated in a firm, none of them shall knowingly represent a client when any one of them practicing alone would be prohibited from doing so by Rules 1.7, 1.8(c), or 1.9. A lawyer employed by the Public Counsel Division of the Committee for Public Counsel Services and a lawyer assigned to represent clients by the Private Counsel Division of that Committee are not considered to be associated. Lawyers are not considered to be associated merely because they have each individually been assigned to represent clients by the Committee for Public Counsel Services through its Private Counsel Division.

(b) When a lawyer has terminated an association with a firm, the firm is not prohibited from thereafter representing a person with interests materially adverse to those of a client represented by the formerly associated lawyer and not currently represented by the firm, unless:

(1) the matter is the same or substantially related to that in which the formerly associated lawyer represented the client; and

(2) any lawyer remaining in the firm has information protected by Rules 1.6 and 1.9(c) that is material to the matter.

(c) A disqualification prescribed by this rule may be waived by the affected client under the conditions stated in Rule 1.7.

(d) When a lawyer becomes associated with a firm, the firm may not undertake to or continue to represent a person in a matter that the firm knows or reasonably should know is the same or substantially related to a matter in which the newly associated lawyer (the "personally disqualified lawyer"), or a firm with which that lawyer was associated, had previously represented a client whose interests are materially adverse to that person unless:

(1) the personally disqualified lawyer has no information protected by Rule 1.6 or Rule 1.9 that is material to the matter ("material information"); or

(2) the personally disqualified lawyer (i) had neither substantial involvement nor substantial material information relating to the matter and (ii) is screened from any participation in the matter in accordance with paragraph (e) of this Rule and is apportioned no part of the fee therefrom.

(e) For the purposes of paragraph (d) of this Rule and of Rules 1.11 and 1.12, a personally disqualified lawyer in a firm will be deemed to have been screened from any participation in a matter if:

(1) all material information which the personally disqualified lawyer has been isolated from the firm;

(2) the personally disqualified lawyer has been isolated from all contact with the client relating to the matter, and any witness for or against the client;

(3) the personally disqualified lawyer and the firm have been precluded from discussing the matter with each other;

(4) the former client of the personally disqualified lawyer or of the firm with which the personally disqualified lawyer was associated receives notice of the conflict and an affidavit of the personally disqualified lawyer and the firm describing the procedures being used effectively to screen the personally disqualified lawyer, and attesting that (i) the personally disqualified lawyer will not participate in the matter and will not discuss the matter or the representation with any other lawyer or employee of his or her current firm, (ii) no material information was transmitted by the personally disqualified lawyer before implementation of the screening procedures and notice to the former client; and (iii) during the period of the lawyer's personal disqualification those lawyers or employees who do participate in the matter will be apprised that the personally disqualified lawyer is screened from participating in or discussing the matter; and

(5) the personally disqualified lawyer and the firm with which he is associated reasonably believe that the steps taken to accomplish the screening of material information are likely to be effective in preventing material information from being disclosed to the firm and its client.

In any matter in which the former client and the person being represented by the firm with which the personally disqualified lawyer is associated are not before a tribunal, the firm, the personally disqualified lawyer, or the former client may seek judicial review in a court of general jurisdiction of the screening procedures used, or may seek court supervision to ensure that implementation of the screening procedures has occurred and that effective actual compliance has been achieved.

## RULE 1.11 SUCCESSIVE GOVERNMENT AND PRIVATE EMPLOYMENT

(a) Except as law may otherwise expressly permit, a lawyer shall not represent a private client in connection with a matter in which the lawyer participated personally and substantially as a public officer or employee, unless the appropriate government agency consents after consultation. No lawyer in a firm with which that lawyer is associated may knowingly undertake or continue representation in such a matter unless:

(1) the disqualified lawyer is screened from any participation in the matter and is apportioned no part of the fee therefrom; and

(2) written notice is promptly given to the appropriate government agency to enable it to ascertain compliance with the provisions of this rule.

(b) Except as law may otherwise expressly permit, a lawyer having information that the lawyer knows is confidential government information about a person acquired when the lawyer was a public officer or employee, may not represent a private client whose interests are adverse to that person in a matter in which the information could be used to the material disadvantage of that person. A firm with which that lawyer is associated may undertake or continue representation in the matter only if the disqualified lawyer is screened from any participation in the matter and is apportioned no part of the fee therefrom.

(c) Except as law may otherwise expressly permit, a lawyer serving as a public officer or employee shall not:

(1) participate in a matter in which the lawyer participated personally and substantially while in private practice or nongovernmental employment, unless under applicable law no one is, or by lawful delegation may be, authorized to act in the lawyer's stead in the matter; or

(2) negotiate for private employment with any person who is involved as a party or as lawyer for a party in a matter in which the lawyer is participating personally and substantially, except that a lawyer serving as a law clerk to a judge, other adjudicative officer, arbitrator, or mediator may negotiate for private employment as permitted by Rule 1.12(b) and subject to the conditions stated in Rule 1.12(b).

(d) As used in this rule, the term "matter" includes:

(1) any judicial or other proceeding, application, request for a ruling or other determination, contract, claim, controversy, investigation, charge, accusation, arrest, or other particular matter involving a specific party or parties, and

(2) any other matter covered by the conflict of interest rules of the appropriate government agency.

(e) As used in this rule, the term "confidential government information" means information which has been obtained under governmental authority and which, at the time this rule is applied, the government is prohibited by law from disclosing to the public or has a legal privilege not to disclose, and which is not otherwise available to the public.

## RULE 1.12 FORMER JUDGE OR ARBITRATOR

(a) Except as stated in paragraph (d), a lawyer shall not represent anyone in connection with a matter in which the lawyer participated personally and substantially as a judge or other adjudicative officer, arbitrator, mediator, or law clerk to such a person, unless all parties to the proceeding consent after consultation.

(b) A lawyer shall not negotiate for employment with any person who is involved as a party or as lawyer for a party in a matter in which the lawyer is participating personally and substantially as a judge or other adjudicative officer, arbitrator, or mediator. A lawyer serving as a law clerk to a judge, other adjudicative officer, arbitrator or mediator may negotiate for employment with a party or lawyer involved in a matter in which the clerk is participating personally and substantially, but only after the lawyer has notified the judge, other adjudicative officer, arbitrator, or mediator.

(c) If a lawyer is disqualified by paragraph (a), no lawyer in a firm with which that lawyer is associated may knowingly undertake or continue representation in the matter unless:

(1) the disqualified lawyer is screened from any participation in the matter and is apportioned no part of the fee therefrom; and

(2) written notice is promptly given to the appropriate tribunal to enable it to ascertain compliance with the provisions of this rule.

(d) An arbitrator selected as a partisan of a party in a multimember arbitration panel is not prohibited from subsequently representing that party.

## RULE 1.13 ORGANIZATION AS CLIENT

(a) A lawyer employed or retained by an organization represents the organization acting through its duly authorized constituents.

(b) If a lawyer for an organization knows that an officer, employee, or other person associated with the organization is engaged in action, intends to act or refuses to act in a matter related to the representation that is a violation of a legal obligation to the organization, or a violation of law which reasonably might be imputed to the organization, and is likely to result in substantial injury to the organization, the lawyer shall proceed as is reasonably necessary in the best interest of the organization. In determining how to proceed, the lawyer shall give due consideration to the seriousness of the violation and its consequences, the scope and nature of the lawyer's representation, the responsibility in the organization and the apparent motivation of the person involved, the policies of the organization concerning such matters, and any other relevant considerations. Any measures taken shall be designed to minimize disruption of the organization and the risk of revealing information relating to the representation to persons outside the organization. Such measures may include among others:

(1) asking reconsideration of the matter;

(2) advising that a separate legal opinion on the matter be sought for presentation to appropriate authority in the organization; and

(3) referring the matter to higher authority in the organization, including, if warranted by the seriousness of the matter, referral to the highest authority that can act in behalf of the organization as determined by applicable law.

(c) If, despite the lawyer's efforts in accordance with paragraph (b), the highest authority that can act on behalf of the organization insists upon action, or a refusal to act, that is clearly a violation of law and is likely to result in substantial injury to the organization, the lawyer may resign in accordance with Rule 1.16 and may make such disclosures as are consistent with Rule 1.6, Rule 3.3, Rule 4.1, and Rule 8.3.

(d) In dealing with an organization's directors, officers, employees, members, shareholders, or other constituents, a lawyer shall explain the identity of the client when it is apparent that the organization's interests are adverse to those of the constituents with whom the lawyer is dealing.

(e) A lawyer representing an organization may also represent any of its directors, officers, employees, members, shareholders, or other constituents, subject to the provisions of Rule 1.7. If the organization's consent to the dual representation is required by Rule 1.7, the consent shall be given by an appropriate official of the organization other than the individual who is to be represented, or by the shareholders.

## RULE 1.14 CLIENT UNDER A DISABILITY

(a) When a client's ability to make adequately considered decisions in connection with the representation is impaired, whether because of minority, mental disability, or for some other reason, the lawyer shall, as far as reasonably possible, maintain a normal client-lawyer relationship with the client.

(b) If a lawyer reasonably believes that a client has become incompetent or that a normal client-lawyer relationship cannot be maintained as provided in paragraph (a) because the client lacks sufficient capacity to communicate or to make adequately considered decisions in connection with the representation, and if the lawyer reasonably believes that the client is at risk of substantial harm, physical, mental, financial, or otherwise, the lawyer may take the following action. The lawyer may consult family members, adult protective agencies, or other individuals or entities that have authority to protect the client, and, if it reasonably appears necessary, the lawyer may seek the appointment of a guardian ad litem, conservator, or a guardian, as the case may be. The lawyer may consult only those individuals or entities reasonably necessary to protect the client's interests and may not consult any individual or entity that the lawyer believes, after reasonable inquiry, will act in a fashion adverse to the interests of the client. In taking any of these actions the lawyer may disclose confidential information of the client only to the extent necessary to protect the client's interests.

## Rule 1.15 - Safekeeping Property

(a) Definitions:

(1) "Trust property" means property of clients or third persons that is in a lawyer's possession in connection with a representation and includes property held in any fiduciary capacity in connection with a representation, whether as trustee, agent, escrow agent, guardian, executor, or otherwise. Trust property does not include documents or other property received by a lawyer as investigatory material or potential evidence. Trust property in the form of funds is referred to as "trust funds."

(2) "Trust account" means an account in a financial institution in which trust funds are deposited. Trust accounts must conform to the requirements of this rule.

(b) Segregation of Trust Property. A lawyer shall hold trust property separate from the lawyer's own property.

(1) Trust funds shall be held in a trust account, except that advances for costs and expenses may be held in a business account.

(2) No funds belonging to the lawyer shall be deposited or retained in a trust account except that:

(i) Funds reasonably sufficient to pay bank charges may be deposited therein, and

(ii) Trust funds belonging in part to a client or third person and in part currently or potentially to the lawyer shall be deposited in a trust account, but the portion belonging to the lawyer must be withdrawn at the earliest reasonable time after the lawyer's interest in that portion becomes fixed. A lawyer who knows that the right of the lawyer or law firm to receive such portion is disputed shall not withdraw the funds until the dispute is resolved. If the right of the lawyer or law firm to receive such portion is disputed within a reasonable time after notice is given that the funds have been withdrawn, the disputed portion must be restored to a trust account until the dispute is resolved.

(3) Trust property other than funds shall be identified as such and appropriately safeguarded.

(c) Prompt Notice and Delivery of Trust Property to Client or Third Person. Upon receiving trust funds or other trust property in which a client or third person has an interest, a lawyer shall promptly notify the client or third person. Except as stated in this rule or as otherwise permitted by law or by agreement with the client or third person on whose behalf a lawyer holds trust property, a lawyer shall promptly deliver to the client or third person any funds or other property that the client or third person is entitled to receive.

(d) Accounting.

(1) Upon final distribution of any trust property or upon request by the client or third person on whose behalf a lawyer holds trust property, the lawyer shall promptly render a full written accounting regarding such property.

(2) On or before the date on which a withdrawal from a trust account is made for the purpose of paying fees due to a lawyer, the lawyer shall deliver to the client in writing (i) an itemized bill or other accounting showing the services rendered, (ii) written notice of amount and date of the withdrawal, and (iii) a statement of the balance of the client's funds in the trust account after the withdrawal.

(e) Operational Requirements for Trust Accounts.

(1) All trust accounts shall be maintained in the state where the lawyer's office is situated, or elsewhere with the consent of the client or third person on whose behalf the trust property is held, except that all funds required by this rule to be deposited in an IOLTA account shall be maintained in this Commonwealth.

(2) Each trust account title shall include the words "trust account," "escrow account," "client funds account," "conveyancing account," "IOLTA account," or words of similar import indicating the fiduciary nature of the account. Lawyers maintaining trust accounts shall take all steps necessary to inform the depository institution of the purpose and identity of such accounts.

(3) No withdrawal from a trust account shall be made by a check which is not prenumbered. No withdrawal shall be made in cash or by automatic teller machine or any similar method. No withdrawal shall be made by a check payable to "cash" or "bearer" or by any other method which does not identify the recipient of the funds.

(4) Every withdrawal from a trust account for the purpose of paying fees to a lawyer or reimbursing a lawyer for costs and expenses shall be payable to the lawyer or the lawyer's law firm.

(5) Each lawyer who has a law office in this Commonwealth and who holds trust funds shall deposit such funds, as appropriate, in one of two types of interest bearing accounts: either (i) a pooled account ("IOLTA account") for all trust funds which in the judgment of the lawyer are nominal in amount, or are to be held for a short period of time, or (ii) for all other trust funds, an individual account with the interest payable as directed by the client or third person on whose behalf the trust property is held. The foregoing deposit requirements apply to funds received by lawyers in connection with real estate transactions and loan closings, provided, however, that a trust account in a lending bank in the name of a lawyer representing the lending bank and used exclusively for depositing and disbursing funds in connection with that particular bank's loan transactions, shall not be required but is permitted to be established as an IOLTA account. All IOLTA accounts shall be established in compliance with the provisions of paragraph (g) of this rule.

(6) Property held for no compensation as a custodian for a minor family member is not subject to the Operational Requirements for Trust Accounts set out in this paragraph (e) or to the Required Accounts and Records in paragraph (f) of this rule. As used in this subsection, "family member" refers to those individuals specified in section (e)(2) of rule 7.3.

(f) Required Accounts and Records: Every lawyer who is engaged in the practice of law in this Commonwealth and who holds trust property in connection with a representation shall maintain complete records of the receipt, maintenance, and disposition of that trust property, including all records required by this subsection. Records shall be preserved for a period of six years after termination of the representation and after distribution of the property. Records may be maintained by computer subject to the requirements of subparagraph 1G of this paragraph (f) or they may be prepared manually.

(1) Trust Account Records. The following books and records must be maintained for each trust account:

A. Account Documentation. A record of the name and address of the bank or other depository; account number; account title; opening and closing dates; and the type of account, whether pooled, with net interest paid to the IOLTA Committee (IOLTA account), or account with interest paid to the client or third person on whose behalf the trust property is held (including master or umbrella accounts with individual subaccounts).

B. Check Register. A check register recording in chronological order the date and amount of all deposits; the date, check or transaction number, amount, and payee of all disbursements, whether by check, electronic transfer, or other means; the date and amount of every other credit or debit of whatever nature; the identity of the client matter for which funds were deposited or disbursed; and the current balance in the account.

C. Individual Client Records. A record for each client or third person for whom the lawyer received trust funds documenting each receipt and disbursement of the funds of the client or third person, the identity of the client matter for which funds were deposited or disbursed, and the balance held for the client or third person, including a subsidiary ledger or ledger for each client matter for which the lawyer receives trust funds documenting each receipt and disbursement of the funds of the client or third person with respect to such matter. A lawyer shall not disburse funds from the trust account that would create a negative balance with respect to any individual client.

D. Bank Fees and Charges. A ledger or other record for funds of the lawyer deposited in the trust account pursuant to paragraph (b)(2)(i) of this rule to accommodate reasonably expected bank charges.

This ledger shall document each deposit and expenditure of the lawyer's funds in the account and the balance remaining.

E. Reconciliation Reports. For each trust account, the lawyer shall prepare and retain a reconciliation report on a regular and periodic basis but in any event no less frequently than every sixty days. Each reconciliation report shall show the following balances and verify that they are identical:

(i) The balance which appears in the check register as of the reporting date.

(ii) The adjusted bank statement balance, determined by adding outstanding deposits and other credits to the bank statement balance and subtracting outstanding checks and other debits from the bank statement balance.

(iii) For any account in which funds are held for more than one client matter, the total of all client matter balances, determined by listing each of the individual client matter records and the balance which appears in each record as of the reporting date, and calculating the total. For the purpose of the calculation required by this paragraph, bank fees and charges shall be considered an individual client record. No balance for an individual client may be negative at any time.

F. Account Documentation. For each trust account, the lawyer shall retain contemporaneous records of transactions as necessary to document the transactions. The lawyer must retain:

(i) bank statements.

(ii) all transaction records returned by the bank, including canceled checks and records of electronic transactions.

(iii) records of deposits separately listing each deposited item and the client or third person for whom the deposit is being made.

G. Electronic Record Retention. A lawyer who maintains a trust account record by computer must maintain the check register, client ledgers, and reconciliation reports in a form that can be reproduced in printed hard copy. Electronic records must be regularly backed up by an appropriate storage device.

(2) Business Accounts. Each lawyer who receives trust funds must maintain at least one bank account, other than the trust account, for funds received and disbursed other than in the lawyer's fiduciary capacity.

(3) Trust Property Other than Funds. A lawyer who receives trust property other than funds must maintain a record showing the identity, location, and disposition of all such property.

(g) Interest on Lawyers' Trust Accounts.

(1) The IOLTA account shall be established with any bank, savings and loan association, or credit union authorized by Federal or State law to do business in Massachusetts and insured by the Federal Deposit Insurance Corporation or similar State insurance programs for State chartered institutions. At the direction of the lawyer, funds in the IOLTA account in excess of $100,000 may be temporarily reinvested in repurchase agreements fully collateralized by U.S. Government obligations. Funds in the IOLTA account shall be subject to withdrawal upon request and without delay.

(2) Lawyers creating and maintaining an IOLTA account shall direct the depository institution:

(i) to remit interest or dividends, net of any service charges or fees, on the average monthly balance in the account, or as otherwise computed in accordance with an institution's standard accounting practice, at least quarterly, to the IOLTA Committee;

(ii) to transmit with each remittance to the IOLTA Committee a statement showing the name of the lawyer who or law firm which deposited the funds; and

(iii) at the same time to transmit to the depositing lawyer a report showing the amount paid, the rate of interest applied, and the method by which the interest was computed.

(3) Lawyers shall certify their compliance with this rule as required by S.J.C. Rule 4:02, subsection (2).

(4) This court shall appoint members of a permanent IOLTA Committee to fixed terms on a staggered basis. The representatives appointed to the committee shall oversee the operation of a comprehensive IOLTA program, including:

(i) the receipt of all IOLTA funds and their disbursement, net of actual expenses, to the designated charitable entities, as follows: sixty seven percent (67%) to the Massachusetts Legal Assistance Corporation and the remaining thirty three percent (33%) to other designated charitable entities in such proportions as the Supreme Judicial Court may order;

(ii) the education of lawyers as to their obligation to create and maintain IOLTA accounts under Rule 1.15(h);

(iii) the encouragement of the banking community and the public to support the IOLTA program;

(iv) the obtaining of tax rulings and other administrative approval for a comprehensive IOLTA program as appropriate;

(v) the preparation of such guidelines and rules, subject to court approval, as may be deemed necessary or advisable for the operation of a comprehensive IOLTA program;

(vi) establishment of standards for reserve accounts by the recipient charitable entities for the deposit of IOLTA funds which the charitable entity intends to preserve for future use; and

(vii) reporting to the court in such manner as the court may direct.

(5) The Massachusetts Legal Assistance Corporation and other designated charitable entities shall receive IOLTA funds from the IOLTA Committee and distribute such funds for approved purposes. The Massachusetts Legal Assistance Corporation may use IOLTA funds to further its corporate purpose and other designated charitable entities may use IOLTA funds either for (a) improving the administration of justice or (b) delivering civil legal services to those who cannot afford them.

(6) The Massachusetts Legal Assistance Corporation and other designated charitable entities shall submit an annual report to the court describing their IOLTA activities for the year and providing a statement of the application of IOLTA funds received pursuant to this rule.

(h) Dishonored Check Notification.

All trust accounts shall be established in compliance with the following provisions on dishonored check notification:

(1) A lawyer shall maintain trust accounts only in financial institutions which have filed with the Board of Bar Overseers an agreement, in a form provided by the Board, to report to the Board in the event any properly payable instrument is presented against any trust account that contains insufficient funds, and the financial institution dishonors the instrument for that reason.

(2) Any such agreement shall apply to all branches of the financial institution and shall not be cancelled except upon thirty days notice in writing to the Board.

(3) The Board shall publish annually a list of financial institutions which have signed agreements to comply with this rule, and shall establish rules and procedures governing amendments to the list.

(4) The dishonored check notification agreement shall provide that all reports made by the financial institution shall be identical to the notice of dishonor customarily forwarded to the depositor, and should include a copy of the dishonored instrument, if such a copy is normally provided to depositors. Such reports shall be made simultaneously with the notice of dishonor and within the time provided by law for such notice, if any.

(5) Every lawyer practicing or admitted to practice in this Commonwealth shall, as a condition thereof, be conclusively deemed to have consented to the reporting and production requirements mandated by this rule.

(6) The following definitions shall be applicable to this subparagraph:

(i) "Financial institution" includes (a) any bank, savings and loan association, credit union, or savings bank, and (b) with the written consent of the client or third person on whose behalf the trust property is held, any other business or person which accepts for deposit funds held in trust by lawyers.

(ii) "Notice of dishonor" refers to the notice which a financial institution is required to give, under the laws of this Commonwealth, upon presentation of an instrument which the institution dishonors.

(iii) "Properly payable" refers to an instrument which, if presented in the normal course of business, is in a form requiring payment under the laws of this Commonwealth.

## RULE 1.16 DECLINING OR TERMINATING REPRESENTATION

(a) Except as stated in paragraph (c), a lawyer shall not represent a client or, where representation has commenced, shall withdraw from the representation of a client if:

(1) the representation will result in violation of the rules of professional conduct or other law;

(2) the lawyer's physical or mental condition materially impairs the lawyer's ability to represent the client; or

(3) the lawyer is discharged.

(b) Except as stated in paragraph (c), a lawyer may withdraw from representing a client if withdrawal can be accomplished without material adverse effect on the interests of the client, or if:

(1) the client persists in a course of action involving the lawyer's services that the lawyer reasonably believes is criminal or fraudulent;

(2) the client has used the lawyer's services to perpetrate a crime or fraud;

(3) a client insists upon pursuing an objective that the lawyer considers repugnant or imprudent;

(4) the client fails substantially to fulfil an obligation to the lawyer regarding the lawyer's services and has been given reasonable warning that the lawyer will withdraw unless the obligation is fulfilled;

(5) the representation will result in an unreasonable financial burden on the lawyer or has been rendered unreasonably difficult by the client; or

(6) other good cause for withdrawal exists.

(c) If permission for withdrawal from employment is required by the rules of a tribunal, a lawyer shall not withdraw from employment in a proceeding before that tribunal without its permission.

(d) Upon termination of representation, a lawyer shall take steps to the extent reasonably practicable to protect a client's interests, such as giving reasonable notice to the client, allowing time for employment of other counsel, surrendering papers and property to which the client is entitled, and refunding any advance payment of fee that has not been earned.

(e) A lawyer must make available to a former client, within a reasonable time following the client's request for his or her file, the following:

(1) all papers, documents, and other materials the client supplied to the lawyer. The lawyer may at his or her own expense retain copies of any such materials.

(2) all pleadings and other papers filed with or by the court or served by or upon any party. The client may be required to pay any copying charge consistent with the lawyer's actual cost for these materials, unless the client has already paid for such materials.

(3) all investigatory or discovery documents for which the client has paid the lawyer's out-of-pocket costs, including but not limited to medical records, photographs, tapes, disks, investigative reports, expert reports, depositions, and demonstrative evidence. The lawyer may at his or her own expense retain copies of any such materials.

(4) if the lawyer and the client have not entered into a contingent fee agreement, the client is entitled only to that portion of the lawyer's work product (as defined in subparagraph (6) below) for which the client has paid.

(5) if the lawyer and the client have entered into a contingent fee agreement, the lawyer must provide copies of the lawyer's work product (as defined in subparagraph (6) below). The client may be required to pay any copying charge consistent with the lawyer's actual cost for the copying of these materials.

(6) for purposes of this paragraph (e), work product shall consist of documents and tangible things prepared in the course of the representation of the client by the lawyer or at the lawyer's direction by his or her employee, agent, or consultant, and not described in paragraphs (2) or (3) above. Examples of work product include without limitation legal research, records of witness interviews, reports of negotiations, and correspondence.

(7) notwithstanding anything in this paragraph (e) to the contrary, a lawyer may not refuse, on grounds of nonpayment, to make available materials in the client's file when retention would prejudice the client unfairly.

## RULE 1.17 SALE OF LAW PRACTICE

A lawyer or legal representative may sell, and a lawyer or law firm may purchase, with or without consideration, a law practice, including good will, if the following conditions are satisfied:

(a) [RESERVED]

(b) [RESERVED]

(c) Actual written notice is given to each of the seller's clients regarding:

(1) the proposed sale;

(2) the terms of any proposed change in the fee arrangement authorized by paragraph (d);

(3) the client's right to retain other counsel or to take possession of the file; and

(4) the fact that the client's consent to the transfer of that client's representation will be presumed if the client does not take any action or does not otherwise object within ninety (90) days of receipt of the notice.

If a client cannot be given notice, the representation of that client may be transferred to the purchaser only upon entry of an order so authorizing by a court having jurisdiction. The seller may disclose to the court in camera information relating to the representation only to the extent necessary to obtain an order authorizing the transfer of a file.

(d) The fees charged clients shall not be increased by reason of the sale. The purchaser may, however, refuse to undertake the representation unless the client consents to pay the purchaser fees at a rate not exceeding the fees charged by the purchaser for rendering substantially similar services prior to the initiation of the purchase negotiations.

## RULE 2.1 ADVISOR

In representing a client, a lawyer shall exercise independent professional judgment and render candid advice. In rendering advice, a lawyer may refer not only to law but to other considerations, such as moral, economic, social, and political factors, that may be relevant to the client's situation.

## RULE 2.2 INTERMEDIARY [RESERVED]

## RULE 2.3 EVALUATION FOR USE BY THIRD PERSONS

(a) A lawyer may undertake an evaluation of a matter affecting a client for the use of someone other than the client if:

(1) the lawyer reasonably believes that making the evaluation is compatible with other aspects of the lawyer's relationship with the client; and

(2) the client consents after consultation.

(b) Except as disclosure is required in connection with a report of an evaluation, information relating to the evaluation is otherwise protected by Rule 1.6.

## RULE 2.4: LAWYER SERVING AS THIRD-PARTY NEUTRAL

(a) A lawyer serves as a third-party neutral when the lawyer assists two or more persons who are not clients of the lawyer to reach a resolution of a dispute or other matter that has arisen between them. Service as a third-party neutral may include service as an arbitrator, a mediator or in such other capacity as will enable the lawyer to assist the parties to resolve the matter.

(b) A lawyer serving as a third-party neutral shall inform unrepresented parties that the lawyer is not representing them. When the lawyer knows or reasonably should know that a party does not understand the lawyer's role in the matter, the lawyer shall explain the difference between the lawyer's role as a third-party neutral and a lawyer's role as one who represents a client.

## RULE 3.1 MERITORIOUS CLAIMS AND CONTENTIONS

A lawyer shall not bring or defend a proceeding, or assert or controvert an issue therein, unless there is a basis for doing so that is not frivolous, which includes a good faith argument for an extension, modification, or reversal of existing law. A lawyer for the defendant in a criminal proceeding, or the respondent in a proceeding that could result in incarceration, may nevertheless so defend the proceeding as to require that every element of the case be established.

## RULE 3.2 EXPEDITING LITIGATION

A lawyer shall make reasonable efforts to expedite litigation consistent with the interests of the client.

## RULE 3.3 CANDOR TOWARD THE TRIBUNAL

(a) A lawyer shall not knowingly:

(1) make a false statement of material fact or law to a tribunal;

(2) fail to disclose a material fact to a tribunal when disclosure is necessary to avoid assisting a criminal or fraudulent act by the client, except as provided in Rule 3.3 (e);

(3) fail to disclose to the tribunal legal authority in the controlling jurisdiction known to the lawyer to be directly adverse to the position of the client and not disclosed by opposing counsel; or

(4) offer evidence that the lawyer knows to be false, except as provided in Rule 3.3 (e). If a lawyer has offered, or the lawyer's client or witnesses testifying on behalf of the client have given, material evidence and the lawyer comes to know of its falsity, the lawyer shall take reasonable remedial measures. (b) The duties stated in paragraph (a) continue to the conclusion of the proceeding, including all appeals, and apply even if compliance requires disclosure of information otherwise protected by Rule 1.6.

(c) A lawyer may refuse to offer evidence that the lawyer reasonably believes is false.

(d) In an ex parte proceeding, a lawyer shall inform the tribunal of all material facts known to the lawyer which will enable the tribunal to make an informed decision, whether or not the facts are adverse.

(e) In a criminal case, defense counsel who knows that the defendant, the client, intends to testify falsely may not aid the client in constructing false testimony, and has a duty strongly to discourage the client from testifying falsely, advising that such a course is unlawful, will have substantial adverse consequences, and should not be followed. If a lawyer discovers this intention before accepting the representation of the client, the lawyer shall not accept the representation; if the lawyer discovers this intention before trial, the lawyer shall seek to withdraw from the representation, requesting any required permission. Disclosure of privileged or prejudicial information shall be made only to the extent necessary to effect the withdrawal. If disclosure of privileged or prejudicial information is necessary, the lawyer shall make an application to withdraw ex parte to a judge other than the judge who will preside at the trial and shall seek to be heard in camera and have the record of the proceeding, except for an order granting leave to withdraw, impounded. If the lawyer is unable to obtain the required permission to withdraw, the lawyer may not prevent the client from testifying. If a criminal trial has commenced and the lawyer discovers that the client intends to testify falsely at trial, the lawyer need not file a motion to withdraw from the case if the lawyer reasonably believes that seeking to withdraw will prejudice the client. If, during the client's testimony or after the client has testified, the lawyer knows that the client has testified falsely, the lawyer shall call upon the client to rectify the false testimony and, if the client refuses or is unable to do so, the lawyer shall not reveal the false testimony to the tribunal. In no event may the lawyer examine the client in such a manner as to elicit any testimony from the client the lawyer knows to be false, and the lawyer shall not argue the probative value of the false testimony in closing argument or in any other proceedings, including appeals.

## RULE 3.4 FAIRNESS TO OPPOSING PARTY AND COUNSEL

A lawyer shall not:

(a) unlawfully obstruct another party's access to evidence or unlawfully alter, destroy, or conceal a document or other material having potential evidentiary value. A lawyer shall not counsel or assist another person to do any such act;

(b) falsify evidence, counsel or assist a witness to testify falsely, or offer an inducement to a witness that is prohibited by law;

(c) knowingly disobey an obligation under the rules of a tribunal except for an open refusal based on an assertion that no valid obligation exists;

(d) in pretrial procedure, make a frivolous discovery request or fail to make reasonably diligent effort to comply with a legally proper discovery request by an opposing party;

(e) in trial, allude to any matter that the lawyer does not reasonably believe is relevant or that will not be supported by admissible evidence, assert personal knowledge of facts in issue except when testifying as a witness, or state a personal opinion as to the justness of a cause, the credibility of a witness, the culpability of a civil litigant, or the guilt or innocence of an accused;

(f) request a person other than a client to refrain from voluntarily giving relevant information to another party unless:

(1) the person is a relative or an employee or other agent of a client; and

(2) the lawyer reasonably believes that the person's interests will not be adversely affected by refraining from giving such information;

(g) pay, offer to pay, or acquiesce in the payment of compensation to a witness contingent upon the content of his or her testimony or the outcome of the case. But a lawyer may advance, guarantee, or acquiesce in the payment of:

(1) expenses reasonably incurred by a witness in attending or testifying

(2) reasonable compensation to a witness for loss of time in attending or testifying

(3) a reasonable fee for the professional services of an expert witness;

(h) present, participate in presenting, or threaten to present criminal or disciplinary charges solely to obtain an advantage in a private civil matter; or

(i) in appearing in a professional capacity before a tribunal, engage in conduct manifesting bias or prejudice based on race, sex, religion, national origin, disability, age, or sexual orientation against a party, witness, counsel, or other person. This paragraph does not preclude legitimate advocacy when race, sex, religion, national origin, disability, age, or sexual orientation, or another similar factor is an issue in the proceeding.

## RULE 3.5 IMPARTIALITY AND DECORUM OF THE TRIBUNAL

A lawyer shall not:

(a) seek to influence a judge, juror, prospective juror, or other official by means prohibited by law;

(b) communicate ex parte with such a person except as permitted by law;

(c) engage in conduct intended to disrupt a tribunal; or

(d) after discharge of the jury from further consideration of a case with which the lawyer was connected, initiate any communication with a member of the jury without leave of court granted for good cause shown. If a juror initiates a communication with such a lawyer, directly or indirectly, the lawyer may respond provided that the lawyer shall not ask questions of or make comments to a member of that jury that are intended only to harass or embarrass the juror or to influence his or her actions in future jury service. In no circumstances shall such a lawyer inquire of a juror concerning the jury's deliberation processes.

## RULE 3.6 TRIAL PUBLICITY

(a) A lawyer who is participating or has participated in the investigation or litigation of a matter shall not make an extrajudicial statement that a reasonable person would expect to be disseminated by means of public communication if the lawyer knows or reasonably should know that it will have a substantial likelihood of materially prejudicing an adjudicative proceeding in the matter.

(b) Notwithstanding paragraph (a), a lawyer may state:

(1) the claim, offense, or defense involved, and, except when prohibited by law, the identity of the persons involved;

(2) the information contained in a public record;

(3) that an investigation of the matter is in progress;

(4) the scheduling or result of any step in litigation;

(5) a request for assistance in obtaining evidence and information necessary thereto;

(6) a warning of danger concerning the behavior of a person involved, when there is reason to believe that there exists the likelihood of substantial harm to an individual or to the public interest; and

(7) in a criminal case, in addition to subparagraphs (1) through (6): (i) the identity, residence, occupation, and family status of the accused; (ii) if the accused has not been apprehended, information necessary to aid in apprehension of that person; (iii) the fact, time, and place of arrest; and (iv) the identity of investigating and arresting officers or agencies and the length of the investigation.

(c) Notwithstanding paragraph (a), a lawyer may make a statement that a reasonable lawyer would believe is required to protect a client from the substantial undue prejudicial effect of recent publicity not initiated by the lawyer or the lawyer's client. A statement made pursuant to this paragraph shall be limited to such information as is necessary to mitigate the recent adverse publicity.

(d) No lawyer associated in a firm or government agency with a lawyer subject to paragraph (a) shall make a statement prohibited by paragraph (a).

(e) This rule does not preclude a lawyer from replying to charges of misconduct publicly made against him or her or from participating in the proceedings of a legislative, administrative, or other investigative body.

## RULE 3.7 LAWYER AS WITNESS

(a) A lawyer shall not act as advocate at a trial in which the lawyer is likely to be a necessary witness except where:

(1) the testimony relates to an uncontested issue;

(2) the testimony relates to the nature and value of legal services rendered in the case; or

(3) disqualification of the lawyer would work substantial hardship on the client.

(b) A lawyer may act as advocate in a trial in which another lawyer in the lawyer's firm is likely to be called as a witness unless precluded from doing so by Rule 1.7 or Rule 1.9.

## RULE 3.8 SPECIAL RESPONSIBILITIES OF A PROSECUTOR

The prosecutor in a criminal case shall:

(a) refrain from prosecuting a charge that the prosecutor knows is not supported by probable cause;

(b) make reasonable efforts to assure that the accused has been advised of the right to, and the procedure for obtaining, counsel and has been given reasonable opportunity to obtain counsel;

(c) not seek to obtain from an unrepresented accused a waiver of important pretrial rights, such as the right to a preliminary hearing, unless a court first has obtained from the accused a knowing and intelligent written waiver of counsel;

(d) make timely disclosure to the defense of all evidence or information known to the prosecutor that tends to negate the guilt of the accused or mitigates the offense, and, in connection with sentencing, disclose to the defense and to the tribunal all unprivileged mitigating information known to the prosecutor, except when the prosecutor is relieved of this responsibility by a protective order of the tribunal;

(e) exercise reasonable care to prevent investigators, law enforcement personnel, employees, or other persons assisting or associated with the prosecutor in a criminal case from making an extrajudicial statement that the prosecutor would be prohibited from making under Rule 3.6;

(f) not subpoena a lawyer in a grand jury or other criminal proceeding to present evidence about a past or present client unless:

(1) the prosecutor reasonably believes: (i) the information sought is not protected from disclosure by any applicable privilege; (ii) the evidence sought is essential to the successful completion of an ongoing investigation or prosecution; and (iii) there is no other feasible alternative to obtain the information; and

(2) the prosecutor obtains prior judicial approval after an opportunity for an adversarial proceeding; (g) except for statements that are necessary to inform the public of the nature and extent of the prosecutor's action and that serve a legitimate law enforcement purpose, refrain from making extrajudicial comments that have a substantial likelihood of heightening public condemnation of the accused;

(h) not assert personal knowledge of the facts in issue, except when testifying as a witness;

(i) not assert a personal opinion as to the justness of a cause, as to the credibility of a witness, as to the culpability of a civil litigant, or as to the guilt or innocence of an accused; but the prosecutor may argue, on analysis of the evidence, for any position or conclusion with respect to the matters stated herein; and

(j) not intentionally avoid pursuit of evidence because the prosecutor believes it will damage the prosecution's case or aid the accused.

## RULE 3.9 ADVOCATE IN NONADJUDICATIVE PROCEEDINGS

A lawyer representing a client before a legislative or administrative tribunal in a nonadjudicative proceeding shall disclose that the appearance is in a representative capacity and shall conform to the provisions of Rules 3.3(a) through (c), 3.4(a) through (c), and 3.5(a) through (c).

## RULE 4.1 TRUTHFULNESS IN STATEMENTS TO OTHERS

In the course of representing a client a lawyer shall not knowingly:

(a) make a false statement of material fact or law to a third person; or

(b) fail to disclose a material fact to a third person when disclosure is necessary to avoid assisting a criminal or fraudulent act by a client, unless disclosure is prohibited by Rule 1.6.

## RULE 4.2 COMMUNICATION WITH PERSON REPRESENTED BY COUNSEL

In representing a client, a lawyer shall not communicate about the subject of the representation with a person the lawyer knows to be represented by another lawyer in the matter, unless the lawyer has the consent of the other lawyer or is authorized by law to do so.

## RULE 4.3 DEALING WITH UNREPRESENTED PERSON

(a) In dealing on behalf of a client with a person who is not represented by counsel, a lawyer shall not state or imply that the lawyer is disinterested. When the lawyer knows or reasonably should know that the unrepresented person misunderstands the lawyer's role in the matter, the lawyer shall make reasonable efforts to correct the misunderstanding.

(b) During the course of representation of a client, a lawyer shall not give advice to a person who is not represented by a lawyer, other than the advice to secure counsel, if the interests of such person are or have a reasonable possibility of being in conflict with the interests of the client.

## RULE 4.4 RESPECT FOR RIGHTS OF THIRD PERSONS

In representing a client, a lawyer shall not use means that have no substantial purpose other than to embarrass, delay, or burden a third person, or use methods of obtaining evidence that violate the legal rights of such a person.

## RULE 5.1 RESPONSIBILITIES OF A PARTNER OR SUPERVISORY LAWYER

(a) A partner in a law firm shall make reasonable efforts to ensure that the firm has in effect measures giving reasonable assurance that all lawyers in the firm conform to the Rules of Professional Conduct.

(b) A lawyer having direct supervisory authority over another lawyer shall make reasonable efforts to ensure that the other lawyer conforms to the Rules of Professional Conduct.

(c) A lawyer shall be responsible for another lawyer's violation of the Rules of Professional Conduct if:

(1) the lawyer orders or, with knowledge of the specific conduct, ratifies the conduct involved; or

(2) the lawyer is a partner in the law firm in which the other lawyer practices, or has direct supervisory authority over the other lawyer, and knows of the conduct at a time when its consequences can be avoided or mitigated but fails to take reasonable remedial action.

## RULE 5.2 RESPONSIBILITIES OF A SUBORDINATE LAWYER

(a) A lawyer is bound by the Rules of Professional Conduct notwithstanding that the lawyer acted at the direction of another person.

(b) A subordinate lawyer does not violate the Rules of Professional Conduct if that lawyer acts in accordance with a supervisory lawyer's reasonable resolution of an arguable question of professional duty.

## RULE 5.3 RESPONSIBILITIES REGARDING NONLAWYER ASSISTANTS

With respect to a nonlawyer employed or retained by or associated with a lawyer:

(a) a partner in a law firm shall make reasonable efforts to ensure that the firm has in effect measures giving reasonable assurance that the person's conduct is compatible with the professional obligations of the lawyer;

(b) a lawyer having direct supervisory authority over the nonlawyer shall make reasonable efforts to ensure that the person's conduct is compatible with the professional obligations of the lawyer; and

(c) a lawyer shall be responsible for conduct of such a person that would be a violation of the Rules of Professional Conduct if engaged in by a lawyer if:

(1) the lawyer orders or, with the knowledge of the specific conduct, ratifies the conduct involved; or

(2) the lawyer is a partner in the law firm in which the person is employed, or has direct supervisory authority over the person, and knows of the conduct at a time when its consequences can be avoided or mitigated but fails to take reasonable remedial action.

## RULE 5.4 PROFESSIONAL INDEPENDENCE OF A LAWYER

(a) A lawyer or law firm shall not share legal fees with a nonlawyer, except that:

(1) an agreement by a lawyer with the lawyer's firm, partner, or associate may provide for the payment of money, over a reasonable period of time after the lawyer's death, to the lawyer's estate or to one or more specified persons;

(2) a lawyer who purchases the practice of a deceased, disabled, or disappeared lawyer may, pursuant to the provisions of Rule 1.17, pay to the estate or other representative of that lawyer the agreed-upon purchase price;

(3) a lawyer or law firm may include nonlawyer employees in a compensation or retirement plan, even though the plan is based in whole or in part on a profit-sharing arrangement; and

(4) a lawyer or law firm may agree to share a statutory or tribunal-approved fee award, or a settlement in a matter eligible for such an award, with a qualified legal assistance organization that referred the matter to the lawyer or law firm, if (i) the organization is one that is not for profit, (ii) the organization is tax-exempt under federal law, (iii) the fee award or settlement is made in connection with a proceeding to advance one or more of the purposes by virtue of which the organization is tax-exempt, and (iv) the client consents, after being informed that a division of fees will be made, to the sharing of the fees and the total fee is reasonable.

(b) A lawyer shall not form a partnership or other business entity with a nonlawyer if any of the activities of the entity consist of the practice of law.

(c) A lawyer shall not permit a person who recommends, employs, or pays the lawyer to render legal services for another to direct or regulate the lawyer's professional judgment in rendering such legal services.

(d) A lawyer shall not practice with or in the form of a limited liability entity authorized to practice law for a profit, if:

(1) a nonlawyer owns any interest therein, except that a fiduciary representative of the estate of a lawyer may hold the stock or interest of the lawyer for a reasonable time during administration;

(2) a nonlawyer is an officer, or a corporate director or limited liability company manager thereof; or

(3) a nonlawyer has the right to direct or control the professional judgment of a lawyer.

## RULE 5.5 UNAUTHORIZED PRACTICE OF LAW

A lawyer shall not:

(a) practice law in a jurisdiction where doing so violates the regulation of the legal profession in that jurisdiction; or

(b) assist a person who is not a member of the bar in the performance of activity that constitutes the unauthorized practice of law.

## RULE 5.6 RESTRICTIONS ON RIGHT TO PRACTICE

A lawyer shall not participate in offering or making:

(a) a partnership or employment agreement that restricts the right of a lawyer to practice after termination of the relationship, except an agreement concerning benefits upon retirement; or

(b) an agreement in which a restriction on the lawyer's right to practice is part of the settlement of a controversy.

## RULE 5.7 RESPONSIBILITIES REGARDING LAW-RELATED SERVICES

(a) A lawyer shall be subject to the Rules of Professional Conduct with respect to the provision of law-related services, as defined in paragraph (b), if the law-related services are provided:

(1) by the lawyer in circumstances that are not distinct from the lawyer's provision of legal services to clients; or

(2) by a separate entity controlled by the lawyer individually or with others if the lawyer fails to take reasonable measures to assure that a person obtaining the law-related services knows that the services of the separate entity are not legal services and that the protections of the client-lawyer relationship do not exist.

(b) The term "law-related services" denotes services that might reasonably be performed in conjunction with and in substance are related to the provision of legal services, and that are not prohibited as unauthorized practice of law when provided by a nonlawyer.

## RULE 6.1 VOLUNTARY PRO BONO PUBLICO SERVICES

A lawyer should provide annually at least 25 hours of pro bono publico legal services for the benefit of persons of limited means. In providing these professional services, the lawyer should:

(a) provide all or most of the 25 hours of pro bono publico legal services without compensation or expectation of compensation to persons of limited means, or to charitable, religious, civic, community, governmental, and educational organizations in matters that are designed primarily to address the needs of persons of limited means. The lawyer may provide any remaining hours by delivering legal services at substantially reduced compensation to persons of limited means or by participating in activities for improving the law, the legal system, or the legal profession that are primarily intended to benefit persons of limited means; or,

(b) contribute from $250 to 1% of the lawyer's annual taxable, professional income to one or more organizations that provide or support legal services to persons of limited means.

## RULE 6.2 ACCEPTING APPOINTMENTS

A lawyer shall not seek to avoid appointment by a tribunal to represent a person except for good cause, such as:

(a) representing the client is likely to result in violation of the Rules of Professional Conduct or other law;

(b) representing the client is likely to result in an unreasonable financial burden on the lawyer; or

(c) the client or the cause is so repugnant to the lawyer as to be likely to impair the client-lawyer relationship or the lawyer's ability to represent the client.

## RULE 6.3 MEMBERSHIP IN LEGAL SERVICES ORGANIZATION

A lawyer may serve as a director, officer, or member of a legal services organization, apart from the law firm in which the lawyer practices, notwithstanding that the organization serves persons having interests adverse to a client of the lawyer. The lawyer shall not knowingly participate in a decision or action of the organization:

(a) if participating in the decision or action would be incompatible with the lawyer's obligations to a client under Rule 1.7; or

(b) where the decision or action could have a material adverse effect on the representation of a client of the organization whose interests are adverse to a client of the lawyer.

## RULE 6.4 LAW REFORM ACTIVITIES AFFECTING CLIENT INTERESTS

A lawyer may serve as a director, officer, or member of an organization involved in reform of the law or its administration notwithstanding that the reform may affect the interests of a client of the lawyer. When the lawyer knows that the interests of a client may be materially benefitted by a decision in which the lawyer participates, the lawyer shall disclose that fact but need not identify the client.

## RULE 6.5 NONPROFIT AND COURT-ANNEXED LIMITED LEGAL SERVICES PROGRAMS

(a) A lawyer who, under the auspices of a program sponsored by a nonprofit organization or court, provides short-term limited legal services to a client without expectation by either the lawyer or the client that the lawyer will provide continuing representation in the matter:

(1) is subject to Rules 1.7 and 1.9(a) only if the lawyer knows that the representation of the client involves a conflict of interest; and

(2) is subject to Rule 1.10 only if the lawyer knows that another lawyer associated with the lawyer in a law firm is disqualified by Rule 1.7 or 1.9(a) with respect to the matter.

(b) Except as provided in paragraph (a)(2), Rule 1.10 is inapplicable to a representation governed by this Rule.

## RULE 7.1 COMMUNICATIONS CONCERNING A LAWYER'S SERVICES

A lawyer shall not make a false or misleading communication about the lawyer or the lawyer's services. A communication is false or misleading if it contains a material misrepresentation of fact or law, or omits a fact necessary to make the statement considered as a whole not materially misleading.

## RULE 7.2 ADVERTISING

(a) Subject to the requirements of Rule 7.1, a lawyer may advertise services through public media, such as a telephone directory, legal directory including an electronic or computer-accessed directory, newspaper or other periodical, outdoor advertising, radio or television, or through written communication not involving solicitation prohibited in Rule 7.3.

(b) A copy or recording of an advertisement or written communication shall be kept for two years after its last dissemination along with a record of when and where it was used.

(c) A lawyer shall not give anything of value to a person for recommending the lawyer's services, except that a lawyer may:

(1) pay the reasonable costs of advertisements or communications permitted by this Rule;

(2) pay the usual charges of a not-for-profit lawyer referral service or legal service organization;

(3) pay for a law practice in accordance with Rule 1.17; and

(4) pay referral fees permitted by Rule 1.5(e);

(5) share a statutory fee award or court-approved settlement in lieu thereof with a qualified legal assistance organization in accordance with Rule 5.4(a)(4).

(d) Any communication made pursuant to this rule shall include the name of the lawyer, group of lawyers, or firm responsible for its content.

## RULE 7.3 SOLICITATION OF PROFESSIONAL EMPLOYMENT

(a) In soliciting professional employment, a lawyer shall not coerce or harass a prospective client and shall not make a false or misleading communication.

(b) A lawyer shall not solicit professional employment if:

(1) the lawyer knows or reasonably should know that the physical, mental, or emotional state of the prospective client is such that there is a substantial potential that the person cannot exercise reasonable judgment in employing a lawyer, provided, however, that this prohibition shall not apply to solicitation not for a fee; or

(2) the prospective client has made known to the lawyer a desire not to be solicited.

(c) Except as provided in paragraph (e), a lawyer shall not solicit professional employment for a fee from a prospective client known to be in need of legal services in a particular matter by written communication, including audio or video cassette or other electronic communication, unless the lawyer retains a copy of such communication for two years.

(d) Except as provided in paragraph (e), a lawyer shall not solicit professional employment for a fee from a prospective client in person or by personal communication by telephone, electronic device, or otherwise.

(e) The following communications shall be exempt from the provisions of paragraphs (c) and (d) above:

(1) communications to members of the bar of any state or jurisdiction;

(2) communications to individuals who are

(A) the grandparents of the lawyer or the lawyer's spouse,

(B) descendants of the grandparents of the lawyer or the lawyer's spouse, or

(C) the spouse of any of the foregoing persons;

(3) communications to prospective clients with whom the lawyer had a prior attorney-client relationship; and

(4) communications with (i) organizations, including non-profit and government entities, in connection with the activities of such organizations, and (ii) with persons engaged in trade or commerce as defined in G.L. c. 93A, §1(b), in connection with such persons' trade or commerce.

(f) A lawyer shall not give anything of value to any person or organization to solicit professional employment for the lawyer from a prospective client. However, this rule does not prohibit a lawyer or a partner or associate or any other lawyer affiliated with the lawyer or the lawyer's firm from requesting referrals from a lawyer referral service operated, sponsored, or approved by a bar association or from cooperating with any other qualified legal assistance organization. Such requests for referrals or cooperation may include a sharing of fee awards as provided in Rule 5.4(a)(4).

## RULE 7.4 COMMUNICATION OF FIELDS OF PRACTICE

(a) Lawyers may hold themselves out publicly as specialists in particular services, fields, and areas of law if the holding out does not include a false or misleading communication. Such holding out includes

(1) a statement that the lawyer concentrates in, specializes in, is certified in, has expertise in, or limits practice to a particular service, field, or area of law,

(2) directory listings, including electronic, computer-accessed or other similar types of directory listings, by particular service, field, or area of law, and

(3) any other association of the lawyer's name with a particular service, field, or area of law.

(b) Lawyers who hold themselves out as "certified" in a particular service, field, or area of law must name the certifying organization and must state that the certifying organization is "a private organization, whose standards for certification are not regulated by the Commonwealth of Massachusetts," if that is the case, or, if the certifying organization is a governmental body, must name the governmental body.

(c) Except as provided in this paragraph, lawyers who associate their names with a particular service, field, or area of law imply an expertise and shall be held to the standard of performance of specialists in that particular service, field, or area. Lawyers may limit responsibility with respect to a particular service, field, or area of law to the standard of an ordinary lawyer by holding themselves out in a fashion that does not imply expertise, such as by advertising that they "handle" or "welcome" cases, "but are not specialists in" a specific service, field, or area of law.

## RULE 7.5 FIRM NAMES AND LETTERHEADS

(a) A lawyer shall not use a firm name, letterhead, or other professional designation that violates Rule 7.1. A trade name may be used by a lawyer in private practice if it does not imply a connection with a government agency or with a public or charitable legal services organization and is not otherwise in violation of Rule 7.1.

(b) A law firm with offices in more than one jurisdiction may use the same name in each jurisdiction, but identification of the lawyers in an office of the firm shall indicate the jurisdictional limitations on those not licensed to practice in the jurisdiction where the office is located.

(c) The name of a lawyer holding a public office shall not be used in the name of a law firm, or in communications on its behalf, during any substantial period in which the lawyer is not actively and regularly practicing with the firm.

(d) Lawyers may state or imply that they practice in a partnership or other organization only when that is the fact.

## RULE 8.1 BAR ADMISSION AND DISCIPLINARY MATTERS

An applicant for admission to the bar, or a lawyer in connection with a bar admission application or in connection with a disciplinary matter, shall not:

(a) knowingly make a false statement of material fact; or

(b) fail to disclose a fact necessary to correct a misapprehension known by the person to have arisen in the matter, or knowingly fail to respond to a lawful demand for information from an admissions or disciplinary authority, except that this rule does not require disclosure of information otherwise protected by Rule 1.6.

## RULE 8.2 JUDICIAL AND LEGAL OFFICIALS

A lawyer shall not make a statement that the lawyer knows to be false or with reckless disregard as to its truth or falsity concerning the qualifications or integrity of a judge or a magistrate, or of a candidate for appointment to judicial or legal office.

## RULE 8.3 REPORTING PROFESSIONAL MISCONDUCT

(a) A lawyer having knowledge that another lawyer has committed a violation of the Rules of Professional Conduct that raises a substantial question as to that lawyer's honesty, trustworthiness or fitness as a lawyer in other respects, shall inform the Bar Counsel's office of the Board of Bar Overseers.

(b) A lawyer having knowledge that a judge has committed a violation of applicable rules of judicial conduct that raises a substantial question as to the judge's fitness for office shall inform the Commission on Judicial Conduct.

(c) This rule does not require disclosure of information otherwise protected by Rule 1.6 or information gained by a lawyer or judge while serving as a member of lawyer assistance program as defined in Rule 1.6(c), to the extent that such information would be confidential if it were communicated by a client.

## RULE 8.4 MISCONDUCT

It is professional misconduct for a lawyer to:

(a) violate or attempt to violate the Rules of Professional Conduct, knowingly assist or induce another to do so, or do so through the acts of another;

(b) commit a criminal act that reflects adversely on the lawyer's honesty, trustworthiness, or fitness as a lawyer in other respects;

(c) engage in conduct involving dishonesty, fraud, deceit, or misrepresentation;

(d) engage in conduct that is prejudicial to the administration of justice;

(e) state or imply an ability to influence improperly a government agency or official;

(f) knowingly assist a judge or judicial officer in conduct that is a violation of applicable rules of judicial conduct or other law;

(g) fail without good cause to cooperate with the Bar Counsel or the Board of Bar Overseers as provided in Supreme Judicial Court Rule 4:01, § 3, last sentence; or

(h) engage in any other conduct that adversely reflects on his or her fitness to practice law.

## RULE 8.5 DISCIPLINARY AUTHORITY

(a) A lawyer admitted to practice in this jurisdiction is subject to the disciplinary authority of this jurisdiction, regardless of where the lawyer's conduct occurs. A lawyer may be subject to the disciplinary authority of both this jurisdiction and another jurisdiction where the lawyer is admitted for the same conduct.

(b) [RESERVED].

## RULE 9.1 DEFINITIONS

The following definitions are applicable to the Rules of Professional Conduct:

(a) "Bar association" includes an association of specialists in particular services, fields, and areas of law.

(b) "Belief" or "believes" denotes that the person involved actually supposed the fact in question to be true. A person's belief may be inferred from circumstances.

(c) "Consult" or "consultation" denotes communication of information reasonably sufficient to permit the client to appreciate the significance of the matter in question.

(d) "Firm" or "law firm" denotes a lawyer or lawyers in a private firm, lawyers employed in the legal department of a corporation or other organization, and lawyers employed in a legal services organization. The term includes a partnership, including a limited liability partnership, a corporation, a limited liability company, or an association treated as a corporation, authorized by law to practice law for profit.

(e) "Fraud" or "fraudulent" denotes conduct having a purpose to deceive and not merely negligent misrepresentation or failure to apprise another of relevant information.

(f) "Knowingly," "known," or "knows" denotes actual knowledge of the fact in question. A person's knowledge may be inferred from circumstances.

(g) "Partner" denotes a member of a partnership and a shareholder in a law firm organized as a professional corporation.

(h) "Person" includes a corporation, an association, a trust, a partnership, and any other organization or legal entity.

(i) "Qualified legal assistance organization" means a legal aid, public defender, or military assistance office; or a bona fide organization that recommends, furnishes or pays for legal services to its members or beneficiaries, provided the office, service, or organization receives no profit from the rendition of legal services, is not designed to procure financial benefit or legal work for a lawyer as a private practitioner, does not infringe the individual member's freedom as a client to challenge the approved counsel or to select outside counsel at the client's expense, and is not in violation of any applicable law.

(j) "Reasonable" or "reasonably" when used in relation to conduct by a lawyer denotes the conduct of a reasonably prudent and competent lawyer.

(k) "Reasonable belief" or "reasonably believes" when used in reference to a lawyer denotes that the lawyer believes the matter in question and that the circumstances are such that the belief is reasonable.

(l) "Reasonably should know" when used in reference to a lawyer denotes that a lawyer of reasonable prudence and competence would ascertain the matter in question.

(m) "State" includes the District of Columbia, Puerto Rico, and federal territories or possessions.

(n) "Substantial" when used in reference to degree or extent denotes a material matter of clear and weighty importance.

(o) "Tribunal" includes a court or other adjudicatory body.

## RULE 9.2 TITLE

These rules may be known and cited as the Massachusetts Rules of Professional Conduct (Mass. R. Prof. C.).

# Appendix Z  Expert Witness Practice Consultants

Steven Babitsky, Esq.
*SEAK, Inc.*
PO Box 729
Falmouth, MA 02541
Phone: (508) 548.9443
Fax: (508) 540.8304
E-mail: Sbabitsky@aol.com
www.seak.com

Rosalie Hamilton
Expert Communications
140 Island Way, #288
Clearwater, FL 33767
Ph. 727.467.0700
Fax 727.467.0800
E-mail: rhamilton@expertcommunications.com
www.expertcommunications.com

James J. Mangraviti, Jr., Esq.
*SEAK, Inc.*
PO Box 729
Falmouth, MA 02541
Phone: (508) 548-7023
Fax: (508) 540.8304
E-mail: seakincjm@aol.com
www.seak.com

# Index

# INDEX

# INDEX